Catholic Press Association

FIRST PLACE

Popular Presentation of the Catholic Faith

Catholic Q & A [The New Question Box]
by Father John J. Dietzen,
wins first place.

There seems to be nothing about the faith that Father Dietzen does not treat somewhere in this compellingly readable book. A well laid out question-and-answer form, with questions divided into subject categories, makes this a book one can dip into or (very tempting!) read from cover to cover.

Father Dietzen combines impressive knowledge with deep pastoral sensitivity. Long may he and his writing continue to inform and inspire seekers about the faith.

ᦁ

Contact us for special discounts on bulk quantities of
Catholic Q & A for large gift orders, classrooms,
graduating student classes, and other groups.

Special sales department:

phone: 212-868-1801 x109
fax: 212-868-2171

Catholic
Q&A

Catholic
Q&A

ANSWERS TO
THE MOST COMMON QUESTIONS
ABOUT CATHOLICISM

John J. Dietzen

A Crossroad Book
The Crossroad Publishing Company
New York

From *The New Question Box*

The Crossroad Publishing Company
16 Penn Plaza, 481 8th Avenue
New York, NY 10001

Book design by Ann Aspell

Printed in the United States of America.

First printing of the Crossroad edition 2005

Library of Congress Cataloging-in-Publications data is available.

ISBN 0-8245-2309-1

2 3 4 5 6 7 8 9 10   12 11 10 09 08 07 06 05

*This book is dedicated with affection and gratitude to my family,
those who have always been and those who have become my family
through the years, and to the thousands of readers whose questions,
insights and searching faith are a continuing source of
admiration and inspiration.*

CONTENTS

intentions / sabbath day / liturgical music / priest as presider / tabernacle/ bells / altar stones / candles/ incense / chalice / Real Presence / posture at Mass / women in ministry / homilies / translations of the Mass / language of the Mass in history / transubstantiation / sign of peace / crossed arms at Communion / *epiklesis* / doxology,.

x

dispensation from form / physical abuse in marriage / Natural Family Planning / birth control / onanism / sterilization / sterility / marriage of cousins / polygamy and church law / children and the Mass / responsibilities of parents / children and cults / homosexual children / impotence / *sanatio in radice.*

Note on the General Instruction of the Roman Missal

The recently completed revision of the Roman Missal, including the General Instruction of the Roman Missal (GIRM), is now in effect for the Universal Latin church. The official English translation of the new missal, including the GIRM, was issued in 2003 by the Secretariat for the Liturgy of the United States Conference of Catholic Bishops. GIRM references in this volume follow the translation.

PREFACE

The question column from which this book is compiled began more than thirty years ago, in the late 1960s, when the church was barely setting out on the journey of renewal mandated by the bishops of the Second Vatican Council. Its purpose was to assist Catholic people — most of whom had little knowledge of the concerns, processes, hopes, vision, leadership, and conclusions that the bishops shared in the remarkable years of that council — to assimilate what had happened there.

Decisions the bishops reached about the life and direction of the church in the modern world, and the practical consequences of those decisions, needed to be viewed thoughtfully in light of the church's experience through Christian history and its authentic theological traditions. The column, and later the several editions of *The New Question Box*, were attempts to make that happen.

That need still exists, but it has changed. People of varying temperaments and background view change, especially change in something as deeply meaningful as their faith, in different ways. Some deal with it more easily than others. Some see the Spirit moving us in ways others would reject.

From my pastoral work, and from the wide range of correspondence I receive from around the country, two things are clear. First, at the opening of the Council, Pope John XXIII explained that its purpose would be not to change Catholic doctrine, but to find better, more human and effective ways of proposing it to people. That work of adapting the church's method of living and evangelizing in a way most likely to influence the modern world is even now barely underway. And second, most Catholics are more knowledgeable and discriminating than they were 35 years ago. They see their faith not only as institutional, but more as a relationship with God, with Jesus Christ.

Perhaps one question and response in this book expresses well two possible trends. The writer complains that I too often do not give simple yes or no answers that "most of us poor Catholics can understand and follow." That is one way to look at Catholic life.

However, in my experience, most Catholics are not all that "poor." Fifty years ago, in the seminary, I realized that any doctrine or teaching is lifeless until I have asked myself the question, what does this mean for me? How should my life be affected because of it?

A huge number of Catholics today feel somewhat the same. Thirty years ago, the principal topics in my mail concerned marriage, divorce and remarriage. Today the predominant subject is holy Scripture. What are its meanings? How can they lead us to a deeper knowledge and relationship with Jesus? Teachings tend to be lifeless and ineffective until one can understand and relate to them personally, and envision how these realities will positively affect friendship with Jesus Christ, which so many Catholics and other Christians increasingly desire. They know that no friendship, with God or anyone else, grows without patience, sincere pursuit of greater understanding and knowledge, prayer, genuine care for the other, and continual reflection.

All this cannot be said, of course, in every column, or on every page of this book. But the purpose of both is to assist and support readers in this pursuit, and to recognize how Catholic life, in all its living expressions of worship, faith and service, can enhance that kind of intimacy with God.

This latest edition will, I hope, make easier a joyful, dedicated living of our faith in that same spirit. It is therefore written from a pastoral viewpoint, responding to some large and small questions facing the church and the whole People of God today. In brief, I have tried to assist and encourage a frame of mind in which Catholic Christians can function with fidelity to the teachings of the church and to God-given intelligence, common sense and faith, and with confidence that any risks are taken in the security of the enduring love of a faithful God.

While repetitions are avoided as much as possible, they are sometimes necessary to give proper context to specific subjects. I ask the readers' indulgence when that occurs. Where necessary, historical background on questions of conscience, belief and practice has been presented to deepen understanding of how and why the church reached the positions it assumes today.

I am grateful to the many diocesan newspaper editors who have carried my column through the years; to the thousands of readers whose questions and faith have been an inspiration and encouragement, and to the bishops, priests, religious and lay people around the country whose wisdom and advice are a constant help and support. My gratitude to you all.

—*John J. Dietzen*
Peoria, Illinois
2005

INTRODUCTION

For more than a quarter of a century, Father John J. Dietzen of the Diocese of Peoria has been the foremost question and answer columnist in the Catholic press in the United States.

Ordained in 1954, he has served his central Illinois diocese as director of the Office of Family Life, an editor of the diocesan newspaper, *The Catholic Post*, officer and board member of the Catholic Press Association, chairman of the Respect Life Board, and member of the Catholics for Life department of the Catholic Conference of Illinois. A teacher, lecturer, retreat master and participant in ecumenical dialogues, he was also pastor of two large parishes: St. Mark's in Peoria from 1973 until 1983, and then Holy Trinity in Bloomington, from which parish family he retired in 1998.

The question column, initiated in the *Catholic Post*, has been syndicated by Catholic News Service since 1975 and appears in Catholic newspapers in all parts of the United States and Canada. A collection of his columns, published in book form with the title *The New Question Box*, won first place in the "Popular Presentation of the Catholic Faith" category of the 1992 Catholic Press Association Book Awards.

In his wide-ranging research for answers to questions submitted by his readers, Father Dietzen draws on major authoritative sources such as the Bible, canon law, the *Catechism of the Catholic Church*, papal encyclicals, conciliar decrees, and documents issued by the U.S. Catholic Bishops and Vatican offices. He also credits his many friends and correspondents, among them national, archdiocesan and diocesan officials, for providing information when needed.

Father Dietzen's vast experience as scholar, journalist and pastor — along with mail his column draws from all parts of the country — give him a unique sense of the church today, and his love and support for his faith and his readers are evident in his responses.

This collection of his columns marks the 15th printing of this volume since it first appeared in book form in 1981; it has been retitled *Catholic Q and A: Everything You Always Wanted to Know About Catholic Life and Faith*.

Once again we invite readers into these pages to enjoy both the questions and Father Dietzen's informative, pastoral responses, and pray they find here the answers to their own spiritual searching, and the sense of courage, confidence, and peace of heart and mind that a deeper knowledge of their faith will bring.

ABBREVIATIONS FOR REFERENCES:

CCL   Code of Canon Law

CCC   Catechism of the Catholic Church

GIRM General Instruction of the Roman Missal

CHAPTER 1

THE BIBLE

∾

Church and sacred Scripture

A priest we know said recently the church existed before the Bible, at least before the New Testament. I realize this is true. But today, he added, we can do without the Bible, but we cannot do without the church. This is more than my understanding of our faith can absorb. Could you tell me in more detail what he meant?

As you say, the church certainly existed before the New Testament was completed. Many Christians were born, lived and died before the last book of the Bible was even written somewhere at least 60 or 70 years after Jesus died. The Bible was not solidified in its present combination of books until centuries later.

The statement that the church could do without the Bible is, in my view, at least ambiguous. In a way, of course, he is right. Theoretically the church could do without the sacraments of baptism, penance, holy orders and possibly even the Eucharist. Who are we to say that the church could not have been formed in a variety of other ways than Jesus actually arranged?

The church which really exists, however, is unthinkable without all of these elements and it is just as unthinkable without the Bible. Surely, the living community of faith with its leaders (particularly the pope and other bishops) will be the living carrier of the message and life of Christ to the world until the end of time. There is one sense, then, in which this living family of Christ will always be the final interpreter of the biblical word of God. It is equally true, however, that Scripture enshrines the teachings of the Lord and of the apostles with a special clarity and universality, so that it will be for all time the norm against which the church measures all its actions and its faith.

Whatever we propose as "might have been," the real church would soon be lost without Scripture. This is why the church has always venerated the Bible just as she venerates the body of Christ. "From the table of both the word of God and of the body of Christ she unceasingly receives and offers to the faithful the bread of life, especially in the sacred liturgy" (Dogmatic Constitution on Divine Revelation of Vatican II). The council document goes on to say that "all the preaching of the church must be nourished and ruled by sacred Scripture."

With this view of Scripture, it is impossible to understand how the church could get along without it. As that same constitution of the Vatican Council says, "It is clear that sacred tradition, sacred Scripture and the teaching authority of the church, in accord with God's most wise design, are so linked and joined together that one cannot stand without the others. All together and each in its own way under the action of the one Holy Spirit contribute effectively to the salvation of souls." (No. 10)

Bible is norm of faith

We are told that the Bible, the Old and New Testament, is "normative" for Christian belief. What does that mean? Catholics, and I think other Christians also, accept certain truths or doctrines that are not found stated in the Bible, for example the Assumption and the Immaculate Conception. If that is true, how can we say the Bible is the "norm" for our religion?

The Constitution on Divine Revelation (*Dei Verbum*), promulgated at Vatican Council II, affirmed that the church has always, and will always, regard the Scriptures, along with sacred tradition, as the supreme rule of faith.

"All the preaching of the Church," it claims, "must be nourished and ruled by sacred Scripture." The Bible, in other words, is a controlling presence in our understanding and reception of God's revelation, what God wished to teach for our salvation. (par. 21) This is what is meant by the Scriptures being normative for Christian belief. In a somewhat shorthand way, it means that no truly Christian teaching can contradict the Bible, which is not the same, however, as saying that every authentic Christian belief must be found in the Bible.

If the Scriptures are, as we believe them to be, the word of God transmitted to us in human language under the guidance of the Holy Spirit, then those Scriptures are without error. Properly interpreted, there can be no contradiction between the Scriptures and any authoritative teaching of the church, which by definition we believe would be inspired by that same Spirit.

Since holy Scriptures are written under the direction of the Holy Spirit, we believe that they must also be read and interpreted under the Spirit's guidance. Three criteria are generally indicated to guarantee that kind of interpretation: First, the interpretation must reflect the unity and content of the whole of the Bible. Second, it must be in accord, in harmony, with the living tradition of the whole church, as the Holy Spirit inspires and supports it down through the centuries. And third, the interpretation must respect what is called the "analogy of faith," the coherence and harmony which exists between the different teachings of the faith. Again, one Christian teaching cannot contradict another teaching, or at least one of them must be wrong.

Something the same can be said for other truths about which someone may object, "Where do you find that in the Bible?" If it does not contradict what is in the Bible, and if it generally fulfills those criteria for interpretation — in other words, if it is coherent with other teachings of faith, consistent with the living tradition of Christianity, and does not conflict with the content and unity of the Bible — then a particular teaching may be accepted without violating the normative role sacred Scripture plays in the Christian religion. This, of course, has happened frequently in the history of Christianity.

The explanation of the place of Scripture in the church may be found a bit more fully in the Vatican II Constitution mentioned above (especially sections 12 and 21), and in the article on sacred Scripture in the *Catechism of the Catholic Church*.

Biblical literary forms

I am sick and tired of hearing that the Bible is full of allegories and parables. If the word of God does not suit your ungodly lay and scientific concept of the world and of God, don't snipple here and there to your liking. Don't you believe the Bible is the word of God?

I'm sorry you are sick and tired of hearing it, but the plain fact is that much of the Bible is made up of allegories and parables — and poetry, fictional short stories, speeches, fables, and numerous other forms of literature.

You are, of course, free to believe what you wish about the Bible, even take it as word-for-word history if you can figure out how to do that. But the church's teaching is clear: The "truth" the Bible expresses is to be found in the meaning that the sacred writers intended when they wrote that particular part of Scripture. And to arrive at that truth, one must investigate whether that writer was producing straight history, a fable with a moral lesson involved, poetry, war stories, fictional tales, legal documents, allegories, or other kinds of writing. Only then do we discover most accurately what God is saying to us.

I like the example of George Washington and the cherry tree. The "truth" of that story is not in the facts of the plot, but in what it says about George. Should a historian some day prove there never was a cherry tree at his childhood home, our answer would be, so what? The story is not about a cherry tree, but about the honesty, integrity and nobility of the character of our first president. Furthermore, the man who thinks it is a tale about cherry trees and horticulture will miss the whole point.

Similarly the man who thinks, for example, that the story of Jonah is mainly about man-swallowing whales and storms at sea will miss the real "truth" of the story which the author intended — that God's love is universal, and the many other revelations which that book so enchantingly unfolds. In that particular instance, it makes not one whit of difference whether the whale carried our hero around for three days, or whether there even was a Jonah in the first place.

As Vatican Council II teaches, it is in all these ways, including some sections of straight history, "that the books of Scripture must be acknowledged as teaching solidly, faithfully and without error that truth which God wanted put into the sacred writings for the sake of our salvation" (Constitution on Divine Revelation, par. 11).

This "truth" in the sacred writings is in human language, however, and is therefore always limited. It must be searched out with much prayer, skill, and a faith sensitive to Catholic Christian tradition. One of the most exhaustive and carefully nuanced documents on the Interpretation of the Bible in the Church is a 1993 publication of the Pontifical Biblical Commission, with that title. In both the Old and New Testaments, it notes, "God made use of all the possibilities of human language, while at the same time accepting that his word would be subject to the constraints caused by the limitations of this language. Proper respect for inspired Scripture requires undertaking all the labors necessary to gain a thorough grasp of its meaning." (Conclusion)

Proper understanding of the written word of God is naturally of primary importance to Catholics. Those really interested in what the church teaches on the subject might read the two documents just quoted, the Vatican II Constitution on Divine Revelation, and the statement of the Pontifical Biblical Commission. Both are available from the United States Conference of Catholic Bishops in Washington, D.C.

Bible only for experts?

You mentioned that in reading the Bible it is important that we have some idea of what the writer intended when he wrote a particular book, and how the people understood it then. How can an ordinary person be expected to know all this? Shouldn't we read the Bible unless we do know these things?

Reading the Bible in a spirit of prayer and faith in God's word is always good and fruitful. In fact, someone who approaches Scripture with this attitude will reap far more benefits than one who has a lot of technical knowledge about the Bible, but no faith.

However, at least a little information about the background of the Bible and its books can make the reading of Scripture more beneficial and prevent much confusion and misunderstanding. Very little of the Bible is "straight" history as we think of it. Most of it is poetry, parables, personal or community reflections on memorable events, legal documents, visions or other manifestations of what were interpreted as God's reactions to human happenings, prophecies veiled in extremely mystical symbols — and even efforts by ancient theologians to put together in a cohesive way this whole series of revelations and experiences.

Since, in addition, all of what is now in the Bible was handed down by writing or word of mouth during a period of thousands of years, it's obviously an advantage to know, for example, what kind of writing each book was meant to be, and even to know some of the historical circumstances of the time. A parallel might be a 1935 newspaper being read today by an older man and a high school freshman. The paper would be far more intelligible and significant to the man who experienced those years than to the 14-year-old who knows only the words he sees on the paper.

Difference in Bibles

Could you please tell us the main difference between the English Catholic Bible and the King James version? I know there is a difference, but why do some people of other faiths say that Bibles are all the same?

There are today only two major differences between what we might call Protestant and Catholic Bibles.

First, Catholic Bibles contain all or part of several books in the Old Testament that do not appear as canonical books in the Protestant biblical tradition. These books are Tobias, Judith, Baruch, First and Second Maccabees, Ben Sirach (Ecclesiasticus), Wisdom, and parts of Daniel and Esther. For reasons we won't go into here, biblical scholars refer to these as the deutero-canonical (second canon) books, or apocrypha, because of varying positions among Jews of the Old and New Testament periods concerning them.

Second, Protestant Bibles generally do not include much in the way of footnotes, explanations or introductions. The Protestant tradition that the Holy Spirit alone guides each individual in his or her reading in Scripture has caused publishers of Bibles to shy away from anything which in their view would put some sort of human intervention between the reader and the Holy Spirit.

Catholic Bibles have not hesitated to include such materials, giving background to entire books or passages, describing the audience to which the book was addressed, and so on. More and more Bibles published under Protestant auspices tend to include similar notes to assist the readers in understanding what the biblical writers were dealing with.

Apart from these, there is generally no great difference between Protestant and Catholic Bibles. In past centuries, certain biblical passages were translated quite differently, colored by doctrinal positions of the two groups. The science of choosing and translating biblical manuscripts, however, is now so highly developed that any slanting of translations in this manner is simply out of the question for reputable biblical scholars of any faith.

New translations of the Bible are underway all the time. The King James version, published in the Protestant tradition, is one of the early English translations (1611) which, however, retains much of its popularity because of the exceptional style and language which have made it a classic of English literature.

The most authoritative current English translation in the Catholic tradition is the revised *New American Bible*, prepared under the auspices of American and other English-speaking bishops. The best current Bibles in the Protestant tradition, I believe, are the *Revised English Bible*, and some other excellent ones, notably the *New Revised Standard Version*, which had a Catholic edition including the apocrypha, and the *New International Version*.

All these, of course, are published in a wide variety of sizes and editions, but the titles I have mentioned, among others, indicate the actual biblical translations contained in the books.

Apocryphal books

When were the apocryphal books (those in Catholic Bibles but not in Protestant Bibles) removed from the Scriptures?

All early English Bible translations, including the King James Version, contained the apocrypha. The Coverdale Bible (1535), the Great Bible (1539) and the Geneva Bible (1560) all included the apocrypha in a separate section between the Old and New Testaments. The same was true of the King James Version in 1611. Only in 1644, under Puritan influence, were these books excluded. The first Bible printed in the New World, in 1783, also omits the apocrypha.

Interestingly, the Geneva Bible accepted these nine books, even though the thorough-going Protestants who published it added marginal notes identifying the Bishop of Rome with the Scarlet Woman in Revelation. King James abhorred such comments, which was one reason he commissioned a new translation by some of the leading Scripture scholars of his day. The new translation is what we know as the King James Bible.

The Latin Vulgate Bible

In your column on various Bibles, you didn't mention a famous one that I have heard about, the Vulgate. Why did you leave it out? Isn't it one of the more important Catholic Bibles?"

The answer to which you refer responded to a reader's request for information about English Bibles. The Vulgate is in Latin.

Back around the year 400 A. D., there was still no complete or scholarly Latin edition of the Bible, based on the languages in which the books were first written. The Hebrew Scriptures (our Old Testament) had been translated into Greek long before. And most of the New Testament was written in Greek.

To make the Scriptures more available to everyone, Pope Damasus (366-384) commissioned St. Jerome, the most learned biblical scholar of the day, to translate the Bible from the original languages into the everyday language of the "common people" (in Latin: *vulgus*).

A revised edition of the Vulgate was published under Pope John Paul II in 1986. In his introduction to the revision, the pope said it provided the church with a Latin text which recognized the developments in Scripture studies and provided a much better text for service in the liturgy.

Were Adam and Eve real?

My son came home from high school the other day and said his teacher told them Adam and Eve never existed. This goes down to the fundamentals of our faith, doesn't it? Did they, or didn't they? If there were two people who started the human race, how do we explain the different races?

We don't know whether or not there were two original human beings from which all the rest of us descended. And if there were, we surely do not know their names.

One thing is certain: We will never find out from the Bible. Holy Scripture simply was not written to pass on to us such details of anthropology as this. Whether there were two "first parents" or 200, or exactly where they came from, has little to do with the spiritual and theological intent of the biblical story of Adam and Eve — which was put together in the form we have it only a few hundred years before Christ.

That story, which we find in the first chapters of Genesis, is meant to convey to us some of the most important truths of our faith — that the world, including the human family, owes its existence to the one true God; that this world as it came from God was good and was meant for human happiness; that whatever misfortunes there are on earth come from people's own stubbornness and sinfulness; that even in the beginning God had a plan to eventually save us from that sinfulness.

I don't know why this should be so "fundamental" for your faith. The great facts about God and our relation with him are the real message of holy Scripture. As for the rest, scientists generally agree that any certainty about such things that happened way back in the dawn of history, tens or hundreds of thousands of years ago, is well nigh impossible.

The position of the church on this subject was made clear in the encyclical *Humani Generis* of Pope Pius XII (1950). In it the Holy Father insisted that the theory that there were more than two "first parents" of the human race should not be taught as an established fact. And that's where the matter stands.

Concerning the origin of the races, neither the Bible nor Christian revelation gives us much to go on. Some of the more fundamentalist Christians profess to see hints in the Scripture about how the races started. But the church's position, once again, is that this type of question must be answered by the sciences of anthropology and paleontology, not by theologians or Scripture scholars.

Many Adams, many Eves?

You say we may accept the possibility that there were more than one Adam and Eve who originated the human race. I have no big problem with this, but do have two questions. How do you explain scriptural references such as St. Paul's remark, "Through one man (Adam) sin entered the world" (Romans 5, 12)?

And isn't it true that many church councils, such as the infallible Council of Trent, and several church documents refer to Adam as "the first man?"

One critical point to remember in considering both your questions is that neither Scripture nor the council you mention were addressing themselves to the question of polygenism (that is, whether there were many first parents). Therefore one must be careful in claiming they answered a question that, up to that time, had never even been approached seriously.

To your first point, preachers and other orators quite commonly use the device of referring to well-known historical characters to make a point, with absolutely no intention of declaring judgment on the actual existence of these characters. When a priest in a homily, for example, refers to the Prodigal Son or the Good Samaritan, he is not professing a belief that these particular individuals of Jesus' parables ever really existed. They fit the point to be made, and that's all their mention really means.

Jesus did this, St. Paul did it, and conciliar decrees and other official church documents do the same. As mentioned above, these documents were not directly concerned with polygenism. But if reference to the scriptural story of creation helped explain or support their teaching, they rightly had no hesitation in using it.

In *Humani Generis* Pope Pius XII explained some doctrinal and scriptural problems with polygenism (some of which have been resolved in the last 50 years, incidentally), and says that no Catholic should hold that opinion (polygenism) as a fact since "it is not apparent" how this opinion is compatible with certain Catholic beliefs.

Humani Generis labels the belief in more than one Adam and Eve a conjectural opinion. It does not call that opinion erroneous or heretical.

By the way, there is no such thing as an "infallible council." A particular truth may be taught as defined doctrine. But the fact that some truths are taught solemnly in a conciliar or papal document doesn't mean that everything is, even if it's in the same sentence.

Temptation of Adam and Eve

In the story of Adam and Eve and the devil, or the snake, the devil says, "That's not true; you will not die. God said this because he knows that when you eat (the fruit of the tree of knowledge of good and evil), you will be like God." Why would Satan want them to be like God and have God's knowledge?

Clearly, the devil in this creation story (Gn. 3) did not intend for Adam and Eve to become like God. His words were a plain lie, but a very seductive lie with just enough truth in it to make it sound attractive.

Until the fall, according to this story, the couple were on extremely intimate terms with God, even walking with him in the cool of the evening (Gn. 3:8). This closeness and intimacy resulted from their recognition of the order of creation: God was God and they were not. As long as they acknowledged this fact, a wonderful harmony and openness existed between them, and between them and God, a happiness and communion we can hardly comprehend. It was this harmony, this happiness, that the devil set out to destroy.

The temptation could be put like this: "Why should you be subject to this God when you can show him you are as good and powerful as he is? God gives you this commandment to hold you under his thumb. But if you disobey, if you act against what God says, you will prove you are his equal. That's what God is afraid of, not that you will die, but that you will discover that you are like him."

In their pride, of course, Adam and Eve forgot, or ignored, the fact that no matter how much they pretended otherwise, they were in reality not God's equal. Like a child who won't believe a sharp knife will cut his finger, they suffered the consequences. By rejecting their relationship as creatures to Creator, they destroyed the harmony of creation, and their whole world began to disintegrate.

They became alienated from themselves ("I was afraid because I was naked"), from God ("The man and his wife hid themselves from the Lord God"), and from one another ("The woman you put here with me" gave it to me), and their children killed each other. One division and hatred after another piled up until their very speech became a sign and instrument of estrangement (chapter 11).

It is into this awful mess that the Lord enters (Gn. 12) and begins, with Abraham, the long story of his redemptive love once again bringing us together, reconciling us to each other and to God.

As in so many other elements of the creation story, the sin of Adam and Eve is really the story of ourselves. Every serious sin committed since then follows the same pattern of pride, rejection of God's dominion, more or less deliberate blindness to what is really happening, disintegration and alienation, and finally a need for the forgiving and healing grace of Jesus Christ.

Was it devil or serpent?

My question has to do with the story of the fall of man in Genesis. In that story the serpent tricks Eve into eating the fruit; she gives some to Adam. Later God banishes them from Eden and the serpent is cursed.

It seems to me the serpent is being punished for something the devil did. I don't believe God would punish one creature for the misdeeds of another. So what am I misunderstanding about the story?

It would help you considerably, first of all, to do some serious reading about biblical interpretation, including how we might understand the Genesis stories of creation. A good start would be the introductory pages of the *New American Bible*, published under the auspices of the bishops of the United States. These pages reflect Catholic teaching about the need to recognize various literary forms in the Scriptures, for example in the "description" of the creation and fall of the human race to which you refer.

Briefly, and to the point, while some Christians disagree with us, we do not understand these stories as describing a strict, straight history of how the world and human beings began. For example, you speak of the curse placed on the serpent for tempting Adam and Eve, that from this time onward he would move by crawling on his belly (Gn. 3:14). Did you ever stop to wonder how serpents moved around before the curse?

I'm not being facetious at all, only emphasizing that such things are not always as simple as they seem and that a little good, serious and reputable Catholic reading on the subject will help you.

Does Bible give earth's age?

I am a sponsor in our parish catechumen class. A priest told us in one session that someone once determined from the Bible that the earth was only about 6,000 years old. I find that fascinating! But he had no further details. Have you heard of this?

It is fascinating, especially in the light of the information we have today about the history of the earth and of the human race. Your priest might have been speaking of at least two people. During the 17th century, Archbishop James Ussher of Ireland, after much careful adding up of figures from the Book of Genesis, determined that the world was created in 4004 B. C.

Some time later, a Dr. John Lightfoot of Cambridge University, England, claimed to prove that the exact moment of the creation of Adam was "October 23, 4004 B. C., at 9 o'clock in the morning." I suppose there is someone somewhere who still believes that. To my knowledge at least, even those who reject any evolutionary explanation of the creation of the world would find it difficult to swallow these figures.

Big Bang Theory of Creation

According to Stephen Hawking's A Brief History of Time, *the Catholic Church has declared that its teaching does not conflict with the Big Bang theory of creation. That means billions of years may have passed. Yet, at our Christmas celebration, the priest said that only a few thousand years have passed since the creation of the world. Can you clear up this confusion on the church's position?*

None of the teachings of the Catholic Church conflict with the so-called Big Bang theory of the origin of the physical universe.

We believe that this material cosmos — all the galaxies and universes, the existence of which are revealed by astronomical and other sciences — came into existence by the personally willed action of an uncreated Creator we call God.

According to the Big Bang theory, all material creation began with an infinitesimal particle of matter and energy, with a density we might call nearly infinite. The intensity of energy within this particle caused it to explode and expand into the material cosmos which now exists. Evidence for the universe having its origin something along these lines is enormous, though it can never be absolutely conclusive.

As I said, nothing in our faith prevents our believing that God could very well have created the universe in this manner. In fact, certain aspects of this theory seem to point to the existence of a Creator more clearly than some scientists are comfortable with.

Certainly, the existence of this creation, with all its mind-blowing combinations of order and randomness; of plan and arrangement, from the smallest particle to the farthest space, alongside an almost fluky indeterminateness that makes the unexpected happen all the time — that all this might have begun with one tiny, dense particle can point us perhaps more than anything else to the incomprehensible "size" and beauty of the God we believe in.

Of course, if one is a Bible fundamentalist believing that everything in the Scriptures, beginning with the Genesis story of creation, is literal historical fact, all the above would be rejected out of hand. (See preceding question.) But such theories have no basis in, and certainly are not required by, Catholic dogma or teaching.

Many Catholic parishes proclaim the ancient martyrology announcement of the birth of the Savior as a solemn introduction to the Christmas liturgy. I suspect that's what your priest was doing. This proclamation, in several sentences situating the birth of Jesus in human history, has been in use hundreds of years, and makes no pretense at scientific accuracy. It is, however, a wonderful and moving statement of the Incarnation, when the Son of God embraced this material creation of his and took on our human flesh and nature.

Age of the human race

I read recently about some people finding human skeletons that are supposed to be over three million years old. A friend and I were discussing the article and she said that, according to the Bible, the whole world is only about 6,000 years old. I'm sure we don't believe that. At least I don't. But what can you say to someone like that? Is there any reason we can't believe that the human race is three million years old?

You raise a lot of big questions. Answers will vary greatly depending on one's understanding of the Scriptures, of religion, of God — and even of science.

There is absolutely nothing in Catholic faith that would prevent accepting any age for the human race. The Bible was never meant by God to be a course in archeology, paleontology, or even of history, in our usual understanding of that word. It is a story of God's saving plan for us, wounded and crippled by our own selfishness and pride, and how that plan unfolded. It is a book of faith, not of technical information.

This goes especially for the first 11 chapters of Genesis, which "cover" the whole history of the world up to God's call of Abraham as the father of the Hebrew people somewhere around 1800 B. C. The great Jewish theologians who put those stories together (creation, the flood, etc.) several centuries before Christ, had many ancient myths and legends to go on, but basically they knew even less about the details of the origin of the world than we do.

This bothered them not in the least. Their purpose, under the inspiration of God, was to make believers, not scientists, out of their people. There's no reason at all you cannot believe men and women were strolling the earth three million years ago -- if you're satisfied with the scientific evidence.

To the other part of your question: If someone insists that every fact, figure, name and event in holy Scripture is technically, scientifically, and historically accurate, don't waste your time arguing about such things as the age of man. You're simply on different wavelengths about the meaning of biblical truth.

What did God do before creation?

The first verse of Genesis says, "In the beginning, God created the heavens and the earth." My question is: What did God — Father, Son and Holy Spirit — do before Genesis 1:1? We know God had no beginning, but always was and always will be. Is there anywhere in Scripture that tells us what was going on with God in the eons before creation of the heavens and the earth?

There is nothing, it seems to me, that so dramatically confronts us with the infinite abyss of mystery between us and the Creator God as the question about what went on "before" creation of the universe. I hope I can respond without becoming too complicated, but it will help to review a few truths.

First, nothing at all happened "before" God created the universe. That word "before" implies time, and time begins with God's creation of what St. Paul, in a wonderful Greek phrase, calls *ta panta*, the everything.

Time is traditionally defined first, and most fundamentally, as the measure of motion. The earth revolves on its axis once, and we call it a day. It moves once around the sun, and we call it a year. Light travels about 5.6 trillion miles from one place to another, and we call it a light-year of time. In other words, unless one material (created) object is moving in relation to another material object, there is no such thing as time in the sense we know it.

To put it another way, it is meaningless to speak of any time before creation. There were, therefore, no eons that God had somehow to fill "until" (another time-connected word) he created "the everything."

As St. Thomas Aquinas explains, God and eternity are outside of time, where things change from moment to moment. Eternity embraces everything that is in one unchanging, instantaneous moment. (*Summa Theologiae* I, 10, 4) If all this boggles the mind, it's no wonder. We're dealing here with infinite mystery, with eternal, totally unlimited being, and we have absolutely nothing adequate to compare it with in human experience or language.

To place all of this in perspective, nothing I say here is new in Catholic teaching. The *Catechism of the Catholic Church* says it again. Human language will never measure up to the invisible, incomprehensible, unknowable One. Our words will always stand on this side of the mystery of God (42).

Again, as St. Thomas puts it, God's actions, like creation and redemption, create a relationship with him that begins at a certain point in time, but his existence is independent of everything he creates. All this simply says there is no before or after with God, no past or future. With him, everything, including all ages of creation, is one eternally present moment.

The mystery of God's eternity touches the very heart of our spiritual lives. The more profound and alive our awareness of the transcendent beauty, holiness and wonder of God becomes, the more eager we can be to answer his invitation to share these unfathomable riches, here and in eternity.

Evolution "more than a hypothesis"

Several years ago, Pope John Paul said there was enough scientific evidence to believe in evolution. Is this true? I thought we always believed that evolution is against our faith.

As long ago as 1950, Pope Pius XII, in the encyclical *Humani Generis*, maintained that the church has no problem with the study of evolution by scientists and theologians. The research, he said, which "inquires into the origin of the human body as coming from pre-existent and living matter," creates no difficulty for Catholic belief, as long as we accept that the spiritual "part" of our nature, what we call the soul, is immediately created by God (n. 36).

In his Oct. 22, 1996, address to the Pontifical Academy of Sciences, to which you refer, Pope John Paul II said that new knowledge leads us to recognize that the theory of evolution is more than a hypothesis. He makes two important points. First, we must use extreme caution when we attempt to find answers to scientific questions in the Bible. Four years before that, he spoke to the same group about the church's condemnation of Galileo. (All are aware, I hope, that the renowned 17th century scientist and astronomer was charged with heresy for claiming that the earth revolves around the sun, not vice versa. His theory was said to contradict Scripture, which speaks rather of the sun moving, going up and coming down around the earth. See, for instance, Jos. 10:12-13.)

In that 1992 address, the pope attributed Galileo's condemnation to the fact that the majority of theologians did not recognize the "distinction between sacred Scripture and its interpretation," which led them "unduly to transpose" doctrine and scientific investigation. The Holy Father's 1996 address, in relation to evolution, repeats this warning against interpretations of Scripture "that make it say what it does not intend to say." Scripture scholars and theologians, he says, cannot do their job properly unless they keep informed about what is happening in the sciences.

Second, the evolution theory, as any hypothesis, needs always to be tested against the facts. As information gathers that fits the theory, its explanation of how life developed on our planet becomes more and more probable. According to Pope John Paul II and, I believe, most Catholic officials and theologians, the facts converging from many fields of knowledge (anthropology, geology, psychology, and so on) create a progressively "significant argument in favor of this theory." (The complete text of this message is available from Origins, CNS Documentary Service, 3211 Fourth St. N.E., Washington, D. C., 20017-1100. Ask for the Dec. 5, 1996, issue)

None of this denies creation by God. It says simply that God apparently did his creating quite differently than those people assume who take Genesis as a scientific explanation of how the universe came to be. How God created it in the beginning, or how the energies placed in the cosmos by the Creator work to move all things toward greater and greater complexity — or simplicity — is not part of our faith.

Evolution and the soul

I enjoy your column each week, but one you had recently on evolution puzzled me. You said that one is free to hold at least some belief in evolution and still be a good Catholic in no conflict with the doctrine of the church.

Animals do not have souls, right? But human beings do. So how can we have evolved from apes, gorillas, monkeys, or so-called missing links? Aren't they animals?

As you correctly point out, there is something that makes us human that cannot be explained by the material part of us that might be derived from other living beings through some sort of evolution. This non-material, spiritual element that is essential to our human personality is what Catholic tradition, following the terminology of one Greco-Roman philosophy, has called the soul.

Since the soul has no parts, one cannot break off a piece and pass it on in the way our parents, for example, pass on the material for our bodies from their own. This is one reason the church has taught, and still teaches, that while our bodies may evolve from other bodies, the spiritual part of us could only come into existence through a direct creative act of God. Each of our souls comes, as it were, fresh from the hand of our Creator.

Tradition has seen at least hints of this teaching in holy Scripture. For example, at death "the dust returns to the earth from which it came, and the spirit returns to the God who gave it." (Ecc. 12:7) And, "We have had our earthly fathers (literally the fathers of the flesh) to discipline us and we respected them. Should we not then submit all the more to the Father of spirits and live?" (Heb. 12:9)

In our own time this position on evolution was repeated by Pope Pius XII in his encyclical *Humani Generis* (1950). The teaching of the church, he says, "does not forbid that, in conformity with the present state of human sciences and sacred theology, research and discussions on the part of men experienced in both fields take place with regard to the doctrine of evolution, inasfar as it inquires into the origin of the human body as coming from pre-existent and living matter — for Catholic faith obliges us to hold that souls are immediately created by God."

Should theology be based on science?

I am a CCD instructor and need some answers. You are probably tired of the subject of evolution, but I have taught and wrote that an ape cannot be in the image and likeness of God. The Bible speaks so often about the story of creation, that I don't see how I can be wrong. When the pope came out with his statement on evolution, (that evolution is more than just a hypothesis and that many disciplines independently are leading us to accept it), I was left virtually defenseless.

Why don't we read the Bible literally as do fundamentalists? The first remark of some Protestant recruiters is that we don't believe in the Bible so we cannot be Christians. Are there books and journals on these subjects?

For whatever reasons, not a few otherwise intelligent people seem to think that any question, any searching, no matter how complicated or profound, should have answers they can absorb and understand in 30 or 60 minutes, just about the length of an "in-depth" television program.

That is not true. If we ask serious questions, then we must be willing to do serious study to find appropriate answers that will satisfy us. This is especially desirable before we start to condemn or accuse others of error because they disagree with what we "know" to be the fact.

I have previously referred readers to the introductions and textual notes in the *New American Bible* (especially the St. Joseph edition), published under the auspices of the bishops of the United States. A thoughtful, careful study of these alone would give at least a good start toward resolving your concerns about how the Catholic Church interprets Scripture.

Second your problems with evolution prove again how we need serious reflection before we build religious doctrines on matters that pertain primarily to the natural sciences.

Some years ago, the publication *First Things* (a monthly "Journal of Religion and Public Life") printed an intriguing dialogue on some relationships of modern physics to theology. One participant noted perceptively that "we had better not base our theology on a desperate hope for continued ignorance" on matters of nature we cannot at present explain.

He makes a good point. In spite of painful experience, many have still not learned that lesson. For 15 centuries, Christians built their Scripture interpretations and theology of creation on the assumption that we would never know more about the universe and our solar system than what we read in the Bible.

Along came Galileo, proving our assumptions were wrong, and it took centuries before we could theologically adapt to the fact that there is more out there than human beings ever dreamed or could imagine. The same thing happened, and continues to happen, with evolution. We assumed that human knowledge about the origins of life would never go beyond the Bible stories. So we built a theology and philosophy of creation on that assumption of continued ignorance.

Then came the totally unexpected converging discoveries of many natural sciences. As Pope John Paul II said, that convergence "of the results of work that was conducted independently is in itself a significant argument in favor of this theory" of evolution.

We are free, of course, to refute that science if we do it on scientific grounds. But to frantically attempt to shore up our religious convictions by refusing to recognize observable facts is ultimately fruitless. It is to deny that truth is one, as our Holy Father reminded us. One truth can never contradict another truth.

Good science can never contradict good theology. For some reason, that seems a particularly difficult and painful lesson to learn.

Which Divine Person is Creator?

My question is about the Holy Trinity. Which Person in the Trinity is the Creator? St. Paul writes about Jesus, "In him were created all things in heaven and on earth" (Colossians 1:16). Yet in the creed we say "I believe in God the Father almighty, creator of heaven and earth." Then in the hymn to the Holy Spirit, we sing "Come Holy Ghost, creator blest" Are they all "creators"? How do we explain this?

We must realize that we do not have, and as limited creatures, could not possibly have, a thorough "explanation" of the nature or the works of the Holy Trinity. The reason is that we are dealing here with the greatest and central mystery of the Christian faith.

Practically everything we know of the Trinity has come from the church's theological and spiritual reflection on two sources: How Jesus talked about the relationships between himself and the Father and the Holy Spirit, and how Christians, individually and collectively, experience the Father, Son and Holy Spirit in their lives.

Jesus, for example, speaks of sending the Spirit. In numerous passages, we read how the very early Christians are quite conscious that their actions are undertaken under the guidance and direction of the Holy Spirit. (See Acts 10:44, 11:12, 13:2 among many other examples)

Gradually, in somewhat different ways in the East and West, the church began to explore the connections between the Trinity's life and actions *ad intra*, as they were sometimes called, God's inner life, and God's actions *ad extra*, what God does outside himself, in creation.

This brings us closer to the answer to your question, insofar as we can have one. While they relate in some mysterious way with each other as "Persons," the Father, the begotten Son, and the Spirit who proceeds from both, share equally the one divine nature. Each is distinct, but each is truly God. From this perspective, every action of God that involves creation, including creation itself, is co-equally the action of all three Persons. Since there is only one God-substance, none of the three act independently. Whatever is done outside of their co-existent relationship, all do. Thus, it is proper and necessary, to say that the Father, Son and Spirit are involved in the work of creation, and in all that sustains and affects that creation.

At the same time, as God reveals himself in the Scriptures, specific divine actions are attributed to one or other of the three Persons. External actions of God are seen as appropriate to a particular Person in view of that Person's "place" in the inner life of the Trinity. The Father, because he is without source or origin in the eternal Trinity, is associated with power and creation. The Spirit, who is viewed as the union of love between the Father and Son, is associated with holiness, comfort, all those human experiences that result from the fire and joy of love. The Son is seen as the Word generated from eternity, not as a creature, but as sharing the God-nature with the Father. To him are attributed qualities such as filial love of the Father. In him, as the word made flesh, the kingdom of God is revealed as present in our human existence.

While only the Son took on our human nature and entered eternal glory through the paschal mystery of his death and resurrection, all three Persons were, and are, involved and active in the saving life and work of Jesus. It is impossible here to give extensive biblical references to all these truths. But some serious study of passages in the Old and New Testaments will yield a multitude of examples of these ways of speaking about the one God, and the internal communal life and external actions of the Holy Trinity.

Moses and the Bible's first five books

In a recent column you said the church formerly defined that the Pentateuch (the first five books of the Old Testament) were written by Moses. Now, you say, the church says this part of the Bible was not written by Moses.

You have a great problem if you deny Moses was the author of these books. Either (1) Christ was ignorant of the true author when he quotes Moses in these books, or (2) he lied or (3) we cannot trust John's or Luke's words when Jesus quotes Moses.

There is at least a fourth possibility which you neglected to mention:

Jesus, according to the Gospels, was simply reflecting Hebrew tradition by referring to Moses as the author of the five books to which you refer, and had no intention of deciding a technical question of authorship for future Scripture scholars.

Even though a few passages apparently do go back to somewhere around his lifetime, numerous parts of these five books indicate one way or another that Moses, who lived probably in the 13th century before Christ, was not their author. To take just one particularly superficial instance, Moses could not have described his own death and burial (Deuteronomy 34).

Your question and comments are a good reminder that we need to understand remarks of this nature made by Jesus or other biblical figures in the way the people would have understood them at that time.

Let me give just one example from the Gospel according to Matthew (12:40). Jesus says, "Just as Jonah was in the belly of the whale three days and three nights, so will the Son of Man be in the heart of the earth three days and three nights."

There is no reason to conclude that by these words Jesus was declaring his belief that the man Jonah was actually swallowed by a large fish, spent three days living and breathing in the whale's insides and then was spat out on the beach. He was simply using a story, a parable from the prophets with which his listeners would have been familiar, to make a point about his own death and resurrection.

One more point. If you are at all familiar with biblical literature, you know that attributing certain writings to a popular figure, perhaps long dead, was a common literary device. King Solomon, for example, who died about 920 B. C., was the pre-eminent wise man in Hebrew tradition, renowned even beyond the borders of his kingdom, as we read in 1 Kings and 2 Chronicles. Later writers in the Jewish wisdom tradition did not hesitate to name Solomon as the author of their work, even though it was written centuries later.

The Book of Proverbs (1:1) identifies itself as "the proverbs of Solomon," and the Song of Songs says (1:1) it was composed "by Solomon." Yet both of these Old Testament works were written or put together, at least in the form we now have them, more than 400 years after the old king's death.

No deception or dishonesty was intended or suspected here. Everyone recognized it as a perfectly understandable way of uniting one's work with traditions that preceded it. In the same manner, no one had a problem calling Genesis, Exodus, Leviticus, Numbers and Deuteronomy the "books of Moses" since they all intended to clarify and enlarge on the law and covenant which God originally revealed to this heroic figure of Hebrew history.

Noah and the Ark

During my young years I thought that everyone and everything perished during the great flood except Noah and his family and animals (two of each). His family and the animals survived because he took them with him on the ark. Now my granddaughter, who taught Bible school at her Catholic church, tells me the story of the great flood and Noah was only a myth, or words to that effect.

We cannot read stories of the Bible, especially those which go back tens or hundreds of thousands of years into prehistory, as if they were written by modern scientists or historians. Just as Jesus used parables (which are fictions to convey a truth he wanted to teach), other parts of the Bible can do the same.

Except for those Christian groups who are biblical literalists (meaning that they accept every part of the Bible as literally true, as if they were scientific and historical documents in our modern sense of the word) almost no one today would, for example, view the story of Noah and the Ark as literally and historically accurate.

This by no means says that the story is not true. The truth of the story is not in whether or not the details are accurate, but rather in the knowledge it reveals to us of God's power, man's capacity for both good and evil, God's desire to forgive and save us, and so on. Sometimes, in fact, when we concentrate too much on the technical details of stories like Noah, we tend to miss the real message which God is telling us if we listen in the right way.

A point you mention in your question is one proof that the Noah story was never intended to give intricate details. You note that Noah took two of each animal into the ark with him. This is true according to one part of the flood story (Genesis 7, 8-9). Later on, however, we are told there were seven pairs of clean animals taken into the ark (Genesis 7, 25). This seeming contradiction posed no difficulty for the writer who finally put the story together as we have it, because his purpose was not to count animals or days of rain. Under the inspiration of the Holy Spirit, he had a far more profound message than that.

Did Abraham commit adultery?

I don't understand the story in the Bible about Abraham. He had a wife, Sarah, but he also had a son (Ishmael) by a slave girl before the son of his real wife. Now, wasn't Abraham committing adultery?

If you check the book of Genesis (chapter 16), you'll note that the slave girl, Hagar, was actually Abraham's concubine. In the Old Testament, however, a concubine was more than a mistress in our sense of the word. She was an actual wife, but of some lower status than the wife (or wives) who enjoyed the full legal status of wife.

The possession of concubines seems to have constituted a kind of transition practice between polygamy (having more than one wife), which was quite common in the ancient world, and monogamy (one wife). No one seems very sure of the exact difference between a wife and a concubine. Probably much depended on the particular time and culture. But having children by concubines was considered completely proper and legal.

The practice continued for centuries after Abraham, who lived about 1700 B. C. In fact, among the Jews as well as other ancient cultures (and in some localities even into modern times) the best barometer of a man's wealth was the number of concubines in his harem. About 925 B. C., a major indication that King Solomon was the richest man in the world was that he had 700 wives and 300 concubines — which has got to be some kind of record! (see I Kings, chapter 11)

The Rachel story in Scripture

Some post-abortion counseling centers have the name of Rachel. The Scripture readings on the feast of the Holy Innocents in December made us wonder about her. The Gospel spoke of Rachel weeping for her children. Is there a connection between these Rachels?

Rachel, the favorite wife of Jacob (Israel), was among the most attractive and endearing women in the Old Testament. She was the mother of his two children, Benjamin and Joseph, ancestors of two of the "12 tribes" who, according to Hebrew tradition, constituted the people of Israel. Biblical chronologies of that period are extremely uncertain, but she probably lived somewhere around 1,500 years before Christ.

The town of Ramah was on the edge of the territory assigned to the tribe of Benjamin, about five miles north of Jerusalem. The site even today has the Arabic name er-Ram. In 597 B. C., Nebuchadnezzar, king of Babylon, conquered the entire area. He eventually destroyed the city of Jerusalem, including the great temple of Solomon. Over the next ten years, nearly the entire population was resettled in Babylon and various other locations in the Babylonian empire, beginning a 60-year exile that would drastically affect the history of the Hebrew people.

The book of Jeremiah (chapter 40) describes how Ramah was the staging area where Jewish captives were gathered before their dispersion for resettlement. Thus, in the passage you quote, Jeremiah pictures Rachel mourning the tragedy befalling "her children," descendants of her sons Benjamin and Joseph.

"In Ramah is heard the sound of... bitter weeping! Rachel mourns her children, she refuses to be consoled because her children are no more" (Jer. 31:15). The Gospel of Matthew quotes this passage in the story of the massacre of infants in Bethlehem after the birth of our Lord (Mt. 2:18).

The words quoted about her in Jeremiah and the Gospel make Rachel an appropriate symbol for mothers attempting to cope with the death of their unborn children.

Why are things "unclean?"

The more I read the book of Leviticus, the more confused I become. Why are perfectly normal functions and things considered unclean? Where did all these strange laws about food, lepers, death, and so on originate?

According to Jewish law, contact with four categories of things rendered an individual unclean, that is, unfit to participate in any worship. These four categories included leprosy, dead bodies, certain foods that were labeled unclean, and sexual functions. Nearly anything that had to do with sexual intercourse, sinful or lawful or not, was considered unclean.

This uncleanness was not necessarily something spiritual, and generally had nothing to do with holiness. In fact, usually it could be taken away by simply washing oneself. But the system was severely adhered to among the Jews. We learn from the Gospels that at least some groups of Jews, such as the Pharisees, insisted on the most rigid observance of all such laws, a position for which they are frequently attacked by Jesus.

No one has ever been able to give a satisfactory explanation of the origin of these Hebraic regulations. It seems clear that they relate somehow to similar laws observed by pagan cults among whom the Jews lived, but every explanation suggested appears to have as many arguments against it as for it.

Jesus' primary objection to the whole system centered on its focus on externals. As he said, it isn't what a man eats or what he touches that really counts, it's what is in his heart and what comes out of that heart that determines how good a person he is.

Circumcision

Circumcision puzzles me. I understand the medical reasons why circumcision may be recommended. But what could circumcision possibly have to do with religion? The Bible says that Jewish men were to be circumcised. And the Bible says Jesus was circumcised. Is there any reason?

Not too many years ago I would have had to say no one knows the answer to your question. Perhaps that is still true, but there is the possibility of an answer in what we have learned from some ancient inscriptions.

It is quite possible that circumcision is closely related to human sacrifice, a practice apparently widespread in some ancient cultures of the Middle East.

Some years ago, archeologists in the Near East discovered a text supposedly written by a priest of the Phoenician culture. According to this writing, a god named El, to prevent destruction of his city, sacrificed his son to his father, a god named Heaven. El then circumcised himself and commanded that all his followers should themselves be circumcised to avoid destruction of the city.

The rite of circumcision, in this tradition at least, seems to be a substitute and symbol for human sacrifice, a part of the body is substituted for the whole.

Ancient cultures saw an intimate relationship between the individual and the entire tribe or community. Thus the fact that this sacrifice involved part of the organ of procreation proclaimed that the whole nation or clan, present and future, was consecrated to the god it worshiped.

In this context it is easy to see why the descendants of Abraham came to view circumcision as a fitting and necessary expression of their covenant with the God of Israel.

Does Israel belong to the Jews?

In connection with the present fights between Jews and Arabs, the claim has been made by some Jews that the land of that area belongs to them. They say God gave it to them. Do you agree? How could they claim such a thing?

In the Old Testament, as God formed Abraham and his descendants into his "Chosen People," he is believed to have particularly destined them for the territory which we now know as the state of Israel. The cohesiveness they would develop in relation to this land would be an important part of the many ways God would develop the theological and social conditions necessary to prepare for the coming, and for the work, of Jesus.

Some (most?) Jewish people feel this divine plan still gives a foundation for their claim to the land. My conviction, and, I believe, the position of any official statements by the Catholic Church, is that the Old Testament theological claim has little or no relevance to the present situation. Settlement of the problems must be on the same basis of political and social justice as might lead to the solution of any other such dispute — and that would include consideration of the history involved during the past 2,000 years as well as in the time before Christ.

Who is Yahweh?

I recently purchased a prayer book that often uses the word Yahweh *for God. I see this word many times today, but I went to 12 years of Catholic school and never heard it once. What does it mean and why is it used so much now?*

The word *Yahweh* represents the best effort of modern Scripture scholars to reproduce the most holy Jewish title for God. In ancient Hebrew tradition, this sacred name was never used except in solemn ceremonies.

According to biblical tradition, it is the name God gave himself when he spoke to Moses in the burning bush in Exodus 3.

The word already was used, however, in some parts of the earliest chapters of Genesis. In whatever way it originated, the word seems to come from the Hebrew verb "to be" and generally is translated as something like "he who is" or "I am he who is" — expressing the total superiority of this living God over all creation.

Instead of the forbidden word *Yahweh*, Jews usually referred to God in their daily conversations and prayers by the word *Adonai*, Lord. In Hebrew writing, when they wished to refer to God, the consonants of *Yahweh* were used (YHWH) with the vowels for *Adonai* (AOA). This indicated that the word *Adonai* should be used in the reading.

However when the earliest English Bibles appeared, the translators made one word out of that combination, ending up with the hybrid "Jehovah," a word which really never appeared in any language.

Yahweh is a strange word to us, even though we use the first part often in our Catholic worship. The word "alleluia" literally means "praise to Yahweh" or "praised be God."

While the precise pronunciation for it is lost somewhere in history because of the Jewish prohibition against saying it aloud, it does hold an honored place in tradition as the unique name for the one living God of Israel and of Christians.

Bible books, chapters and verses

In the early years of Christianity, along with the books of our New Testament, there were many Scriptures which are called non-canonical and are not in our Bible. Who decided, and when, which books were to be in the New Testament Bible?

Theoretically, the answer is clear and relatively simple. We believe that, under the inspiration and guidance of the Holy Spirit, the living church gradually discovered which of the many sacred writings of very early Christianity were to be in the "canon."

The Greek word *canon*, in this context, means a norm or standard. The biblical canon, then, constitutes those books which were inspired by God, and which were believed to constitute the norm or rule for Christian faith and moral life.

Many letters, Gospels and other writings circulated among the early churches. Various lists or canons surfaced, and Christians eventually recognized certain Scriptures as normative, that is reflecting Christian faith and presenting a model or guiding standard for any authentic Christian church.

By about the year 400, popes and councils had endorsed a basic list. Certain confusions remained, however, all the way up to the Council of Trent, which in 1546 finally defined those books to be recognized as the church's sacred, canonical Scriptures.

It sounds easy. In reality the process was not at all so simple and neat. For one thing, a number of supposedly important books were just "lost." The letter of his own that Paul mentions in 1 Corinthians 5:3, and a document containing quotations from Jesus in Aramaic, supposedly written by the apostle Matthew, simply disappeared somewhere along the line.

Others encountered much opposition, partly because some origin or presumed connection with the apostles was considered essential for acceptance. Even way back then, leading Christian scholars questioned whether Hebrews and Revelation were really written by Paul and John respectively, thus casting doubt on their apostolic origin.

Complicating things further was the fact that numerous changes and additions were made after the original forms of the Gospels were written. Sometimes these came from sayings of Jesus that were passed down orally well into the second century.

The story of the woman taken in adultery (John 8), for example, was most probably inserted into the fourth Gospel about 100 years after the Gospel was first composed; in other words, not too much before the year 200. No wonder some of the great early fathers of the church differed among themselves about which books should be on the canonical list.

Who divided the New Testament?

Who divided the New Testament into chapters and verses?

The division of the Bible into chapters was, as far as we know, the work of Stephen Langton (died 1228), a professor at the University of Paris and later archbishop of Canterbury. Old Testament verses were numbered by a Dominican priest, Sanctes Pagnini, in 1528, and New Testament verses by a Parisian printer, Robert Etienne, in 1555.

Composition of the New Testament

To settle an argument, how long did it take to write the New Testament?

If you're talking about the actual writing and putting together of the books of the New Testament as they are in our Bible, the earliest was the first letter to the Thessalonians, written around the year 50 or 51, about 20 years after Jesus' death. All of Paul's letters were written, obviously, before his death, probably before the year 67.

The Gospel of Mark, the earliest of the four Gospels, dates from perhaps the year 65, though all the Gospels made use of documents, liturgical rites, and other traditions which existed in the Christian communities before that date.

The last books were probably the three letters of St. John and the book of Revelation, all of which were perhaps written sometime around the year 100, or later.

Thus, the basic composition of all the books covered a period of somewhere around 50 years.

Who wrote the Gospels?

During a sermon on the radio, a Protestant minister said that the Gospel of John was not written by the apostle John the Divine, and that Catholics and Protestants agree on this. Don't we have to believe that the New Testament was written by the apostles? If not by them, then who did write the Gospels?

It has long been known by Scripture authorities of all Christian faiths that several books of the New Testament were not actually written by the persons traditionally thought to be their authors. The Gospels of Matthew and John are almost certainly two New Testament books of this nature.

There's nothing surprising here. In ancient times a literary work commonly bore the name of the person out of whose teaching the work was formed, even if the man himself did not write it — or perhaps was no longer even alive. The book would still be recognized (and even named) as the teaching of that particular "master" or famous person, though developed, edited, and expanded upon by others perhaps over a period of many years.

This, of course, has no bearing on whether or not the books of the Bible were inspired. The church has never made doctrinal declarations about the authors of the books which make up the Bible.

Chronology of biblical books

What is the chronology of the books in the Bible? Is there a list that details this chronology? I understand Isaiah was written in three parts, before, during and after the exile in Babylon. Is that true? When Herod Antipas "ruled" Galilee, who ruled Judea, Syria and the other provinces? Can you suggest sources for us to get the answers?

We recently heard of one Gospel not mentioned in the Bible that describes the boyhood of Jesus, one by St. Thomas. Are these Gospels available somewhere? Even the little history of the Jews I have learned helps me understand the Sunday readings and has deepened my faith. We'd love to have a Bible class, but none is available in our area.

First let me say I am awed by the number of questions I receive similar to yours. For years, a third to a half of all questions sent to me concerned marriage, remarriage, annulments and church rules about such subjects. Today that "first place" easily goes to questions concerning holy Scripture. The serious, even scholarly hunger for knowing and applying the biblical word of God is one of the wonderful encouraging signs of faith alive in our Catholic Church.

Several early Christian "gospels" are not in our New Testament. One alleges to describe some bizarre miracles performed by the child Jesus.

The most famous Gospel of Thomas is a series of 114 "sayings" of the "living Jesus." The entire text of this Gospel was discovered only in 1945, among other texts in an ancient library along the Nile in northern Egypt. This Gospel goes back probably to the year 100 at the latest, and is perhaps the most significant archeological find in the history of New Testament scholarship. Its importance in the developing study of the life and words of Jesus can hardly be exaggerated. The text is available in several publications.

I make these comments, among other reasons, to stress that, while such early Christian writings can be helpful, and may even derive one way or another from the author to whom they're attributed, they are not, and will not become, part of our Bible. We believe that the books of Scripture, as tradition and teaching of the church have handed them down to us, are complete.

Numerous excellent resources exist today for every area of biblical interest. Three come to mind for a start. One is the *New American Bible*, the "official" scripture published under the auspices of the bishops of the United States. The texts, notes and commentaries are marvelous and thoroughly reliable in their reflection of our faith.

Next would be the *Catholic Study Bible*. It contains the NAB text and materials, and much additional background on the whole Bible and on individual books (Oxford University Press).

If you're really hungry (and have about $70), the flagship one-volume of English-speaking Scripture scholarship is the *New Jerome Biblical Commentary*. The best scholars in the world contributed major, readable articles on everything from the Genesis creation stories to the Dead Sea Scrolls and current approaches in biblical study. It also includes introductions and verse-by-verse commentaries for all the books of the Bible (Prentice Hall).

Excellent Bible group study programs are available, too. Many appreciate the program, "Scripture from Scratch" (videos and printed materials from St. Anthony Messenger Press.)

I'm happy you are part of this remarkable activity in the church. Bishops, priests, all of us, require serious involvement in the Scriptures, as St. Augustine said, lest any of us become "an empty preacher

of the word of God outwardly, who is not a listener to it inwardly"
(Sermons 179).

Why is Matthew first?

We know that the Gospel according to Mark was written before the Gospel according to Matthew. Then why is the Gospel according to Matthew the first one in the New Testament, before Mark? Every Bible we have looked at puts Mark second and Matthew first.

I would not necessarily agree with your certainty about the priority in time of Mark over Matthew. It is true that most Bible scholars feel the evidence points increasingly to the conclusion that Mark came first. That's as far as we can go.

Sometime during the century after our Lord's death and resurrection, his "good news" of salvation (the Gospel) emerged as a collection of four documents, called the Gospel "according to" Matthew, Mark, Luke and John. Matthew led the list, as he still does, for some significant reasons. For one, that Gospel seems to have been the first of the four to be accepted by one of the major Christian communities, probably Antioch.

It is difficult for us to appreciate the influential role this Gospel played for early Christians. It served as a sort of catechism, or summary of Christian beliefs, which laid out for the faithful and others who read it what it meant to be a follower of Christ. Those who count such things point out that almost all Christian writers of the second century refer to Matthew more than any other Gospel. Perhaps the greatest of them, St. Irenaeus, in his work *Against Heresies*, quotes Matthew more than all the other Gospels combined.

One reason for this is the sheer range of content in Matthew. It contains nearly all the narrative material in the Gospel of Mark, but much more, such as material about the infancy and resurrection appearances of our Lord. It also settles several questions that could be raised in the Gospel of Mark. Matthew makes clear, for example, that Jesus was not baptized for his own personal repentance. Matthew also explains how the rumor got started that Jesus' own disciples had stolen his body from the tomb.

The Sermon on the Mount (chapters 5-7) all by itself could easily explain why the "first Gospel" came to be accepted at that time as the best practical expression of Christian beliefs and ideal behavior. Another explanation for Matthew's first place in the list of the four Gospels is that early Christians generally considered it the first to be written, largely for reasons outlined above.

That traditional order of placement continues in current editions of Scripture, even though it may not match the order in which the Gospels were written.

Sexually inclusive language in the Bible

Our Scripture study group is a real joy. We hope you can enlighten us on sexually inclusive language. Couldn't the Bible use words that include women as well as men? I think most of us wonder why there is such a problem including both sexes whenever possible?

As you must be aware, while the questions you raise are complicated, they are interesting and useful questions. I would offer three observations which seem worth serious consideration by your group.

First, any language in daily use by a group of people undergoes continuous change. New words and meanings, even new grammatical structures, are always developing. When I was growing up, "gay" meant joyful, exuberant, happy. A "pusher" was one who demonstrated personal initiative, until the drug culture changed that.

There's no doubt that words like "man" and "mankind" now carry at least some different sense than previously when a more universal meaning was understood and accepted. Even dictionaries define "man" with different nuances today than they did two generations back.

In today's social ferment, this shift is to be expected, especially since English, in grammar and vocabulary, is linguistically one of the more sexist languages, broadly expressing gender stereotypes to the detriment of one sex or the other. We always need to respect this reality and the transitions I mentioned when we write or speak, and perhaps especially when one language is translated into another.

Second, holy Scripture is a special case. Here it is not enough simply to translate passages into modern, current English or any other language. We believe that God's revealing of himself, as recorded in Scripture, was not an ethereal, timeless, unattached event outside the daily gritty limitations, and even sinfulness, of the people themselves. Revelation happened in specific cultures, with all their peculiarities and weaknesses, and that's the way it has come down to us.

We may abhor the slavery taken for granted by Paul and numerous Old Testament writers. We may be embarrassed by the way women were grouped with oxen and asses in the Ten Commandments (Exodus

20:17). But we are unfaithful to Scripture, and to revelation, if we divorce these sacred writings from their historical contexts, and "correct" Jeremiah, or the authors of Deuteronomy, or Luke, or Paul, as if they possessed the same moral and social and political sensitivities we have.

In other words, biblical translations must be faithful to Catholic teaching regarding God's activity "in human history as it unfolds" (U. S. Bishops' Criteria for Evaluation of Inclusive Language in Scripture Texts Proposed for Liturgical Use, November 1990).

The revised New Testament of the *New American Bible* (Catholic) explicitly deals with the need for gender-inclusive language. The introduction explains that discriminatory language should be eliminated when possible, but "the text should not be altered in order to adjust to contemporary concerns." Thus, for example, it retains the word "brothers" in its inclusive sense, since no corresponding English word includes both sexes.

Particular care is required when we attempt to treat gender-related language about God, and the persons of the Holy Trinity, sensitively and with fidelity to the scriptural text.

One final consideration. Our language, the way we speak about people, events and ideas, is far more rooted in our real culture than we usually realize. Scholars of linguistics generally accept as a "given" that language rises out of the social behavior in a culture, not vice-versa. In other words, as long as society continues its economic, social and political sexual discrimination, genuine sex-inclusive language will never take hold among us. (Incidentally, the way this applies to racial discrimination is another, but similar, story.)

Some may not like to hear it, but experience tells us that if we want language to change, society must change. The fact that our sensitivity to language discrimination is far greater than it was 50 years ago shows that our culture is beginning to move. When we have moved a lot more, we will, I believe, be much more comfortable with appropriate gender-related language, and with how we relate to the language of the Bible.

Interpreting the Gospels

Last Holy Week the Gospel of Mark about the denial of Peter was read at Mass. In the Gospels of Matthew, Luke and John, the denial of Peter was three times, but in Mark two times. The Gospel of Mark confuses readers. Why not correlate the three into one Gospel so as to have the true meaning?

All the Gospels speak of Peter's three denials, including the Gospel of Mark (14: 68, 70 and 71).

Your question, however, raises a significant point that occurs frequently in the mail I receive. Perhaps it is one aspect of the conviction among many Catholics and other Christians that everything in religion should be black and white, without ambiguity, including the Bible itself. Any evidence that this is not always so is met with disbelief, if not (as apparently in your case) confusion.

The problem you experience is not uncommon. When we read the New Testament, especially the Gospels, we easily tend to think we are reading a life of Christ much like any modern biography. We feel that the first job of Matthew, Mark, Luke and John was to get the facts straight or, as you say, "correlate" the different accounts to get to the "true meaning."

We know, however, that the Gospels were never intended to be that. Aside from the fact that scientific historical scholarship as we are familiar with it is a relatively modern invention, details of fact were of no critical concern to the gospel writers. Their intention was rather to explain the meaning of the message of Jesus, what he stands for and what his followers are expected to be.

Since that is what the evangelists set out to do, we are doomed to failure if we expect something else. Evidence for the truth of what I am saying abounds in the New Testament.

We know, for example, that the Eucharist, or the Breaking of the Bread, held a high place in the minds of early Christians. One would assume that at least here they would have their "facts straight." Yet the quoted words of Jesus in the institution of the Eucharist at the Last Supper are different in all three Synoptic Gospels (Matthew 26, Mark 14, Luke 2). John does not refer to the Eucharist at all at the Last Supper, at least in this direct way.

The differing readings perhaps reflected variations in the liturgy from one place to another in those early decades of the church. Whatever the reasons, the gospel writers had no problem adding or subtracting ideas they thought necessary to express what they wanted to say about Jesus.

What I am saying is not a minority opinion of a few biblical scholars. It is the official position of the Catholic Church about the formation and character of the Gospels. In 1964 the Pontifical Biblical Commission issued an instruction on the historical truth of the Gospels. From the many things handed down to them, says the commission, the gospel writers "selected some things, reduced others to a synthesis and explained yet others as they kept in mind the different situations of each of the churches.

"They selected the things which were suited to the varying situations of Christian believers and to the purpose they had in mind, and adapted their narration of them to the same situations and purpose ... The truth of the story is not at all affected by the fact that the evangelists relate the words and deeds of the Lord in a different order and express his sayings not literally but differently, while preserving their sense."

Thus, as the instruction indicates, the first principle of the church in interpreting the Scriptures is: Seek out the meaning intended by the evangelist in narrating a saying or a deed in a certain way or in placing it in a certain context. What did the writer intend to say? That is the first question to ask.

Insofar as the gospel authors knew about each other's writings, as Luke and Matthew seem certainly to have known about the earlier Gospel of Mark, they obviously had other concerns besides meshing their facts. Their message was much bigger, much different and much deeper for their readers than that.

Pope John Paul II summarized Catholic teaching on this subject in his letter of Jan. 6, 2001, on the beginning of the third millennium. "The Gospels do not claim to be a complete biography of Jesus in accordance with the canons of modern historical science. From them, nevertheless, the face of the Nazarene emerges with a solid historical foundation." (n. 18)

Perpetual virginity of Mary

How did the church come up with the idea that Mary remained a virgin after the birth of Jesus? Wouldn't it be a "sin" for Mary not to have relations with Joseph while they were married? This would not make her any less of a person or saint; she was still chosen to be the mother of God. Also, in the Magnificat Mary says, "My spirit rejoices in God, my Savior." So how did the church come up with the fact that she was born without original sin?

It is true, of course, that the Catholic Church professes the doctrine of the perpetual virginity of the Virgin Mary, a belief, incidentally, which was shared by several major figures of the Reformation, including Luther, Calvin and Zwingli.

From the earliest expressions of this teaching, however, in the first centuries of Christianity, it is clear that the spiritual and theological implications of her virginity were essential and integral to an authentic understanding of what that virginity was about.

Her physical virginity was a reality, we believe. But the meaning of that reality goes beyond biology and physiology. It was most of all an expression, a living out, of her radical, total love for God, and her full surrender to his will. As with all her unique gifts from the Father, the gift of her virginity must be seen in the light of Mary's supreme vocation of being the mother of Jesus Christ, the Mother of God.

Thus, in the perspective of the earliest Fathers of the church, the virginity of Mary is significant first of all as a privilege of Jesus himself. His conception in her womb by the power of the Spirit reflects the eternal "conception," born of the Father before all ages, as the creed says, and his mission to regenerate, recreate, the whole human race through his new covenant. It is in this context that Mary is the "new Eve," mother of a new creation of the human family, and a unique sharer in her Son's victory over sin and its effects in the world.

The tradition of the subsequent virginity of Mary during her whole life, which is an even older patristic tradition than the virgin birth, is based on the same Christian insights. The marriage of Joseph and Mary was unique, in many ways a mystery. Spouses in marriage vow to each other the right to genital expression of their love when that "right" is sought in timely and appropriately loving ways. There is no absolute obligation, however, even as we understand marriage today, for either partner ever to exercise that right. The Gospels (including Luke 1:34, where Mary says "I have no relations with a man") and the whole Christian tradition, seem to assume that's what happened with Joseph and Mary.

Finally, when proclaiming the dogma of the Immaculate Conception in 1854, Pope Pius IX made clear that all Mary's gifts, including this one, were given to her through Christ. She was preserved from all sin, he said, "in consideration of the merits of Jesus Christ, savior of the human race."

Thus Jesus is, as the Magnificat proclaims, her savior as he is our own.

The name of Jesus

As my children and I were discussing Christmas, one of them asked why Mary and Joseph named their baby Jesus. I told them that was the name

God wanted the baby to have, but they weren't satisfied. Nothing more came to mind, so we decided to ask. Was there any special meaning to that name?

As you say, according to the Gospels the name "Jesus" came from God through an angel to Mary (Lk. 1:31) and in a dream to Joseph (Mt.1:21). The name in other forms, Joshua in particular, has a long history in Hebrew culture.

Jesus is the Greek form of Joshua, a name which in Hebrew means "God (Yahweh) helps," or more popularly "God saves." It is this second meaning that Matthew picks up on, reporting that the name was bestowed on Jesus "because he will save his people from their sins." For Matthew it also carried the connotation, always a central theme in that Gospel, that the salvation Jesus brings is a community, a "church" event. Jesus would save "his people."

Second, the name was not unique. People often named their children Jesus in those days. Paul refers to a Jewish Christian of that name (Col. 4:11), and it appears in other literature of the same period. The same remains true today in some places.

The implication is that Jesus received a very common name, one that did not immediately separate him from the human family, but helped to identify him with it.

Jesus in Roman literature

Jesus Christ is surely one of the greatest figures in history. Is he mentioned anywhere other than in the Bible?

I assume you are asking about early Christian history, around the time the New Testament was being formed. For us Christians, who believe that the coming of Jesus was the pivotal point in human history, it's difficult to imagine how little interest he aroused apart from his own small community of followers. From any viewpoint other than faith, he was, after all, merely the leader of a tiny offshoot group of Jews in a spectacularly insignificant corner of the Roman Empire.

The first historical mention of Jesus outside the circle of Christians apparently was by Flavius Josephus, a Jewish historian who eventually won the close friendship of Vespasian and other Roman emperors. This historian's works, especially *The Antiquities of the Jews*, completed about the year 94, were highly prized resources by St. Jerome and other early church fathers.

Toward the end of the book, Josephus describes how, under the procurator Albinus, there was brought before a group of judges "the brother of Jesus, who was called Christ, whose name was James" (Book XX 9.1) This would have been James the apostle, one of the three disciples closest to our Lord, who died as a martyr in the year 44.

An earlier mention of Jesus in the *Antiquities*, as a miracle worker who rose three days after dying, was almost certainly added later by a Christian "copy editor."

The first mention of Jesus by a pagan writer seems to be that of the Roman historian Tacitus, about 110 A.D., who speaks of Christians "whose founder, one Christus, was put to death by the procurator Pontius Pilate when Tiberius was emperor (*Annals* XV. 44). Another historian, Gaius Suetonius, in his *Life of Claudius* (perhaps about 120 A.D.) writes, "Since the Jews made continual disturbances at the instigation of Chrestus, he (Claudius) expelled them from Rome." This is generally accepted as referring to the early Christians and to Christ, though the timing is rather faulty. Claudius was emperor some years after Christ.

Was Jesus born on Christmas?

One night our study club realized that no one knows exactly when Jesus was born. How did we come to celebrate December 25 as the anniversary of his birth? Do we know what year he was born?

Strange as it seems, we have no idea of the date of Christ's birth. The Gospels are no help. From information given especially in the Gospel of Luke, scholars generally believe that Christ was born between the years 8 and 6 B. C. Though our present calendar was supposedly based on the year of Christ's birth as year one, the science of historical scholarship was not sophisticated enough for them to come to a precise determination, thus the difference of six or eight years.

Numerous theories have been put forward to explain December 25 as Christmas Day. The most likely one, however, the one most generally accepted by scholars now, is that the birth of Christ was assigned to the date of the winter solstice. This date is December 21 in our calendar, but was December 25 in the Julian calendar which predated our own, and January 6 in the Egyptian calendar. This latter date is still followed by some Eastern-Rite Christian churches.

The solstice, when days begin to lengthen in the northern hemisphere, was referred to by pagans as the "Birthday of the Unconquered Sun." During the third century, the Emperor Aurelian proclaimed December 25 as a special day dedicated to the sun-god, whose cult was very strong in Rome at that time. Even before this time, Christian writers already had begun to refer to Jesus as the Sun of Justice. It seemed quite logical, therefore, that as Christianity began to dominate the religious scene in the Roman Empire, the date of the "newborn sun" should be chosen as the birth date of Christ.

Were there Magi?

At Christmas time, a priest speaking on television said maybe there were no Magi who came to the crib of Christ. This story is in the Gospel. What does the church say about our belief in the Three Kings? Is it possible that the story did not really happen?

First, we're not speaking here about anything which is part of our required belief as Catholics or Christians. Particularly does it not involve any belief in "three kings." The Gospel of Matthew, the only one that tells this story, does not call them kings, nor does it say how many there were. Eastern Catholics, for example, traditionally speak of 12 kings, not three.

The answer to your question involves many technicalities of biblical interpretation referring to the literary form, or style of writing, used in this Gospel. We are fairly certain, from careful study of the Gospel and other documents written about the same time, that Matthew contains several examples of what is called *haggadic midrash* — that is, stories used to spin out and clarify the meaning of a particular event or teaching.

Such stories were intended to convey as clearly as possible the truth of the mystery being considered. They were not meant by their author to be taken literally, in our sense of the word, and were quite common among Jews as effective teaching tools.

One may believe that the story of the Magi happened exactly as it is described in the Gospel, or that it is partly made up but based on some actual journey of Magi to Jerusalem about the time of the birth of Jesus, or even that the story is legendary and intended to call attention to the fulfillment of the prophecies referred to by Matthew.

Any of these understandings is compatible with the Catholic understanding of the meaning and divine inspiration of the Bible.

The "historical Jesus"

Our parish Bible class is studying St. Luke this semester, in conjunction with the current Sunday readings. Some materials we use refer to the "historical Jesus" as if he is different from the Jesus we know. I have, I think, an idea of what is meant, but am not clear enough to explain it to the class. Is it possible to discuss the subject without becoming confusing? Could you explain simply who the historical Jesus is?

The "search for the historical Jesus," as it is sometimes called, has been a significant movement in biblical studies since early in the 20th century. Properly and carefully explained, it can help us understand some important elements of the church's teaching about the New Testament, the Gospels particularly.

For starters, your group must be aware of the Catholic teaching that the four Gospels were formed in three time periods or stages. First came the personal ministry of Jesus himself, what he actually said and did, what concerns he had to deal with, what types of people he was trying to motivate. A good way to put it, perhaps a little over simply, is to ask: If a video camera had followed him around, what would it have recorded?

Second came the period of proclamation, when the apostles and other early disciples preached Jesus to the earliest Christian communities, roughly between 35 and 70 A.D. How did they reinterpret the words and actions of Jesus in a variety of new cultures, new situations, new languages? How would the saving message, the "good news" of the risen Lord take root in new believers?

The final stage was the actual writing of the Gospels, a period covering roughly the years 65 to 100 A.D. During these years, "from the many things handed down," the Gospel writers "selected some things, reduced others to a synthesis, others they explicated as they kept in mind the situation of the churches." Thus they compiled a narrative concerning the Lord Jesus "with a method suited to the peculiar purpose each (author) set for himself." Their purpose, then, was not to compose a "biography" of the Savior, but to create a portrait of Jesus that would establish a base of faith in the risen Christ.

(This church teaching, including the above quotes, is found in the Pontifical Commission's Instruction on the Historical Truth of the Gospels, 1964, and in other documents.)

It is important to emphasize here our Christian belief that all this happened under the guidance and inspiration of the Holy Spirit, the Spirit Jesus promised would be with his community of believers through the ages (Jn 14). In no way, therefore, may we fear that the "truth" about Jesus and his message became diluted or confused by the time the Gospels were written.

On the contrary, the process leading up to their writing made the four Gospel portrayals of Jesus clearer and infinitely more revealing than would have been possible (from our human perspective at least) had they been written the day after the resurrection. Again, it all occurred with the Spirit hovering over the infant church as it was evolving.

From here on, the answer to your question is brief. The "historical Jesus" is the "actual" Jesus who walked this earth, the one we might discover hidden behind the words and events of the present Gospels — the circumstances of his life, how people lived and worked in those days, what social, economic, religious and political realities affected their lives. Scholars, with varying motives and degrees of faith, ask: If we search, scientifically and historically behind the words of the Gospels, what "real" Jesus, what words and actions of Jesus might we better understand?

That's a valid and potentially illuminating question. However such a study might enlighten and inspire us, it will never replace or detract from the Jesus we know and love by faith, the Jesus passed over to us by the Spirit, the Jesus of the Gospels.

Did Jesus know he was God?

Recently in a homily I heard a priest comment that "according to Scripture scholars, Jesus came to the realization that he was God over the course of his life." I heard the same idea years ago in a theology class at a Catholic college. The reaction was: If Jesus didn't know for sure that he was God, why should we follow his teachings? What is the official church teaching on this matter? Why do we stress the humanity of Jesus?

Your question involves one of the two pivotal mysteries of our faith. (The other is the Trinity.) We believe that Jesus is truly God and truly human.

How can one person combine in himself all the attributes of an infinite God and at the same time all the attributes (except sin) of a very finite human nature? That is mystery. It is the question Christians have wrestled with since the beginning and which we continually attempt to understand further, always realizing that a full explanation is beyond the reach of our intelligence.

Whatever we say must respect both of those natures or we undermine something essential in what we mean by professing Jesus as Savior. We cannot deny any facet of God as present in Jesus. On the other hand, our faith and the New Testament itself affirm that Jesus was not just dabbling here and there with being human. He possessed a perfect human nature, including a real human mind, a real human will, a real human body, with all that those things necessarily imply.

Some people, in the early centuries especially, spoke of Jesus' mind in such a way that it nearly destroys the humanity of that mind. They seem to say that, particularly in a crisis, he possessed a kind of trap door that connected his mind to God's, in effect making his mind not human but divine.

How far can one go with this without ultimately claiming that Jesus did not really, but only seemed to, have a human intelligence, a human nature? Even the New Testament seems clear about the distinction. Luke tells us that as Jesus lived in the home of Nazareth he "advanced in wisdom and age and favor before God and man" (2:52). Hebrews tells us, among many other statements regarding the nature of Jesus, that he learned "obedience from what he suffered" (5:8).

You might well remark: How can one say those things about God? We don't know. But obviously Luke and the author of Hebrews felt comfortable saying them about Jesus.

We must be extremely careful that our ways of speaking do not imply a denial of the divinity of Jesus. We must, however, be just as careful not to say anything that would imply a denial of his human nature. It is not a matter of "stressing," but admitting that he was truly a human being as well as truly God.

As I said, the union of those two natures in our Lord is a mystery. We may try to delve into a mystery, but we must never attempt to solve it by taking part of it away. This we would do if we denied something in Jesus that is necessary for a true human nature.

As for the reaction you report in your question, the mystery of the Incarnation always has been a stumbling block to discipleship with Jesus. And I don't imply agreement with everything any priest says about Jesus when I say that. Each of us confronts a test of faith, however, when we meet the full implications of that mystery. For some today, as for the people of his home town when he came back to visit, he is still "altogether too much for them."

Did Jesus learn?

I still wonder if it is right to say "Jesus learned obedience through suffering." Wasn't he born obedient? When the devil tempted him on the mountain for 40 days, wasn't he being tried for weakness? It seems to me that our Blessed Lord died giving glory to God his Father, who is our Father. Jesus didn't have to learn obedience; he was God!

As I said in the answer to the previous question, the quote you give did not originate with a modern writer. It is straight out of the letter to the Hebrews in the New Testament. It is, in fact, only one of many statements in that letter and elsewhere in the Bible which stress a truth many Catholics have a hard time believing — that Jesus was really, truly human, with all that implies in body and spirit.

From my own experience, it seems that the denial of the humanity of Jesus is easily one of the most serious errors of faith in our day. For historical reasons, we have so concentrated on the fact that he is God that we have greatly underplayed the truth that "He is like us in everything except that he did not sin." (Hebrews)

The remarks in Scripture about Jesus growing, learning, suffering, crying, struggling with weakness and fear, and so on, were as vital to the early Christians as they are to us. These Christians realized, as we should also, that our belief that Jesus is truly human is just as important as our belief that he is God. If either were not true, his saving life, death and resurrection would be only an empty gesture. If, for example, Jesus is only God and not man, it might prove God's benevolence toward us, but we would not be the saved people we believe we are. Jesus could only accomplish salvation, as we believe in it, by being fully and actually one of us.

The quote you give simply repeats, therefore, what the Bible says about Jesus' humanity, a most important truth if we are to appreciate properly the mystery of the Incarnation and his role as our Savior. All passages about Jesus going through the same processes of development and struggle as other men (as long as we eliminate any moral weakness or sin) reflect this essential element of our faith. We not only can believe, we must believe it, if we are to be faithful to our Christian traditions.

Did Jesus only pretend to be human?

The other day a priest referred to Jesus as a human being, as you did in one of your columns. I've always been taught that Jesus is one being, one person, the second person of the Blessed Trinity, that he is indeed not a human person, but a divine person. I accept fully and unconditionally the mystery of the Incarnation and all that the church teaches about the two natures and wills.

Years ago, a nun gave the comparison of a king who fought with his soldiers, himself wearing the uniform of a private. He was a real private without in any way renouncing his royalty. He was a soldier like the rank and file, and at the same time a king. This seems an apt comparison, doesn't it?

Only up to a point. The comparison has too many similarities to an ancient heresy called Docetism, which cropped up in the early centuries of the church. Named from the Greek word, *dokesis*, meaning an appearance or something imagined, Docetists asserted that Jesus was not really human. He seemed to be a man, through some sort of illusion, but he really was not.

Thus, the king in your comparison was not really a private; he only appeared to be. It seems to imply, therefore, that when God came to earth, he was not really a human being, not really a man; he only appeared to be. And that is absolutely not what we believe about Jesus.

The popularity of that kind of comparison, and the discomfort many Catholics and other Christians still demonstrate when someone insists that Jesus was and is completely, perfectly human, seem to indicate that the Docetists' concern remains quite alive in the church. Isn't it totally beneath God's dignity — almost blasphemous — to believe that God, without ceasing to be God, literally became a human being?

The answer of our Catholic faith is, loud and clear, "no." In some mystery of providence, God found it fitting to his plan of creation — and to his plan of revealing his eternal love for us — that the second person of the Trinity become a member of the human race.

This is precisely what the church means when it says that Jesus is one person, the divine person of the eternal word of God, with both a divine and human nature. He is completely and totally God, and completely, totally man.

Are they real words of Jesus?

Our Catholic newspaper had a recent article about a new book identifying the real words of Jesus in the Gospels. I thought we already have the words Jesus spoke. Or aren't we supposed to believe the Gospels when they tell us Jesus said something?

First, I should correct your word "identifying." With no tape recordings or video tapes of Jesus, and only comparatively few and often conflicting records such as the Gospels to go by, it is all but impossible to identify with certainty the exact words of Jesus. Almost always, the best we, or the experts in biblical research, can do in such questions is say that the evidence points to this or that reading as more probable than another. Much research of this type is going on, by the way, and it can add immeasurably to our understanding of Jesus and his life and message.

We are able here barely to touch on your assumptions about what Jesus says in the Gospels, but a few reminders may help. First, even the Gospels themselves, as we have them, often differ significantly in their quotes of Jesus. For example, the Lord's Prayer is different in Matthew and Luke (and both of them differ from the one we use), and the words of the institution of the Eucharist at the Last Supper differ from Gospel to Gospel.

Second, most ancient texts from which our modern Bibles are translated have nothing like quotation marks, or even periods. Punctuation of the kind and complexity we use was unheard of. In those manuscripts, phrases and sentences simply run into each other, on the assumption that the reader will make sense of the words. When a verse reads, "Jesus said such and such," did the author mean that to be a direct quote, or rather simply the idea that Jesus expressed, what we would call an indirect quote? The answer comes down finally to an educated judgment by the person doing the translating.

Third, and perhaps most important, the people who listened to Jesus, and those who eventually put the Gospels and other Scriptures into the form we have them, weren't nearly as interested in such grammatical details as we are. The precise words that were used, or the syntax, were far less significant than the meaning. For them, the more important concern was that the mind and teaching of Jesus be faithfully passed down, and then translated from a form of Aramaic (the daily language of Jesus, though he probably knew some Greek and Latin) to Greek, and eventually to other languages.

The book you mention may or may not contribute much to our knowledge of the New Testament and what Jesus actually said and did. However, the Gospels as we have them contain their own spiritual power as the Word of God. The most important traits we bring to them are openness to that Word, and faith.

Jesus' brothers and sisters

I am a college student assigned to read part of the New Testament. We are reading texts that indicate James and others were "brothers" of Jesus. Did he have brothers and sisters? In research, we found one explanation indi-

cating they were from the lineage of Joseph. Could Joseph have had a child with someone else?

The Gospels of Matthew (13:55-56) and Mark (6:3) mention the names of four brothers of Jesus: James, Joses (Joseph), Judas (Jude), and Simon — and some unnamed sisters. Other references to brothers of the Lord occur elsewhere in the New Testament. In the Bible, "brother" in conversation may often refer to a close friend, or fellow member of a group. Brother as a family reference, however, as here, seems nearly always to have meant a blood relative.

Various explanations have been offered about who these brothers and sisters might be. Through the centuries, Christians have held that Mary was always a virgin, which would rule out the possibility of their being her children.

After careful study of other tentative explanations, the predominant theory today, I believe, in sofar as there is one, is that those brothers and sisters of Jesus were children of Joseph by a previous marriage. As unfamiliar as this may sound to us, it is not a new idea, nor does anything in the Gospels or in official Catholic teaching conflict with this possibility.

Early Christian documents, among them the second-century Gospel of Peter and the *Protoevangelium* of James, identify the "brothers" of Jesus as children of a union before Joseph's marriage to Mary. While these "Gospels" are not in our canon of Scripture, they are valuable windows to the thoughts and beliefs of the first 100 to 200 years of Christianity. And their view of the matter still seems most probable.

If the theory is true, and Joseph was deceased before Jesus began his public life, it helps explain also why Mary would have accompanied these brothers and sisters, and perhaps even raised them. As most of us are aware, there has been a long-standing assumption in Christian devotion that Joseph was somewhat older than Mary. If that is true, an earlier marriage could explain the "brothers and sisters." As I indicated, this explanation in no way reflects negatively on the church's doctrine concerning the perpetual virginity of the mother of Jesus and that she had no other children.

Obviously, I am speaking here about official Catholic doctrine. Some later private revelations, from the Middle Ages to modern times, began to stress the opinion that Joseph, like Mary, lived a virginal life before and after Christ's birth. Perhaps this led to the decline of the old "previous marriage" theory. Whatever the case, private revelations to saints or other visionaries about details of Joseph's life may be fascinating. They are not, however, a necessary part of Catholic belief.

Jesus and his Father

In the Gospel of Mark (13:32) Jesus says something I do not understand about his relationship to the Father. We know Jesus and the Father are one with the Holy Spirit. Yet Jesus says that no man and no angel, not even the Son (meaning apparently himself) knows the hour of the passing of heaven and earth. How could Jesus say something like that?

We find numerous remarks like this in the Gospel which seem to be incompatible with the fact that Jesus is the second person of the Trinity and therefore shares in all the knowledge of God. No full answer is possible since we are dealing here with the mystery of the Trinity itself and of the Incarnation. Two general directions of answers, however, are possible. First, Jesus could be speaking here solely in the context of his human nature, which is limited, as is all human knowledge and understanding. How human limits coexist with divine omnipotence and infinity is, of course, the mystery of the Incarnation.

Another explanation can be that Jesus is speaking not so much of his own personal relationship with the Father, but rather of his mission to reveal to the human family all the truths regarding God that would contribute to the development of our relationship with him here and in eternity. This may be one reason why such seeming contradictions appear often in the Gospel of John, which was written rather late and therefore is able to reflect much more the Christ who is the risen Lord and head of the church, as distinct from the Jesus who walked the earth with the apostles.

In fulfilling his mission as Lord and Savior, Jesus knows much which he cannot tell us — not because of some unworthy motive on the part of God, but simply because we could not grasp such knowledge or use it creatively even if it were given to us. Jesus made clear that he considered it part of his own responsibility to determine how much of what he knows of the Father he should make known to us.

Why didn't Jesus cure more people?

Why didn't more people request cures of Christ who apparently never refused such requests. It seems to me that the path to his temporary home would have been thronged with people who heard of this miraculous healer. Why were there any sick left in Israel?

As you might suspect, you are not the first to be puzzled by this question. Through all the centuries since Christ, Christians have noted and meditated on the fact that if Jesus cured one person, he could have cured everyone. Furthermore, since his powers of healing were not limited to time and space, he theoretically could have cured everyone in the world and put an end to all human suffering.

The fact that he did not eliminate all pain and evil from our human condition certainly cannot be attributed to his lack of power, or to his lack of compassion and love. He overwhelmingly showed both of these, most of all by his own suffering, death on the cross, and resurrection.

It seems clear, then, that the healing miracles of Jesus had other larger purposes beyond the relief of pain. For one thing, Jesus saw his healing actions (and other physical miracles such as giving back life to those who had died) as signs of his supreme power over all evil. To him they were witnesses to the fact that neither physical suffering nor the worst of human sinfulness could ever be larger than the power of good, the power he embodied as God. On occasion he makes this connection quite explicitly, as in the healing of the paralyzed man in Luke, chapter 6.

Another conclusion Christians have drawn from Jesus' approach to human suffering is that he did not come to take it away, but rather to give it meaning — or at least to help his people understand that there is a need for it. It is as if he said: "If I don't take away all your suffering, it is not because I cannot do so, or because I do not love you enough. Buried deep inside the human heart, there is the mystery that fulfillment — perfection — comes from the passage through death to life. The best I can do is tell you this, show you that it applies even to me, and then ask you to follow me and trust me."

If this answer does not sound as final and perfect as you would like, we must remember that we are dealing here with one of the oldest questions human beings have wrestled with: Where does evil (physical and moral) come from, and why is it here? Among the many reasons for Christ's miracles, one is that they were his way of helping us deal with this question. If he could not give us a perfectly satisfying answer, he at least helps us to see that in the mystery of God's providence there is an answer, an answer that is revealed, if only dimly, most of all in his own death and resurrection and in our following him in this paschal mystery.

Treat others like outcasts?

My family had quite a discussion on the meaning of the Gospel one Sunday. What is the interpretation of the passage where Jesus speaks about attempting to correct our "brother" by ourselves or with a few others, or finally by the church itself. If he doesn't listen, we are told to treat him like a "Gentile or a tax collector."

This passage occurs in a section of St. Matthew's Gospel in which Jesus describes several aspects of his kingdom as embodied in the church, that is, in the assembly of his people on earth. Gentiles were non-Jews and therefore heathens as far as the Jews were concerned. Tax collectors, and especially publicans, were in those days considered (often rightly) as sinners, extortionists and traitors. Both groups were held in contempt as outcasts, people to be avoided.

The seemingly harsh words of our Lord must be understood in relation to what immediately follows. Jesus says that when two or three are gathered in his name, he is there, and will grant whatever they ask. Part of his point is that the spirit of charity, prayer, and trust hopefully should prevent any conflict from reaching the point of division which it might reach if approached with only a cold, legalistic attitude.

Another factor in understanding the passage, forgiveness, comes up in the very next verse. Peter asks Jesus if one must forgive his brother up to seven times, which Peter obviously considered as excessively generous. Jesus replied that our forgiving, without demanding undue retribution or revenge, must be unending, at least if that's the way we want God to treat us.

Call priests "Father"?

Some Protestant friends have told me that Catholics do wrong in calling priests "Father." This is against the teaching of the Bible, according to them. How do we explain what we do since it does say in Matthew 23:9, "Call no one your father on earth, for one is your father in heaven."

The practice of using the title Father is not new. It goes back to the earliest centuries of Christianity and has been in use ever since, though the name is traditionally applied more commonly to monks than to secular priests. Protestants abandoned its use gradually after the Reformation.

The reasons for calling the priest Father are simple and very natural. He is the usual minister of those sacraments that, in the name of Christ and his church, give us the new birth and life of grace — baptism, the Eucharist, penance and so on. By his continuing care, instruction and support, he nurtures the life of God which we share as Christians in a manner parallel to the role of our natural fathers.

For this reason St. Paul does not hesitate to call himself the father of his Christian converts. "Although you may have 10 thousand others to teach you about Christ," he told the Corinthians, "remember that you have only me as your father." (1 Co. 4,15 — *Living Bible* translation) He also twice calls Timothy his son because he had brought Timothy's family to the faith of Christ. (Phil. 2,22 and 1 Tim.1,2)

Understood literally, this section of the Gospel of Matthew would mean we were forbidden to call our natural fathers by that name, or to call our instructors teachers. The whole context makes clear that Jesus was not hung up on the word father or teacher, but that he condemned the practice of some leaders in heaping titles on themselves out of pride and self-importance.

As one of the most respected Protestant biblical commentaries remarks, "If one takes this command literally, the titles 'doctor' and 'professor,' as well as 'rabbi' and 'father' are forbidden to Christians in addressing their leaders." (*Interpreter's Bible*; vol. 7, on the Gospel of St. Matthew)

The "unforgivable "sin

In the Gospel of St. Matthew (12:31), Jesus speaks of a sin "against the Holy Spirit" which will never be forgiven in this world or in the next. What is this unforgivable sin?

St. Augustine, St. Thomas Aquinas and many others believed that by the "sin against the Holy Spirit" Jesus meant the sin of final unrepentance, which is the refusal to repent of one's rejection of God through a serious sin, even at the moment of death. This probably is still the most common view since it is a total, final rejection of all the helps the Holy Spirit offers us to turn away from evil and toward God.

Perhaps another way of saying the same thing is that anyone who deliberately and maliciously refuses the helps which the Holy Spirit gives to keep us from sin in the first place, sins against the Holy Spirit. As St. Thomas says, many gifts of the Spirit are meant to help us avoid sin in our lives. The gift of hope keeps us from despair. The gift of fear of the Lord keeps us from presuming in the wrong way on God's mercy and love, and so on.

All these gifts, he tells us, are effects of the Holy Spirit within us.

When we refuse to hope, when we refuse to acknowledge the majesty and power of God in our lives, we in effect say we do not need the Holy Spirit, which puts us in deep spiritual trouble. Repentance is impossible because when we're in that frame of mind there cannot be even enough humility for us to admit that we have sinned and need repentance at all.

Whatever the meaning of this Gospel passage may be, the one all-essential truth to remember is that, if we have sinned, God our Father is always there with open arms to welcome us back, and the Holy Spirit is always ready to help us go there.

What is a levirate marriage?

Recently we had in the Sunday readings the weird story about the woman with six or seven husbands, and the question of whose wife she would be in heaven (Mt. 22:23-33). I looked up the passage in my Bible. The reference, it said, was to a "levirate" marriage, but gave no further explanation. What is a levirate marriage?

Levirate marriage was a legal tradition, common in some ancient cultures, by which a man's brothers were required to marry his widow if he died without a son. The name comes from the Latin word *levir*, brother-in-law. The Hebrew people were among those who considered this a serious family obligation imposed by God through Moses.

While certain basics remained, other elements differed through the centuries. In some instances the obligation to produce a son for the eldest son might fall even on his father.

A curious early tale, for example, in Genesis 38, involves Judah, one of the 12 sons of Jacob the patriarch. Judah's son, Er, died before his wife, Tamar, bore him children. Judah then gave Tamar to son number two, Onan, who wasn't especially eager to continue his brother's family line. Onan "knew that the descendants would not be counted as his; so whenever he had relations with his brother's widow, he wasted his seed on the ground, to avoid contributing offspring for his brother."

After the Lord struck Onan dead, Judah was understandably not anxious to pass Tamar on to the next son, Shela. He kept putting her off until she realized her father-in-law had no intention of following the law. Disguising herself as a prostitute, she enticed Judah himself, had relations with him and conceived a child. When Judah learned she was pregnant and was preparing to punish her for her immorality, she produced sure evidence that he was the father. When informed of the truth, Judah said, "She is more right than I am," since she wanted to observe the law, even when Judah was unwilling.

Much later, when women could inherit from their father, the levirate custom applied only when there were neither male nor female children (Nm. 27:8; 36:6-7). All this sounds bizarre to us, of course. What could have been the source of such customs?

Possible explanations involve the compelling need among ancient peoples and tribes to protect the inheritance of possessions, most of all of land. Intermarriage with another clan, or failure to keep their land intact through the eldest son who, as our Hebrew Scriptures mention often, inherited everything, ate away at the lifeblood of the family. Arab nomads in some areas continue that levirate tradition even today. For the Jews, however, the predominant reason was simply to assure that the deceased father would have an heir who could continue his family.

By the time of Jesus, the levirate law very possibly was already history, at least among his people. This fact would not have prevented religious leaders of that day from debating at length such questions as we find in Matthew's story, which Mark and Luke thought worth passing on as well. Other passages dealing directly or indirectly with levirate marriage are in Deuteronomy 25:5-10, and Ruth 4.

What was Matthew's wedding garment?

Would you please tell us what is meant by the story of the wedding feast and wedding garments in the Gospel of Matthew? My husband seems to think it means only certain people are called to be saved. How could a good king condemn people for coming improperly dressed to a wedding feast they didn't even know about?

The parable to which you refer (Mt. 22:1-14) relates the last of three stories Jesus tells in answer to a challenge put to him by Jewish leaders: "On what authority are you doing these things?" and to their rejection of him and his teachings. Jesus in effect responds: God sent you the prophets, including John the Baptist and a whole stream of emissaries, including his own Son, but you refused to hear God's voice in any of them. Therefore, others from outside the Chosen People, new or old, are being called to take a place in the kingdom of God.

Comparing God's reign to a luscious, rich banquet is a common theme throughout the Scriptures, one which Matthew makes good use of here. (See Isaias 25, for example) Many elements of this story stretch the imagination beyond all credibility. What king, for example, leaves a banquet waiting, goes off to war, kills enemies and burns cities, and then comes back to finish the party?

In other words, we're dealing with a parable which is clearly an allegory. It relates through these images the history of God's saving work on earth, concluding with the universal invitation to fill the banquet hall with everyone, "the bad as well as the good."

Understood this way, the question about wedding garments is easily answered. In early Christianity, conversion to faith in Jesus Christ was commonly referred to as putting on a new set of clothes. St. Paul says that all who have been baptized have clothed themselves with Christ. (Gal. 3:27). This was a symbolic way of stating that those who identify themselves with Christ in baptism accept the responsibility to "wear" his way of living, to authenticate their relationship with the Lord by their deeds.

Just as with parables, it is fruitless and usually misleading to look for specific spiritual meanings in every detail of an allegory. The central meaning of this one is not hard to find. Now, in the new and final covenant between God and the human family, we are invited to clothe ourselves in the patience, meekness, kindness and compassion of God (Col. 3:12). Our condition at the end will depend on how faithfully we have worn that clothing.

Events of the week before Calvary

Our interfaith Bible study group is studying what happened in the days before Calvary. John (12:1) says something about "six days before Passover," and follows with events of different days. One day describes the discussion of the withered fig tree, another the anointing of Jesus at Bethany, and so on. Is there any clear explanation of what took place each day preceding the crucifixion?

The Gospels give us little information about time frames for these final days of Jesus' life, and differ widely from one Gospel to another about what happened when. It's impossible to put them together in a neat chronological package.

The Gospels do not agree even on the day of the Last Supper, and therefore of the crucifixion. Matthew, Mark and Luke put it at Passover, the first day of the feast of Unleavened Bread (Matthew 26:17), which would be the 15th day of the Jewish month of Nisan. John says the supper was before the feast of Passover (13:1), the day of preparation (18:28 and 19:42), in other words on the 14th day of Nisan, one day earlier in the week.

Scholars differ on the possible motives for, and significance of, this difference. But they pretty much agree that John's dating is probably correct. The sequence of some events of that week is not the same from one Gospel to another. For example, Matthew and Mark place the anointing of Jesus by the woman at a dinner in Bethany sometime after his entry into Jerusalem. John has it the day before that entry (Jn 12:12). There are just too few specific clues in any of the Gospels, or all of them put together, to map those final events of Jesus' earthly life in chronological order.

These variations should not surprise us. The Gospels were not meant to be biographies of Jesus in our modern sense. The authors intended primarily not to write history, but to explain the meaning of the message and person of the risen Lord, what he reveals, what he has accomplished and what he expects his followers to be. Each had his own theological perspective and obviously did not hesitate to rearrange places and times and other details if that would help achieve his purpose.

The "disciple Jesus loved"

There are several places in the New Testament where one of the apostles or disciples is referred to as "the one Jesus loved." Who was this? And why is his name never mentioned?

The Beloved Disciple — or "the disciple whom Jesus loved," depending on the translation — is referred to often in the fourth Gospel. This person, the most intimate friend of Jesus according to that Gospel, became the major source for Christian belief in what is called the Johannine community, the community (or communities) of John, out of which came the Gospel according to John.

We know from that Gospel, and from the letters of John, that this group of believers underwent internal and external crises and conflicts. The Gospel reveals, for example, the mounting tensions between those Christians and the leaders of Judaism.

In chapter 9 we hear the story of the man born blind, whose sight is miraculously bestowed by Jesus. That passage refers explicitly to a major event in the final separation of the Johannine Christians from their Jewish connections, the decision by Judaism, somewhere around the year 90, to eject from the synagogue anyone who professed Jesus as Messiah (9:22). Other tensions developed inside the community. In the first letter of John we find harsh denunciations, unequaled in the New Testament, of one faction by another. In the course of their censures, they describe forcefully what true followers of Jesus Christ should believe and how they should act.

The Beloved Disciple was their inspiration and authority for all this. Even after his death (see 21:23), his teachings continued to inspire their development of the lofty theology about Jesus, which makes the fourth Gospel so unique. Perhaps most intriguing, this disciple appears, at least with that designation, only in the final days of Jesus on earth — at the Last Supper (13:23), on Calvary (19:26) and in Galilee after the resurrection (21:20).

In the final major work before his death, *An Introduction to the New Testament*, Sulpician Father Raymond Brown, often called the dean of New Testament scholars, summarized three answers to the possible identity of the beloved disciple.

First, it could have been a known New Testament figure. Zebedee's son, John, is one possibility, but others have been suggested. Any answer would be only a guess. Second, some scholars propose he is a pure symbol, the model of a perfect disciple. The fact that he is never given a name, and appears alongside Peter in situations where the other Gospels mention no such figure, could lend support for this view. Third, the beloved disciple could have been a minor person in earlier synoptic traditions, too unimportant to be remembered in the first three Gospels, but who later became an important figure in the Johannine community and the fourth Gospel. This third view appears to be the one held by most scholars.

No Eucharist in John's Gospel?

Why does St. John's Gospel not even mention the institution of the Eucharist at the Last Supper? We believe that, in chapter 6 of that Gospel, Jesus was referring to the promise of the Eucharist when he spoke of eating his flesh and drinking his blood. If John believed those words as we do, it's strange he did not tell us when that promise was fulfilled.

As everyone familiar with the New Testament knows, the Gospel according to John is different in a number of major ways from the other three Gospels. Reasons for these differences are not always easy to find, though much has to do, apparently, with the fact that the fourth Gospel was completed some decades after the others.

An even larger reason is that John's approach to Jesus and his message reflects a level of theological reflection unknown in Mark, Matthew and Luke. For example, John is the only Gospel to tell us the mother of Jesus was present at the crucifixion. The other evangelists name women being there, but not Mary. If she was there, were they ignorant of the fact, which doesn't seem likely, or didn't they think it was important? Or did John speak of her on Calvary because of a theological relationship between her and the church, represented by "the beloved disciple"?

Maybe John knew the story of the institution of the Eucharist was already well known from the other evangelists, so he wished to explain further what the Eucharist meant. Thus he told a Last Supper story the others omitted: Jesus washing the feet of the disciples. We probably will never have certain answers to such questions.

What do Christ's sufferings lack?

St. Paul says somewhere we should make up in our sufferings what was lacking in the sufferings of Christ. I thought Christ's atonement was sufficient and superabundant. He did it all! How could we add anything to that?

The passage (Colossians 1:24) has puzzled Christians for centuries. Taking for granted, as you said, that our Lord's sacrificial death and resurrection was absolutely and totally sufficient for the redemption of the world, two kinds of explanation seem most common.

One relates this verse to the context in which Paul speaks of his own role as a missionary of the Good News of Christ. Each new receiver of that message, and each suffering Paul undertakes for the sake of the people and the church, moves the church that much closer to its fulfillment in the preaching of the Gospel to the whole human race.

Another interpretation addresses the sufferings themselves, sufferings of Paul and other Christians until the end of the world. Jesus makes clear that the sufferings of his followers, the church, are *his* sufferings. Those who persecute his disciples persecute him! (Acts 9:4) Thus the fullness of our Lord's saving work, the completion of the mission given him by the Father, will arrive only when the last "daily cross" of which he spoke has been borne faithfully by each disciple and by the community of believers, his body on earth.

What was "lacking in the sufferings of Christ" was thus not an insufficiency in his redemptive actions. Rather, it claims that his work will not attain its complete effect until all his disciples have carried their cross with him.

Did Jesus despair on the cross?

In the Gospel of St. Matthew, chapter 27, Jesus cries out on the cross, "Eli, Eli lama sabachtani" — "My God, my God, why have you forsaken me?" In what language did Jesus speak? Is it possible he said rather, "My God, where are you?" The Jesus I know would never say he was forsaken since he loved and trusted his Father throughout his life.

There is no doubt that Jesus suffered much of our human desolation, grief, aloneness, and possibly even bafflement, at the time of his passion. It was an agonizing torture so severe that it caused a bloody sweat and brought him close to a feeling of almost total dereliction. We say "close" because in the cry itself is the expression of profound faith in the midst of all the pain —"My God, my God!"

This exclamation of our Lord has long been seen as a prayer using Psalm 22, a graphic passage which parallels the suffering of Jesus on the cross, and which begins with these words. The same psalm is quoted just before this passage of Matthew (verse 43), and the following verses about Jesus' thirst recall the later words of that same psalm, "My throat is dried up like baked clay, my tongue cleaves to my jaws... they have pierced my hands and my feet."

If it is true that Psalm 22 was involved in this cry, the words become one of the most significant acts of faith, love and victory uttered by our Lord.

Did Jesus forgive on the cross?

Jesus is quoted in Luke 23:34, "Father forgive them for they know not what they do." A footnote in the New American Bible indicates the words do not occur in the oldest manuscripts of Luke or other earlier Greek manuscripts. Why then did the church include that portion of the Bible? It is significant because forgiveness of his crucifiers from the cross has become an accepted part of Catholic theology and spirituality.

The need to make some choices between ancient manuscript readings is not uncommon. Determining which possibility is most probable involves many factors. Which one best reflects the style and language of that writer, the literary devices he uses? Does the time the manuscript was written explain why changes were introduced? What is most consistent with other passages, other words or actions of Jesus, for example?

So here, the *New Jerome Biblical Commentary* notes that the internal evidence (evidence from the text itself) weighs heavily for the authenticity of this passage (p. 719). Luke balances Stephen's prayer of forgiveness (Acts 7:60) with that of Jesus. Unlike the other synoptics, Luke presents Jesus as speaking at every main section of the crucifixion, as here at the moment of crucifixion.

Other manuscripts might have left out these words for several reasons. The later destruction of the Jewish temple might seem to indicate that Jesus' prayer of forgiveness was ineffective. Or maybe the omission resulted from anti-Jewish sentiment. Whatever the reasons, the passage remains part of the canon of the Gospels accepted by the church.

Did Jesus rise from the dead?

I find it hard to believe a recent column in our local paper. The author says most New Testament scholars do not believe Jesus rose bodily from the dead. According to him, "One Catholic seminary instructor says he does not know of any credible Bible scholar who would hold for a bodily resurrection of Jesus." Is this true?

The resurrection of Jesus from the dead is the core of our faith. As St. Paul says, if Jesus has not risen, we Christians are to be pitied. On the other hand, any thoughtful reader of the Gospels is aware of major puzzles in the different stories of the resurrection and events which followed.

Our Lord's resurrection was not simply a "return to life" as he possessed it in human form before his death. He was seen and not recognized by his closest friends, and then recognized (Jn. 20:14). He appeared and disappeared instantaneously (e.g. Lk. 24). The Gospel stories themselves differ considerably from each other on many details of the events on the first Easter Day and the days following.

Paul himself, who tells us he saw the risen Lord, in comparing our resurrection to that of Jesus, says that what dies is a physical body, but what is raised is a spiritual body, imperishable, glorious and undying (1 Cor. 15).

One obvious task of biblical scholarship is to compare and analyze all this New Testament information and theology, and develop possible explanations in the context of traditional Christian faith. With very rare exceptions, those explanations in recent times do not include denying the bodily resurrection of our Lord.

As one of numerous illustrations, we might refer to the most prestigious and scholarly one-volume English commentary on the Scriptures, the *New Jerome Biblical Commentary*, compiled by major Catholic Scripture scholars in the English-speaking world. In a section on the resurrection of Jesus, four of these theologians, whose names are familiar to any serious student of the Scriptures, clearly defend the bodily resurrection of Jesus. They strongly reject the rationalistic and liberal criticism of the 19th century which in one way or another attempted to discredit the resurrection.

Their position is obvious throughout, perhaps most explicitly in the context of these various "qualities" of the risen Lord. "If the New Testament," they write, "stresses that what was seen was a radically transformed Jesus, it was Jesus who was seen," the Jesus with whom the disciples had walked, talked, ate and lived during his public life. Among some circles it is considered clever these days to discredit genuine scholarship of any kind, including biblical studies. Unfortunately, sometimes honesty and truth get buried in the process.

When you see these extravagant kinds of statements, don't panic. Try to check them out. Does the author really know what he is talking about? Does he perhaps have a personal bias or prejudice? "Don't believe everything you read" is still good advice.

The risen body of Jesus

Your column has been a great help to my faith. I have several questions. Did Christ's physical body really rise at the resurrection? If so, is it in a physical place? If not, what happened to it? Why didn't anyone witness the resurrection? Will our bodies rise in the same way?

It depends, first of all, on what is meant by Christ's "physical body." If by that you mean that the bodily cells which lay in the tomb were raised back to life, the answer is most probably no, surely not necessarily. The resurrection of Jesus was something far beyond the simple resuscitation of a dead corpse, as seems to have been the case, for example, with Lazarus (Jn. 11). Lazarus eventually died again. Jesus did not, and will not.

As his appearances to the disciples after his resurrection make clear, Jesus in his risen life has a new dimension of living, different than he had before. It is without question the same Jesus they knew before the crucifixion. He has a body. They touch him. He eats with them. He speaks with them. Yet there is a mysterious difference in the way he looks, the way he comes to them, the way he wants them to recognize him, the way he "is."

While he and his Spirit clearly enter and affect our lives on earth, he himself is now personally beyond change, beyond corruption, beyond death, beyond history. He is in an eternal state of being with the Father that is unlimited, outside of our time and space. In those days with his disciples after being raised from death, and so today, Jesus is in eternity with the Father. As St. Paul puts it, without end "he lives for God" (Romans 6). What "is sown corruptible. . . is raised incorruptible. . . . It is sown a natural body, it is raised a spiritual body" (1 Co. 15).

So, to answer your question, Christ's physical body was raised up in the resurrection. But we need to understand that in the right way. Is it in a physical place? We would say yes, insofar as it is a physical body. He did not become an angel, or pure spirit. When we try to say "where," we are beyond our depth. Human experience on this earth just doesn't give us a lot of help on that.

Why didn't anyone witness the resurrection? We don't know. Maybe because it wasn't "witnessable" in any human way of speaking. Sometimes, I believe, Christians envision the resurrection as Christ's corpse suddenly jerking to life and breaking out of the tomb. If we believe the witness of the Gospels and the other books of the New Testament, that's not what happened.

It comes down to two facts significant for the early Christians. The tomb was empty, and major people in the early Christian community saw and experienced Jesus as alive and working with his people. These facts firmly established their conviction that Jesus lives, that he is Lord of the church and of the world.

As for our own resurrection, our Catholic faith echoes the explicit teaching of St Paul: What happened to Jesus will happen to us. What dies is a corruptible, weak, natural body; what rises is an incorruptible, powerful, spiritual body. As we have borne the image of the earthly Jesus, we shall also bear the image of the heavenly one (1 Cor. 15:42-49).

In this Paul expands on what we repeat in our major professions of faith. The Apostles Creed and the Athanasian Creed explicitly say "resurrection of the body." The creed of Nicaea/Constantinople, which we use each Sunday at Mass, speaks of the "resurrection of the dead," but clearly means also resurrection of the body. As the *Catechism of the Catholic Church* says, the "how" of all this exceeds our imagination and understanding; it is accessible only to faith. (1000)

Was one Emmaus disciple a woman?

Our question is about the two disciples who met Jesus on the road to Emmaus and ate with him (Lk. 24:13-35). Could they have been husband and wife? It appears they shared a home. One of them, Cleopas, is a man, but his companion's gender is not indicated. Is there any Catholic tradition to shed light on this?

There is no tradition exactly, but the possibility you mention has been raised often. You offer one reason. Another, perhaps stronger, is the statement in the Gospel according to John (19:25) that among the women standing by the cross of Jesus was the wife of Clopas — same name, but different form, as the man described in Luke 24.

Both Gospels seem to assume the name would be recognized by other disciples. And John would likely have been familiar with the story in Luke's Gospel, written a number of years earlier.

Naturally, we cannot know for sure. But there appears to be some likelihood that the two disciples on the road were husband and wife, both close to our Lord, who had suffered a devastating loss (so they supposed) in the death on Calvary and were now sadly heading back home.

Slavery in the Bible?

Is it true that the Bible accepts the idea of slavery? St. Paul has been quoted that Christians should submit to slavery and not try to change things, as if he were really in favor of it.

Not everything that we see people doing in sacred Scripture, even very holy people, represents the highest ideal of human activity. The Old and New Testaments unfold the gradual understanding of the full implications of God's word as he reveals it to us. Obviously, this understanding even now has a long way to go.

It is true that early Christians were a lot more tolerant of slavery and other social evils than we would be. Perhaps it is better to say that they accepted it as a fact of life that could not change quickly, and they tried to live with it, being as faithful to the ideals of Christ as they could.

Gift of tongues

What is the gift of tongues? Do you believe in it? What do you think of the Pentecostal Movement, where people are supposed to have the gift of tongues?

The gift of tongues is one of the special manifestations of the presence of the Holy Spirit in an individual or group by which the individual (or group) speaks in a language that no one present can understand without a corresponding gift for "translation." It was not uncommon even in the early days of the Christian Church; St. Paul treats the subject at some length in 1 Corinthians, chapter 14.

There is some dispute whether the gift of tongues as experienced then, and apparently in a number of instances today, is a miraculous ability to speak a foreign language, which could have some missionary symbolism, or an ecstatic expression of syllables totally meaningless to anyone except another person similarly inspired to "interpret" the tongues. Maybe it is a combination of both, or even two separate gifts entirely.

Speaking in tongues may be a special gift by which the Holy Spirit's presence and power becomes evident in a group. One difficulty, of course, as St. Paul points out, is that self-deception is quite easy. An individual, or others, may believe he is speaking in tongues when the vocal expressions result only from a hyper-emotional state. The test of genuineness, according to Paul, is whether the experiences increase faith, serve a constructive purpose, and bring peace to the group rather than confusion.

Participation in charismatic (sometimes called Pentecostal) prayer activities seems to have helped many to a better life of faith and closeness to God. Supposedly, the gift of tongues has been experienced in some charismatic meetings, but it is by no means essential or common to them.

Did St. Paul believe end was near?

Can you enlighten us on the meaning of 1 Thessalonians 4:14, "Then we who are alive and remain shall be caught up together with them in the clouds to meet the Lord in the air, and thus we shall always be with the Lord."

Does this refer to what some Christians call the rapture? Does the Catholic Church teach this?

The first letter to the Thessalonians was written by St. Paul about the year 50, 20 years or so after the death and resurrection of our Lord. This means that it is the earliest Christian document in the New Testament, and was written during a period when Christians still believed the end of the world was near, that it would come, in fact, before the death of some people alive at that time. St. Paul clearly shared that expectation, as the passages such as the one you quote indicate.

These words echo the same apocalyptic language about the end of time that we find, for example, in the Gospels. Bizarre and graphic images of trumpets, clouds, earthquakes and other natural disasters were common in the religious literature of those times. They were never intended, or understood, to provide a pictorial description of the world's end. They rather emphasized the cosmic changes that would be involved in the end of time and that the entire event would be at God's initiative, a continuation of his majestic lordship over all creation.

As years went on, Christians gradually realized that the Lord had much bigger and longer-range plans for the world and the church. Thus, we do not find this same sort of suspenseful language in the later writings of Paul and other Christians.

The millennium

What is the meaning of the passage in the book of the Apocalypse that says the reign of Christ will be 1,000 years? Does this mean anything at all to us, or does it really mean that his reign in the world is 1,000 years?

One is bound to be hopelessly confused about the book of Revelation if he forgets that this is a book of visions and complicated, and often totally mystifying, symbols. Several groups, some quite large, in the history of Christianity took that passage (Revelation, chapter 20) literally. They believed in an actual millennium (from Latin *mille anni,* 1,000 years) during which Jesus would reign, and then take the saved into heaven after the final defeat of the devil.

Among ancient people large numbers were frequently symbols of an unmeasurable, infinite time. Perhaps the idea of a final 1,000 years is based on a non-biblical book called the *Secrets of Enoch* in which the world is described as 7,000 years old — with the present time being the final 1,000 years.

With few exceptions, millenarists became rare after the first thousand years came and went after Christ, and it became evident that there must be another meaning to the passage.

Armageddon

A member of another religion spoke to us about a battle of Armageddon, supposed to happen at the end of the world. She said it is in the Bible, but didn't explain any further except that they believe it will be a terrible conflict to separate good people from the bad. Do you know what she was talking about?

The book of Revelation (chapter 16) speaks of a battle in the last stages of the world involving the devils and the kings of the world — "the great day of battle of God, the sovereign Lord." This event is to occur at a place called Armageddon.

As with so many parts of this highly symbolic book of visions, it is not easy to place what is said in any kind of clear historical or geographic context. The usual interpretation is that the word comes from the Hebrew *har Mageddo*, or mount of Mageddo. Mageddo was an ancient fortress-city of Palestine overlooking the main pass through the Carmel mountain range. Thus it occupied a key position along the primary military and commercial route between Egypt and the rich countries of the Fertile Crescent.

Mageddo was captured and recaptured numerous times in its long history and became somewhat synonymous with a battlefield. For this reason, it would be a likely symbol for the "ultimate conflict" between God and his friends and the followers of the devil.

The end of the world

When will the world end? Does the church teach anything about it?

The thousands of false predictions which have excited the world at one time or another ought to convince us, even if nothing else does, that God hasn't let us in on his plans for the date of the end of the world.

Whether it is 100 or 100,000 years away, we don't know. The Bible, at best, only speaks of situations which will be present before the end of the world. Even then, it is usually hard to discover what the Scripture writers really mean.

However, those who parade around with signs declaring "The end is near" do have a point. Neither Scripture nor the church is concerned with satisfying our idle curiosity, but rather with reminding us that the day we leave this earth, not the day it burns up, is the end of the world for you and me.

Fundamentalists and Bible interpretation

I enjoy discussing matters of our faith with others, but I find talking with fundamentalists frustrating. One said he takes the Scripture as it stands with no interpretation; this according to him is how the Holy Spirit guides us, all in plain black and white. No scientific or historical discov-

ery should have any significance in all this, according to them. Does the Holy Spirit really influence us this way?

If by interpretation we mean choosing one explanation, meaning or reading of the sacred texts over another, then it is utterly impossible to read the Bible intelligently without interpreting it. Let me suggest just two of numerous possible examples of what I mean.

Mark's Gospel says Jesus was baptized by John the Baptist (Mk. 1:9), but Luke has John in prison when Jesus came to be baptized (Lk. 3:20-21). Which is right? Luke says Joseph and Mary lived in Nazareth before Jesus was born. Matthew clearly assumes that they lived in Bethlehem, and only "went and dwelt in a town called Nazareth" after their return from Egypt (Mt. 2:23). Since both cannot be right in each of these instances, what reasons does one offer for accepting one meaning or explanation over the other? That is interpretation, at least of some sort.

It helps also to remember that a major difference between traditional Catholic Christianity and fundamentalism is our attitude toward the created world. Christian tradition from the beginning has taken creation very seriously and sacredly. Whether it is material (bread, wine, water, oil, words, actions) or spiritual (our minds and wills, our passions and emotions), we believe that all creation, rightly used, can be a channel of God's power and grace.

The more exclusive other-worldly approach tends to consider things of this world, especially as they are affected by human action, unworthy of God. None are capable of being sacraments, points of contact between God and ourselves through and in which God can work his love.

For us, to reject science, history, discovery, is to reject the Holy Spirit. To accept what we learn with our minds, enlightened by faith, honors the God who made us and the Spirit who enlightens us. In other words, we believe that to use what we have been able to learn about the times in which the authors of Scripture wrote, what problems they faced and what they meant to say, is affirming, not denying, the Holy Spirit.

Everything is obviously possible for God. We believe, however, that the normal and ordinary way the Holy Spirit works in us, individually and as community, is not by shining a mysterious light into our eyes or by some other miraculous intervention. Rather when we do our best to use well the gifts he has given, his power is at work immeasurably in ways we cannot even imagine (Eph. 3:20), enriching our minds and wills as we reflect on him and try to love him more deeply.

As you suggest, this approach to creation and to the Scriptures will not always result in the black-and-white, us-against-them type of answers we might sometimes desire. We believe, however, it is still the best way to honor God and to respect this world which has come from his creating hand.

"Where is it in the Bible?"

I am having some difficulty with a fundamentalist. Could you give me the passages in the Bible where Jesus instituted the seven sacraments?

Many Catholics (and most other Christians) who involve themselves with fundamentalist, literalist, cultic Christian groups find themselves confused and embarrassed when they are aggressively confronted with a question such as, "Where do you find this in the Bible?" They panic and run to their priest, or to me, and say, "We must be wrong because I can't find this belief in Scripture!"

The truth is that we, and all Christians, have many important beliefs that are not found in the Bible. Jesus did not write a Bible, nor did he tell his apostles to write one. He founded a church, a community of believers to which he promised his Spirit, with whom he promised to remain and to keep in the truth until the end of time. (See Matthew 28 and John 15 and 16) Out of that community of believers came the Bible. It is part of Christian tradition, not apart from it.

Thousands of Christians were born and died before all the New Testament was even written. They received their faith not from a "book," no matter how sacred, but from the group of those who were Christ's disciples long after he died, the group we call the church. To put it bluntly, we do not believe, and Christians never have believed, that everything we believe, all the doctrines and truths of our faith, are explicitly in the Bible.

We do believe wholeheartedly that the Bible is the Word of God. As I explained in the answer about the Bible as the norm of faith, we believe that nothing the church believes or holds as revealed by God can ever *contradict* the holy Scriptures. That is what the church means by saying that the Bible is the norm of faith for all time. We must measure our beliefs and practices against that Word. Nothing we believe can ever contradict or deny it. But we believe, as the church has believed since the beginning of Christianity, that the Holy Spirit guides us in our Christian belief and life above all in and through the community of faith, not exclusively by the book which that community of faith produced during the first hundred years of Christianity.

I said before that all Christians hold beliefs, essential beliefs, that come from outside the Bible. That includes even the most fundamentalist "bible-Christians." For example, when such Christians point to the Bible and say, "You must accept this because it is the word of God," ask how they know that book is the word of God. Because the book says so? Anyone can write a book and declare in it somewhere that it is the word of God. But that declaration doesn't make it so.

Even for Christians who "accept nothing that isn't in the Bible," the most basic of all their beliefs that the Bible is the divine word must come from outside that book. It must be authenticated by someone, or some group, that points to it and says: This is God's word. Accept it and believe it. Of course, the same community that points to the book and authenticates it in the power of the Spirit is that very community of faith that Jesus founded and promised to be with, the community we call the church.

So don't panic when asked these questions. If anything, the thing to panic about is that perhaps you do not know enough about your faith to really explain what and why you believe what you do. You need to study! I'm not trying to dodge your question about the sacraments. I'm just saying that, even when attempting to explain the sacraments, I cannot try to defend my own Christian faith with a fundamentalist approach I don't accept in the first place. Neither should you.

CHAPTER 2

THE CHURCH

❦

People of God

Why is there now so much talk in the Catholic Church about the "people of God?" I presume the phrase means to include us. Is it the same as "the church?" If so, why not just say so?

The term "people of God," used prominently by Vatican Council II, is a much broader name than "church," particularly if we mean it in the very limited sense of Roman Catholic Church.

The phrase comes from the Old Testament, where the people of Israel frequently are called the people of God, a group set apart by God as recipients of special blessings from him.

In the New Testament, the death and resurrection of Jesus and the proclamation of this great event by the preaching of the Gospel gave rise to a new "people of God," brought together not by their own initiative, but by God's own action. (The Greek word for church, *ekklesia*, means literally a group called out, or called apart.)

The church, in the sense of the recipients of God's saving work in the world through Christ, obviously can be looked at in different ways. As any mystery, no one description or definition can convey the entire meaning. The phrase, "Mystical Body of Christ," for example, is a metaphor developed by St. Paul in his theology of Christ and his people. As generally understood, however, it focuses on the more specific claims an individual may have for union with Jesus, such as baptism, membership in the "organized" church, explicit belief in certain doctrines, and so on.

"People of God" focuses rather on the more general claims that give to mankind a right to God's mercy and other blessings — the Incarnation, and the death and resurrection of Jesus. This seems to be the reason for the frequent use of that name in and since Vatican Council II.

Priesthood of the laity

I became a Catholic three years ago. They told us we would continue learning for many years, since there was time during those months to discuss only a small part of Catholic beliefs. I am finding this true. Recently a longtime Catholic gave me a book that speaks of the "priesthood of the laity." We never talked about that, and none of my other books mention it. Can you help?

The response involves some knowledge of the use of the words "priest" and "priesthood" in the New Testament. The Greek word for priest, *hiereus*, is never used in the New Testament to designate an official of the church. It is applied to Jesus himself in the Letter to the Hebrews. Sometime afterward, probably around the year 200, it began to be applied to Christian bishops and later to presbyters or elders. I'm sure you understand that the priests referred to in the Gospels, for example, are priests of the Old Testament, not of the Christian church.

In the latter part of the first century, some decades after our Lord's death and resurrection, the whole Christian people are called by St. Peter "a chosen race, a royal priesthood, a holy nation, a people of his own" (1 Pt 2:9). At a certain period in our century it was not uncommon to find this reality expressed as "the priesthood of the laity."

That is not an accurate phrase, however, since Peter's words apply not to the laity but to all Christians, regardless of their official status or ministry in the church. The priesthood he speaks of, which is to announce the praises of God, do good works by which God would be glorified and offer spiritual sacrifices acceptable to God through Jesus Christ (1 Pt 2:5, 9, 12), is one shared by all faithful followers of Christ. The more limited sense of an ordained priesthood identifies a particular role that the ordained fulfill, especially in the eucharistic and other sacramental worship of the Christian community.

"The one, true church?"

Can we as Catholics still say that the Roman Catholic Church is the one, true, Catholic and apostolic church? And that we alone possess the truth?

Understanding these qualities in a very carefully defined way, as the church understands them, the answer would be yes. However, I'm afraid that in the sense you mean (and as many Catholics and most Protestants probably think the church means them) the answer would have to be no.

When we call the Catholic Church "true," for example, it does not mean that we believe that we alone possess the truth. Catholic theology not only holds that other churches can profess and teach truth, but also that the Holy Spirit is working within them in a real way with its light and love. This is especially true in Christian churches, but can be true of other religions as well — most certainly and obviously, of course, of the Jewish faith, which shares many essential traditions with Christianity.

Any sincere Catholic does believe that in the Catholic Church there are certain channels of truth and grace and intimacy with Jesus that normally are not present in the traditions, liturgy, and life of other churches. If he did not believe this, one would assume he would belong to another church — or none at all. The same would presumably be true of any sincere Methodist, Baptist or Lutheran — for the same reasons.

Our beliefs in this matter were stated well and often in Vatican Council II, and many times since. We believe that "the one true religion subsists in the catholic and apostolic church"; that truth imposes its demands on the human conscience "by the power of its own truth" and not by coercion, and that the Spirit's gift of truth must be honored wherever it is found. (See Declaration on Religious Freedom, Art. 1, which is quoted here, and the Decrees on Ecumenism, Art. 2, and on the Church, *Lumen Gentium*, Art. 15. See also chapter on ecumenism.)

Didache

What is the Didache, which you mention sometimes in your column? Where can I obtain a copy? I am interested in the travels and teaching of the first apostles.

The complete text of the Didache is available now in the Ancient Christian Writers series (vol. 6, Paulist Press). But don't expect it to add much to your knowledge of the travels and teachings of the individual first apostles. This isn't what the document is all about.

The full name of the work is *The Teaching (didache) of the Lord to the Gentiles Through the Twelve Apostles*. Written in Greek, it apparently originated in Syria in the first half of the second century A. D., somewhere around the year 125. Despite the name, its 16 chapters contain much more than a list of apostolic teachings. Included among other topics are sections on church structure, some sacramental liturgies (including a remarkably familiar description of what we now call the liturgies of the Word and the Eucharist at Mass), and even policies concerning charitable and social works of mercy.

The Didache was almost completely unknown until little more than 100 years ago, in 1883, when a metropolitan of the Greek Orthodox Church published an 11th century manuscript. Since then the document has become the major source of information about the early church in the generations immediately after the first apostles.

The Christian creeds

During the study of the creed in our RCIA (Rite for the Christian Initiation of Adults) group, one candidate questioned the need for two creeds, the Apostles' Creed and the Nicene Creed we recite at Sunday Mass. When were these two creeds written? Why are there two? Are there others? Do other denominations use these creeds?

A creed (from the Latin *credere*, to believe) is a list of religious doctrines held by a particular group. Some are shorter, hitting just the basics; others are longer and more detailed. Thus, while we are more familiar with the two you mention, Christians have had several of both kinds over the past 2,000 years.

The first ones, which we find already in the New Testament, contain only a few words. In his letter to the Philippians, for instance, St. Paul tells us that the climax and summation of our Christian response to the Incarnation and the saving death of Jesus is: Jesus Christ is Lord (2:11). We find this proclamation of faith reflected or alluded to elsewhere in the New Testament dozens of times.

Another was "God has raised him (Jesus) from the dead." This formula, too, is repeated often in the Acts of the Apostles, and inferred repeatedly in other places.

This does not imply that other important beliefs are not contained in the Scriptures. Paul makes clear, however, that these two were (and still are) the core of Christian faith. "If you confess with your mouth that Jesus is Lord," he says, "and believe in your heart that God raised him from the dead, you will be saved" (Romans 10:9).

As time went on, a variety of urgent circumstances prompted Christians to develop more detailed and specific lists of their beliefs.

Under what conditions, for example, should Christians allow others to become members of their faith community? What "bare bones" truths, handed down from the apostles about Jesus and his teachings, should new Christians be required to profess before being accepted for baptism?

By the beginning of the third century, catechumens approaching the waters of baptism needed to respond "I believe" to three fundamental questions, framed in words very similar to the Apostles' Creed. With minor differences, these same questions, or "baptism promises," form part of our baptism liturgy to this day.

Some time later, perhaps in the fourth century, the formula of faith based on these questions, the Apostles' Creed, pretty much reached its final form.

Another circumstance giving rise to creedal statements was found in the various doctrinal controversies within the Christian communities. Through most of the fourth century, the church wrestled fiercely against teachings which began with a priest named Arius directly attacking fundamental beliefs about the divinity of Christ and the Holy Trinity. Bishops and theologians at the first ecumenical council in Nicaea (325) developed a more extended profession of faith aimed particularly against Arius and his followers.

Fifty-six years later, the ecumenical council of Constantinople (381) modified that profession somewhat, ending up with what we commonly call the Nicene Creed.

These creeds were formed many centuries before the Protestant Reformation. Both of them, the Apostles' Creed particularly, have a place in the worship of many, if not most, Protestant congregations today.

It is worth noting that these early creeds and other expressions of faith during the first 1,000 years of Christianity are seen today as having increasing importance in the movement toward Christian unity, especially between the Eastern and Western Catholic Churches.

Most of us, I believe, do not recognize the enormous significance of the creed we profess together each Sunday. Framing the foundational truths of Christian faith as they do, they are among the most majestic achievements of those who have gone before us as followers of Christ.

Ecumenical Councils

I recently read a remark by a prominent writer that the second Vatican Council was actually the first really ecumenical council. I understood that there were many before this one. What did he mean? When will the next council be?

It's true that there were many ecumenical councils before Vatican Council II. It's also true, if one wishes to be geographically and numerically literal, they were not truly ecumenical — that is, worldwide. Possibly the most significant council in more modern times, for example, at least in its long range influence on Catholic life and belief, was the Council of Trent. It started in 1545, after eight years of agonizing preparatory work, with only 25 bishops and four cardinals at the opening Mass. Dragging out for 19 years, with 25 separate sessions, it never enjoyed, for various political and religious reasons, the presence of more than a small minority of those eligible to attend.

More recently the first Vatican Council opened in 1869 with about 700 bishops, out of about 1,050 eligible, on hand, and 500 of these were from Europe. At some sessions, only around 100 bishops were present.

During Vatican II, however, about 2,900 bishops and prelates were invited. More than 2,500 attended the opening in 1962 and 2,400 the closing in 1965. Based on numbers and on areas of the world represented, it was by far the most "ecumenical" council in history.

It is not primarily the numbers or geography that makes an ecumenical council. The other councils were ecumenical insofar as their actions were at least accepted and approved by the Bishop of Rome, and were applicable to the whole church.

Since these councils are called only when the need arises, the next one may be 10 or 100 years from now.

Theology or dogma?

Our study club had a disagreement over something in the book we are discussing — a reference to the "theology of St. Paul." Some of us found no problem with the words, but others claim the phrase is misleading. There is, after all, only one theology that is true, isn't there — at least only one that we as Catholics can accept?

I think you are getting theology mixed up with dogma. They're two different things.

Theology can mean any development or discourse on ideas relating to God. More specifically, it is an organized *system* of thought which tries to synthesize the truths we have about God from reason or from revelation. It is an individual's, or group's, insights on how the doctrines of Christianity, for example, hang together, how they fit with other aspects of human life and knowledge, and so on.

In that sense, there are many "theologies" which are perfectly respectable and acceptable in Catholic tradition, even though they may profoundly disagree with each other. St. Augustine, for instance, developed a theological system which St. Thomas Aquinas often radically disagreed with in his own theology 800 years later. Today nearly 800 years after St. Thomas, theological systems frequently take basically different avenues toward explaining the meaning of Christian truths than he did.

St. Paul was a man of faith and insight who developed his own theology, putting together the teachings he received from Christ, and enriching his and our understanding of them.

At different times in Christian history, other "schools" of theology placed their emphases differently than he did. A good example is the place Paul gives to the resurrection as the central event establishing Jesus as the Son of God with the power of the Savior. During perhaps most of the centuries since Paul, the theological tendency has been to identify this key event as the Incarnation itself, rather than the resurrection.

Such differences may appear academic, but they significantly influence the direction of Christian spirituality and belief. Many "difficulties" with modern theology, for example, result from the fact that it leans heavily toward the resurrection emphases of St. Paul — which, however, vastly enriches our understanding of the real meaning of the Incarnation of the Son of God.

What are theologians trying to do?

Maybe you can tell me what the theologians are trying to do, destroy the church? As far as I can see, they are undermining the faith of good people.

This considerably abbreviated query was preceded by several other obviously rhetorical questions concerning current developments in the church. Perhaps this final comment wasn't really meant to be answered either. But its spirit is evident often in letters that cross my desk.

Theology is a specialized and intricate science, and theologians are specialists in that field. Through the centuries, the church has depended heavily on the research and writings of trained experts in this science — theologians like St. Jerome, St. Thomas Aquinas, St. Augustine, St. Alphonsus Ligouri, and thousands of other great and lesser lights. Most of them, incidentally, were "prophets without honor" through much of their own lifetime.

When I say the church has depended on them, I include bishops and popes. While they are the official teaching body in the family of Christ, bishops are not often theologians with highly advanced training, particularly in critically important fields of scriptural and doctrinal theology, or in specialized technical areas of ethics.

Of its nature, theology is a speculative, open-end science. Part of its business is to be at the cutting edge of Catholic thought as the church's understanding of Jesus and his message develop through the ages. As with mothers, fathers, or priests, there are capable and less capable ones. A theologian may be right or wrong, or in between. His expertise may be in one field rather than another. Above all, his theories and opinions are only as good or as bad as his reasons for them.

When anyone condemns or ridicules "the theologians," therefore, I can't avoid the suspicion that he has never seriously studied what specific theologians have to say on a subject, or he is seeking someone to blame for things he doesn't understand or approve of. Or possibly both of these.

Blanket blaming of parents, teenagers, intellectuals — or theologians — for our discomforts and crises is easy, but rarely contributes anything toward our understanding or the search for truth.

What is the magisterium?

I am a fairly recent convert to the Catholic faith, but I keep coming across a word in our Catholic paper which I never heard during my instructions. What (or who) is the "magisterium?"

The word "magisterium" comes from another Latin word, *magister* (teacher); it means the power, or duty, of teaching and leading.

Before our Lord died, he promised his followers that the Holy Spirit, whom he would send, would bring to their minds all that he had told them. Magisterium is the word we use to indicate the authority and responsibility the church has in fulfilling that promise of Christ, the responsibility and charismatic power to be the faithful interpreter of God's word to mankind. It is, in other words, the human instrument Jesus uses to keep his people from serious and dangerous mistakes in their understanding of God and of man's salvation.

This responsibility is personalized and focused in the Holy Father, and in the bishops of the world together with him — a tradition Catholics believe continues the pattern set by Jesus in placing this responsible authority in Peter, and in the other apostles with him. Because they are in this way the official interpreters and guardians of revealed truths, the bishops and the pope are also often referred to as the church's magisterium.

This duty is not carried out in a vacuum. As Pope Paul VI noted some years ago, the magisterium reveals no new truths, but is to be a "faithful echo" of the Divine Word and of Holy Scripture. In this, pope and bishops need the input, support, and assistance of all others in the church. These include laity and clergy — who, by the witness of their daily lives help toward a deeper understanding of the teachings of Jesus — theologians, and other teachers.

The magisterium is one always-living way our Lord honors his promise to his followers to guide them into all truth. (Jn. 16:13)

When does the pope speak infallibly?

According to Catholic teaching, when does the pope speak infallibly? Is it in an encyclical, or in some other way? Could you give an example of such a teaching?

While he was still here on earth with his disciples, Jesus told his followers that he would be with them always and that the Spirit he would send would keep them always in the truth.

It is Catholic belief that this promise is fulfilled in part by the fact that, under certain conditions, the Holy Father, as the focal point of Catholic unity and faith, is invested in a special way personally with this promise of Jesus to keep the church free from error.

This unique certitude of truth — infallibility — is present, we believe, when the pope speaks precisely as chief shepherd and teacher of the church on matters of divine faith or morals, and clearly intends to exercise his role in the church in that solemn manner. This is the service he is called on to offer his fellow Catholics as chief bishop in the church.

The infallible nature of a teaching depends not on the type of document in which it is included, but on the intention of the Holy Father made clear in the statement itself. Theoretically, it could be on the back of an envelope.

One doctrine considered to be taught with such infallibility was that of the Assumption of Mary, declared by Pope Pius XII in 1950. Toward the end of a long encyclical, (*Munificentissimus Deus*), analyzing the history of the doctrine of the Assumption through the centuries, Pope Pius defined the teaching with these solemn words: "We have poured forth prayers of supplication again and again to God, and have called upon the Spirit of Truth. Now, for the glory of Almighty God, who has lavished his special affection upon the Virgin Mary; for the honor of her Son, the undying King of the Ages and Victor over sin and death; for the increase of the glory of that revered mother; and for the joy and exultation of the entire church:

"By the authority of our Lord Jesus Christ, of the Blessed Apostles Peter and Paul, and by our own authority, we pronounce, declare, and define it to be a divinely revealed dogma that the Immaculate Mother of God, the ever Virgin Mary, having completed the course of her earthly life, was taken body and soul into heavenly glory."

Popes elected by people?

A book used by our study club comments that popes were formerly elected by the people. Can you enlighten us? We assumed that the popes were chosen by the bishops or clergy before they were chosen by the cardinals.

Your book is right. During most of the history of the church, most bishops, including the bishop of Rome, were chosen in some way by the people.

During the first ten centuries, the choice was made by a commonly accepted procedure involving the clergy and laity of each particular diocese. Civil leaders had an increasingly larger hand in the choice, sometimes simply picking a person they felt would be favorable to their own policies. Thus, the emperor of the Holy Roman Empire was for centuries the most powerful factor in the choice of the pope.

Only in 1059 did Pope Nicholas II place the election of the pope in the hands of the cardinals. (Cardinals, as we know them, did not exist in the church much before this time.)

The Third Lateran Council (1179) decreed that a two-thirds vote of the cardinals is required for election of the pope. Pope Gregory X, to further lessen political influences on papal elections, ruled in 1271 that the cardinals should be isolated under lock and key during the proceedings — a provision all but ignored in many elections since then.

In 1945, Pope Pius XII revised the procedures, requiring a two-thirds majority plus one for election. In 1975, Pope Paul VI again revised the procedures somewhat, but did not substantially change the policy for papal elections today. Pope John Paul II did the same in 1996.

A woman pope?

A friend of mine told me that a woman was declared pope sometime in the church's past. Her name was Katherine. I know that a woman cannot become a priest, much less a pope, at least not legally. But could a woman be named pope incorrectly?

The legend of Popess Joan (not Katherine) recurs regularly, especially in anti-Catholic tracts which usually speak as if they have discovered something new. Perhaps your friend has encountered one of these.

The story of Popess Joan is a weird tale which first appeared in the 13th century, nearly 300 or 400 years after she was supposed to have lived. She disguised herself, so the story goes, so effectively that she became a priest, a cardinal in the Roman Curia, and finally pope. She reportedly reigned for two-and-one-half years as Pope John Angelicus, sometime between the years 800 and 1100.

Her sex was discovered when she gave birth to a child during a papal procession near the Colosseum. The legend is given no credibility by historians.

Any married popes?

A book we are discussing refers to the fact that some popes have been married, but doesn't go into detail. Is this true? Have we had married popes?

Of course we have had married popes, beginning with St. Peter, though we don't hear anything about his wife after the references to her mother in the Gospels. (See, for example, Mark 1, 30)

The same is true with other popes. Records are sparse, so we know little about their married life before or after they became head of the church. We do know that one married pope, St. Hormisdas (514-523), was the father of another pope who is honored as a saint, St. Silverius (536-538).

To my knowledge, the last married pope was Adrian II (867-872). At least for a while after being named pope, he apparently lived with his wife and family at the Lateran Palace in Rome, even though an unmarried clergy was by this time common in the Western church.

Anti-popes?

A magazine article I read referred to someone as a possible "anti-pope" and implied that he would not be the first one in history. Were there really anti-popes? I thought there could only be one pope at a time.

It has happened more than once that strong political or religious factions in the church have not liked the man chosen as pope, or perhaps thought he was chosen unlawfully, and so picked their own man and called him pope.

These are complicated messes usually, and difficult to untangle. While there is technically only one pope at a time, historians sometimes have a hard task sorting out which is which.

A classic example was during a considerably hairy time for the church in the third century when Pope Callixtus and a popular anti-pope, Hippolytus, spent a good deal of their adult lives condemning each other. Today both are honored as martyrs and saints.

There hasn't been an anti-pope for more than 500 years.

Why pope lives in Italy?

Why does the pope live in Italy? Couldn't we just as easily have a leader who lived in the U.S.A. or China?

Nothing says the pope must live in Italy. As you may know, even before John Paul II, there were other popes of other nationalities. And during one period of nearly 100 years, all the popes lived in France.

However, no matter who he is or where he lives, the pope holds his position as the Bishop of Rome.

To discuss fully why this is so would require many books. Briefly, the Bishop of Rome has held the position of pre-eminence among other bishops in the church from its earliest years, since this is where St. Peter spent the last part of his life and where he died.

We possess letters and other indications that, even before the last of the twelve apostles died, the Bishop of Rome was recognized as the authority over all other areas of the church. Probably the most famous of these is the letter of St. Clement, the third pope after Peter, to the Church of Corinth, Greece, in the year 95.

Other more specific ruling and teaching prerogatives that we attach to the Holy Father's position developed in Catholic doctrine and practice in later centuries.

If pope becomes incapacitated

Rumors are that Pope John Paul II has Parkinson's disease. What happens if he becomes incapacitated mentally or physically? If he could no longer fulfill his responsibilities, who would substitute for him? Also, must the College of Cardinals elect one of their own to the papacy? Or could they choose someone else, even a lay person?

According to the *Code of Canon Law* (332), if the Roman Pontiff resigns his office, it is necessary for validity that the resignation be made freely and be properly manifested. It is not required, however, that the resignation be accepted by anyone.

The first and most obvious requirement, therefore, is that the decision be made by the pope himself, no one else. Furthermore, that decision must be clearly disclosed, in writing, for example, or perhaps by declaring his intention to the College of Cardinals. Once the Holy Father makes that choice manifest, it takes effect automatically.

With modern medical advances bringing increased longevity, it is likely the church will sooner or later need to face such problems. Until now, however, resignation has not been a major concern.

In 1294, a saintly Benedictine monk was elected pope against his will. After a tumultuous few months as Pope Celestine V, he resigned his office, the first and, according to most historians, perhaps the only pope to do so. The church thus has little experience with papacies ending in any way except death.

In 1999, Vatican sources indicated that Pope John Paul may have already provided for his eventual incapacity. He might even stipulate that if his physical condition were to deteriorate to a certain point, it be considered equivalent to resignation.

Anyone, even a layman, may be elected pope. He would immediately be ordained bishop, however. When elected, a pope by definition becomes the Bishop of Rome.

Did early Christians have priests?

In a Bible discussion group recently, we talked about the priesthood. Someone said she thought the Bible said nothing about priests — meaning priests as we know them in our church. Is this true? Didn't the early Christians have priests?

The New Testament speaks of three main ministries in the church: bishops, deacons and presbyters (elders). The exact function of these ministers, especially of the presbyters, is not perfectly clear, although bishops had the predominant supervisory responsibility.

The Greek word for priest, *hiereus*, is not used in the New Testament to designate an official of the church. It is applied to Jesus himself in the Letter to the Hebrews. In other places it refers to Christians in general to describe their special character as the people of God.

There is some likelihood that presbyters performed functions which we relate to priests, although their ministerial relation to the church is far less clear than that of the bishops and deacons.

The word *hiereus* only came into use in the Christian Church about 150 years after Jesus' death and resurrection as the Eucharist came to be more and more recognized as a renewal of the sacrifice of Calvary, as well as a meal. In the religious traditions of that time, a sacrifice was offered by a priest. Thus Christians began to confer that title on the minister who presided at the Eucharist.

Can a priest marry?

We learned that a close priest friend is planning to marry. This disturbed me greatly because I believed that the priests who did this were not good priests anyway, and I always thought he was a good priest.

What is his status in the church now? What should be our attitude toward him? Can we in good conscience retain his friendship?

Many Catholics still do not realize that it is possible for a priest to be released from his promise not to marry. Unlike marriage, whose nature and permanence are established by God himself, the celibacy of the priesthood is something the church could change and has changed in various ways through the centuries.

Jesus established the priesthood to serve his people in various ways, but he never made it his absolute rule that priests could not be married. In fact, married priests have been common in some parts of the world since the beginning of Christianity.

If a priest simply ignores the solemn promise he has made to remain unmarried, it would be wrong. It is possible for him, however, to petition the pope to release him from that promise; in that case, he could marry and remain in good standing in the church as a layman.

Without his telling you, there's hardly any way you can know what his status is now, since these matters are naturally handled privately. If you are a close friend, ask him. I think it is only fair that you should know, as it inevitably affects your feelings toward him.

Whatever the answer is, it doesn't mean he was not a good priest. If he did abandon his promise of celibacy without a dispensation, he possibly cut corners and neglected prayer a lot more than he should have, but God is the judge of that.

As for continuing your relationship with him, it can never be anything but right to be a friend to anyone — a thoughtful and honest friend. Try to understand and have the courage to be, and say to him, what you believe is best for him and for the others you must think of.

Married converts ordained priests

According to some news reports, the Catholic Church seems to have no problem letting Episcopalian converts come into the church to serve as priests while still married and with families. Yet, it holds that allowing Catholic priests to marry and minister to the people as priests is not possible. These policies seem to be contradictory. How can they be held at the same time?

Catholic policies permitting married converts to become candidates for the priesthood are recent and are still developing. Some basic criteria, however, seem to be emerging.

The largest number of married Roman Catholic priests in our country are former Episcopal priests. Their situation is somewhat, but not entirely, unique. As was true with the Oxford Movement in England during the 1800s, the present generation of Episcopal priests who leaned toward Roman Catholicism generally felt they should remain within the Anglican tradition and work toward corporate reunion with Rome. Later, many decided to apply individually as married candidates for ordination in the Roman Catholic Church.

They were formed within the Catholic system, they argued, and embraced Catholic tradition and teaching. Some of the group, especially among those who longed for the larger reunion of the churches, even accepted the primacy of the Bishop of Rome. Their position was that both in marrying and in their movement to the Roman Catholic Church with hopes of ordination, they acted in good faith.

The Vatican Congregation for the Doctrine of the Faith accepted this reasoning, it seems. It recognized these Episcopal priests and their families as acting in good faith, and approved their reception into the Roman Catholic Church and eventual ordination as married men. They were, in other words, dispensed from the promise and commitment of celibacy.

A well-known former Lutheran minister, now a Catholic priest, has pointed out to me that the Catholic self-understanding of Anglican clergy applies also to the many Lutherans who consider themselves "evangelical Catholics." Such Lutherans, he said, see themselves as temporarily separated from Rome and working for reunion. With this understanding, which is grounded in the Lutheran Augsburg Confession of 1530, he believes Lutherans could be received on the same basis as Episcopalians, with married men having the same possibility of ordination to the priesthood.

On the other hand, people who are raised Roman Catholic are presumed to know and be committed to the Catholic discipline of a celibate priesthood. Thus, they may choose to marry or be ordained, knowing that one of these sacraments precludes the other.

It appears that Roman Catholic policy for ordaining married converts to our faith still needs time to develop, and many factors, perhaps some yet unforeseen, will enter the discussion.

Sexual orientation and ordination

I would like the bottom line on whether the Catholic Church can knowingly ordain homosexual men to the priesthood. Some fellow parishioners say, "What's the difference? If they do their job and remain celibate, it's not an issue for contention and debate."

Others say it is an issue because the person is not whole, has set aside God in this part of his life, is not reconciled in this important physical aspect of his personality, and would be a negative example blocking God's grace to others. I'd greatly appreciate your answer.

First, I need to say that your description and your judgment of homosexuality in men (or women) are highly questionable, to put it mildly, and certainly do not reflect the attitude and position of the church in the matter.

To say that such persons have set aside God, are not reconciled in their physical makeup and block God's grace to others is at best rash judgment and furthermore simply does not fit experience.

In my 47 years as a priest, I have been acquainted with a good number of homosexual priests. I'm not sure how many people they ministered to were aware of the fact, and as far as I know these priests were not sexually active. Nearly all of them have been good, highly effective, prayerful and dedicated in their ministry.

To answer your question, nothing in church law automatically precludes a bishop from "knowingly" ordaining a homosexual. For validity of orders, the only requirement is that the candidate be a baptized male (canon 1024).

Other requirements, of course, must be fulfilled if the ordination is to be licit, or lawful. These include a period of probation, during which the necessary education and formation programs take place and adequate evaluation of the candidate's qualities can be completed.

Also, there must be no impediment in the way (for example, according to the present general law of the church, a valid marriage is an impediment to ordination), and the individual must be considered useful for ministry in the church. These are all spelled out in a number of canons.

When these conditions are fulfilled, a bishop may ordain the individual, whatever his sexual orientation.

History of celibacy

In light of the present controversies concerning celibacy in the priesthood, do we have any examples of a celibate life in the Old Testament? And when was celibacy for the priesthood made mandatory in our church?

To my knowledge, the only major Old Testament figure who was celibate was the prophet Jeremiah, who lived around the beginning of the destruction of Jerusalem and the Babylonian exile (sixth century B. C.). He was told by the Lord (Jer. 16:1-4) not to marry as a sign to the people that children then being born would die in the tragedies to come.

The very idea of a celibate life for men or women was generally repugnant to the Hebrew culture as it was to most cultures at that time. For a woman to be unmarried and childless was shameful. For men and women, marriage and a house filled with children was seen as a mark of God's blessing.

The first general law in the Western church obliging the clergy to a celibate life appeared in the later part of the fourth century. This occurred through the decrees of several popes beginning with Pope Damasus (366-384) and local councils in Africa and Europe.

During the next 700 years, the marriage of priests, deacons and bishops was unlawful in the Western church. The movement toward a clerical celibacy culminated for the universal church in the 12th century at the First and Second Lateran Councils, when such marriages were considered not only illicit but also invalid.

Much later, at the Council of Trent in 1563, the law of clerical celibacy was reaffirmed. However, against enormous opposition, the council declared that priestly celibacy was a matter of church law, not divine law. This means that the church could change its legislation concerning celibacy and priests would no longer be obliged to observe it. The church did this for deacons at Vatican Council II when it instituted a married permanent diaconate.

The road of clerical celibacy has been rocky through the centuries, particularly in the early Middle Ages and again in the period before the Protestant Reformation. Rocky or not, it seems clear the church is not prepared to alter easily a practice which has been so intimate a part of its life for the past 17 centuries.

How did the Roman collar begin?

What is the origin of the Roman collar for clergy? When and where did its use begin? I am a priest and have looked everywhere for the answer, without success.

I am not surprised you found the search difficult. Throughout the centuries right up to our own time, regulations and customs concerning clerical dress differed greatly from one time or place to another, and usually are hard to trace.

For at least the first five centuries of the church there were no special rules for clergy dress. What customs existed then, and for at least 1,000 years after, usually were based more on the cleric's occupation (teacher, philosopher) or more specific vocation (monk, hermit, ascetic) than on general church law.

Even the Council of Trent in the 16th century simply required "that (Catholic) clerics always wear a dress conformable to their order, that by the propriety of their outward apparel they may show forth the inward uprightness of their morals" (Session 14). Later in that same century, Pope Sixtus V designated the cassock as fulfilling the "propriety" of Trent, and apparently intended to require clergy always to wear this robe in public. Until recently, the cassock still was the usual street dress of clergy in Italy and, to a lesser degree, in Spain and France.

The Roman collar was not used in the United States or in England until the 1800s. You may recall seeing portraits of early American priests or bishops with a kind of white "choker" around the neck. About the middle of the last century, Bishop (later Cardinal) Nicholas Patrick Wiseman decreed several ways in which his diocese in England should imitate the Italian (Roman) Church, including that priests must wear the Roman collar. Another significant innovation of Bishop Wiseman, incidentally, was that priests should be called Father. Before that the title was used, if at all, only in reference to members of some religious orders, such as Benedictines and Franciscans.

In the United States, the Council of Baltimore (1884) ruled that in public, priests should wear the Roman collar, along with a dark coat that reached to the knees.

As I indicated, one finds significant differences from country to country. In England both Catholic and many Protestant clergy wear the Roman collar. In Germany, among many other countries, many, or most, Catholic priests wear a dark suit and tie. If one sees a clergyman with a Roman collar, there is a good chance it will be a Lutheran pastor.

Present canon law requires that clergy "cultivate a simple style of life and are to avoid whatever has a semblance of vanity," and are to "wear suitable ecclesiastical garb in accord with the norms issued by the conference of bishops and in accord with legitimate local custom." (canons 282 and 284)

Illegitimacy and priesthood

Many years ago I read that a boy born out of wedlock could not be a candidate for the priesthood in the Catholic Church. Is this true?

In the former *Code of Canon Law,* illegitimacy was among the "irregularities" that prevented reception of holy orders. This law did not intend to punish anyone; it was one manner in which the church attempted to protect the dignity of public worship.

Even then, there were procedures present to allow the ordination of an illegitimate child. The present code does not include this obstacle to holy orders. It is, therefore, no longer in effect.

Deacons and holy orders

A recent article celebrating Vatican II's restoring permanent deacons in the church states, "In its effort to update the life of the church, Vatican Council II made allowance for the diaconate 'to be restored to its own permanent position in the hierarchy' (Lumen Gentium 29), also making it possible for married men to be conferred this sacrament." Is the diaconate considered the sacrament of holy orders? When a seminarian receives the order of deacon, and then priesthood, does he receive the sacrament twice?

One might put it that way, I suppose, since the sacrament is conferred in two distinct ceremonies. It is more proper and theologically correct, however, to speak of three degrees of the sacrament of orders.

St. Hippolytus, a Roman priest who died in 236, left us a valuable work entitled The Apostolic Tradition, with information about Christian worship and structure in his time. The bishop is the *sacerdos* (priest), says Hippolytus, elected by the people and ordained by imposition of hands by another bishop. The bishop, among other functions, presided at the Eucharist and proclaimed the Word of God.

Presbyters (elders or priests) were ordained by the bishop, with other priests laying on hands with him. They stood with the bishop as he presided at the eucharistic celebration, and themselves presided at the Eucharist with the bishop's permission.

Deacons were ordained by the bishop alone, since he determined the specifics of their service to the local church.

With the restoration of the permanent diaconate in the last 40 years, the Catholic hierarchy described by Hippolytus remains in basic outline the one we know today.

The *Catechism of the Catholic Church*, summarizing this tradition, speaks of two degrees of ministerial participation in the priesthood of Christ, the episcopacy and the presbyterate, and a third degree, the diaconate, to serve liturgical and other needs of the local community as determined by the bishop. "Catholic doctrine teaches that the degrees of priestly participation (episcopate and presbyterate) and the degree of service (diaconate) are all three conferred by... the sacrament of Holy Orders" (1554 and 1596).

A letter of St. Ignatius of Antioch, martyred in Rome about the year 107, emphasizes the importance of all three degrees of holy orders, bishops, priests and deacons, in the life of the church. "Without them," writes Ignatius, "one cannot speak of the church."

Duties of permanent deacons

Since 1971 a number of men have been ordained permanent deacons in our archdiocese. Please enumerate the duties they perform in church as permanent deacons. This point is not clear to many Catholics. Do the deacons receive remuneration for acting in this capacity?

Before I answer your question directly, it should be noted that liturgical functions of the deacons, especially at the celebration of the Eucharist, are intended to be a climax and a symbol of the other service they render to the community outside of the liturgy. This point is made constantly by those who work in the training and supervision of the deacon programs.

The following liturgical functions are among those assigned to deacons by the church:

1. to function as deacon at celebrations of the Eucharist,
2. to function as celebrant of the sacrament of baptism (anyone may administer the sacrament of baptism in emergencies; deacons are officially appointed ministers of that sacrament by the church),

3. to take holy Communion to the sick in their homes, hospitals and other health care facilities,
4. to serve as celebrant of Benediction of the Blessed Sacrament (this includes wearing the proper vestments, exposing the Blessed Sacrament, and giving the blessing with the sacred vessel containing the Eucharist),
5. to officiate at services for the dead and at burial rites,
6. to officiate at marriages,
7. to administer the sacramentals of the church according to the rite indicated by the church, including blessing religious articles, and the blessing of throats on the Feast of St. Blase, and
8. to bless and distribute ashes on Ash Wednesday. (see *Moto Proprio* on the Order of Deacon, Pope Paul VI, 18 June, 1967)

The 1984 *Book of Blessings* indicates a number of blessings at which a deacon may preside. It adds that whenever a priest is present, it is more fitting that he preside and that the deacon assist by carrying out those functions proper to the diaconate. (n.18)

Deacons may also preach at celebrations of the Eucharist and other ceremonies. However, this function as well as the faculty to officiate at marriages must be granted to them by the bishop of the diocese.

Many, probably most, permanent deacons receive no regular payment for the services they give. Policies concerning remuneration are established by the diocese and the institution in which the deacon serves.

Young lady wants to be priest

I know Pope John Paul II says women cannot be ordained. But my problem is, I really think I have a vocation to be a priest and help people the way priests can. One of my teachers said I shouldn't feel that way since the pope says no, but I do. I want to do what God wants, and I pray about this a lot. I am 14 years old. My mother suggested I ask for your help.

You deserve congratulations for reflecting and praying so much, and looking for God's will about what you will do with your life. You and your parents should be happy about that. I would suggest at least two important truths for you to think about.

First, there is nothing wrong with your wanting to be a priest. Other great and holy women have had the same desire. Surely you have heard of St. Theresa of the Child Jesus (also known as St. Theresa of Lisieux, or the Little Flower), one of the most popular and influential women of modern times. Carmelite Father James McCaffery, and other scholars of the life of St. Theresa, tell us that she wanted desperately to be a priest. She could never understand why that was not allowed.

According to her sister Celine, the source of much of our knowledge about her, even as Theresa was dying (at the age of 24) she told her sister, "If I could have been a priest, I would have been ordained at the June ordination." As she spoke of the "wonders we shall see in heaven," Theresa said, "I have a feeling that those who desired to be priests on earth will be able to share in the honor of the priesthood in heaven."

St. Theresa, incidentally, was never shy about protesting laws and policies she thought were wrong. She disagreed strongly, for example, with church regulations of that time severely restricting reception of holy Communion. Several years after her death in 1897, Pope Pius X relaxed those regulations and encouraged frequent and even daily Communion. He acknowledged St. Theresa as the one who inspired and enlightened him to do so.

Second, it is important in our spiritual lives to remember that sometimes we may have strong desires, for really good and holy things, that for whatever reason are impossible to fulfill. In those situations we have to bypass that desire, accept in love the hurt that results, and go about our work of becoming a saint in other ways. There is nothing weak or second-rate in acting this way. We do what we can to change what we believe needs changing, but we don't let these limitations make us bitter or keep us from being useful and happy.

Again, St. Theresa is a perfect example. She made clear more than once her disagreement with the restrictions placed on women, but she didn't let that stop her. She went on doing what she could do and became a saint who accomplished more good during her life and after her death than most of the rest of us dream of. On the 100th anniversary of her death, Pope John Paul declared Theresa a doctor, a preeminent teacher and saint of the church. So she is an excellent model.

Since this is the only life you have, keep exploring how to use your talents as best you can in every way open for you.

Women's role in church

Women in the Catholic faith are encouraged to participate in church activities which include serving on school boards, parent-teacher organizations, parish councils, liturgy committees, and other planning groups.

Others play a vital role in religious education as nuns, CCD teachers, or just plain Mom. Women have been the backbone of many right-to-life groups. They are also asked to be readers at Mass and distribute Communion.

And yet, although girls serve in most other places, even now, our daughters are not permitted to serve Mass in their parish. Does the church really teach that women are inferior? One priest I asked said that was nonsense, but I wonder.

Yours is a difficult question to deal with because the story of the ministry of women in the church can be confusing.

From your question I assume you know that female Mass servers are permitted by general law of the church. In a March, 1993, letter, the Vatican Congregation for Divine Worship and Sacraments told bishops they may allow female altar servers. The practice is now common in many, probably most, countries.

However, women are not eligible for ordination to the diaconate or the priesthood, or for installation into the ministries (formerly minor orders) of lector (reader) or acolyte. Other liturgical regulations, however, allow women, at least in some circumstances, to perform nearly all the functions of both reader and acolyte.

In his Apostolic Letter on the reform of Minor Orders (Aug. 15, 1972), Pope Paul lists the duties of Lector (reader) as: reading the Scripture and responsorial psalm, presenting the intentions of the prayer of the faithful, directing singing and other participation by the faithful, preparing other Scripture readers, and "instructing the faithful for the worthy reception of the sacraments." All these can be and are done by women.

Acolytes serve as special ministers of the Eucharist, and as assistant to the deacon and priest during the eucharistic liturgy. They may also expose the Blessed Sacrament for adoration, and instruct others in their function in the liturgy. Again, of these four acolytes' duties, church law allows three of them to be performed by women.

Concerning the inferiority of women, there are some embarrassing theological traditions that must be faced, because they cannot help but have some influence on the discussion about women's role in the church.

For example, one of the latest series of Latin theology textbooks was published within the past few decades by an American theologian. The volume on the sacrament of orders reflects a long theological trend when it says that women should not be allowed to have the office of teacher because of their "natural condition of inferiority and subjection." Being weaker, they "are inept for the heavy labors of the social and ecclesiastical life." Their moral feebleness "is manifest in the lightness of judgment, in credulity, and in the fragility of spirit by which she is less able to reign in the passions, particularly concupiscence."

This was written in 1962, but the idea is not new. St. Thomas Aquinas said several times that women are by nature mentally and morally weaker than men, and that women are naturally subject to men.

Past views on women

In speaking of the role of women in the church, you remark that St. Thomas Aquinas wrote that women are inferior morally and mentally to men. One friend who is supposed to know a lot of theology told me he does not believe St. Thomas would ever say anything like that. Can you tell me where statements like this are found?

Anyone familiar with the history of Christian thought would know that statements along these lines are not unusual. To place the question in proper context, however, we need to understand two historical facts of life.

First, for much of the history of the human race, until modern times in fact, prevailing biological teaching was that in human procreation women provided only a "nest" and growth material for new life. The "active" part was the male seed which totally determined the nature of the new person.

Furthermore, it was believed that if the male seed was perfect, a male was born. If it was significantly defective, a female baby resulted, whose physical, mental and moral prowess would inevitably be less than a man's.

Second, again until fairly recent times (indeed theologians are still wrestling with how this attitude fits with what we know about human activities) in anything having to do with physical processes like generation of the species, these processes as they occur in animals, and "why" animals do them, were generally considered to provide the best insight on how and why they should happen in human life. Particularly did this affect Christian moral viewpoints on the purposes and moralities of sexual activity between men and women.

Knowing this helps us understand, even if we cannot agree with him, that St. Thomas (who died in 1274) was simply reflecting the best science of his day when he said that a woman is a misbegotten or defective male. (*Mas occasionatus* I,99,2 ad 1; all references I give here are to the *Summa Theologiae*.)

"The active power which is in the male seed is intended to produce a perfect image of itself, a masculine sex," he said. "When a female results it is either because of a weakness in this active power or because of some indisposition of the materials, or even from a change produced by an outside factor — for example, from south winds, which are humid." (I,92,1 ad 1) St. Thomas, incidentally, received that idea about the south winds from Aristotle.

Clearly such erroneous biology easily leads to other equally bizarre conclusions. Thomas says, for example, that women need the virtue of sobriety more than men "because there is in them a greater proneness to concupiscence. . . sobriety is more required in women because there is not sufficient strength of mind for them to resist these concupiscences." (II,II,149,4)

These supposedly scientific conclusions led to spiritual implications as well. A woman cannot be validly ordained to the priesthood, said Thomas, regardless of her qualifications, since "no status of prominence can be signified in the feminine sex, because woman has the status of subjection, and so cannot receive the sacrament of orders." (Supp. 39,2)

Similarly, a woman should not baptize, even in an emergency, if there are men around to administer the sacrament. (III,67,4c)

Unfortunate and faulty as one might find statements such as these, it seems to me one should not condemn too heartily Thomas and other great thinkers who accepted what was almost universally believed to be scientific fact. It illustrates, however, the kinds of history we need to sort out to understand better the relationship of men and women in human society and in the church. Ultimately the answer for us appears in the fundamental equality between men and women as taught by Jesus and the rest of the New Testament, a position these theologians found almost impossible to integrate with what they "knew" to be scientifically true.

Finally, to prove that the theologians of no particular religious denomination hold a monopoly on being occasionally wrong, I offer the classic analysis of Martin Luther (*Table Talks*) on the place for women:

"Men have broad shoulders and narrow hips, and accordingly they possess intelligence. Women have narrow shoulders and broad hips. Women ought to stay at home; the way they were created indicates this for they have broad hips and a wide foundation to sit upon."

How do I join the church?

I am a 17-year-old Protestant. However, I feel that I belong in the Catholic Church. I have been reading about the church and going to Mass. Should I recite the creeds and prayers along with the church members? How can I be sure that I am ready to become a Catholic, and how do I go about joining?

I have thought and prayed about this for over a year. My heart tells me I'm headed in the right direction.

Your letter was a cool breeze on a warm day. As a Catholic who loves our church and our faith a great deal, I'm always pleased when someone like you wants to share it. And I'm happy for you. Obviously you even now feel God working in your heart through the contacts and experiences you have with the Catholic faith.

My first advice is that you talk with a priest, or perhaps to a Catholic friend who might lead you to a parish program for someone like yourself. While we are always happy that someone wishes to join our faith, we are concerned, as you are, that this decision be made with sufficient understanding of what it means to be a Catholic. Our faith is not simply a list of doctrines we accept. It is a way of life based on friendship and intimacy with Jesus, a special relationship with God and others. This relationship is enlightened and supported by the Scriptures and by our shared life of prayer and worship and service.

Every Catholic parish has some process to help people know when, as you say, they can be sure they are ready. For most parishes today that journey of faith involves what is called the Rite of Christian Initiation of Adults (RCIA). Over a period of several months you will pray and learn, share your faith and doubts and questions with others, and have plenty of time, guidance and companionship as you weigh the decisions you will need to make.

In the meantime keep going to Mass every Sunday. Listen and participate attentively. You may stand, kneel, join the prayers, and do whatever everyone else does, except receive Communion. That should wait until you finally become a Catholic. Please talk to someone about your desires soon, if you have not already done so, and get moving with your plans.

Belonging to a parish

I live in one state and work in another. I am registered in the parish where I live. Three years ago I decided to go to Mass every morning. The only church I could attend and still make it to work was close to my job. Now I'm beginning to wonder which church is really mine.

Since on weekdays no collections are taken, I have not been contributing to that church. I give my fair share to my home church. Should I quit my church and register in the one I attend on weekdays?

Many Catholics find themselves in your situation. They belong to one parish but for various reasons attend another through the week.

Don't worry about it. I'm sure the priest at your workday church is pleased to have you there. If you wish to do so occasionally, give something to show your appreciation for the opportunity to attend Mass there. But nothing more is required.

More importantly, perhaps you need to reflect with some seriousness about what it means to be a member of a parish. You may be among those Catholics who feel that "belonging to a parish" means hardly more than where you go to Mass and place your envelope in the Sunday collection.

If everyone acted on that principle, no parish would be worth much. Church law defines a parish as a "specific (stable) community of Christian believers" (canon 515). If that means anything, it means that every parish is a fellowship of believing Catholics who help each other and the rest of the community to live out the Gospel of Christ together.

Are you single, married, a parent? Whatever your present state of life, the priests, staff and probably many other people in your parish are trying to serve you and everyone else, liturgically and in other ways. They need your help.

As a general rule, the pastor in the parish where you reside is primarily responsible for you. For a serious enough reason, however, you might register in another parish.

I suggest you pick out the one where you can honestly and generously use your talents and make it, in fact, your parish.

Can we change parishes?

My husband and I have some serious problems with our parish. In some ways we enjoy it, but we feel we, and particularly our children, are missing important things in the church today. Part of it is the liturgy, but it goes beyond that to a spirit that we feel is just not where the church is today.

We want to do what is right, but are not sure where we stand as far as parish membership is concerned. Is it possible to join another parish?

Your concerns are vital ones for many in the church today. The solution is not easy, but a few thoughts may help.

For centuries a "Christian community" meant a small area in which a group of people lived and shared nearly everything together, including prayer and worship. Our Catholic traditions and laws concerning parishes developed in such situations.

In today's mobile society, however, it is often hardly more than a legal fiction to say that members of the parish are "neighbors." A person's community is more likely to be based on work, education, recreation, social life, and even on religious and apostolic activities, including the liturgy.

Today the church allows wide varieties in parish liturgies. The spirit of parishes will differ depending on how both priest and people understand the church and what they believe a Christian community should be.

Current regulations of the church seem to recognize all these factors. Parishes are indeed generally territorial. This means that the local parish priest is responsible for the care of all the faithful in that territory. Church laws spell out those responsibilities and the care with which pastors must carry them out. (See for example CCL nos. 515-519)

However, the laity also have rights and obligations which are relevant here. They have the right to present their desires and needs, especially their spiritual needs, to their pastors. (CCL no. 212) According to their knowledge, competence and position, they have the right and sometimes the duty to make known their views concerning the good of the church not only to their pastors but also (with respect for the common good of everyone) to others in that parish community or elsewhere. (CCL no. 212)

They are obliged to assist in the necessary works of the church — its worship, apostolic mission, charities, the care of its ministers, and its care of the poor (CCL no. 222).

They have a right to the spiritual helps of the church, especially the Word of God and the sacraments, and a liturgy carried out as the church allows and prescribes to help them pursue their proper form of spiritual life and to grow in Christian and human maturity. (CCL nos. 213, 214, 217)

Good and faithful Catholics might perceive these rights and duties (and others pointed out in the law of the church) differently from the pastoral vision and style they experience in their own local parish. The difference may be such that they feel they cannot honestly and charitably fulfill these obligations and rights in that particular parish community.

For these reasons, policies and attitudes are, in practice, much more flexible than formerly. In a sincere concern for the health of the whole church family, however, it seems to me a Catholic should preserve some sense of responsibility toward the people of the parish in which he lives, even though he may join and participate in another parish community.

What is canon law?

Frequently you refer to the canon law of the Catholic Church. Where can one get a copy? Is it even available to everyone? So much of what happens is explained simply by "it is canon law." I would be interested in reading it and having it to check on.

The *Code of Canon Law* is the basic set of regulations that govern the life of the Catholic Church, from electing a pope to receiving the sacraments. As an institution made up of human beings, the church has always had rules, or canons (Greek for precept, law) of some sort. We find them even in the New Testament.

As human society changes, laws change also, including those of the church, requiring frequent revisions and reorganizations of one kind or another over the past 2,000 years. Perhaps the most famous is the 12th-century *Concordance of Discordant Canons*, in which a monk, Gratian, attempted to reconcile all prevailing legislation.

Surprisingly, the first real *Code of Canon Law* was published only in 1917. When Pope John XXIII convoked Vatican Council II in 1959, he requested a revision of the code, which was completed under Pope John Paul II in 1983. It is this code which presently governs Catholic life in the Latin Church. Another code exists for Eastern Catholic churches.

The code is available from the Canon Law Society of America (Washington D. C. 20064). It is not extremely long and, as legal documents go, is nearly a gem of simplicity and clarity. I should warn anyone who is considering buying it, however, that while it is easy to read, it is far from easy to apply correctly. It compacts into 1,752 canons the legal experience of hundreds of years, and like any tightly written legal document is highly complex.

Canons interrelate broadly with each other. Innocent-sounding phrases one might easily ignore can be crucial for a right understanding and interpretation of the law. In other words, it is not for nothing that men and women spend years of study and training to properly apply the code in the daily life of the church.

The *Code of Canon Law* can be interesting reading, even fun (if one enjoys that sort of thing). Just be aware of the limitations. A careful, serious reading of canon law does not make one a canon lawyer, any more than a reading of the Internal Revenue Code makes one an expert on income tax.

Precepts of the church

I accompanied a young woman acquaintance to her Rite of Christian Initiation of Adults program. At no time were what we used to call the "six precepts of the church" mentioned. Do we still have them?

The juridical obligations and rights of all members of the Catholic Church are in the *Code of Canon Law* and generally described in one section (206-223). The following section (224-231) spells out specific responsibilities and rights of lay people.

These regulations reflect what our faith already teaches about our obligation to work cooperatively to build and sanctify the Body of Christ. They can be briefly summarized as follows:

1. To lead a full sacramental life, especially to participate in the Mass each Sunday and holy day, sharing at the same time in holy Communion; and receive the sacrament of reconciliation regularly, at appropriate times.
2. To provide proper religious education for oneself and one's children, especially by use of Catholic schools and other educational programs.
3. To observe the marriage laws of the church.
4. To strengthen and support the church, including one's own parish community and clergy, and the worldwide church.
5. To practice penance and self-denial in the Spirit of Christ, including fast and abstinence on days appointed by church leaders.
6. To share in the missionary spirit and apostolic work of the local and universal church.

It is just coincidence that this group numbers six. In the RCIA program these duties and rights were probably not listed in one neat order, but I'm sure they were all explained at appropriate times.

Religious life for divorced

What opportunities are there in the church for a divorced Catholic man or woman who would like to dedicate his or her life to God in a religious community?

What you suggest is not at all impossible. Each religious congregation or order has its own regulations and procedures in such matters. Anyone interested in such work should contact the desired religious community and ask about the possibilities of sharing in their apostolate.

Religious communities

I am aware there are numerous orders of priests, such as Jesuits, Franciscans and Oblates, and other orders of sisters. I'm curious as to how many there are, their names, and why there are so many.

I'm not sure anybody anywhere knows how many orders (or congregations or institutes) of religious men and women exist in the world. Just one reason is that, while there is a central agency in the Vatican dealing with this part of the church's life (Congregation for Religious), religious communities may spring up and flourish under the authority of local bishops long before they appear on any kind of permanent and centralized list where they might be counted.

Hundreds of religious institutions of men (groups which live a more or less common life under rules to which they commit themselves) are part of today's church, along with probably a few thousand institutions for women.

All such orders developed in response to what their founders perceived as needs of the church at that time — prayer, preaching, teaching, care of the sick, missionary work, and so on. Some have continued for more than a thousand years; others gradually died out as the need declined or as responsibility for those needs was assumed by others.

According to the *Official Catholic Directory* published by P. J. Kenedy and Sons, sisters from approximately 360 different religious congregations presently serve in the United States, though the motherhouses (headquarters) of many are located in other countries. Included in this group are close to 50 different Franciscan orders. Some have hundreds of members, others less than a dozen.

Also in the United States are nearly 100 religious orders of priests, comprising 40 percent of all the priests in the nation. The others are diocesan (secular) priests, who are ordained for service in their respective dioceses. Twenty-four additional religious orders in the United States are composed entirely of brothers, having no priest members at all.

And this says nothing of several hundred Protestant religious congregations in our country and in Europe, some of which have contributed immeasurably to the efforts toward Christian renewal during the past 40 years.

For more specific information, write directly to a particular religious order, or to either the National Sisters' Vocational Conference, 1307 S. Wabash Ave., Chicago, IL, 60605, or the Conference of Major Superiors of Men, Suite 601, 1302 18th St., N. W., Washington, D. C., 20036.

Handicaps to vocations?

My brother tells me that if someone has a physical illness this is a sign that the individual doesn't have a religious vocation. What about handicapped men and women who are otherwise healthy?

Religious orders of men and women vary in the types of work they do in the church. Mental and physical qualifications would vary accordingly. A foreign missionary needs different abilities than a high school teacher, and both of these differ from a contemplative order which demands its own physical and mental qualities.

Certain illnesses or handicaps naturally make life in a religious community difficult or impossible.

I suggest you write to a priest, brother, or sister whom you know, perhaps in the religious order that you are considering, and ask their advice. With some asking around, and prayers, you might find just what you're looking for.

Will there by sisters much longer?

With all the changes and confusion in the religious life, do you think sisters will be around much longer?

Yes, I think sisters will be around for a long time. There has been, and will always be, an important place in the church for the witness of the celibate life for men and women, and of those with life commitments of Christian obedience and poverty. They help to convey, as good husbands and wives do in their vocations, important and unique messages of God's love and fidelity that men and women will always need.

In the 1980s, Pope John Paul II wrote to the American bishops of the need for the pastoral care provided by religious men and women. Among the essential elements of the religious life, he noted, are consecration to Jesus Christ, apostolic works, personal and liturgical prayer, public witness, a structure calling for religious authority based on faith, and a special relationship to the church. These elements, said the Holy Father, make the religious life a great gift of God to the local church and to the church throughout the world. They are, however, lived in different ways from one institute to another.

Ever since Abraham, God's will has been worked out through our humble, prayerful, and patient willingness to change. There's no reason it should be different for sisters.

Secular institutes as a vocation

I read your column about a single Catholic woman inquiring what vocation might be open to her. Perhaps you could have mentioned the secular institutes. There are over 160 in the world, and we have a National Conference of Secular Institutes in the United States.

I am grateful to the spiritual director of the Don Bosco Volunteers, a secular institute for women, for reminding me of this relatively new Catholic vocation. The roots of such a vocation go back centuries, but the institutes were officially recognized only in 1947 by Pope Pius XII. Secular institutes have since been praised and encouraged by other popes. Pope John Paul II noted in 1988 that members "offer proof that temporal realities, lived with the power of the Gospel, can give life to society, making it freer and more just."

The present *Code of Canon Law* defines a secular institute as "an institute of consecrated life in which the faithful, living in this world, strive for the perfection of charity and endeavor to work for the sanctification of the world especially from within" (canon 710).

Depending on their particular constitutions, this vocation is open to single lay people or sometimes to diocesan priests or deacons who feel called to a more intense consecration of their lives to God. Information is available from the U. S. Conference of Secular Institutes, Box 4556, Washington, D. C., 20017.

When a Catholic leaves the church

Please explain Catholic teaching about those who leave the Catholic Church. I think if someone chooses another faith, it is something they must determine in their conscience. I remember hearing when I was young that anyone who leaves the Catholic faith cannot be saved. Can we possibly believe that?

As Catholics, we believe that the fullest abundance of those aids to salvation intended by Jesus Christ exist in our church. This includes the sacraments and other liturgical worship, unity of faith, and the communion of prayer and teaching. One would assume that members of other churches, if they take their faith seriously and conscientiously, believe something similar about their own church, or they would join another.

Catholic doctrine, however, is clear today about the relationship between membership in the church and salvation, and about individual responsibility. Both Vatican Council II and the *Catechism of the Catholic Church* phrase it very precisely.

In the Dogmatic Constitution on the Church (14), the bishops of the council put it this way. Whoever, "knowing that the Catholic Church was made necessary by God through Jesus Christ, would refuse to enter her or to remain in her, could not be saved." The catechism (846) repeats the same idea.

That sentence needs to be read carefully. It says in other words: Whoever knows, believes in conscience, that he or she has a responsibility before God to join or remain in the Catholic Church, must do so.

We know, of course, that generally people who are not Catholic have no sense or conviction of such a responsibility. Because of lack of education or a variety of other possible reasons, the same can be true of some people who were born Catholic or who entered the church later in life. Ultimately, therefore, it is a matter between them and God, a matter of accountability to their conscience, if they turn away from the Catholic faith.

Pope John Paul II repeated this teaching even more clearly in his message for the World Day of Peace (Jan. 1, 1999), on respect for human rights. In the section on religious freedom, which he called the heart of human rights, he said "no one can be compelled to accept a particular religion, whatever the circumstances or motives." The inviolability of religious freedom, he continued, "is such that individuals must be recognized as having the right even to change their religion, if their conscience so demands. People are obliged to follow their conscience in all circumstances and cannot be forced to act against it."

Salvation outside of church?

A magazine published by a group using the name of a famous shrine of our Blessed Mother insists that to save your soul you must be a Catholic, and quotes Vatican Council II as saying: "Outside the church there is no salvation." The article also says that anyone who is a Catholic must remain a Catholic or be lost forever. Is this quotation correct? Do you have an answer?

The substance of the quote you give is from the Second Vatican Council (Constitution on the Church, no. 14) and from other Catholic documents. However, one must understand that statement as the church clearly means it. And, as the church explains it and believes it, the statement does not mean that those who are not members of the Catholic Church are unsaved or "lost."

As noted above, Catholics believe the fullest riches of the means intended by Christ for our salvation exist in our church. These include the sacraments and liturgical life, unity of faith, communion in organization, and other elements of Catholic spirituality.

However, the Catholic Church explicitly and strongly teaches that many essential elements of salvation, including the saving guidance and presence of the Holy Spirit, are also at work in other churches. This goes particularly for other Christian denominations, but applies to non-Christian religions and even to those people struggling to live a good life who do not even know of God or Jesus Christ.

Thus the Catholic Church sees these others as related to us in the saving mission of Christ. Baptized Christians who live their faith in the Scripture and in Christ, and who often receive sacraments within their own churches, are "in some real way joined with us in the Holy Spirit, for to them also he gives his gifts and graces, and is thereby at work among them with his sanctifying power. Some indeed he has strengthened to the extent of shedding their blood" as martyrs (Constitution on the Church, no. 15).

Far from being lost outsiders, the Catholic Church sees all people justified by faith through baptism as "incorporated into Christ. They therefore have a right to be honored by the title of Christian, and are properly regarded as brothers in the Lord by the sons of the Catholic Church" (Decree on Ecumenism, no. 3).

As for non-Christians who have no knowledge of Christ, or perhaps even of God in any explicit way, our church believes they, too, are under the saving love and care of God, and share (even if they are unaware of it) in the redemptive merit of our Lord's death and resurrection. The Constitution on the Church (no. 16) affirms: "Those also can attain to everlasting salvation who through no fault of their own do not know the Gospel of Christ or his church yet sincerely seek God and, moved by grace, strive by their deeds to do his will as it is known to them."

This repeats traditional Catholic teaching when it adds: "Divine providence does not deny the help necessary to salvation to those who, without blame on their part, have not yet arrived at an explicit knowledge of God, but who strive to live a good life, thanks to his grace."

You ask whether those who are Catholic must remain Catholic until death or be lost spiritually. As I said in the previous question, just as many outside the church, so many Catholics — because of lack of training and education or opportunity for true commitment — may have little or no real Catholic belief. Ultimately, of course, it is a matter between them and God if they turn away from their Catholic faith.

What makes a good Catholic?

My friends and I are confused by an increasing number of organizations and movements we are supposed to join to be better Catholics. Some make us suspicious, especially one or two groups tied to appearances of the Blessed Virgin Mary, or so they say.

Some look good. Others scare us because they claim we cannot become "good, loyal Catholics" except the way they tell us. They sound terribly narrow. We've had priests involved in some of them and have been told they are the only priests we can trust to hear our confessions or give us advice. How can we tell what to think?

Your concern is a healthy one, shared by many Catholics these days. I might suggest a few basic guidelines from our Catholic tradition.

First, however, we must remember that ours is a big church. Historically, when it is at its best and most alive, there's always room for a whole rainbow of ways for people to pray, to think, to live out their faith and grow in holiness.

Just because something does not appeal to us or may even seem a little out of place doesn't mean there is anything bad about it. Without respect and room for these differences and honest varieties within the appropriate framework of faith, the church stagnates.

But to your question. One danger sign to look for is any position which rejects what the church is doing and teaching today. Many groups, some of them, as you say, related to alleged supernatural apparitions, refuse to accept the teachings of the church since the Second

Vatican Council. In their opinion, these teachings and practices conflict with what they see as some "golden age" of the past. We believe on the contrary that the same Spirit who was with the church in the past is with it now.

Another red warning flag is any claim that this or that group is the "elite" of the church, that they are the real and genuine Catholics, that anyone not with them or who sees things differently is somehow a second-level Catholic.

I, too, have known some who have their own priests who are supposed to be, for one reason or another, the only ones who "understand" them and are good enough to minister to them. These types of organizations (one might sometimes call them cults) have been around since the beginning of Christianity. We read about them already in the New Testament. It seems to be a common temptation for any religious society. In my 47 years as a priest, I have led or been involved with dozens of spiritual and apostolic movements. All of them have accomplished much good. But nearly every one went through a stage when it needed to fight the temptation to consider itself something like an eighth sacrament, to believe no one is a genuine, full Catholic until he or she has done their "thing," or seen things their way.

Of course, groups and societies who pursue this course always have the highest motives to "purify" the church. But, unchecked, such attitudes often have led to gross intolerance and arrogance. When sufficiently large, they have caused serious injuries, persecution and hurt to the Body of Christ through the centuries. But still they surface every generation or so.

The sacraments, the Gospels and the basic prayer and spiritual efforts taught in continuous church tradition still are sufficient to make good, loyal and complete Catholic Christians. One archbishop noted this a few months ago, specifically in connection with one of the several dozen alleged apparitions currently popular. But his remark is valid in other matters as well.

"One can become a saint," he wrote, "and fully participate in the life of the church, without giving credence to such apparitions; they are not part of the deposit of faith. In fact, basing one's piety on them can often be narrow and illusory."

The third and best criterion of all in evaluating the genuineness of these movements and societies is the old standby: What are their fruits, their results? Are they bringing to the Catholic community (parish, diocese, universal church) greater hope, unity, charity, kindness, peace and other fruits of the Spirit listed by St. Paul? (Galatians 5:22)

Or do they seem to be arousing mistrust, secretiveness, elitism, hostility and bickering, division and oppression?

You can guess which ones St. Paul and Christian tradition recommend.

How to grow in Catholic understanding

How are convert parents to help their children through a Catholic grade school when they themselves are still learning? I took instructions more than 10 years ago. What I learned then was not all retained, and I can't remember being taught such things as May Crowning or first confession and first Communion (child style).

I feel that to be better Catholic parents, we need to be better educated. I know from retreats I've been on that there are different ways of believing. My fear is not to know enough about my religion to answer my children's questions.

You ask some good questions. They express the concern of thousands of other Catholic parents as well.

In all our classes and programs for people preparing to enter the Catholic faith, we attempt to prepare them for the very frustrations you feel. Most lifelong Catholics don't realize how the "feel" for a multitude of practices, devotions, feasts and customs has become part of their bones through the years.

An inquiry class or RCIA program cannot possibly cover all these concerns. They must be lived through, perhaps several times, and not just learned about if one is to understand them.

Several remedies are available to you. The first and perhaps most important is to give yourself the opportunity to experience as many as possible of the things you hear about in your parish or elsewhere that will acquaint you with the daily life-style of being a Catholic.

This doesn't mean you must accept or even like everything you see. As I said previously, ours is a big church with a long, rich and profusely varied tradition. The tradition is good, but everything cannot be for everyone. The Eucharist, the sacraments, fidelity to the Christ who reveals himself in the Gospel — these are the essentials. Ways of prayer, preferences in liturgical celebrations, customs which bring the great themes of our faith into our home, these will vary from one person to another, one home to another, and for that matter from one parish or diocese to another. So be patient, but give yourself a chance.

Another help for "born" Catholics as well as converts is to have a good Catholic dictionary or similar resource in your home. Some excellent ones are on the market, briefly explaining most points of Catholic history, belief, and practice you could ever want to know about.

Also, take advantage of every opportunity your parish gives you to cue in on what is happening to your children. Every good parish and school has sessions for parents, especially at times like first confession, first Communion and confirmation.

Finally, don't be surprised at your need to know more. In today's church, a constant effort to keep up on what's happening, and why, is absolutely essential for any priests or parents who don't want their children or parishioners leaving them behind.

Does the church change?

What you say in the previous answer is encouraging. But many Catholics I know seem to feel everything in the Catholic Church is tradition. Nothing can change, so there's no need for any kind of "keeping up."

The Catholic Church does have a rich and living tradition. But anyone who reads newspapers must see that the church changes in many ways through the years. The church is not a museum. It is a living community of believers who face in each generation the responsibility to apply the Gospel and the traditions of the church to new experiences and new demands.

History proves that sometimes the church as a whole tends to forget this. For a long time, for example, the church seemed to act as though it could live and teach in the 19th and 20th centuries pretty much as it did in the 15th century, a neglect that helped make Vatican Council II, which Pope John intended to move the church toward dealing more realistically with modern society, such a jolt for the Catholic world.

Individual Catholics can do much the same. The assumption that what one learned 30 years ago will do for the rest of one's life, if it was ever valid, surely isn't valid today.

Unless we are to be strangers to the church our children will live in and that we ourselves will be a part of 30 years from now, consistent, prayerful reading about how and why this church is trying to meet the challenges of today's society is absolutely necessary. Many Catholics feel alienated and frustrated these days because they haven't realized this. The Holy Spirit will keep you moving in the right direction with your children.

The Baltimore Catechism

The Baltimore Catechism *we hear so much about — where did it come from? And why isn't it used as much in religion classes as it used to be?*

The *Baltimore Catechism* was the result of the desire of the American bishops in the late 19th century to have a concise summary of Catholic doctrine. It was written at their request in 1885, after the Third Plenary Council of Baltimore, from which it receives its name.

One of many so-called "national catechisms" having the same purpose, it followed basically the tradition and format of the famous *Roman Catechism* written by three Dominican theologians after the Council of Trent, around the year 1565. The *Roman Catechism* was not meant for general use by the faithful, but only as reference material for "pastors and others who hold the office of teaching."

For several centuries after that, such catechisms largely replaced holy Scripture and a living liturgy as a primary means of transmitting the faith. Biblical research, and its practical application in the understanding of Christian life and belief, was minimal in the church for various reasons. Official rites, the Mass and sacraments especially, also became less meaningful and useful as a help to teaching a living faith.

More recently, as a result of the unprecedented expansion of knowledge about holy Scripture, and of the liturgical renewal of this century, most catechetical books are based more on the Bible and on a revitalized liturgy. For this reason, these are increasingly relied upon for catechism courses and other types of religious formation of young people and adults.

Understanding the Catholic catechism

I have been attending Mass for a long time and am interested in joining the Catholic Church. After studying the Catechism of the Catholic Church, *however, I am led to believe the Catholic Church would not accept me.*

I am 40 years old, have been married and divorced twice, but have no plans for marriage now. As I understand the catechism, you are required to have a marriage annulled after a divorce before you can receive the Eucharist. I need to know if that is even possible for me.

Trying to arrive at answers from the catechism to questions like yours can be difficult and frustrating. Small parts of a proper answer, all of which must be considered together, will necessarily be scattered in various sections of the book. This is particularly true in matters of church law and discipline. Some knowledgeable Catholics, even some priests, have drawn confusing conclusions by not taking everything essential into account.

I say all of this to assure you that, judging from your letter, conversion to the Catholic faith, including sharing the Eucharist, is possible for you now.

There is no need here to go into detail. Should you ever begin to consider another marriage, you should immediately make an appointment with a priest and explain your circumstances. He will determine which of several possible avenues, only one of which might be an annulment, would be best to pursue and then help you with the required procedures. Since you are not contemplating another marriage now, however, there is no obstacle to your entering and fully participating in the Catholic faith.

Coming back to the faith

How does a person who has been away from the church for years redeem herself and get back to the faith? Or is that even possible? It would be like starting all over again, re-learning prayers and how to act at Mass.

How does one make a confession after all these years? I could never remember all the sins since my last confession.

Believe me, coming back (including confession) is not nearly as complicated or as difficult as it appears to you now. In fact, if you have decided that you wish to return to full practice of your faith, the hardest part is already done.

Make an appointment with a priest you have confidence in, perhaps one you know is considerate and thoughtful, and ask his help. It isn't necessary that you even know him. He will guide you. If you are ready and have made all the decisions necessary, it may all be done in one visit with him — except for catching up, as you say, on a lot that you may have missed through the years. But with your good will, that will come. The important thing is to take the first step.

What does excommunication mean today?

One reads in history about persons and groups being excommunicated or placed under interdict. We read little about it in modern times. What does canon law say about excommunication and interdict? In what circumstances are these measures applied?

Excommunication and interdict are two of the sanctions, or "punishments," which Christian people have applied to those who seriously violate the Christian or Catholic rule of life.

In practice, for the average Catholic both of these sanctions are basically the same. In either case, the individual is forbidden any liturgical ministry in the Mass or other public worship of the church and may not receive or celebrate any of the sacraments. Other consequences refer mostly to those who hold some public office in the church.

The occasional need of the Christian community to isolate serious offenders from participation in community activities dates back to biblical times. The gospels and the letters of the New Testament refer on several occasions to situations in which the offender should be expelled from their midst. (See, for example, I Corinthians,5)

Excommunication and other sanctions were more significant and powerful in past centuries when the church and at least some civil governments had a more intimate relationship than they have today. Partly for this reason, church laws regarding sanctions were more complicated and severe than they are today.

Our present *Code of Canon Law* provides automatic excommunication for only seven serious offenses in the church: desecration of the Blessed Sacrament; doing physical violence to the pope; absolving an accomplice in sin; a bishop consecrating another bishop without a mandate from the pope; direct violation of the seal of confession; procuring a successful abortion, and rejection of the church through apostasy, heresy, schism.

Many circumstances, such as the age of the individual (no automatic excommunication applies to individuals under age 18), and fear or ignorance present at the time of the action, affect whether or not an excommunication is actually incurred. No church penalties at all apply to anyone under age 16. (see canons 97, 1323, 1324)

It is also important to remember that application of such severe sanctions, whether in the New Testament itself or in the church's laws, are intended both for the good of the community and for the direction and healing of the one who has sinned against that community.

No excommunication, interdict or other sanction is permanent and irrevocable. It always includes the invitation to repentance and return, and holds out promise of forgiveness from God and the Christian community, the church.

It should be obvious from what I've said that, while our present laws are much simplified, this part of the church's legislation remains complex because the church wants to make them applicable only in the most serious cases and only when absolutely necessary for the common good of the Catholic people.

Specific cases should be taken up with one's parish priest or confessor.

Catholic Church and the UN

Has the Catholic Church ever condemned the United Nations? How can so many priests and bishops defend it?

Catholic leaders, especially those who speak officially for the whole church, have consistently promoted the existence and growth of the United Nations (UN) and urged that its international authority be strengthened.

Since the UN was founded, Pope Pius XII, John XXIII, Paul VI and John Paul II have recognized its limitations and weaknesses, but insisted it is still the best hope for world peace and order. This position is confirmed by the encouragement and support the church has offered to all the major agencies of the UN since World War II.

What is incardination?

Our new associate pastor was incardinated into our diocese. What does that mean? I thought once you were ordained you remained within your diocese. What would prompt such an occurrence? What are the procedures?

Every diocesan priest is incardinated (affiliated) with a particular diocese, to serve under the bishop of that diocese.

However, sometimes family, health or other reasons make it appropriate for a priest to move from one diocese to another. This is arranged through and with the two bishops involved and in consultation with the priest himself. This may occur not only after ordination, but while the student is preparing for the priesthood.

CHAPTER 3

THE MASS
EUCHARISTIC LITURGY

❧

The word "Eucharist"

I'm in the dark about the word "Eucharist." It is used both for holy Communion and for the Mass. Why can't we simply say Mass and Communion?

The word "Eucharist" comes from the Greek word *Eucharistein*, to return thanks. It is one of the most ancient designations for the Eucharist among Christians, since that was its primary purpose — to remember with thanks what God has done for us in Jesus Christ.

That name is much more specific and meaningful than "the Mass," which is simply an English corruption of the Latin words which formerly ended the Mass, *Ite missa est.*

The church is returning to use of the word in many ways. Our celebration of Mass is divided, for example, into the Liturgy of the Word and the Liturgy of the Eucharist.

The long prayer which the priest says, and to which the people respond, which contains the narration of the institution of the Eucharist is called the Eucharistic Prayer. It begins with "Let us give thanks to the Lord our God," to which the people respond "It is right to give him thanks and praise."

Why are Masses different?

It used to be that we could attend Mass at any church and it was the same at all of them. Now it's different at all of them. Why? Couldn't they all use the same books to be uniform?

During the first 15 centuries of the church's life, the Mass was not the same in all the churches. Especially in the first several centuries, the celebration of the Eucharist was just that — a celebration. Actions, words, music, the whole atmosphere of the Mass was different according to who was there, the condition and circumstances of their lives, and so on.

For a variety of reasons, the Mass gradually ceased being an event that the people participated in as members of the Body of the risen Christ. It became rather a sacred ceremony carried out by the priest, actions the rest of the people only watched reverently.

By the time of the Council of Trent in the 1500s, much early history of the Mass which we are aware of today had been completely forgotten. The bishops at that council, however, were faced with numerous attacks against the Mass and the Eucharist from leaders of the new Protestant Reformation. They understandably responded to these attacks by taking one form of the Mass — the form used in Rome at that time — and declaring it the *only* form of the Mass allowed in the Western Church. Every action and prayer was spelled out in minute detail. No options were offered. No variations were permitted.

Long before the Second Vatican Council, church leaders were aware that this kind of frozen liturgy was blocking the growth of real liturgical prayer and worship and that something had to be done to provide more flexibility and wider local options. The purpose wasn't variety for variety's sake. It was to enable people of different ages and times and temperaments and circumstances to make the Mass a genuine, living worship-celebration of their Christian life.

Variations are specifically allowed and suggested in the official instructions on the Mass. Numerous options for Scripture readings are offered. Several prayers or exhortations are accompanied with the notation that the priest should "use these, or similar words." Wide leeway is given in such things as music and actions. The sign of peace, for instance, is to be given "according to local custom."

When you're present for a Mass that is different than you're used to, why not relax, try to get into the spirit of it and share in it as well as you can? A little adaptability, and trying to share what others are feeling could be a real act of charity toward those around you as well as to yourself.

Multi-cultural liturgies

I have read that the church is allowing strange customs at Mass in foreign countries — Hindu ceremonies in India, tribal dances in Africa, and even ancestor worship in China. I know things are changing, but will the Mass be the same from one place to another at all any more?

The Mass will always be the same in its essentials — reading and reflection on the Word of God, the renewal of the offering which Jesus made to the Father on Calvary, and the Communion of his body and blood as the sign and source of the one Body of Christ. In other words, it will always be a sacrificial offering, and a sacred meal.

Apart from these essentials, however, eucharistic worship will depend on the culture, customs, language and temperaments of the people who offer it.

Certain historical circumstances have caused most of us to think of the Mass as unchanging and "universal" in the wrong sense. Serious and irreparable damage has been done to the church because of small-mindedness and short-sightedness in this matter. A few hundred years ago, for example, an imaginative missionary effort that might have brought all of China into Christianity collapsed because officials in Rome insisted, among other things, that all Masses be in Latin and that priests wear Western-style dress and vestments.

This attitude, long under serious question, was officially corrected by Pope Pius XII. When the church attempts to call a people to a better way of life under the inspiration of the Christian religion, he said in one of his encyclicals, "she does not act like one who recklessly cuts down and uproots a thriving forest. She grafts good stock upon the wood so that it may bear even better fruit." The policy of using anything in local cultures, even religious customs, that can conceivably be meshed with Christian beliefs is now well established.

Chinese, incidentally, do not "worship" ancestors. They, and other Oriental cultures, have traditionally a profound reverence and honor for them. A misunderstanding of this custom has been another costly mistake for the church.

Why call Mass a memorial?

Why do priests call Mass a memorial? Isn't it still true that the Mass is primarily a sacrifice? My interpretation of "memorial" is for someone who is deceased. Certainly Christ lives! We receive the living risen Christ. Isn't this a downgrading of our belief?

We often refer to the Mass as a memorial carried out "in memory of his death and resurrection" (second Eucharistic Prayer). However, this designation for the celebration of the Eucharist is not new. It goes back to the earliest records we have of prayers offered at the eucharistic celebrations.

Obviously, the word memorial in this context does not mean

something for the dead. It simply means something done in memory of someone or something. In fact, this is the reason Jesus himself gives us in the Gospel for the celebration of the Eucharist, "Do this to remember" me and what I have done for you.

In the Mass the entire purpose is to remember what Jesus has done in his sacrificial death and resurrection, to give thanks for it, and to renew the offering of ourselves, united to this eternal sacrifice of Jesus to the heavenly Father.

Far from being downgrading, remembering — with thanks and praise — is what the Eucharist is all about.

Did Jesus offer the only sacrifice?

Our question has to do with the Mass. How do we respond to Protestant friends when they cite Hebrews 10: 11-18, which says we no longer need priests to offer sacrifice (during Mass) because Christ died once and for all.

According to Hebrews, "there is no longer any offering for sin." Since Jesus died and sacrificed his life once and for all, they say there should be no "priests" now, no possibility or need for more sacrifices than Jesus Christ has offered. How do we answer that?

Your Protestant friends are right in claiming that Jesus Christ offered the one perfect sacrifice, offering his body once for all (Hb 10:10). It is the teaching of the Letter to the Hebrews, and Catholic doctrine, that no new or additional sacrifice is necessary or possible for the salvation of the world.

A new or additional sacrifice, however, is not the same thing as a re-offering of the one sacrifice of Christ, which is what the Catholic Church believes takes place at the celebration of the Eucharist at Mass.

The Letter to the Romans (8:43) tells us that Jesus, in his crucified and risen body, stands at the side of the Father always interceding for us, in other words, always offering to the Father his death and resurrection on our behalf.

As the *Catechism of the Catholic Church* explains it, our celebration of the Eucharist echoes this continual re-offering of the paschal mystery, the dying and rising of Christ. The eucharistic celebration is not a different or additional sacrifice. Rather, we call it a sacrifice because it re-presents— makes present again — the sacrifice of the cross. It is a remembrance, a memorial of that event, and makes it "in a certain way present and real." (1363)

To put it another way, the sacrifice of the Eucharist and the sacrifice of Christ on Calvary are one single sacrifice. The difference is in the manner of the offering. In the words of the Council of Trent, the Catechism teaches that in the eucharistic liturgy "the same Christ who offered himself once in a bloody manner on the altar of the cross is contained and is offered in an unbloody manner" under the sacramental symbols of bread and wine. (See catechism, especially 1362-1367)

You may explain this to your friend, of course. It is often difficult, however, for those Christians who have had little encounter with religious sacramental symbols to grasp this understanding of the Eucharist. Catholics, and members of other denominations who have a more extensive belief and experience with sacramental forms of worship, generally will find it easier.

Catching up with the church at Mass

For reasons I won't explain, I was out of the church for nearly 40 years and just came back to confession and Communion several months ago. I never realized how much I missed it. I'm trying to catch up, but one thing that bothers me is that the Mass is not in Latin the way I remember it.

Your letter intrigued me. About 1970, when I began writing this column, questions like yours concerning our vernacular liturgy were frequent. Now, more than 30 years later, I realize it's been many years since the last such question.

I believe the reason is simple. The vast majority of Catholics have become so accustomed to participating and praying, by both listening and responding in their own language, and aware of the insights of faith they receive in this way, that they can hardly imagine the Mass otherwise. This is why, with almost no exceptions, every effort to "revive" the Latin Mass as the norm for public worship has had, at most, minimum success.

Increasingly my own conviction is that if Vatican Council II had accomplished nothing else, hearing God's Word and offering the Eucharist in the language of the people would have made it worthwhile. From there, the Holy Spirit can keep our vision clear and lead us to whatever is good.

Consider our Eucharistic Prayers, for example. They are, as are all other parts of the Mass, first and pre-eminently our worship of the Father in and with Jesus Christ. But they are also a "school" in which we encounter week after week the essential truths and challenges of our faith. The Trinity, the Incarnation, the redemptive, forgiving mission of Jesus; the meaning of Christ's eucharistic presence as in every age he forms his church into "one body, one spirit" in him (Eucharistic Prayer II); the communion of saints; the pastoral structure of the church expressed by petitions for the pope and local bishop in every eucharistic prayer; the "royal priesthood" (1 Pt 2:9) of all the faithful assembled, the people of faith who "offer to you, God of glory and majesty, this holy and perfect sacrifice" (Eucharistic Prayer 1); the second coming — all these truths, and more, are recalled in every Mass.

And we recommit ourselves to all these beliefs in the great Amen, and in the Communion we receive.

It's no wonder that from the earliest decades Christians viewed weekly sharing in the Word and Eucharist as the life-breath of their faith. A believer could not drink in those words and actions, and respond to them year in and year out, without their taking deep root in the heart. The point is that ordinarily all this could not conceivably happen without the intimacy and immediacy of communication in one's own language. This is what most Catholics have today come to discover from their own personal experience.

After trying all kinds of substitutes for centuries, including eventually vernacular translations of the missal, the church has returned to its ancient tradition of celebrating the eucharistic mysteries in the language of the people who are there.

I hope these ideas help you and others like you who missed a lot. Give yourself time, and listen patiently to what is happening when you are present for Mass,

Sabbath changed to Sunday?

Why was the Sabbath changed from Saturday to Sunday? Is there a chance it might be changed back someday? Seventh Day Adventist pamphlets deal with this subject, and they are so convincing that I've decided to go to Saturday evening Mass until this is explained.

The first Christians changed the "Sabbath" day to Sunday for a variety of reasons. First, the fact that the resurrection of Jesus is recorded in Scripture as occurring on the first day of the week had much to do with making this the most appropriate day to celebrate the Eucharist commemorating that event. Christians also changed other days of observance, including fast days, from those prescribed by Jewish law to emphasize their departure from the traditions of Israel.

When the Seventh Day Adventist Church was formed about the middle of the last century, the four men and one woman who became its nucleus were somehow convinced that Saturday, not Sunday, should still be the "holy day" of the week. It is one of the lesser ways the teachings of that church depart from general Christian tradition. There's no reason to suspect our Sunday observance will change.

A sin to skip Mass?

Is it still a mortal sin to miss Mass on Sunday? We have relatives who go only when they feel like it. Their excuse is that there is no more sin since Vatican II.

I am sometimes tempted to believe that one of the biggest mistakes of the church was to make a "law" that we must go to Mass on Sunday.

For too many Catholics, the obligation to participate in Mass each Sunday is in somewhat the same category of church law as abstaining from meat on the Fridays of Lent, or even of attending Mass on holy days of obligation. It obscures the significance of the Sunday Eucharist for Christians.

To speak of the presence or absence of a church regulation as a primary motive for participation in the Sunday Eucharist radically misses the point. In early Christian times, centuries before it was a church "rule," participation in the Eucharist each week was considered automatic.

Assuming one was not ill, only two reasons could explain an individual's routine absence. He had either decided not to be a Christian any more, or his knowledge of the faith was seriously deficient and more instruction was needed.

Sunday Eucharist, in other words, constituted the life-breath of the Christian person and community. Both the New Testament and earliest Christian writings point out this truth. (See, for example, Acts 20:7, "On the first day of the week, when we gathered for the breaking of the bread. . .")

The church has realized in the past few generations that many Catholics lost touch with this essential Christian tradition, if indeed they were ever aware of it. To participate in the Sunday Eucharist because "I have to" may be understandable at certain stages of growing up. A Catholic adult at age 30 or 50 should have moved beyond that.

To answer your question, the law is still there and perhaps is still necessary for most, or all, of us to have the opportunity to grow to a fuller appreciation of this central element of our faith.

The *Code of Canon Law* recalls our tradition: "Sunday is the day on which the paschal mystery is celebrated in light of the apostolic tradition and is to be observed as the foremost holy day of obligation in the universal church." It then provides, "On Sundays and other holy days of obligation the faithful are bound to participate in Mass" (canons 1246 and 1247).

Vatican Council II did not, and had no intention to, minimize the essential role of the Sunday Eucharist in the life of the church.

Need a reason for Saturday Mass?

I have heard that a Catholic may fulfill his Sunday Mass obligation on Saturday evening only if he cannot get to Mass on Sunday morning. Is this true? If so, it's news to me.

It's news to me, too. The Vatican Instruction on Eucharistic Worship which deals with this privilege places no such restrictions on one's right to fulfill the Sunday obligation on Saturday evening.

The *Code of Canon Law* (1248) simply says: Anyone satisfies the precept to participate in the Mass by assisting wherever it is celebrated in the Catholic rite either on the day (Sunday or holy day) itself, or in the evening of the preceding day.

Mass and Communion for the aged

I am 81 years old and was told by a priest that I was excused from Sunday Mass if I didn't feel up to going. Also, someone told me I never had to go to confession, and I could receive the sacraments. Is this true?

At your age, you are excused if you do not feel able to attend Mass on a particular Sunday. In fact, if you cannot go without danger of getting sick, or serious danger of perhaps falling and hurting yourself, you are completely excused from Sunday Mass.

The only time one must receive the sacrament of penance before Communion is when he or she is conscious of a deliberate mortal sin. I am sure you may go to Communion whenever you have the opportunity, even if you do not get to confession.

If you are unable to go to Mass for a few Sundays, or even longer, call your parish and ask someone to bring you Communion. Many parishes have ministers of the Eucharist who might bring Communion to your home each Sunday. If the priest himself comes, you could use that opportunity to receive the sacrament of penance.

Hour for Saturday Mass

What is the earliest hour of the day on Saturday that I may hear Mass and fulfill the Sunday obligation? Some churches in our area have Mass at 4 p.m. and I have heard that this is too early.

It is the responsibility of the bishop of each diocese to determine the time on Saturday afternoon when Sunday obligation Masses may begin. In most dioceses it is 4 p.m. or 4:30 p.m., but ask your parish priest what the rule is in your own diocese.

Normally it is safe to say that any parish Mass regularly scheduled on a Saturday afternoon is intended to be within the guidelines set by the bishop for fulfilling one's Sunday obligation.

Shopping for Saturday Mass?

Does a Saturday Mass which doesn't have the Sunday liturgy, such as a wedding, funeral, or jubilee Mass, still fulfill the Sunday obligation? There seems to be a difference of opinion on this.

I hate the thought of "shopping around" because it certainly seems to negate the spirit of the Mass. But that's what I feel like I'm doing when I must check with the priest first to see if the Mass "counts" or not. This problem also came up in the last Easter Vigil.

The Instruction of the Vatican on Eucharistic Worship of May 25, 1967, which provides for anticipating the Sunday Mass obligation on Saturday evening, says that when a parish Mass is scheduled on Saturday for that purpose, the liturgy for the Sunday should be celebrated. It does not, however, make the actual Sunday liturgy a *condition* for fulfilling the Sunday obligation. Catholics may fulfill that obligation at a wedding or funeral Mass, for example, presuming, as you said, that it is within the required time period for your diocese.

All of the above is irrelevant to Holy Saturday. The Mass at the Easter Vigil is liturgically *the* Easter Mass even more than the one the following morning.

Masses for the people

When I was younger I was told that Sunday Masses were said for the people who attended. Today Mass on Sunday is usually offered for somebody who has died, or for an anniversary. Have the rules changed?

Pastors of parishes (and also bishops) are obliged to offer the Eucharist once every Sunday and holy day, and a few other special days, for all the people committed to their care. (canons 388 and 534) This responsibility is referred to as the *Missa pro populo*, or "Mass for the people."

Televised Mass and Sunday obligation

If the pope's blessing with a plenary indulgence can be obtained by all who follow the rite on television or radio, why can't the obligation of Sunday Mass be fulfilled by watching a Mass on television at home on Sunday morning?

For that matter, why can't we confess over the telephone?

The answer is basic and simple: The Mass is not a private prayer; receiving a blessing is, even though there are public and communal aspects to any blessing.

Many Catholics still do not realize that the obligation of Sunday Mass is not to hear or watch someone else do something, but to be there to do it oneself, and share it with our fellow Catholics. The Eucharist is an action, a celebration, of the Catholic community and cannot be substituted for by seeing a television program.

If one cannot be present for Sunday Mass with one's parish or other community, a television or radio Mass may assist in uniting one with it in spirit, or in realizing one's desire for union with Christ in the Eucharist. But such listening or viewing is never a substitute for being there.

Confession, too, is a personal dialogue and presence with Christ and the Catholic community on earth as represented by the priest. This personal confrontation with the people of God, with the priest as their ordained representative, is essential to the sacrament.

Televised or telephoned confession could not fulfill the requirements for the sacrament of forgiveness of sins.

Holy day Mass obligations

Holy days of obligation were always somewhat confusing, but never as much as now. One year All Saints is a holy day, the next year it is not. Please explain what holy days are still in effect, and how to know whether or not we are supposed to attend Mass on those feasts.

In November, 1991, the then National Conference of Catholic Bishops of the United States approved a proposal that affects the observance of three holy days.

Whenever Jan. 1 (the Solemnity of the Mother of God), Aug. 15 (the Assumption of the Blessed Virgin), or Nov. 1 (All Saints) falls on

Saturday or Monday, the obligation to attend Mass is canceled.

That decision resulted from confusion about when the two Mass obligations, Sunday and the holy day, could be fulfilled. Could it be with two Masses in one day? Could the holy day obligation be fulfilled at an anticipated Sunday Mass on Saturday evening? And so on.

As a number of bishops have noted, perhaps there is no less confusion with the new system than with the old. Nevertheless, that is the present legislation.

In 1999, the Vatican allowed each province in the United States to decide whether it wished to transfer observance of the feast of the Ascension to the following Sunday, the Sunday before Pentecost. Many of the dioceses in our country now celebrate the Ascension on that Sunday.

The two other holy days observed in the United States are the solemnities of the Immaculate Conception on Dec. 8, and the Nativity of our Lord on Dec. 25. These are always holy days of obligation, even when they fall on a Saturday or Monday.

Canon law lists several other holy days, but conferences of bishops may abolish some of them, or transfer them to a Sunday. In the United States, for example, the feasts of Epiphany and the Body and Blood of Christ (Corpus Christi) are transferred to the nearby Sunday, and are not holy days of obligation..

The bishops could rescind Jan. 1, Aug. 15 and Nov. 1 as holy days of obligation altogether. They have considered that possibility several times, but until now have not thought it opportune to do so.

Mass in a private home?

If Communion can be brought to a sick person, can Mass be offered for them at home, too? My father is confined to a wheelchair except when he goes to the doctor. Would it be possible for a priest to have Mass in his home sometime? It would mean much to all of us.

The church has indicated that bishops may allow Masses outside of churches and chapels — in homes, for example. One of many circumstances in which such Masses are explicitly approved is the gathering of family and friends in the homes of the sick or aged who cannot otherwise participate in the eucharistic celebration.

Some regulations for these celebrations preserve the propriety, serenity, and sacred character of the Mass. (See Instruction for Masses for Special Gatherings, May 15, 1969.)

Home Masses for the sick, and for other gatherings and events, are not uncommon in our country. In most dioceses, Mass may be offered in homes at the discretion of the pastor of the family in whose home the Mass is to be celebrated.

Mass stipends and intentions

During Mass in our parish, the priest reads the petitions after the Gospel. He concludes with, "and for John or Jane Doe for whom this Mass is being offered."

We as a family look forward to participating in the sacrifice of the Mass. But when the priest says the Mass is "being offered for John Doe," I wonder, is the principle purpose for the parishioners being there to offer it for John Doe? Would it not be more appropriate for the priest to say, "for John Doe, who is remembered at this Mass?"

Also, certain names appear repeatedly in the church bulletin listing Masses for the coming week. One may get the impression that these people are going to get to heaven in a hurry. How about deceased persons who have no one to offer Masses for them?

For more than 1,000 years, Catholic people have had the custom of stipends for the church's ministers and other needs of the Christian community. However, the church has carried on an almost continuous struggle to avoid any semblance of commercialism and misunderstandings about the meaning of such offerings.

Language which is at least open to misunderstanding has been common; the example you give is a good one. Among our primary beliefs about the celebration of the Eucharist is that its reach and intentions are as broad as the first offering of that sacrifice by Jesus on Calvary.

As our Eucharistic Prayers make clear, every offering of this sacrifice includes not only the whole church but the whole human family, living and dead. Even should he wish to do so, no priest could narrow down that worldwide embrace as Jesus renews his sacrificial offering in the person of his church on earth.

When a priest accepts a stipend, he accepts the responsibility to include that intention in his prayers at Mass. This is the meaning of the church's law which states: "It is lawful for any priest who celebrates or concelebrates Mass to receive an offering to apply the Mass according to a definite intention." (canon 945)

For this reason, a statement that the Mass is "being offered for" an individual, or to include that name specifically in the prayers for the dead during the Eucharistic Prayer, is generally considered inappropriate since it places undue attention and emphasis on that particular intention rather than on the entire church.

No one "buys" major ownership, as it were, in a particular offering of the Eucharist. If any announcement of the special intention is to take place, perhaps your suggestion is a good one liturgically and theologically, "John or Jane Doe is being remembered at this Mass."

What I have said above should respond to your other question about apparent advantages of the rich over the poor in the celebration of the Eucharist.

Several stipends for Mass?

Is there a law that forbids two or three intentions at a Mass? I think most people would not object to two or more intentions for a Mass rather than wait two or three years before having the Mass celebrated.

Only one stipend or offering may be accepted by a priest for any one Mass.

Canon 948 says, "Separate Masses are to be applied for the intentions for which an individual offering, even if small, has been made and accepted."

In other words, what you are suggesting is, at least lawfully, out of the hands of individual priests. The reason, which is obvious, is to avoid abuse in offering and accepting Mass stipends.

Pius V's Mass trampled?

Would you please explain why the Latin (Tridentine) Mass of Pope St. Pius V was not translated into English or other native tongues, but rather trampled underfoot? I understand there was a curse on anyone who would change the Mass.

At the Second Vatican Council, the bishops of the world laid down the rules for the revision of the Mass. These requirements are found in the Constitution on the Sacred Liturgy, *Sacrosanctum Concilium*.

The revised missal, they said, should be drawn up so that both texts and rites "express more clearly the holy things they signify"; that the several parts of the Mass should be clear as to their nature and purpose and how they are connected together; that the active participation of the faithful be more easily accomplished; that the "treasure of the Bible be opened up more lavishly so that richer fare may be provided for the faithful at the table of God's word," and that a rite for concelebration by many priests be incorporated into the new missal.

In other words, just as Pius V saw the need for action in the 16th century, Paul VI, along with the rest of the bishops, among whom was the future Pope John Paul II, felt strongly that the so-called Tridentine Mass lacked too many of these elements to serve well the liturgical and spiritual renewal of modern Catholics.

Are you aware, by the way, that the Tridentine Mass as approved by Pius V in 1570 has not been in use by the church for nearly 400 years? Only 34 years after that approval, Pope Clement VIII issued changes and said that his was now the definitive edition. Several subsequent popes did the same, right up into the 20th century, resulting in the Mass we had before Vatican II.

Obviously, the Tridentine Mass held in such veneration by some Catholics isn't that at all. In fact, the "new" Mass we have today is far more traditional in the church.

When Pius V issued his edition of the Roman Missal, he pleaded that it be an instrument of liturgical unity. Pope Paul VI did the same after Vatican II. The "variations and adaptations" allowed for in the new rite were themselves a basis for hope, he said, that the revisions "will be received by the faithful as a help and witness to the common unity of all."

Sincere Catholics will do everything possible to make that happen.

Why was Mass in Latin?

A recent issue of our Catholic paper quoted a cardinal who said that before Vatican Council II "our historical sense was somewhat blunted," giving as one example the lack of awareness that the Mass had not always been celebrated in Latin. I had never thought of this. In what other languages has the Mass been celebrated before the changes we have today?

I agree with the cardinal's assessment. Judging from my own experience and from my mail through the years as author of this column, the greatest single reason for rejection and lack of understanding of the current developments in the church is a severely limited knowledge of our history as a church.

Without a sense of history, one easily falls into the trap of assuming that what has been since we were born has always been. As one woman said to me, protesting our use of English at Mass: "If Latin was good enough for Jesus, why isn't it good enough for us?" The fact that Jesus and most of the early members of our faith quite possibly didn't even know Latin, didn't phase her, if indeed she ever considered it.

To answer your question, the Mass, even before Vatican II, has been celebrated in numerous languages. In the beginning, the language of the liturgy was almost certainly Aramaic, used by Jesus and the disciples and early Christian converts.

Before long, however, the common liturgical language was Greek, the tongue most common in the world as Christianity began to spread. Other languages such as Syriac, Arabic and Coptic, one of the few "relic" languages of ancient Egypt, have been and still are used in Catholic churches of the East.

During the third century, the Roman church began to adopt Latin as its quasi-official tongue. This was understandable for many reasons. At that time and for nearly the next thousand years, every literate person understood Latin. Civil and church business was conducted in Latin. It was natural that the liturgy should be in Latin.

At the time of the Council of Trent (mid 1500s) and for years after, use of local languages during the liturgy was considered "Protestant." To suggest a greater openness to vernacular languages (as many bishops did at Trent) was to become suspect of disloyalty or heresy. Even during these centuries, nevertheless, many languages such as Armenian, Greek, German, Chinese, Mohawk Iroquois in the United States, and others, were officially approved from time to time.

The move to return to local languages for our liturgy developed slowly during the past 100 years or so. The rationale for that development has been explained by recent popes and by the bishops of Vatican II. In that council's Constitution on the Sacred Liturgy, the bishops expressed their desire to change those features which may have "crept in which are less harmonious with the intimate nature of the liturgy" or which have grown less functional.

Among these was the language itself. Texts and rite should be restored, they said, "so that they express more clearly the holy things which they signify. Christian people, as far as possible, should be able to understand them with ease, and take part in them fully, actively, as befits a community" (no. 21). Christians always insisted that their liturgical rites be in a language that conveys the reverence and mystery of what we celebrate. Experience proves that this can be accomplished with careful and dignified use of the language of the people.

Latin wasn't a dead language

In your answer about the Mass in Latin, with all your jargon you did not mention the real reason the Mass was in Latin.

No one who presents himself as an authority on the Catholic faith with a question and answer column could be unaware of the fact that the "dead," and therefore unchanging, Latin language was deliberately adopted so the church's dogma would be uniformly interpreted around the world, so the words of Christ would remain free from the vagaries of local semantic influence and trendy philosophical interpretation. You know this. It demands further response.

I don't know where you received your information, but it is inaccurate. As I explained, in the early centuries of the church, the typical language for liturgical and certain other Christian usage and activities was Greek. As the church, particularly in Europe, became more involved and even identified with Roman, and therefore Latin, culture, Christian authorities gradually realized that to continue Greek as the "official" language of the church would be to lose effective touch with people for whom Greek was more and more a foreign language.

In the West (as distinct from the Eastern or Oriental churches) almost anyone who could read and write knew Latin. It was the language of commerce and most social intercourse.

This is why, in the fourth century, most effectively under the influence of Pope Damasus, Latin gradually became the language most commonly used by the church, even in the liturgy. With the dissolution of the Roman Empire in the fifth century and later, local cultures and languages in both southern and northern Europe began to predominate until eventually Latin itself became a dead language.

How and why it continued to be the official language of the church in most of the Western world until the 20th century is another story. It is worth remembering, however, that Latin became the "Catholic" language not because it was dead, but because it was one people could understand.

Why is priest "presider"?

Prior to the beginning of Mass, we hear an announcement that Father Doe is the "presider for the Mass," rather than the customary "celebrant of the Mass." In the lexicon of the church, are these two phrases synonymous, or is the sacramental priesthood being confused with the priesthood of the people?

The designation of the priest as presider or presiding priest is used for at least two good reasons which tie closely together. First the priest is not the only celebrant of the Eucharist. It is proper, in fact necessary if we are to remain faithful to Christian tradition, to say that the entire community gathered around the altar in faith is celebrating that faith by hearing God's Word and by offering the Eucharist.

This is repeated countless times in the liturgy, especially in the eucharistic prayers. The first Eucharistic Prayer (the so-called Roman Canon, which was the only one used for some centuries before Vatican II), for example, makes abundantly clear that while the priest is doing the speaking, he is acting and speaking for all.

"All of us gathered here before you. . . offer you this sacrifice of praise," it says.

"Father, accept this offering from your whole family," it repeats later.

And, "We, your people and your ministers. . . offer to you, God of glory and majesty, this holy and perfect sacrifice."

Second, the priest is appropriately and accurately described as the presider at the celebration, because he, as the dictionary says, occupies the place of leader and directs the proceedings.

The General Instruction of the Roman Missal defines this as precisely what the priest was ordained to do: "Within the church the priest also possesses the power of Holy Orders to offer sacrifice in the person of Christ. He therefore stands at the head of the faithful people gathered together, presides over its prayer, proclaims the message of salvation, joins the people to himself in offering the sacrifice to God the Father through Christ in the Spirit, gives his brothers and sisters the bread of eternal life, and shares in it with them.

"At the Eucharist he should, then, serve God and the people with dignity and humility; by his bearing and by the way he recites the words of the liturgy he should communicate to the faithful a sense of the living presence of Christ." (GIRM 92)

Thus, instructions for Mass continuously refer to the priest as presider, and to the bishop as president, the one who presides, when he celebrates the Eucharist with his people. (See, for example, GIRM 4, 5, 22 and 93)

In the liturgy and theology of the church, the sacrament of orders gives the priest a leading and indispensable role in the celebration of the Eucharist. In fulfilling that role, however, he is not doing something for the community, as the word "celebrant" might seem to indicate. He is doing something *with* that community, of which, before he is a priest, he is also a member through baptism.

Thus, while there is nothing wrong with the word celebrant as long as it is properly understood, designating him as the presiding priest describes more accurately his role in the eucharistic liturgy.

Why Masses for the dead?

When someone dies and has received all the rites of the church, and we know that he or she has led a good Christian life, what do you think of having Masses offered for the deceased? If we believe in God's mercy and love, do you think that year after year we should continue to offer Masses for them?

There are many reasons Masses may be offered for a deceased person. First, as all prayer, the intention may be to ask God's blessing and grace on that person during his or her life. God is not bound by limits of time. Past, present and future are all *now* to him. We put ourselves in that sphere of reference of eternity in our prayers.

The church does this all the time. In the funeral liturgy, for example, and in anniversary liturgies years after the individual is deceased, prayers ask God to give that individual the blessing of a holy and peaceful death.

Another reason is that our prayers and other good works can help the deceased in satisfaction for sin that may be due upon death. Exactly how this works out in God's providence we naturally do not know. But it is still valid and solid Catholic belief.

Finally, our Masses and prayers can express thanks and praise to God for the life of a person we have loved and still love. Many men and women who firmly believe their loved ones are in heaven, and who may even pray to them as among the saints of God, still have Masses offered for them. These Masses are expressions of faith and hope, a part of their remembering, and of their joy over the eternal happiness of someone they love.

"Privileged" funerals and weddings?

I've been to many Catholic funerals and weddings, and frankly am mystified often by the differing numbers of priests attending such events. At some, many priests are present; at others not even the pastor is there to officiate. How do you explain this different treatment for different people?

As former pastor of fairly large parishes, I am sensitive to the concerns you bring up. No matter how simple and often obvious the answer may be, misunderstandings sometimes arise and rash judgments often result.

Usually the answer is apparent when one knows the background. With almost no exceptions, the explanation is either that the individual has worked, often in a very quiet way, in agencies or institutions that involve contact with many priests. Or that the family itself includes some priests or just close friends who are priests. Such details would usually not be known to persons who are not familiar with the family.

As for which priest performs a wedding or funeral, in most parishes that depends on which priests are free to do so, and who is able to work best with the family in making arrangements for the wedding or funeral. I have always found people understanding and thoughtful in such situations.

Mentally handicapped at Mass?

Often our parish Mass is attended by a group of mentally handicapped teenagers. Why do these poor people have to attend Mass? Surely they do not understand what is going on and are not interested in being in church. Are they obliged to attend Sunday Mass?

In my opinion you underestimate the ability of many mentally handicapped people to understand and participate in the liturgy, or other activities for that matter.

A group from our local association for retarded citizens regularly attends Mass. I frequently celebrate Mass myself with mentally and physically handicapped children and adults. My experience is that, while their intellectual grasp might not equal that of others, their joy, their awareness of the presence and love of God and their simple human warmth are unmistakable.

Much of this results from the unusual degree of tenderness and care given by their parents and family, and from the love of the many remarkable people who volunteer to help them. But it's real nonetheless.

Such children probably would be excused from Sunday Mass. By no means does it follow, however, that they cannot receive much from, and offer much to, those who celebrate the Eucharist with them.

Must priest offer Mass?

At our parish there are five Masses on Sundays and three priests in the parish. How many Masses is a priest allowed to say in one day? Also, isn't it a rule that a priest must say Mass every day?

By general church law, priests may offer no more than one Mass each day, though bishops can permit them to offer two Masses on special feasts and Sundays when necessary.

The basic principle in all such matters is that the reasonable needs of people must be met, especially where Mass and the sacraments are concerned. It is not uncommon for priests to offer two Masses on weekdays, for example when a funeral Mass must be added to the daily Mass schedule.

Many priests also frequently offer three Masses on Sundays to fulfill a minimum schedule of Masses in a parish church. The church has no strict law about when a priest is required to offer Mass, but urges frequent celebration of the Eucharist. Canon law says, "Remembering that the work of redemption is continually accomplished in the mystery of the Eucharistic Sacrifice, priests are to celebrate frequently; indeed daily celebration is strongly recommended, since even if the faithful cannot be present, it is the act of Christ and the Church in which priests fulfill their principal function."(CCL 904) In fulfilling their responsibilities to the people of their congregation, parish priests celebrate the Eucharist almost every day, under normal circumstances.

Candles at Mass

We help in arranging for Mass. At one time the candles used in the liturgy were to be blessed and contain at least 51 percent beeswax. I understand this is no longer true. May candles used at Mass be of other materials? How many should there be at Mass?

The General Instruction of the Roman Missal (GIRM), found in the front of the official Sacramentary (missal), contains the basic instructions for the celebration of the Eucharist.

At least two candles (or four or six, especially on Sundays or holy days) should be placed on the altar or around it in such a way, however, that they do not block the view of what is happening on the altar. (GIRM 117 and 307)

There are no specific regulations about the ingredients for candles.

Incense causes breathing problems

Is it possible to do away with incense since it bothers so many people? I myself have asthmatic bronchitis. I start coughing, my throat gets dry, and sometimes I must leave church. Others tell me their reactions are worse than mine.

I guessed that incense manufacturers would have tried to address that problem with some sort of non-allergenic incense. I learned, however, that, though one or two have tried, there is no such product that works decently. They all use natural resins (frankincense, myrrh and others) which, according to their experts, cannot be synthesized or modified without ending up with some not very pleasant odors.

One manufacturer told me the only answer is to use good incense, but use less of it. The less smoke, the fewer harmful effects for people like yourself. Maybe your priest would be helped by knowing the severity of the problem for you. I know from my mail the problem you have is widespread, and for some people it is physically serious.

Chalice

Is it true that the chalice at Mass is no longer required to be gold, or gold plated?

The inside of chalices and other vessels used for the consecrated wine and hosts at Mass should be gold plated if they can rust, or if they are made from less valuable material.

Sacred vessels should be of a material considered locally as having some value and appropriate for sacred use. Chalice bowls should be non-absorbent, but the base may be of any other solid material worthy for use in the Eucharist. Regulations for the shape of the vessels are broader also. It is required only that they have a form that is in keeping with the local culture and with their purpose in the liturgy. (GIRM 328, 330)

Location of the tabernacle

I have a strong devotion to the holy Eucharist, and I cannot understand why the tabernacle has been relegated to a side chapel in some new churches. It has even been moved in some older churches. Can you explain?

I admire your reverence for the eucharistic presence of our Lord. As in so many things today, however, it is good to try to learn why something is happening before you reject it.

The General Instruction of the Roman Missal prescribes that the tabernacle should be in "a part of the church which is noble, worthy, conspicuous, well decorated and suitable for prayer." (314) The tabernacle in which the Blessed Sacrament is reserved should not be on the altar on which Mass is celebrated. (315)

The tabernacle should be placed, according to the judgment of the diocesan bishop, either in the sanctuary, apart from the altar of celebration, or "in another chapel suitable for adoration and the private prayer of the faithful, and which is connected with the church and is conspicuous to the faithful." (315)).

The introduction to the Roman Ritual for Holy Communion and Worship of the Eucharist Outside of Mass repeats this theme.

"It is highly recommended," it says, "that the place (for reservation) be suitable also for private adoration and prayer so that the faithful may readily and fruitfully continue to honor the Lord, present in the sacrament, through personal worship. This will be achieved more easily if the chapel is separate from the body of the church," especially where other activities during the day might be distracting (9).

The instruction *Eucharisticum Mysterium*, one of the church's chief decrees on worship of the Eucharist, repeats the admonition that eucharistic reservation should be a place of honor for private devotion, but apart from the main body of the church. (No. 53)

The purpose of all this is to distinguish the two manifestations of the eucharistic presence of our Lord, the celebration of the Eucharist in communal worship at Mass, and the reservation of the Eucharist for Communion to the sick and dying, and for private prayer. In the first of these, the focus is the altar of sacrifice. In the second, the focus is the tabernacle. Having them separate and honoring that distinction in prayer and worship helps keep focus on whatever eucharistic activity occupies us at the time.

Perhaps it helps to understand what the church is thinking here if we recall what it says about tabernacles not being on the altar itself, another frequent recommendation in liturgical instructions. "In the celebration of Mass the principal modes of Christ's presence to his church emerge clearly one after the other," declares *Eucharisticum Mysterium*.

"First he is seen to be present in the assembly of the faithful gathered in his name; then in his word, with the reading and explanation of Scripture; also in the person of the minister; finally, in a singular way under the eucharistic elements. Consequently, on the grounds of the sign value, it is more in keeping with the celebration that Christ not be present eucharistically in the tabernacle from the beginning on the altar where Mass is celebrated. That presence is the effect of the consecration and should appear as such" (55; see also GIRM 315)

In other words, since signs and symbols are of supreme importance in liturgical worship, care should always be taken that they not be mixed or confused.

Churches which follow Catholic guidelines in this matter are not "relegating" the eucharistic presence anywhere. They are attempting to honor both aspects of our eucharistic life in the manner they deserve.

A place for altar stones?

A parish in our city recently built a new church. Formerly each altar where the holy sacrifice of the Mass was offered had to have an altar stone with the relics of one of the saints. But we noticed this otherwise beautiful altar did not have one. Are such relics required anymore? If not, why not?

The practice of placing relics of saints in the altar still continues, but care must be taken that there is solid evidence of the authenticity of such relics. (GIRM 302)

In the early church, the eucharistic sacrifice was offered over the tombs of martyrs since they were in a special way witnesses to Jesus Christ by their willingness to die for him. Later the practice developed of having a martyr's body, or part of it, placed in every altar as a continuation and reminder of that tradition.

As time went on, the altar began to lose its identity as "the table of the Lord." It sometimes seemed to become overpowered by statues of angels and saints and other structures.

In its present liturgy, the church is trying in every possible way to make the altar table the central and prominent feature of a church building, as it should be.

The Introduction to the Rite for the Dedication of an Altar, promulgated in 1977, requires that the altar be constructed away from the wall so the priest can easily walk around it, and that it be in a central location where it will draw the attention of the whole congregation. In any new church, statues, pictures of saints or relics may not be placed on or over the altar.

Newer regulations maintain that policy. If an older church has an altar already so positioned that it makes participation by the people difficult, or if it cannot be moved without detriment to its artistic value, then another fixed altar may be erected and dedicated. Sacred celebrations should be performed only on that altar. In order that the people not be distracted from the new altar, the old altar should not be decorated in any special way. (GIRM 303)

According to the *Code of Canon Law* (1237) relics are limited to fixed altars, that is altars which are attached to the floor so they cannot be moved.

Requirements for liturgical music

The priests in our parish ask us not to sing some music we have used for years. They say it isn't liturgical. It seems to me that if we have done it and it makes people happy, there's nothing wrong with it. Why would priests act this way?

A complete answer to your question would be far beyond the space available here. Your concern is too important, however, not to respond at least in some way.

My first reaction to your letter (which was considerably longer than the part I quoted) is that your parish is lucky to have the priests you describe. While individual judgment always enters into music, it sounds as if they know what they're doing.

The fact that a musical composition sounds passable and that it makes people — choir or congregation — happy, does not in itself make it sacred music. As Pope John Paul said some years ago, "It cannot be said that all music becomes sacred from the fact and at the moment in which it is inserted into the liturgy."

The church has explicit and clear criteria on what music may be used in liturgy, and how it should be used. These criteria appear in the section on sacred music (chapter 6) of the Constitution on the Liturgy of Vatican Council II, and in numerous documents by the U. S. bishops. Briefly, music must meet three tests before it should be used in the Eucharist or other official liturgies.

1. The first is artistic; it should be basically good music in both composition and performance. In my judgment, of the three tests this is the one most offended against in many parishes. Whether traditional or modern, organ or guitar, choir or folk group, music does not become appropriate for the liturgy simply because the notes hang together and the composer or performers have well-intentioned hearts.

2. Second, music must be liturgically correct. That means the music must fit the liturgical seasons and feasts; must be appropriate to the ceremony and the part of the ceremony in which it is used, and must give opportunity for the congregation to participate in those parts of the Mass which are theirs. A solo "Our Father," for example, or a response to the preface ("Holy, Holy, Holy") sung by a choral group alone, would offend against this requirement.
3. Third, the music must be pastorally appropriate. That doesn't mean it has to be something the pastor likes, but that it be music which will help this particular congregation at this particular time pray and worship God well together.

A host of concerns enter here: The musical experience and proficiency of the people, the economic, social and family cares they bring to that celebration of the Eucharist, and so on.

Since we're all human, few parishes measure up fully to all of these requirements all or even most of the time. But as St. Augustine once remarked about liturgical music (1,600 years ago — it's no new problem), "Do not allow yourselves to be offended by the imperfect while you strive for the perfect."

What can you do? If you're serious, get a copy of the booklet, "Music in Catholic Worship," by the American Bishops' Committee on the Liturgy. A good study of this still insightful and readable document is a minimum for any competent Catholic musician or music director. It's available from USCCB Publications, 3211 Fourth St. NE, Washington, D. C., 20017.

Keep familiar songs in liturgy

Perhaps you'd comment about how we are subjected to so many new songs in church. We hardly learn one when another comes along. We like to sing, but seldom is a song around long enough for us to learn and enjoy it.

Your feelings are shared by others and they deserve to be seriously considered.

Two fatal dangers lurk in all liturgy planning. One is to have everything always new, the other is to have everything always old. Real liturgy, whether it is family, patriotic or religious, always has a core that remains the same. An individual family may have its own traditional and consistent manner, for example, of celebrating birthdays. In the Mass we have a basic core of actions and words that we call the Liturgies of the Word and Eucharist.

Even outside that core, however, there needs to be a degree of continuity and familiarity and enjoyment. Some ability to be comfortable and free in singing chants or hymns is essential for genuine community worship. I believe most mistakes and frustrations with our liturgical worship are caused by forgetting that truth.

The other error, always having everything the same, can be just as harmful to active and intelligent prayer. Even within a good and healthy family birthday "liturgy," the celebrant still may choose the meal or the flavor of the cake.

Well-prepared and musically decent new hymns, used long enough for people to enjoy praying with them, are essential for a community that wants a living liturgy. Obviously there can be no strict rules about this. So much depends on the nature of the worshiping community. Its age and culture, even its understanding of and commitment to good liturgy, all enter the picture.

What is essential is that everyone be sensitive to both sides of the scale. If you feel one or other of these considerations is lacking in your community, surface your concern and discuss it with those responsible for the liturgies and other services in your parish.

Stand, kneel or sit?

During a vacation in Europe we were surprised that many churches have chairs rather than pews. No one knelt at any time during the Mass, except for a few American tourists. We felt we were correct in following the congregation.

The local people in the churches you speak of were following the general law of the church about postures during Mass. People are to stand from before the Prayer over the Gifts (said by the priest just before the preface of the Eucharistic Prayer) until the end of Mass.

Exceptions are that they should sit after Communion if there is a time for meditation, and they should kneel at the Consecration unless prevented by health, lack of space, large numbers or other reasonable cause. (GIRM 43)

In 1969, the American bishops adapted this rule for the United States, providing that people should kneel from after the Sanctus ("Holy, Holy, Holy") until after the Amen at the end of the Eucharistic Prayer (Appendix to the GIRM, 21)

The faithful may receive Communion either standing or kneeling, as established by the conferences of bishops. When they communicate standing, it is recommended that they make an appropriate gesture of reverence before receiving the sacrament. (GIRM 160) In response to this instruction, the bishops have established standing as the posture in the United States, and a bow of the head as a gesture of reverence.

Unless the bishops of other countries adapt the missal in a similar way, the regulations for the universal church which I indicate above would apply for the people there.

For many centuries Christians never knelt at Mass, which may explain the situation in older churches you encountered. During one long period of the church's history it was forbidden to kneel at Mass, and standing was the obligatory and normal posture on Sundays and during the Easter season. Congregations in many countries and dioceses basically continue that sort of tradition, as you have seen.

More on posture at Mass

Recently we visited another parish where the congregation only stood or sat. There was no kneeling during the entire Mass. This upset me. There seems to be no humility while standing during every part of the Mass. What is right?

It may help your blood pressure if you remember that many liturgical practices, even those which we often consider absolutely essential, differ widely from time to time and from place to place. When larger churches and basilicas were built, standing was the normal posture through the entire Mass. In Rome and other ancient and modern cities, numerous Christians churches still do not have seats, let alone kneelers.

Even to the present, all four major Eucharistic Prayers refer to the people as "standing" around the altar (using the Latin *circumstantes*, those standing around, or the verb *astare*, to stand near). I don't demean kneeling at Mass, but it's worthwhile to keep things in perspective.

Even in the Western world, kneeling and genuflecting have been part of the Mass for only a few hundred years. Before that, kneeling was primarily a sign of penance and contrition.

As the missal says, a common posture observed by all is a sign of the unity of the assembly and its sense of community. It expresses and fosters the spiritual attitude of those who take part in it (GIRM 42). The previous question explains the regulations for the United States.

Bow or genuflect?

I have seen people, including priests, bow toward the altar and the Blessed Sacrament instead of genuflecting. Shouldn't we genuflect if we really believe in the presence of Jesus in the Blessed Sacrament?

Genuflection, bending one or both knees as an act of reverence, happens to be the act of reverence Catholics of our time and country are most accustomed to. But a profound and devout bow can be just as reverent. Until perhaps 300 years ago, bowing was the common way of showing reverence to the Eucharist, or to the crucifix. It was considered proper, in fact, for young girls to curtsy to the Blessed Sacrament.

Our practice of genuflection derives mainly from practices of imperial Rome and later courts of Europe.

Entrance procession exalts priest?

One of our liturgy leaders would like to eliminate the entrance procession at weekend Masses. She thinks it makes the priest look like an emperor and appear better than everyone else.

She wants the priest to sit somewhere in church, then walk up to start Mass. I think the entrance procession gives dignity that the liturgy should have. What is proper?

I, too, have seen what you describe. In my view, it misses the purpose of the entrance procession and song in our liturgy. This same misunderstanding is reflected in the opening instructions one still occasionally hears from cantors: "Let's stand and greet our celebrant as we sing hymn 91, 'How Great Thou Art.'" The procession and song are not to greet or honor the celebrant, however great he may be, but to unite the minds and hearts of the assembly as they begin their community worship of God. Having ministers simply emerge to perform their liturgical functions misses a golden opportunity (if the entrance rite is done well) to add dignity and focus to what is about to take place.

These are not my ideas; it is the ancient understanding of the entrance rite reflected in present liturgical documents. Our major guide to the celebration of Mass put it as well as any. After the people have assembled, it says, the entrance song begins and the priest and ministers approach the altar.

"The purpose of this chant is to open the celebration, foster the unity of those who have gathered, introduce their thoughts to the mystery of the liturgical season or festivity, and accompany the procession of priest and ministers." (GIRM 47)

I also need to say something about another facet of your question. Of course the priest is no better than anyone else. But as you say, people knowledgeable in their faith are aware that the ordained priest is not merely one who happens to walk up and start Mass. He has a unique function as leader of the community's eucharistic worship. As one who is sacramentally designated to act in the name of Christ and his body, the church, the priest is the official presider at the eucharistic liturgy and has as his primary duty the proclamation of the Gospel of God to everyone (Vatican II, Decree on the Ministry of Priests, 4). Priests "exercise this sacred function of Christ (announcing the divine Word to all) most of all in the eucharistic liturgy" (Constitution on the Church, 28; Decree on Priests, 13).

This is not the place to prolong that point, but we need to avoid falling into a trap here. Some priests today seem to feel that they exalt themselves by belittling the non-ordained, especially lay people — the "you can't do what I can do or be where I can be" syndrome. In the other direction, however, one finds some lay people who apparently feel that minimizing the role and ministry of the ordained is somehow a path to "equal status."

It seems to me this is at very least not helpful. As we struggle to recognize and utilize more perfectly the gifts each of us enjoys, our common dignity and equality before the heavenly Father is too well affirmed and proven by our faith for us to allow ourselves to resort to such tactics.

Why does priest kiss the altar?

Why does the priest kiss the altar? Some do it after the last blessing at Mass and some do not. Is there some reason?

For Catholics, the altar is not merely a piece of furniture. It is loaded with precious symbolism.

Along with the pulpit, where the Word of God is proclaimed, it is the focal point of our meeting with God the Father in and through Jesus Christ. If the Liturgy of the Eucharist is the central event which brings us to the Father "through him (Christ), with him and in him," the altar around which this happens holds a place of primary honor and dignity.

The General Instruction of the Roman Missal explains: "The altar on which the Sacrifice of the Cross is made present under the sacramental signs is also the table of the Lord to which the People of God is called together to participate in the Mass, as well as the center of the thanksgiving that is accomplished through the Eucharist." (296)

The church extends this by referring to the altar not only as the place of renewing the sacrifice of Jesus, but as Jesus himself. The fifth Easter preface to the Eucharistic Prayer proclaims, "As he gave himself into your (the Father's) hands for our salvation, he showed himself to be the priest, the altar and the lamb of sacrifice."

This is why the church sees the altar (not the crucifix, or even the tabernacle containing the Blessed Sacrament) as the central and focal point of those buildings where we gather to celebrate the Eucharist. It is also why tradition has called for the bishop, priest and deacon to venerate the altar, usually with a kiss. Instructions for the Mass direct the priest and other ordained ministers to kiss the altar at the beginning and end of Mass. (GIRM 49 and 90)

Reverence for Gospel

Just before the reading of the Gospel at Mass, the priest touches his head, his mouth and his breast. Then most of the people do the same. What does this mean?

The priest and people make a small sign of the cross on their forehead, their lips and breast. The action is a prayer that the Good News of the Lord which they are about to hear may be always in their minds, on their lips and in their hearts.

Sing the Alleluia

Our parish liturgy planning group needs information about the Alleluia. Some feel it should never be used unless it is sung at Mass. Others say it is better to say it than not have it at all.

According to the Lectionary, the official ritual of the church for the Liturgy of the Word, "the Alleluia or the verse before the Gospel must be sung, and during it all stand. It is not sung by the cantor who intones it or by the choir, but by the whole congregation together" (no. 23). Other liturgical documents, for example the General Introduction of the Roman Missal (62), and the decree of the Congregation for Divine Worship governing chant at Mass (1972, n. 7) just assume that the Alleluia is sung. The instruction of the American Bishops' Committee on the Liturgy, "Music in Catholic Worship," says, "If not sung, the Alleluia should be omitted" (n. 55).

The reason for emphasis on singing the Alleluia is twofold. First the dignity and reverence due the proclaiming of the Gospel calls for special attention. This is also why incense and lighted candles are often used at that time.

In addition, the word "alleluia," which loosely translated means "praise to Yahweh," is the great acclamation of joy and praise to God in both the Old and New Testaments. Reciting the Alleluia would be the liturgical equivalent to reciting instead of singing "Happy Birthday to you" at a birthday party.

Holding hands at Our Father

At some of our Masses we hold hands during the Our Father. Now someone tells us this was forbidden several years ago. Is this true?

No. In 1975 the Sacred Congregation for Divine Worship was asked whether the congregation might hold hands during the Lord's Prayer *instead* of offering the sign of peace. The answer was no. "The Sign of Peace is filled with meaning, graciousness and Christian inspiration," it said. "Any substitution for it must be repudiated." Nothing was said prohibiting the practice of holding hands during the Lord's Prayer. It is neither prescribed nor prohibited.

Hear or read Scripture?

Our parish has booklets for people to use at Mass. Until recently these booklets contained the readings from the Bible for Sunday Mass. Now they do not.

For those of us raised with the notion that the ideal was to use a missal and follow the priest at Mass, it is puzzling when we're told we should not be reading at Mass, even the readings from the Bible.

The main reason for our puzzlement is that we have largely lost sight of the fact that *hearing* the Word of God is a liturgical act, an act of public worship. When the Mass was in Latin, meaningful hearing of the Word was, of course, impossible. After English translations of the Mass became permissible around the beginning of the 20th century, we followed what the priest was saying by reading the English version.

When the lector (reader, deacon or priest) proclaims the Word of God at the celebration of Mass, he performs an act of worship; and we perform an act of worship by *listening* attentively and prayerfully to that Word. Thus, the church's directives discourage whenever possible the printing of the Scripture texts in Mass booklets.

The liturgical instructions for Mass put it well. "When the scriptures are read in the church, God himself is speaking to his people, and Christ, present in his own word, is proclaiming the Gospel. The readings of God's word must therefore be listened to by all with reverence." (GIRM 31)

Obviously, this doesn't mean that private reading of Scripture is unimportant or discouraged. It's simply that the solemn proclamation of the Word during Mass is not the place for it.

Can women be lectors?

If women are allowed to be lectors (readers) at Mass, why are there churches where only men have this privilege? We are in a small parish and have women lectors. Visitors sometimes tell us they do not like the idea, that only men are allowed in the sanctuary.

Except for functions reserved to priests and deacons, women have the same right to liturgical ministry as do men. This includes leading the singing, directing liturgical participation, acting as commentator, reading Scripture, serving as extraordinary ministers of the Eucharist, and assistance at the altar as server.

By decree of the Congregation on Divine Worship, only those qualifications may be required of women as are required of men — worthiness of life, and so on. The same decree also requires that when women do read the Scripture, they do so where the other readings are proclaimed so that a single place is reserved for all biblical readings. It is no longer stipulated, as it once was, that women remain outside the sanctuary. Whatever a woman does, she should do in the appropriate location.

Difficulties with homilies

How does one tell a Catholic priest his homilies are as boring as hades? Does an adult congregation have to be told that an Epistle to the Philippians was written to the people of Philippi? For attention-getters do we have to be shown an apple or a banana? On various Sundays we have had a man's hat, a flashlight, a picture of a lamb and U. S. currency (money to burn).

I'd bet that for most priests who read this, the first gut reaction will be: You're damned if you do, and damned if you don't.

I realize what you're saying, having been subjected myself to some condescending and childish talks in my life. But with all the wailing about the quality of unprepared homilies today, I think you have to at least give your priest credit for trying.

As a priest who wants to meet the minds and hearts of a rainbow of people on Sunday mornings, I can assure you that any priest who exercises the time and ingenuity on his homilies that yours does would welcome whatever critiques and suggestions you might offer.

I and most other priests, I believe, appreciate reactions from our parishioners. Feedback on his homilies is one of the things a priest needs most and receives least. Sometimes it is difficult to implement suggestions for one reason or another, but we're grateful for them anyway.

So tell the priest how you feel. He may or may not be able to do anything about it, but I wager he thanks you.

Is creed necessary?

A young priest who has been in our area for about five years never says the Profession of Faith, neither the Apostles' nor Nicene Creed. He says the creed is reserved for special occasions. I feel I have not fulfilled my Sunday obligation if I have not attended a complete Mass.

The presence of a creed does not determine the validity of one's participation in the Eucharist. The praying of the Profession of Faith is not an essential part of the Mass on Sunday or any other time.

The official instructions for the Mass, however, provide that the creed be recited by the priest and people at least on Sundays and special feasts. There is no liturgical basis for regularly neglecting that part of the Mass.

"Maker" or "creator"?

What is the reason for changing the word "creator" to "maker" in our Profession of Faith at Mass? The word "maker" has a downgrading and untrue implication of the beginning of the world. Why the change in the Nicene Creed?

The change was made because the word "maker" is a more exact translation of the Nicene Creed, both in the original Greek and in the Latin versions.

The creed, which resulted mainly from the first ecumenical council at Nicaea in Asia Minor, uses the Greek word *poietes.* The usual Latin translation of that is *factor.* Both words literally mean maker rather than creator.

As long as we're on the subject, this same reason explains some changes in the wording of several parts of the Mass during the past 20 or 30 years. The new wording is a more exact translation.

I get some questions, for example, asking why in the same creed we now say "we believe" when the Latin of the so-called old Mass said *credo*, "I believe."

The reason is that the authentic texts of the Council of Nicaea use the plural both in Greek and in Latin for that verb. "We believe" is a more correct translation than "I believe."

"The Spirit, the Lord"

In the creed at Mass, why do we say we believe in "the Spirit, the Lord?" What is the significance of this, since that title is always reserved for Christ?

In the church's tradition, the title "Lord" (in Greek, *Kyrios*) most often refers to Jesus, but not always. Christ enjoys that title most appropriately as the God-Man, the unique mediator between God and creation, and therefore Lord of the world.

The title has also been used for the Holy Spirit, since the Spirit shares in the divine nature of the Father and Son, and therefore in all the prerogatives and attributes they have as God.

The church in the East (Constantinople), with its heavily Spirit-oriented mysticism, speaks of the Spirit as *Kyrios* more than does the West (Rome), and usually relates this title to the Third Person's work as Giver and Generator of life. Some early Eastern forms of the Apostles' Creed, as well as the Creed of Nicaea (year 325) we use at Mass, illustrate this tradition.

The reference to the Holy Spirit as Lord was not in the original creed of the Council of Nicaea; it was added by the Council of Constantinople half a century later.

Jesus' words at consecration

The words of consecration in our Mass are different than they were in my old English missal in the old Mass. Isn't the consecration supposed to contain the words that Christ used at the Last Supper?

Jesus never spoke English. Words we have can be only a translation of the Aramaic he used, an effort to put the meaning of what he said into another language.

If you look at the Gospels and St. Paul's description of the Last Supper in the First Letter to the Corinthians (chapter 11), you will find that even they differ in the words ascribed to Jesus in the institution of the Eucharist. The reason is that the exact words of Jesus were not that important to the writers of the Gospels, who probably reflected the words used in the eucharistic liturgy at the time and place of the writing of that part of the New Testament.

It's the same today. In the Eucharistic Prayer, which, as the name implies, is essentially a prayer of thanksgiving and remembrance, the important concern is that the words give the meaning Jesus intended, as this meaning is handed down to us in Scripture.

Shed for all, or many?

In the consecration at Mass, the English translation heard in our churches says that the blood of Christ "will be shed for all so that sins may be forgiven."

In the Gospel of Matthew it says that at the Last Supper Jesus said all should drink of his blood "which is being shed for many unto the forgiveness of sins."

Who made this diabolical mistake by inserting the word all instead of many as the Gospel says.

I can go you one better. Even the present Latin text of the Mass says *pro multis,* which literally means for many, but which is translated in the English as "for all."

The English translation is a proper one, which is clear (if not simple) from the original languages involved.

The Greek text of Mark and Luke for these verses from the Last Supper uses the words *hyper pollon* (for many). Matthew uses a different preposition in the text you mention, but the meaning is the same. However, in the Gospels there are many so-called semitisms, ideas written in Greek in the Gospels but based on previous texts written in a semitic language, in this case Aramaic or Hebrew.

The significant factor is that Hebrew and Aramaic have no equivalent word for "all." Hebrew *rabbim,* which means "many," also has the meaning of "all" — "the many who form the whole." Numerous examples of this appear elsewhere in the Bible, both in the Old and the New Testaments. In Matthew 20:28 Jesus says he gave his life for the ransom "of many," the meaning is clear; he gave it for all humanity, not just some. The Catholic *New American Bible* explains this verse in these words: "Many does not mean some are excluded, but is a semitism designating the collectivity who benefit from the service of the one, and is equivalent to all."

We know, furthermore, that this all-inclusive meaning of "many" was well understood by early Christians. John's Gospel, for instance, while it devotes five chapters to events at the Last Supper, gives no description of the institution of the Eucharist on that night, as do the other Gospels. John's main eucharistic texts are in chapter six where Jesus "foretells" that he will give his disciples his flesh to eat and his blood to drink. There, in the climactic phrase, Jesus declares that the bread he will give is his flesh "for the life of the world" (John 6:51).

The same universal meaning is kept in Spanish *por todos*, Italian *per tutti*, French *pour la multitude,* and other languages.

Our English words at Mass, therefore, are the most accurate translation of this important passage that biblical scholarship can give us.

What is "epiklesis"?

I have a new missal and find it very helpful in understanding many things about our parish Mass. Several words, though, I can't understand. What is "epiklesis?" It is mentioned several times but never explained.

I imagine you find the word in the explanation of the Eucharistic Prayers, or perhaps alongside the Eucharistic Prayers themselves.

Epiklesis is a Greek word that means an invocation, or more literally, a calling-down. It is the name given to that part of the Eucharistic Prayer in which God the Father is asked to send the Holy Spirit on the bread and wine that these may become the body and blood of the Lord, and that the spiritual effects of the body and blood will be received by those who offer it.

From earliest times these prayers of thanksgiving have contained such an invocation under this title.

Doxology or Amen?

Should the people say the "through him, with him" prayer with the priest at the end of the Eucharistic Prayer, or not? In some places they do, in others they do not.

The prayer called the doxology — literally, prayer of praise — at the end of the Eucharistic Prayer should not be said by the assembled people, only by the priest. The people's part is the solemn response,

"Amen," which should normally be sung, or at least recited actively by all present.

The word "Amen" goes back to Jewish people in the pre-Christian era. It means "All this is true, we believe it," a profound and reverent affirmation of all that was just said and done. As such, it is a magnificent conclusion to the Eucharistic Prayer by all present who share in the offering of that Eucharist.

In the book of Revelation (Rev. 3:14), Jesus himself is called "the Amen, the faithful witness" of the Father, the one who reflects and affirms perfectly all the Father wishes to be and to say to human beings.

Considering the half-hearted, timid manner with which most congregations respond with this great "Amen" at Mass, whether it is sung or recited, it is understandable that many feel the whole doxology should be said by everyone just to keep that solemn moment from falling flat. But that is not the way it should be.

Sign of peace

How and why did the kiss of peace, or shaking hands, at Mass originate? Do you think our Lord shook hands with the apostles when he said, "My peace I leave with you, my peace I give you?"

How can this practice be avoided by those who find it obnoxious?

The kiss, or sign, of peace is among the oldest rites connected with the Mass. At least five times, the New Testament speaks of Christians greeting each other with a "holy kiss" or a "kiss of love." We're certain that by around the year 150, the kiss was probably already in use as an expression of unity and peace among Christians, and constituted a regular part of the eucharistic liturgy.

For centuries the *Pax* (peace) as it was called was exchanged by everyone at Mass. Toward the late Middle Ages, the practice was observed only by the attending clergy, and other signs (embraces and so on) often substituted for an actual kiss. This continued until our present time when the kiss, or sign, of peace once again is prescribed in some manner for all the faithful.

The church's instructions for Mass indicate that, before the breaking of the bread, each person offers a sign of peace to those nearby, by which the church asks for peace and unity for herself and for the whole human family, and the faithful offer a sign of their communion with the church and their love for each other before receiving Communion together. (GIRM 82)

In spite of your misgivings and suspicions, the sign of peace has deep roots as a fitting external expression of the Christian meaning of the Mass and holy Communion. In the beginning, the rite took place early in the Mass, but later found its way to the time around Communion, the sacrament which we still refer to as "the sign of unity and the bond of love."

The church's long adherence to the kiss of peace as a significant element of the Mass might reasonably suggest that anyone who finds that part of the Mass annoying needs greater understanding of the Eucharist. A handshake, an embrace, or a kiss, may not be the best possible signs of peace. Imperfect as they may be, however, they carry a message that we need to understand if we are to celebrate the Eucharist together as Christ intended it to be celebrated.

Bells during Mass?

Can you tell us whether or not bells are to be used at Mass? Our former pastor discontinued them and we thought our new pastor would start them again. But he says we don't need them anymore. If they were important and nice to have in the past, why not now?

According to present liturgical instructions, a minister may ring a bell shortly before the consecration, and at the elevation of the eucharistic bread and chalice. In other words, it is permitted, but not required at that time. No mention or provision is made for ringing bells at Communion time or other parts of the Mass. (GIRM 150)

To answer your question, good reasons lie behind the change, but as is always true with folk customs, they're not easy to untangle. Ringing bells during Mass apparently began in monasteries during the Middle Ages. Only choir monks attended the conventual (community) Mass in mid-morning. Others out in the field followed the progress of the Mass through the chapel bell.

One event which occasioned increased use of bells was the introduction of the elevation of the host and chalice after the consecration, around the year 1200. These elevations came to be seen, even into our own time, as the main part of the Mass. At one time some fervent Catholics walked from church to church just to watch the elevation. Bells were rung to express elation and to let everyone know "Jesus is now here" and all present could look at him.

In 1972, the Vatican congregation responsible for liturgy related the use of bells to the level of liturgical education in the parish. Where this education has been adequate, it noted, there is no need for this kind of signal. If sufficient liturgical instruction is in fact lacking, bells should be rung at least at the two elevations to elicit joy and attention. (Notitiae, 1972, 343)

Today, we have a deeper awareness than did the people of those days that, while Jesus becomes present to us in a new way under the form of bread and wine in the Eucharist, he doesn't come fresh, as it were. As we gather to celebrate that Eucharist, we *are* the Body of Christ long before he becomes present to us as our food and drink, and as our sacrifice to the Father.

Also, we now express that joy over the Lord's eucharistic presence with our own voices, especially in the acclamation after the Consecration, and in the great Amen at the end of the Eucharistic Prayer. As in many other ways, we now do ourselves what we formerly could only watch, or listen to, someone else doing.

Crossed arms at Communion

Please explain something I see in churches recently. At Communion time some people come up with arms crossed. The priest does not give them Communion, but says a prayer. What is this about?

The practice you describe is observed in many parishes today. Catholics not receiving Communion, and children and people of other faiths who wish to do so, approach the communion station with the rest of the congregation. As they reach the priest, they cross their arms over their breast as a sign they do not wish to receive Communion.

The priest or other eucharistic minister places his or her hand over the head or shoulder of the individual and says a brief blessing or prayer, for example: "May Jesus keep you always in his love. Amen."

Priests and people who take advantage of this opportunity see several good points to recommend it. Perhaps most of all it gives Christians of other faiths, who cannot normally receive Communion at a Catholic Eucharist, a way of sharing in the Communion part of the Mass in some manner.

Many non-Catholics are present in some churches each Sunday. Some are alone, and some have come with Catholic spouses or other Catholic family members. Most of these participate fully in the Mass in every other way.

While we cannot invite them to the Eucharist itself, we can do more than ignore them after the buildup of the Eucharistic Prayer by allowing them to share some expression of our care and common Christian identity during this intimate part of the eucharistic celebration.

To my knowledge, two main objections have been offered against this practice. It is suggested that having people come forward for a eucharistic blessing confuses the liturgical sign of the reception of the Eucharist, thus reducing the significance of receiving holy Communion itself.

Having experienced this practice for several years, it seems that's not what happens. If anything, it increases the awareness of the great privilege and reality of receiving the Eucharist, whether the individuals are children, adults who are preparing to embrace the Catholic faith, or others who for one reason or another cannot or do not receive the Eucharist.

A more practical objection is that people who become accustomed to the practice in one parish will be confused or embarrassed when their request for a eucharistic blessing is not recognized or accepted in another. This is naturally a serious concern for any thoughtful pastor. Whether or not this disadvantage outweighs the advantages is a matter of pastoral judgment. Some Oriental Rite Catholics routinely approach Communion with arms crossed, for example, which might cause a bit of confusion in some parts of the country.

It is interesting that Pope John Paul II himself offers such a blessing. In 1989, on a visit to Sweden, he gave the blessing to Lutheran Archbishop Bertil Werkstrom of Uppsala and Lutheran Bishop Henrik Svenungsson of Stockholm when they joined the Communion line at his Mass in Stockholm; the pope even recalled the event with obvious emotion in his general audience address more than a year later, on Jan. 23, 1991.

Transubstantiation

Years ago we were taught that transubstantiation was a basic belief of our faith. Today we hear no reference to it in our homilies. Is it still a valid part of Catholic doctrine?

The word itself may not be used as much in catechism and other instruction classes or homilies. But that has nothing to do with our belief in this essential doctrine of Christianity.

The reality behind the word, the true presence of our Lord Jesus Christ, "body and blood, soul and divinity," under the appearance of the eucharistic bread and wine, is and always will be at the heart of our Catholic Christian faith.

Every Liturgy of the Eucharist at Mass literally overflows with this reality. Most obviously in the words of Consecration during the institution narrative of the Eucharistic Prayer, we hear the words of our Lord himself, "This is my body... this is my blood."

Every time you receive Communion, you make an explicit profession of faith in this mystery by your "Amen," as the eucharistic minister holds up the host and declares the "body of Christ."

The word "transubstantiation" was used in connection with the Eucharist for the first time at the Fourth Lateran Council in the 13th century. It is not used as frequently today, however, because it is too much of a Latin mouthful, and we are able to express what we believe about this sacrament without resorting to such (for us) unfamiliar and arcane terminology.

The *Catechism of the Catholic Church* is a good example. By the words of Christ and the invocation of the Holy Spirit, it says, the bread and wine mysteriously become the body and blood of Christ (1333). Later the catechism speaks at some length about what happens when Christ becomes present in the Eucharist. A "conversion" of the bread and wine into another reality takes place. The church believes, it says, that the word of Christ and the Spirit have power to make this change happen (1373-5).

The word "transubstantiation" doesn't occur at all in this explanation except at the end, and then only as part of a quote from the Council of Trent (1376). Big words may have theological value, but they really don't tell us much more about the what or the how, or take us any deeper into the mystery.

The Real Presence after Mass

Please explain how and when the church came to the conclusion that the Real Presence of our Lord continues after the celebration of the Eucharist. It does not seem to be logical or the purpose of the sacrament for the Lord to continue his presence outside of the sacrifice of the Mass.

From earliest decades, Christian communities understood that the real presence of the risen Lord in the eucharistic bread and wine endured after the eucharistic celebration itself. This celebration might take many forms, including some apparently that did not include what we call the words of consecration in the institution narrative of the Mass. One example is the Eucharistic Prayer in the Didache (*The Teaching of the Twelve Apostles*) written in the first part of the second century, one of the most valuable documents we possess from early Christianity.

Nevertheless in whatever form the Eucharist was celebrated, it was assumed that union with the Christian community could be enhanced if people who could not be present received the Sacred Species later. Around the year 150, the Christian philosopher and martyr, Justin, tells how portions of the bread from the Eucharist were taken to those who were absent.

Deacons and others routinely took Communion to the sick, prisoners, and others who were not able to be at the community celebration.

Another example is the Communion service during the liturgy of Good Friday. Since the year 800, Communion has been received in this ceremony using hosts consecrated at a previous Mass. (See the chapter on Ecumenism for additional information on Christian beliefs about the eucharistic presence of our Lord.)

CHAPTER 4

HOLY COMMUNION

Communion under both species?

Several Protestant friends have asked me a question I can't answer. At the Last Supper, Jesus commands us to take and eat his body and drink his blood. Why don't we do that? Please don't tell me that's changing; it doesn't explain why it was not done up to now. And don't tell me it's not practical or convenient. If this is what Jesus wanted, who are we to say it's too time-consuming?

Your question is a good one, and frankly I'm not sure there is an answer that will satisfy your friends. As usual, however, a little history helps to put it into better perspective.

For most of the history of the church (about 12 centuries), Communion under both species was standard at Mass. Much theological and spiritual significance was placed on the symbolism of receiving the Lord in Communion under the form of both bread and wine.

Even during this time, however, all the way back to the earliest years, Christians clearly understood that one did not have to receive both forms in order to truly receive the living Lord. Never was there some sort of gross supposition that in the bread one received the dry body of Christ, which later became alive with the blood when one drank from the chalice.

Communion under one species was, therefore, not at all unusual from the beginning. The Eucharist would be taken to the sick at home, for example, under the form of bread alone, and no one doubted that the individual received the whole sacrament. Infants or young children, and the sick who could not swallow food, were given Communion only in the form of wine.

Around the 12th century, a few groups began to claim that one did not truly receive the Eucharist unless one received the form of both bread and wine, a trend which prompted the church, for polemical reasons, to look more favorably on Communion under one species. Later, as some Protestants began to promote the idea that the whole Christ is not present under only one species, the church increased its emphasis on the ancient truth: Anyone who receives only the form of bread or wine receives the living Christ in Communion.

For this reason, church law eventually went so far as to forbid the people to receive from the chalice at Mass. Thus, the practice of receiving only the host became common not to deny that both species was the ideal, but simply to make clear the rejection of the error that demanded both species.

Today, of course, the danger of that doctrinal error is long past, so the church has resumed its insistence that receiving under both species is the ideal, symbolically whole way to receive the Eucharist. The point appears numerous times in official liturgical documents. The General Instruction of the Roman Missal puts it very well: "Holy Communion has a more complete form as a sign when it is received under both kinds, bread and wine. For in this manner of reception a fuller sign of the Eucharistic banquet shines forth. Moreover, there is a clearer expression of that will by which the new and everlasting covenant is ratified in the blood of the Lord, and of the relationship of the Eucharistic banquet to the eschatalogical banquet in the Father's kingdom." (GIRM 281)

A major instruction on the liturgy of September, 1970, repeats that Communion under both kinds "is the more perfect expression of the people's participation in the Eucharist."

From all this at least two points seem clear. First, anyone who says we must both eat the bread and drink from the cup in order to truly receive the Eucharist contradicts the belief and practice of Christians from the beginning.

Second, anyone who believes that Communion by bread alone is the normal way of Catholics, and that Communion also from the chalice is merely a dispensable liturgical frill, is out of touch with the long eucharistic tradition of the church, not to speak of present liturgical directives.

For us Catholics (and one would hope for all Christians), it comes down to this: Jesus, living in his church, is the best interpreter of those teachings and commands assigned to him in the Gospels.

Is the Eucharist also sign and symbol?

A speaker at a recent religion conference made, I think, some strange remarks about the Eucharist. Insisting on the real presence of our Lord, she went on to shout quite vehemently that the Eucharist is not a symbol, it is the real body of Christ. It doesn't "stand for" anything.

In high school and later, we learned that Christ is truly present in the Eucharist, but the sacrament is also a sign of many things, including the promise of life in heaven. That has stayed with me and has always been special in my life.

I know the church hasn't changed on this. Do you have any explanation for what she was talking about?

You seem to remember your theology very well. The church's literature, theology and liturgy through the centuries are loaded with references to the Eucharist as a symbol, a sign in which what is visible and touchable points to another reality that cannot be seen.

We would expect this, in fact, since the Eucharist is by its very nature a symbol. As St. Thomas puts it in the hymn "Adoro Te Devote," by faith we believe the true God is hidden (*latens Deitas*) under the external forms (*figuras*) of the bread and wine. What we see and touch indicates a reality that is invisible.

I cannot imagine someone even a little versed in theology not being aware that this way of speaking is common in our tradition. In the very celebration of the Eucharist, the consecrated wine is called "the blood of the new and everlasting covenant," a visible symbol of the new bond created by Jesus between us and the Father.

Eucharistic prayers call the celebrating of the sacrifice and sacrament a memorial, a sign which causes us to remember what the Lord has done, as the words of Jesus command us in the Consecration. And our liturgy continually refers to what you remember learning: The Eucharist is a sign and promise of life with God. As the prayer after Communion on the feast of Corpus Christi says, Jesus gives us his eucharistic body and blood "as a sign that even now we share your life."

The *Catechism of the Catholic Church* contains numerous references to the symbolisms in the Eucharist. One of them points out that the first Christians already saw the Breaking of the Bread as a symbol, a sign, by which they "signified" their oneness in Christ (1329).

All this in no way denies or diminishes our belief in the "true, real and substantial" presence (Council of Trent's words) of Jesus Christ under the appearance (another "sign" word) of bread and wine. The woman you speak of seems to have fallen into a trap that has caused the church enormous grief through its 2,000 years, the tendency to deal with mysteries with an either-or, rather than a both-and, approach.

In any genuine mysteries we're speaking ultimately of The Mystery, the Supreme Being who will never be totally comprehensible to us. When we attempt to tie all the loose ends neatly, we end up in a doctrinal swamp.

Many early Christians, for example, got way off track by emphasizing the humanity of Christ in such a way that they denied his divinity; others so focused on the fact that he is truly God that they ended up denying he is also truly human.

It took the church centuries to work its way through that maze. One of the lessons learned was that we should never try to explain one mystery by explaining away another. We do well to remember that when dealing with the mysteries connected to the Eucharist.

Catholics believe in real presence?

On a religious television program recently, the hostess said Catholic schools no longer teach that Jesus is truly present in the Eucharist, that it is only a symbol. How can this be? If this is what our schools are teaching, why do we have them? She said surveys show most Catholics today do not believe in the Eucharist. I find that hard to believe.

I assume your report was accurate, since I heard from others as well, apparently after the same broadcast. I, too, find these "facts" hard to believe. I don't know on what she bases her accusation, but there is nothing I've ever seen to support it. The schools in every parish I have worked with, or know of, are clear and thoroughly Catholic in their teaching about the Eucharist. To make this kind of broad accusation, undermining and defaming Catholic schools around the country with such falsehoods, contributes nothing helpful to the faith and life of Catholic people.

As for the surveys, I'm not at all sure the eucharistic faith of Catholics is more deficient today than it was years ago. First, there were no such surveys at that time to measure against. Second, no matter how fair surveys on this subject attempt to be, it is impossible to capsulize our beliefs about the Eucharist in a few brief questions. It took the church 15 centuries to arrive at the language of the Council of Trent (session 13) describing the true and substantial eucharistic presence of our Lord, and even that is being refined and clarified to this day.

Our belief in the real presence — "body and blood, soul and divinity," as the old catechism formula put it — needs to be carefully understood; it can be, and has often been, misinterpreted. In ancient times, and up to the present, people not of our faith often misunderstood what we mean by eating the body of Christ, and viewed it as some sort of cannibalism.

Thoughtful Catholics may not know all the technical theological terminology, but they know what they believe. They tend to be cautious of language that could be open to a caricature of our faith. We are, after all, dealing here with a profound mystery no human words will ever adequately express.

And finally, it's simply reality that some Catholics thrive on deploring what they see as a crisis of faith so they can lay the blame on whatever it is they currently don't like in the church — English liturgy, women lectors, Latin Masses, lay eucharistic ministers, and so on. Many factors always affect the quality of people's faith, in the Eucharist as in everything else. Fortunately, our Eucharistic Prayers at Mass plainly express what the Eucharist is and why. From the words of consecration to the calling down of the Holy Spirit and the many acts of thanksgiving, when these prayers are proclaimed intelligently and listened to carefully, the true faith is present and alive.

Likewise, when the faithful make their act of faith at Communion by saying, "Amen, I believe it" after being offered "the body of Christ," they declare quite clearly what they believe. It is worth remembering that for centuries, when the Mass was once before in a language people could understand, long before Catholic schools or CCD classes, the Eucharist, with the Liturgy of the Word, was a primary place where faith was planted and nourished. Maybe we need to look there a little more closely.

Intinction

Your column in our Catholic paper said in relation to the different ways of receiving Communion under both species, that "intinction is a liturgically correct method of distributing holy Eucharist."

In training to become a eucharistic minister in our diocese, I was told this form of receiving the Eucharist is not acceptable. Some documents were apparently cited in support of this. I would appreciate your clarification on this matter.

I know of no official document which forbids Communion by intinction — dipping the host in the cup and then giving it to the communicant. It is still theoretically an acceptable way of giving Communion.

However, at least two things urge strongly against its use. First, it is a much less appropriate and symbolic way of receiving under both species than actually drinking from the cup. More seriously, distributing Communion by intinction removes the option of receiving Communion in the hand. A host that has been dipped in the chalice could only be placed on the tongue of the recipient.

Thus, practically speaking, the training and information you received was correct. (see GIRM 287)

AIDS from the Communion cup?

As a health-care worker I occasionally care for AIDS patients. These patients are usually in isolation. I know there have been no documented cases of AIDS passed by tears or saliva, but the Communion cup frightens me in this respect.

I was excited about receiving Communion under both the bread and the wine when it began. However, now my husband asks me not to take the wine, and he doesn't either, due to the threat of AIDS. Has this problem been considered in parishes?

Some years ago (in 1987) I responded to a similar question. At that time I quoted the best authorities in the country supporting the opinion that no evidence exists indicating that AIDS may be contracted through something like a common communion cup. That position seems to be even stronger now.

As most people are aware, acquired immune deficiency syndrome (AIDS) is caused by a virus which invades, among others, one group of cells vital to the body's system of defense. The virus destroys virtually all these cells. Infections and other problems, which we would normally fight off easily, become devastating and eventually fatal.

The methods by which the disease is transmitted from one person to another are commonly known. Scientists agree that what is called casual contact is not among them.

In April, 1987, the Health Letter of the Harvard Medical School strongly rejected the theory that people who live in the same household as an AIDS patient, using the same utensils, linens, and so on, may communicate the disease to others in their community. "Studies of household contacts have not found any evidence of transmission," it said. Certain types of sexual relationships and people who share drug needles run high risk, according to the document. Apart from this, "those whose physical contact with others is non-sexual have virtually no risk of getting the disease."

Later, a Federal Center for Disease Control spokesman I consulted confirmed to me that no evidence exists linking transmission of AIDS from one person to another with the types of contact connected to drinking from a common communion cup.

During 1988, the surgeon general of the United States attempted to put the best current knowledge together in an informative brochure on AIDS, which he sent to every household in the country.

"You won't get the AIDS virus," said the study, "through everyday contact with the people around you in school, in the workplace, at parties, child-care centers or stores. You won't get it by swimming in a pool, even if someone in the pool is infected with the AIDS virus... You won't get AIDS from saliva, sweat, tears, urine or... a kiss.... It can't be passed by using a glass or eating utensils that someone else has used."

To be sensitive and alert to the dangers of AIDS only makes sense. The best scientific research available, however, still indicates that using a common communion cup at Mass is not one of those dangers.

Diabetics and alcoholics

You point out that Christ's body and blood are present in both host and chalice. However, once bread and wine are consecrated, the host cannot be dipped in "wine."

No one need receive under the appearance of wine, but only alcoholics should avoid it (due to taste and odor). No diabetic, for example, could be harmed by drinking the blood of Jesus.

It is common in Christian tradition to refer to the eucharistic species as bread and wine when the context shows clearly that the consecrated body and blood is intended. This occurs over the centuries in poetry, prayer and theology.

Even one of our Eucharistic Prayers (IV) speaks of the consecrated species as "this bread and wine." So we need not be oversensitive about the terminology.

As for alcoholics and diabetics, the precious blood of the Eucharist not only tastes, looks and smells like wine, it has all the chemical qualities and effects of wine. Some diabetics and alcoholics are understandably warned by their doctors not to drink from the cup at Communion time.

Communion at home during Holy Week?

Is there a rule about what to have ready when the priest or Communion minister comes to my home for Communion? Also, can I go to Communion on Holy Thursday and Good Friday?

The official ritual of the church for Communion outside of Mass says that when Communion is given anywhere outside of a church "a suitable table is to be prepared and covered with a cloth; candles are also to be provided" (no. 19). This would, of course, include at home.

The same ritual says that people who are sick may receive Communion any time on Holy Thursday and Good Friday. On Holy Saturday it may be received only as viaticum, that is, if the person is dying (no. 16)

This is indicated also in the Sacramentary for the liturgy of those days. The introduction to the Good Friday celebration notes: Holy Communion may be given to the faithful only at the celebration of the Lord's passion, but may be brought at any hour of the day to the sick who cannot take part in this service.

Selection of Eucharist ministers

What are the rules for selecting lay people to be eucharistic ministers? Some believe there are guidelines and others believe it is more or less up to the pastor. If there are norms for selecting these lay people, what are they?

The norms for special eucharistic ministers were established by Pope Paul VI in 1973 in his instruction on facilitating reception of Communion, *Immensae Caritatis.*

In this instruction the pope designated that such ministers should be chosen in the following order: reader, student of a major seminary, male religious, woman religious, catechist, man or woman. However, this order may be changed according to the prudent judgment of the local bishop.

In practice, most bishops in our country and others have not demanded this absolute preference of men over women or religious over lay people. As the pope indicates, however, the decision is up to each bishop.

Beyond this, Pope Paul states that "a special minister of holy Communion must be duly instructed and should distinguish himself or herself by Christian life, faith and morals, striving to be worthy of this great office; cultivating devotion to the holy Eucharist and acting as an example to the other faithful by piety and reverence for this most holy sacrament of the altar. Let no one be chosen whose selection may cause scandal among the faithful."

Several methods are possible to keep the final choice from being an arbitrary one on the part of the pastor. All parishioners may be invited to volunteer, for example, or suggestions might be sought and tabulated from members of the parish council or other significant organization.

Dislike eucharistic ministers

Dear Readers:

I received a letter from a lady who said that if she had to receive Communion from a lay person she would not receive at all. Return mail, much of it more than a little emotional, proved two things: That the church of the past 75 years or so succeeded remarkably in instilling practices aimed at reverence for the holy Eucharist, and that this very success has created confusion, and plain error, in the beliefs of many Catholics.

The following excerpts represent recurrent themes in the protests mailed to me, and my responses.

From Missouri: You mention that the church has excellent historical, theological and liturgical reasons for allowing lay persons to distribute Communion. Whatever that means, if they exist now, they also existed in the 1920 and 1930s, if Jesus is really present in the Eucharist. If touching the host in the 1930s was such a serious matter, why can everybody handle it now?

In all the responses, this was the most common error — confusing belief in the real presence of Jesus in the Eucharist with practices or regulations which often governed our attitude toward it. I, too, was raised with the strong admonition that to touch the host, or even the chalice, unnecessarily was a serious sin.

What we did not realize was that these policies (insofar as they were "rules" at all) were only church rules, and were in fact observed only in certain parts of the world even at that time. Therefore, the church could change them, as it changed the Lenten fast and Friday abstinence.

From Delaware: I will not go to Communion to a lay person. He's no better than I, so why can't I give holy Communion to myself?

You are able to give Communion to yourself, if you choose to receive Communion in your hand. However, a eucharistic minister — priest, deacon, or lay person — will still distribute it to you.

From Florida: All the reverence we had for the host is gone. It seems to be only a piece of bread. Is the church drifting back to the days of Martin Luther?

The church introduced the current eucharistic practices for the very reason that it sensed a need to safeguard truths about the Eucharist that have been lost in recent generations. When it allows a layman or woman to give Communion, as it did for centuries in the past, the church in no way implies a lessening of its belief in, or its reverence for, the eucharistic presence of our Lord.

Martin Luther, incidentally, believed firmly in the real presence of Jesus in the Eucharist until he died.

From Iowa: These two fantastic fingers of the priest were the next thing to God. And now anyone can give Communion? No way!

As gently as I can, I have to say this understanding of the priesthood borders on superstition. A priest is not ordained, nor are his hands (not two fingers) anointed with oil, to qualify him to give Communion, but to designate and empower him to preside at the celebration of the Eucharist — or offer Mass, if you will — with his Catholic Christians.

Fast before Communion?

What exactly is the present rule for the fast before holy Communion? Are the rules the same for the entire world?

At the end of the third session of the Second Vatican Council in 1964, Pope Paul considerably simplified the eucharistic fast. According to this 1964 decree, persons should fast from food and liquids, including alcoholic liquids, for one hour before receiving Communion (not one hour before the Mass at which they receive).

Water does not break the fast, and may be taken anytime. The same goes for medicine.

The reason for this regulation is simply to aid in preparing oneself spiritually and mentally for participating in the offering of the Eucharist at Mass, and for receiving it in Communion. Basically, this regulation applies to the whole church, though there are some variations in different parts of the world.

Because of their special needs, the discipline is considerably relaxed for the sick and aged, as well as for people who take care of them. Thus, the period of the eucharistic fast is reduced to "about a quarter of an hour" for the sick and aged, and their care-givers.

The *Code of Canon Law* says simply that the sick and aging and those who care for them can receive the Eucharist even if they have consumed something during the preceding hour. (CCL 919) Obviously, the intention is that the sick should be given every possible opportunity to receive holy Communion.

Communion with wine for sick

I am a eucharistic minister and take holy Communion to elderly and ill people in their homes. Often, people become too ill to be able to take even a small piece of the host. Is the church giving any thought to allowing eucharistic ministers permission to give a sip of consecrated wine to these people?

What you suggest is already quite common. Many seriously ill patients, even some who are not terminal, are unable to swallow even the smallest piece of anything solid. The church provides explicitly for these people in its instructions on care for the sick. According to the *Ritual for Pastoral Care of the Sick*, sick people who cannot receive Communion under the form of bread may receive it under the form of wine alone.

If the wine is consecrated at a Mass not celebrated in the presence of the sick person, the consecrated wine is kept in a proper vessel and placed in the tabernacle after Communion. The precious blood is carried to the sick in a vessel which is closed in such a way as to eliminate all danger of spilling; something like a small medicine bottle is generally used. If some of the precious blood remains after Communion, it should be consumed by the minister, who should also see to it that the vessel is properly washed (no. 74).

Perhaps even some deacons or priests are not familiar with this provision. It would be enlightening, I think, for all ministers of the sick who at any time might administer the Eucharist to have a copy of this ritual and read carefully the general introduction, and the introduction to the many forms that sacramental care of the sick might take. Inexpensive paperback editions are easily available.

Bread for the Eucharist

What is the church's position on bread for the Eucharist in the Latin rite? Are you aware of any suitable and acceptable recipe for homemade altar bread other than the traditional hosts? Also, if you would, what are the sources for this information? I believe many other Catholics will be helped by knowing the rules and how we can apply them.

I cannot respond to your question honestly or intelligently without first explaining that we have two seemingly contradictory sets of regulations for eucharistic bread.

The Catholic Church has insisted increasingly during recent decades on the vital importance of signs in the celebration of the liturgy, especially the other sacraments and the Eucharist. These signs — oil, water, bread, wine, gestures, words — are of the essence of the sacraments and should reflect as fully and genuinely as possible the reality they purport to be. Dirty water or gummy oil, while perhaps valid for the sacraments, would be grossly inappropriate.

Thus, speaking of the Eucharist, the church has insisted that the bread for the eucharistic celebration should "have the appearance of food." (General Instruction of the Roman Missal, no. 321) In other words, it should look and taste like bread people really use.

On the other hand, the tradition of the Latin rite, at least for many centuries, and present regulations of the church, indicate that no other ingredients are to be added to wheat flour and water in the making of the bread. It is difficult to make bread that way, have it come out looking more like recognizable bread than our customary hosts, and still be serviceable for Communion use.

One is reminded of the little boy who was asked if he believed that the bread had become the body of Christ. He replied, "I believe it is the body of Christ, but I don't believe it was bread."

Early in 1978 the American Bishops' Committee on the Liturgy presented a canonical position paper to the appropriate congregation in Rome searching for some leeway by which unleavened bread could be prepared with a few additives that would make it appear more like real bread.

The following year, Cardinal Francis Seper, the late prefect of the Congregation for the Doctrine of the Faith, responded that "it would not be appropriate to accept the suggestions" of the paper for some additions to the material for eucharistic bread. On May 23, 1980, an instruction by another Vatican office (the Congregation for Sacraments and Divine Worship) repeated basically the same instructions.

Thus, these regulations presently govern the Latin Rite Church in the preparation of eucharistic bread. As you imply in your question, quite different regulations apply to the Eastern Rite Churches.

As a final note: The communications from the Vatican congregations, particularly the letter from Cardinal Seper, speak only of "lawfulness and desirability" of different bread materials. Bread with additions to the wheat and water, therefore, would be valid but not lawful for eucharistic bread.

Reactions to wheat prevent Communion?

In some ways I feel sad that so much attention is given to the form of Communion. As a celiac sufferer who can eat nothing made of wheat, I would be grateful just for Communion.

It is good to read in your columns about a greater awareness of celiac disease. After years of living in a vacuum, we are finally being diagnosed. A friend asked her pastor if she could receive only from the cup. He said, "We will not serve wine in this parish." Do you have any more suggestions?

Celiac, or celiac sprue, disease is a malabsorption condition in which individuals have a specific intolerance to wheat and other grains which contain gluten.

The small intestine cannot absorb food nutrients in the presence of gluten, which means these persons cannot tolerate wheat, rye, barley or oats. They are not affected by other flours like potato, corn or rice. Alleviation of additional afflictions, autism for one, now is found to be possibly related to the elimination or control of gluten in the diet.

Sometimes even a tiny bit of wheat may excite a reaction, causing illness, even death. Complete elimination of these grains from the diet usually allows people with this syndrome to live normal, healthy lives.

As one who is blessedly spared this disease, I had no idea how many celiacs there are, well over 100,000, many of them Catholics with the same dilemma you have. For them the Eucharist is only one of many daily challenges, but that one is a major spiritual concern for any Catholic, since Communion bread must be made of wheat flour to be valid for the Eucharist.

Several times I have suggested the most obvious alternative, receiving Communion only under the form of wine. Many celiacs take advantage of this possibility. Unlike the priest your friend encountered, most pastors cooperate with this need in every way possible, even to providing small cups exclusively for the use of the celiac patient. (Even the minute contact with the wheat particle the priest places in the chalice before Communion can make the wine dangerous for those allergic to gluten.) Wine is not always a solution, however; for some celiacs only wine fermented with particular yeasts, or in particular regions, is safe.

In a 1985 letter to the American bishops, Cardinal Josef Ratzinger, head of the Congregation for the Doctrine of the Faith, again affirmed that bread from which all gluten is removed is not valid for the Eucharist. Manufacturers of communion hosts in the United States and Europe have tried to formulate a wheat bread with no gluten, but without success.

I am grateful to you and the many dozens of other readers who related their experiences, diet suggestions, frustrations and hopes. One thing all agree on; they feel there should be some way they, or their children who have the disease, could receive the Eucharist without endangering their health, if not their lives.

I profoundly wish I could suggest a simple solution, but I cannot. Perhaps in the future there will be an answer. I can only say that many families with one or more celiac sufferers have been able to work out a manageable life-style for everyone involved. For others it is a heavy burden, with apparently no present answer.

Fortunately, good resources are available for celiac patients and their families, particularly through the Celiac Sprue Association, Omaha, NE, 68131-0700. Their web site (www.csaceliacs.org) is also loaded with helpful background and practical information.

How often to receive Communion?

A recent homily in our parish left several of us perplexed. The priest emphasized that we should not go to Communion each time we go to Mass. We should not go to Communion sometimes, he said, so that others who do not go will feel more comfortable. Also, we should not give our children the example of going each time; they should see us go to Mass without going to Communion.

To be honest, these statements hurt us deeply since we go to Communion often and hope our children will want to go also. To us, not going to Communion is like going to a banquet and then not partaking in the best part. I hope you can clear this up for us.

Like you, I find it hard to understand those kinds of statements, assuming, of course, that you reflect accurately what the priest said.

It is true that some priests (and lay people) feel for some reason that many Catholics go to Communion today when they should not. I have, in fact, heard similar ideas expressed by some of my priest friends in Europe. After remarking on the difference between their Sunday Masses, at which perhaps half the people receive Communion, and our own, where almost everyone receives, they revealed their suspicion that if American Catholics were as spiritually honest as they should be, fewer of them would be going to Communion so often.

I am fully aware that the consciences of some Catholics have become dulled to the point that they see no conflict between seriously sinful lives and receiving holy Communion. But I fail to understand how anyone might claim that half, a quarter, or even five percent of our people are walking around in mortal sin. It seems to me this would involve, among other things, some very rash judgments.

Another explanation is possible. There is still more than a little touch of Jansenism loose in the Catholic Church. Jansenism, a heresy quite strong in Europe and America into our own century, taught that few people are worthy to receive Communion more than once or twice a year. That attitude deeply infected Catholic spirituality, and traces of it remain to this day.

Fortunately for all of us, none of whom would ever be worthy to receive under such severe restrictions, the church has long since rejected Jansenism as a distortion of the function of the holy Eucharist in our lives. Put simply, this sacrament is meant to be food and strength for our pilgrim journey in this life; it is not offered as a reward for a holy and sinless life.

I'm with you. Parents, priests and teachers must help children develop a healthy and delicate conscience about sin and its relationship to the Eucharist. But we must also help them understand that the Eucharist cannot be simply an occasional or incidental element in either the Mass or in their lives.

We have no doctrinal or psychological basis for assuming that deliberately refraining from receiving holy Communion will help us effectively fill either of these responsibilities.

Communion more than once a day

Can a person receive holy Communion more than once a day without special permission?

Communion formerly was to be received only once a day. Several years ago those rules were considerably relaxed, allowing Communion more than once.

The *Code of Canon Law* simply says that anyone who has received the Eucharist may receive it again on the same day only during a eucharistic celebration. (CCL 917) In 1984 the Vatican Commission for Interpretation of Canon Law ruled that even at Mass, Communion should not be received more than twice a day.

The church knows from experience that some Catholics are tempted to treat sacred things, even the Mass, in a superstitious manner. I once knew a lady who proudly and piously claimed she attended 11 Masses — at least the "essential parts" — every Sunday.

To prevent people from collecting Communions in a similar fashion was one reason for the church's stricter once-a-day rule in the past, as well as for the clear, if broader, policy today. It trusts that people's deeper and fuller awareness of the meaning of the Eucharist will discourage any abuse and at the same time prompt them to receive Communion whenever it is appropriate — even more than once a day.

First Communion before confession?

My grandchildren attend a parish in our city where children cannot go to confession until after they receive first Communion. I think that is wrong. How can the teachers and priests there do that?

I have come to believe just about anything is possible, but I seriously doubt that any parish follows a policy that forbids first penance before first Communion. It would be extremely difficult to defend such a position.

Recent documents from Vatican congregations remind us that "When he arrives at the age of discretion, the child has the right, in the church, to receive both sacraments (penance and Eucharist)." There should be no "general rule" anywhere requiring reception of holy Communion before the first reception of the sacrament of penance. (On First Confession and First Communion, from the Congregations for the Sacraments and Divine Worship, and for the Clergy, March 31, 1977)

This means that as a child reaches the age of reason, he has a right as a Catholic to be instructed at his own level about the sacrament of forgiveness by his parents or teacher, and he has the right to an opportunity to receive this sacrament.

Perhaps that parish, as many or most other parishes, provides assistance to children and parents to prepare for both penance and the Eucharist, and then urges parents to present their children when they are ready for either one. In other words, in those parishes children are not *required* to receive the sacrament of penance before first Communion.

Children do have a right to receive the Eucharist as soon as they are aware of the basic doctrines and have a desire to receive. There's the famous story of Pope St. Pius X (called "the Pope of the Eucharist") who offered Mass one day for a group of pilgrims. While giving Communion, he came to a six-year-old boy whose parents said, "Holy Father, he is not yet old enough to receive." The pope turned to the boy, held up the host, and said, "Who is this?" The child answered, "That is Jesus."

"He knows enough," said the pope, and gave the boy his first Communion.

The traditional discipline of the church, stated in the Council of Trent and restated in present law, requires sacramental confession before Communion only when one is conscious of a grave (mortal) sin. (canons 916, 988, 989) How this traditional Catholic discipline applies to children receiving first Communion is affected by another law which says parents and pastors should "see that children who have reached the use of reason are correctly prepared and nourished by the divine food as early as possible, preceded by sacramental confession." (c. 914)

Many customs developed concerning the sequence of these two sacraments during recent centuries, especially in light of the practice of very infrequent Communion in the time of the Jansenistic heresies and after. Many Catholics still alive remember when even outstanding members of the faith received Communion two or three times a year, and confession automatically preceded Communion every time. Naturally, first Communion would be no exception.

As the congregations indicate, children have a right to both penance and the Eucharist, and this right must be honored in accord with solid traditional doctrine of the church concerning these sacraments.

Can infants receive Communion?

Our new Catholic neighbors have several children, teenagers and up. Their mother told me that all their children received first Communion when they were infants, before they came to this country. How is this possible?

If her children did indeed receive holy Communion as infants, I suspect the family is a member of one of the Eastern Rite Catholic Churches.

For many centuries, until about the year 1200, babies were given holy Communion immediately after baptism, at which time they were also confirmed. In other words, the three sacraments of initiation — baptism, confirmation and the Eucharist — were commonly ministered all at one time. Certain Eastern churches continue that custom.

When you have a chance, check with your neighbor. If her husband belongs to an Eastern rite, chances are that all the children do also (CCL 111), in which case they would have received their Christian initiation according to that rite.

Communion for semi-comatose

Can a semi-comatose person receive Communion? My son was in an accident which resulted in a badly broken leg. Three months later he had surgery to remove the body cast, but something happened. Now he can open his eyes and move his head. He hears, but we do not know if he understands, though we feel he does. Doctors say he has brain damage, but we will not know how much he can understand until he comes out of the coma.

As his mother, I feel he should be given the benefit of the doubt that he knows what is going on, at least to a degree, but just cannot communicate his feelings. Why should this young man be denied Communion? Those I talk with all seem to give me a different answer. The situation has been going on for nearly a year.

Not having talked with any of the priests or doctors involved, I can answer only from the information you give. Judging from what you have described, I feel as you do, that there is some reason to suspect your son might have enough consciousness to be aware, at least to some degree, that he is receiving Communion and that there's nothing lost in trying.

I'm assuming from what you say about Communion that he does take some food or drink through the mouth. The Eucharist should never be administered intravenously but, if he can eat or drink anything, he could receive the Eucharist.

As you hint in your letter, it is by no means an unusual medical experience for a patient to be able to hear and understand certain things without being able to respond in even the slightest way — a hand squeeze or blink of an eye, for example. This fact, of course, remains unknown until the patient recovers fuller consciousness.

I suggest you sit down again with one of the priests who knows the situation and discuss it thoroughly. Your son's tragedy must be a terrible suffering for you as well as for him, and I'm sure any priest will be willing to do all he can to help you both.

What is spiritual Communion?

What exactly is a spiritual Communion? I am a convert, and an older Catholic tells me that we receive the same graces from this as from actually going to Communion. Is this true?

A spiritual Communion is a conscious, serious internal act of desire to receive holy Communion, or more specifically, to have the union with our Lord that normally accompanies the proper reception of this sacrament. It can be made in one's own words or thoughts, and those who prayerfully desire Communion with Jesus in this way enjoy the blessings and helps of the sacrament itself.

One hears less about spiritual Communion today because of the comparative frequency with which the Eucharist is actually received at Mass. Spiritual reception of Communion began to be quite common 800 or 900 years ago when holy Communion was received rarely, perhaps only a few times during one's lifetime. In this kind of atmosphere, formal spiritual Communions could naturally play a much larger role in one's spiritual life.

Such Communion "by desire" is still good, of course. But much of its spiritual significance is absorbed today by the richer understanding of the sacrifice of the Eucharist, and its proper influence in our daily prayer and work.

Particles of the Eucharist

Isn't there danger of desecrating the host from particles falling on the lips, hands, clothing, pews, or floor after Communion? What should one do about such fears?

It is Catholic doctrine that Jesus Christ is present in the Eucharist as long as the reasonable appearance of bread and wine is there. The traditional theological phrase is that Christ is present "under the species of bread and wine." The Latin word *species* means "that which can be seen," or "that which makes manifest."

Thus, when the species of bread or wine are no longer there, as for example in almost microscopic crumbs, the body of Christ is no longer present. The church wants us to deal with the sacraments with the eyes of faith, but also in a common sense, human manner. Don't worry about tiny particles that "may" have fallen and adhered to clothing or fingers. This kind of scrupulosity is unnecessary and actually distracts from the attitude of love and devotion that should surround our reception of the Eucharist.

Should only priests give Communion?

I was taught in a Catholic school that the priest's hands, and his right thumb and forefinger, were especially blessed for handling the body of Christ and dispensing Communion. If this is so, how can nuns and lay people give Communion?

I am still not sure about the idea of receiving the body of Christ in my hands. It seems to me it should be placed on one's tongue. Can you clear this up? I don't necessarily dislike it; I just don't understand.

Contrary to what many Catholics report they were taught, it was never true that the priest's thumb and finger were anointed in order that he might "handle the body of Christ." The symbolism of placing oil on a person, whether at baptism, confirmation, or ordination, is not intended as a particular sanctification of that part of the body. It signifies that the entire person is consecrated and dedicated to an exalted position as a member of the family of Christ.

Jesus himself is said to be anointed by the Father; in fact, that is the meaning of the word Christ, one who has been christened or anointed to a role and mission of particular dignity.

Certainly a focal part of that mission for the ordained priest is to preside at the eucharistic liturgy and make possible for the rest of the Christian people, and celebrate with them, the unbloody renewal of the death and resurrection of our Lord. The anointing, however, is not directly related to giving Communion anymore than it is to the forgiveness of sins, or any other priestly function. This point is particularly clear from the fact that for 1,200 years or so, it was common for any Christian to give Communion to any other Christian. People took Communion in their hands at Mass, gave it to each other, and even took the Eucharist home to family or friends who could not be present at Mass.

Within the past several centuries, in an effort to counteract certain heresies which denied the real presence of Jesus in the Eucharist, the church gradually built up the detailed prohibitions we learned about not touching the host. When I was small (in the 1930s), we were taught that it was seriously sinful to touch not only the host itself, but even the chalice and ciborium in which the host and consecrated wine were contained.

We now know, however, that such prohibitions did not reflect (as we then assumed) what the church had "always" done, and that they involved nothing essential to Catholic doctrine or practice.

You are never, of course, forced to receive Communion in your hand if you do not wish to do so. There's always the option to receive either way. Frankly it seems to me that the hand is no less holy than the tongue. The incredible fact is that Jesus gives us his body and blood as our spiritual food and drink in the first place. From that viewpoint, at least, to make a big deal out of which part of our body touches the host first appears to me to be supremely ridiculous.

Communion on the tongue?

When and why did the church originate receiving Communion on the tongue? It does not seem likely that the bread was distributed in this manner at the Last Supper.

You are right. Communion was received in the hand for about the first 1,000 years of Christian history. It was only in the late Middle Ages, generally in the 10th and 11th centuries, that the change was made, about the same time that the use of unleavened bread became common in the celebration of the Eucharist. The reason seems to have been a feeling that receiving directly in the mouth was somehow more reverent.

By this time, the practice of receiving Communion very infrequently, perhaps once a year or less, had become well accepted. Reception of the Eucharist by anyone but the priest had become so rare that missals of that period don't even mention Communion for lay people. Related to this decline, various customs developed with the intention of emphasizing the separation and distance between God (Jesus Christ) and ourselves. Receiving Communion on the tongue was one of them. The elevation during Mass, introduced into the liturgy much later (about the year 1200) was another.

The same reason, a sense of reverence as well as history, inspired a return to Communion in the hand in our own century. Sticking out one's tongue is not usually considered a sign of respect in our age; extending one's hand was again seen as a sign of openness and acceptance of the gift God gives us in the Eucharist.

Our present ritual for receiving in the hand is patterned after that prescribed in the Jerusalem Catecheses about the year 400. Not everyone has the same feelings about this, of course. Thus the church today provides the option for each communicant.

The "reverence" of outstretched hands

A member of our parish tells us he has it on good authority that when Communion is received standing, liturgical law requires that one genuflect before receiving. That's news to me. I've only seen it done two or three times. Is that now a rule for going to Communion?

I don't know who his authority was supposed to be, but there is no such requirement. The General Instruction of the Roman Missal says only that communicants should make a suitable reverence before responding "Amen" to the words "the body of Christ." It has the same notation twice. (160) This reverence might be a genuflection, of course, but it could also be several other actions, such as a bow.

The point has been made, very fittingly I believe, that the most expressive act of reverence before Communion is the one the vast majority of people already use, holding out their hands.

For most of the human race, outstretched hands are a powerful symbol of nearly all those things we want to say to God as we come to receive the body of Christ. Whether it's a child standing before his parents, a starving mother in Rwanda, or ourselves before the eucharistic Lord, open hands held out to someone express our desire and need for what that person has to give.

Open hands also proclaim other feelings in our hearts at that time: Our hunger and reverence for the gift we ask, our trust that the giver will give it, humility in acknowledging total dependence on what we will receive, praise and thanks for the generosity of the one who offers the gift, and much more.

As a priest, I admit to being deeply moved by this eloquent gesture every time I give Communion. It's hard to imagine any other action capable of carrying such a weight of spiritual meaning for approaching Communion. As a bonus, it is also unobtrusive and does not call attention to oneself.

Some may object that this sounds fine, but how many think of all this every time they receive the Eucharist? It's true, of course, that we need to be always more conscious of why we do what we do. But one might make that same objection about a kiss or hug. What husband and wife reflect consciously on the deep meanings of these actions every time they say hello or goodbye? Whether they do or not, however, the meaning remains and inevitably achieves its effect when such acts are done in a context of love and devotion.

It's the same with open hands extended in prayer and hope. This nearly universal gesture in its own way accomplishes what it symbolizes, humbleness and hunger.

Is Communion in the hand "evil"?

You say that extending our hands to receive Jesus could be a meaningful symbol of trust, openness and desire for the Eucharist, among other things. Don't you know you are contradicting Mother Teresa? According to a magazine I receive, a priest in New York asked Mother Teresa what is the most destructive and evil thing in the world today. She answered, receiving Communion in the hand. Why are you and the church at odds with such a holy person?

I received several letters quoting the same priest and the same periodical about Mother Teresa. I continue to be amazed by people's gullibility. Can you honestly imagine Mother Teresa, who saw and cared for the worst misery this earth can contrive, saying that Communion in the hand is the biggest evil in the world?

After a while, the volume of mail prompted me to ask an official of her community about it. Her answer: The Missionaries of Charity respect the freedom given by the church to receive Communion either on the tongue or in the hand. Their usual practice is to receive on the tongue, but they are free to receive in the hand.

Obviously Mother Teresa did not consider it the greatest evil. Regardless of that, some will continue to believe anything, no matter how ridiculous, if it's what they want to believe.

Priest receives Communion last?

When my family sat down to dinner, my father always waited to be served until his wife and children had taken what they needed. I've seen other families do this, too.

Why does the priest "eat," receive Communion, first at Mass? As the host, shouldn't he give Communion first to the parishioners and then receive himself? It may be a trivial question, but I have seen this done twice, and it impressed me.

I have also attended Masses when the priest received Communion last. The practice could seem appropriate and commendable if one judged it from the perspective you suggest. In my judgment, however, and obviously in the judgment of the church through the ages, there is something lacking in that perspective.

The "host" at the eucharistic sacrifice and sacrament, the one who invites and welcomes and feeds us, is not the priest celebrant, but the same one who was host at the Last Supper, Jesus Christ himself. The Eucharistic Prayers, in fact the whole Liturgy of the Eucharist, clearly assume this truth more often than one could count.

The banquet is his, accomplished by the power of his Spirit, just as the eternal banquet in the kingdom of God, which eucharistic communion prefigures and anticipates, belongs to him. In every consecration it is Jesus who says, "Take this and eat." It is he who forms those who are nourished by his body and blood into "an everlasting gift" to the heavenly Father (Eucharistic Prayer III). And it is his Spirit who gathers "all who share this one bread and one cup into the one body of Christ," making those who receive it "a living sacrifice of praise" (Eucharistic Prayer IV).

Obviously, the liturgical tradition of the church bends over backward to be sure the fact is not missed, that the origin and soul and climax of the Eucharist is the risen Lord himself.

Your question is not trivial at all. Some funny things are said occasionally today about "whose" Mass it is we celebrate. The proclamation we hear just before Communion helps keep everyone's attitudes and actions in proper perspective: "Happy are those who are called to his supper."

Communion after remarriage

If even non-Catholics can go to Communion sometimes in our church, why is it that divorced people cannot? We are members of the church, we believe in the Eucharist, and we're trying to do what's right. It hurts very much not to be able to receive the Eucharist, and we need it maybe more than the others do.

I hope you are aware that simply being divorced is no obstacle to holy Communion. I assume from your letter that you are remarried; if you are not, nothing prevents your reception of Communion if the usual other conditions are fulfilled.

If one is divorced and remarried, it becomes an entirely different problem.

By present church law, divorced and remarried Catholics are unable to receive the Eucharist. Without getting too complicated, it must be noted that the church is seriously concerned about moving toward a more understanding and open stance in relation to such Catholics. It recognizes the difficulty and delicacy of the effort to accomplish this without compromising its belief in the permanence of marriage, as well as its convictions about the Eucharist being a sign of unity and faith which has, at least to some degree, been broken by the individual's remarriage in contradiction to the laws of the church.

It seems to me we are experiencing an increasing awareness of the need to recognize that at least many divorced and remarried Catholics are in the present circumstances of their lives still members of the church who spend themselves generously for their spouses and their children. They are doing all they are morally capable of doing to live as good Catholic Christians.

The American bishops acknowledged the urgency of this question and the possibility of its being resolved when they requested the removal of excommunication for divorced and remarried Catholics. The church cannot recognize the second marriage as valid, they said, nor does their move concerning excommunication "of itself" (an important phrase) permit remarried Catholics to receive Communion. This "most difficult question — return to full eucharistic Communion — can be resolved," explained the bishops, "only in a limited number of instances, depending on particular circumstances."

Bishops of many other countries share this very serious pastoral concern.

Clearly, much more reflection on the subject can be expected. In the meantime, I suggest you take the bishops' advice to remarried Catholics: "Take the next step by approaching parish priests and diocesan tribunals to see whether their return to full Eucharistic Communion is possible" by this route.

(Quotes are from the statement of the American bishops when they petitioned the pope in May, 1977, to rescind the excommunication of divorced and remarried Catholics which had been in force in the United States since 1884.)

Rash judgments about remarried

You stated that by present church law, divorced and remarried Catholics are unable to receive the Eucharist. You give the impression that this is just church law.

I thought it was divine law that we had to be in the state of grace to go to Communion. People who were validly married, got divorced and are now remarried are objectively in the state of mortal sin. That condition lasts until they are willing to give up their sinful relationship. How can you say such people may at some time be able to receive Communion?

You are right in everything you say. You omit, however, some critical additional truths which you have apparently forgotten.

One essential requirement for serious (mortal) sin is that individuals deliberately remain attached to that sin, or deliberately remain in a sinful situation from which they are morally capable of removing themselves. Those last words are important. They mean that the person must have not only a theoretical possibility, but a real honest-to-God choice available for getting out of the situation that is objectively sinful. If he does not have such a choice, it cannot automatically be declared that he is in what you call the "state of mortal sin."

The very case you protest, in fact, that of a divorced and remarried Catholic, might present one of the more apt examples of such a condition. Let's suppose a Catholic woman is divorced and remarried contrary to the laws of the church. Fifteen years later, she knows she has done something wrong and wants to do everything possible to get straight with God. By now, however, there are four growing children living in what appears to be a good home with a reasonably happy and stable mother and father. By every human appearance and judgment, at least, the children are dependent upon both parents for the right fulfillment of their basic social, physical, psychological and perhaps even religious needs.

I know of almost no moral theologians and very few, if any, parish priests who would claim that this woman has a serious moral obligation to break up her home, take her children (if she can) and divorce her husband so she can get back to Communion. In fact, most agree today more than ever that the very suggestion of such a solution is grotesque.

(I will not discuss here such solutions as a brother-sister relationship between the husband and wife, which are increasingly recognized as having limited validity in such situations. At any rate, they are private matters between the couple and are therefore irrelevant as to how that marriage looks to outsiders.)

From this it should be obvious that to view all couples in a divorced and remarried relationship as living in mortal sin is plain and simple rash judgment. Admittedly not all such relationships are the same or equivalent to the one example I give, but this type of situation is by no means uncommon.

We should be careful not to pass judgment. It is well to remember Christ's words: "Be compassionate, as your Father is compassionate. Do not judge, and you will not be judged. Do not condemn, and you will not be condemned. Pardon, and you shall be pardoned." (Luke 6:37)

The absolute prohibition against divorced and remarried Catholics receiving the sacraments is a church law, or, if you wish, the church's interpretation and application of a divine law. In taking this stand, the church must consider many factors, such as preserving clearly its teachings on the permanence of marriage, and the meaning of the Eucharist as an expression of faith and unity with the church.

The fact remains, however, that this prohibition is open to change or mitigation by the church, with no violence done to divine law concerning the Eucharist.

As for those of us who are not directly involved in a situation like this, we should remember that every case is different and there may be many aspects of a case that for reasons of justice or privacy cannot be explained to anyone else. In other words, we ought to just plain mind our own business and remember that God is perfectly capable of watching out for his own interests.

It should be enough for us to hope, and be thankful, that a fellow Christian may be able to work out something that can give peace of soul to himself and his loved ones.

Former Catholics who receive Communion

Our son and his wife left the Catholic Church a few years ago. They have two sons, now ages 10 and 12. These boys were baptized Catholic, but never made their first Communion. Recently they visited in our home, and all four of them received Communion, including from the cup. The daughter-in-law says this is a matter between them and God. How do we respond to that?

I assume you and, from what you tell me, probably your son's family are basically aware of the Catholic Church's policy on interfaith Communion in the church (see chapter on ecumenism). So let's talk about the personal issues that concern you.

You might remind them that they left the Catholic Church on their own initiative, which, if it says anything, says they wanted to separate themselves from Catholic belief and worship. Thus, what they are doing directly abuses the hospitality of the church and is at very least a thoughtless discourtesy. One would not act in such a way with former friends. No one would say, "I don't want to be part of your life," and then drop in for a meal whenever he or she felt like it.

Of course you cannot physically stop them if they persist. You do, however, have a right to tell them how their actions hurt you and violate what you believe. You can also ask them some obvious and honest questions:

- If you choose not to be a Catholic and say you don't believe what we believe, why do you feel you can drift in and out?
- If you believe the Eucharist is the body and blood of Christ, why aren't you Catholic?
- If you do not believe in the Catholic faith, why do you act as if you do?
- If you do believe, how can you not raise your children Catholic?

Whatever you do, just explain, don't accuse them. No "How could you do this to us?" Or even, "How could you do this to God?" You cannot know their hearts, but questions such as these may help them become more honest and above board with themselves than they seem to be right now. Of course, these concerns need to be addressed sensitively and lovingly, so your family doesn't become even more alienated, not only from the church, but perhaps even from you.

Easter duty

Is the obligation of the Easter duty (going to confession and Communion between the first Sunday of Lent and Pentecost) still in effect? What happened to that very strict ruling?

Basically the obligation of annual Communion during the Easter time still exists. According to church law, all the faithful who have received first Communion should receive the Eucharist at least once a year. Unless something serious stands in the way, this should be done during the Easter time which, as you mention, lasts from the beginning of Lent to Pentecost. (CCL 920)

The obligation for the sacrament of penance during that period is still as it always has been, binding only if it is necessary for an individual to be able to receive the Eucharist.

The *Code of Canon Law* (CCL 989) states that all who have reached the age of reason are obliged to confess any serious sins once a year. In this law, however, as in past similar statements, the church does not intend to impose a new obligation for confession, but simply to prescribe a time within which mortal sins should be confessed so that, if for no other reasons, the Eucharist might be received. Thus, the law does not apply to anyone who is not aware of an unconfessed mortal sin.

It bears repeating, though, that this law deals with the minimum required. By no means does it recommend receiving the sacrament of penance only once a year, or only when one is conscious of serious sin. The healing, forgiving and strengthening powers of this sacrament are such that it should be, in some way, a regular part of our spiritual lives as Catholics.

Treating people with compassion

Could you please tell us confused Catholics whether the church requires one to be in the state of grace before taking holy Communion? I continually see hundreds go to Communion, but only tens go to confession. Am I to assume:

1. *Confession is no longer required after mortal sin before receiving Communion?*
2. *People go to Communion knowing they are not in the state of grace.*
3. *The rules have been changed by the church concerning confession, Communion and grace.*
4. *The church quietly is closing its eyes and saying little or nothing, as in our parish.*

My suspicions are strengthened by the once or twice a year drive to get people to the confessional, while never mentioning weekly or monthly confessions or the need for them.

I understand your question, and am sorry that a preoccupation with the number of people that go to Communion as opposed to those going to confession troubles you so. Times when pastors published the number of Communion hosts dispensed and the number of people who went to confession, or who attended novenas or offered spiritual bouquets of certain prayers, are long gone.

Of course church rules have not changed about either sacrament, and the church is not "quietly closing its eyes" and saying nothing. I would suggest, as gently as I can, that you might be leaning toward rash judgment of the people you feel "go to Communion knowing they are not in the state of grace."

I might suggest further that you ease up on your worry. God sees what is in their hearts, as he does indeed see what is in yours. Try to see these people in a more compassionate light and make no judgment about the state of their souls. That's up to God.

Communion for mentally handicapped

A child in our neighborhood is attending school for the mentally handi-capped and cannot remember her prayers, so she never made her first Communion. She is 12 years old. May she receive Communion when she attends Mass on Sunday with her guardian?

The more basic question is why she has not made her first Communion. Mentally handicapped children often cannot memorize prayers. By no means does it follow that he or she cannot grasp enough of the meaning of Communion to receive this sacrament. If she is attending school, she surely is able to achieve some knowledge of Jesus and understand that she receives him in Communion.

I hope you will encourage her guardian to talk with a priest. If someone can pray very simply with her and help her understand at her own level what she is doing, she should be receiving the Eucharist regularly.

Communion for Alzheimer's patients

I am the major care-giver for an Alzheimer's patient in our family and need to know whether he can receive Communion. I get conflicting an-swers; one priest is reluctant to bring him the sacrament because "he doesn't really know what is going on." My brother is, as they say, in the later mid-stages of the disease, and of course is regressing regularly. But I am convinced he is sometimes more aware of "what is going on" than we think. Is there a rule about this? I think that, even in his condition, re-ceiving Communion would be a big help.

Your instincts and experience agree with all that is known about Alzheimer's sufferers, especially in the later and final stages. The loss of memory and cognitive abilities, which so distresses and frustrates care-givers like yourself, is not the whole story of what can be going on deep inside.

Even when they cannot speak intelligibly or rationally, or grasp verbal communications, many, perhaps most, of these patients can experience through their senses much that seems to open up parts of their lives that seemed lost in permanent darkness.

Just before a recent Christmas, a group of 60 Alzheimer's patents attended a church service in California. Many of them could not say their own names, but from somewhere inside they found the words to sing "Silent Night" and "Joy to the World."

Experiences that reach the senses of hearing and touch sometimes seem especially able to surface memories long lost to consciousness. In my own experience, Catholics in the later stages of the disease may unexpectedly remember the sign of the cross, or accompany someone praying the Our Father or Hail Mary. Visiting familiar places like their church, hearing stories of where they have been and what they have done, is often a big help.

In light of all this, it seems presumptuous to refuse Communion to Alzheimer's patients as long as they are physically able to receive. There is no way one could legitimately presume that the patient is incapable of receiving the Eucharist with sufficient awareness and spiritual benefit.

When it comes to the sacraments, the church's position is, and has been, to always give people the benefit of any doubt, and leave it to God to sort out. We are ignorant of too many factors to take that judgment on ourselves.

Finally, I hope you are taking advantage of every opportunity to keep yourself fed, spiritually and emotionally. Caring for Alzheimer's patients is arguably the most draining and exhausting task one can have, and it cannot be done without a load of continuing help and support.

Fortunately, varieties of printed and other resources are available for such assistance. Most larger communities today list an Alzheimer's Association chapter in the phone book. National headquarters are at 919 N. Michigan Ave., Chicago, IL, 60611-1676. Phone 800-272-3900. Their web site is www.alz.org.

Communion should be ministered

As a parish priest I see conflicting practices concerning Communion under both species. I've seen the chalice left on the altar; each person came, picked up the chalice and drank from it. At other times, Communion ministers have given the chalice to the people. Do you know if both of these practices are correct? What is the rule?

The chalice should never be left on the altar for each individual communicant to pick up and drink. The theology and entire symbolism of the Communion rite require that the Eucharist be "ministered" to the individual communicants.

Regulations on giving Communion are clear on this. It is no more correct to receive Communion from the chalice this way than it would be to receive the bread by just picking it up from the ciborium on the altar.

The church is so conscious of the need for ministering the Eucharist that it provides an emergency procedure when not enough ministers are present at a particular Mass. When sufficient eucharistic ministers are lacking for some reason, the priest may appoint suitable persons who in case of necessity would distribute Communion for the occasion. (*Immensae Caritatis*, 1973, instruction of the Sacred Congregation for Divine Worship and General Instruction of the Roman Missal 162) A brief commissioning ceremony for that particular situation is given in the same document.

Just as the minister of the host holds the host and says, "The body of Christ," the minister of the chalice presents the cup to the communicant and says, "The blood of Christ." The communicant answers, "Amen."

Ministering the Eucharist

I am an extraordinary eucharistic minister. During a recent workshop we were told that when we give Communion we should look at the person, smile and say "the body of Christ," then wait until the person says "Amen" and give the host.

One priest, however, says we should not even have eye contact. He quoted someone who said, "Look at the host. You came to receive the body of Christ, not to visit with the celebrant. The gift is more important than the one who delivers it."

Liturgical regulations require that Communion be "ministered," not just picked up from the altar, for example, precisely because this or any other sacrament is not only a transcendent divine activity, it is also a human interaction between two members of the Body of Christ.

We must continually reflect both of those realities, Pope Paul VI said, "if we wish to keep the celebration of the sacraments from deteriorating into an almost superstitious formalism" (Address to Rome priests, 1970)

Any eucharistic minister, priest or otherwise, always should be keenly conscious of a truth that has awed theologians from the early fathers of the church on: The person to whom we are ministering the Body of Christ is already the Body of Christ, both individually and ecclesially. The church itself is present already both in the minister of the sacrament and in the recipient, says the Rite for Anointing the Sick (no. 40).

St. Augustine, commenting on the "tremendous import" of St. Paul's words that we, though many, are one bread, one body, says to his people, "By the grace of redemption, you are already that which you receive" in the Eucharist. In Communion, in other words, the Body of Christ gives the Body of Christ to the Body of Christ.

In light of truths like that, how can we possibly pretend detached uninvolvement when we invite a fellow member of our faith community to one of the greatest experiences of faith either of us can ever have?

Perhaps a core of the problem is your last statement about the gift being more important than the one who delivers it. Who, after all, is the one who "delivers" it if not Christ himself? That also is a truth held most sacred in Christian tradition. Jesus Christ is present in the sacramental liturgy in the person of his minister, says Vatican Council II, quoting Augustine, "so that when a man baptizes it is really Christ himself who baptizes."

"Rightly then," the council continues, "the liturgy is considered as an exercise of the priestly office of Jesus Christ" (Constitution on the Liturgy, no. 7).

Thus perhaps the best question a minister of the Eucharist might ask is: How would Jesus himself do it if he were the one standing here in his own physical person? I can't believe he would do it without visibly expressing in some genuine way the warmth, joy and intimacy of life he shares with the one standing before him.

Give name before Communion?

Some priests and other ministers of holy Communion use the name of the communicant before saying "the body of Christ" or "the blood of Christ." I have done this myself at retreats where I know the names of everyone. I do not feel it is pastorally appropriate at a parish Mass where the priests or ministers do not know the names of all who will receive Communion.

The practice seems to create an "in group" and "out group" and thus to be divisive at the very time we should be most united. I find it especially "cruel" at a school Mass and only a few in each class are named, usually the more popular and endearing children.

What is the official stand on this, or what seems appropriate to you as one more aware of pastoral practice than I am. If at any time we ought to be treated alike and no distinctions made, it is at Communion. I have also seen priests carry on conversations with people who approach them for Communion, even stoop down to speak playfully to children while holding the Communion plate in the other hand. Any comment on that?

Apart from the general and specific liturgical principles concerning integrity of the liturgy text, I know of no regulation that would directly govern this situation. Some feel these principles are broad enough to accommodate the practice you speak of, others do not.

Directives which guide our behavior as liturgical ministers indicate that we are not to minister the sacraments like robots. Along with the other sacraments, holy Communion should be administered in a human, friendly, warm and responsive manner, consistent with that sense of dignity, reverence, and as you well note, impartiality, which should always characterize any minister of the liturgy.

It seems to me the practice of giving names at Communion goes a little over the edge of inappropriate familiarity and camaraderie at Communion time. Be that as it may, it certainly too often goes over the edge of inappropriate partiality. It may perhaps be appropriate on certain special occasions. As you indicate, however, the wrong impression can easily be, and I know for a fact sometimes is, conveyed. Obviously, nothing should happen during Mass, most particularly at Communion time, which appears to give recognition and affirmation to one group to the exclusion of others. Almost inevitably this is what happens when peoples' names are used at Communion, particularly in a parish or other broad community Mass.

This is the main reason I never do it, and appears to be the reason you as a pastor are sensitive and concerned. The same ideas are relevant to the last part of your question. This type of interplay does nothing for the sanctity of the Communion rite.

In an increasing number of parishes and dioceses in the country, young children and others who are not receiving Communion, non-Catholic spouses and parents for example, approach the Communion minister with arms crossed over the breast to receive a brief blessing. This means a great deal spiritually to a lot of people. The simple ceremony, however, should be brief and straightforward. It should never degenerate into the kinds of things you describe. I have a suspicion that what you observed was not this type of Communion blessing. Those I have seen always reflected an obviously sincere dignity and reverence.

When host is dropped

Does the Catholic Church still have the dry sink where the dropped host was put directly into the ground? It seems now the priest picks it up and keeps on going.

It was never suggested, or even proper, for a consecrated host to be disposed of in the sacrarium, which is the proper name for the sink you speak of. Many churches have such a place leading directly into the ground to dispose of holy water, for example, which should not be poured into the common sewer.

The consecrated Bread and Wine, however, are never treated that way as long as the appearance of bread or wine is still present. If the priest does not feel comfortable distributing a host to someone after it has fallen to the floor, he may keep it and consume it himself later.

CHAPTER 5

BAPTISM AND CONFIRMATION

ᕙ

Qualifications for baptism sponsors

I have several questions referring to Catholic baptism. Must there always be two Catholic adults to act as godparents, or is one Catholic adult and one non-Catholic sufficient? Or is either one required to be a Catholic? Is there any age requirement?

The rules of the church in these matters are very clear. At least one Catholic sponsor is required at a Catholic baptism. According to the Rite of Baptism, the requirements for a single sponsor are mainly that the sponsor:

1. be mature enough to take the responsibility to testify to the faith of an adult convert, or to profess with the parents the church's faith when a child is being baptized;
2. be able to help the parents as necessary to bring up the child as a good Christian;
3. have received the sacraments of baptism, confirmation, and the Eucharist;
4. be a member of the Catholic church who is living a life in harmony with that faith and with the role of sponsor;
5. be at least 16 years of age, unless an exception is made for a special reason, and,
6. not be the father or mother of the one to be baptized. (CCL 874)

   If there is only one sponsor, that sponsor may be a man or woman, regardless of the sex of the child. If there are two, it should be one of each sex. (CCL 873)

Sponsors for Catholic, Protestant baptisms

I've heard that Catholics may be sponsors at Protestant baptisms, and Protestants at Catholic baptisms. Is that true? We get differing answers from priests.

When only one Catholic sponsor is assigned, a baptized non-Catholic Christian may stand in place of the second sponsor. However, this non-Catholic is not a godparent in the canonical sense of the word; he or she is officially referred to as a "Christian witness" to the baptism.

Similarly, a Catholic may stand in as a Christian witness for a person being baptized in another Christian denomination, along with a sponsor of that denomination.

Since all the above is explicit Catholic policy around the world, you shouldn't be receiving conflicting information from priests. Perhaps some of them are not familiar with church regulations on the subject, particularly in the Introduction to the Rite of Baptism itself and in the Directory for Ecumenical Matters of March 25, 1993, n. 92-98.

Though parents do hold the primary obligation for the religious upbringing of their children, baptismal sponsors are by no means without their own responsibilities unless the parents die. The baptism ceremony, in fact, directly asks the godparents if they are willing to help the parents in their duties as mother and father. This help may be given in various ways: By moral support to the parents, by staying close to their godchild in showing interest in his spiritual development, by perhaps a small gift on the anniversary of birth or baptism.

The Introduction to the Rite of Baptism beautifully states that the godparent is added spiritually to the immediate family of the one to be baptized and to represent Mother Church. As occasion offers, he or she will be ready to help the parents bring up their child to profess the faith, and to show this by living it.

Baptism sponsors

I could not believe what I read in your column concerning requirements for sponsors at confirmation and baptism. In the 1920s when I was a child, I was called by the priests next door to us to be a godmother for a dying baby, or for a baby whose parents knew no one to stand up at the baptism.

The priest assured me I had no obligation. It was an act of love and compassion. In the 1950s I was sponsor for a poor little girl who knew no one to be her sponsor. The priest said, "God will give you graces." According to what you say, I could never have been a sponsor in those situations.

You were thoughtful to offer your help and support in these situations. I'm sure the priest appreciated it, as I have when similar situations arose in my own pastoral ministry.

The responses I gave reflect the procedures for the sacraments defined by the church for normal circumstances. Even today the church leaves much to the judgment of the people involved in emergencies or in the special types of cases you describe.

We must remember, too, that the situation today is vastly different than it was in the 1920s or 1950s. In those days the assumption was much more common, whether or not it was actually justified, that parents would exercise their responsibilities amidst a relatively supportive community of relatives, friends and others of their faith. These so-called support groups often made the obligations of godparents much simpler.

However valid these assumptions may have been previously, the church today, both clergy and laity, recognizes that such close supportive relationships are simply not available to most families. It is this awareness which prompts the church to be far more concerned about, and to examine more carefully, the intentions and commitments of parents and sponsors in the sacraments of Christian initiation.

Godparent by proxy

We have a baptism coming up in our family. The ones we would like as godparents cannot be at the ceremony since they will be in the military in Germany at that time. Is it possible to have a proxy godparent who would stand in for them?

Previous church law (before 1983) mentions the possibility of proxies at baptism. But no longer. Neither official liturgical books or other church laws now provide for official "proxies" at baptism.

This does not necessarily mean that godparents must be present at the baptism ceremony. While the ritual calls for certain responses from godparents during the baptism, their primary responsibilities toward the child (or adult) can be accepted and carried out without their physical presence at that time.

Even if not present, they must fulfill all requirements for baptism sponsors, and the baptizing minister must have absolute assurance that they intend to accept and fulfill their obligations to the child. Their names will be recorded in the parish baptism record.

Sponsors are not required for validity of baptism. The introduction to the baptism rite for children says: Each child may have a godfather and godmother. Canon law states that insofar as possible the one to be baptized is to be given a sponsor.

Thus, as long as the actual sponsors are qualified and explicitly committed to their responsibilities, there seems to be no reason against another one or two people standing in for them at the ceremony itself, even though they would have no official designation as proxies.

Orthodox godparent

A friend of mine who is Russian Orthodox was recently godmother for her Catholic friend's baby. Is this permissible?

As I explained earlier, in place of a second Catholic baptismal sponsor, a Christian of a Protestant denomination who may be a relative or friend of the family may serve as a Christian witness of the baptism with a Catholic sponsor. A Catholic can do the same for a member of a Protestant denomination. In both cases, of course, the responsibility for the Christian education of the person baptized belongs primarily to the godparent who is a member of the church in which the person is baptized.

An even closer participation is permitted when the person to be baptized is a member of one of the separated Eastern churches, which would include the Russian Orthodox. A member of one of these churches may be godparent, together with a Catholic godparent, at the baptism of a Catholic infant or adult. (Directory Concerning Ecumenical Matters of March 25, 1993, n. 98)

Your friend therefore acted quite properly in being godparent at the baptism, at least according to the regulations of our church. In all such instances the individuals involved from other faiths should be sure that their action is not contrary to the regulations of their own church as well.

Are godparents obsolete?

Recently, I was godmother for a relative's baby. I was disappointed at the baptismal ceremony. As godmother I had no part or say while the baby was being baptized. The mother and father held the infant and stood in the center while the godparents stood beside them.

I don't see why godparents have to be chosen since they are not doing their traditional part.

Apparently you have not had an opportunity to attend a baptism for a good many years. Throughout the renewed ceremony for baptism, the primary responsibility of the parents in the training and education of their children is emphasized far more strongly than in the older rite.

As you indicate, normally the parents hold the child and they make the primary promises for the Catholic upbringing of the child who is baptized. Don't you agree that this is precisely the way it should be?

It may be true that in the ceremony itself godparents take a less active role, though there are several actions and promises that involve them personally. Their primary function always has been, and still is, to support and assist the parents in every way possible as the child grows toward full Christian manhood or womanhood.

If anything, a thoughtful and faithful godparent means more to parents than ever before. Heaven knows, mothers and fathers today need all the help they can get in giving example, support and guidance to their children in the critical years of development. Godparents who take their responsibilities seriously are badly needed by both parents and children.

Maybe you did not get to hold the baby at baptism. I hope you remain conscientious about the much bigger responsibility that is still there.

Changing sponsors

Our child's godfather is no longer Catholic, or Christian of any kind as far as we know. We would like to replace him with another friend of our family. Is that possible?

When a godparent abandons the Catholic faith, the child's parents might understandably wish another person to become godparent, one more likely to care for the child's spiritual welfare.

The Congregation for the Sacraments has acknowledged that very possibility, stating that the bishop of a diocese may officially designate a substitute sponsor, whose name could be inscribed on the official baptismal register. This ruling was sent to bishops in both the United States and Canada. (Reply of November 13, 1984; in 1985 Roman Replies of the Canon Law Society of America)

There may on occasion be a good reason for this kind of official change of godparent. However, as I explained previously, a loving, concerned friend or relative can usually do just as much good for the child without going through all this formality.

Bringing baptized child to church

Some friends recently had a baby who became dangerously ill shortly after birth. A nurse baptized her at the time. Now the baby is to be taken to church for another baptism ceremony. We and the baby's parents are converts to the Catholic faith, and don't quite understand this. We thought that once baptized, always baptized.

There is no second baptism involved here at all. You are correct in that once an individual is baptized a Christian, there is nothing to "add" to it except living out that commitment. A second baptism would do nothing the first valid baptism didn't already do.

About 600 years ago, the church began the practice of "supplying ceremonies" of baptism. As you know if you have attended a Catholic baptism, the liturgy for this sacrament involves many important prayers and symbolic actions.

In the constraints of an emergency baptism, most of these other parts of the rite must be omitted. All there is time for are the essentials, pouring the water and saying the words of baptism. The ceremony for your friends' baby will provide all that was missed.

Your concern is a valid one, however, because people frequently misunderstand this ceremony.

For example, the old form for supplying baptism ceremonies included what is called the exorcism, a graphic excoriation directly addressed to the "accursed devil," ordering him to depart from the children being baptized. Consequently, it was not uncommon for people to believe that emergency baptism was not really effective and that children remained "under the power of Satan" until the exorcism was pronounced later.

In the present baptism ceremony, this "exorcism" has become a prayer addressed to God, asking him and thanking him for the victory over sin and the powers of darkness which we share with Christ through baptism.

At the request of the bishops at Vatican Council II, the Congregation for Divine Worship in 1969 issued a revised Rite for Bringing a Baptized Child to the Church, which makes clear that the child is already a fully baptized member of the church. The whole tone of this new ceremony is different. There is no exorcism. At the beginning, parents are asked, "What do you ask of God's church now that your child has been baptized?" The answer: "We ask that the whole community will know that he/she has been received into the church."

In other words, everything — the anointing, giving of the baptism candle, and so on — is designed to announce and rejoice over the public reception of this new member. Far from superfluous, it is a wonderful way to acknowledge and celebrate an aspect of this sacrament that is easily overshadowed in the usual celebration of this sacrament. By baptism we become, and are accepted as, members of a community of believers, the Body of Christ on earth.

Illegitimate child's father

Our unmarried teenage daughter had a child more than a year ago. Our pastor, a Catholic social worker, and a lawyer said the father's name need not appear on the birth certificate or the baptism certificate.

We moved shortly before the baby was born. The parish priest at the new church insisted that our daughter name the biological father or he would not baptize the child. She was upset, but wanted the child baptized so she named the father.

This still upsets her and she would like to have this man's name removed from the official church record. The biological father was not Catholic and has, in fact, never even seen the child.

You had the correct advice in the beginning. The father's name does not need to appear on the birth certificate or the baptism certificate. To my knowledge, all states require the name of only one parent on the birth certificate.

Neither is the name of the child's father required on the baptism record. In fact any name could be given, which could easily result in serious injustice to innocent people, so in such circumstances the father's name should never be on a baptism record.

There really appears to be only one thing that can be done and that is to write to the bishop and explain the situation. It is possible, however, that at this time even the bishop could not have the name removed.

Blessing after childbirth

What has happened to the "churching of women" ceremony? Years ago in my parish it was given often during the year, but no parish that I know of does it now. Is it still given anywhere?

Part of your answer lies in the history of the ceremony. The churching of women, or the Blessing after Childbirth, apparently entered Christian practice as a carryover from the Jewish ceremony of purification. Under Jewish law, a number of actions incurred spiritual contamination or uncleanness. Among these were any actions involving sexual functions, legal or illegal. A woman was unclean after childbirth, for example, seven days if the child were a boy, and 14 days if the child were a girl. (Leviticus, chapter 12) This uncleanness was formally removed by an appropriate rite of purification. (The purification of Mary after the birth of Jesus is still celebrated by the church as part of the feast of the Presentation on Feb. 2)

In its Christian form, the ceremony took more the theme of thanksgiving to God for the safe birth of the child and petition for God's blessings on the mother and child.

One reason the blessing after childbirth is not more widespread among Christians is that many of its features, prayers and blessings are already implied or included in the rite of baptism. The newly revised baptismal rite contains numerous references to the parents and to what is in their hearts and prayers concerning their new child.

The Catholic Book of Blessings (n. 236) includes a blessing for mothers unable to be at their children's baptism so they might "benefit from the blessing that in the rite of baptism prompts the mother and all present to thank God for the gift of the newborn child."

Baptism by immersion

In discussing renovation plans for our church, the priest is determined to put in a baptismal font large enough for adult immersion. Referring to the difference between immersion and the usual pouring of water, he said: "A strong sacrament makes for a strong Christian. A weak sacrament makes for a weak Christian."

Are you going to tell me that the hundreds of souls who have been baptized here by pouring water were weak Christians? Many parishioners are upset by that statement.

The basic truth I believe your priest was driving at is accurate. His conclusion about the quality of an individual's faith, however, I believe went considerably beyond what he could possibly know. The *Catechism of the Catholic Church* reminds us of an important truth about the sacraments.

All sacramental celebrations are "woven from signs and symbols. In keeping with the divine pedagogy of salvation (that is, God's way of teaching us about his work of saving the human race), their meaning is rooted in the work of creation and in human culture" (No. 1145).

From the beginning, the church has taken that idea seriously. The genuineness and recognizability of material elements used in the sacraments (oil, water, bread, wine, words) are essential if they are to be what they should be, real "signs" of what Jesus Christ accomplishes in us through these rituals.

During the first 800 or 900 years of Christianity, for example, bread used in the Eucharist was the same, or nearly the same, as people ate at other meals. The symbolism of Christ "feeding" us spiritually in this sacrament was obvious. Similarly, Christians were familiar with a number of images about the meaning of baptism. Through it we "put on a new self," like a new garment (Colossians 3:10). We are "enlightened" and taste "the good word of God" (Hebrews 6:45).

The central image, however, was the one indicated by Jesus in the Gospel of John (3:5): We are "born of water and Spirit."

That's the way Paul saw baptism. We were "buried with him (Jesus) through baptism into death, so that, just as Christ was raised from the dead by the glory of the Father, we too might live in newness of life" (Romans 6:4).

Immersion of people being baptized (standing in water, which is then poured over the head of the baptized) was seen as a fuller expression of this burial and rising to new birth. It continued in the church until about the 14th century. Early Christian art and literature reveal that, already in those first decades, baptism by pouring water over the head ("infusion") was also acceptable.

Over the centuries, attempts to define what was "absolutely essential" in the sacraments caused loss of many of these stronger symbols. Eucharistic "bread" became small white wafers, for example.

The church today is attempting to revive awareness and use of genuine, meaningful signs in sacramental liturgies. Eucharistic bread, for instance, should look like "actual food." The same with baptism. Immersion is "more suitable as a symbol of participation in the death and resurrection of Christ" (Christian Initiation, General Introduction, 1969, no. 22).

Most everyone I know who has witnessed this form of baptism has been deeply moved by its powerful symbolism of the meaning of baptism, and of our initiation into the family of Christian believers. Both immersion and infusion are lawful for the Catholic celebration of baptism.

Baptism by pouring only, while it does not carry the same weight of sign and symbolism as immersion, is not what one could call a "weak" sacrament. Neither, as the church's experience proves, does it necessarily produce weak Christians.

Baptism at home?

My husband and I are expecting the birth of our second child. My husband is not baptized, but is deeply religious and attends Mass with the family each Sunday. He feels unable at this time to join the Catholic faith because of personal reservations; I respect his wishes.

We were left with the feeling of celebration after our first child's baptism three years ago. Now we are becoming more active in the parish, but our Catholic friends are scattered all over the city.

We asked the priest who married us, a close family friend for many years, if he would baptize our baby in our home. He agreed, pending approval of our parish pastor. Our pastor, however, says that a baptism can only be conducted in the parish church except in an emergency. What is your opinion?

For us Catholics, our community — or parish — church holds a place of special reverence. It is more than simply a handy building in which to do our religious business. It is literally the home of a parish family, a group of believers who together share their faith in their worship of God, in the celebration of the Eucharist and the other sacraments.

A church building is, therefore, a sign and symbol that reminds us of many things about our religion, not least of which is the responsibility we have for each other in developing and supporting the faith we share together. Admittedly no parish does this perfectly, but it is what we are about and what we aim at trying to be with and for each other.

This explains the church's centuries-old bias for locating important events of our faith in the community's special place of worship. This same conviction is behind its present rules for the celebration of baptism.

These rules are really not that hard to find; they are in the Introduction to the Rite of Baptism for children which any priest, certainly any parish, owns. The regulations that bishops, priests and others are expected to follow are contained there.

According to these guidelines, "so that baptism may clearly appear as the sacrament of the church's faith and of admittance into the people of God, it should normally be celebrated in the parish church."

The bishop, after consulting the local parish priest, may permit baptisms to take place at a baptismal font in another church or public place of worship within the parish boundaries.

The Rite of Infant Baptism states: "Outside a case of necessity, baptism is not to be celebrated in private homes" without the bishop's permission. (n. 12) Except in an emergency or some other pressing pastoral reason, baptisms are not to take place even in hospitals. When such an emergency occurs, the parish priest is responsible for being sure that the parents are "suitably prepared beforehand."

Most priests with whom I am acquainted try to be as considerate and permissive as possible in such situations. However, they do have a responsibility to consider the faith of the individuals involved and the faith of the whole parish family, and to respect the church's instructions for the administration of the sacrament.

Your priest friend will surely be welcome at the ceremony. I hope his presence and the increased familiarity you have gained with some of the people in the parish will help make the baptism of your new baby the joyous celebration it should be for everyone.

Is infant baptism wrong?

Our newspaper had a short article about baptism. Apparently there is a new ceremony for baptizing adult converts. But the article quoted some Catholic authority that infant baptism is wrong and that we shouldn't do it any more. Is this true? Surely we aren't going to stop baptizing babies now?

There is a beautiful rite for initiating an adult into the Christian faith which naturally includes the sacrament of baptism.

I have read quotes of the remarks probably referred to in your letter concerning this new rite. The introduction to the ceremony indicates that this rite is the norm for all initiations into the church. One noted liturgist has, it seems, interpreted this to mean that anything except adult baptism is abnormal.

According to the quote I have seen, he said, "The normative nature of adult initiation means that departures from the norm, while necessary for serious reasons, are always abnormal. Hence indiscriminate infant baptism, while common, is abnormal and should be stopped."

Infant baptism of the children of Christian parents has been a practice of the church almost since its beginning. The psychological and spiritual community of the Christian family was recognized very early. Even though the child was too young to believe on his own, his parents knew they were a "new creation."

Their Christianity was not an incidental frosting on their personality. They believed, as St. Paul said, that for them "To live is Christ." It was only natural, therefore, that their child share from its earliest days in their faith and love — and their baptism.

According to our earliest records, as in Acts 2, perhaps only adults were baptized, though we can't be sure of that. Very soon afterward, however, infants were included, at least as whole families were brought into the church, which seems to have been rather common.

All Eastern and most Western churches consider infant baptism as coming from the very beginning of the Christian era. The great theologian Origen, for example, about the year 280, and St. Augustine (about 400) considered infant baptism a "tradition received from the apostles." St. Irenaeus (about 180), a close friend of St. Polycarp, who in turn knew St. John and the practices in the time of the apostles, took it for granted that infants and children should be baptized along with adolescents and adults. The discoveries of modern psychology concerning the deep spiritual and religious involvement between parents and children seem only to strengthen the wisdom and validity of that tradition.

If, then, our author means to say that the practice of infant baptism in itself is abnormal, I believe he must yet bring forward a good deal of evidence and argument if he expects to make his case.

If, however, by "indiscriminate infant baptism" he simply means that we should not pour the baptismal waters over everyone that comes along, I can only agree with him. But I don't know any priests who do that.

Baptized without permission

My husband became a born-again Christian about two years ago and is deeply involved in the Charismatic Movement.

Friends of ours who are Christian Scientists had a baby recently. My husband baptized their baby without their knowledge. I feel he disrespected their personal beliefs. I think they should know, but have mixed feelings about telling them. Your opinion would be appreciated.

Your husband is apparently operating out of a very superstitious understanding of the sacraments. Be that as it may, he surely acted against the rights of the parents and the child in this circumstance. No child should be baptized in such a situation unless his or her parents agree and intend to raise the child as a Christian. Even then, they should be directed to a priest or another Christian minister for the proper preparation, performance and recording of the baptism.

I see no good that could come from your telling the parents at this point. You might or might not wish to inform them if, in the future, they plan to have the child baptized, but probably it could cause only hard feelings if you told them now.

Baptism without father's consent

My daughter is married to a Moslem. He refuses to get married in the Catholic Church. They now have a baby and my daughter wants him baptized. Is there a way that my daughter can receive the sacraments and baptize the baby without his consent? Someone told me it can be done.

It is possible something might be done to help your daughter in this circumstance and that the child might receive the sacrament of baptism. Exactly how this might happen must be worked out between her and the priest in her parish, or perhaps with the advice of another priest in the area with whom she may be acquainted. Please urge her to talk with her priest as soon as possible and follow his counsel.

Should priest delay baptism?

During the last few years I've heard of priests hesitating or even refusing to baptize children. Recently my nephew told me that when he and his wife took their first child to the priest for baptism, the priest gave them a hard time. He told them he would have to talk to them a few times about their own practice of the faith before he would baptize the baby.

I don't know what my nephew will do, but I do know that other parishes do not hold up baptisms like this. Isn't there a church law that says children are to be baptized as soon as possible after birth? Does the priest have any right to postpone baptism this way just because the parents don't go to Mass as often as they should?

The heart of your question and of the priest's approach with your nephew lies in the last part of your last question. Whenever a Catholic couple (or the Catholic partner in an interfaith marriage) is seriously deficient in the practice of religion, the parish priest has not only a right but an obligation to delay the baptism of their child until he can help the parents straighten out their own faith.

True, the church insists on the parents' obligation to have their children baptized "within the first three weeks" after birth. (CCL 867) The law assumes, however, that the parents are practicing Catholics prepared by their teaching and example to bring their children up as good active Catholic men and women.

Thus the same law requires that immediately after birth, or before, the parents go to their parish priest to request the sacrament of baptism for their child and to be properly prepared for it.

The church, in fact, insists that a priest cannot lawfully baptize a child unless he has a solidly-founded hope that the baby will be raised properly as a member of the Catholic religion. If evidence for this hope is lacking, he should delay the baptism and explain to the parents why this is being done. (CCL 868)

The Rite of Baptism emphasizes the point. At least twice during the ceremony, Catholic parents openly proclaim that they accept and believe the faith in which the child is being baptized, and that they are willing to give the example and teaching necessary for that child to be raised in the faith.

Under normal circumstances, this promise cannot be made by supposedly Catholic parents unless they themselves are faithful to the practice of their faith, and are not simply bringing that child for baptism out of a sense of family tradition or a vague feeling that "it's the right thing to do"—which is often true today with parents who do not go to Mass regularly or otherwise are weak in their beliefs, or are not faithful in practicing what they say they believe.

The church is concerned that parents not be placed in the position of making a profession of faith that they do not honestly and fully accept. Thus, the parish priest is directed to work with the parents who are not yet ready to profess that faith completely and to assume the responsibility of educating their children in the faith, and then to decide upon the right time for the baptism.

I realize that such regulations may startle many Catholics. But being realistic, we are in a situation different from the one we were in when the church instituted the practice of almost automatic baptism of children of baptized Catholic parents. Frankly, in this as in numerous other aspects of our faith, the church today is trying to pull us (both clergy and laity) away from viewing the priest as simply the administrator of a religious club, who is there to respond and satisfy religious needs, as it were, on demand.

Anyone who knows the history of the church of the past two or three hundred years is aware that by automatic baptisms, first Communions, and so on, whole populations of people were left at an almost primitive level of Catholic faith. One generation of baptized non-practicing Catholic parents followed another. Few, if any, were required to deal honestly with their own need for God, and to open themselves to the possibility of growth to anything like a full Christian Catholic life. As someone put it well, a church which never says "no" to parents who are seriously deficient in their belief and practice of their faith will never allow them to become deeply believing parents.

I believe your nephew and his wife are fortunate to have a priest who is trying to help them question seriously who and what they are as Christians, and to be certain in their own hearts that the baptism of their child will be what it was meant to be, a genuine recommitment of all their family to their Catholic faith.

"Immediate" baptism?

How can you be so stupid? In spite of what you say, no priest has any right to refuse or delay the baptism of a baby any time. Whatever happened to original sin? How can you condemn a baby for something it didn't do? No priest better ever hesitate to baptize a grandchild of mine just because his parents don't go to Mass the way they should, or I'll give him a piece of my mind.

I must admit a number of people wrote protesting what I said in that column, but you have an unusually delicate way of expressing the point.

To answer the question implied by your letter, there has been a change in the church's attitude toward baptism of children. The assumption that parents are practicing Catholics, and that the child is actually being baptized into a genuine Christian community which includes the child's family, is no longer possible. It is too often contradicted by the facts.

Baptism of a child (or an adult) is not an individual matter between the person and God. It is an action of the whole Christian community welcoming that child as part of a family that belongs to that Christian community, and it is the child professing its belief (through parents and godparents) in that family of faith, and wishing to become a part of it.

This is not something incidental to baptism; it is essential to it. Admittedly it is an aspect of baptism that was not stressed in the past because it didn't need to be. Today the situation is different. A highly respected canon lawyer made the point a few years ago at a meeting of the Canon Law Society of America. Speaking of the right to baptism (and the other sacraments of initiation, Eucharist and confirmation), he said, "Surely human beings have a right to enter that community and participate in it. But they have no right to enter it to destroy it. The community itself has the right of self-preservation and growth. It has the right to be what God intends it to be. And this right of the community conditions the right of individuals to enter it."

In other words, before an individual is baptized, the parish — and the whole Christian community — has a right to know that the commitments made in that ceremony are honest.

This is not only for the good of the church, but also for the good of the child. You may have forgotten that in baptism the individual baptized makes some awesome promises to participate as a full active member of the Christian people as he grows in that community. It is unfair for parents to commit a child to that kind of responsibility when they have no intention of properly assisting that child to grow in faith, and enable it to fulfill those promises honestly and sincerely in later years. Parents who do not practice their faith have no right to make commitments on the part of the child that they are not willing to help that child fulfill. It's basically as simple and as direct as that.

We still believe in original sin, but the baby is in no way being condemned for something it didn't do. The church does not teach that unbaptized children or adults will lose their soul, or will even be, through no fault of their own, deprived of the presence of God in eternity. We know that Jesus commands baptism for his followers, and that this is the normal way for entry into the kingdom.

God never assured us, however, that he has revealed all his plans to us, or that he does not have ways of bringing his life and grace to human beings in other ways than through baptism. Certainly the church has never taught, for example, that unbaptized pagans who possibly never even heard of God or of Jesus are automatically deprived of eternal salvation. It has, on the contrary, taught that God has ways which man does not know, and these are his own secrets to reveal or not as he wishes.

He gives his church the responsibility of directing its own life in a way that will help that community to remain faithful to what he commands and to the life-style that he has revealed, including procedures for administering and receiving the sacraments.

The shift in the church's perspective is solidly established in our present legislation and policies concerning the sacraments. In addition to numerous references to this policy in the Introduction to the Rite of Baptism itself, the Congregation for the Doctrine of the Faith

(June, 1970) insisted that a well-founded hope for a Christian education of a child must be present or the child should not be baptized.

In other words, the church is making every effort to lead us to a richer and fuller understanding of the church as the family of Christ, and how all of her activities, most especially the sacraments, must reflect that vision.

Parents responsibility at baptism

Your answer about possible hesitation to baptize babies has me really disturbed. I have a grandson a year old who has not been baptized, but my hands are tied. The infant's father, my son, has become one of the hordes who have ceased attending Mass. He's in a mixed marriage but there's no interference from his wife. He was educated in Catholic schools through college. I feel a condition such as this needs deep consideration before a decision to delay baptism of the baby. It could mean complete severance from the church. Why don't you consider this?

I certainly do consider it, and any priest who has to deal with this kind of situation considers it very carefully. Receiving people into the church, whether infants or adults, is one of the greatest joys of the priesthood. We do not lightly pass up that opportunity.

We do have, however, an obligation to the Christian Catholic community and to the parents of children who are presented for baptism. We must not perpetuate a lukewarm or nonexistent connection with the church by supposedly Catholic people simply because they want a baptismal ceremony.

Somewhere along the line, parents of children must decide where they stand with God and with their religion. We do them no service by pretending that being half in and half out is no problem as long as they come around to the church for baptisms.

I, and other parish priests, do not simply refuse to baptize people. We spend many hours and sometimes weeks working with parents, trying to help them to come to a decision about whether they can honestly present their children for baptism and commit themselves to the kind of life that will be necessary if their children are to be raised as Christians and Catholics.

Frankly, from my experience, I believe the likelihood of greater severance from the church is most remote. By our working with parents in this way, many parents have come to realize that they must stop playing games with their faith and with God and lay their life on the line as Catholics and Christians.

Others have not come to this conclusion yet, but I have known of no one who has ended up more separated from the church than they were before.

Understanding, and the proper kind of encouragement, incidentally, from grandparents and friends can be a great assist to fathers and mothers who are contemplating the baptism of their children, and prompt the kind of personal commitment this ceremony will demand from them.

What happens to unbaptized children?

What is the thinking of the Catholic Church on the destination of a child who dies before it can be baptized? Could it be baptized after death in any way?

The death of a child before baptism, sometimes even before birth, is always a hurtful and confusing experience for believing Christian parents. It may help to keep in mind a few matters about our faith.

All sacraments, including baptism, are for the living; they cannot be received by someone who has already died. If death is in any way doubtful, of course, baptism could be administered in case the person is still alive.

That is not the whole story, however. Jesus clearly told us that baptism is the sacramental "sign" way by which people enter into his life, his community of faith. Christians have always pondered what exactly this means, since billions of people die without baptism. Multitudes of these have never even heard of God or of Jesus.

If God loves all people and wishes them to be saved, how does that happen? As the question applies to very young children, theologians have offered numerous possible explanations through the centuries. Whatever the theory, however, one fundamental conviction is considered beyond doubt: God offers the grace of salvation to everyone who does not place a deliberate obstacle to that grace.

Obviously, that includes children who die too young to have consciously chosen any obstacle to God's love. St. Augustine, in fact, uses precisely this principle to support his teaching that God gives the grace of baptism, and therefore salvation, to such children.

The *Catechism of the Catholic Church* approaches the same idea from another direction. Baptism is necessary for salvation, it says, "for those to whom the Gospel has been proclaimed and who have had the possibility of asking for this sacrament." Little children have not had that possibility.

In other words, God has told us much about his plan for salvation, and he expects us to believe and follow what he says. But there is also much he has not told us. As Pope John Paul II put it in his book, *Crossing the Threshold of Hope*, God is unendingly at work in the sacraments, "as well as in other ways that are known to him alone" (Page 134).

As the catechism teaches, "God has bound salvation to the sacrament of baptism, but he himself is not bound by his sacraments" (1257).

Are unbaptized children in purgatory?

Although it is 13 years since my child died, I am still haunted by what the hospital chaplain told me. Our child died before birth, so could not be baptized. As you have explained in your column, the sacraments are for the living. I can understand that.

What I didn't expect was his answer to my question: What happens to these children? He said unbaptized people, including children, spend forever in purgatory, with no hope of entering heaven. I love the church and am convinced the priest was wrong. But what he said still hurts.

It's difficult to believe any priest could say that, especially the part about purgatory. Sometimes we don't hear things well, particularly in moments of great stress. If what you said is accurate, however, I apologize to you and others who have written with similar stories. The fact is, we know very little about such matters except the one overriding certainty that people who die without baptism are in the hands of a loving, merciful and saving Creator.

I hope you re-read the previous question and answer carefully. As we learn in many other matters of faith, it is often possible to be fairly certain about what God has done, is doing, or can do. When we pretend to be certain about what God cannot do, however, we quickly find ourselves way out of our depth in mystery. I hope this is of some help for you. God created your child out of love. That love, we trust, has touched your child with the same precious blood of Christ that offers salvation to the rest of us.

What happened to limbo?

Four years go we had a daughter who died suddenly just a few hours after birth. Your answer about the destiny of children who die before baptism was a real comfort and encouragement for us and, I'm sure, for others who have had a similar experience. It's what we always knew in our hearts, but it was good to hear what you said and the words of our Holy Father.

Whatever happened to limbo? Years ago we were taught that unbaptized infants go there. It's not heaven, we were told, but at least "they are happy." You didn't mention this. Any reason?

It's true there was much talk about limbo in the past. Some Catholics probably still think of it along with heaven and hell, as a third possible eternal "place to go" after death. The fact is, however, that the church never did have much to say officially about limbo (Latin for "fringe" or "border").

For centuries it was assumed that God took care of unbaptized infants in his own way. Certain theologians once held that unbaptized infants suffered some type of pain, but by the 12th or 13th centuries that idea was pretty much abandoned.

Later on, limbo became the subject of heated theological debate when a heretical sect called Jansenists taught that all infants dying without baptism are condemned to the fires of hell.

In 1794, Pope Pius VI condemned this teaching. He said, in effect, that one may believe in a limbo, a "middle state" of happiness that is not heaven with God, and still be a Catholic (Errors of the Synod of Pistoia, no. 26). That remains the only significant mention of limbo in any Catholic document. Obviously, it's a long way from saying that limbo belongs anywhere in official Catholic teaching.

As you have surely noticed, one seldom hears the word anymore. The *Catechism of the Catholic Church*, which touches on everything seriously connected with Catholic faith, doesn't mention it. The reason seems to be that limbo implies some sort of two-tiered final goal for human beings. One is eternal life with God. The other is a "natural" happiness apart from God (limbo) where people "go" who for no fault of their own do not reach the top level.

The catechism clearly teaches otherwise. There is only one final goal, one desire of happiness for all humanity, life with and in the God who created us. We may attain that goal or we may reject it by our own fault, but there is no half-happiness somewhere in between. God has raised us to a supernatural life, a sharing in his life far beyond our natural capacity. Having done that, there is, so to speak, no going back.

The desire for this happiness, says the catechism, is part of our nature, a gift of God, a vocation addressed to every human being. The ultimate goal then of human existence, of every individual and of everything people do, is the same: To share in the very happiness of God (1718-1719).

Whatever mysteries we must negotiate in exploring answers to questions about what happens to the unbaptized, we will need to find those answers without resorting to something called limbo.

Parents left the church

My son, an excellent Catholic before this, married a non-Catholic divorced woman who had two children, and they had two sons of their own. My son is willing to have his sons baptized, but won't raise them as Catholics; he doesn't go to Mass even on Easter and Christmas.

I am wondering if it would be all right to have the children baptized in some other religion. That way they would at least be Christians.

A child should not be baptized into any Christian community unless at least one of his or her parents is committed to that faith and intends to raise and educate the child in that religion.

Merely having children baptized does not make them fully Christian unless they are entering a Christian community (their family and a larger Christian community) that will nurture that Christian faith and make it a reality in their lives as they grow.

From your letter it seems obvious that your son and his wife do not consider themselves Catholic. In fact, unless you have omitted something important, it doesn't seem that they have any religion at all. Arranging for the children to go through a baptism ceremony will not solve either their parents' problems or their own.

Parents married out of church

I have a niece who was married to a non-Catholic; they were divorced after a year and she wanted to marry a Catholic. The priest told her nothing could be done, so they got married by a justice of the peace. I know their marriage is not valid according to the laws of the Catholic Church. Now they are expecting a baby. Will their child get to be baptized a Catholic? Could we be godparents?

As I stressed in previous pages, being baptized as a Catholic means much more than simply that a priest performs the ceremony. The newly baptized commits himself personally or through parents and godparents to a life of faith, worship and mutual support within the Catholic community. His fellow Catholics oblige themselves to the same for him.

Are the parents you describe able to make such a promise? It is possible they can, if they themselves are committed to living as full a Catholic life as circumstances permit. One point in their favor is that both have at least some Catholic background and roots in the Catholic faith. That doesn't remove all the problems, but it does give them a bit of a head start in a difficult task.

Normally you should be able to assume that if the baptism is taking place in the Catholic Church, all requirements are present and you would be free to act as godparents. In fact, in such a situation, particularly if the child's family is close to you, you may be able to bring a significant amount of support to them in raising their child in the Catholic faith.

If you have any other specific doubts, I suggest you talk with the parish priest who will plan the baptism with the child's parents. The final decision rests with the parents and with their priest.

Children of unmarried mothers

I have a friend whose daughter is pregnant and not married. She and her boyfriend do not wish to marry until they finish high school in about a year. Can she have the baby baptized in the church without being married? Also, can she give the baby the father's name even though they are not married?

It is possible for children of unmarried mothers to be baptized. As in any other baptism, however, several requirements (which I have explained in previous questions) must be met before the priest could baptize the child as a Catholic.

I would strongly advise your friend's daughter to think twice before naming the baby after the father. They're still very young and much can happen in the next year, or before they decide finally whether or not to marry.

To answer your question, however, the laws are generally very liberal about names. One may choose nearly any name one wishes for himself or for a child as long as the choice does not injure the rights of others.

State laws differ in a few instances, however, so the girl involved should check with a lawyer and with the boy involved before she acts.

Protestant baptisms recognized

In your question column you stated that long before Vatican Council II the Catholic Church accepted baptism of certain Protestant churches, including the Disciples of Christ. I was baptized in 1962 in the Catholic Church. Either you or the priest who baptized me are misinformed. In spite of my insistence that I had been baptized properly previous to 1962, I was required to receive a conditional baptism. This caused a hurtful situation for me and my family.

Several people wrote after that column appeared with stories similar to yours. You would encounter a much different situation if you were joining the Catholic Church today.

The statement to which I referred, which assumed the validity of baptism of most Protestant congregations, appeared in a reply from the Holy Office, Dec. 28, 1949. It resulted not only from a better awareness by the Catholic Church of baptism in these other churches, but also to at least some degree from a more developed theology and practice concerning baptism in some Protestant denominations.

Today conditional baptism (or, as it is sometimes erroneously called, re-baptism) of converts to our faith is relatively rare. Usually, if a convert has belonged to one of the major Protestant denominations, conditional baptism is given only if the fact that the person was baptized is uncertain, or if the individual himself or herself has a serious reason to doubt the validity of the previous baptism.

Present regulations of the church, in fact, forbid conditional baptism of converts without a reasonable doubt and serious investigation of the previous baptism. (Rite of Reception of Baptized Christians into Full Communion with the Catholic Church, no. 480, and 1993 Vatican Directory on Ecumenism, nos. 94-95 and *Code of Canon Law,* 845)

Saints name for baptism?

Is it any longer required to have a saint's name for baptism?

The Rite of Baptism does not require the parents to choose the name of a saint for their child.

However, the tradition of naming children after one of the saints is still good and admirable. Among other things, it is one way of reminding them that they are part of a long Christian line and puts them early in touch with the heroes of our faith.

Enrollment for baptism?

Friends of ours had a child several months ago and asked to have him baptized. As they explain it, the priest told them he could not baptize the baby since neither of the parents is a practicing Catholic. (The husband is not Catholic; the wife is, but admits she doesn't go to church very often.)

However, the priest told them he would enroll their baby, and perhaps baptize him later. I've never heard of that. What does it mean?

The church has pointed out numerous times during the past generation that children should not be baptized in the Catholic Church unless there is solid reason to anticipate they will be raised as Catholics. Normally this means at least one of the parents, if not both, are practicing their Catholic faith.

In 1970, the Sacred Congregation for the Doctrine of the Faith repeated this position. If neither parent is a practicing member of the church, and (as would usually be true in this case) there are not sufficient reasons for the priest to proceed with the baptism, one option open to him and the parents is the following: A priest may "enroll" the child (presumably as a member of the parish, and as a candidate for future baptism) with a view to its being baptized later; he would then meet with the parents several times to prepare them for the responsibilities assumed in the baptism of their child. (Notitiae 1971, 69)

Some parishes follow this procedure. Apparently your friends' parish is one of them.

Can only a bishop confirm?

I read with interest your answers to questions in our paper. Born and raised a Protestant, I desired for a long time to be a Catholic and converted in 1976.

The priest in the parish gave me instructions for about six weeks, then administered the rite of confirmation. Since that time, some close Catholic friends have wondered whether a priest can administer confirmation, or can only the bishop do this? Now I am not sure if I am truly a Catholic. Am I?

No need to worry. If you followed the instructions and procedures your priest suggested, you are a full-fledged member of the Catholic faith.

Until a few years ago, the sacrament of confirmation was ordinarily administered only by a bishop. Now, however, a parish priest may administer this sacrament in several circumstances, one of which is the reception of an adult convert into the church. After the baptism (or after the profession of faith if the person is already baptized), the rite of reception into the church calls for the priest to minister confirmation to the new Catholic. This seems to be what happened in your case.

Responsibilities of sponsors

I have heard that it is now possible for the same person who was sponsor at baptism also to be sponsor at confirmation. Is this correct? Does the confirmation sponsor have to be a Catholic?

According to the present regulations concerning confirmation, it is not only permissible but desirable that the godparent at baptism also be the sponsor at confirmation. The reason is obvious. The responsibility assumed by the sponsor at confirmation is the same as that of the sponsor at baptism, that is, to help the candidate for the sacrament to live up to his or her baptismal promises under the influence of the Holy Spirit. Having the same sponsor on both occasions emphasizes this responsibility more effectively. There may, however, be a different sponsor for confirmation. Included among the qualifications for the sponsor are that he or she be spiritually qualified, be sufficiently mature to undertake the responsibility involved, and be a Catholic who has already received the three sacraments of baptism, confirmation and the Eucharist.

Confirmation name needed?

Our daughter will be confirmed soon and nothing has been said about a confirmation name. Is it still proper to have a special name at that time?

It is no longer required to have a confirmation name different from the one given at baptism. The use of the person's baptismal name is allowed at confirmation since this better expresses the close relationship between these two sacraments, both of which are part of the process of Christian initiation and commitment.

Candidates may choose a new name for confirmation if they wish. I'm sure this will be explained in your parish.

Supplying ceremonies

I have a 23-year-old daughter, partially handicapped mentally and physically, who was born with hydrocephalus. When she was in the hos-

pital she was confirmed by a Ukrainian priest. Now she wants to be confirmed by a bishop, have a sponsor and pick a confirmation name like her brothers and sisters.

Could she possibly be confirmed the next time this sacrament is scheduled at our parish?

The Ukrainian (sometimes called the Ruthenian) rite is among those rites in full communion with the Roman church, under the pastoral jurisdiction of the bishop of Rome. Probably the one who confirmed your daughter was a priest of this rite.

If so, the confirmation she received was presumably valid. If it was, she would not be confirmed again since, like baptism, this sacrament is not repeatable.

Even so, however, there are simple ways in which she could share in the solemn ceremony of confirmation. She could choose a confirmation name, which she had not the opportunity to do previously, and someone close to her could serve as sponsor.

Such participation might be compared to "supplying the ceremonies" for baptism after a baby, for example, has been privately baptized in an emergency. The child may be brought to church later, and the entire solemn rite of baptism is celebrated with the sole exception of the pouring of the water.

Considering the spiritual significance such a celebration would apparently have for your daughter and your family, I feel certain your parish priest and your bishop would be anxious to work something out so she can be confirmed with her group.

You must talk with a priest in your parish, however, first to ascertain the above facts, and then to explore possibilities appropriate for your daughter and for the parish community.

Just for the record, some branches of the Ukrainian rite are not Roman Catholic, but Orthodox. The chances that the priest who confirmed your child was from one of these branches are slim, and in any case would not change what I said above.

Parents sponsors?

In your column you once said that parents could be sponsors for confirmation. They have served as such in our parish for several years, but now our pastor said that, according to the bishop, parents should not be sponsors now. Who is right?

The Introduction to the Rite of Confirmation expresses the preference for the godparent of baptism to be the confirmation sponsor. Or another person may be chosen. In this same paragraph the document says, "Even the parents themselves may present their children for confirmation." (n.5)

In light of this, it was judged, particularly before the 1983 *Code of Canon Law*, that parents may be sponsors. But the words don't say that. Parents may be "presenters," not sponsors.

The new Code requires confirmation sponsors to fulfill the conditions given for sponsors at baptism (CCL 893). Fathers and mothers are prohibited from serving as baptismal godparents (CCL 874).

The situation is confused since no confirmation sponsor is absolutely required in the first place. The confirmation ritual and canon law, respectively, specify that "ordinarily" and "insofar as it can be done" a sponsor should be chosen for the candidate. So there may be no sponsor at all.

At any rate, the present law of the church on confirmation sponsors is the following: (1) The baptism godparent is preferred. (2) Another person may be chosen. (3) In either of these cases, or if there is no sponsor, a parent may "present" the individual for confirmation.

More than one confirmation sponsor?

Our granddaughter will be confirmed soon. She wants both my wife and me as sponsors, and doesn't want to hurt our feelings by choosing one. Our parish priest said no, another priest said it would involve too many people, and the bishop said canon law does not allow it. We hope you can give us an answer.

All three persons you consulted are correct. Canon law just assumes that one person, at most, will serve as confirmation sponsor. (canon 892-893) As a practical consideration, particularly in larger parishes, it could complicate procedures, and even create problems of space, if those confirmed had more than one sponsor.

As I said above, a confirmation sponsor is not absolutely necessary at all. You and your wife might explain to your granddaughter that you thank her for wanting both of you, and that neither of you will be hurt if the other is asked.

Deciding to be a sponsor

My niece lives with her father, who is divorced and remarried. I believe this girl will ask me to be her sponsor at confirmation. Would it be all right if I accepted? She often does not go to Mass and there are things I could not change; nor could I be responsible for her being brought up as a Catholic.

One can never be sure as a sponsor, or even as a parent, how children will turn out in their religious practices and convictions. But the situation you describe prompts more than the usual concern by someone asked to be sponsor.

I suggest you first talk with the priest in her parish to find out what the children are being told about the relation of confirmation to their future lives as Catholics, and what else is expected of them as candidates for this sacrament.

Then talk with your niece. Depending on her age, you may be able to help her begin to make some realistic, personal decisions.

If her relationship to the church is as tenuous as you indicate, and continues that way, it would not seem to make much sense for you to commit yourself (which is what you do as sponsor) to help her to do something she doesn't want to do in the first place.

What the sacrament would mean to her then I don't know, but it might be unfair and perhaps meaningless for her to ask you to be her sponsor under these conditions.

CHAPTER 6

MARRIAGE AND FAMILY LIVING

∾

Origin of marriage vows

Would you know where the words of the marriage vows originated: "I take thee. . . till death do us part." Did they come from Christ or officials of the church?

The language of the marriage vows did not come from Christ. In fact, the words or actions by which marriage consent is expressed by the bride and groom have varied greatly from one time to another, and even today from country to country and from one Catholic rite to another.

The only essential in our Christian context is that the couple declare to each other in some external way their intent to join now in a permanent marriage union with faithfulness to their spouse. This declaration may be in words or, as in some rites, almost entirely in symbolic actions — such as drinking from the same cup, conferring of the wedding rings, etc. The significance of these actions is as clearly understood by all the participants as words would be.

Form of marriage vows

Our family attended a wedding with wedding vows I have never heard before. The couple said something rather long about their love and how they wanted to live together for life, but no other vows. Is it possible now for a couple to use their own words and make up their marriage vows?

The ritual for marriage in the Latin rite of the church contains one form of consent at a wedding: "I, Joseph, take you, Jane, to be my wife. I promise to be true to you in good times and in bad, in sickness and in health. I will love you and honor you all the days of my life." Instead of a statement by the couple, the priest may put it in the form of a question: "Do you, Joseph, take Jane. . . ?"

In November, 1969, the American bishops approved a second form with which we in the United States are more familiar: "I, Joseph, take you, Jane, for my lawful wife, to have and to hold, from this day forward, for better or worse, for richer, for poorer, in sickness and in health until death do us part." If the couple prefer, this form also may be put as a question asked by the priest. One of these forms must be used at all marriages of Catholics in the United States; the bride and groom, therefore, are not free to compose their own vows, nor does any priest have a right to compose his own.

The reasons for this should be obvious when we realize that marriage vows (anytime, but in a special way between two Christians) are not a private affair between the couple; they have importance and implications for the whole community.

The U. S. Bishops Committee on the Liturgy explains it this way:

"While the couple may well find language of their own to express very profoundly the consent and covenant which they undertake, this is a central ritual and ecclesial act and they have a responsibility to the community of believers assembled, that is, the church before which they manifest their consent, to use language clearly and certainly conformable to the church's faith and understanding of the sacrament."

In practice, this requirement works no hardship on the couple, since there are numerous other chances for them to express their faith and understanding of their vows during the wedding ceremony. One most obvious and frequently used is the opportunity for the couple to compose their own prayer to be recited together or separately either shortly after they declare their vows or during the meditation period after Communion. This may be what you heard the couple say.

If a couple unexpectedly employs other language of consent or commitment than that provided in the rite, no matter how appropriate that language may be, the presiding priest should see that one of the approved forms is used also.

He might do this very simply by using one of the two question forms I mentioned above. (Bishops' Committee on the Liturgy Newsletter, August-September, 1981)

Required marriage preparation

In connection with the approaching marriage of a relative, I was told that there would be no instructions for the couple by the priest. Aren't priests required to give instructions or help to people before and after they are married?

By church law, parish priests are under heavy obligation in this part of their pastoral life. The *Code of Canon Law* (1063) binds a pastor to assist all the faithful of that community in preserving and increasing the holiness of Christian marriage.

He is to accomplish this in several ways: By instructing children, young people and adults on the meaning and duties of Christian marriage and parenthood; by instructing brides and grooms before their wedding concerning the holiness and responsibilities of marriage; by a meaningful celebration of the marriage liturgy, bringing out how the couple signify and participate in the unity and fruitful love of Jesus and his church, and by helping married couples themselves protect and increase the holiness of their family life.

The parish priest is not required to provide all this instruction and assistance personally. The range of areas in which the couple needs assistance is vast. It involves instruction and counseling on finances, interpersonal communications, in-laws, sexual expression of their love, the care and upbringing of children, and other elements significant in the early years of their marriage and throughout their married life.

Parish priests today rely heavily on Pre-Cana Conferences, Engaged Encounters, and other programs for those preparing for marriage, and a whole range of aids for husbands and wives in their relationship with each other and their children.

Preparing for marriage

My daughter and her non-Catholic fiance attended Sunday afternoon classes with other couples at a distant church. These classes were boring because my daughter had taken college courses which covered all segments of married life. The hundred or more questions they were asked to answer were personal and none of the priest's business. If my daughter refuses to answer these questions, can our pastor refuse to marry them?

All dioceses in our country have some form of required preparation programs before marriage. In more and more places these programs take two forms. One is some type of pre-marriage class or series of conversations with trained married couples about early married life. These classes take many forms, from a series of lectures in a Pre-Cana program to weekend conferences for engaged couples.

Understandably, the quality of these programs varies from time to time and place to place, depending on leadership and participants. Not everything will appeal to everyone. I have found, however, that much depends on the attitude of the people attending. Usually couples who attend with an open mind and who feel they still may have something to learn find these courses useful in some way. At least they appreciate the church's concern that they be given all possible help to prepare them for a good and happy marriage.

The other element common to most marriage preparation requirements is an inventory to help the couple evaluate their agreements and strengths and weaknesses in important aspects of the early years of marriage. Some couples naturally profit more than others from such programs. But, in my experience, all of them, including those most highly educated, recognize full well why the church expects couples preparing for marriage to participate in them. They are grateful that everyone involved, including the parish priest, is concerned enough and loves them enough to want to help.

Your daughter and her fiance should talk with their parish priest if they do not wish to particpate in the required programs.

"Promises" in a mixed marriage

Your answer concerning the marriage of a Catholic with a non-Catholic sounded so simple. Why didn't you mention that the Catholic party must sign a statement that the children of that marriage must be raised Catholic? Some young people are surprised to learn that such papers must be signed before the marriage can take place before a Catholic priest. If one of the parties does not agree to this, the marriage cannot take place.

What you say is only partially true. Formerly, both the Catholic and non-Catholic partners signed promises to raise the children Catholic. This practice was changed by Pope Paul VI in a document on interfaith marriages (*Matrimonia Mixta*) in 1970.

While the procedure is different, the intent of the church is the same, to prevent as much as possible serious harm to the marriage because of religious differences between the husband and wife. Let me explain.

The procedure today is this: The non-Catholic partner signs or promises nothing. The Catholic partner signs two statements. The statements are basically as follows:

1. I reaffirm my faith in Jesus Christ and intend to continue living that faith in the Catholic Church, and
2. I promise to do all in my power to share my faith with our children by having them baptized and raised as Catholics.

The priest helping the couple prepare for the wedding is required to sign a declaration that the non-Catholic partner has been informed of this affirmation and belief of the Catholic.

Normally, the priest will explain what these beliefs mean to the Catholic, and how such beliefs affect a Catholic's life, and then urge the couple to be sure before their wedding that their respective faiths and convictions can be preserved and honored in their marriage.

Several points need to be noted about the "promises" made by the Catholic. First of all, they add nothing to what a Catholic already believes if he or she is a committed and knowledgeable Catholic. When an individual presents himself to a Catholic priest for marriage as a Catholic in the Catholic Church, the priest and the church assume that individual is a Catholic — which means there are some things that person is honestly convinced of and adheres to as his or her personal faith. Among these are the two statements given above. Any Catholic who does not hold these as basic beliefs is either ill-informed about his religion, or is very shaky in his faith.

Why then are the declarations asked at all? One reason is as a reminder. But more importantly, they are meant to help the couple identify differences in their religious beliefs or expectations from the marriage so these differences can be dealt with and resolved before the marriage takes place.

In other words, while the church knows what a good Catholic believes, it does not pretend to know the religious beliefs of the non-Catholic. It presumes, however, that the non-Catholic has some beliefs about God, family, marriage, and other religious matters. And it is concerned that these beliefs of the two people be confronted by them before the marriage so that any critical differences may be ironed out.

Ultimately, this must be done by the two people themselves, acting from the base of their own convictions. They must be sure that any conflicts of belief (for example, about their own personal religious obligations, the baptism and education of their future children, and so on) can be resolved without either of them being asked to compromise what their conscience tells them are serious moral obligations before God. If such resolution proves impossible, the couple could not enter the marriage with a good conscience.

The entire procedure is another expression of the church's concern for the faith and conscience of the Catholics, but also of the non-Catholics, whose convictions are, one would hope, just as serious to them as ours are to us.

Banns of marriage

Are the banns of marriage announced anymore? Before several marriages of friends they were not given in church at all. Will they be announced only if the family asks?

The banns of marriage are announcements of an intended marriage with the expectation that anyone aware of impediments to that marriage will make the fact known. Present law of the church does not require banns, but bishops' conferences may include them among appropriate inquiries which are to precede marriage. (CCL 1067) American bishops do not prescribe them at this time.

Can cousins marry?

Would you please explain what relatives are forbidden to marry, and how this is figured? A cousin of mine is engaged to another cousin, actually a second cousin. I didn't think this was permitted in the Catholic Church. Many people do not know relatives farther back than grandparents or second cousins.

You are referring to an impediment to marriage that in church law, and in state laws, is called consanguinity — literally, common blood.

There are two kinds of consanguinity. One is the direct line, meaning the relationship between an individual and his or her parent or grandparent.

Such a direct line relationship is a serious impediment to marriage. No permission (dispensation) for a marriage between two such people is possible.

The other kind of consanguinity is indirect or collateral. This is the relationship, for example, between brothers and sisters (second degree), first cousins (fourth degree), and so on.

According to general Catholic Church law, any collateral relationship, up to and including fourth degree (what we usually call first cousins), is an impediment to marriage. (CCL 1091)

As with the direct line, no dispensation can ever be given by the church for a marriage between brother and sister. In the other cases, however, the church, through the bishop, can (and fairly often does) dispense for a serious enough reason.

Marriage between first cousins is more common in some cultures of the world than it is in our own. In these situations, dispensations by the church for such marriages are also relatively common.

Church laws forbidding marriage within certain degrees of consanguinity are based on social and health reasons which are rather obvious. While a few ancient cultures apparently allowed some type of marriage relationship between brother and sister and even between parent and child, some of these relationships were forbidden by every major code of law with which we are familiar, even those which predate the Jewish law of the Old Testament.

Incidentally, yours is one part of the country (Pennsylvania) in which there are relatively large numbers of Oriental Rite Catholics. Laws which govern these branches of our church vary somewhat from Latin rite canon law, particularly in the method of computing degrees of relationship. But, in practice, the impediments and the possibilities are similar to those I have explained.

Is premarital sex wrong?

I am a Catholic dating a Protestant girl. We are in our 20s and considering marriage in the future. Is it wrong to have sexual relations with the one you intend to marry? We have talked of having sexual relations, but I'm confused. I want to do what is right, and we need an answer that will help us both. I know one of your answers may be if we love each other enough, we will wait. We both want to be sure.

Catholic moral teaching remains, and is likely to remain, that sexual relations before marriage are wrong. Within the limits of space here, I can mention only a few, but I believe important, thoughts that may help.

First, you must realize that your desire for sexual union with the woman you love is not only normal, it is the way you ought to feel about her. Any man or woman who plans to marry and doesn't strongly want sexual intimacy with his or her partner is in trouble. They need either a medical examination or psychiatric counseling — or a serious re-examination of their choice of partner.

This desire is, however, no basis all by itself for judging whether sexual intercourse is morally right or wrong. As all Catholic-Christian moral doctrine, this teaching of the church was not pulled out of thin air. The church only confirms by its own insight and belief what is common human experience — complete sexual intimacy between people who are not married is hurtful individually and socially in ways that are usually not even dreamed of beforehand. It is therefore sinful.

The total giving of themselves that sexual intercourse involves implies an acceptance of responsibility and permanent, committed trust of another that you are simply not able at this point to profess honestly. No matter what you say you mean to each other, you do not have the assured and promised commitment to one another that marriage, and only marriage, brings with it.

The vows you one day profess (if you marry each other, and that's still a big if) are no mere legal formality to make official what was already there before. As your family and friends and church will witness by their presence, the promises you make that day will transform your relationship for the first time into more than merely a private arrangement between the two of you. Only then will you have established the permanent, public responsibility to and for each other that makes sexual intercourse an honest, truthful expression of what you are together.

Contrary to what one regularly hears today, there is absolutely no evidence that sexual intimacy before marriage increases the chances for a happy union after the wedding. In fact, the contrary is true, for some very practical reasons.

Especially outside the context of a married community of life, many of the joys, adventures and excitement of sexual experience and fun can easily (much more easily than you might believe) become monotonous. There may accompany this experience at least some sense of guilt. Sexual intimacy can thus become seriously blunted in its potential for helping couples work patiently and tenderly through the tensions, uncertainties and new responsibilities of the first years of marriage.

Sexual intimacy also tends to become almost obsessive, especially when divorced from other needs and responsibilities which accompany normal daily married life. Once sex is begun, it can become a kind of hovering presence for a young man and woman. When they meet for a date, they know how the evening will end. All ingenuity in finding and learning other ways of enjoying each other, of having fun together, of communicating their hopes and concerns and ideals, even of exploring how they can make some gift of themselves to others who need them — all this easily becomes crowded out and ignored. Sex is always available, and requires little in the way of thought, personal effort or unselfishness.

Your ideals and your love for each other appear deep. I hope you will keep them that way and think through your moral decisions in this light. The payoff in happiness and peace of mind will be worth whatever it costs.

Cohabitation no impediment to marriage

In answer to a question concerning cohabiting couples, you left out the fact that the sacrament of matrimony can be validly received only when both parties are in the state of grace. The probability that cohabitation involves sexual relations means the sacrament of penance is necessary before the marriage.

Many Catholics still have two confusions about the marriage of couples who have been living together. One mistaken notion is that cohabiting couples are impeded by church law from entering a Catholic marriage. While many elements in their lives need to be addressed and dealt with before they marry, living together does not in itself prohibit their marriage in the church.

The Catholic Church has limited and specific impediments to marriage — lack of age, impotence, perpetual vows of chastity, a previous marriage, and others. Cohabitation is not one of these impediments.

Second, Catholic teaching is that an individual who, while conscious of a serious sin, receives the sacrament of marriage or the Eucharist, for example, still receives the sacrament validly, though unlawfully and sinfully. Living together before marriage is contrary to a Christian way of life, and is not acceptable in Christian morality. It is an objectively hurtful, sinful situation, regardless of how the couple involved may view it at the moment.

Certainly you are aware that if a person receives Communion while conscious of an unforgiven mortal sin, that person receives the sacrament validly. He or she truly receives the eucharistic body of Christ the same as anyone else. The fact that the reception is sinful does not make it any less a sacrament.

Somewhat the same is true in marriage. Christians who celebrate the sacrament of marriage in a state of serious sin — whether that sin involves embezzlement, malicious and destructive gossip, gross abuse of others, immoral sexual behavior or any other seriously wrong action — receive the sacrament of marriage.

As with the Eucharist, the effect of the graces of the sacrament are inhibited by the spiritual condition of those who receive it. But they are married nevertheless. They need not, indeed cannot, be "re-married" after whatever mortal sin they are aware of is forgiven.

None of the above diminishes the responsibility of a cohabiting couple, and the priest or other parish minister working with them, to deal in every way possible with the negative spiritual, emotional, sacramental and marital implications of their lifestyle before marriage.

Engaged couple shares bedroom

When a couple is engaged, one set of parents of the couple see no wrong in the couple moving into the boy's bedroom. The other parents believe this is seriously immoral. In this case, doesn't the parish priest have the obligation to tell the couple and the condoning parents that it is wrong, and to help guide them back into the Christian lifestyle?

I understand your hurt, disappointment and frustration over what this young couple is doing. In addition to being wrong, this arrangement makes difficult, if not impossible, the joy and mutual support that living together can bring when experienced within the commitment and covenant of husband and wife.

The trust and faithfulness these discoveries help build in the context of marriage pay rich dividends in future years. You want this, of course, in the fullest degree possible for your son or daughter.

You wonder what you can do. At this point, not very much, at least in the light of the few details you have given. Obviously, no parents are obliged to condone or allow such an arrangement in their home. Nor should they.

As for the other parents' feelings, or the priest's, have you discussed this with them? And I mean personally? Much misinformation and misunderstanding in situations like this result from second or thirdhand sources.

Talk to the individuals involved. Don't be ashamed of your position or hesitate to enforce it. At the same time, make your love and care for these young people as clear as you can. Ultimately, God is their judge, not you.

Parents respond on live-ins

Dear Readers:

A mother wrote saying that her daughter had moved into an apartment with a young man. She asked for help on how to deal with the situation. How could she keep the door open and still make her own feelings clear? Should her daughter's friend be invited to family functions?

The response was overwhelming, not only in volume but in the evidence it gave once again of the faith in God and of the beautiful, almost primitive, parental instinct of love and protection that guides good mothers and fathers.

By far the majority insist that parents have a right and responsibility to make clear they believe that what is being done is wrong, and why; but absolutely no shunning, no keeping them out of family gatherings, even if that means inviting the live-in partner also and showing basic Christian kindness to him or her as well. Everyone who mentioned the subject agreed that the couple should not be permitted to share a bedroom in the parents' home.

Not more than one or two percent of the parents pushed a hard-nosed approach: These "children" made their choice; they're out, and they can come back when they change their ways. None of this group, incidentally, gave evidence in their letters of having faced the situation personally. There was much difference of opinion about under what circumstances parents should visit the young couple's home. Many made the point, however, that parents should offer no support, financial or otherwise, to the upkeep of the couple's home.

Some of the most encouraging and inspiring notes were from adults now happily in good and strong marriages (with their former live-in partner or someone else) who expressed gratitude for their parents' patience, faith and goodness during a period they know now was a tremendous test of those parents' love. These children, now with children of their own, admit they would never have kept their faith, or perhaps their emotional balance, if their parents had not stayed with them.

I will allow one Rhode Island couple to speak for nearly 300 others who expressed similar convictions:

"First and foremost we have to remember that our children, a gift from God, pass through us. We do not own them. Second, we are admonished by God not to judge or we will be judged. So at this point, it is obvious we do not have much control except perhaps a negative approach like shunning them, which I think is against all Christ's teachings.

"The answer sounds simple, but it is not, because of the heartbreak that comes from watching those we love do harm to themselves and others... The true solution is to do and accept the above, having faith that God will see us through, keeping the doors open and encouraging love and communication, with the understanding between God and us that he will make the final judgment and enlighten us and our children to understand our responsibilities."

Be tough on live-ins

I am a regular reader of your column and a disgruntled Catholic. With responses such as the one you set forth (see above) dealing with live-in sin and immorality, it is no wonder that the youth of our country have lost all sense of sin. You almost condone the immorality of cohabitation outside of marriage. I have had experience of a couple living together, but I did not water down the morality of the church to please the sinners. It's about time priests start preaching the moral principles and teaching of the church for a change, and stop promoting all the crackpot teaching of post-Vatican II theologians. It's high time you priests in the modern church got with it.

Many parents have written or phoned me since that column, thanking me for the help it was to them as good Catholics in attempting to deal with an extremely complicated and painful family situation.

You are asking me to answer a question that was not asked. The parent who wrote knew very well the situation was morally wrong; I agreed with her. She wanted to know not whether the couple should be living together or not, but rather how good parents handle the situation with charity and fidelity to what they believe, and with honesty to everyone.

You apparently had your own way of dealing with the problem. Other parents have different methods and follow them without any denying or watering down their convictions about the moral character of what their children are doing.

The parents who approached the situation more tenderly and patiently than it seems you did are not morally corrupt, and it is wrong and rash for you to imply that they are. The fact that many of their children are now in good marriages and raising good families says a lot for the validity and goodness of their methods.

Does baby prevent a marriage?

My 22-year-old grandson and his steady girlfriend are expecting a baby in three months. They are both Catholic, and have received all necessary sacraments up to now. The priest told them a couple who have a child out of wedlock cannot get married in the church. I'm sorry about the circum-

stances, but am happy about my new great-grandchild. So is the baby's father, who has a fine new job to support his family.

There is no basis in Catholic teaching or policy for the statement allegedly made by the priest. At least two possibilities occur to me that could explain what happened. The couple, who are dealing with a number of stressful circumstances, may simply have misunderstood the priest. If so, it's unfortunate they didn't get the matter straightened out at the time. Or the priest may have perceived some serious problems in their relationship and unfortunately chose to tell them they couldn't (in his view of the situation) get married.

Unwise and confusing as this may be, occasionally some priests, perhaps out of desperation but without explanation or advice about further steps, use this route to discourage couples from marrying. Please suggest to your grandson that they approach another priest to assist their preparation for marriage.

Marry "in the church"?

My daughter plans to marry a divorced Protestant. He was baptized in the Baptist Church. Since they were told that they cannot marry in the Catholic Church, should my daughter obtain special permission from the bishop to marry in a Protestant church? May a priest be present at the ceremony and give them some special blessing?

When the priest said your daughter and her fiance cannot marry in the church, he meant that they cannot be married according to the laws of the church, not simply that they cannot have the ceremony in the church building. A dispensation from the bishop to marry without a priest, in a Protestant church or elsewhere, is possible only when a couple are free to marry each other validly within the framework of Catholic marriage laws. Therefore, without a declaration of nullity or other procedure (which apparently your parish priest considers unlikely) no such permission could be given, nor would a priest be present.

As a possible help to others, I should point out that your question, and your daughter's situation, is just one more illustration of the need to consider these facts of life before, not after, a person gets seriously involved with another with the possibility of marriage. The church's basic teachings and regulations concerning marriage are clear, long-standing, and readily available.

If an individual's Catholic faith is personally valuable and essential, some principles and rules for personal guidance on dating and courtship must be set for oneself long before things have come to the point of planning the marriage.

Marriage ceremony in the park?

May a marriage be performed by a priest outdoors? Our daughter and her fiance, non-Catholic, would like the ceremony in a local park, a lovely area where weddings are popular. Is this possible? We've been told it is not, but that sometimes the priest will allow it.

The general law of the church requires that a marriage between two Catholics, or between a Catholic and a baptized non-Catholic, be celebrated in a parish church unless specific permission is granted by the bishop for the marriage to take place elsewhere. The reason is that our churches, our buildings of prayer and worship, are sacred places where most sacred events should take place. The sacramental marriage of Christian people — two Catholics, or a Catholic and a baptized Christian of another denomination — is one of them.

Thus, not only because it is an act of worship, but because a wedding is an especially solemn public act of our faith, the parish church is the preferred location. Exceptions to this rule are possible at the discretion of the local bishop. One reason, for example, could be when one or both partners, Catholic or otherwise, have so little connection with or respect for their Christian faith that a church wedding would be meaningless for them, perhaps even for their families. The policy for your diocese would be the one set by your own bishop.

If the non-Catholic party in an interfaith marriage is not baptized, the marriage would be a true marriage, but not a Christian sacrament according to Catholic theology. This wedding may be celebrated either in church or some other suitable place, which might be an outdoor location. These regulations are found in the *Code of Canon Law* (1118).

Cohabiting grandparents?

My non-Catholic father-in-law is a 68-year-old widower dating a 66-year-old Catholic widow. They have a total of eight childen and 12 grandchildren, are devoted to each other, go on vacations together and have their own homes. Their problem is they don't want to get married. I believe both previous marriages were not too happy, and they're afraid to tie the knot again.

Our problem is how to explain things to the grandchildren. Is their cohabitation wrong? She does not receive Communion at Mass. He feels responsible and has asked me about it because I am Catholic.

Though I realize you want to be considerate and tolerant of someone so close to you, I don't understand why you would have a question about this. The fact they had unfortunate first marriages, though apparently fairly long and in many ways fruitful ones, is good reason to be cautious about a new union. But it does not excuse them from behaving in a morally and spiritually unhealthy way for each other and their families. Whether they wish to or not, they must accept responsibility for how their behavior affects the attitudes and consciences of their children and grandchildren toward marriage and other relationships.

Work with them as you would with your own children in similar circumstances. Sixty-eight and 66 may be approaching upper age, but they're not dead. They need to talk this over together thoroughly. Since he has asked your help, perhaps you can share your moral and other concerns honestly with them, and encourage them to do the same with each other.

Marriage ceremony without Mass

Our daughter plans to marry soon. She informs us that they want a wedding in a large church in our city, but she and her fiance, both Catholic, want no Mass because they do not practice their faith. She already set a date with the pastor, but did not tell him she did not want a Mass. Will the priest perform the ceremony without a Mass?

It is not unheard of today for a couple, both from Catholic homes, to approach the time of their marriage having little faith in the church or sometimes even in God. They may be good young men and women otherwise, but are perhaps going through a religious crisis that they probably should have dealt with in adolescence.

When that happens, it often does seem more proper and honest for the couple to have a marriage ceremony without the Eucharist, which for them would have little or no meaning. In fact, many priests speak to couples about this option when it is clear they hold little interest in having a nuptial Mass.

My own approach, and I think that of most priests, is to use the time available before the marriage to discuss with the couple the need for making some firm decisions at this juncture of their lives about what life, God, the church, the sacraments and the Eucharist mean to them, if anything. With responsibilities for each other and perhaps soon for their children, they no longer have the luxury of floating aimlessly in these critical areas of a mature life.

I have no idea what the policy of that particular pastor is. I would urge your daughter to meet with him soon and level with him about her feelings and plans.

A sacrament without believing?

I am disturbed by an answer you gave about marriage. You said that non-Catholics are considered to have a sacramental marriage if they are validly baptized Christians. Is this true if they do not believe the marriage is a sacrament? And suppose the ceremony is witnessed by a clergyman who also does not believe it is a sacrament? You seem to answer in the affirmative.

This would seem to make the sacraments simply magic. I suggest you reconsider your answer.

The answer I gave is correct according to present Catholic belief and practice. The questions you raise are serious, however, and are, in fact, being studied by theologians and canon lawyers.

The position of the church concerning sacramental marriages is in some ways confusing. According to our theology, marriage is the only sacrament that individuals can receive not only without knowing it, but even without believing in it — in fact, even deliberately rejecting a belief in the sacramentality of their marriage. Your question pinpoints a precise situation in which such an anomaly might occur.

At least part of the solution seems to lie in a clarification of the meaning of the word sacrament. That there is a significant and profound difference between the marriage of non-Christians and the marriage covenant and life of two Christians who meet and live with each other as committed members of the family of Christ, would not be denied, I believe, by anyone. St. Paul said in his Letter to the Ephesians, the marriage of a man and woman who are already brother and sister in the family of Christ is itself a sign — a sacrament — of the love that flows between Christ and his church.

So the church is attempting to polish its understanding of Christian marriage.

The problem, incidentally, arises not only in the situation you describe. A similar question might be asked of a marriage which involves individuals who call themselves Catholic, but whose beliefs and practice of the faith are nearly non-existent. How realistic or honest is it to call such a marriage a sacrament — that is, a proclamation and commitment to living out their faith as members of the Body of Christ? Your question is an excellent one. Frankly, I'm surprised more people don't ask it.

Common-law marriage

My daughter-in-law discussed with me the wedding plans of her son, my grandson. I asked who would officiate at the marriage; she said no one. The "groom" told his mother they intend to perform the ceremony themselves. I've never heard of this. She further said they have checked, and it is indeed done in Colorado, where they live.

Surprisingly to many people, I'm sure, this so-called common-law marriage could well be a valid civil union. In common-law marriage, if a man and woman are legally able to marry each other and fulfill certain conditions, they are considered legally married, even without a ceremony or formal civil record.

Such marriages were common in the United States in frontier days. An attorney friend graciously researched present state-to-state laws on the subject. To my surprise and hers, 12 states, including Colorado and the District of Columbia, still recognize common-law marriages.

Requirements differ, but common-law marriages occur generally when a heterosexual couple (common-law marriages don't apply to same-sex unions) cohabit for a significant period of time, intend to be married and present themselves to other people as husband and wife — using the same last name, calling each other "my wife" or "my husband," filing joint tax returns, and so on.

The couple must also live in a state where such marriages are recognized. No state defines the period of time required for a common-law marriage to exist. Once it exists, however, the couple must, for example, go through a formal divorce if they want to end the marriage.

So your grandson and his friend have apparently received accurate information. Other states recognizing common-law marriages, as of this writing, are Alabama, Iowa, Kansas, Montana, Oklahoma, Pennsylvania, Rhode Island, South Caroline, Texas and Utah — and New Hampshire for inheritance purposes only. Other states have Full Faith and Credit statutes accepting the married status of a couple coming from a state which recognizes common-law marriages.

Any couple contemplating this avenue for their life together will need good legal advice concerning all conditions for a common-law marriage and its implications. Catholics need to remember, too, that these state laws do not repeal or diminish the canonical requirement that Catholics must enter marriage before a priest or deacon for that marriage to be recognized as valid in the church. By church law, the publicly expressed consent of the two partners makes a marriage union. Nothing, including cohabitation, can substitute for that consent. (canon 1057)

Marriage not always "before priest"

Can you please explain why the bishops are allowing some Catholics to marry in a Protestant church? Is this another example of where American bishops are acting against our Holy Father? I cannot in conscience attend the wedding I am invited to unless I am sure this is really approved by the Catholic Church.

The requirement that Catholics be married before a priest, which is the cause of your confusion, is a good example of truths and rules which many people think are essential to our faith, but are not.

Christians through the centuries considered marriage of their brothers and sisters in the faith as sacred, and placed high value on those marriages taking place somehow in the context of their Christian community.

But no particular "form" of marriage (how and before whom it should take place) was required for validity of the marriage until about 400 years ago. At that time (1563) the Council of Trent ruled that a marriage must take place before one's pastor or bishop in order to be valid.

However, because of some technicalities of church law, mostly involving promulgation of this rule and another by Pope Benedict XIV about 200 years later, Trent's regulation did not apply to much of the world until early in the 20th century.

Among the places where it did not apply were large areas of the United States, including major centers of Catholic population like Chicago and New York, and nearly all the Northwest states. Until 1908, in those parts of the world, a marriage of Catholics before a judge or even a minister of another religion would be held valid by the Catholic Church, with no dispensation needed. Only 93 years ago, a Vatican decree (*Ne Temere*) finally extended these provisions to the entire world.

This sounds complicated, but it should prove that the church is acting well within its tradition and authority when it gives bishops the power to dispense their people from the Catholic form of marriage which is presently in canon law.

Marriages "out of the church" may be valid

My oldest daughter was baptized and raised a Catholic. Later she joined another Christian denomination, and recently married a young man in that church. I refused to attend because I felt I had to make clear I did not approve of her entering an adulterous and invalid relationship.

When my second daughter married, I was not invited because of the prior situation, and she has cut me out of her life. I'm sorry about this, but what could I have done and be true to my beliefs?

First of all, I'm sorry for the hurt you are suffering because of these difficult family situations. I must say again, my own pastoral experience convinces me that more lasting good is accomplished when we preserve ties of love and family friendship as much as possible. You may strongly disagree with what your children do, but you still love them I hope, and they need to know that by your actions as well as words.

There is no black and white, one-size-fits-all solution for these dilemmas. To insist only one way is possible to stand for the truth in such complicated circumstances reveals either pride, or a deep need for moral decisions which are absolutely certain, with no tinges of gray or risk. Such attitudes open the way to, among other things, rash judgments about a person's state of soul.

Second, and in some ways perhaps more important if your letter describes the circumstances accurately, at least your elder daughter was probably not entering an "adulterous and invalid relationship" according to Catholic Church law. Canon law (1117) states that a person who leaves the Catholic Church "by a formal act" is no longer bound to the "form" of marriage, the obligation to be married before a priest for a valid marriage.

Exactly which behaviors might constitute such a formal act are not entirely clarified, but it is widely held that one such act would be what your daughter did, officially join another faith. In other words, her actions may have hurt and mystified you, but assuming they are otherwise free to marry, she has likely entered a marriage the Catholic Church itself considers valid and (if both are baptized) sacramental.

The church's flexibility here is another evidence that we cannot be God's surrogate in judging others. Being faithful to what we believe is one thing. Making our personal peace and serenity depend on what someone else does is something else entirely. As a famous retreat master remarked in one of his conferences, "The first step toward peace of heart is resigning as general manager of the universe." And we don't need to resign from our principles to do that.

Should family members attend this wedding?

On a supposedly Catholic television program recently, the speaker, a priest, speaking of Catholics marrying out of the church, said any Catholic attending such a marriage commits a sin.

We had a similar situation in our family. A Catholic cousin married a non-Catholic woman in her church. We decided we should attend. We made sure he knew what we thought about his action and that we were disappointed. But we told him we would be there because we love him and hope for his happiness. He thanked us and said he understood. We still think we did the right thing. Was that speaker giving a law that every Catholic must follow?

It would be impossible to bring valid reasons for the judgment the speaker made. One would need to prove that attending such a wedding is either sinful cooperation in wrongdoing, or gives genuine scandal.

Neither of those conditions is necessarily fulfilled. Whatever sin might be connected to the action was not supported by the presence of family like yourselves. You made your position clear to your cousin, and I imagine to your children and others, so there was no scandal that could fairly be taken by anyone over what you did. And your presence did not facilitate the marriage; from what you have written, it seems certain the wedding would have happened whether you were there or not. Your "cooperation," if any, was not sufficient or proximate enough to outweigh the good you wished to achieve by being there.

Marriage performed by former priest

I was recently present at a marriage that took place on a boat dock. What seemed most strange was that the officiating "minister" was a man who had been a priest, left the church, and is now married. We were told he still had authority to perform the ceremony. Can this be true legally?

You don't mention the religion of the couple, but church law is clear where Catholics are involved. Catholics normally must be married by a bishop, priest or deacon in good standing in the church if that wedding is to be valid in the Catholic Church.

Does a former priest have authority in civil law to assist validly at a marriage?

A priest has civil authority to officiate at marriages because he is an official of the Catholic Church. Thus, a priest who has left the church would seem to lose it. The reality, however, is not that simple. Apparently few states require a clergy member to be in good standing with his or her religious community in order to perform a wedding ceremony.

The Uniform Marriage and Divorce Act, produced partly under the auspices of the American Law Institute, has been adopted to some degree by most states. It recognizes a marriage if the minister is officially acknowledged by any religious denomination. This would seem to rule out priests who are no longer recognized officials of the Catholic Church. On the other hand, the act recognizes a marriage, even if the person officiating was not legally qualified, "if either party to the marriage believed him to be so qualified."

At least two major states (one of them my own, Illinois) use the same terminology in their marriage legislation. Others do not. In other words, there is no pattern that I've been able to learn that would apply to all the United States. Anyone for whom it becomes an issue would be wise to consult an attorney.

Bible and interracial marriage

Two years ago I became friends with a man with whom I work. We have developed a close relationship and are beginning to talk of marriage. Does the Bible speak of interracial relationships? I'm a Caucasian and he is Black, but with each other we don't see color.

There is nothing in the Bible specifically about interracial marriage. However, you would want to examine carefully all the concerns faced by any other couples preparing for marriage. In addition, you need to ask yourselves specifically how you will deal together with the social and perhaps economic implications for your biracial family if you marry.

Another major factor is how supportive and accepting your families will be for you and your children, and what the "climate" is for interracial families where you live.

You will, I'm sure, be asked by your parish priest to participate in the usual marriage preparation programs for your diocese, which will be helpful. Some books and other writings by couples in an interracial marriage are available in libraries and through the Internet. They should suggest some helpful insights for you.

Dispensation from form of marriage

A Catholic friend of mine is marrying a Jewish girl in a civil ceremony presided over by a justice of the peace. I've spoken to two priests on his status with the church after his marriage, and received two different answers. Will he or will he not be a Catholic in good standing after this ceremony?

The Catholic "form" of marriage requires that Catholics be married before a priest or deacon to be validly married. Bishops may dispense Catholics to be married by someone else, a minister of another church, justice of the peace, and so on. This is referred to as a Dispensation from the Form of Marriage. (CCL 1127-2) The petition for this dispensation is made through the priest who is arranging the marriage. Catholics who marry with this dispensation remain in good standing with the church.

Son left church, still bound by form?

Our son has become a "born again" Christian and plans to marry in his new church. Do we, as parents, go to the ceremony or stay away? It used to be wrong to attend such affairs, but now we don't know. Our nephew was in a similar situation recently, and his parents received all kinds of answers, including "absolutely not" and "do as you like." I'm confused.

First, it should be some consolation and support for you to note that, as I explained in a previous question, a Catholic is now obliged to be married before a priest only if he or she has not formally rejected the Catholic faith. (CCL 1117) The church, therefore, recognizes that people may leave the church, not consider themselves Catholic any more, and perhaps even embrace another faith, and should not then be bound to the Catholic form of marriage. Your son appears to be in that situation.

If he is, and if they are otherwise free to marry, his marriage would, in the opinion of canon law scholars, be a real marriage, even according to church law. While you regret his loss of the Catholic faith, this fact might affect your own acceptance of him, and of his marriage.

I am sure you wonder about the possibility of scandal. What will your action say to your son, and to the rest of your family and friends, about your own attitude toward his leaving his old faith and changing to the new religion? On the other hand, basic charity and your parental love urge that you let him realize you are not ostracizing him from your family, and that you keep lines of communication open to him.

If you feel that merely going to the wedding would indicate your approval in a way that would compromise your own faith convictions seriously, then you should not go. You may, however, as have other parents in this situation, be able to make your position clear, and attend the wedding without being misunderstood.

The solution you reach will depend on these and other facts, such as the nature of your relationships within your family, who else will know about it or be at the wedding, and your judgment as to how your friends would understand your presence there. Other children in your family, especially younger ones, are also a consideration. You naturally do not wish to confuse or mislead them about your faith and what it demands of them and you.

Perhaps today there is less danger than before in the attendance of parents at such affairs because of the widespread confusion and radical religious searching in many of our young people. One wonders on occasion, to put it bluntly, if they ever had any faith to lose, and this through no moral fault on the part of the parents. Emotional spiritual maturity of the kind required for a genuine, internal faith commitment seems to arrive late for many young people today.

Think and pray about it, decide, and don't fret over your decision.

Marriage in Protestant church?

Recently a Catholic friend was married to a divorced man in his Presbyterian church by a Presbyterian minister. We understand that a Catholic priest attended and blessed the couple after they were married. Does the Catholic Church recognize this marriage as valid and can she receive the sacraments of penance and Communion? If so, we would like an explanation.

There are two ways the marriage might take place in light of his previous union. First, there could have been an annulment of that first marriage. This means, as is discussed more at length elsewhere, that some impediment existed from the beginning of that first marriage so that in the eyes of the church, and possibly of the state as well, there was never a marriage at all.

The other way is through a procedure called Privilege of the Faith. Privilege of the Faith processes are used to dissolve the marriage of a baptized Christian and a non-baptized person so that the partners in that marriage may marry again.

The Privilege of the Faith process is somewhat similar to another procedure called the Pauline Privilege (see Paul's first Letter to the Corinthians, chapter 7). This process is used to allow a second marriage when neither partner in a first marriage was baptized.

None of these procedures are new, though the average Catholic doesn't usually hear about them until it involves a friend or member of the family. The marriage you speak of probably involved one of these processes, along with a dispensation from the form (see previous question), and would be legitimate according to Catholic marriage laws. There is no reason the Catholic wife could not receive the sacraments.

Non-Catholic marriages are valid

I am a widowed Catholic who married a twice-divorced Protestant in a civil ceremony. He was baptized and married in the Lutheran Church. I was informed by my parish priest that my marriage could not be blessed, nor could I receive the sacraments unless my husband pursued a petition of annulment.

If the church, in fact, does not recognize marriages performed outside the church, why is it necessary to have a marriage annulled which, in the eyes of the church, was never valid in the first place?

You are mistaken, as are apparently countless others both Catholic and non-Catholic, in your assumption about non-Catholic marriages.

It is true that every baptized Catholic who has not formally rejected the Catholic faith must be married before a priest (or bishop or deacon) to be married according to the laws of the Catholic Church.

That rule does not apply to people of another faith, or who have no religion at all. If neither marriage partner is Catholic and both are free to marry (if neither has a previous marriage, for example), and they were married before a qualified minister or judge, the Catholic Church recognizes this as a true, valid marriage.

If two Buddhists marry, for instance, before a Buddhist monk, we acknowledge that as a true marriage bond. Even more, if both non-Catholic partners in a marriage are validly baptized Christians, such as two Lutherans or Methodists, we Catholics view that union as not only a valid marriage but a Christian sacrament.

Hundreds of Catholics, and others who become involved in a serious relationship with Catholics, cause themselves much frustration because they do not remember this simple but essential truth. Most priests with even a little parish experience have had couples approach them to be married with the nonchalant remark, "He was married before, Father, but it doesn't count because he's not Catholic."

The church honors every marriage, Catholic or not, as a sacred union that cannot be simply brushed off. Any previous marriage by one of the partners planning a wedding must be dealt with in an appropriate way by the church before the planned marriage can take place. In this matter there is no difference between one part of our country, or the world for that matter, and another. They are provisions of the theology and law which govern the Latin Rite Church.

A Jewish-Catholic wedding

I attended a Jewish-Catholic wedding in which much of the Catholic liturgy was omitted. While it took place in the Catholic church, there was nothing Catholic about it, no sign of the cross, and the name of Christ was never mentioned. A Protestant friend who attended made the statement that it could have been performed in the courthouse. Can you explain? There was a time when the Catholic Church didn't sway one inch, and now the pendulum has swung the other way.

The kind of wedding you describe always presents a dilemma to the church, to the priest in a parish, and usually also to the families.

The Catholic is marrying someone who, apart from what Christians share in our Jewish heritage, is alien to Christian culture and traditions. By the time they are preparing the wedding, there is little chance that religious differences will affect their plans for marriage one way or the other.

In such circumstances, the church, through its pastors and others, attempts to strengthen the moral and spiritual commitments of the couple about their marriage, to respect the beliefs of both parties and their families, and to treat the Catholic with the charity and concern that any member of the church deserves. At the same time, we, the church, must be faithful to ourselves and not contradict our own beliefs.

The marriage ceremony you describe is common, and represents one pastoral attempt to respect all these responsibilities. None of our beliefs is denied; the ceremony utilizes elements of our faith which we hold in common with Jewish tradition — which elements are, of course, extremely rich. (The same policy often is followed by priests and other Christians who participate in prayer at events where both Christians and Jews are present.)

The solution is not ideal for anyone concerned. But assuming the couple are to be married with the blessing of the church, the alternative would be a dispensation from the bishop for them to be married by another clergyman or a civil judge. I imagine you agree this would be no improvement over the manner your priest handled the wedding.

Sanatio in radice

When a bishop grants a sanatio in radice, *is a record kept in the bishop's (chancery) office? Is the couple granted the* sanatio in radice *entitled to a copy of the bishop's approval for their personal records, or does this remain in church records only?*

A *sanatio in radice,* often simply called a *sanatio,* is the validation of a marriage that already has taken place. The validation is accomplished in such a way, however, that any impediment to the marriage that may have been there is dispensed or corrected, and the renewed consent of the couple is not required. According to church law, it is as if the marriage were valid from the beginning.

Suppose, for example, a Catholic man were marrying an unbaptized woman. Without a dispensation, such a marriage would not be valid in church law. Suppose further that by some oversight (which may have been unknown even by the priest and the couple) the necessary dispensation was never granted before the marriage ceremony.

By the process of *sanatio in radice* (a Latin phrase meaning "a healing at the root"), the necessary dispensation would be given perhaps months later, but the marriage is considered valid from the wedding day.

A record of such actions is kept in the chancery. If the couple request it, a copy of the record of the action may be sent to them.

Keeping vows in abusive marriage

This past Sunday the Gospel said, "What God has joined together let no man separate." In his homily, the priest described a woman whose husband frequently and severely beat her and the children. People told her to leave him and to go her mother's home. She said she would rather die than break her marriage vows. Our priest seemed to hold this woman up as an example of strength in marriage.

If we interpret the words of Jesus the way the priest did, aren't we saying that Jesus condones beating women, and that he would condone even the death of women at the hands of their husbands?

Let's pass by for now the priest's attitude and talk about the wife in his homily. I admire such a woman's desire to be generous and faithful, but something serious about marriage vows got lost somewhere.

When they were married, this woman promised to love her spouse for better or worse, for richer or poorer, until death. What love is shown in being a cooperator in her spouse's violence against her and their children?

Blunt as it may sound, this is objectively what she is when she deliberately remains in such a destructive, violent situation. Any husband who behaves this way toward his family is seriously sick. He suffers from a gross personality disorder which he is acting out on the nearest persons available. He is missing something essential in his commitment and relationship to his wife and children. To accept and adapt to such behavior is not what marriage vows mean.

Fidelity to the promise to "love for better or worse" means, in this instance, doing everything possible to stop abusive behavior, not only for her sake and the children's, but for his sake as well. Genuine "tough" love will get the message across: "This will not continue. For your sake as well as for ours, you need help. Get it." If he will not, her promises to love him, as well as the obligation to love herself and the children, do not require her to continue in a situation that allows his abusiveness to go on.

Someone may protest: There are hard things in every marriage; you learn to put up with them. True. The reason you put up with them, however, in marriage or any other good relationship, is that you are helping each other grow emotionally, spiritually and mentally.

That is clearly not happening here. The man is hurting both himself and his family. And the mother, if she is capable of any alternative, is permitting harm not only to herself and the children, but to her husband as well.

Marriage vows are meant to be kept. But if the spouse is brutally and destructively abusive, part of keeping those vows is to do whatever is possible to end the circumstances that make that abuse possible. If removing herself and the children is the only way to take one's spouse out of an atmosphere that is destroying him and everyone else, the other spouse is being faithful, not unfaithful, to his or her marriage vows by following this course.

It may be the harder path, but the alternative is to make both of them dependent, in a most unhealthy way, on each others needs and weaknesses. People in this kind of painful life need our prayers for wisdom and courage for themselves, and for understanding in those around them, especially their families and religious leaders.

Further help for abused

Your column on abusive marriage and marriage vows meant much to me in dealing with my own feelings and memories. I have sent your column to others, including my own daughter, who endured 17 years with a husband who physically abused her. It is sad to need to talk about these things, but you gave us the courage to do it.

My other children and I have discussed your answer and we want you to know you have helped our family answer some difficult questions. Can you suggest further reading to learn more about how to understand this problem and how to deal with it?

Many excellent books give helpful insights on spousal and parental abuse. Two that stand out in my mind, though they're not "how to" books directly on the subject, are by Dr. M. Scott Peck (published by Simon and Schuster). One is the popular *Road Less Traveled.* The other, *People of the Lie,* is not so well-known, but has helpful information and insights about what is really happening in abusive violence.

Another excellent, more hands-on, book is *Codependent No More,* by Melody Beattie (Harper & Row). The subtitle describes it well: How to Stop Controlling Others and Start Caring for Yourself. Someone in a situation similar to yours referred me to it several years ago. Since then I have learned it is widely used in Al-Anon and other support groups. These titles, and other excellent books on the subject, are available through any bookstore.

Witness at civil marriage?

Is it permissible for a practicing Catholic to be the main witness at a wedding between a divorced Catholic and a Protestant in a civil ceremony?

It is wrong for a Catholic to be a witness at a marriage ceremony which is invalid and wrong according to church law. (Attendance at such a marriage is another matter, discussed in other questions.) It is possible, though unlikely according to your letter, that the marriage will be in accord with church legislation. This would have required action by a Catholic marriage court relating to the first marriage, and a dispensation for the new marriage to take place in another church or court. If you're not certain, your parish priest can help you find out.

Impotence: an impediment to marriage

An article I read referred to a couple who could not marry because the man was impotent. Later the bishop intervened and granted a dispensation so that the marriage could take place in a Catholic church. When I was in Catholic high school we learned that impotence was an impediment to a valid marriage. A person cannot make a contract he cannot fulfill. Impotence is as much an impediment as insanity, close blood relationship or previous marriage. I would certainly like an explanation.

You seem to remember your high school marriage class well, but for those who don't, we should note the difference between sterility and impotence.

An individual is sterile, in the legal sense of the word, when he or she is incapable of conceiving a child because of a defect in the natural internal process of generation, in the elements of that process that are involuntary. A man who produces no sperm, for example, or a woman who has no ovaries, is said to be sterile. Impotence, on the other hand, is the inability to have sexual intercourse because of a physical or emotional defect.

You are correct that impotence is an impediment to a valid marriage. And one detail is critical in this case, however. In order to be an impediment to marriage, impotence must be absolute in the sense that it is permanent, with no hope of rehabilitation that might in the future make sexual relations possible.

The bishop and other officials of the diocese involved received medical opinions from some of the best authorities in the country that such absolute impotence is very rare. Rehabilitative techniques for people who suffer from paralysis-related impotence (as the man did in this case) are improving all the time. All experts consulted suggested that these improvements hold out some hope for the man involved here. Where there is such hope, impotence is legally doubtful and the couple have a right to marry.

The bishop gave no special permission or dispensation. He followed basic principles of church law (and, incidentally, of some civil laws) and told the couple they were free to marry in the Catholic Church.

Still "husband and wife" in heaven?

I recently lost my wife of 37 years. She suffered seven months before God decided she had suffered enough. How can people in heaven be happy if they can see how miserable those left behind are? If there is no marriage in heaven, it wouldn't seem she is preparing a place for me. And if she can see me, she must know I am not happy and can never be happy again without her.

The sadness and pain you feel over the loss of your wife's presence is shared by millions of others who have experienced the death of a spouse or close friend. From the limited vision we enjoy in this earthly life, some realities always appear to be incompatible. Intense suffering and happiness are two of them. How can you or your wife be happy, when you are so miserable?

The answer, when we are able to receive it, is that things will look infinitely different when we eventually view them from God's perspective, with the eyes of eternity, the way your wife sees them now.

Suffering, whether physical, emotional or spiritual, does fit in God's plan of creation and salvation. If there were no other proof, we have Jesus Christ's life, death and resurrection to assure us.

From the Gospels, we know the Father was intimately present to Jesus always, even in the midst of his passion. Yet he did not remove that suffering. He knew that, even for his Son, it had an intimate and essential role in what enables us to come to a full and good human life.

Perhaps it all comes down to being humble enough to acknowledge that some realities of human existence lie beyond our comprehension in this life, the life your wife now understands in a way once impossible for her. She is with you in the communion of saints, supporting you. She is also brilliantly aware that in spite of all our doubts and fears, it will all fit together when we see all things as they really are.

It is true, of course, that there is no married life in heaven, certainly not in the reproductive dimension we experience here. However, several decades ago, Pope Pius XII had some enlightening and consoling words to say about that. Speaking to married couples, he noted that, while marriage itself may not endure in heaven, married love will continue. What does that mean? First of all, part of heaven will be our conscious intimacy and communion with those who were dear to us here on earth. Beyond that, however, is the fact that our personalities, our ways of loving and being which we will carry into eternity, are molded largely by the people with whom we shared this earthly life. You are a significantly different person than you would have been had you not married, and a different person than if you had married some-one other than the woman you did. In other words, your love for her and hers for you has intimate effects in both of you that, in all their goodness, will never end.

Sex and old age

I have a question we discussed recently. Are sex and intercourse permit-ted after the child-bearing possibility is eliminated because of age?

The inability to have children is not a moral or spiritual obstacle to sexual relations. Many couples (I would hope most of them) find their sexual relationship full and enriching well into the older years. Not only is there nothing wrong with it, this is the way it should be, and what they should attempt to be for each other if possible at any age.

Marry after 50 years living together?

Can a couple who lived for 50 years as man and wife, and raised five children as Catholics with a Catholic school education, now be married in the Catholic Church? No one knows they never married. They would rather die than let their children and family know the truth.

This question so intrigued me that I talked personally with the couple involved. How could they possibly carry this off for 50 years? How explain no wedding pictures? Anniversaries?

A few details are disguised to protect their privacy, but the story is basically true. They lived together a while when they were young, be-came committed to each other for life, started receiving the sacra-ments and chose a "wedding date" which they observe each year.

Now to the couple who wrote, I have two bits of advice for which you will need an attorney and a priest. The attorney can tell you, for one thing, whether or not common-law marriages are, or were, recog-nized in your state. (A common-law marriage is one for which no ceremony was ever held, but which is recognized as legal if certain requirements are met.)

Your attorney will also advise you about legal implications (inher-itance, rights concerning medical decisions, and so on) arising from the lack of documentary proof of your marriage.

Your parish priest, or any other priest in your area, should be able to guide you toward a Catholic marriage, and will do it confidentially.

Polygamy and church law

Recently I read that it was not until the late Middle Ages that a papal encyclical banned polygamy. What is the history of polygamy in the church prior to its being officially prohibited?

There is no evidence that the Catholic Church, either in its theologies or official teachings, ever approved one husband having more than one wife at the same time.

Several reasons may explain the confusion you encountered. One is the divine approval of polygamous marriages in the Old Testament. Christian theologians through the centuries have speculated on how that could be. Some said polygamy is only illicit because of an explicit command by God. A more common position is that having several wives is against the natural law but was permitted in the Old Testament by God for special reasons. In either case, none defended polygamy as a morally lawful option since the time of Christ.

Several hundred years ago the church made some strong statements against polygamy that might seem to imply this teaching was something new. These declarations, however, were to repudiate a position held by some Protestant reformers that at very least leaned heavily toward occasional permission to have more than one wife. The political leader, Philip of Hesse, for example, consulted Martin Luther and Philip Melancthon about his desire to take a second wife. They gave their approval since "what was permitted in marriage in the law of Moses, the Gospel does not take away." The Council of Trent in 1563 opposed that position.

Even into the 20th century some writers unfriendly toward the Catholic Church claimed that popes permitted bigamous unions for royal officials.

The allegation was repeated several times, for example, that Pope Clement VII declared himself prepared to grant a dispensation to King Henry VIII for bigamy. To my knowledge, no historian today seriously embraces that position.

Parents reject daughter

If a girl has entered an enforced marriage, it is obvious she has committed a sin against purity. If an accusing person (a parent of the girl) states that because she has done wrong she will never be forgiven and may never come home again, and that they never want to see her, is the parent "judging" or "condemning?" Is condemning or judging justifiable?

Your statements cry out for comment on a number of aspects besides your actual question. For example, under no circumstance, including pregnancy, is there such a thing as an "enforced marriage." Until the marriage ceremony itself, both partners are free to marry or not. In fact, in some instances the circumstances of the girl's pregnancy might increase the urgency that they *do not* marry. Anyone who encourages such a couple in the belief that they "have to get married" is guilty of a sinful and grave injustice.

Young couples whose sexual activity leads them into an unmarried pregnancy generally never stop to think of the many people they hurt and the lives they distress in addition to their own. Among those who suffer much are, in most instances, their own parents. Even so, I find it difficult to grasp how supposedly emotionally stable parents can react to their child in the manner you describe, though I know from unhappy experience that it does happen. The Gospels, beginning with the Sermon on the Mount, abound with clear statements from Christ that this attitude toward a sinner is unjustified and sinful.

Any sin committed by the two people may have been repented and forgiven long before anyone knew of the pregnancy. If God has forgiven, by what contortions of conscience could anyone assume the right to withhold forgiveness, to play God in this brutal way? And this at a time when unselfish support and love from the parents is needed more than ever!

There is, after all, still such a thing as hating the sin, which we must, and loving the sinner, which we also must.

Pregnant, afraid of parents

A recent conversation I had with a young Catholic girl disturbed me greatly. While she knew abortion was "morally wrong," the young woman said that if she ever became pregnant she would choose abortion. "My parents would kill me," she said, "or make me feel so bad I would want to kill myself."

Her parents happen to be active pro-life people. How many other young women are recommending or having abortions, knowing the spiritual consequence, to escape the wrath or heartbroken reaction of their parents or other family?

No unmarried young woman looks forward to facing her parents and saying, "I'm pregnant!" The agony, the fear, the mortification must be terrible for both parties. But mistakes in life do happen and we as Catholics are taught love and forgiveness. I hope these women believe that, and that their parents can find the strength to love by that rule.

Every life is a gift from God. If not for that young woman, then per-haps for deserving and loving couples awaiting adoption. Pro-life support should begin at home, surely not by encouraging sexual activity, but by discouraging hypocrisy and, more importantly, saving lives.

Maybe everyone else already knows this. But I had to say it.

Everyone else does not know it. What you have said needs saying more than you know. Thanks for writing.

Adult children no longer go to Mass

During our 40 years of marriage, my husband and I had rough times, but we felt we had a good family. Three of our children survived. They all had a good Christian education and training. Our sons went to Mass often and served Mass sometimes nearly daily. Our daughter was in the con-vent nearly 10 years and left. She married, divorced, and is now living with a man. Our children are basically good, but none of them goes to church anymore. I feel I must have done something wrong. Can you give me any idea on how to deal with all this?

We must acknowledge there comes a point when adult children be-come responsible for their own lives. It is a time when parents, after having done their reasonable best for their sons and daughters, allow that responsibility to shift to their children's shoulders.

They need not agree, or pretend to agree, with all those children do. But a great load is lifted once we accept the fact that they are now adult persons in their own right and must answer for their own lives. We need not, and should not, feel a responsibility to provide solutions for everything, even for our families. We continue to put our best ef-forts into God's hands, relax, and allow his grace and love to go to work in the people we care for.

Furthermore, parents (and for that matter, anyone who has re-sponsibility for others) should find consolation in knowing that noth-ing done out of love for another person is ever lost. From our human experience, and particularly as Christians with the example of Christ before us, we believe in the transforming power of love. The effects of our loving actions may not always appear in the way, or at the time, we wish. They are there nevertheless, and will show themselves in times and places we never expect — and perhaps will never even know about.

Sociologists agree that children possess an uncanny instinct for absorbing and retaining the values they perceive in their parents. Once again, however, these effects may not reveal themselves in ways that will easily lessen the pain of disappointment and sense of failure on the part of parents.

In other words, when our work of being parents and nurturing does not produce the visible results we would wish, by no means does it follow we did something wrong, or that our work was a failure.

Battle with teenagers over Mass

My teenage children think I'm wrong in forcing them to go to Mass on Sundays. They are 14 and 16, and say they "don't get anything out of it." We battle every Sunday. Can you help me put the record straight? What can I do?

What record? Its all in your question, and it sounds frustrating and unhappy for both you and your children. Looking at it only from your direction right now, it's important for parents and any others responsible for growing children to keep clearly in mind what they are aiming for, long range, in the religious training of their children. I'm sure your primary goal is to help them toward a mature, living faith and trust in God, and a reverence for the Eucharist in the community of Catholics that will be with them in their adult lives. Your purpose is not simply to be able to congratulate yourself after 20 years that you've been able to get them through those church doors every Sunday morning.

There is still time to reconsider seriously what you want to achieve with your children in the matter of religion. This may involve asking yourself some confronting questions such as what your own faith means to you, and why you are so concerned that your children share it. Why do you go to Mass yourself?

If you're to support and guide your children, make yourself be specific in your answers. Perhaps a conversation with a priest or a good teacher who deals regularly with teenagers would help you. It's too bad this wasn't done more thoughtfully before — like 10 or 15 years ago.

More on teenagers and the Mass

Dear Readers:

My response to the mother who wrote saying she had a battle every Sunday morning with her teenage children about going to Mass hit tender nerves. Here's a sampling of readers' reactions:

*From **Texas**: You are wrong in saying something has seriously broken down in a home when teenage children have to be battled and forced to go to Mass. Catholic education must share in the fact that, of our eight children, only one still practices her religion. You're as frustrated as we are.*

*From **Illinois**: Your answer is typical of the parish administrator who can't be bothered with pastoring, who doesn't inquire into the possibility that the "turned off" teenager may be his fault.*

From Florida: I don't know what ivory tower you've been living in. Children who went to church with enthusiasm in their earlier years seem to undergo a personality change in adolescence. "As the twig is bent by the peer group, so the tree shall grow."

*From **Ohio**: In a good Catholic high school my daughter was taught she did not have to go to church every Sunday. Where have you been? Don't you know what they are teaching these days? Many parents are having the same problem, and it starts at school, not at home!*

My only further response to these and others who wrote is that it is useless, and usually inaccurate, to assign blame for the religious floundering of young people today. The parent asked what she could do about the problem, not what churches or schools could do. I tried to answer her.

Home, church and school are closely interrelated, and normally reflect each other. I still believe, however, that the home is the major factor in what a person becomes as an adult — which may be quite different, incidentally, from what he or she is as a teenager.

As for what is being taught in schools, have you ever gone straight to the teacher involved and asked what exactly is being said and taught? I have, several times. It can be a helpful and enlightening experience.

Finally, I pass on what one reader claims would have been the "correct answer" to the question. I disagree with some of it, especially the first sentence, which he himself contradicts at the end. But it makes many good points. Here it is:

"Until large numbers of priests learn to make their liturgies the meaningful and beautiful services they can and should be, there is nothing you can do. Your best efforts are nullified by the lifeless, sterile and cold liturgical services conducted by so many of our priests. You might try searching in your area for a parish where the priest does something more than

go through a ritualistic ceremony which not even he seems to believe in. So many priests refuse to treat the Mass as a celebration. They resent and often refuse to offer the sign of peace, and are horrified by a kiss in the sacred confines of the church.

"CCD classes are devoted to catechism-like teachings by rote, with no attempt to understand what their students need and want. These comments do not apply to all; they do apply very often. Keep trying. In the meantime, don't blame yourself. Do your best to inculcate Christian values in your children; continue to love them, encourage them and pray.

"Because of God's gift of free will, they cannot be forced into being practicing Catholics. Continue to give good example. Let them know that you yourself are aware of their problem, but are trying, through the Mass and sacraments, to stay close to God and his church."

Little children disrupt Mass?

I implore you to tackle an aggravating problem that pastors and columnists alike are apparently afraid to approach. That problem is lack of common sense among parents of small children at Mass. They fail to control fussing kids even during the homily. In churches that provide quiet rooms, pastors often refuse to require parents of small children to use them.

If you were a pastor who wished to deal with this in a genuinely Christlike manner, how would you do it? Before giving your answer, it might be worth considering a few facts. I agree with you that some parents are not as considerate as they might be when their small children disturb everyone in the vicinity. But they are by no means always the neglectful, inconsiderate parents you seem to assume.

Perhaps more often than not, those parents, sometimes single parents or Catholic partners in a mixed marriage, have exerted more effort and patience and plain determination to be there for Mass than any of the rest of us. They're doing their best. Their faith brings them. They're already hassled enough in their lives. They've come to ask the help of God (and perhaps our understanding), and are usually the first to take it personally as just one more put-down if we priests do what you seem to suggest. I know this for a fact from my own experiences with people.

I don't condone or appreciate blatant thoughtlessness any more than the next person. I do know, however, that most parents of small children are thoughtful about this, and I'm proud of the patience and understanding of the rest of the people in church when things don't always go smoothly. To some this may sound like a simplistic approach, but my feeling is that it is natural for little children to stew and fuss and sometimes cry. But (unless, of course, they drown out the best part of my homily!) I'd rather have them there than not there, especially if their parents could not come without them.

Nurseries and cry rooms may help, though I'm not sure how much. Any parish priest will tell you they're not the whole solution. College students in our community often told me they liked to come to parish Masses rather than liturgies for students only. With old people and babies and everything in between, Mass is, as one student said, "more the way it ought to be." Maybe she caught on to something the rest of us have forgotten.

Children and cults

We are parents who would like your insights about children and cults or fundamentalist sects. Our area has experienced tragedies that disturb and worry us, not only with collegians and teenagers, but even younger children. Sometimes problems are out of hand before parents even know about it.

From my experiences with families in this frightening circumstance, and from research of others, there are at least two essentials for parents to consider. These may provide a base for your group's deliberations.

First, we need to be sure our children have a solid spiritual framework for their lives. Nearly always, cults or fundamentalist evangelicals who labor aggressively and successfully to recruit participants are filling a spiritual vacuum in those who become their adherents. Being certain our children (or we ourselves) "have the answers" and "know the truths of the faith" is not enough. We must work with them at every stage of development, talk over what their faith means to them in the daily business of living, how it helps to bring sense and understanding and Christian perspective to their routine personal crises and challenges.

This requires that they be well acquainted with the Gospels and are beginning (or are well along the road as they grow) to be aware of a personal relationship with Jesus Christ. It is especially when these are lacking that cults or revivalist sects find fertile and ready ground for their message.

A fatal mistake is to assume that spiritual growth is taking place in our children simply because they go to Mass every Sunday and attend Catholic school or religion classes. Failure in these, of course, only compounds the problem and, for Catholics, nearly guarantees a serious religious crisis sometime in the future. Essential as these fundamental practices of faith are, they cannot produce a vibrant and significant faith life unless that life is actively and consciously nurtured at home, somewhat along the lines I've indicated.

Where is your children's faith? What do they believe? What do prayer, church, Christ mean to them? If we don't bring them to ask themselves those questions, eventually somebody else will. All this implies, of course, that we have developed a level of serious communication with our children, which takes us to number two.

Part of the lifeblood of such cults is a high degree of secrecy. They need to exist in a shadow world. The reason is simple. In varying measure, they depend on and demand, as much as possible, control of the minds and emotions of their adherents beyond that of other religious organizations. Therefore they must attempt to control what their members hear and read and think. Adherents must be insulated as much as possible from outside influences that might introduce "dangerous" ideas or doubts. Secretiveness, concealment of their tactics, their plans, even their membership, thus becomes a major strategy, a necessary discipline to which all are gradually introduced.

What this says is, we urgently need habits of trust and openness with our children. If we have from early on become accustomed to discussing faith and God and religion with them, we have a big head start. When we perceive that they're becoming withdrawn about religious conversations or experiences, when we hear remarks like, "You wouldn't understand; it's my business," or when they consistently avoid the subject, it is time to be concerned and do something about it. Nothing healthy or good is happening when children, of any age, feel this need to be furtive.

Clearly, such openness between parents and children cannot begin at the age of 16 or 14, or even 10. So both of these suggestions relate closely to each other. At least this is a start. I wish there were a simpler, easier answer, but I don't believe there is.

Should affairs be confessed?

My husband and I have been married about 40 years. Before we were married I had an affair. After we were married, my husband, who was in the service, asked if I had sexual relations before our marriage. I confessed.

When my husband is sober and working, he's a fine person. But when he is drunk, he accuses me of having affairs and other things I would not think of. I have never cheated on him, and have kept my marriage vows.

My doctor said my husband was using me to deal with his own guilt. He has never told me he loves me; he has written it, but never said it. It's getting too much for me.

Your letter is one more proof of something that cannot be said often enough. Such confessions by husbands and wives generally accomplish nothing except to threaten the atmosphere of that relationship for the rest of their lives.

This is particularly true when one partner prompts, or tries to force, a confession from the other.

So many negative factors are at work here that aggresive questioning about such matters gives reason to wonder about the love or emotional stability of one's partner. A normal person would usually not want to know such information, and even more would not wish to inflict the pain that such a confession causes someone he loves. These things are and should be kept between oneself and God. You cannot go back and relive your life, but maybe what I've said can help put your situation in better perspective.

I agree with your doctor. Your husband's attitude through all these years says more about him than it does about you. It seems to me you are handling the situation as well as possible. His continued lack of consideration, to put it mildly, hurts you deeply. I understand that. But your own persevering patience, love, prayer, and understanding will enable you to go on coping with it.

You cannot do this alone. Friends or counselors whom you can trust are essential. I can't be too insistent in recommending Al-Anon, a group related to Alcoholics Anonymous but consisting of the spouses and children of people who are addicted to alcohol. Members can help you cope with the Jekyll-Hyde personality your husband displays and help you understand how to depend on God and others for help.

Al-Anon or Alcoholics Anonymous should be listed in your phone book. If not, write to Al-Anon Family Group Headquarters, Box 182, Madison Square Station, New York, N. Y., 10010.

Homosexual children

We have four grown children, all raised Catholic with a Catholic education, and we enjoy a good, loving relationship with all of them. Today, the two who are the most gentle and caring, and most spiritual, are self-

proclaimed homosexuals. Both of them, one son and one daughter, claim to have known from an early age they were different. As their mother, I believe this is true.

I don't know the details of their personal lives, but does my church tell me that if these two are not able to abstain, they are going to hell? How can God, who gave them such beautiful gifts and strong human urges, reject them? Our one comfort and help has come from church ministries, all of which gave the teaching of the church on the "ideals" of behavior.

I have always sought and loved a God who is compassionate and merciful, a God we cannot understand or know everything about. Have I been wrong?

No, you are not wrong. You are facing the same fears and frustrations as thousands of other parents in this circumstance.

One of the most caring and helpful documents ever issued by the bishops of the United States is titled Always Our Children. First published in September, 1997, and revised shortly after, it was intended primarily for parents of homosexuals. It considers, as gently and as honestly as possible, many crucial points for families of homosexuals. It is impossible to relate here in detail what they say, but their opening summary of what they desire to offer mothers and fathers is itself constructive. Their message, the bishops affirm, speaks of:

"Accepting yourself, your beliefs and values, your questions and all you may be struggling with at the moment, of accepting and loving your child as a gift of God; and of accepting the full truth of God's revelation about the dignity of the human person and the meaning of human sexuality. Within the Catholic moral vision there is no contradiction among these levels of acceptance, for truth and love are not opposed. They are inseparably joined and rooted in one person, Jesus Christ."

God does not love someone any less because he or she is homosexual, says the letter, and that love is always and everywhere offered to those who are open to receiving it. St. Paul's well-known passage is quoted, that nothing can separate us from the love of God that comes to us in Christ Jesus (Romans 6:39).

The bishops repeat the church's teaching that same-sex genital behavior is objectively immoral. Whether such activity is subjectively sinful, however, whether an individual actually sins personally in engaging in these activities, depends on several factors.

Traditionally, a grave sin must involve a serious matter, and must be done with full knowledge and deliberate consent. (The *Catechism of the Catholic Church* discusses these briefly in paras. 1856-61) Whether and how these conditions may be present in an individual circumstance is often extremely difficult to unravel, even for the individual involved, let alone for anyone else.

As the bishops significantly note, sexual orientation, heterosexual or homosexual, is only one component of our self-identity. "Our total personhood," they note, "is more encompassing than sexual orientation. Human beings see the appearance, but the Lord looks into the heart."

Sometimes the best approch may be a "wait and see" attitude, while you try to maintain a trusting relationship and provide various kinds of support, information and encouragement. The bishops' revised message includes numerous suggestions and insights which, in my experience, have proven helpful to parents of homosexual children. It is available from the U. S. Conference of Catholic Bishops Publication and Promotion Service. Phone 800-235-8722. Ask for Always Our Children, publication 5-131.

Husband is homosexual

I have been married for 28 years. We have four children, two living at home. My husband has waited until now to begin acting out his homosexuality. I've been suspicious for years, but I love him. My life has been turned inside out and I don't know what to do.

You have not indicated the ages of your children still living at home, but if they are still minors, or otherwise will follow your suggestions, you need to get them help. This collapse in the sexual structure of their family, and their perceptions of that collapse, require outside professional assistance. You also need counseling and advice to help you clarify and keep healthy your own emotions and feelings, as well as to understand from your perspective what was going on in your marriage.

Fortunately or unfortunately, such experiences are common enough that support groups exist for persons as yourself, and even for your children. And I don't exclude even your adult children from the need of some support and understanding. You may call Catholic Charities or any other major social service organization to learn the names of people to contact.

The above must be your first and immediate priority. I know you love your husband and want to help him. No one can be helped in such circumstances, however, unless he or she genuinely desires help and will work to receive it. Given the years this problem has been going on in the context of an apparently normal family life, I suspect he will not be open to, or capable of, the kind of assistance you and the rest of the family need to put your lives back together. Finally, don't be afraid to talk to your parish priest or another clergyman in whom you can have confidence, and ask his help. He may have some helpful insights, and at least can direct you to the other kinds of counsel available for you.

Evolving theology of marriage

I am a woman, 57 years old, planning to be married but naturally unable to have children. An article I read recently claimed the Catholic Church has taught that marriage relations are allowed only if the couple can and want to have children. Surely that cannot mean we should not have intercourse because we cannot have children? Can't it be just a loving union of two middle-aged people who care for each other?

I'm afraid the answer to your question is more involved than you expected. The church's theology of marriage and of married intercourse developed slowly through many centuries, and is in fact still evolving. It always has seen marriage relations as good, but in explaining why, the church has had to choose between a variety of apparently contrary explanations.

One conviction it adhered to almost exclusively for centuries, was that having children is good, and having children is what makes marriage and sexual intercourse in marriage good. For many centuries, in fact, general Christian teaching was that sexual intercourse was sinful when conception was impossible.

Before going further, two facts are significant. First, throughout history until within the last two centuries, little was known about the biology of procreation. Theologians and scientists commonly believed that the "seed" of life came entirely and exclusively from the male. In intercourse the incipient human being was transferred to the woman's body where it grew until birth. This affected moral teaching, of course, since destruction of this seed was considered at least in some way homicide.

Second, from the age of St. Augustine (fourth century) nearly until our own time, the one recognized factor justifying sexual intercourse was the possible conception of a child. This philosophy, which prevailed to some degree all through these centuries, developed in reaction to some of the gnostic and dualist ("spirit is good — material things are evil") theories of those days, which one way or another threatened Christian life and doctrine. For this reason, and because it always involved a vehemence and delight which "goes beyond the bounds of reason," intercourse could be "justified" only by an intention for procreation.

These points may sound complicated and academic but they carry practical consequences which affect an honest response to your question. St. Gregory the Great, who died in the year 604, for example, followed the general teaching in his Pastoral Rules (3.27) that married people should have sexual relations only to have children, and added that if any pleasure is mixed with these relations, they sinfully transgress the law of marriage — though the sin was not serious.

Only under the powerful influence of Albert the Great (13th century) did this position concerning pregnancy begin to be reversed. The debate in those days was vehement, since it began a major break with the tradition that no other morally legitimate reason existed for intercourse than the intention to have children.

Even so, as late as the 15th century the famous preacher, St. Bernardine of Siena, referred to the "modesty" of animals during gestation as an indication that married people should not have intercourse at all during pregnancy. (Seraphic Sermons 19.1)

Only in the last 300 years or so, particularly through two highly respected theologians, Thomas Sanchez and St. Alphonsus Liguori, has the expression of affection and married love been increasingly acknowledged as valid and morally acceptable in intercourse, even when conception of a child is impossible.

All the recent popes have expanded on this theme, particularly since the landmark encyclical on Christian marriage by Pope Leo XIII (1880).

As the saying goes, this may be more than you wanted to know. Obviously, the history of this subject in the church is complicated, and all kinds of contrary opinions existed at the same time. But the above brief sketch may explain the background of what you read, and why you need not be concerned about your forthcoming marriage. The possibility of having children is not a factor you need to consider.

Origin of teachings on birth control

I know there is much controversy about birth control today and the church is officially against it. I'm puzzled, though, on how it came to teach what it does. Was it originated by a pope, or a council? What is the scriptural basis for it?

As far as we know, Jesus never taught anything explicitly on the subject of birth control. The church's position on birth control, as most of its other moral teachings, developed gradually. Questions confronted people at various times, and the church responded.

From the time of St. Paul, Christian teachers placed great emphasis on virginity, often even within marriage. Largely as a result of this emphasis, a number of strange sects arose who attacked marriage from any of several directions. Some were materialistic and sensual; others were quite "spiritual," claiming that marriage, and especially sex, were evil and beneath the dignity of enlightened Christians. To counteract these groups, the church had to answer the question: If virginity is so ideal, how does the church avoid being in the position of condemning marriage and sexual procreation?

The manner in which Christian teachers and theologians answered this question proved critical in the church for nearly 14 centuries. One option open to them was the one suggested in St. Paul's Letter to the Ephesians: Sexual intercourse is closely associated with married love and is, among other things, important for the growth and development of that love.

However, under pressures from the social structure of the time and from the great emphasis on virginity in the church, and in order to compromise with the contempt for sexuality among the "spiritual" heretical groups, theology and preaching took a different direction. Sexual intercourse can be good and holy, said Christian teachers. But what makes it good and holy is procreation, the desire for a child. Thus enjoyment of sexual relations, or having intercourse as an expression of love for one's spouse, is sinful unless the couple desires to conceive a child.

Additional support was claimed for this attitude by an appeal to "nature." The obvious physiological function of any organ (including sex organs) was the only one considered "natural," divorced from any relation to the whole person. As some early preachers and doctors of the church put it, the natural way is the way animals do it — and animals have sexual union to procreate other animals. Human beings, therefore, should do the same.

St. Augustine, who died in the year 430, crystallized this attitude toward sex in his writings. His approach generally predominated in the church until about 150 years ago; contraception was included in the lists of sins (penitentials) drawn up by various theologians since about the eighth century. Until modern times, official teaching on the subject has been generally informal and local, but has followed the attitude I just explained. As I noted in the previous response, Pope St. Gregory the Great (590-604) taught that married couples may have intercourse to have children, but if any enjoyment is mixed with it, they sin against the "law of marriage."

As anyone knows who has read St. Thomas Aquinas, Chaucer or Dante, this rather severe approach came under considerable neglect, not to say disregard, through the centuries. Only since the 19th century, however, thanks largely to one of the great theologians of modern times (St. Alphonsus Liguori), has respectable Catholic theology accepted the fact that married love and affection possess an essential significance in sexual intercourse.

Traditional teaching on contraception has been adhered to in all papal documents. But the essential role of the love and affection between husband and wife in sexual relations is increasingly emphasized, especially by Popes Pius XI, Paul VI and John Paul II. Both the Old and New Testaments tell us much about the meaning of sexuality and sexual relationships between men and women. No one seriously claims today, however, that scriptural texts can solve the birth control controversy one way or the other.

Catholic teaching on the subject was summarized and repeated in the historic encyclical letter of Pope Paul VI, *Humanae Vitae* (1968). The Holy Father surveyed the traditions of the church in its respect for the conjugal and parental designs for marriage, noted the many ways nature itself causes "a separation in the succession of births," and concluded by reiterating the position of the Catholic Church: "Nonetheless, the Church, calling men back to the observance of the norms of the natural law, as interpreted by her constant doctrine, teaches that every act of marriage intercourse must remain open to the transmission of human life." (n.11)

Popes, bishops, theologians and others have urged that people faced with decisions in this matter be helped with compassion, love, understanding, patience and acceptance. After *Humanae Vitae*, the American bishops, among many bishops' conferences, urged "those who have resorted to (contraception) never to lose heart, but to continue to take full advantage of the strength which comes from the sacrament of penance, and the grace, healing and peace in the Eucharist."

We must, therefore, have utmost concern and care for the ambiguities and tensions experienced by couples facing sometimes heart-breaking decisions. It needs to be said clearly, however, that whatever its controversial aspects, the church's position on this subject comes straight out of its reverence and respect for the gift of human life.

The question here is different from that of abortion or infanticide, where human life is already begun. Yet the church firmly believes, as Pope John Paul II has written, "that human life, even if weak and suffering, is always a splendid gift of God's goodness. Against the pessimism and selfishness which cast a shadow over the world, the Church stands for life. In each human life she sees the splendor of that 'yes,' that 'amen' who is Christ himself. To the 'no' which assails and afflicts the world, she replies with this living 'yes,' thus defending the human person and the world from all who plot against and harm life." (Exhortation on the Family, 1981; no. 30)

Purposes of marriage

Your background on the church's position on birth control is informative. The natural sex drive has a beautiful result, a new life. Isn't a secondary but nonetheless beautiful result of sex between husband and wife the relief of the sex urge, resulting in bodily peace, feelings of love and mental balance between the couple? What are the church's views on this?

In his encyclical on Christian marriage (*Casti Connubii*, 1930), Pope Pius XI taught that the mutual fulfillment and holiness of husband and wife is itself a "primary purpose" of the marriage vocation.

Vatican Council II, in all its statements on marriage, avoided the "primary-secondary" approach completely. All essential aspects of marriage — openness to children, mutual affection, sexual relations and the rest — depend on and support one another. "While not making the other purposes of matrimony of less account," says the council, "the true practice of conjugal love, and the whole meaning of family life which results from it, have this aim: that the couple be ready with stout hearts to cooperate with the love of the creator and the savior, who through them will enlarge and enrich his own family day by day." (Church in the Modern World, n. 50)

Pope John Paul II expanded on this theme in his Exhortation on the Family quoted above. "The fruitfulness of conjugal love," he wrote, "is not restricted solely to the procreation of children, even understood in its specifically human dimension. It is enlarged and enriched by all those fruits of moral, spiritual and supernatural life which the father and mother are called to hand on to their children, and through the children to the Church and the world." (n. 28.)

Onanism

In your history of the church's teaching about contraception, you failed to bring in the Bible. Look in the book of Genesis about contraception: "A detestable thing, a conjugal blasphemy that offends the highest attribute of the Father, Creation."

First, I'm not sure where you found the quote, but it is not from Scripture. Among a few things wrong with it, creation is certainly not the highest attribute of the heavenly Father. His greatest attribute, by his own frequent declaration, is his merciful, forgiving love.

Scripture was not included in the brief history to which you refer because it has little, if anything, to say directly that is helpful regarding the morality of contraception. Indirectly, of course, it says much about the meaning and value of life, the relation of children to the love and hopes of parents, the lordship and authority of God, the importance of generosity and faith, and so on, all of which play a role in any moral decisions including this one.

Presumably your reference to the Bible is to Genesis, chapter 38. Onan's brother died. According to law in the Old Testament, Onan was bound to marry his brother's widow, Tamar, and have children by her if possible. The "levirate" law prescribed that these children would legally be not his, but his brother's. For this reason, says Genesis, whenever Onan had relations with his brother's widow, "he wasted his seed on the ground, to avoid contributing offspring for his brother. What he did greatly offended the Lord, and the Lord took his life."

The passage has often been wrongly interpreted as an explicit condemnation of contraception, and even more of masturbation. It is commonly acknowledged, however, that not the "wasting of the seed," but the refusal to observe a most serious family and tribal law was primarily responsible for Onan's condemnation and punishment.

What is Natural Family Planning?

Concerning the church's teaching about contraception, how does Natural Family Planning (NFP) fit into this picture? Couples we know who teach NFP claim it is not rhythm or contraception, but something entirely different. Is that true?

While the word once referred mainly to a method of counting the days before or after menstruation ("calendar rhythm"), rhythm is, in fact, a generic term to designate any method which attempts to avoid or regulate pregnancy by avoiding intercourse when it is thought the woman is in the fertile part of her menstrual cycle. Various methods have been explored through the years to help couples avoid pregnancy by limiting intercourse to the infertile times of that cycle. NFP is one (and most probably the best) of those methods, even though it did not exist, at least under that name, until relatively recently.

Two critical elements determine the effectiveness of any "rhythm" method. One is the scientific-medical clarification of when the fertile time of a woman's monthly cycle occurs. In previous ages that time was thought to be immediately before or immediately after her "period." We now know that is not true. Under normal conditions an ovum (egg) is released from a woman's ovary about 14 days before the beginning of menstruation and lives approximately 24 hours after its release. It is during those 24 hours that fertilization (pregnancy) can take place, if the male sperm unites with the ovum. The sperm is capable of fertilizing an ovum for about 72 hours, perhaps more. Thus, there are, in very round numbers, about four days during each menstrual cycle when intercourse could result in pregnancy.

The other significant element in the effectiveness of any "rhythm" method is determining exactly when that 24-hour period with a fertile ovum occurs, thus providing basic information about when intercourse must be avoided if the couple wishes to avoid pregnancy. Once these core days have been identified as accurately as possible, certain additional factors may be considered to determine finally the "safe" days of that menstrual cycle. Of course, the system can be used in the opposite way if the couple wishes to have a child.

Numerous factors can be tested at home to attempt to determine that time. They include the woman's temperature, identifiable pains or feelings in some parts of her body that consistently accompany certain phases of her cycle, the "thickness" of vaginal secretions that vary at different times of the month, and others. Women naturally differ in their cycles. Sickness, and stress, for example, also affect any of these physiological events.

The effectiveness of any method depends on the motivation and commitment of a couple who want it to work. A good deal of patience, perseverance and discipline are required to perform these tests regularly and to abide by the findings.

Natural Family Planning combines several of the above criteria. For those couples who are sufficiently motivated and seriously want it to succeed and who are faithful to its regimen, it has a very high rate of success as a method of family planning. NFP training programs are available today in almost all dioceses and major cities.

Did church condemn NFP?

We are friends with several couples and were discussing Natural Family Planning. One older couple told us they remember when the church condemned any kind of rhythm method for family planning. We younger couples said we didn't believe that, but they insisted. Is what this couple said true? If so, how do you explain it?

Basically, your older friends are correct, but that is to oversimplify. The subject is a long and complicated one in Christian tradition.

First, let's again make our subject clear. We're speaking of any method by which a couple attempts to limit their sexual relationships to infertile times in the "rhythms" of a woman's menstrual cycle. The first people we know of, in Western civilization at least, to see the contraceptive possibilities in this method were fifth century B. C. Greek physicians. While their timing of fertile periods was faulty, it was as good as any would be until about 175 years ago.

The most important early Christian theologian to deal with the subject was St. Augustine, who severely condemned the use of infertile periods to avoid conception. He berated the Manichaeans for telling people to watch "the time after purification of the menses when a woman is likely to conceive and at that time refrain from intercourse," lest a child be conceived. This proves, he said, "that you consider marriage is not to procreate children but to satiate lust." It makes "the woman no more a wife but a harlot" (*De Moribus Ecclesiae Catholicae et Manichaeorum,* c. 18).

The question did not become too relevant morally until the 1840s, when French physician Felix Pouchet was thought to have pinpointed the fertile period more exactly. Soon this raised serious questions for theologians and priests in confession. After much controversy the matter was presented in 1880 to the Sacred Penitentiary (a Vatican agency) for answers.

The reply, which one way or another governed most official Catholic thinking on the subject for decades, concluded: "Spouses using the (rhythm) way of marriage are not to be disturbed and a confessor may cautiously insinuate the opinion in question to those spouses whom he has in vain tried to lead from the detestable crime of onanism."

In other words, to suggest limiting intercourse to the infertile periods was allowable if that was the only way to stop people from using other contraceptive techniques. Controversies on the matter pretty much died, however, when the Pouchet method proved mostly unreliable anyway.

In the 1920s, scientists in Austria and Japan (Knaus and Ogino) discovered radically new data on the fertile periods, data generally confirmed by today's science and used as the basis for most current "rhythm" programs. This data inspired further questions and development of Catholic teaching on the subject, though some major moral theologians continued to hold that rhythm could only be allowed as the lesser of two evils.

Certain Catholics today attempt to interpret those past positions as not unfavorable to the general use of the woman's sterile period for birth control. There is no question, however, that they were understood commonly by leading Catholic clergy and lay people, theologians and otherwise, as forbidding the practice.

Some of my own friends and later co-workers in family life offices around the country were shocked and scandalized when in 1951 Pope Pius XII completely opened the door to the rhythm method. "Observing the non-fertile periods alone," he said, is entirely moral if there are serious medical, eugenic, economic or moral indications, "which often occur" (Address to Italian Catholic Union of Midwives, Nov. 26, 1951, no. 36). One physician, nationally acknowledged for his expertise on the subject, spoke for many others in the 1950s when he said that any rhythm method is against the natural law, since it intentionally arranges for specific acts of sexual intercourse to be rendered infertile, thus separating the husband-wife love aspect of sexual intercourse from its potential to beget children, the same argument St. Augustine used against rhythm 16 centuries earlier.

This controversy over the morality of rhythm only abated, in fact, in face of the mushrooming contraceptive and abortion movements of the 1960s and 1970s. Since then, the door opened by Pope Pius XII has swung wide open to complete approval and encouragement by the church of this form of family planning.

Today the church's teaching is quite explicit. Utilizing the rhythm of the woman's menstrual cycle, by NFP for example, couples may, with sufficient reason, intentionally and morally attempt to arrange their sexual lives so their actions of intercourse will be infertile and not result in pregnancy.

But "each and every marriage act (intercourse) must remain open to the transmission of life." (Pope Paul VI, *Humanae Vitae* 1968, No. 12)

Sterilization

If a young Catholic woman with three children, who has unsuccessfully used the rhythm method, had her tubes tied, has she committed a mortal sin? Has her husband sinned, especially if he agreed with her in wanting no more children?

Can she go to Mass and the sacraments? Do you think the Lord tries to understand the reasons why we do what we do? Many young couples need these answers, and I'm number one on the list. I'm 28 years old.

Let's take your questions one at a time. First, and maybe the hardest to respond to: Did you commit a sin? The Catholic Church teaches that any kind of direct sterilization (such as tubal ligation or vasectomy) is objectively seriously sinful. This means that such an action in itself, considered in isolation (if that were possible) from the circumstances of the individuals involved, is a serious offense against God, our Creator, since it deliberately destroys one of the major functions of our body.

Whether an act of sterilization is subjectively sinful — that is, did the person involved actually commit a grave sin? — is a far more difficult question. Involved are such circumstances as these: Did this person realize fully that the action was seriously sinful for him or her when it was done? Were there alternatives that the individual was emotionally, intellectually and spiritually capable of choosing and carrying out? Worded more theologically, was the person morally free-willed when he acted as he did? Were other circumstances present to diminish full responsibility for possible sinfulness in what was done?

While these are routine questions in determining moral responsibility for our actions, it is usually hopeless, fruitless and sometimes even harmful to attempt to untangle them after the fact, even for the person directly concerned. Usually the individual has a pretty good idea of how his action fit in with what his conscience told him was right and wrong. Once the thing is done, the right thing is to put the matter in the hands of our Lord, ask his forgiveness for any sinfulness of which one may be guilty, and move on.

How about your husband? Encouraging and assisting another in doing something seriously wrong can itself be seriously sinful. However, the same questions discussed above would apply to him as well as to you.

Can you go to Mass and receive the sacraments? By all means! Not only can you, you should do so. As a mother and wife, and with your concern over your actions, you need the healing and forgiving love of Jesus which we experience in the sacrament of penance and the Eucharist. Don't put it off. If you feel it will help, go to a priest you feel will be compassionate and honest with you, and talk with him.

Scripture and sterilization

Is there any Scriptural text in either the Old or New Testament which directly or indirectly condemns sterilization of a man or a woman as a means of birth control?

We could not expect to find a text in Scripture directly condemning such operations. When the Bible was written and for centuries afterwards, sterilization procedures of the kind you ask about were not dreamed of. However, you are surely aware that the Bible insists numerous times that human life, including one's own, is a gift of God and in his hands, not ours. As St. Paul puts it, "None of us lives as his own master and none of us dies as his own master. While we live we are responsible to the Lord, and when we die we die as his servants. Both in life and death we are the Lord's." (Romans 5, 7-8) This clearly means more than that we cannot kill ourselves or others. We must respect the limits of our rights over the parts and functions of our bodies — proportionate to how intimate a particular part of our body is related to the wholeness of our person and our life.

Rarely, if ever, may we look to Scripture to solve specific cases involving modern technology. Bioethics, for example, presents us today with baskets full of moral questions which the writers of the books of Scripture could not have imagined. That does not mean, however, that the Bible does not proclaim some truths on the subject.

Sterility

What would be a wife's position if her husband had a vasectomy without her knowledge or approval? Would she be practicing some sort of sinful birth control by having sexual intercourse once she has been informed of the surgery?

Your question might more basically be phrased: May a married couple have intercourse even though they know their union cannot result in children because of a condition of sterility? Such a condition may be present naturally (as when one partner is unexplainably sterile), after a hysterectomy, at an older age when child-bearing years are past, and so on. No moral obstacle to sexual relations exists in these circumstances. The possibility of the wife becoming pregnant and bearing a child is not a moral requirement for intercourse.

Regardless of how it started, you have a condition of sterility in your marriage which, at least on your part, did not and does not now imply any sinful intention or deliberate wrong action. There is no reason you are required to abstain from sexual relations.

However, you cannot ignore another element in the situation. Your married life, including your sexual life, is not carried on as two individuals isolated from each other. Since the cause of the sterility in your marriage was deliberate, it is important that you help your husband heal any sinful conscience, and resolve any other concerns that might negatively affect your relationship with each other.

In vitro fertilization

A magazine we receive had a long article recently about "in vitro" fertilization. According to the author, this happens more often than we think. Is the church still against this way of conceiving babies? I know it's different, but if it helps couples conceive a child, what is so bad about it?

Technologies in the reproduction of human life are developing rapidly, but at least until now nothing has happened to diminish serious moral concerns about in vitro fertilization (IVF), or about the many other procedures for fertilization and pregnancy independent of sexual intercourse.

IVF is one method now possible to conceive a child without sexual relations between a man and woman. In this procedure, the gametes (woman's ovum and the male sperm) are united, and conception occurs in a laboratory container where the first stages of new human growth occur. Soon the developing embryo is transferred to another environment, usually the mother's (or other woman's) womb, for continuing development. Such fertilization is called heterologous if the gametes come from people who are not married to each other, and homologous if the cells come from a husband and wife married to one another.

The church considers in vitro, literally "in glass," fertilization morally unacceptable for at least three fundamental reasons. First, from the time the ovum is fertilized, a new separate human life has begun which has its own identity and dignity. Commercial, scientific and other procedures often performed on lives begun in vitro violate the respect and physical and spiritual reverence owed to these lives.

Second, IVF methods normally involve producing a number of zygotes (fertilized ova). Some or all are usually placed in a womb; all but one or a few of them usually die one way or the other. In some procedures this would involve direct killing of human life; in others it may not. At very least it wrongly places new human beings in high risk of death.

And third, this process for initiating human life is a subversion of the dignity and unity of marriage, and of the integrity of natural and necessary parental relationships with children as they come into the world. This aspect of the moral character of IVF may seem less tangible, but it is an important and profound one. In the tradition and teachings of the church, as well as in the vast majority of human social traditions through history, sexual relations in the context of the marriage relationship are the only setting worthy of bringing into existence and nurturing new human life.

Heterologous fertilization, of course, brings in the additional questions of marriage fidelity and parental identity and responsibility. But even homologous fertilization deprives human procreation of the dignity which is proper and natural to it.

Explanation of the church's teaching on these matters may be found in the March, 1987, Instruction on Respect for Human Life in Its Origin and on the Dignity of Procreation, issued by the Congregation for the Doctrine of the Faith. It says of this procedure, "In conformity with the traditional doctrine relating to the goods of marriage and the dignity of the person, the church remains opposed from the moral point of view to homologous 'in vitro' fertilization. Such fertilization is in itself illicit and in opposition to the dignity of procreation and of the conjugal union" (11, 5).

It needs to be clearly stated here that when IVF or any other kind of artificial human fertilization does happen, the resulting life is no less human and no less to be accepted and cared for with love. This, of course, underlies the first and second points I made above.

For us who were raised when there was only one way for a baby to be conceived and carried to term in the womb of its own mother, it boggles the mind to realize that today there are at least 30 different combinations of methods whereby all this can happen. And each has its own array of religious and human, and therefore moral, questions.

For the reasons given, the church's concerns about IVF and related procedures remain basically as they have been. They are not likely to change unless future technological developments somehow address and mitigate them.

CHAPTER 7

DIVORCE, ANNULMENT AND REMARRIAGE

ᕠ

Summary of Catholic marriage rules

I know you receive and answer a lot of questions concerning marriage. Some people divorce and remarry in the church, some cannot, and some have marriages annulled. Frankly it's confusing to me, maybe because I've really never seen a list of all the rules in one place. Is it possible for you to tell us what these rules or laws are? I think it would help me and probably many others to understand some of the situations in our families.

The marriage legislation of the church is long and involved, reflecting at once its concern for the sacredness of marriage and its concern for the people in painful or impossible marriage situations.

From my experience, however, the following summary of the church's present marriage laws should go far in answering questions about specific cases, as they would apply normally to our country.

1. Every baptized Catholic who has not formally rejected the Catholic faith must be married before a priest (or bishop or deacon) in order to be validly married according to the laws of the Catholic Church. Without a dispensation from the bishop, any marriage that does not take place this way is not valid in the eyes of the church. (See CCL 1108, 1116, 1117)
2. If neither marriage partner is Catholic and both are free to marry (for example, if neither one has a previous marriage), the Catholic Church recognizes the union as a true, valid marriage. Thus, contrary to what some people still believe, the church considers the marriage between two Hindus, for example, or two Baptists or Lutherans, as real valid marriages.
3. Furthermore, if both non-Catholic partners in a marriage are baptized Christians, the Catholic Church views that marriage

as a Christian sacrament. They receive the sacrament of marriage and have what Catholic theology calls a sacramental marriage.

Because they are Christians, their marriage carries with it that special reflection of the covenant of love that Jesus has for his people, his church. As the Second Vatican Council beautifully put it: "Christian partners are strengthened, and as it were, consecrated, by a special sacrament for the duties and dignity of their state. . . . The spirit of Christ pervades their whole lives with faith, hope and love." This unique character of all Christian marriages has special significance in our marriage laws, as the next point makes clear.

4. While the church does claim authority to dissolve certain marriages "in favor of the faith," it considers any sacramental marriage, in the sense explained above, beyond its reach or power to dissolve.

Thus, if it is certain that two people in a valid marriage were truly baptized in any Christian church, there is no possibility of the church's dissolving that marriage to allow either of the individuals to marry again. (Remember that "dissolving" a marriage is different from an annulment, which is a declaration that there was never a valid marriage at all, as will be discussed later.) This rules out such procedures as the Pauline Privilege or Privilege of the Faith which might be used in other circumstances, and which we'll talk about next.

Remember that in any case involving someone who has been married before and who now wishes to marry someone else in the Catholic Church, all pertinent facts (such as baptism, previous marriages and divorces, etc.) must be substantiated by appropriate documents and, if necessary, by testimony of people in a position to know. This is one way the church attempts to assure that the persons involved do not get into a new situation that will hurt them again, perhaps even worse than before.

The church does, as I said, claim authority to dissolve certain marriages so that the partners may be married again. This is what happens in most situations where a person who is Catholic marries for a second time.

If one or both partners in a valid marriage is not baptized (wherever that marriage took place), such a marriage may be dissolved by the church so that a later marriage may be true and valid. This procedure is based on a passage in St. Paul (1 Corinthians 7:12-15) in which Paul discusses marriages and remarriages of new converts to Christianity.

For at least 1,500 years, the church has interpreted this teaching as giving it the right to dissolve marriages of unbaptized people "in favor of the faith" — that is, for the good of their faith.

Such procedures may be of two kinds:

1. Pauline Privilege, named after St. Paul. This method is used to dissolve the valid marriage of two non-baptized persons if one of the partners wishes to become a Catholic and marry a Catholic. These cases are usually decided by the marriage tribunal of the local diocese.

2. Privilege of the Faith. Through this approach, the church dissolves a valid marriage of a baptized person (whether that individual is Catholic or Protestant) with a partner who is not baptized. Here, one spouse is baptized at the time of the marriage; in the Paul Privilege procedure, both are unbaptized. Normally, Privilege of the Faith cases are decided by officials in Rome.

Finally, one more word about annulment, which is a formal declaration that what seemed to be a valid marriage was never really a marriage at all. Note carefully that this is different from dissolving a marriage that is truly already in existence.

In most annulment procedures, it makes no difference whether the people involved are Catholic or Protestant, baptized or not. What must be proven is that some condition was present in the couple's relationship that would rule out the possibility of authentic, valid marriage promises.

One example of such a condition would be if one or both spouses intended never to have any children in their married life. Another example would be an emotional or psychological instability so serious in one of the partners that he or she simply was incapable of genuine, full commitment to the kind of life together that marriage involves.

Annulments are discussed more fully under other questions.

Divorced persons still Catholics

I married a Catholic in the Catholic Church. Five years later I completed instructions and was baptized, but not confirmed. Seven years after that, we were divorced.

My question is: In the eyes of the church, was I a Catholic at the time of my divorce? Because I am divorced, am I now a Catholic? I have not remarried. Is it proper for me to go to Mass and receive Communion?

There's probably not a parish in the country which can claim to have the kind of assistance and support for divorced men and women that it should have, and would like to have. So perhaps some basis exists for the feeling of being "left out" to some degree. But the fact is, divorce does not remove anyone from full membership in the church.

We Catholics make no secret of our convictions about the permanence and indissolubility of marriage. But it's also obvious that personal tragedies can develop in a marriage which make it emotionally, spiritually, and perhaps even physically dangerous if the husband and wife remain living together. One or both of the spouses has no alternative except to legally separate for his or her own health and the health of any children.

When such separations involve good and sensitive people, they are never an easy way out. They carry terrible burdens of hurt, fear and frustration which may never be completely healed or forgotten. There's just no way that the church could say to such suffering people, "You're out."

Yes, you were a member of the church after you were baptized and you are still a member of the church after your divorce. There is nothing to prevent your receiving the sacraments of penance and the Eucharist.

After the breakup of a marriage, unless outright gross infidelity of one kind or another is part of the history, a realistic and helpful assigning of guilt is probably impossible and unnecessary.

For whatever faults there were on your part, ask God's forgiveness, including through the sacrament of reconciliation, and receive the Eucharist regularly. You will need it and all the other help you can get to fulfill your new responsibilities to yourself and others.

Communion after divorce

I am a recently divorced Catholic. I understand that I can no longer receive the sacraments. For years I was taught that when you went to Mass, you should always receive Communion. Now, of course, I don't do this.

Should I still go to Mass? I can't participate fully because I cannot receive the sacrament of holy Communion. So why bother?

Let me first say again what I have said many times. You can receive the sacraments, including penance and holy Communion, right now! It continues to astound me that many Catholics, and those not of our faith, have the wrong notion about this.

The church knows that, given the human weaknesses we have, sometimes situations in a marriage demand that one of the parties seek a divorce to escape the physical or emotional abuse one partner is inflicting on the other, and perhaps on the children.

Even when circumstances are not that disastrous, and a civil divorce happens, the partners, if they are Catholic, may receive the sacrament of penance, confess any seriously sinful responsibility for the collapse of the marriage, and go to Communion.

This is no new church teaching. Perhaps because Catholic teaching about the permanence of marriage had become so ingrained, Catholics and others concluded: So if you get a divorce, you can't go to Communion.

Access to the sacraments, according to the practice of the church, becomes an issue only if a Catholic contemplates another marriage. In this case one needs to talk with the parish priest, or other parish minister, to explore what methods are possible to make that happen. I hope you, and any others in your position, will no longer deprive yourselves of these avenues of grace and strength.

Your final three-word question is an exceedingly serious one, and not easy to answer adequately, at least for me. Your instincts and convictions about the intimate connection between the celebration of the Eucharist and holy Communion are entirely valid. Certainly I, and most Catholics I believe, would agree with you in not being able to imagine going to Mass and regularly being unable to receive the Eucharist.

On the other hand, the Mass, the celebration of God's word and of the Eucharist, is still the focus and apex of our Catholic liturgical life. Catholics, for example, who remarry out of the church are not canonically excommunicated. As Pope John Paul II said years ago, "The church remains their mother, and they are part of her life" (Address to laity in San Francisco, Sept. 18, 1987).

Whoever we are, and in whatever circumstances, sharing in the eucharistic sacrifice, though incomplete without Communion, remains a high priority of that bond with the rest of the body of Christ.

Getting back to sacraments

A mother wrote to you that her divorced and separated daughter would like to return to the Catholic Church but was afraid she would not be allowed to receive the sacraments. I hope she accepts your suggestion that she talk with her parish priest and follow his advice.

I am a divorced Catholic who remarried outside the church. The last two years of the second marriage (I am now divorced again) I attended Mass on a regular basis without receiving the sacraments. Those two years of watching my fellow parishioners receive Communion while I sat were difficult and humbling. I came to realize how much we can take this weekly God-given gift for granted.

After divorcing my second husband, I tearfully approached an unfamiliar priest in an unfamiliar city. This priest was literally a godsend to me. After a long discussion and tearful confession (my first in five years) I started annulment proceedings. The following Sunday I received my first Communion in five years. Before Communion, the congregation read aloud "Footsteps." I could hardly see the words on the sheet through my tears.

As I approached Father for Communion, he looked at me and said, "Cathy, receive the body of Christ." I couldn't even respond as the tears were welling up in my heart again, as they are now reliving that day.

For the past year, every time I receive Communion I feel the glory and peace of partaking in this sacrament.

Please tell this young woman and all the people in the same situation to continue in their faith by going to Mass, whether or not they are able to receive the sacraments. I pray for them that they may find the peace that I have found through God's grace.

God has given me a very special gift, my fiance. With God's help, I plan to finally make a marriage work. I thank him every day. The priest is happily helping us through the preparations and, God willing, will unite us this next summer in the sacrament of marriage.

You give good advice. I'm sure your experience will give hope and courage to many. Thanks for writing.

Divorced and remarried

A columnist in our local paper recently discussed the remarriage of divorced Catholics and whether they could go to Communion. Several times she quoted a priest whom she named and identified as a "widely known Catholic authority on separation and divorce."

After explaining that such people were no longer excommunicated from the church, the priest said that Communion is "not a gold star, not a badge for having it all together... We say that the meal (Communion) is not supper for those who have it all together, but for those to whom the

Lord is reaching out in their struggles. This is not a relaxation of formal rules, but a greater degree of understanding of the Eucharist, that it is a meal of healing, of reconciliation for people trying to do their best under the circumstances."

What is your opinion of his attitude?

It is true, divorced and remarried Catholics are not excommunicated. That says nothing about the validity of their new marriage. It simply says that they are still members of the Catholic Church, except that they have done something seriously wrong in violation of its laws and, perhaps in most cases, divine law.

Generally, if one is a Catholic (which a remarried Catholic still is), the only other requirement for receiving the Eucharist is that he or she is not deliberately in the state of mortal sin.

Note that this does not say they have not committed a serious sin. Perhaps they have, if all necessary conditions were present. But being in the state of sin means that one deliberately continues in a sinful situation which he is morally able to abandon. This means that the individual is physically and emotionally and spiritually able to leave that situation without causing even more serious harm.

Church law puts it this way: Catholics "obstinately persevering in manifest (open, public) grave sin are not to be admitted to holy Communion." (canon 915)

To use an obvious example, a remarried man, for instance, may have extremely serious responsibilities of every kind to his present family. Even though all this may have come about because of sinful actions, those responsibilities are there now. If he simply cannot leave his home without serious physical, mental and even spiritual harm to his present wife and children, I know of almost no one who would claim he must break up that family in order to get himself straight with God.

The illustration points out that such situations are possible and that unknown circumstances can make it dangerous to judge another.

Your priest's final phrase, "trying to do the best under the circumstances," must be understood seriously and correctly. Like the expression, "follow your conscience," it can mean many things. But understood rightly in the light of the teachings of the church, it summarizes one's responsibilities before God quite well.

It should be noted, to avoid misunderstanding, that, for ministering the sacrament of the Eucharist, the position in place for the Catholic Church remains that enunciated by Pope John Paul II in his 1981 encyclical on the family. "The church reaffirms her practice, which is based on sacred Scripture, of not admitting to eucharistic communion divorced persons who have remarried. They are unable to be admitted thereto from the fact that their state and condition of life objectively contradict that union of love between Christ and the church which is signified and effected by the Eucharist." (n. 84)

Excommunication and remarriage

I still don't understand a few things about the possibility of divorced and remarried Catholics returning to the sacrament of Communion.

Does the church now consider second or third marriages all right, since these people are no longer excommunicated? If not, how can the church say it is possible for them to receive Communion if they are living in sin?

I realize this matter sounds extremely complicated and confusing to most Catholics.

First of all, be clear on one point. In eliminating the excommunication of divorced and remarried Catholics, the American bishops' statement about excommunication (1977) does not indicate acceptance of these second marriages as valid and sacramental. The fact that persons in this situation are no longer excommunicated means that they remain members of the church and may share in many ways in its life and worship. (Actually, many remarried Catholics were doing this already, which only increased confusion over the significance of the bishops' action, which they intended as an expression of concern and care for these members of our faith.)

To your second question, it is true that divorced and remarried Catholics are living in an objectively sinful situation according to the church's laws, which reflect its beliefs in the permanence of marriage. For this reason, the general rule of the church is that they cannot receive Communion.

However, whether the individuals involved are as you put it, "living in sin" as far as their own souls are concerned, is something only God can know and judge. It is possible they are not, if, for example, they sincerely wish to do everything necessary to get right with God, but find it morally impossible to leave the present spouse without serious emotional, spiritual, or physical harm to others. This is simply good traditional moral theology.

Applying, then, our traditional theology of the Eucharist, it becomes clear that receiving Communion may be considered in some instances. As the bishops said, the lifting of the excommunication does not "of itself" permit divorced and remarried Catholics to receive the sacrament of penance and the Eucharist, but the possibility is not ruled out.

A daughter and her parents' divorce

About two years ago my parents separated, then divorced six months later. My father had another girlfriend at the time, who also had divorced her husband. In the meantime I found out he had seen other women in the 21 years of my parents' marriage, and was dating this woman long before their separation.

I was told yesterday by my father that he plans to marry this woman. I am devastated. He says she is going to convert to Catholicism and they are going to be married in the Catholic Church. I cannot see at all how this marriage can even take place. Is there something I can do?

I nearly passed by your letter because it involves heavy matters for a daughter like you to be forced to deal with. However, you seem old enough to understand the hard things that need to be said, and which may be helpful to others in circumstances like yours.

Do you know what an annulment is? Briefly, it is a declaration that some circumstances existed throughout the marriage that made a marriage between those two people impossible.

We know that some people, even adults who may say the marriage vows beautifully, and even to some degree live a decent marriage, may in fact be so emotionally immature and unstable that a true marriage covenant with anyone is impossible.

I have only your letter to go on. And in no way do I pretend to anticipate decisions of marriage tribunals. I'm simply trying to help you to understand what may be going on here by telling you that, from what you have said, it may be questioned whether your father is capable, or has ever been capable, of the genuine commitment marriage requires. The promiscuity you describe during an entire marriage would seem to indicate a terribly immature personality. Such an individual may be sincere in entering a marriage, yet just not possess enough emotional or psychological maturity to commit to the community of life we believe marriage to be.

From your letter it appears that your father has introduced some sort of case to your diocesan tribunal, though if I were you I would not be too sure until I checked. If he has, the priests and other experts involved must and will make judgments on the information they receive from competent people in and out of the families.

It needs to be repeated that granting an annulment does not automatically allow an individual to enter a new marriage in the Catholic Church. When serious emotional incompetence is established as the grounds for an annulment, the annulment decree insists that no new Catholic marriage take place unless and until appropriate psychiatric therapy has brought that person to a level of emotional maturity sufficient for a real marriage. Otherwise the same problem would make the second marriage as invalid as the first.

Officials of the Catholic Church involved in these processes have the same concerns and fears and reverence for marriage as you. They do not take these responsibilities lightly. We hold marriage sacred. It is only because we do honor it as a radical commitment and dedication of one's whole self to another person that cases such as your father's are dealt with carefully and respectfully for everyone concerned.

Your father seems to be a confused and emotionally mixed-up person. If you discover that he has, in fact, initiated a case with your diocesan tribunal office, please feel free to contact that office and talk with one of the priests or other personnel there. As a concerned daughter, I'm sure they will do their best to help you understand what is going on. In the meantime, continue your prayers and keep your own obviously high ideals.

Anointing of the sick after remarriage

Can a Catholic who has remarried without an annulment receive the sacrament of the anointing of the sick? As chaplain of our Catholic medical center, I tell other staff that to receive the Eucharist or anointing, the patient must be in the "state of grace." If there is no annulment, no sacraments should be administered except in danger of death.

I am pressured to anoint these remarried people. I feel it more appropriate that confession and the Eucharist be the healing sacraments if the patient is properly disposed to receive them and their marriage status allows it. What do you think is the right course of action?

Some reasons exist in our Catholic tradition for the policy you pursue. We sometimes refer to this sacrament, formerly Extreme Unction, as a "sacrament of the living." This means it is to be received only by someone who is, as you say, in the "state of grace." This "state" is, of course, an internal condition of one's soul, one's personal relationship to God. It is not always or automatically determined by one's external or public status in the church.

Important references to this sacrament might seem to presuppose that one who receives it is in sacramental communion with the church. The decree of Vatican Council II on the liturgy, for example, in its brief outline for reform of rites for the sick, orders that "a continuous rite be drawn up, structured so that the sick person is anointed after confessing and before receiving Viaticum," the Eucharist. (nn. 73-75) This seems to imply that those who receive anointing of the sick should be at least spiritually capable of receiving the sacraments of penance and the Eucharist.

Canon law, however, says only that "the anointing of the sick is not to be conferred upon those who obstinately persist in manifest serious sin." (1007) This adds another important dimension to the situation.

Those two words, manifest (Latin, *manifesto*) and obstinately (*obstinate*) have a heavy meaning in church law. Manifest means that the individual's sin is a matter of some public knowledge. People obstinately persist in serious sin when they stubbornly reject the teachings and laws of the church, and continue in some sinful situation from which they are morally (emotionally, spiritually) and physically capable of removing themselves. All priests with any significant parish experience know that there are people, for example in a second marriage not recognized by the church, who cannot at this moment remove themselves from that situation without injustice to others, particularly their present spouse and children. Such Catholics would not be "manifest" and "obstinate" sinners in the technical sense. Canon law would seem to say they could receive anointing of the sick.

Church law uses the same terminology for those who should not be admitted to holy Communion (c. 915). The American Canon Law Society, in its first commentary on the 1983 code, notes that this restriction obviously applies to anyone excommunicated or otherwise separated formally from the communion of the church.

"Other categories of manifest and grave sins are not so neatly discernible," they continue. "The minister cannot assume, for example, that the sin of public concubinage arising from divorce and remarriage is always grave in the internal forum. Any prudent doubt about either the gravity or the public nature of the sin should be resolved by the minister (of Communion) in favor of the person who approaches the sacrament." (*The Code of Canon Law: A Text and Commentary*, 1985; p. 653)

Is divorce against the commandments?

I am a high school CCD teacher and have a question based on our text. In the teacher's guide on the sixth commandment, it lists divorce and unreasonable denial of marital rights among the main sins against this commandment. I don't understand this. What sins are involved when people divorce?

First, the basic moral questions to be asked in contemplating a divorce are: What are the real reasons? Is there a genuinely honest cause for what I'm doing? Sincerely responding to these questions is a long way from: "I'm just not interested anymore. I simply want to get out."

Every priest with even a few years of parish experience is only too familiar with the inadequate manner in which many couples, some Catholics included, prepare themselves for marriage. For this and other reasons, everyone, priests included, is aware today that numerous marriages have over the years become radically dysfunctional. They manifest serious physical or emotional abuse, totally impossible expectations on the part of one or both partners, and other evidences of a harmful relationship. This type of condition may exist from the very beginning of a marriage.

In these violent circumstances, a legal divorce may not only be allowed, it sometimes becomes an outright obligation on the part of the innocent party in order to protect the emotional, spiritual and perhaps physical health of one or both partners, and perhaps also of the children. Pursuing a divorce in this kind of situation, which is not nearly as rare as most couples in more stable marriages suppose, is understandably not sinful.

This is not to say that some sinfulness, at least objective sinfulness, is not almost always involved in what leads up to the divorce. That sinfulness may have little to do with the sixth commandment, or sex. The tragic destructiveness I mentioned above has much more to do with charity, personal respect and trust, fidelity to promises and plain caring. It is violation of these virtues by one or both spouses, not the legal action at the courthouse, that constitutes the major part of any "sin" involved in divorce.

In Catholic doctrine and law, marriage is a personal covenant commitment between a man and a woman, establishing between them a partnership, a community of the whole of life. Those are awesome words. We need to consider them seriously when we speak of these matters, and not reduce them, and possibly sins involving them, only to external actions and omissions. Insofar as they relate to Christian marriage, this applies to the Ten Commandments as well.

Marriage to a foreigner

My friend is a Catholic and in love with a man from another country. Some time ago he was married just to remain in the United States. Is there any hope for getting married soon?

If it can be proven that this man entered into a marriage primarily for the reason you indicate and did not intend a real marriage commitment to his first wife, this fact would be an obvious basis for a possible annulment of his first marriage.

This type of case has become, if not common, at least frequent during the past generation, particularly involving refugees from Latin America and Caribbean nations. But each case must be handled individually by the tribunal of the diocese in which the individuals live.

Please suggest to your friend that she ask her parish priest for his advice and assistance as quickly as possible.

If spouse is not baptized?

Can a marriage between a Catholic and a non-Catholic be dissolved because the non-Catholic was never baptized?

In his long discussion of marriage and celibacy in the first Letter to the Corinthians (chapter 7), St. Paul says that if the non-Christian spouse of a recently baptized Christian is willing to continue living together in harmony, there must be no divorce. If the non-Christian spouse is unwilling, however, the couple may separate for the good of the faith and presumably for the benefit of both.

Since the fourth century — for about 1,600 years — Christian tradition has (sometimes with considerable hesitation) seen this as a biblical basis also for allowing a divorce and remarriage in the situation you suggest. In church law it is called the Privilege of the Faith.

The procedure is not an overnight one, however, and sometimes can become quite complicated, involving problems of previous marriages, the question of whether or not the husband and wife were baptized Christians, and so forth. Each case is different and is handled separately through agencies set up in the church for that purpose.

Married a transvestite

A friend married a transvestite — a person who dresses in clothes of the opposite sex — but didn't find out until after they had been married for some time. She tried living with him, but after a few years she was in such a state the doctor recommended divorce.

She is a good Catholic, but would like to remarry. Could this be grounds to have the marriage annulled? Priests I have questioned doubt it.

It may be possible for such a marriage to be annulled. A major element in the case is the depth and extent of the psychological disorder from which her husband suffers. In certain instances, this type of person is so emotionally crippled that true consent to marriage, with the relationships and responsibilities this implies, is not judged possible.

Only appropriate psychiatric and legal consultation can determine that. A decision concerning the nullity of the marriage would then be made based on the results of such investigations.

Suggest that your friend discuss the matter personally with a priest in her area, and follow the procedure he suggests.

Lack of Form

A problem has recently surfaced within our family which has us all puzzled. Our daughter was married by a justice of the peace early last year. The marriage was a tragedy for many reasons, and they are now separated. She is filing for divorce. Our parish priest tells us we must provide copies of baptism, confirmation, and other certificates, and after a hearing she will be granted an annulment. How can this be? If the Catholic Church does not recognize her marriage and she cannot receive the sacraments in this unrecognized marriage, how can it issue an annulment? We'll appreciate any light you can shed on this.

An annulment is a declaration (by the church or civil authorities) that no marriage ever existed. Numerous reasons might exist for such a declaration, ranging from purely legal impediments through such conditions as a serious lack of proper intention for marriage, or psychological inability to commit oneself to marriage.

In your daughter's case the annulment would be granted because of what is technically called "lack of form." This means that a Catholic was not married before a priest and therefore, according to church law, the marriage is invalid. One needs to prove that he or she was a baptized Catholic who never formally rejected the church, and that the marriage ceremony never took place before a priest. (CCL 1117) The documents you are to obtain are mainly to substantiate those facts.

It is possible for a Catholic to be validly married before a minister or justice of the peace if a dispensation for such a marriage has been received from the bishop of the diocese. You give no indication, however, that your daughter obtained such a dispensation.

Judging from your letter, your daughter is free to receive the sacraments of penance and the Eucharist.

Time for marriage cases

Your column is great, and I hope you can help me. Why does a tribunal take so long to decide a Privilege of the Faith case involving a single Roman Catholic man, aged 57, marrying a divorced Methodist woman, aged 47, whose first husband was an unbaptized atheist? A pre-Cana conference priest said six months to a year is possible for a waiting period.

My dear fiance is thoroughly confused, as ordinarily four months is the only waiting time required.

I'm always cautious in making predictions about the time required for completion of a marriage case. To begin with, most cases require a number of documents and perhaps testimonies from people familiar with the couple involved; these alone may require several months, depending on the location of the witnesses and their willingness to assist in the case.

Add to this the time required for action by the local diocesan tribunal and possible (as in all Privilege of the Faith cases which involve a previous marriage in which one of the spouses was baptized) action by the appropriate officials in Rome, and you are talking about a long time.

The priests and other personnel in the tribunals I know are conscientious, hard working and knowledgeable people. With almost no exceptions, they are also extremely sensitive to the human realities and pain behind the names on the papers they work with.

Because they are concerned and aware of the anxieties of the people involved, I also have found them most understanding and helpful when anyone asks for information on the status of a particular case. There is nothing wrong with your contacting the tribunal yourself.

What is the Roman Rota?

Our daily paper carried a story not long ago about the Roman Rota. We have also seen it mentioned several times in reference to reform in the church. What is it — and why do some apparently think that it is a problem?

The Roman Rota is the name of the highest standing "court" in the Catholic Church. It goes back about 800 years, and at one time had enormous power. Appeal from its decisions even to the pope himself was impossible without the establishment of a special papal commission.

Today the Rota hears all types of cases, most of them dealing with marriage, almost always on appeal from a lower church court. It is made up of about 18 judges (called auditors), who are divided into groups of three to hear and decide cases.

In general, objections to the Rota reflect the belief of many that a decentralization of court procedures would be desirable; for instance, it might be arranged that most judicial cases which now must go to Rome for final action would be handled instead entirely within each country.

Among other things, it is argued, such decentralization would reduce considerably the time required (often several years) to obtain a decision from the overworked offices in Rome.

Annulments explained

In response to a question about annulments, you said:

"If one spouse proves to have an emotional deficiency so serious that a true married life was and is psychologically impossible for him or her, the marriage tribunal would be required to declare that no marriage ever existed even though the couple went through the marriage ceremony, lived together for several years, and had several children in the meantime."

Why don't all the so-called Catholic periodicals get together and submit a proposal to Rome that the phrase, "I take you for richer or poorer, for better or worse, in sickness and in health," be eliminated from the marriage vows?

It is because the church considers marriage vows so serious and essential that it requires couples who enter marriage not only to be sincere, but to have at least a minimum ability to know what the words mean and be able to live by them.

A 12- or 14-year-old girl or boy may love someone very much and be quite sincere in wanting to get married. The church says, however, as do most states and countries, that no matter how sincere such a child may be, he or she lacks the experience of life and the emotional and psychological maturity to realize the implications of those vows. He therefore lacks ability to commit himself to a genuine community of life that we call marriage, even though he may say the words clearly.

Surely you are aware that this kind of immaturity and lack of capacity for commitment are quite possible in someone considerably older than 12 or 14. These defects, however, are not always easily discernible; they may, in fact, only become evident some time after the couple begins to live together as husband and wife.

It will help, perhaps, if we recall that religious orders of men and women are allowed to call a candidate to final perpetual vows not only when that candidate has reached a sufficient age, but also only after some years of thought, study and prayer, and after a lengthy time of living the responsibilities that life will require.

Yet we regularly accept young couples for marriage when they have known each other but a few months, and almost nothing is known about whether either of them understands or knows what marriage means, or whether they can live up to the responsibilities of marriage..

I'm not suggesting trial marriages; in my opinion there is no such thing. Nearly every diocese in the country provides an increasing variety of helps to assure a young couple that they are prepared as much as possible for a valid, honest Christian marriage.

I only suggest that given the fact of our upset and confused culture today, we should not be surprised, or for that matter scandalized, that some couples are simply incapable of marriage with each other, and that this fact becomes inescapably clear through proper investigation.

While annulments in the Catholic Church today often derive from this sort of psychological incapacity, other reasons are also possible. Among these would be a clear intention by one of the partners contradicting an essential value of marriage, such as permanence, fidelity or openness to children.

One last remark. I strongly urge you and everyone else to resist the temptation to harsh and rash judgments about annulments and those who receive them. Believe me, annulments are no "easy way out." Behind every one lies a sad story of tragedy, broken hopes, defeat and heartbreak.

But there is another story of faith, love and deep concern for what is right that is able to sustain the individuals involved through the long and often painful annulment process. God is the only one who knows our hearts and he is, after all, the final judge.

Annulment and physical abuse

Some years ago we brought our daughter and her 18-month-old child from Florida to live with us. A neighbor of our daughter had called to tell us she had taken our daughter to get stitches in her chin. Her husband had been abusing her for over a year. She tried to stay with him, since she felt she should live with her husband.

Now it seems there is no hope for that. We understand that the diocesan marriage court decides if there are grounds for a marriage annulment. Could you suggest what action we might take?

You do not give many details, but I have found that whenever there is serious physical abuse, particularly early in marriage, there are often also other serious psychological problems that make an annulment worth investigating.

Contact your parish priest, explain the situation, and ask his advice. He will guide you through the procedures which, as you indicate, are the responsibility of the marriage court of your diocese. If it is impossible to contact a parish priest near you, you may write directly to the diocesan marriage court and explain the circumstances. They will help arrange at least an initial interview to begin the process.

When one spouse wants no children

My daughter, a Catholic, has been married to a Catholic man for four years. For two years he gave excuses for not wanting to start a family; then he told her there would be no children in their marriage at all. He left her, was unfaithful, and now wants to return to her. But he still says there will be no children. She feels there is no point in getting back together if children are going to be ruled out completely. What can I advise her to do?

In our Christian tradition, in most civil law traditions, and in the laws of our church, openness to at least the possibility of children has been considered an essential element of any valid marriage.

This does not mean that the couple must positively intend to have children. Nor does it rule out the possibility of marriage between a couple who are sterile, for whatever reason.

Openness to the possibility of children does mean, however, that neither of the spouses has a deliberate intention not to have children. If either spouse does have such an intention, saying in effect, "I do not want any children in this marriage and do not intend to have any," an essential condition of marriage is lacking in their union.

From what you have told me, that seems to be the clear state of mind of your daughter's husband. This could not be known for sure, however, without the proper kind of investigation.

I suggest you ask your daughter to go to her parish priest, or another priest with whom she can talk, and explain the situation. If it can be established that her husband has, in fact, deliberately ruled out an essential element of marriage, the church would declare that marriage annulled — that is, that no real and valid marriage ever existed between these two people.

Is annulment "Catholic divorce?"

A Protestant lady and I had a conversation about a local divorce and remarked that it would be terrible for the children. When I mentioned that Catholics do not believe in divorce, she looked at me and replied, "Yes, I know. You call it annulment." Another lady remarked, "Divorce or annulment, what's the difference?" Can you give me any help on what to say?

Judging from the number of letters I receive asking almost the same question, the confusion on this topic among Catholics as well as Protestants is extensive.

A good deal of the confusion, in my opinion, results from the mish-mash of information about annulments and the Catholic Church presented in the news media. There is a huge difference between divorce and annulment. Even complete ignorance of church law and a slight knowledge of civil law will apprise anyone of that fact, since annulment is as much a reality in civil or state law as it is in canon law.

Let's suppose a fairly rich man tires of his marriage and wants to make sure his wife gets no alimony, as she might after a divorce. It is not uncommon in this or other circumstances for the man to petition the court for an annulment, a declaration that for some legal reason there never was a marriage in the first place. This (supposedly) would eliminate any financial claim she might exercise had there been a real marriage and a simple divorce.

One could not, I think, convince that man or his wife or the judge that there is no real and significant difference, but only a semantic one, between a divorce and an annulment.

It is not possible to expand further here, but the Catholic Church's understanding of annulment is basically similar to that of civil law. The church does indeed, with Paul in the New Testament, believe that any Christian marriage is a sacrament of the church and is unassailable even by the church. In other words, it cannot be ended by any sort of "divorce."

It also believes, however, that circumstances can be present which might only become absolutely clear years later, but which made a true marriage — that is, a full Christian commitment to a common life of love and all that means in a husband-wife relationship — impossible for those two people.

When the church is asked by one of the parties to study this possibility and determine as much as is humanly possible whether or not a real marriage was present, it must in justice respond to that request as fairly and honestly as it can. This is what it does in an annulment procedure.

Where to file for annulment?

I have two questions concerning annulments. Does a petition for annulment need to be filed in the state where the marriage took place? Would the other spouse be contacted or notified of the reasons for the annulment?

Normally the petition for any marriage case, including an annulment, should be initiated with the priest in the parish where the petitioner or respondent lives at that time, or where the marriage took place. A case may be initiated, however, in any of three locations: The diocese where the wedding took place; the diocese where the petitioner lives, and the diocese where the other spouse lives.

Unless it is clearly impossible to locate the other partner in an annulment process, he or she is always contacted during the investigations and is notified of the tribunal's action if an annulment is granted. If the other partner is uncooperative and refuses to respond to any inquiries about the case, that does not prevent the case from continuing to its conclusion.

Concerned about his violence

I just finished reading one of your columns dealing with annulment and the psychological inability of one or both of the spouses to make a marriage commitment. That is where I am.

My wife and I have been married almost 17 months, but it really has been rough. At the Engaged Encounter, I told my then fiance that I couldn't make the commitment. There were many tears, but she wouldn't take no for an answer. I felt obligated to marry her.

Every once in a while I'll explode and heap a lot of pain upon her. I never hit her, but I have come extremely close. I once dragged her across the room and dropped her. I shook my fist in her face, told her to go back where she came from, and threw water on her. The last time I got mad it was murderous anger that burst out. It scares me. I've tried to get psychological help, but most people say I have to go with my wife to receive any marriage counseling. She is not open to that and chides me for running to a priest and counselor.

I had previously left a religious order on the grounds that I couldn't decide. Please pray for us and give us any advice you can.

I have mailed what assistance I could to the man who sent this letter, but it seems to me that a lot of readers need to hear what he has to say. This man, and probably also his wife, are a good lesson for the many Catholics who complain about annulments and say the church is getting soft.

My experience as a pastor, and the mail that comes to me from readers of the question column, prove that this couple is not unusual. Their situation, in fact, is not as violent and vicious as some other marriage relationships.

With any sincerity at all, one would have to honestly question whether this couple — this man at least — could possibly be truly married in the sight of God, with a real commitment to the kind of common life and love that marriage promises involve.

The danger in dealing with this subject is that we might seem to imply that any marriage with extremely serious problems between a husband and wife is almost certainly invalid and could be annulled. It is not my intention to say that. I don't believe it.

Any marriage between two reasonably normal people will encounter occasional and sometimes long-lasting strain, tensions, and differences that will call upon every bit of unselfishness, patience, forgiveness and plain generous love the individuals can muster. There will perhaps be times they could wish to get out of the marriage, feeling they just weren't "meant for each other."

These are the times when commitment, grace, perseverance, and keeping a Christian perspective on life are especially called for. These are the times that enlarge the hearts of faithful spouses beyond what they dreamed possible.

In relating this man's feelings, then, I'm not making generalizations, nor am I attempting to anticipate the decisions of a marriage tribunal after its long and careful investigation. I do hope, however, that this sad letter will help us recognize that annulment cases are not only, or even mainly, from people who are just looking for an easy way out of a marriage.

Awareness of the daily tragedies of situations like this can help us be as charitable, forgiving, and supportive as possible to the people in these circumstances and to the church authorities who are trying to help them.

Marriage case fees

I have assisted some individuals, divorced and remarried, in going to a priest to seek the possibility of an annulment. I especially am concerned about the fees that some couples have quoted. There was never a fee several years go when I was involved in a similar case. Has there been a change?

Dozens of hours of work, often including considerable consultation with professional people (physicians, psychiatrists, psychologists and others) are required to complete most annulment processes. These procedures, with added overhead costs of the offices and personnel involved, can be very expensive.

All dioceses that I know of indicate a fee requested from individuals petitioning an annulment to help cover these expenses. Normally these fees do not cover the total cost, but they help a lot and make such procedures available for as many individuals as possible. They are not a "payment" for a favorable decision in a marriage case, nor are they a condition for the completion of the case. In most instances with which I am familiar, fees are normally collected after the decision is made and are, in fact, excused (or sometimes paid by the parish involved) if the individuals are too poor to afford the fee.

Children legitimate after annulment?

If a man and woman have been legally married for a number of years and an annulment is obtained for whatever reason, are the children born to this couple considered illegitimate?

If the man and woman in question were free to marry in the first place, any children born during their legal union are considered legitimate.

Such a union is called a "putative" marriage; that is, everyone thought it was a marriage and there was no overt reason to think otherwise. The fact that some condition was present throughout the marriage that enabled it to be annulled years afterward does not change the fact that this couple was thought to be married by everyone, including even themselves. Their children are legitimate for all purposes of church law and, to my knowledge, also of civil law.

Angry over annulment

For the past five years I have attempted to assist a sister whose 26-year marriage with two children was dissolved by a tribunal on the grounds that they were psychologically incapable of a real marriage commitment. Her spouse was immediately married by a Catholic priest to another woman.

I find it difficult to understand why the church allows her tribunals to dissolve marriages this way. My sister remains single and lonely because she cannot believe the church so easily allows her remarriage. Please explain this to me.

An annulment does not "dissolve" a marriage. It is a declaration by trained authorities in the Catholic Church that no marriage ever existed between those two people. This has nothing to do with the length of time they were married, or how many children they have.

The church does not reach this conclusion as you say "so easily." Declarations of nullity come only after lengthy and intensive investigations, with every possible piece of helpful information obtained from both parties, their families, and their friends. These investigations, along with interpretation and analysis, sometimes take several years. Your sister and you must know this since she was herself part of this process.

If your sister remains unable to reconcile herself to this decision, please ask her to discuss it with a priest in her parish, or even with your diocesan tribunal. She clearly needs help to situate herself honestly and comfortably in her present spiritual situation, and move on with her life in a healthy way.

Civil record of annulment?

When a diocese grants an annulment, does the court house remove the record of a marriage from the books?

Actions of church tribunals affecting marriages are distinct from civil actions and therefore do not affect civil records. An annulment granted by a church body would not be recorded in the court house.

As a practical matter, however, church tribunals never undertake an annulment process until a civil divorce (or on occasion a civil annulment) has been finalized. In other words, a marriage ceases to exist in civil law long before a decree of annulment would be granted by a diocesan tribunal.

Need for counseling after annulment?

You have written several times that an annulment of a marriage is possible because of the psychological inability of one or both of the spouses to make a marriage commitment

Any party found "guilty" of such deficiencies by the tribunal, in my opinion, should be refused permission to enter another marriage if these deficiencies make them incapable of honest marriage consent. However, this is not the case. Once an annulment is granted, both parties are free to remarry with the blessing of the Catholic Church.

It is not true that once an annulment is granted both parties are automatically free to marry in the Catholic Church. The previous marriage is no longer an obstacle. The church does, however, recognize the very difficulty you raise.

When a serious psychological problem is discovered in an annulment process and there is no evidence this deficiency has been overcome in the intervening years, the annulment decree itself states that the individual involved may not attempt another marriage in the Catholic Church until appropriate psychiatric counseling and therapy is completed.

Divorced "worthy" to take up gifts?

What do you think of divorced Catholics who are now remarried to divorced persons taking up the gifts to the altar at Mass? These people were married in the Catholic Church the first time, with a Mass.

It is usually safe, and appropriate, to assume the pastor is sufficiently aware of the circumstances of such a family, and has made a prudent judgment on the matter. Unless there is serious reason to think otherwise, I think the proper and Christian attitude for the rest of us is:

1. happiness that the people involved are still trying to keep active in their religion and their spiritual lives, and gaining some consolation and help from their parish in what must be an extremely painful situation;
2. satisfaction that, while these persons may not be free to receive the sacraments of penance and the Eucharist, some ways have been found for them to share in the worship of God as much as possible;
3. and, the details of the divorce and remarriage and of how things were worked out for their activities in the parish should not be of excessive concern to the rest of us.

No one knows the full background in these cases except the individuals themselves, God, and perhaps to some degree the parish priest. And it is really nobody else's business. Only God knows how guilty a person is in his or her heart for what happened in the past, or how much they may regret whatever wrong has been done.

We should regard these people, then, with the same respect and kindness we owe others, and encourage them to participate in every parish activity that is open to them.

CHAPTER 8

RIGHT AND WRONG

∾

Knowing right from wrong

I always thought that when we have to decide whether something is right or wrong, we are supposed to follow our own conscience. I mentioned this in a group recently, and the priest said it was not true. According to him, we are obliged to follow the teaching of those in authority, especially in the church. Who is right?

Possibly much of your confusion arises from the fact that the word "conscience" can mean many different things.

You are correct in believing that our personal moral decisions must be made on the basis of what we ourselves honestly believe is right. Whatever another may say or do, God holds us responsible for our moral actions, and that responsibility cannot be shifted to someone else. We must reach our decision and then trustingly be able to stand before God and say, "I may be wrong, but to the best of my ability, I sincerely believe this is what I should do."

The *Catechism of the Catholic Church*, quoting Cardinal John Henry Newman, calls one's conscience the "aboriginal vicar of Christ," the voice of Christ before all others. Deep in a person's consciousness is a law he or she must obey, a voice calling him to love, to do good and avoid evil, says the catechism. Interestingly, the catechism notes that forming a good conscience is a long process, "a lifelong task." It would be easy to form one's conscience if one's only and final obligation was to follow the instructions or commands of someone else, an attitude which caused horrendous havoc during our own lifetimes.

Conscience is the individual's "most secret core and his sanctuary," says the catechism, "there he is alone with God." (n. 1776, quoting Vatican II, The Church in the Modern World, 16)

Probably no one has articulated the Catholic tradition more

clearly and unambiguously than the most prominent Catholic theologian of our generation, Cardinal Joseph Ratzinger. Over every other authority, he said, there stands the ultimate tribunal, "one's conscience, which must be obeyed before all else, if necessary even against the requirement of ecclesiastical authority."

How conscience is formed, he continued, cannot be left out of the question. But in the last resort, conscience is "transcendent," "beyond the claim of external social groups, even of the official church." (Commentary on the Documents of Vatican II, ed. Vorgrimler, 1968; on *Gaudium et Spes*, part 1, chapter 1)

What the priest possibly was attempting to tell you was that an honest conscience is not, as many people today appear to believe, a kind of blind instinct or spontaneous feeling. This could come more from selfishness or cowardice than from any good motive.

The church has spoken explicitly on this subject often in recent decades. The bishops at Vatican Council II summarized it well in their Declaration on Religious Freedom (no. 2): "Every man has the duty, and therefore the right, to seek the truth in religious matters, in order that he may with prudence form for himself right and true judgments of conscience. . . In all his activity a man is bound to follow his conscience faithfully. . . He is not to be forced to act in a manner contrary to his conscience. Nor, on the other hand, is he to be restrained from acting in accord with his conscience, especially in religious matters." (nos. 2 and 3)

A genuine Christian conscience is the product of persevering effort in charity, faith, maturity, reflection, prudence and prayer. It involves giving proper weight in these reflections to what our common sense tells us, to the principles given to us by our Lord in the Gospels, and to the insights and teachings presented for the guidance of our Christian lives by those who have responsibility as teachers in the church.

When is "sin" sin?

What exactly is meant by the moral principle: Sin is in the will, not in any external act. Over 30 years ago, in a religion class to youth in their early 20s, a priest recommended that we memorize that principle as a way to deal with personal sin. Unfortunately, he didn't explain it. What is the story?

It is true that every sin is first and primarily in our will, not in what we do. The essence of any sin is that it is a deliberate (that is, freely and consciously embraced by our free will) act against the law of God.

This means that even before any external action takes place, our will, which is meant to be turned in love and reverence toward God, says: "In this I will not obey; in this I will do what I want, not what God wants." When that happens, as Jesus himself tells us, we have already sinned.

The seriousness of the sin depends on how serious a matter we're dealing with and on other factors. But our experience of sin — our own and others' — confirms that this is the way sin happens.

Here, as is so often true, the sin of Adam and Eve offers remarkable insight into all the sins of the human family that followed. The Tempter's appeal was not to the enjoyment of the "fruit of the tree of knowledge of good and evil." Rather the devil claimed that only God's jealousy was behind his command; if they disobeyed God, they then would prove themselves to be God's equal. "God knows well that at the moment you eat of it your eyes will be opened and you will be like gods!" (Gen. 3:5)

As always, there was just enough truth to the temptation to make it attractive. By refusing to obey him, wouldn't they prove God was not above them, that they were just as "big" as he was?

The tragedy was that it was all pretense and lie. They were, after all, not the equal of their Creator. And when they forgot that, their world fell apart.

Thus the core of their sin and ours, the moment when it happens, is when our will says: "Here and now, I come first, not God. It is my will that must be done, not his."

This is not to say there is no sin in the external deed which follows that act of the will. There is more malice, hurt and destruction (in other words, more sinfulness) in actually murdering someone than in desiring and planning the action without carrying it out.

Incidentally, it is this truth that sin is first and mainly in the will, not in the action, that the church would have us be most concerned about today in the sacrament of reconciliation. Deeds are important. But it is the sinfulness in our hearts, the sinful leanings in our will that lead to those deeds, that must be dealt with above all if we are to renew our lives, reduce our faults and grow in holiness.

Making moral decisions

If the church can't or won't say what is a sin, can we ask if there really is any sin? It would seem that everyone, including Hitler, could rationalize their doings.

Unfortunately, there is, no doubt, such a thing as sin. The church can and does make absolute statements about sin. However, maybe our expectations of what exactly the church can or should say about God's laws are wrong.

Above all, we cannot think of "the church" as a sort of answer machine for every question about life and morality. The church is a living community of people struggling and working at every point through history to understand and respond to God's laws — especially the primary law of Christ to love God above all and to love our neighbor as ourselves. The bishops and pope have the primary teaching responsibility through the charism of their office, but they, too, are part of this pilgrim church. History has always taught, as it does now, that the black and white answers some people seem to demand are often not possible, or at least that such answers are not at all evident.

Also, we must remember that what we call God's laws often deal with matters of "natural law" — that is, those laws or principles of action that people must follow in order to be truly human, to provide for the right kind of physical, emotional, intellectual and spiritual growth that will make them more perfectly alive and whole as human beings. Among these would be, for example, the principles underlying the Ten Commandments.

As I explained in more detail in the second chapter, the church, again mainly through its college of bishops and the Holy Father, guides us in applying these principles to our daily lives. In carrying out such guidance, the church is faced with an ever-changing array of social, scientific, economic, political and psychological realities — all of which in some way affect what is the truly "human" or moral way to act in specific instances.

Our traditional moral principles tell us that circumstances which partially determine what is morally right or wrong change not only from one part of the world or one culture to another. They also change from one time to another.

The classic, but by no means only, example concerns accepting interest on invested money. For centuries the church taught repeatedly that this was seriously wrong because the custom seemed to threaten the economic stability of families and society. One ecumenical council (the Council of Vienne) decreed that anyone who taught that taking interest was not a sin should be punished in the same way as a heretic.

That position gradually changed as the requirements and nature of large economic systems became evident. The change occurred, however, only at the cost of long confusion and disagreement among bishops, theologians, priests and others about the legitimacy of the practice.

Christ promised us all the guidance we will need to make good, sincere moral decisions. We would do well to remember that promise, and remember that, even in the midst of what seems like confusion, Jesus always keeps that promise. If occasionally there is more gray area than we find comfortable or desirable, perhaps that is his way of telling us to be a little more self-reliant and a little more open to his grace and to the fact that we still have a lot to learn.

Finally, a key word in your question is "rationalize." People rationalize morally when they know what they want to do, know their motives are doubtful if not downright evil, and yet fish around for some phony justification to delude themselves and others. This is pure dishonesty right from scratch, and has nothing to do with genuine moral decision-making.

Why keep the commandments?

If a person has to keep the Ten Commandments to get to heaven, why did Jesus Christ die on the cross and shed his blood for us? Romans (3:24) says we are "justified freely by his grace through the redemption that is in Christ Jesus." Isn't it by the blood of the Lord, and not by the observance of the law, that we are forgiven our sins and have eternal life?

You're right. We do not keep the law of God and Jesus Christ in order to "buy" God's love and our sharing in his life. These are free, unmerited gifts.

Jesus does tell us, however, what we must do because we are his disciples, part of his family. Several times he corrected his followers when they tried to act, or even prompt him to act, against that lifestyle. (See, for example, Matthew 7:21,19:17 and chapter 25, and John 9:21.)

In other words, there are certain ways we Christians do things. And Jesus tells us we must live our lives according to that way or we just won't fit into the kingdom.

Does God punish us?

I am a teacher. While my subject is not the Bible, I do receive a lot of questions about the Scriptures. One of my students pointed out that the Book of Exodus says, "I the Lord your God am a jealous God inflicting punishment for their father's wickedness on the children of those who hate me, down to the third and fourth generation."

Does this mean my son and his children will be punished for what I do?

One of the fascinating phenomena in the Bible, particularly as we go through the history of the Old Testament, is the gradual purification and elevation of humanity's understanding of, and relationship with, God.

This is true even, perhaps especially, among the Jewish people from Abraham to Christ. More than once, for example, we read how in war the Hebrew armies annihilated their enemies, men, women and children, and even the dumb animals. This was said to be done with the blessing and sometimes at the command of God himself.

Every Christian, and probably most pagans today, would find such vindictive slaughter utterly appalling and thoroughly at odds with every Christian principle. Even in later centuries of the Old Testament, during the period before the coming of Christ, such an attitude toward one's enemies was considered incompatible with a proper understanding of God and his love for all people.

A similar development occurs in the subject you mention. Among many cultures, including the ancient Jews, a theory prevailed that guilt and innocence, holiness and sin, were tribal. If the patriarch sins, all the tribe are enemies of God — or the gods. If the patriarch is good and just, the entire tribe shares his holiness regardless of the behavior of any individual.

Denial of this type of tribal identity occurs more and more frequently as time goes on in the Old Testament. Perhaps the most dramatic refutation of this attitude is the prophet Ezekiel, whose awareness of and reverence before the majesty and infinite holiness of God is surpassed by no other prophet. At one point (chapter 18) he describes the erroneous understanding of God expressed by an old saying, "Fathers have eaten green grapes, thus their children's teeth are on edge." So ingrained was the tribal concept of guilt that Ezekiel had to defend himself (and God) against the accusation that treating people individually was unfair. The Lord is forced to say, "Is it my way that is not fair, or rather is it not that your ways are unfair?"

Before we too easily judge such ancient ideas harshly, we might ask ourselves how often we have heard others, or perhaps ourselves, remark in the face of tragedy, "What have I done to deserve this?" Unfortunately we still tend to make God in our own image and likeness, which may be the reason the image of a vengeful God, half-judge and half-executioner, dies very slowly in the human heart.

Is it possible to forgive?

Through the years I have been very badly hurt by several people, especially when I was younger. I know there is a mandate from God that we are to forgive those who offend us, even those who do grave injustice against us. I am finding it so difficult to forgive these people deep in my heart. What can someone like myself do?

The volume of mail I receive on this subject surprises me. People, obviously very good people, find themselves spiritually frustrated and guilty because they, as you, feel they cannot forgive and don't know what to do about it. From my own pastoral experience, it seems that a large part of the problem stems from the old admonition to forgive and forget. In most cases, especially when the hurt has been grievous, it is impossible to forget, even after many years.

The mistaken supposition then is that one has not forgiven the wrongdoer. We forgive others by letting go of resentment and the desire to take revenge, to inflict harm in return on those who have violated us. Memory of what happened may remain. It is normal and healthy to be angry when someone does violence to us or to someone we love, and that anger may reappear when the memory of injuries recurs.

But again, that does not rule out forgiveness. Anger, just as the other normal human passions, is necessary and proper. It's how we respond to anger that is important. When we cease to harbor the desire for vengeance, when we give up our need to get even, to punish the other person for what he or she did, we are well on the road to forgiveness.

Two very ordinary actions can be signs that, however much we still hurt, we are in the process of forgiving. First, we can pray for the other person. When we do that, we are also, even if we don't realize it, praying for our own healing. And second, we can be willing to treat the other person with civility and charity. We don't need to seek him or her out, and we don't need to be friends or buddies. But we should be open to simple Christian decency if the situation presents itself.

I know that many who say they cannot forgive have already reached this point. If not, it is something to aim for, and much more sensible than attempting to suppress our memories.

What is obscene?

My question has to do with morality I suppose — the meaning of "obscene." Obscene means something lewd or impure. But now I see it used to describe other things. A remark in our paper said that a recent speech by a high government official was obscene. How do you explain that?

The definition you give is the common one, but it is not the real, basic meaning of the word. The adjective comes down to us from ancient Greek (and perhaps Roman) drama. In many Greek plays there were hideous crimes committed: eyes were put out, parents killed their children and vice versa, and the bloodiest monstrosities were perpetrated. However, these were always done *ab* or *ob scaenam* — literally, off the scene, or off the stage, because they were considered too loathsome, too cruel, too dehumanizing to be openly laid out before decent and civilized audiences.

Thus, whatever is repulsive, cruel, or otherwise excessively shameful in man's dealing with his fellow man, came to be labeled as obscene. Sexual immodesty is, therefore, just one type — and perhaps one of the lesser types — of obscenity abounding in the world.

A good example from Scripture, incidentally, is Isaias' prophetic description of Jesus in his Passion. This future Servant of God, said Isaias, would suffer so violently that he would become as "one of those from whom men hide their faces." In that sense what was done to Jesus, and the whole episode of his subjection to it, was truly "obscene."

Sin in anger?

Is it a mortal sin to use God's name in vain in a fit of anger?

The traditional three requirements for a mortal sin are still good ones:

1. Serious matter. The action must be one which is completely incompatible with a respect and love for God.
2. Sufficient reflection. One must realize when he is doing the action (or refuses to do it in a sin of omission) that if he does what he is contemplating, he is deliberately rejecting God's love and friendship. In other words, he must be fully aware that what he is contemplating is a mortal sin.

3. Full consent of the will. Realizing all this, he still deliberately wants to go ahead and do it anyway. Considering these requirements, it is difficult to see how the action, as you describe it, could ever be a mortal sin.

Alcoholic beverages

By what authority does the Catholic Church approve drinking when the holy Scriptures are so clear regarding the Lord's attitude toward it? Has no one ever questioned this before? With all the heartache, sin, and irresponsibility that drinking causes, how can one honestly believe that it is approved by the Lord?

Certainly it has been thought of before. A number of Protestant sects, as you must know, consider any drinking of alcoholic beverages a sin.

It is impossible, however, to use the Bible in any way as a basis for this belief. There is no denying that the misuse of alcohol causes enormous suffering and is wrong. Indeed, the Scriptures say as much several times. But Scripture also has numerous good things to say about wine and encourages its proper use for everything from celebrations to bodily health.

There is no scholarly basis for saying that the word most often used in the Bible for wine (in both Greek and Hebrew) means anything else than fermented, alcoholic "fruit of the vine." That includes the wine miraculously presented by Jesus to the bride and groom at Cana, as well as the wine St. Paul tells Timothy to take occasionally for the good of his stomach. (1 Tim. 5:23)

Defense attorney's duties

Several trials which have been widely publicized have made me wonder about what a Catholic lawyer is allowed to do. Many times, from things that come out during a trial, it sure seems to me the lawyer must have known the person who hired him was guilty.

Suppose a lawyer does know, is really sure, that a person committed the crime he is being tried for. Could the lawyer take the case and try to get his client off? Isn't it wrong for a lawyer to lie and say things he knows are not true, just because he is the defense attorney?

It is wrong for an attorney to lie, especially in circumstances such as this. But that doesn't really answer your question.

In our system of justice, a person is legally (even if not morally) innocent until proven guilty. An attorney may take up the legal defense of an individual he knows is morally guilty and attempt to block a conviction.

To accomplish this, the defense attorney may use any legal means that are just. For instance, he may attempt to hide information that would be detrimental to the client, and he may attack or take advantage of weak points in the prosecution's case.

At least two actions, however, would be wrong and professionally unethical. One would be an attempt by the lawyer himself to falsify information or documents, or lie about the case or anyone connected with it.

The second is where perhaps the greatest danger lies for an attorney who is trying to prove to a jury something he knows is not true. He has no moral or legal right to deliberately attempt to confuse or intimidate a witness into giving testimony that the witness really knows is not true. It goes without saying that the attorney acts immorally in bringing a witness who has the deliberate intention of perjuring himself.

Another consideration is the character of the defendant himself. An attorney would act immorally, for example, if he designedly brought about the freedom of a psychopathic individual who would clearly constitute a menace to people around him, without in some significant way attempting to alleviate that danger.

Gossip

When does an injury to another person by true gossip become sinful? If the information is strictly true and has taken place, where is the injury or the sin?

In my experience as a priest, no sin of speech (perhaps no sins of any kind) are more destructive to our social relationships than the one you mention — and the feeling that simply because a thing is true about someone else, we are free to say whatever we like about it, whenever we like, and to whomever we like.

One who thinks and acts this way is grossly in error. When the topic of our loose gossip is true, we're dealing with the sin of detraction and contumely (insult). To lie about others, attributing to them faults and bad actions we know are untrue, is even worse, a sin of calumny or slander.

One commits the sin of detraction when he makes known the faults of another without a very good reason for doing so. It can be a serious moral offense if it does great harm to that other person's reputation by having his or her faults spread about when they otherwise would not be.

The same sin is committed when the other person is refused ordinary decency and respect, whether face to face in private, or in public, such as in newspapers or on television. Even when the other person's faults are public knowledge, it still can be a sin against charity to speak unnecessarily about those faults.

Occasionally there may be good reasons to tell another's faults, to a child's parents, for example. It is wrong, though, to imagine that just because a story about another is true, one is at liberty to spread it around. A person's good name is among his most precious possessions, and the fact that one gets a kick out of being always there with the latest tidbit is no justification for tarnishing that good name. A person's faults are a matter between himself and God. The rest of us should keep our noses out.

Scripture has many strong condemning words for gossips. In Psalm 101, God doesn't mince words: "The slanderer of his neighbor in secret — him will I destroy."

Already in his own time, St. Paul recognized the poisonous effect of this kind of conversation. He found himself forced to warn against it frequently. His advice to Titus is still valid: "Tell them not to speak evil of anyone." Which means in blunt language: "If you can't say something good about someone, keep quiet."

Catholic social teaching

I have seen many references to "Catholic Social Doctrine." I don't remember anything like this from the catechism, or in religion classes. What does it mean?

The phrase "Catholic Social Doctrine" signifies the large body of official Catholic teaching dealing with such "social" matters as economic life, rights and responsibilities of private property, political systems and their relationships to the individual citizen, labor unions, war and peace, and many others. These teachings have developed over many centuries, but have been made more specific during the past century, especially in formal teachings of the modern popes.

Pope John XXIII summarized the basics of this complex body of doctrine in one of his great social encyclicals, *Mater et Magistra*. First, he says, all aspects of economic life in a nation must be regulated not for "the special interests of individuals or groups, nor (by) unregulated competition, economic despotism, national prestige or imperialism, nor any other aim of this sort. Rather, all forms of economic enterprise must be governed by the principles of social justice and charity."

Second, all social institutions (governments, welfare programs, international bodies such as the United Nations, etc.) must aim "to achieve in social justice a national and international juridical order, with its network of public and private institutions, in which all economic activity can be conducted not merely for private gain but also in the interest of the common good" of all people.

These principles may sound trite and simple, but their violation lies at the source of most social evils of our age. Major social documents have come during the last century from nearly every pope and from many national conferences of bishops. Some of the most significant of recent popes are the encyclicals Peace on Earth of Pope John XXIII (1963), The Development of Peoples of Pope Paul VI (1967), and On Human Work of Pope John Paul II (1981).

Catholic teaching about the death penalty

There is much discussion in our state about the death penalty. The Catechism of the Catholic Church (no. 2266) repeats the "traditional teaching of the church" that public authorities have the right to punish crimes with penalties commensurate with the crime, "not excluding in cases of extreme gravity, the death penalty."

I'm really struggling with this issue. The pope and our own bishop seem to say the church is totally against the death penalty. I cannot be the only one confused. Where do we stand?

Some confusion is understandable considering the movement in the church's position, as reflected by Pope John Paul II and most bishops, over the past several years.

First, the catechism itself is now much more explicit. A new article (no. 2267) in the revised edition repeats the traditional position, but then adds, "If non-lethal means are sufficient to protect and defend the security of persons, then public authorities must limit themselves to such means." Today, it continues, the state has other ways to make a guilty person incapable of further harm, "without definitively taking away from him the possibility of redeeming himself." Cases in which execution of the offender is necessary "are very rare, if not practically nonexistent." During his 1999 visit to St. Louis, Pope John Paul II repeated his appeal to build "a consensus to end the death penalty, which is cruel and unnecessary."

Anyone who has followed events of the past several years can understand why the pope, plus an endless stream of bishops and other Catholic leaders, have come to such a hard line about the evils of the death penalty. The major reasons may be summarized as follows:

—The death penalty is applied with gross inequity. For example, 12 percent of the prisoners on death row are in Texas, which has about 7 percent of the population and leads the country by far in number of executions. Everywhere in the United States, those on death row are predominantly the poor and racial minorities.

—No evidence exists that the death penalty is a deterrent to crime. As the Texas bishops and, incidentally, the nation's chiefs of police point out, states which have the death penalty have no lower rates of crime than states without it.

—Many condemned to death have been later found innocent. At a recent conference at the Northwestern University Law School, reports showed that since 1976, when the Supreme Court reinstated the death penalty, more than 500 persons have been executed. As of last year, of the 75 individuals scheduled for execution, one out of seven had their sentences reversed because of new evidence. Based on this percentage, it is reasonable to assume that nearly 500 persons out of approximately 3,500 now on death row are innocent and may be found innocent before or after they are executed for the crimes for which they were convicted.

As the only developed nation in the world which has the death penalty, the United States is in the unenviable company of countries like Iraq, Iran and China.

There are other reasons, but one that church leaders (Catholic and others) often point to in their opposition is the dehumanization of a society that officially kills any of its members, for any reason. One mother, whose child was viciously murdered, opposed the death penalty for the murderer, saying, "There has been enough killing."

Too often plain revenge is the real motive behind wanting the death of a perpetrator of a vicious crime. And, at least in the estimation of the pope, that is not a worthy Christian motive for any action.

As Archbishop Charles Chaput of Denver wrote at the time of the Timothy McVeigh trial for the Oklahoma bombing, the death penalty accomplishes nothing but "closure through bloodletting, violence against violence."

The hope of the bishops and the pope is that we can be, and are, better people than that.

What about conscientious objection?

I know the Catholic Church in the United States has a position on conscientious objection. Do these statements of the American bishops give a moral way out of going into the armed forces?

The United States bishops have made clear that refusal to participate in a war's violence and killing can flow directly from traditional Catholic "religious training and belief." They support this claim from a number of official sources, including positions taken by the entire Catholic Church in Vatican Council II.

Some years ago, the world Synod of Bishops in Rome addressed this question. "It is absolutely necessary," they said, "that international conflicts should not be settled by war, but that other methods better befitting human nature should be found. Let a strategy of nonviolence be fostered also, and let conscientious objection be recognized and regulated by law in each nation."

Thus, the American Catholic position is not at all radical. It says in another way what our bishops insisted on in another pastoral letter (1968). Human beings will keep using war and violence to solve their problems until enough young people simply refuse to participate in them.

Beware of convicting others of sin

I cannot agree with people who contend that one is free from sin if he personally feels no guilt and has a clear conscience on the matter. I'm referring to such serious sin as abortion. As far as I'm concerned, it is childish to base our reactions on personal feelings. Too many have this attitude of permissiveness. They feel, in their particular instance, their actions are perfectly acceptable.

You're probably right in believing that many of us too easily excuse ourselves from moral responsibility even in matters of serious sin. In today's legal and social atmosphere, one area in which this can easily happen is in the direct killing of an unborn human being, which is certainly an enormous and sinful injustice.

However, we must be very careful that we never confuse the objective sinfulness of an action with the degree of guilt an individual has incurred in doing it.

To put is bluntly, there's no way you can possibly know to what degree a person is guilty of the sin of abortion.

Even the woman herself may find it almost impossible to sort out the motives and emotions and pressures which allowed her to do what she did. At any rate, her guilt, whatever it is, is a matter between her and God.

Admittedly, this is a delicate situation to deal with if a person is trying to be helpful to another. An honest acknowledgment and acceptance of one's guilt is always a first necessary step to forgiveness and healing, or it will only rise again to plague her in perhaps much more serious ways later on.

So, gentle reminders of the seriousness of what has been done, of our responsibility for our actions, and of the ready, forgiving love of Christ are always in place. But we should never pretend we know what is really going on in another person's soul.

Wrong for jury to judge?

I am a jury trial judge and must decide which prospective jurors may be excused from serving. Among the frequent excuses is the claim that Jesus said, "Judge not and you will not be judged." Often it is asserted by Jehovah Witnesses, but sometimes also by Protestant ministers. Recently to my surprise, a Catholic woman told me the same thing. This lady was unique, since many Catholic priests and nuns have served as jurors cheerfully and with dedication.

Could you explain how I might reply to people who invoke this passage?

The passages to which you refer (mainly Matthew 7:1 and Luke 6:37) are always interpreted as warnings against harsh and self-righteous criticism of others, not against a clear and open stand on moral issues that affect society.

Jesus himself teaches this attitude, and in this he is in harmony with Old and New Testament tradition. From the ancient prophets (one might particularly cite Amos, Isaiah and Jeremiah) to the Gospels, God's people have been told they must eradicate the injustices in society that cause injury, injustice and even death to the poor, the helpless, and other innocent people.

They must not, in other words, be neutral about what is happening. They are commanded not only to condemn evil done to others, but to do everything possible to eliminate that evil from human society.

Jesus stood clearly in the spirit of that tradition. The Sermon on the Mount, the criterion for the final judgment given in Matthew 25, and numerous other occasions on which the Lord spoke of the responsibility to see that justice is guaranteed for a brother or sister who is suffering unjustly, all indicate that he was not neutral to all this. Nor did he expect his followers to remain simply weeping bystanders.

Obviously, therefore, Jesus did not discourage every kind of judging in the passages your potential jurors invoke. The context shows that while we must not be vindictive and cruel, we must recognize, and help society recognize, and put an end to social injustices that seriously disrupt our life together.

It may help your jurors also to recognize that, in making legal judgments, we in no way pretend to determine how that person stands personally with God. We have no way of knowing a person's deepest soul and thus no way of knowing whether, or how much, that person is subjectively guilty of sin before God. That surely is not ours to judge.

The purpose of the court is only to determine, under proper instruction from the judge, whether the individual is guilty before the law of the crime of which he or she is accused.

Those are two very distinct kinds of judgments which not only jurors, but the rest of us, too, need to keep clearly in mind.

No more fast and abstinence?

I am puzzled by a book on Catholic spirituality which claims Friday "penance" is not merely a suggestion. A Catholic commits sin if he or she allows a Friday to pass without an act of penance. The author refers to Pope Paul VI's constitution on the subject and says a person is guilty of mortal sin by not observing a notable number of Fridays without a proportionate grave reason.

We're told we should do some kind of other penance in lieu of abstaining from meat on Friday, but I've never heard the obligation expressed in terms of sin. I know the rules about fast and/or abstinence during Lent. My question in a nutshell: Is it really a mortal sin not to do any other kind of penance on the other Fridays of the year?

The source you quote has a confusing way of expressing the present discipline of the church concerning penance on Friday. In his 1966 document *Poenitemini*, changing the regulation about abstinence from meat on Fridays, Pope Paul VI did not replace one kind of "sin" with another. He was pointing out "the implications and importance of the Lord's command to repent," since all members of the church "are in continuous need of conversion and reform." He refers to the tradition of Catholic spirituality that this penance takes many forms, from fasting and abstinence, to prayer, fulfilling the daily duties of our vocation, and patiently bearing the hardships and uncertainties of each day's struggle. Much depends on one's circumstances, he notes. Richer people will need more self-denial. The poor can offer their suffering to the Father, in union with the suffering of Christ.

In its section on the subject (1427-1439), the *Catechism of the Catholic Church* lists numerous other forms of interior and exterior penance. Habitual failure to observe some kind of regular penance, in the sense given by Pope Paul and the catechism, is a sinful violation of the commands given by our Lord in the Gospels. Christian tradition and Pope Paul tell us that. It is in that context of the Lord's call to a life of penance and conversion that the pope calls "substantial observance" of the designated days of penance a "grave obligation." In that sense your author is correct.

Your concern is also valid, however. If an individual is observing even minimally the habitual practice of penance the pope describes, it is hardly conceivable that he or she could go through a whole day without some kind of prayer, patient fidelity to life's obligations, an act of charity or any of the other forms of penance prescribed by Jesus and the church.

Nine months after *Poenitemini,* our bishops made that document's provisions specific for the United States, abrogating our obligation of Friday abstinence from meat, except during Lent. Without making it a "law," they recommended abstinence from meat on all Fridays as a praiseworthy, voluntary not obligatory, act of self-denial.

In other words, go back to the command of Christ: "If anyone wishes to come after me, he must deny himself and take up his cross and follow me" (Luke 9:23), and ask yourself what, if anything, that means to you.

Fast and abstinence rules

Could you define the Lenten obligations of fast and abstinence? Many Catholics differ about what the two words mean.

The rules are so simple any more, it's hard to see where there can be any confusion worth worrying about. In most places in the United States today, Catholics over 14 years of age must *abstain* from meat (and soup or gravy made from meat) on Ash Wednesday and all Fridays of Lent.

On two days — Ash Wednesday and Good Friday — those over 18 and under 59 should *fast.* This means only one full meal, and only liquids like milk and fruit juices between meals. The size of the full meal, and the two lesser meals, depends on the individual's physical needs.

One is excused from the whole obligation if his health or work would be seriously affected by this fast or abstinence. The Lenten emphasis today is much more on prayer, the liturgy, good works and voluntary self-denial, than on complicated and severe regulations about food. You might check with your pastor to be sure of the regulations for your diocese.

Degrees of wrong in sin

Please help this convert with something that just doesn't seem to add up. Why does the church put marrying outside the church in the same (mortal sin) category as something like murder? Aren't there degrees of wrongness even among the commandments?

You have some excellent insights on the meaning of sin. As you imply, if our life of grace is a relationship with God, that relationship can be affected, even seriously, in varying degrees.

First, you are right (and in agreement with Christian moral tradition) in seeing degrees of wrongness in acts and intentions which are seriously sinful. Thus, to say that something is a mortal sin, assuming that all necessary reflection and intentions are there, does not imply that it is "just as bad" as any other serious or mortal sin.

Sin is not measured in pounds or inches. It is an injury, sometimes a destruction, of our relationship with God; it involves actions and decisions that affect that relationship.

As in other aspects of faith, we learn much about our friendship with God by comparing it with our relationship to another human being. Some things can weaken that relationship (a "venial sin"); some actions can destroy it.

A husband, for example, might destroy his relationship with his wife by some sort of serious infidelity, until repentance and forgiveness follow. He could also destroy it by deliberate, vicious emotional abuse that strangles her spirit and perhaps even her sanity. There's no question that the second is more destructive and therefore more sinful.

According to biblical and traditional understanding of the Christian life, the same is true in our relationship with God. Some wrong actions, serious in themselves, may be objectively less destructive of our relationship to our Creator and Lord than other sins. Certain objectively sinful actions are also more subject to circumstances (fear, lack of awareness and so on) which can diminish or exclude actual personal sin.

In at least one sense, sins which are purely church laws are often, if not always, in this later category. They may undermine, or destroy to some degree, the social fabric and health of the church as the Body of Christ. But they are normally not as immediately and directly destructive of human society and human beings as violations of the Ten Commandments and other precepts of the natural law.

Sunday rest

What does it mean to "keep holy the Sabbath day" today? I am a senior citizen and try to live by the commandments. I go to Mass unless I'm sick, and say my daily prayers. The problem is that I do some knitting to keep busy.

Several ladies reproach me for this, saying it is sinful to do these things on Sunday. I don't do it for money, but just to relax, and for therapy. Is watching television less sinful than knitting?

You may be aware that the "forbidden" work idea developed in a radically different agricultural-labor society. It is futile and misses the point entirely to discuss (as we used to do) whether crocheting, gardening or changing the oil in the car are allowed on Sunday.

Our aim is rather to have our home and activities reflect, on that day above all, the peace, joy, contentment and love that should be ours because of what Jesus has done for us.

Go ahead and knit — or crochet, or watch television, or do anything else that makes you relax, feel useful or just keep busy, if that is what you like to do. The commandment to keep holy the Sabbath day has nothing to do with these kinds of things for us Christians.

If you go to Mass when you can, and keep up your prayers and other relationships with God as you are able, none of these activities is wrong for you on Sunday. Do them and enjoy them.

Whatever obligations the church has asked us to observe on Sunday are meant as an aid to keeping the spirit of reverent reflection, worship and rest. Vatican Council II calls Sunday "the original feast day" and urges that its observance should always be proposed and taught "so that it may become in fact a day of joy and of freedom from work." (Constitution on the Liturgy, 106) The *Catechism of the Catholic Church* (2185-2187) and the *Code of Canon Law* say the same: "They (the faithful) should avoid any work or business which might stand in the way of the worship which should be given to God, the joy proper to the Lord's day, or the needed relaxation of mind and body." (CCL 1247)

Sacraments after vasectomy

Under what conditions could a man receive the sacraments of penance and holy Communion if, after sincere consideration of his conscience, he determined that a vasectomy was not wrong for his circumstances and, in fact, had such surgery performed?

Putting the question precisely as you did, the answer would have to be that nothing prevents such a person from receiving the sacraments. One does not commit a mortal sin unless in doing the action he believes and reflects sufficiently on the fact that here and now he is doing something that is seriously against God's law. Your statement implies that the individual in question is doing just the opposite; as he sees it, he is saying sincerely to God: This is what I believe you want me to do. Such a person is obviously not guilty of sin, and therefore has no reason to mention the fact in confession or to keep from holy Communion.

The joker in the whole question is in the words "sincere consideration of his conscience." If you recall another question about conscience, you know that an honest conscience necessarily includes many factors, not the least of which is the moral guidance given by our Christian faith, and by the church.

It also includes at least one most essential "consultation," the one with one's spouse. Even apart from any Christian morality, consideration of such decisions in isolation from or against the wishes of one's wife would be in itself a grave offense against justice and charity.

"Sincere consideration of one's conscience" with prayer, faith, and trust, is within the ability of each of us. It seems to me, however, that some of us are occasionally tempted to make it more spontaneous and simple than it in fact is, especially in matters of large, long-range importance. I would suggest that you have not fulfilled that responsibility until you have discussed the subject with a knowledgeable priest.

Should this vasectomy be reversed?

I am engaged to a man who, prior to our engagement, had a vasectomy. Even though I am postmenopausal, my fiance has offered to have the operation reversed — at his own expense, since medical insurance will not pay for the procedure. Is that necessary? I need advice before I push him to an operation that may not be required morally.

I don't believe either of you are morally obligated to pursue this surgery.

First, neither his sterility nor yours is an impediment to your marriage. Lots of people marry validly who, for one reason or another, are sterile.

Just to keep things straight, impotence is another matter. Inability to have sexual relations with one's partner from the beginning of marriage, whether the cause is physical or emotional, makes a marriage between them invalid.

As far as moral obligation is concerned, even were you still able to have children, his obligation to attempt a reversal of the vasectomy would be at least doubtful.

Since you cannot have children anyway, the old moral axiom applies, *Nemo ad inutile tenetur:* No one is obligated to an action that is useless. In other words, even were the reversal successful, your marriage would be no more fertile, as far as children are concerned, than it would be in his present condition.

You don't mention your friend's religious background. Whatever it is, since a vasectomy is objectively a serious violation of one's body, it is important for both of you that he deal with this fact spiritually and prayerfully before God, if he has not already done so.

Endorsing candidates

Is it permissible or proper for a Catholic priest to endorse by name a candidate for public office from the pulpit? To me this is inconsistent with the statement on political responsibility of the U. S. Catholic bishops in 1995.

I presume you're referring to the bishops' plea that all citizens become informed on relevant issues and vote freely according to their conscience. Nothing any priest says can deprive you of that right or obligation.

Promoting (or attacking) specific candidates by name is risky, in my opinion, if for no other reason than that it violates the legal prohibition of such electioneering by tax exempt institutions, which includes our churches.

Such siding with one candidate or another from the pulpit is usually, maybe always, counter-productive and can alienate as many as it converts. Catholic people want and deserve to have their churches free of this kind of political activity.

Just as certainly, however, neither the church nor its pastors can allow themselves to be above, or ignore, the political scene. It is their duty to assist their people — from the pulpit or otherwise — in understanding the Christian and Catholic teachings involved in current issues, and to remind their congregations that they are individually responsible for the moral and social consequences of their political decisions. And that includes the votes they cast.

The bishops, with Pope John Paul II, teach and operate in this fashion on everything from the death penalty and abortion, to human rights and arms sales to foreign countries. As they affirmed during the 1976 presidential campaign, "We are not supporting religious bloc voting, nor are we instructing people for whom to vote. Rather we urge that citizens make this decision for themselves in an informed and conscientious manner, in light of candidates' positions on the issues, as well as their personal qualifications... We shall continue to address the issues facing our nation by all appropriate means at our disposal."

It seems to me that's excellent political procedure for all of us to follow. The American bishops position on political responsibility, and rules for Catholic parishes and institutions on what to do and not do in election campaigns, is spelled out in the brief pamphlet A Call to Political Responsibility (1996) available from the U. S. Conference of Catholic Bishops Printing Office, 1-800-235-8722.

Priests and politics

I've never heard a good answer to this, and it seems to be getting worse instead of better. Why do so many priests feel they have to demonstrate, march, and get involved in all these political causes? It seems to me they ought to leave that up to us lay people.

When was the last time you yourself demonstrated, spoke out courageously, or in some way, as the saying goes, "put your body on the line" for great human needs like peace, racial and social justice, or feeding the hungry? In all candor, the answer to your question may lie in your answer to mine.

Our individual temperaments, abilities and personal inclinations will determine how we each should fulfill this obligation. One doesn't necessarily have to carry signs to be a good Catholic. But if our Christian and Catholic faith has anything significant to offer in forming policies about these great concerns, someone has to shout it from the housetops, or whatever else is needed to get these ideals out in the daylight and prompt people to consider them.

You'll notice that even the pope and bishops find it necessary today to take "political" positions on matters that were not considered the church's business only a generation ago. If in doing this they seem to be moving too much out of the sacristy, perhaps it's because they're trying to teach us that when it comes to justice, peace, and civic responsibility, our faith demands more, and more specific, things from us than we thought.

Can Catholics join the Masons?

We were told in recent years that Catholics may join the Masons if certain conditions are fulfilled. A few years later our local paper reported that the Vatican had reaffirmed its "200-year-old ban against Roman Catholics joining the Masons."

Now I read in our Catholic paper that membership in that organization is permitted only when permission is received from Rome. What is the situation? Are Catholics allowed to hold membership in Masonic organizations or not?

The former (1918) *Code of Canon Law* stated that anyone who joined the Masonic sect or other society which plots against the church or legitimate civil authority incurred automatic excommunication. Even then, however, that proscription was not in fact as absolute and universal as it was usually understood, for the following reason.

These kinds of regulations come under what might be called the penal laws of the church. And the interpretation and application of penal laws (laws which in some way limit human freedom and apply sanctions) are nuanced and limited by many principles which form part of the church's tradition of jurisprudence.

One such principle is that any regulation or censure which would forbid actions otherwise open to Catholics must be interpreted in its narrower sense. Such a regulation usually applies, for example, only where the reason for the law clearly exists in a particular situation. Thus, membership in a particular Masonic group would be forbidden only when that organization does in fact oppose the church or government by open prejudice or persecution, and undermining civil authority.

As recently as 1974, the Congregation for the Doctrine of the Faith reiterated this interpretation in a letter to episcopal conferences concerning membership in the Masons. "In the consideration of particular cases," the letter said, "it must be kept in mind that the penal law is subject to strict interpretation. Similarly, it is sound to teach and to apply the opinion of authors who hold that canon 2335 (old code) refers only to Catholics who enroll in associations which truly plot against the church.

"Nevertheless, in every case the prohibition remains in effect for clerics, religious, and members of secular institutes not to enroll in any Masonic societies." (protocol n. 272-44)

The statements of the same congregation on February 17, 1981, repeated the position that general principles of interpretation of penal laws should be applied to individual cases.

The later statement to which you refer was a declaration on Masonic association by the same Vatican congregation on November 26, 1983. While the document clearly intends to tighten up the church's position on Masonic membership, it leaves areas of considerable confusion and ambiguity which will probably be resolved only with experience.

The declaration, for example, seems to want to stress that nothing is changed, that the church's negative position "remains unaltered" and that joining the Masons "remains prohibited." Yet, as the director of the American bishops' committee on doctrine pointed out, a new regulation seems to be established restricting the power of local bishops. Such bishops, it says, no longer have authority, mentioned explicitly in the 1981 statement, to judge whether a specific Masonic organization could be approved for membership. Apparently even the 1981 statement was understood differently by bishops and by the congregation.

Anyone familiar with the history of Europe and America during the past 200 years is aware that the character of Masonry changes drastically from one place or time to another. Political and anti-religious activities so common to Masonry in Europe and Latin America, have, with some notable exceptions, hardly been evident in most parts of the United States.

Apart from the 32nd degree Southern Jurisdiction of the Scottish Rite, which often has been accused of actions and attitudes prejudicial against Catholics and the Catholic Church, Masonic organizations in the United States generally avoid the more sinister characteristics of international Masonry. In fact, individual American Catholic bishops have publicly praised the spirit and good works of Masonic groups in several parts of the country.

The 1983 *Code of Canon Law* does not mention Masons explicitly. It simply forbids Catholics to join any organization which plots against the church. (CCL 1374) However, the major objection of Christians against Freemasonry has been not only its sometimes anti-Catholic and anti-religious activities, but perhaps even more its beliefs and quasi-religious character, many aspects of which seem contradictory to Christian doctrines.

It was this in particular which inspired the strongest condemnation yet by American bishops of membership in Masonic organizations. A lengthy report from a committee of the National Conference of Catholic Bishops released in June, 1985, calls Freemasonry "irreconcilable" not only with Catholicism, but with all Christianity. "The principles and basic rituals of Masonry embody a naturalistic religion, active participation in which is incompatible with Christian faith and practice. Those who knowingly embrace such principles are committing a serious sin" in professing beliefs which are contrary to Christianity.

The study also describes the "politically reactionary and racist" nature of most U. S. Masonry today. With the exception of one lodge in New Jersey that admits blacks, it says, "all women, men under 21, and blacks are barred from Masonic initiation in regular lodges."

Local bishops or other church authorities may not make a more lenient judgment or dispense in this matter, according to the Congregation for the Doctrine of the Faith.

Clearly, the prohibition against Catholics belonging to the Masons remains serious. This position, incidentally, is similar to that of many other Christian churches around the world which forbid or discourage affiliation with Freemasonry.

Mason-related organizations

My longtime friend is a member of the Order of the Eastern Star and has invited me to join. I know the Catholic Church still officially prohibits men from joining the Masons. But what is the position on women's auxiliary groups? I'd like to join, but would not want to do so if it is forbidden by my church.

As you say, the prohibition against Catholic men joining the Masonic orders remains in existence, even in our country. However, there is a principal of church law which states that any church regulation which restricts the right of a person must be interpreted strictly. That is legal language for saying that such regulations must not be extended to cases other than those actually expressed in them (CCL 36).

Applied to your question, this means that the ban on joining the Masons means just that and nothing more. Thus, the restriction does not apply to the Order of the Eastern Star, which is an adjunct group, not a formal part of the Masons. In fact, as is well known, women are not even eligible for membership in Freemasonry.

The same would hold for the other two major auxiliary groups related to the Masons, Job's Daughters for girls, and DeMolay for boys.

Other concerns naturally need to be weighed in making such a decision. As a 1985 background report for the American bishops noted, for example, "Although the possibility of scandal may exist, the fact remains that these women and young people do not swear Masonic oaths and are not considered Masons."

In any case, the Catholic Church's prohibition against joining the Freemasons would not include these oranizations. Nevertheless, the bishops said, membership in these organizations should be "discouraged."

Habit of masturbation

Several years ago because of the incapacitation of my wife, our sex life was over. We still have a warm and loving marriage of over 30 years, but during the last few years I have fallen into the habit of masturbation.

Because I was unable to control this, I no longer received the sacraments and then gradually stopped attending Mass. I despair of ever breaking this habit. Is there an answer for me?

I'm sure there is. The details will have to be worked out gradually, but a most important part of the answer is to return to the sacraments of penance and the Eucharist. Where there is good will, as there obviously is in your letter, the life and grace available to us in these ways is valuable and powerful.

I suggest you try to find a priest, a confessor, who is willing to take the time and give the attention to assist you. Several explanations are possible for your development of this habit.

Considering your faith and your desire to live a good life, there is serious question about how deliberate, and therefore how sinful, such actions may be on your part. A kind and willing priest will help you sort this out. Be calm and peaceful about it, do the best you can, and trust that God knows where your heart is. I'm sure that with prayer, the Mass and the sacraments, you will find a way to deal with this that will give you peace of mind.

Cloning

Many times in recent years I have read about "cloning," that it is causing serious moral problems. What is it, and what are the problems?

The word comes from the Greek word, *klon*, which means a twig or a cutting, and is used to designate a process which biological science has discovered for duplicating certain organisms.

It is common knowledge now that every cell in a plant or animal carries the special, unique "genetic code" of that individual. For example, the sets of chromosomes that are in the first cell, when the sperm and ovum unite in human reproduction, divide and are duplicated eventually in the billions of cells in an adult body. Certain processes guide some cells to become arms, others to become legs, and others to become blood, but all the original genetic "information" is in each cell.

Not long ago scientists began discovering that it is possible to take a cell from some living organisms and produce a new "beginning" cell that possesses the same genetic makeup as the "parent." This cell would, in effect, grow into an identical twin of the parent body.

Until now, cloning has been successful only with some plants and animals. Some scientists expect the day is not too far distant when it will be possible with humans. Then science could, for example, choose the ideal basketball player, let's say Michael Jordan, and produce 100 Michael Jordans from his own body to form "ideal" basketball teams.

The moral question, as with so many other newly-discovered scientific possibilities, is: Should humankind do something just because it is possible? If so, under what conditions, and with what safeguards? Who will make the decisions? What human, spiritual, psychological, religious values are involved?

Unfortunately, as with many other modern technical developments from sperm banks to nuclear weapons, too many persons consider such concerns irrelevant, or at least superfluous. Their thought seems to be: "Let's try it and think of the consequences later." By that time, irreparable damage could be done to the bodies, psyches, and social structure of the human race. For these reasons, moral theologians of all faiths are wrestling publicly and urgently with such questions.

Genetic engineering

The Catechism of the Catholic Church *clearly suggests that some gene-altering procedures are moral, others are not. It would appear the church accepts some prebirth surgeries, for Down syndrome, for example. Others (for left-handedness? eye color?) seem disapproved. Some day it may be possible to isolate the "gay" gene and alter it. When are such measures approved? Or when do they, as the catechism says, violate the "personal dignity of the human being and his integrity and identity?"*

The same fundamental moral principles apply for prenatal surgery as for surgery on any other human person. Many questions arise. Do the benefits expected outweigh the risks? What burdens (pain, cost and others) will the surgery (or lack of surgery) entail for the patient and others? What degree of hope exists that the surgery will be successful? If it is successful, is the hoped-for result proportionate to the "defect" being corrected?

The unique delicacy, technological complexity and experimental nature of embryonic gene replacement and repair will naturally greatly affect answers. But they are still valid questions. For example, super high-risk procedures would be more acceptable in attempting to correct the chromosomal deficiency in Down syndrome children than they would be to alter eye color.

The catechism makes this fairly clear earlier in the same section you mention. Any procedures on the human embryo are lawful if they "respect the life and integrity of the embryo and do not involve disproportionate risks for it, but are directed toward its healing, the improvement of its condition of health or its individual survival" (quoting the 1987 Vatican document, The Gift of Life).

We will need more information than we presently possess, I believe, especially in the fields of psychology and genetic biology, before we can properly apply these norms, for example, to altering the sexual orientation of the embryo.

Transsexual surgery

We hear so much these days about transsexual operations. Is this a moral procedure — to change a man into a woman, or a woman into a man?

Your question allows of no easy or simple answer. But a couple of things will be significant factors in any such decision.

First, let's suppose we are dealing with a reasonably normal person whose male or female identity is well established — emotionally, physically and psychologically, both internally and in relationship to others. For such an individual to attempt a sex change, even to whatever slight degree that might be possible, would be a gross abuse of his or her person, and morally wrong.

Few, if any, such cases are that clear cut, however. It is possible for an individual to possess a clear genetic sexual identity (male or female chromosomes) as well as major physical male or female sex characteristics, and still suffer from a quite confused sexual identity. The complicated system of internal secretions (hormones), which interact from one organ or gland to another, is subject to all sorts of imbalance; if this imbalance is extensive enough, it may cause serious difficulties in an individual's ability to function in his or her "proper" sexual relationships.

In light of this, many other factors must be considered. Certain surgical procedures are, or soon may be, available to deal with these kinds of pathologies in men or women. For one thing, however, there's room for question in some cases how much "sex change" is really involved. More importantly, procedures are increasingly available to deal with such physical ills by therapy less drastic and questionable than surgery.

One gets the impression that most of these radical "treatments" have been carried out, up to now, with almost no serious consideration of the implications for either the individual or society. That in itself must be deplored. But it is too soon, and too many variables are involved, to conclude at this point that every operation labeled a "sex change" is always automatically wrong.

Consistent ethic of life

I have read and heard much about the "seamless garment," but no one explains it, even the priests who refer to it. Can you tell me what it is?

The "seamless garment" is another name for what is more frequently called a "consistent ethic of life." Both phrases mean that our moral teachings and positions about issues relating to human life should be consistent, and not deny on one issue what we defend on another.

In other words, if one human life is sacred, all human life is sacred, and our political and moral position should reflect that "consistency."

Though the idea is far from new, the specific consistent ethic of life, or seamless garment approach, was proposed by the late Cardinal Joseph Bernardin of Chicago in 1983. Since then it has become a major element in every serious moral discussion, from abuse of the aged and sexual exploitation, to war and the death penalty; from economic oppression of the poor and helpless, to reform of health care, and the massive violence committed today against unborn children.

The "consistent ethic" approach has profoundly affected Catholic thinking in all these areas, perhaps most especially on the subject of just war and capital punishment.

Cardinal Bernardin pointed to three themes that underlie a consistent ethic of life: The theological assertion that the human person is made in the image and likeness of God, the philosophical affirmation of the dignity of the person, and the political principle that society and the state exist to serve the person.

Within this framework, the Catholic bishops of New York contended in their February, 1994, statement against the death penalty that whether one speaks of violent crimes or unplanned pregnancies, "death is never the answer."

Interestingly, the seamless garment argument has led other groups to embrace the Catholic position on the evil of abortion.

Sojourners is a Washington-based group and is the name of their influential magazine devoted to many issues of justice and peace. Some years ago the community abandoned its neutrality on the morality of abortion. The editor explained: "Our deepest convictions about poverty, racism, violence and the equality of men and women are finally rooted in a radical concern for life — its absolute value and the need to protect it. It was only a matter of time before the spiritual logic of these other commitments would lead us to a 'pro-life' response to abortion as well."

The seamless garment, or consistent ethic of life, idea has immeasurably enriched the discussion of issues relating to respect for the sacredness of human life. It surely will continue to do so as its challenges are increasingly accepted, we hope, both by those who presently claim a pro-life position and by those who do not.

Contemplating an abortion

I have a friend who is seriously thinking of having an abortion. To me, it's murder. But what can I say to prevent it? She says my church shouldn't dictate what she can or cannot do.

In my experience, when a situation of real crisis arises in an individual's life, all rational argument on this subject is pretty futile. Deep convictions, faith, and the "feel" the individual has for other children and for life are what will determine her decision.

Participation in dozens of discussions, panels, and ordinary bull sessions with people of all shades of opinion on the question has convinced me of one thing: Very few pregnant women, even those strongly pro-abortion, really believe they are not carrying a human baby. They know, regardless of the line they may give themselves, that what is in their womb is not just a blob, a chunk of material that is as disposable as an appendix or gall bladder; it is a baby, already a boy or girl — her child.

Seen in this light, the words of one mother are, to put it mildly, impressive: "Apart from everything else, maybe I'm just too much of a coward to have an abortion," she said. "I know I'd have to live with it till I die. I don't mean just the abortion itself; maybe I could get over that. But what will happen later? Five years from now, when I see a little girl all dressed up downtown or going to school, I will know she could be my daughter. Fifteen years from now, when I see a neighbor's boy growing into manhood, I would know mine could be just like that. And 30 years from now, when I see a young mother taking care of her home and children, I'd know she could be mine — if I hadn't ended it all before it got started. I know these thoughts would nag me for the rest of my life. And I'm afraid it would drive me crazy."

Maybe the mother who said this is unusually sensitive and perceptive. But we don't really know much about the satisfactions or regrets of women who have had an abortion, five or 25 years later, do we?

Every major city has at least one emergency counseling center helping pregnant women consider alternatives before having an abortion. These may be found in the phone book under such names as Birthright, Alternatives to Abortion, Life-Line, the Society for the Preservation of Human Dignity, Alternatives Inc., Choose Life, Birth Choice Inc., Heartbeat, Right to Life, and Catholic Social Service. Encourage your friend to make use of these services, and pray for her. If she believes in God, urge her to pray before she makes her final decision.

When is embryo human?

I understand that for a long time the church distinguished between an animated (with a soul) fetus and an inanimate (without a soul) fetus. St. Thomas and other theologians held this view. Why did the church change its position so that a fetus is now considered animated at conception?

It is important first of all, in examining Christian teaching and practice, to separate the question about time of animation from that of abortion.

One of the earliest Christian documents we possess, outside of the New Testament, is the Didache, commonly called *The Teaching of the Apostles.* Written somewhere around the year 125, it contains an explicit condemnation of abortion and infanticide.

That condemnation, in one form or another, continued throughout Christian tradition. Not a lot was known about the formation of humans before birth; hence most of the controversies about the time of "ensoulment." But that a human being was developing somehow, and to kill it was wrong, was never disputed by any major theologian or church official.

The question you ask arises solely from the fact that, until modern times, people had very little knowledge about how new life develops in a mother's womb. They knew nothing of how sperm and ovum unite to form a human cell. All the living material of a new human (or other animal) life was believed to be in the male "seed." Females contributed only the "nest" and the material (blood) on which the seed fed and grew.

Similarly, little was known about stages of growth, especially before quickening (first feeling of movement), which everyone throughout the ages understandably viewed as a crucial stage of fetal development. I repeat, however, that even with this minimal knowledge, deliberate killing of unborn human life even in this earliest form was never considered, from any Christian point of view, a morally responsible act.

The change for the church (and for the rest of the human race) came from the discoveries of biological, genetic and psychological sciences during the past two centuries, especially in recent decades. To speak only of genetics, it is now a scientific certainty that the genetic code (DNA) which identifies each species and each individual for life is present already in the very first cells.

As the axiom goes, from the moment the first cell is formed (in the union of the sperm and ovum) until death occurs, the being "becomes what it already is," human. From the beginning, the cells are living and growing. And the life present is obviously not that of a cat or a monkey. It is identifiable as human life. To put it another way, the church now has a clear scientific basis, not available in previous centuries, for its teaching that taking the life of the unborn is evil, and that killing children, born or unborn, is no civilized solution to any problem.

Anyone interested in more details on the history of how abortion has been viewed in the world and in the church will find much interesting and useful information in the excellent book, *Abortion — The Development of the Roman Catholic Perspective*, by John Connery (Loyola University Press).

Douche and abortion after rape

Several years ago in theology class, the priest told us that in case of rape, a woman may have an abortion right away. Can you tell me if this is true?

I'm confident the priest didn't use exactly those words. An abortion, in the sense of direct killing or rejecting a human life that is already begun, is never a morally good act no matter how early in the pregnancy it takes place.

Your teacher was probably referring to the possible use of a douche of the vagina or the uterus of the woman who was raped. After sexual intercourse it takes some time for the male seed (sperm) to pass through the vagina and the uterus and enter the Fallopian tubes where it may unite with an ovum to begin a new human life. Unless and until those two cells join, there is no human cell, and no human life.

Therefore, in the case of rape, for example, a vaginal or uterine douche may be used to attempt to wash out the male sperm before it has a chance to unite with an ovum. Doctors and theologians generally agree that this might be done up to about an hour after the attack. It is not an abortive measure since no human life is yet present.

While this procedure is morally permissible, its effectiveness is not impressive and impossible to predict. (Some research places it about 64 percent effective.) As those who have sought efficient contraceptives have discovered through the years, there's a marvelous persistence in the whole process of human generation, even down to the movement of the tiny reproductive cells after intercourse, a persistence that is not easily frustrated.

Another reason that this procedure is quite uncommon is that hospitals now utilize other pharmaceutical procedures, treating victims of rape with drugs to prevent pregnancy. Some of these are clearly abortifacient, others are not, and many are somewhere in gray areas. Catholic hospitals, and others who desire to avoid abortive measures, have established various protocols, too complicated to discuss here, attempting to assist these victims by using available technologies in a morally acceptable way.

Acceptable abortion laws?

I am much opposed to the Supreme Court decision legalizing abortion and am working with a right-to-life organization. A question has arisen about approving legislation allowing an abortion to save the life of the mother after rape or incest. What is the church's position on this?

The position of the church is as it has been, that deliberate killing of an unborn child is always wrong even if it is intended to save the life of the mother.

However, a Catholic could properly approve and work for legislation along the lines you mention for at least two reasons. First, it is often politically necessary, and moral, to fight for and accept legislation which is at least part of what you would like, when it's clear your entire desired package is just not possible at this time. Accepting laws that would prohibit abortion after rape or incest does not mean one approves abortion in those instances. It only accepts that a perfect law is unattainable at the present. One less perfect might still prevent countless abortions, and at least open a door for fuller legal protection of the unborn.

Second, in practice (and probably even in theory) immoral abortions "to save the life of the mother" are generally not likely to occur.

A pregnant mother may be ill with a serious disease that the doctor must treat immediately. The doctor may know that if he does what is needed to heal the mother, she will lose the baby. An obvious illustration is cancer of the uterus. If in the physician's prudent medical judgment that uterus must be removed before the baby is viable, or the mother will die (or the cancer will likely spread critically), the uterus may be removed. Naturally, with such surgery the baby will die.

Some would incorrectly call this "an abortion to save the mother." It is, however, a moral procedure. The baby is not killed, or aborted, in order to save the mother. It dies when the mother is treated as is medically necessary.

Other medical procedures may be less clear cut, but could fall into the same category.

In practice the problem hardly exists today. In the largest hospitals and clinics in the country which handle especially difficult cases, it has been years since doctors have faced a decision whether to save the mother or the child, if indeed they have ever done so in modern times. Medical management of pregnancy problems, to serve both the child and mother, has made and is still making progress.

Returning to sacraments after two abortions

I was raised a Catholic and married a Catholic, though he wasn't practicing his faith. My problem is that I had two abortions, which I didn't want, but finally had. I know it was very wrong, so I haven't been able to go to confession or Communion for 25 or 30 years. It's driving me crazy now. What can I do?

Abortion is a very serious offense against God and humanity, since it is the taking of a human life. I realize you know this, but I want to emphasize that what I say next is not meant to minimize that fact. The first step to forgiveness is an honest acknowledgment of our sin.

I hope you talk with a priest and receive the sacrament of penance soon. One of the strange things about sin is that it frequently seems to diminish in size when we're tempted, and then afterward it looms so huge that we fear even God can't forgive or heal the hurt. In a way, that is an even bigger mistake than the sin itself.

God doesn't like the sin and certainly doesn't encourage us to ignore his commands. But he does tell us often in Scripture that he considers the forgiveness of sins the greatest of all his works. In other words, he boasts that no sin, no evil, is beyond the reach of his goodness and his mercy. That is a joyous and basic fact of Christian faith.

So, he is there, waiting for you simply to run to him and tell him you're back. Read prayerfully the story of the forgiving father (Luke, chapter 15), then go to confession and receive the Eucharist. You've been away long enough.

Mother or baby?

In my college ethics classes a thousand years ago, I understood that if there were a question of the mother or baby, the mother's life must be sacrificed. Others said that, since the baby is an unjust aggressor, the baby should be sacrificed. Who is right?

While my college and seminary days were somewhat less than a thousand years ago, I doubt that I'm much younger than you. The only thing I remember about that "mother or baby" question is that it is not, was not, and will not be taught by the Catholic Church as even remotely applicable to a medical dilemma during pregnancy — but there have been, and it seems always will be, people who think that's what the church believes.

The history of medical science, biology, and moral theology on the subject is long and complicated, but to claim that a baby in the womb is an "unjust aggressor" in any moral sense of the word is out of the question.

Unfortunately, that term has been used sloppily on occasion in reference to other medical procedures possible during a pregnancy, and which might (or certainly will) result in the death of the unborn child. A classic, though somewhat unreal, example, which I pointed out in a previous question, is a pregnant mother with a uterus her doctor feels must be removed immediately. Such surgery would be morally permissible even though a nonviable fetus would surely die in the process.

There's an old axiom that remains true here: Good moral theology and good medicine go together, with emphasis on the word "good" in both cases. It is wrong and unnecessary to directly take the life of any innocent person, born or unborn.

School policies for pregnant students

The Catholic high school our granddaughter attends has a rule that I find cruel. If one of the female students is pregnant, she must leave the school at the beginning of the seventh month of pregnancy. If she has an abortion, and the fact becomes public, she will be expelled.

I know we want to discourage premarital sex. But my husband and I think this rule does something much more. It almost encourages abortion.

Can't we do better than this? It seems a terrible and sexist way to deal with a tragedy that we all need to face.

First, let me note that the thoughts I am about to offer apply just as much to families, parishes and the whole Catholic community, as much as to schools. Perhaps since situations like this are sadly too frequent, Catholics (and others) have, I believe, become increasingly compassionate and supportive of women with problem pregnancies.

It is my conviction, as pastor and former family life director of my diocese, that such rules, insofar as they still exist (and I don't think they exist in many schools today), are a poor and harmful response to a serious problem.

The concern and sanction seem to be not so much about the sin that may have been involved, or even the pregnancy, but rather the embarrassment caused by the pregnancy beginning to "show." I have sat in living rooms with parents who were urging their pregnant daughter either to abort or separate herself from the family until "things are over." We would surely be perceived as approaching this attitude in such a policy.

This becomes yet more serious when the pregnancy results, as it so often does today, from incestuous rape by a parent, sibling or other relative. Often, if not most of the time, the school, a caring faculty, and a few friends are the only base of hope and emotional (sometimes also physical) safety such young women have.

Surely we need to deal with the problem, but our Catholic credibility is heavily at stake here. As you point out, when we say in effect, "If you are still pregnant by the seventh month, you will need to leave our school" — and that is exactly what will be heard by many — what are we telling them is the alternative?

A policy expelling students who have an abortion could simply be seen as "damage control." If you have an abortion, you cannot say we didn't tell you not to. Again, such will be the message heard, even by many of our own people.

You hint also that such policies say nothing about the boy or man who is at least as responsible for the pregnancy, and often for the abortion, as is the young woman. What happens to them in these kinds of sanctions?

Usually nothing nearly as punitive. This, if nothing else, shows there is something unjust about what is being done here. Wouldn't it be spiritually and pastorally better to acknowledge that we don't have a clear-cut solution, that we all need to keep our respect for each other and pray a lot more over it so our decisions are as Christlike as possible? This is what good Christian parents of such children do. As Catholic institutions which proclaim and profess to live the same faith, can we admit that maybe we also don't have an all-wise, one-size-fits-all solution at this point?

One glaring concern is how we justify this exclusion of women who may have sincerely repented and confessed their sin. How explain this sanction on teenagers who, because of extreme force or fear, or sheer unhinged panic (which a little pastoral experience proves is not uncommon) very possibly have not even committed a subjectively serious sin? What are we punishing? What good are we accomplishing?

It's understandable that we would like some clear and absolute response, but in human realities as delicate and fragile as this, that is never possible.

Allowing administrators and chaplains, in dialogue with the individual's pastor, to handle these cases one by one, with their on-the-scene knowledge and concern for the people involved, perhaps isn't the best of all solutions and has built-in risks. It certainly seems, however, to promise less harm to the good name of our families, our parishes and our schools, and to the spiritual lives of the people involved, than any other solution in sight.

Speaking to teens, adults about sin

I am a high school CCD teacher and have an ongoing disagreement with our pastor and CCD director. To put it bluntly, I think they are too soft and easygoing.

The main thing kids need to know today is what sin is. They need to be told continually what the church says. We have to keep telling people where they are sinning, and if you ask me, this goes especially for teenagers. Father says maybe I "nag on it" too much, and "that's not the way to get them to be good Catholics."

My feeling is that if they can't accept what the church teaches, they should change or leave. You said recently that a first step to forgiveness is acknowledging our sins. So what do you think about this?

I think a number of things about it, but probably should limit myself to responding to your obvious question. Perhaps the only place to start is with the words of Jesus, "I did not come to condemn the world but to save it" (Jn. 12:47).

Translated to your teaching ministry, it might be put this way: Our basic mission as teachers is not to tell the world how bad it is, but to make it holy and, with Christ, bring it back to the Father. It is not primarily to tell people to get out of the church, but to help them to see reasons to stay in.

Thus, it seems to me your question concerns not so much "what" we teach, as how we motivate people to live good and wise lives, specifically as part of the Catholic Christian community.

My 47 years as a priest convince me that the vast majority of people, Catholic or not, are deeply aware they are not perfect, that they have faults and sins, that they are finite and weak morally and otherwise. But they sincerely want to be better.

As one theologian wrote, ethical commands in themselves do not move people to wisdom and goodness. "They have absolutely no need for a rescue team that stands on the beach and bores suicides with the news that they are drowning. They already know that; what they really want to hear is some reason why they shouldn't go ahead and sink."

Pope John Paul II makes the same point beautifully and often in his book *Crossing the Threshold of Hope.* Convincing the world of sin (see John 16:8) is not the same as condemning it for sinning, he says. It "means creating the conditions for its salvation... To save means to embrace and lift up with redemptive love, with love that is always greater than any sin" (pages 57-58).

Teenagers, and adults for that matter, are no different from small children. Telling people constantly how wicked they are, how much they are failing, may make the accusers feel good and righteous, but it does not make men and women into better people.

Jesus talked much about sin. But his approach to changing people's hearts was never to beat them with their guilt. He reminded them that they were precious to God. He did not say, "God loves you, so you can go and do whatever you feel like doing." Neither did he ever say: "Go straighten your life out and then come back and we will talk."

Rather he called them to come, to be his, to share his life with the Father, to remember who they are and act accordingly. He knew God's healing love was bigger than their sins, and intimacy with him would change them.

Sometimes we do need to be prophets, to speak words we know will be unwelcome and resented, and maybe even hurt. But this must always be done humbly, respectfully and with genuine compassion and love for the other.

Our mission, whatever our small role may be in the church, is to use our "moral power" not to crush people, but to give them hope; not to make them cowed, but holy. It seems clear to me, from your considerably longer letter, that this is what your pastor is trying to say. At least it is worth your prayerful reflection, perhaps with the Gospels open in front of you.

Maturing heterosexually

A speaker at our church, describing sexual development in young people, said that one of the signs of maturity is that we become heterosexual. This confuses me. Does that mean that children and adolescents are normally homosexual until they mature? Such an attitude surely seems to go against what we are told today about the emotional and physical sources of homosexual orientation.

We can understand the word heterosexual in two ways. The one with which we are most accustomed refers to someone whose primary and predominant sexual attraction is to the opposite sex. With this meaning, the opposite of heterosexual is homosexual.

The other meaning of heterosexual needs some explanation. At the risk of oversimplifying, we know that human sexual development does not happen in one great leap. A characteristic of early development, around the time of puberty and for some years before and after, is that sexual attraction is mostly self-centered and undifferentiated.

Adolescent boys, for example, tend not to focus their sexual inclinations on developing a committed relationship with only one person. Their orientation or fantasies, or whatever one may call them, rather than being outgoing and self-giving are more directed toward "females" in general, and what girls and women can do or be for them. The term sometimes used for this phase of development is autoerotic.

One's self is at the center. Who the other partner, real or imaged, may be, or how many different ones there may be, doesn't really matter.

Unfortunately we know from experience that some men and women never move beyond this level of sexual awareness and maturity.

Healthy growth into maturity eventually brings the individual out of this sexual self-centeredness. She or he becomes gradually heterosexual (literally: sexually oriented toward another person) and capable of what we call an adult, loving, other-centered sexual life. In this understanding, heterosexual means that a man or a woman has grown beyond being autosexual, self-centered, and is now capable of a mature committed sexual relationship with, and directed toward, another person. Most of what we call "rules of sexual morality" deal with these realities of human growth.

What some people think of as religious or Christian commandments about sex are really what long human experience has proven to be just plain common sense, if we expect to have decent and healthy people and societies. The human race has known for centuries that this kind of sexual maturity in men and women is essential if a community is not eventually to self-destruct. Intense sexual intimacies too early, regardless of desire and instincts, can handicap young people for life, cripple them in a rut of self-centeredness, and lay the groundwork for all kinds of personal, family and social tragedies.

I hope it is obvious that with this response I intend no implications about homosexuality. I simply wish to explain, in response to the question, what heterosexual growth means as we mature.

Abortion and excommunication

I had an abortion 20 years ago and was told the priest could not give me absolution in the confessional. So I never went back because I could not face that.

The years have passed, and it bothers me more every day. I go to Mass all the time, but can never bring myself to go to a priest about it because of what I was told. I'd love to go to Communion this Easter. I hope you will be able to help.

I am sorry you have been away from the sacraments all these years. This is especially sad because apparently it resulted, as unfortunately so often happens, from information you received that was almost certainly false.

It is true that, according to Catholic belief, anyone who procures a completed abortion (not only the mother, but others directly involved in the act) incurs an automatic excommunication. However, several critical conditions must be met before one incurs that excommunication.

For one thing, the person must be at least 18 years old, and know when the abortion takes place that an excommunication will be incurred if the act is carried through. Many people who know that abortion is seriously wrong do not know an excommunication is incurred at the same time.

Furthermore, if circumstances surrounding the pregnancy are such as to cause grave fear and confusion in the mind of the woman, or if she is under severe pressure from family or perhaps close friends, again the excommunication would not be incurred.

Some other conditions are also required, but I hope you get the point.

The information you received that the priest was unable to deal with this excommunication in the sacrament of penance was almost certainly wrong, even 20 years ago. Even if you did incur an excommunication, which as I said is quite doubtful, a priest in your parish or a neighboring parish can nearly always take care of it immediately and finally when you go to confession. You have been away from the sacraments long enough. Please go to a priest and celebrate this Easter as you have been wanting to.

For those interested in checking references, the sections of canon law most relevant here are Canons 1398, 97, 1323 and 1324. Parallel canons in the former code which would have been in effect 20 years ago are worded somewhat differently but are, in practice, basically the same as the 1983 code for this type of penalty.

Post-abortion counseling

Dear Father Dietzen:

In a column regarding abortion, the writer stated, referring to her abortion, "I live daily with the pain and shame of what I did, and six years later still pray for forgiveness."

While your response to her was excellent as far as it went in assuring her that she is not excommunicated, more needs to be said.

As a psychiatrist, I frequently see women who have been to priests repeatedly for confession following abortion, but who are unable to accept and receive the forgiveness that is offered. For women in this situation, it is often essential to have post-abortion counseling from a Christian perspective, with prayer for emotional healing.

Although many professional counselors have not received specific training in post-abortion counseling and may not know how to help, a growing number of professional counselors, psychiatrists, as well as priests and religious, are becoming educated and gaining experience in this very specialized type of counseling.

I would advise women with this type of problem to call the National Office of Post-Abortion Reconciliation and Healing at 1-800-5WE-CARE. Staff at this number can refer women to counselors and support groups throughout the United States.

The video "Dear Children" by Liguori Press is also a powerful tool to explain post-abortion syndrome, and shows through interviews with real people how forgiveness and healing can be experienced. The book Will I Cry Tomorrow? by Susan Stanford, Ph.D., tells the author's own personal experience in dealing with the pain and guilt of abortion, and shows positive steps that people can take to experience God's forgiveness and healing.

I would encourage readers with this type of problem to seek additional help if confession alone has not been sufficient to bring resolution. Although God's forgiveness is freely given in the sacrament, there are often many different emotional issues going on, and further help is necessary.

I am grateful to this doctor for pointing out post-abortion realities that need to be dealt with, and that can encourage women (and men) who are trying to work their way through their recovery. The specific suggestions she makes are among many excellent ones available.

Had abortion, after bad advice

I need to know my standing in the church. I am the mother of two beautiful children and am approaching 40 years of age. About a year ago, I found that I was pregnant. A routine blood test indicated a higher than normal risk of Down syndrome. My doctor insisted on amniocentesis, which confirmed our fears. We explained that we were always against abortion and that I participated often in pro-life rallies.

A counselor didn't suggest abortion, but did tell us that some priests do not look harshly on women who have terminated a pregnancy because of genetic abnormalities, and under the circumstances, the church would accept the decision. She suggested we write a list of pros and cons. After soul searching, the only reason I found for not having an abortion was to save myself living with the guilt. I did what my brain said was right for my family and son. If I had listened to my heart, I would still have been pregnant.

Am I still a member of the Catholic Church? I don't feel right going to confession and asking for forgiveness when I feel that if faced with the same circumstance I would make the same decision. Please help me.

I was moved by your letter. Your kind of story and your feelings are repeated countless times by women who have, or have not, decided to abort their children. Lots of things could be said, but two I believe are most critical.

Assuming you reflect her words accurately, you were badly misled by the individual you approached for counseling. And I think you know that. For starters, not only some, but most priests, I hope, do not "look harshly" on women who have had an abortion. That is by no means the same as suggesting that they consider deliberate killing of any unborn human life anything but a gravely wrong and sinful action.

The church expends huge personal and financial resources to help heal and reconstruct the spiritual and emotional lives of women after an abortion. This says simply that judgment and punishment are not ours to inflict. Those belong to God alone.

In this, as in all other areas of faith and life, our duty is to teach what we believe as clearly as we can, and then try to reflect the kindness and goodness of Christ to those who for whatever reason have not measured up. Again as with our Lord, compassion should never be misunderstood as compromising what is taught to be right and wrong ways to act.

Your counselor was not only wrong about the church's teaching. Her suggested manner of reaching a decision might be acceptable if you're wondering whether to vacation in Alaska or Cancun. It is a poor and dangerous one, however, for arriving at life-or-death moral decisions such as you faced.

Are you excommunicated? From what you have said, almost certainly not. (See previous question on abortion and excommunication.)

As a practical matter, the answer to that question is not really relevant and would be taken care of anyway when you go to confession. What is important is that you get back to the full practice of your faith, including penance and the Eucharist.

You say you would do the same again. But you don't really know that. God's grace can do wonders, and your letter shows that you already have grave doubts about the wisdom of what you did. One thing is sure. Without prayer and the sacraments, you are much more likely to act in the future in ways that will make you unhappy, ways you know are wrong. Please talk to a priest soon. You have waited long enough.

Can medical care be refused?

A few weeks ago I was diagnosed with inoperable liver cancer and have been undergoing chemotherapy. Would refusing chemotherapy be the same thing as committing suicide? I read where a noted entertainer was diagnosed with cancer, yet refused chemotherapy and was going to let nature take its course.

I believe that one should make every attempt possible to extend one's life. If I die, I hope doctors would have learned something to help others in the same situation. Refusing any form of chemotherapy would be like a slap in God's face, for he gave doctors the talents to help others.

I admire you for the courageous and thoughtful manner in which you are attempting to meet these painful life decisions. We need to begin, as you already have, by acknowledging our Christian conviction that, while life is a sacred and marvelous gift from God, death for us is not an absolute evil. Since we believe the end of this life is not the end of existence, we do not cling frantically to each additional moment regardless of the cost or consequences to ourselves or others.

Our Christian faith thus says much about the questions we ask ourselves in times like this. The concerns you have, which are shared by all in similar circumstances, basically revolve around two words, benefit and burden. What benefits will the therapy, whatever it be, bring to you and to others? You do not mention some important details here. Are you a parent with young children? An older person whose family is grown? What likelihood of success does your team of physicians offer? At best, or at worst, what are the reasonable expectations? These questions need to enter into your decision. They must be weighed along with the burdens involved.

Today the cost of medical procedures in these areas easily reach into the hundreds of thousands of dollars. What does this do economically to your family or other loved ones when balanced against the expectations of success? Considering your age and responsibilities, is the sheer pain involved reasonably worth the benefits you might achieve? Consider the other physical and psychological burdens on yourself and those around you. How might your decision affect your chances for anything like a reasonably normal human life?

I recognize these are heavy, almost brutal, questions. But they are the ones we must deal with when faced as you are with decisions about "extraordinary" ways of regaining or maintaining physical health.

I hope all who read this recognize that it barely hints at the complexity and thoroughness with which we must address questions like this. Even should one wish to study the subject, most books are far beyond the time and background of the majority of people. One recently published book, however, I would recommend highly as a readable and morally solid presentation of the kinds of concerns to be considered in situations like yours. It is *Medical Ethics: A Catholic Guide to Healthcare Decisions*, by McCarthy and Caron, published by Ligouri Press (Liguori, MO). I think you will find it helpful.

What is usury?

Is there, or was there ever, a sin called usury?

Yes, there was such a sin, and in fact still could be under certain circumstances. Roughly speaking, the word "usury," which goes back to ancient Rome, means about the same as our word "interest" — money paid for the loan of someone else's money or other property. The Old Testament broadly condemns this kind of charge to another, with some exceptions.

During Christian times the condemnation continued for the most part. St. Thomas Aquinas, for example, taught that it is unlawful to accept money for the use of money, "which is called usury." (*Summa Theologiae* II-II, q.78. art. 1) One exception was permitted even at that time if the lender suffered a loss or opportunity for profit because of the loan.

Obviously the picture changed considerably with the development of our modern economic systems. Theologians in general, and the church specifically, have for some time held the position that taking of interest for the use of money is lawful, as long as the rate is just and not harmful either to the individuals involved or to society.

Today the term usury refers, even in state laws, to actions which exploit individual needs or financial conditions in order to charge interests which are clearly unjust and destructive of another's ability to live a decent and proper life.

CHAPTER 9

PENANCE AND
ANOINTING OF THE SICK

ᐁ

Evolution of private confession

*My friends and I have enjoyed a number of communal penance services
in our church. It is much more meaningful than the private confession
we were used to. I am told private confessions were not practiced in the
church for a long time. When did our individual type confession start?*

You are right that private confession as we have it was unknown in the
church for a very long time. In early centuries, the process of forgiveness for sins was rather public, required a long time, sometimes several
years, and took place under the direction of the bishop.

The move toward private confession to a priest extended over several centuries, but started for the most part in Ireland perhaps about
the time of St. Patrick, who died in 461. Monks, most of them not
priests, traveled the Irish countryside preaching and baptizing and
conducting a simple rite of forgiveness patterned on the type of counseling the monks themselves were accustomed to in their own spiritual
lives.

Penitential books began to appear with appropriate penances for
various sins and were used by the monks in the penance ceremony.

As Irish monks spread over Europe, they took these rituals and
books with them and began to use them in countries where they
settled. But the practice took hold very slowly.

Several bishops and regional church councils condemned what
one council, Toledo in Spain, called the "abominable presumption" of
"asking a priest to forgive them as often as they wish to sin." They
insisted on a return to the ancient and accepted penitential disciplines.
Even as late as the ninth century the practice of private confession
apparently was unknown in Rome.

Gradually the idea took hold, however, and bishops moved from condemning the practice to trying to regulate it. By the time of the Fourth Lateran Ecumenical Council (1215), private confession had become pretty much "the" sacrament of forgiveness in the church.

I must add, however briefly, that these changes and developments in the church's understanding and practice of forgiveness of sin should not surprise us. We know it happened with the other sacraments as the people of God lived through the centuries, and could be equally expected in this case.

There is no question that in its understanding of this sacrament, the church is turning from a rather legalistic approach to one which is more scriptural and liturgical and more centered on conversion of the heart — in other words, more with the focus of the penitential disciplines during the first centuries, but with many insights offered by our experiences of faith in our own age.

What is perfect contrition?

What is an act of perfect contrition?

The theological terms perfect and imperfect contrition have enjoyed differing and sometimes controversial meanings over the past several hundred years. Since the Council of Trent in the 16th century, the difference has been placed mainly in the motive of our sorrow for sin. Perfect contrition is sorrow over offenses primarily because of our love for God and for Jesus Christ, and because sins violated that love. Imperfect contrition looks more toward ourselves, that our sins are shameful and we deserve punishment for them.

The difference between the two perhaps makes more sense in theory than in practice. Even imperfect contrition arises from the help of God's grace and has behind it basic elements of faith, hope and love. Otherwise the shame over breaking God's law and the fear of punishment or separation from him would not be there in the first place.

In both cases the sorrow arises, at least in some degree, out of the virtue of charity, and both include a firm turning away from any serious offense against God.

Penance after mortal sin?

Is it really necessary to go to confession before receiving Communion if one has committed a mortal sin?

Yes. If someone is certain that he has offended God that seriously, he should receive the sacrament of penance before going to Communion, except for emergency situations.

It is true, of course, that such a person re-establishes his or her friendship with God before confession by turning back to him in honest sorrow for the wrong that was done. But going to confession in a case like this is not an empty, superfluous formality.

Any sin, especially more serious sin, injures our relationship not only with God, but with other people, most of all with our fellow Christians. The sin may involve others directly. At least indirectly, our loss of holiness, our self-centeredness in the sin, and the crippling of generosity in prayer and other good things we do for others, all in some way affect the human family we belong to. It is only fair and just then, that we first confess our sin and receive the "public" forgiveness for it from the priest who acts in the name of our Lord and all his people in the sacrament of penance.

After that, sharing of the Eucharist and holy Communion, which is the sign of our mutual friendship with Christ and with each other, makes more spiritual sense.

Can a priest hear confessions everywhere?

A visiting priest-friend of our family told us recently that he could not hear confessions in our church without permission from the bishop. Doesn't a priest have the right to hear confessions anywhere?

Normally he does. According to the *Code of Canon Law,* if a priest has delegation or permission (technically called "faculties") to administer the sacrament of penance in his own diocese, he is able to exercise those faculties anywhere, unless a particular bishop somewhere else specifically denies him those faculties. (CCL 967) Under the previous code, apart from emergencies, faculties had to be obtained for any diocese other than his own.

Is ex-priest bound by seal?

If you tell a serious sin to a priest in confession and he leaves the priesthood, could he repeat it to someone?

No. A priest is bound by the seal of confession for life. Even men who leave the priesthood consider this one of their most sacred obligations, always.

Penance: prayer or action?

The last time I went to confession, the priest gave me a penance to do something which I won't explain here. I asked him what prayers I should say, and he told me my penance was "the action, not the words." Can you explain this?

It's quite simple. The "penance" requested in the sacrament of penance is intended not only to make up for our sins, but to help us remedy the weaknesses that cause our sins and to commit ourselves to a new life. Sometimes the priest may feel that some action — like an act of kindness — will serve that purpose better than "three Our Fathers and three Hail Marys."

The church encourages such penances. In the document outlining the ceremony for this sacrament (Rite of Penance, par. 18), we are told that the satisfaction or penance imposed should "correspond to the seriousness and the nature of the sins confessed, to the extent possible. This satisfaction may be suitably performed by prayer, by self-denial, and especially by service of neighbor and works of mercy through which the social aspect of sin and its forgiveness may be expressed."

Confession an Easter duty?

In response to a question about the Easter duty (chapter 4), you tell us: "The obligation of confession during the Easter season is still, as it always has been, binding only if it is necessary for an individual to be able to receive the Eucharist." I refer you to the church canon: "If anyone denies that each of Christ's faithful of both sexes is bound to confess once a year, let him be anathema." How do you explain your answer in the light of this statement?

The best, in fact the only, way to discover the proper meaning of a moral or doctrinal statement of the church is to examine what the church itself meant to say at the time, and how it interprets that statement.

So here, in spite of the seeming absolute command of yearly confession, in its sacramental practice and regulations, the church has always, at least as far as I can determine, meant this to apply only where a mortal sin had to be confessed. The context of the Council of Trent's canon, and even more the context of the Fourth Lateran Council statement to which you refer, support this interpretation. Moral theologians, old and new, agree almost without exception.

If you wish a specific example close to home, refer to the *Balti-*

more Catechism Number Three, which was for decades before Vatican II the most official and authoritative expression of beliefs and practices of American Catholics. Question 293 asks: "What is meant by the commandment to confess our sins at least once a year?" The answer: "By the commandment to confess our sins at least once a year is meant that we are strictly obliged to make a good confession within the year, if we have mortal sin to confess." (*Baltimore Catechism*, St. Joseph Edition)

I trust you realize this is not what the church recommends; it is simply the bare minimum required. Of course, if one is guilty of serious sin, he would need to go to confession to fulfill the other annual sacramental obligation, to receive the Eucharist sometime during the Easter time.

Any Catholic who understands how the sacrament of penance heals us in our sinfulness and other weaknesses, and how it strengthens and reconciles us to God and to our fellow members of the church, will normally receive this more than once a year, mortal sin or not.

Confession how often?

Is it necessary to receive the sacrament of penance every time one goes to Communion? Once a month? Once a year? What is the latest on going to confession to be able to receive Communion?

You really have three questions. Is it necessary always to receive confession before Communion? What does the precept to go to confession once a year really mean? And how often might one properly receive this sacrament?

The practice of receiving the sacrament of penance before each reception of Communion accompanied the great decline in receiving the Eucharist in the Middle Ages. The high (or low) point came under the influence of the Jansenist heresies beginning in the 16th and 17th centuries.

Due to this rigoristic approach to morality and the sacraments, many aspects of Catholic belief and life were bent all out of shape. Among these was the feeling and practice that reception of the Eucharist, even by cloistered nuns and monks, should be limited to a few times a year.

Ordinary folks were encouraged to receive perhaps only once a year, sometimes less than that. In such confused times it is understandable that people gradually assumed they must go to confession each time before Communion.

This situation prevailed almost into the 20th century when Pope Pius X (1903-1914) urged early Communion for children and frequent Communion for all. As people began receiving Communion each month (remember the monthly Communion Sundays for the Ladies' Sodality or the Holy Name Society?) or even weekly, the "tradition" of confession before every Communion continued.

The church, in fact, still is wrestling with this same history on the question of whether or not confession absolutely must precede first Communion for young children.

This, among others, is a major reason the church today finds it critical to re-evaluate the theology and place of the sacrament of penance in our daily Catholic life. About the obligation to confess at least once a year, see the answer to the previous question.

How often should one celebrate reconciliation with God and "with our brothers and sisters who are always harmed by our sins," as the Rite of Penance puts it? That same rite, which is the official guide of the church for this sacrament, mentions only Lent, obviously the most appropriate time. Others would be Advent and whatever occasions during the year or in one's life invite us to re-examine the direction of our lives and commit ourselves completely to God.

Why not yes or no?

I found your answer about how often to receive the sacrament of penance confusing and evasive. Why must you answer a simple question with an explanation that goes back to the Middle Ages? I would appreciate having you answer the question in language I can understand, such as "Yes, you must receive confession at least once a month or before Communion, or whatever, or no." Please try an answer most of us poor Catholics can understand and follow.

I did not respond to the question the way you wish because an honest answer is just not that simple. For one thing, I disagree heartily that "most of us poor Catholics can understand and follow" only simple yes or no rules.

I believe most Catholics and other Christians increasingly hunger for a deeper personal relationship with God and with Jesus. They are not satisfied any longer with merely "obeying the rules of the club," even in the sacrament of penance.

They are aware that no friendship, whether with another person or with God, happens without sincere efforts toward deeper understanding of oneself and the other, and a deep desire for intimacy. Such a relationship, with God or man or woman, does not come about solely by following a set of regulations.

The purpose of this column, and this book, is to support people in coming to that kind of intimacy with God. My intention is not merely to provide yes-or-no responses, but to help Catholics understand their faith better so they can live it more deeply. I felt the woman herself wanted more than a yes or no. She wanted an explanation.

In my view the simple one-word answer, which Catholics have wanted and received too often in the past, would have been worse than no answer at all. It would have supported the serious misconception that simply following regulations, not understanding how the sacraments play an intimate role in building our friendship with God, is the most important thing.

Many Catholics still would like their faith to be summed up in a list of black and white rules. Relationships simply do not grow that way. They demand patience, sincere pursuit of greater understanding and knowledge, prayer, genuine care for the other person, and continual reflection.

A mechanical view of our religion which sees the practice of our faith as a series of do's and don'ts stunts our spiritual growth and makes a personal loving friendship with God all but impossible.

Scrupulosity

Two priests told me recently in confession that I am scrupulous. Both said I should ignore the times I thought I committed a sin and go to Communion anyway. I don't understand how I can do that. I was always taught we have to go to confession before we receive Communion if we have a mortal sin. Can you tell me what to do?

Yes, I can. And I hope you will do it. Follow the directions the priests have given you!

Scrupulosity means that for any of several reasons an individual has lost his or her sense of good judgment about what is a sin. A scrupulous person tends to see sin where there is no sin, sometimes interpreting the most innocent action as seriously sinful because of "bad intentions" or wrong evaluation of the seriousness of the action.

A priest is, or should be, prepared to recognize signs of scrupulosity in confession, and to help the individual work through them. In some cases where the problem has developed into a deeper neurosis, he may even suggest professional psychological assistance.

Your best course, in fact your only course, is to go to a priest in whom you have confidence and follow his directions completely, even about Communion. And don't float around looking for a priest who will "really understand" your situation. Chances are that one or both of the priests you mention do understand, and are doing the right thing to help you.

One final word: Don't be discouraged. This emotional difficulty always causes anxiety and suffering. But encouraging signs in your letter hint that the problem is not yet too deep. If you pray and follow exactly the course I've outlined, you will either solve the difficulty or learn how to live with it peacefully.

Scrupulosity, or sin?

My husband had a heated reaction to your answer to the scrupulous lady who worried about what is a sin. Other priests had told her she should go to Communion no matter what sins she thought she committed. You said she should follow their advice.

We think you should have insisted that one does not go to Communion with a mortal sin, and then approached the possibility that she may be scrupulous.

In the opinion of at least a few priests, the lady in question is a victim of genuine scrupulosity. It also came through in her letter to me.

Such persons may be totally incapable of judging the seriousness of any sin or even of judging whether there was a sin at all. It can be questionable whether an individual so distraught and emotionally entangled is psychologically capable of serious sin. If you recall, two of the requirements for mortal sin are sufficient reflection and full consent of the will.

My response, therefore, described how a scrupulous person may react. The answer obviously does not apply to anyone not afflicted with this emotional problem.

Right to confessional privacy

Our church has arranged a reconciliation room in part of the sacristy. The people were told that the old confessional will no longer be used.

Some of us are disturbed by one of our priests who does not always observe the right of a penitent to go to confession anonymously. He will bounce out to escort one into the room, or see the penitent out after confession. Confession has never been a favorite sport of most Catholics. This makes it more difficult.

First of all, a priest who refuses to respect the anonymity of penitents who desire it in their confession unjustly violates a serious and clear right of Catholic people.

Regardless of the priest's personal feelings, he never has a right, whether by edict or intimidation, to impose his feelings on others in contradiction to options legitimately offered by the church. This is particularly true in matters relating to the sacraments.

As you indicate, the church's instructions for ministering and receiving the sacrament of penance provide that the penitent should have the opportunity to go to confession face-to-face or anonymously, whatever way he or she wishes. I hope you will try as gently and as honestly as you can to let your priests know your feelings so this sacrament can be for you the healing and helpful experience our Lord meant it to be.

Penance without serious sin

What does one do when he is sent from the confessional and told not to come back until he has committed a mortal sin? Does that mean we should never go to confession? I know a number of elderly people who are facing this problem. I would like to receive this sacrament more often, but I'm confused.

About the only advice I can give to you is to do as the priest says; don't go back — to him — for such a confession. Go to another priest, and there are many of them, who do not have such a rigid view of the nature and purpose of the sacrament of penance.

A confession of this nature is usually called a "confession of devotion," that is, only venial sins or previously forgiven sins are told to the priest. Such confessions have been and still are strongly encouraged by the church. The Introduction to the Rite of Penance stresses the value of "confessions of devotion" as having their own kind of healing power.

Pope John Paul II, in his exhortation on reconciliation and the sacrament of penance (1983) explained that Christians come to sacramental penance for other reasons than regaining the grace lost by mortal sin.

Among the reasons, he said, are a need to check one's spiritual progress, sometimes a need for more accurate discernment of one's vocation, a need and desire to escape from spiritual apathy and religious crisis, and often a need for broader spiritual direction which is readily linked with the sacrament of penance.

Even the second form of celebration, explains the pope, which unites a communal penance service with the opportunity for individual confession, can spiritually assist the Christian whose life reflects not even a hint of mortal sin. He mentions two features here of special importance: The word of God listened to in common, which has a remarkable effect as compared with its individual reading, and a better emphasis on the social character of sin and reconciliation (Apostolic Exhortation on Reconciliation and Penance, no. 32).

Naturally we must never allow such confessions to become mechanical or superficial, or without a true spirit of sorrow. And we shouldn't forget that sins can be forgiven in many other ways — prayer, penance, good works, and especially in the eucharistic sacrifice, which always remains the center of our spiritual lives.

Effect of the penitential rite at Mass

I realize the importance of the sacrament of penance. What is the efficacy of other activities like prayer, and especially the penitential rite at the beginning of Mass? Is it a rite of penance? Does it have reconciliation effect? If not, what is its purpose?

It surely does have reconciliation effect. The church always lives in awareness that, however filled it may be with the gifts of Christ, it is made up of people who unfortunately often fall into sin. Thus the church, "at the same time holy and always in need of purification, constantly pursues repentance and renewal." (Introduction to the Rite of Penance, 3. The references that follow here are to the same document)

Next to the eucharistic sacrifice itself, the flagship, so to speak, of this pursuit of forgiveness and healing is the sacrament of penance. As I explain in previous questions, the teaching of the church is that any grave (mortal) sin should be confessed to a priest in confession (7). But, as the rite puts it, "the people of God (the church) accomplishes and perfects this continual repentance in many different ways," by enduring hardships, doing works of mercy and charity, and trying to adopt more fully the outlook of the Gospel. Certainly not least are the penitential aspects of the eucharistic celebration, which includes the penitential rite you mention and other parts of the Mass, including the Eucharistic Prayer, the creed, and the Lamb of God. The church mentions each of these explicitly as part of the church's pursuit of reconciliation with God, with and through Jesus Christ. (Rite of Penance, 4 and 22)

To answer your question then, the penitential rite at Mass is effective for forgiveness and reconciliation. Unfortunately, we always want to go another step. How much "forgiveness" is available in each of these ways of reconciliation?

Just as we can't put a quantity on grace, on our sharing in the life of God, we can't place a pound or quart label on which of these is "more" forgiving. We are dealing with a God whose love for us goes beyond measure, who asks us to open ourselves to his mercy and redemptive love. We believe the church, guided by the Holy Spirit, tells us how, and helps us to move consciously and reverently into the presence of that mercy. The penitential rite of the Mass is among its ways of doing that.

Lacks courage in confession

Is it possible for a person to save his soul if over many years he has received the Blessed Sacrament while in the state of sin, due to embarrassment over sins omitted in confession? He makes a perfect Act of Contrition with a promise to straighten out and confess these sins, but at the next confession lacks the courage to tell them.

Then the same problem repeats itself, the same sin is committed and no courage. Is there a chance for repentance for this kind of person?

There's always a chance for repentance and for getting oneself straightened out with God. Confession of all serious, mortal sins of which a person is aware is required in confession. No one can excuse himself from that.

It is possible, however, for an individual to get so mixed up emotionally and so unreasonably frightened by the prospect of confessing the sins, that his personal guilt before God is questionable. It may reach the point where even the individual himself is incapable of making a decent judgment about his guilt.

My main concern, however, after studying your letter is your own confusion and fear which could be eliminated or alleviated so easily if you would simply go and talk to a priest. I urge you to do that. It doesn't have to be your own parish priest. The city you live in has a dozen or more who would be anxious to help you get out of your dilemma. Please go and talk with one of them soon.

Pregnant, refused absolution

I have a teenage granddaughter who is unmarried and pregnant. This girl regrets her action and went to confession a couple of weeks ago. She went home upset. After she confessed, the priest refused her absolution, told her she could not receive the sacraments and said she was excommunicated from the Catholic Church. Did he have the authority to do this?

I know from experience, and even more from my mail, that priests can do strange things. I have a strong feeling, however, that in this case there is gross misunderstanding somewhere along the line.

Even if the priest reacted more harshly than he should have, there's nothing in your letter that would bring up the subject of excommunication. The subject is irrelevant to the kind of sins you speak of, and would not even arise in the sacrament of penance.

My guess is that either your granddaughter misunderstood what the priest said, or there is perhaps more to the situation than she has told her family, or than they have wanted to tell you.

If you are still confused, talk it over with a priest — the same priest or another — and explain your concerns. Without violating the confidentiality of the sacrament of penance, he might be able to help you, or at least ease the hurt caused to your granddaughter and her family.

Vatican guidelines for priest confessors

Our Catholic newspaper reported on recent Vatican guidelines for confessors, mostly about birth control it seems. What disturbs me is the statement that generally a confessor is not obliged "to investigate concerning sins committed in invincible ignorance of their evil, or due to an inculpable error or judgment." In such cases "it is preferable to let penitents remain in good faith rather than create a situation in which they would begin formally to sin."

How could any Catholic beyond the age of reason be invincibly ignorant of the church's teaching on artificial birth control? They might not want to believe it. But that's not invincible ignorance.

Before approaching your question, I need to say that something bothers me very much in the mail I receive about this subject. Perhaps it's worth some prayerful reflection.

I have the strong impression that many people are angry mostly because another person is doing something we believe is wrong and getting away with it. There seems to be an anxious need and desire to prove someone else is committing serious sin. St. Paul insists that genuine Christian love is patient, not pompous, and "does not rejoice over wrongdoing" (1 Cor.13). Wrongdoing must be appropriately identified and addressed, but only with humility and sadness over the sinfulness. To be gleeful that we can declare someone in mortal sin, that we can deliberately put them into a state of sin when (because of some ignorance or moral disability) they are not, is a terrible sin against love of God and neighbor.

Instructing the ignorant is still a spiritual work of mercy. And doing something objectively sinful is wrong. It is a cosmic leap to a far different wrong, however, to deliberately attempt to change that objective wrong into a subjective, personal alienation from God. To do this unnecessarily and without serious reason, to do it for example just so others don't slip by without the punishment we think they deserve — that is evil, a prideful intrusion into the relationship between an individual and God.

Contrary to what you and others assume, ignorance of the law, which you reject in this case, is only one of many varieties of invincible ignorance. There may also be ignorance of the fact that I am bound by the law, whatever that law is. For instance, if individuals exercise all the reflection, faith and prayer they can reasonably manage in the circumstances, and if they still cannot see they are bound to a particular obligation, they are in what is, somewhat indelicately, called invincible ignorance. Their action may be objectively wrong, but they are not sinning because they cannot see that they are acting wrongly. (Those serious about understanding this may consult almost any of the classical moral textbooks, for example, Noldin-Heinzel *Summa Theologiae Moralis, De Principiis,* 1952.)

As an example, some noted non-Catholic theologians and philosophers have been, or are today, experts in Catholic doctrine. They know well the church's teaching about necessity of membership in the Catholic Church. In spite of all their study and reflection, however, they have never come to see membership in the church as a personal moral imperative. They know the "law"; they just cannot in conscience conclude that the law applies to them. According to the church's traditional teaching on moral responsibility, they are (again in the embarrassingly disrespectful phrase) invincibly ignorant.

Finally, the directives reflected in the guidelines you mention are not new or revolutionary. They are part of the church's traditional criteria for evaluating responsibility and culpability for moral actions.

Only personal sins are confessed

A young Catholic couple love children and plan to have a family as soon as they are mature enough and personal circumstances permit. They have been using the rhythm method, but they use an artificial method of birth control also. They feel they should express their love at times other than the short infertile period. They don't think they need to confess this, as they do not feel they are sinning. Must they go to confession? I'm afraid they are seriously considering leaving the church if this is so.

Your letter raises a number of points about which I suspect this couple might need enlightened rethinking, not the least of which are their reasons for delaying a family; of course, you don't give many details.

No one is ever required to confess anything that he or she honestly feels is no sin. In fact, when an individual is convinced that what has been done is morally permissible or good, it normally would not be mentioned in confession.

In forming one's conscience on any serious moral question, the guidance of the church on that particular subject, here birth control, and on the whole process of reaching moral decisions must have a significant influence for Catholic Christians. But when one receives the sacrament of penance, it is, among other benefits, for the forgiveness of *sins* — that is, actions which an individual is convinced in his own conscience are wrong, but which he or she goes ahead and does anyway.

Presuming that you reflect this couple's dilemma correctly, they seem to have one of two problems. Perhaps they do not understand confession properly. Or they might not be as sure as they say they are that their course of action is morally right for them, and they feel uneasy enough about it that they feel they should confess it.

Children resist confession

Perhaps you can advise me on a problem I'm having with my daughter. She received first Communion about two years ago and made her first confession about one and a half years later. Although she receives Communion regularly, she resists confession. I have not made a big issue of it, but am hoping to persuade her to go during Lent. Must I force her to go if she resists, or should I let it slide for a while?

We should not be surprised by your daughter's confusion since most adult Catholics are still trying to discover just where this sacrament fits into their lives.

No one, not even a parent, should force another to receive any sacrament. That can do no real good either spiritually or psychologically. On the other hand, you should not "let it slide for a while." I think there is a middle way.

Helping your daughter by your own words and actions to understand a few facts about sin and the sacrament of penance is important. One crucial truth forgotten by many who say confession is useless unless one has committed a mortal sin, is that all sin, even slighter sin, is an offense not only against God, but against all the church. It weakens and diminishes the holiness of all by lessening one's own holiness and spiritual goodness.

When I sin, I injure the Body of Christ and, to the degree of my sin, distort the image of Christ existing in all my brothers and sisters. To be whole, to be honest again, I need not only the "private" telling of my sin to God, I need the church, through its priest, in that living encounter of confession and forgiveness to say to me: "We forgive you. In the shadow of the cross of Christ, let's all undergo a change of heart and try to be again the sign of his loving presence to each other and to the world that we were meant to be."

The special encounter with God's forgiving and healing love in the sacrament of penance brings one directly into the everyday realities of guilt, our need for cleansing from sin, and our identity with the death and resurrection of Jesus in a way nothing else does.

These realities must be thought through and made our own if we expect them to become real to our children. I suggest you use one of the many good books on confession geared to younger people and available from a Catholic bookstore, or through a Catholic catalogue you could borrow from your pastor.

I am happy you want to help your child become more comfortable with the sacrament of forgiveness. One of the great priests and theologians of our time, Jesuit Father Karl Rahner, spoke once of the many Protestant leaders today who recognize the need of regular confession of sins. He added, "With this situation facing us, would it not be very strange if we began to neglect frequent confession out of carelessness and a desire for comfort in the spiritual life?" With thoughtful parents like you, maybe that is changing.

Age for "serious" sin?

We are trying as best we can to help our oldest child prepare for first confession. We haven't received much help. We would really like to know how to help all our children form a good conscience without seeing sin where there isn't any — or at least not anything serious.

If you can help us with this question, it will put some things in focus for us. At what age do you think a child is responsible enough to realize he is committing a mortal sin?

You deserve credit for approaching this task with your child so thoughtfully, and for asking some important questions.

No one is guilty of any sin unless he realizes what he is doing. So what you are really asking is: At what age is a child able to commit a mortal sin?

In practice the answer will differ from person to person. Even theoretically, it might vary widely depending, for example, on what level of moral perception and spiritual growth is psychologically possible at a given age. But a few things can surely be said. (Note that what follows refers to mortal sin; we are not concerned here with lesser, or venial, sins.)

A mortal sin is, as you know, any action by which a person consciously and with full deliberation and determination turns his whole self away from the friendship and love of God. It contains genuine undertones of eternal commitment because in itself the decision is total and permanent, even though repentance and conversion may come later.

Such a decision demands considerable grasp of one's personal worth and identity, an awareness of one's control over the directions of his loves and commitments, and a fairly profound spiritual perceptiveness. In other words, one must be able to give himself consciously, deeply and fully to God before it can make sense to say he can refuse to give himself to God in committing such a serious sin.

We are talking, then, about something which surely surpasses the moral capability of a normal 7 or 8-year-old. We do not allow even a 12-year-old to marry or to profess religious vows. Normally, such a child is insufficiently developed both psychologically and spiritually for that kind of love or that kind of radical decision on the direction of his or her life.

This tells us much about the answer to your question. Since a child cannot reject (in a serious sin) a love and commitment he has not yet been able to make in the first place, something like the same development and age seems necessary before a person can commit a mortal sin. We are probably talking about somewhere in the teens, or maybe for some people even later.

Naturally, one's understanding of mortal sin affects the answer, too. If we insist, for example, that a child can commit a mortal sin at the age of 12 or 14, with all of that age's mental, spiritual and psychological gropings, then it seems we are making mortal sin something considerably less than the catechism and good theology tell us it is. We also threaten to establish a child's whole religious relationship on a rather superficial basis, as if love and friendship with God were something a person can pop in and out of several times a month.

Threaten with sin?

You say that the psychological requirements for mortal sin are possibly not present until the teens. Isn't this just encouraging children to sin? Isn't a threat that they may sin the thing that often helps them behave correctly?

If I understand your question correctly, and I'm afraid I do, it reflects an attitude toward sin and conscience that should be unthinkable, but which has been all too prevalent in much of our past religious education.

First and most important, we have no right to lie to children to make them behave. Particularly we have no right to play God and say, in effect: "Even if they haven't committed a serious sin, it's better that they think they have. It will train them to do what is right."

This attitude is, or at least has been, not uncommon among some well-meaning religion teachers. It is, however, a gross injustice to both God and to the individual we're dealing with, and can do irreparable damage to a young person's understanding of his relationship with God.

The point I made in the previous answer was that until some considerable maturity is attained, a young person psychologically and spiritually cannot adequately comprehend the radical commitments and rejections involved in a mortal sin.

Different rites of penance

Several years ago, a parish nearby had a communal penance service twice a year, before Easter and Christmas. The church was filled every time.

This priest has been gone for years, and I know a number of people who have not been to confession since he left. A short time ago I took an adult religion class. Someone asked about the communal penance service, and Father said it was not allowed. This is a shame. If such a ceremony will get people to meditate and examine their consciences and get closer to God, why shouldn't we let it happen?

The church today has three rites for celebrating the sacrament of reconciliation. First is the rite for reconciliation of individual penitents. This is the one-on-one "private" ritual similar to traditional private confession.

Second is the rite for reconciliation of a number of penitents, with individual confession and absolution. This is the form of communal penance service perhaps most familiar to Catholics today. As the ritual for penance indicates, this form shows more clearly the social or ecclesial nature of penance. Everyone listens together to the word of God, examines the conformity of their lives in light of that word of God, and supports one another by prayer together. One or more priests are present so that individual confession and absolution are available.

Third is the rite for reconciliation of a number of penitents with general (not individual) confession of sins and absolution given by the priest to all at one time.

Your letter is not clear about which rite you are speaking of. If it is the third, with general absolution, your priest is correct. This form of penance is not allowed as a general rule; it may be used only in emergencies or other clearly defined circumstances.

The second form (worship together with opportunity for private confession) is, I believe, becoming more and more common and enjoys practically all the spiritual advantages of the third rite. Our experience where I have been pastor, and that of many other parishes, is similar to yours; hundreds of people attend these ceremonies, obviously convinced that this method of expressing sinfulness and asking forgiveness fits their personal sense of sin and need for reconciliation and healing. It combines, so to speak, the best (at least most of the best) of both worlds, our need to express personally our sinfulness and desire for forgiveness, and on the other hand, our need not only of God's pardon, but of "reconciliation with our brothers and sisters who are always harmed by our sins" (Introduction to the Rite of Penance, n.5).

Finally, I suggest that perhaps you are dismissing the value of individual confession (rite one) too easily. This form has important spiritual advantages, especially when we realize that the sacrament of penance not only looks to forgiveness of the past. It looks particularly to the future, giving us grace to examine the direction of our lives and deal with pride, selfishness, greed and other sources of sin deep inside us.

A regular and healthy celebration of this rite, along with communal penance services, does much to open our hearts to the healing and creative power of God's presence.

Is general absolution rite valid?

My question is about the general absolution ceremonies held in some parishes. Many Catholics who attend these services consider them an important and welcome change in the church. Others call them an abuse, since they disregard the matter and form of the sacrament, and say they therefore do not validly receive the sacrament of penance. Both views cannot be correct. What is the church's teaching about this?

Before anything else, it is important to note that, with one possible exception which I mention later, all three forms are valid for the sacrament of reconciliation. Contrary to what you say some Catholics believe, rites with general absolution do have the necessary traditional matter (confession of sin, expression of sorrow and desire for forgiveness) and form (priest's words of absolution) that makes them true and valid sacraments.

The church's official Rite of Penance (35) states that, in the third rite, a general confession is made by all in the form of an act of sorrow, (for example, the prayer "I confess to almighty God..."), and penitents show their desire for forgiveness by bowing, kneeling, or other approved sign. The priest then gives absolution.

Canon law lists several conditions which must be fulfilled for licit celebration of general absolution (canon 961). One circumstance that makes it lawful is imminent danger of death, with no sufficient time for priests to hear confessions individually.

Another is grave necessity, when sufficient confessors are unavailable to allow individual confessions properly within a "suitable" period of time, and penitents would be deprived for a long while of the grace of the sacrament of penance or the Eucharist. (In 1988, the United States Bishops' Conference interpreted this as one month.)

It is the responsibility of the diocesan bishop to judge whether these required conditions for general absolution are present, considering the criteria agreed upon by the national conference of bishops.

Vatican authorities have expressed concern that too broad a use of general absolution will lead to a lesser importance given to traditional "private" confession, and they insist on strict observance of the limitations church law places on this rite of the sacrament. Nevertheless, canon law continues to approve the third rite of reconciliation when the above requirements are fulfilled.

For a valid reception of absolution given to many penitents at one time, those conscious of serious (mortal) sins must intend to confess those sins in private confession within a suitable period of time. (canon 962) Apart from this instance, however, even when the required conditions are not fulfilled, the third rite of reconciliation with general absolution is still valid, but unlawful (illicit). All present who have the intentions I indicated above, along with other intentions always necessary for confession, receive the sacrament validly, with all the graces which accompany the sacrament of penance.

Generic confession

While my mother and I were discussing the confession rite, she told me that in her parish during a communal penitential rite people come up in groups, kneel down before the priest one at a time, and he gives them absolution. They do not mention their sins and the same penance is given to everyone. I'm not saying this is wrong. But it could have disadvantages. It does bring people back to confession who maybe haven't gone in years. People are even coming from other towns to that church.

The kind of confession you mention is sometimes called generic confession. The penitent says he or she has sinned without indicating the kind of sin, or the number. Such a confession is legitimate if one is not confessing serious, mortal sins, whether at a communal penance service or not.

The indication of having sinned and that one is sorry need not be in words. It could be in action, such as your example of kneeling before the priest, which in the context of the penance service obviously means, "Father, I have sinned, and I am sorry."

This method of confessing has some obvious defects along with obvious and attractive advantages. Most of all, it limits the helpful and healing interaction that should occur between the priest and penitent in the rite of penance. Such confessions are legitimate when only venial sins are involved. Generic confession of serious sins is permissible only in an emergency situation. These sins should be mentioned later when the first opportunity for private confession presents itself.

As long as these distinctions are recognized, the practice you describe has much to recommend it. Apparently a lot of people find something in it spiritually fruitful.

Convert afraid of confession

I am married to a Catholic man and now realize I would like to be a Catholic also. My problem is that before I knew my husband I had an abortion. I realize this is against the teaching of the Catholic Church. If I become a Catholic, would I have to admit in confession that this is in my past? I hope I would not even have to bring it up.

Please do not let this fear deter you from entering the Catholic Church. Many factors will make this problem much smaller, in fact, than it may look to you right now.

Only serious sins, which the individual knew were serious at the time they were committed, must be mentioned in confession. From your letter it would appear that you perhaps did not realize the enormity of the sin of abortion when you were younger.

As you learn more about the Catholic faith and specifically more about the sacrament of penance, I believe you will find that the fears which seem so huge now, even about the sin that bothers you, will pretty much fade away. The options open about where you go to confession and to whom, the strictest secrecy which binds every priest when he ministers this sacrament, and above all, the healing and forgiveness that come to us from Jesus and his church, will in the end make things much easier than you now imagine.

Can't remember my sins

It is hard to remember all my sins when I go to confession. When you can't remember them all, how do you tell them to your priest? I am nine years old and in fourth grade.

I congratulate you on your interest in the sacrament of penance and your desire to receive this sacrament in the right way.

It is important to remember something you already know. This sacrament not only forgives sins, it strengthens us to live good Christian and Catholic lives. The grace which Jesus gives when we go to confession, therefore, helps us to direct our lives along the lines that Jesus wants.

One consequence of this is that we should not bother ourselves too much in trying to remember in detail all the sinful or partially sinful actions we have done. With your attitude, there are surely no serious sins in your life. It's more important that you try to grow in your trust in God and your love, in a practical way, for God and for those around you — your family, your friends, and yourself.

I mention these thoughts only to emphasize that the first thing our Lord wants from us is to be comfortable and happy in our meetings with his forgiving love in the sacrament of penance. Beyond that it would help to read whatever you can find about this and other teachings of your faith. Your knowledge in these matters should grow along with your knowledge of other things as you move toward adulthood.

Worrying about past confessions

I spend a lot of time worrying about past confessions, especially those I made as a child or a young teen. As a child my confessions weren't always honest, but I did try to straighten things out later. After years I recalled another sin much like the ones I had confessed. Is it necessary to go back to confession again? I really worked hard trying to clear the slate.

Isn't it unfortunate that the sacrament of forgiveness, which our Lord obviously meant to be a source of peace and appreciation of his mercy, sometimes becomes a cause of worry and fear?

The first and most important thing to remember about the sacrament of penance, in fact, about all our relationships with God, is that he looks into our heart and knows what is there. As a Father who loves us without limit, he knows and accepts what is there far better than we do ourselves.

It is true that for a good confession we should mention any action of ours which we are sure was a mortal sin. However, God knows we are human; he does not expect us to be computerized data retrieval machines. Our memories slip and sometimes our motives look impossibly mixed-up as we try to evaluate what we have done wrong.

From your letter it seems clear to me that you are like many others who have similar concerns about previous confessions, especially those that go back many years. I don't think there's any question you have tried to be honest with God in your confession and in your sorrow. You are trying to live a good Christian and Catholic life. That is what God sees and that is what is important.

In other words, don't worry about what is past. When you receive the sacrament of penance, renew your sorrow for whatever wrongs you have done in your life, and focus your attention and prayers on the present and the future, which is what this sacrament is all about.

"Integral" confession

We were taught that in the sacrament of penance, if there are no serious sins, it is sufficient and good to mention a past sin or present fault that we are bothered about and want to overcome. That is what I usually do. I now read in a Catholic magazine that this is wrong. We should not "confess just one sin," but every confession must be "integral." What does that mean?

An integral confession, in traditional sacramental terminology, means that all serious, mortal sins committed since one's last reception of this sacrament must be confessed.

Some ambiguity apparently has arisen over a practice in some communal penance services at which each penitent is asked to "mention one sin" at the time of individual confessions at that service. There is nothing wrong with that, if one is speaking of lesser venial sins. It is misleading to imply that only one serious sin might be confessed if there has been more than one.

"Fifth Step" and confession

Last fall I realized that I had an addiction and joined a 12-step program to help me recover. One tool they suggest is writing out my feelings and things I have done wrong; this brought a sense of freedom and helped to get rid of some guilt feelings.

The fifth step involved sharing this information with someone else. In my opinion it would serve as a basis for a really significant reception of the sacrament of reconciliation. Would that be possible and appropriate?

You make a good and strong point. While Alcoholics Anonymous was the first group to identify the "Twelve Steps," the process has proved effective equally in other types of addiction.

I have on occasion talked with individuals as they worked their way through the fourth step ("to make a searching and fearless moral inventory of oneself"), and then assisted them through the fifth step ("to admit to God, to ourselves and to another human being the exact nature of our wrongs"). Sometimes this was done in the context of the sacrament of penance; the occasion became a powerful spiritual sacramental experience for both of us.

Some people might protest that the sacrament of reconciliation should not become a personal psychological assessment or a therapy session. That is true. But neither is it a purely clinical recitation of sinful actions and prayer of absolution. The Introduction to the Rite of

Penance urges exactly the opposite. In order to fulfill his ministry properly and faithfully, "the confessor should understand the disorders of souls and apply the appropriate remedies to them. Discernment of spirits is a deep knowledge of God's action in the hearts of men. It is a gift of the Spirit as well as the fruit of charity."

It is one of the skills the confessor should bring to the sacrament. In receiving the repentant sinner and leading him to the light of the truth, a confessor "reveals the heart of the Father and shows the image of Christ the Good Shepherd" (n. 10). This well fits the role of someone accompanying another person through the fifth step.

Phobic about confession

For many years I have had a phobia about going to confession, along with several other phobias. I have undergone treatment for this, but am still unable to receive this sacrament.

Several years ago I had an extramarital affair. I told my therapist about it, but cannot speak of it to anyone else no matter how hard I try. Because of my inability to confess this to a priest, I have stopped going to church. My therapist believes I am forgiven because of my disability.

Am I? I want so much to be a part of the church again, but I don't know if I have been forgiven by telling another person. Can I receive Communion again?

We are obliged to confess any mortal sins in the sacrament of penance before receiving Communion unless it is just impossible to do so. There are different kinds of impossibility. One kind would be physical, for example if no priest were available for confession during an unreasonably long period of time. Another could be one you appear to be experiencing. In your case the impossibility is not physical, but emotional. I'm assuming, of course, that the information you give about the diagnosis and nature of your affliction is accurate.

You apparently are confident that your therapist is aware of the spiritual seriousness for you of the sacrament of penance, and that you are satisfied in your own mind that you suffer from a disorder that goes beyond the usual "fear" of going to confession. (Few people get a thrill out of telling their sins to someone else, in confession or not.) The type of phobic neurosis you claim to have is possible, especially given the usual context of the sacrament of penance.

If the above is true for you, you would not be obliged to receive the sacrament of penance before Communion. "No one is obliged to do what is impossible," is a fundamental principle of moral theology.

This applies to you if it is psychologically impossible for you to confess this particular sin. Express your sorrow to God as well and as honestly as you can, and try to get back to the sacrament of penance, and Mass and Communion. You've been away long enough.

Can a foreigner go to confession?

A Catholic friend of mine is from a foreign country and does not speak English. She wants to go to Communion, but is hesitant because she cannot go to confession. May she receive the Eucharist without confession, or what should she do?

Your friend's situation is not uncommon. Many people from foreign countries stay here for long visits with family, or take up residence permanently without being able to carry on a conversation in English.

Confession of sins should be made in some manner, but there are other ways than by speech when that is impossible. While specific details may not be expressed so easily, the penitents can, for example, indicate which obligations or commandments have been violated, and by other signs express in some general way their sorrow for their sins and their acknowledgment of having done things for which they wish God's forgiveness.

It is even possible if the penitent so wishes, for him or her to confess through an interpreter, as long as abuse or scandal is avoided (CCL 990). In such an instance the interpreter would be seriously bound to secrecy about the confession.

Help your friend to talk with a priest. Most priests have experience with this and can arrange a comfortable and satisfactory way for her to receive the sacrament of penance.

Returning to confession after many years

It is nearly 20 years since I last went to confession. I ceased going because of a problem with our parish priest and because I doubted, as I believe many others did at that time, that a mortal could absolve my sins. In the intervening years, I have continued to pray, faithfully attend Mass, receive Communion, and have been married.

Now I would like to return. You can imagine my fear after 20 years, and less than positive experiences with this sacrament in my youth. And I know some things have changed. What is my status in the church? What prayers do I need to remember?

You are still in good standing in the church. But you're missing out on one of the sources of holiness and strength in Catholic life. My suggestion is to go ahead and receive this sacrament, and don't worry about the details. Confession wasn't meant to be, and is not, that complicated.

Practically all churches today provide the opportunity for either sitting face-to-face with the priest, or kneeling in the traditional anonymous way. By norms established by the United States bishops (1974 and 1978) the option is up to you, depending on what you feel will be most helpful for you spiritually.

Usually the priest will say a brief prayer before you begin, or read a short passage from the Gospels. Then begin in whatever way you wish. Tell the priest the main things you need to confess, for which you ask the forgiveness of God and the people you have hurt by your sinfulness. The priest may ask you to fill in any gaps, may give you some thoughts to reflect on, and ask you to say some prayers of contrition and perform some act of penance as a symbol of your sorrow and desire to grow in holiness. He will then say the prayer of forgiveness (absolution).

The "changes" in the sacrament of penance are not so much in procedures as in greater attention to the causes of our sinfulness and to our cooperation with the healing grace of God in committing ourselves to greater holiness of life.

While we seek forgiveness for our sins, the grace and orientation of this sacrament looks more to the future than the past. What's done is done. It's part of history; not even God can change that. What he can change, with our cooperation, is our hearts and the trends of our lives that are less than we would like them to be.

Pray about it, choose a priest you can feel comfortable with, and start profiting again from this way of experiencing God's compassion.

Parents approved abortion

I have a heavy burden on my shoulders and I need help. A short time ago, my husband and I agreed with our 15-year-old daughter when she had an abortion. Father, she still sucks her thumb, and even now I don't think she realizes what we have done. I still think we did the right thing.

God says that sinners who are truly sorry will be forgiven, but the thought of going to confession scares me. Having our priest tell me I can no longer go to the sacraments is more than I can face. I am a convert, but my husband, who was born a Catholic, feels this is what will happen. What should I do?

Your family has suffered terribly with this experience, but the hope you are looking for is there if you will prayerfully follow a couple of suggestions.

First, be sincerely honest with yourself. What you did was wrong. But considering the enormous pressures you were under, no one except God can possibly judge how guilty you may have been for what you did.

However, after writing three full pages defending yourself for doing the right thing, you conclude by saying how much you need God's forgiveness for your action. You knew, for example, that loving institutions and people were available to help your daughter through the experience with much less trauma than could result from an abortion, if only you would let them.

This leads us to your first and most important step to hope and healing. When we sin seriously, it is generally impossible to unravel and analyze all the good, bad and doubtful motives that influenced us. In fact, it is usually not even healthy to try to do so after the fact. God does not expect or want this.

We open our hearts to his forgiving love, as did the prodigal son, by humbly and trustingly acknowledging our sinfulness and telling him we are back. This is the big part of the job. Once you do this, with the grace of God, 90 percent of your return journey is completed.

As for your other question, don't stay away from the sacrament of penance any longer. Your husband is mistaken in what he expects the priest to say. Nothing will stand any more in the way of your receiving the Eucharist and the other sacraments.

Sacraments for criminals

Can a murderer, rapist, or a robber who is not Roman Catholic be converted to Catholicism and receive all the sacraments after living a sinful life for 10 or 20 years?

Of course he can. It is hard to believe that some Catholics or other Christians are surprised at this, considering the times Jesus insisted he came "not to call the just, but to call the sinner to repentance."

If one has to be perfect, or sinless, to become or remain a Catholic, we are all in deep trouble. In fact, if we are to have the spirit of Christ, our best efforts at charity, patience, and acceptance should be directed to those who have (at least as far as our human eyes can see) the most to overcome, and who have the most difficult struggle to become what God is calling us to in this pilgrimage on earth.

No one of us has any right to act otherwise than Christ himself, who was overjoyed and went out of his way to lend a healing word when a sinner showed he was ready to try to find his way back. I suggest you reread chapter 15 of St. Luke's Gospel.

Anointing of the sick

I recently attended a church ceremony in which a friend received what we used to call Extreme Unction. Several people received the sacrament, including some who were young and didn't look sick at all. Isn't it necessary to be "in danger of death" to have this sacrament? And what is the proper name for it? I've heard it called several things.

This sacrament for the sick is one that has undergone significant development during the past 50 years. The Constitution on the Liturgy of Vatican Council II (art. 73) recognized this development when it said, "Extreme Unction, which may more properly be called the Anointing of the Sick (its official name today), is a sacrament not only for those who are at the point of death."

Thus, the sacrament is for the sick, but by no means only for the dying. In a scriptural passage which forms one of the main bases for the anointing of the sick, St. James says: "Is anyone sick among you? Let him ask for the elders of the church. They will pray over him, and anoint him in the Name of the Lord." (James 5,14)

According to our ritual for the anointing of the sick, an individual need not be in danger of death, but "dangerously ill" either from sickness or advanced age. In other words, older people are considered eligible for the sacrament if they are notably weakened by the general infirmities of old age, even if they are suffering from no serious specific disease. Moreover, the illness need not be physical.

All this means there could be many explanations for the situation you encountered. People no longer need to be dying, or even look sick, to receive the sacrament of the anointing of the sick.

Reasons for anointing

Recently a serious back problem forced me to have an extremely dangerous operation. It could have left me crippled for the rest of my life. I asked the chaplain in the hospital to give me the sacrament of the sick. It would have given me a great deal of comfort, because I was very frightened.

The chaplain said he would not give it to me because it is given only in danger of death, and as long as I was in the state of grace I didn't need it. Could you explain this? It is not the way I understood this sacrament.

The introduction to the church's Rite of Anointing and Pastoral Care of the Sick (n. 8-12) lists the following who may and should receive the sacrament of the sick:

— those who are dangerously ill due to sickness or old age;
— those who have already been anointed but are now suffering from a different illness, or if the danger becomes more serious in the same illness;
— those who are to undergo surgery because of a serious illness (which seems to have been the case with you);
— old people who are weak from age, even if there is no dangerous illness present, and
— sick children, if they have sufficient use of reason to be comforted by this sacrament.

The ritual notes that "a prudent or reasonably sure judgment, without scruple, is sufficient for deciding on the seriousness of an illness."

Can lay people administer anointing?

I understand that a lay person can baptize and administer last rites when a priest cannot be located. If this is true, please explain the procedure so I will be prepared in the future?

In emergency situations, a lay person can administer the sacrament of baptism. When this occurs, the simplest elements of the rite are used. Water is poured over the person and the words are said: "I baptize you in the name of the Father and of the Son and of the Holy Spirit."

If by last rites you mean the sacrament of the anointing of the sick, only a priest can administer this sacrament. Obviously, however, any lay person may, and should, assist someone who is seriously injured, or ill and possibly dying, by helping the individual to pray with acts of faith and hope and love of God. This should be done, in fact, even when one is visiting another who is seriously ill. Sometimes hearing another person pray can console a seriously sick person who does not have the physical or mental strength to accompany that prayer.

Anointing and viaticum

I appreciate your answer explaining the anointing of the sick. A question was prompted by a priest's remark that this sacrament is not the sacra-

ment of the dying. Does this mean that one who is dying should not receive this sacrament? I can hardly believe that. What did the priest mean?

One who is dying can and should receive the anointing of the sick. The priest might have meant two things. First, he perhaps was making the point that the sacrament of the anointing of the sick is not only for the dying, or those who are in danger of imminent death, as some formerly believed. As I explained, it is only necessary that the individual be "seriously ill," even though there may be no real danger of death.

He might also have meant that the sacrament of the dying is not strictly speaking the anointing of the sick, but rather the Eucharist, which is also correct. Christian tradition gives a special name to holy Communion when it is received by the dying. We call it viaticum, literally something to be with us and help us "on the journey" through death into eternity.

We should, therefore, be certain that friends or relatives have every opportunity to receive Communion whenever possible as they approach death.

The sacrament of the anointing of the sick may be repeated if the individual recovers and then gets sick again, or if, in the same illness, the danger becomes more serious.

Ministry to the sick

For nearly three years I have been a eucharistic minister to the sick. Our pastor now asked me to take charge of our care for the sick, some of whom are at home, others in hospitals and nursing homes.

When the parish group of eucharistic ministers gathered to discuss schedules, some expressed concern that we should do more than just take Communion to the people we're assigned to. Could you help us, or should we just be satisfied taking Communion?

You deserve thanks for what you're already doing. The opportunities you give to the sick in your parish to receive this sacrament, far beyond what was possible in the past, are much appreciated, I'm sure.

Every document of the church in the last generation relating to care of the sick points out the need for special pastoral care, since they are among those who are "in a special way united with the suffering Christ for the salvation of the world." (Vatican II Dogmatic Constitution on the Church, 41)

So, your concern is valid. As you are discovering apparently, several publications deal in one way or another with insights, guidelines and procedures for the care you speak of. They're available at good Catholic book stores, even through catalogues. You might take a look at a few of them.

The most neglected resource on this subject, however, in my view, is the official rite of the church, *Pastoral Care of the Sick*. Most people, even many priests, think of this book as useful only for administering the Eucharist and anointing the sick. It does deal with these, but much more. The various introductions, with a variety of information and spiritual reflections on this ministry, are worth reading and praying over by ministers like yourself and the people you work with.

The first two chapters deal with visits to the sick without the Eucharist. In other chapters, you will find prayers, intercessions and Scripture passages to choose from. If the parish has the money, give one of these rituals to all your people who work with the sick. They are available in small, inexpensive soft-cover editions.

CHAPTER 10

ECUMENISM

∾

Does belief make a difference?

Since Vatican Council II we have heard reference to the "people of God" and talk about the Christian churches. Does this refer to the various Christian denominations? And if it does, does it mean that we now believe that "one religious denomination is as good as another?"

The book of Revelation refers to the seven churches in Asia. Would this be considered the same as the present-day parishes or dioceses? Or is it in reference to the inclusion of Baptist, Presbyterian, and other Christian churches?

You're really asking three questions. First, in Vatican Council II and often since then, Catholic documents refer to other Christian denominations as "churches." By this is meant that they are, as is obvious, members of the family of believers in Jesus Christ and true Christian communities. On Sept. 5, 2000, in the declaration *Dominus Jesus,* the Congregation for the Doctrine of the Faith held that ecclesial communities which have not preserved a valid episcopate and the genuine eucharistic mystery "are not churches in the proper sense." (n. 17)

The second question, concerning common beliefs, is too complicated to discuss in detail here. Very briefly, all Christian churches agree in many major areas of belief about Jesus, God, and his church on earth. Individual Christians must follow their conscience as they understand what God asks in their relationship to him.

However it is overly simple to jump to the conclusion that "one denomination is as good as another," since many denominations differ significantly in major points of doctrine. Catholics, for example, (along with Anglicans and many Lutherans, at least) believe in the real presence of Jesus in the Eucharist. Other Christians may not believe this and we presume they are following the light of their own conscience in rejecting that belief.

It would, nevertheless, be foolish and irrational to hold that it makes no difference whether one believes it or not, whether it is true or not. If Jesus is not present in the Eucharist, we are (even in good faith) believing that what is only bread is really God. On the other hand, if Jesus is truly present in the Eucharist and there to be offered and received as the great sign and means of the unity of his people on earth, then those who reject that belief (again, even though in good faith) are missing one of the most majestic elements of Christian life.

While there is only one God and one Lord, we need to take care that tolerance and acceptance of others, particularly Christians, regardless of our difference of beliefs, do not turn into a position that "it doesn't make any difference what you believe as long as you believe something" — which, if God and religion have any rational meaning at all, is total nonsense.

The churches in the book of Revelation, which was written centuries before Protestant denominations began as we know them, did refer, as you suggest, to the local churches, akin to our present-day diocese or parish. In fact, by the time this book was written, most local churches were apparently already under the responsibility of an "Episkopos" (overseer), as our dioceses are under the responsibility of a bishop.

Are only Christians saved?

Some of my Catholic co-workers told our Jewish co-workers that they can never achieve eternal happiness after death because they have not ac-

---

REGARDING CATHOLIC NORMS FOR ECUMENISM

Current Roman Catholic ecumenical principles and guidelines are primarily contained in the Directory for the Application of Principles and Norms on Ecumenism, issued by the Pontifical Council for Promoting Christian Unity, approved by Pope John Paul II in March, 1993. Familiarity with this document is essential for a fuller understanding of the church's ecumenical theology and practice. Unless otherwise noted, the word Directory in this chapter refers to this document.

---

cepted Jesus into their lives. What does this mean for the millions of good people who lived before Jesus? Or the other millions who never had the opportunity to hear about Jesus or were raised in a non-Christian faith?

What your co-workers are saying is not what the Catholic church teaches. Certain other Christians may agree with them, but Catholic doctrine today is clearly to the contrary.

The *Catechism of the Catholic Church* speaks strongly, as we would expect it to, about the essential place of Jesus Christ and baptism and membership in the church in God's saving plan. Then it adds a most significant and critical sentence: "Hence they could not be saved who, *knowing that the Catholic Church was founded as necessary by God through Christ,* would refuse either to enter it or to remain in it" (n. 846, quoting the Vatican Council Constitution on the Church, 14. Emphasis mine)

If you read the emphasized words carefully, you can see that they would not apply to billions of people on earth now and in the past, including most, if not all, people of the Hebrew tradition.

The idea behind this teaching is more explicit in the following catechism paragraph: "Those who, through no fault of their own, do not know the Gospel of Christ or his church, but who nevertheless seek God with a sincere heart and, moved by grace, try in their actions to do his will as they know it through the dictates of their conscience — those too may achieve eternal salvation" (847).

In other words, God's grace is guiding and saving those who live sincerely and conscientiously good lives, but who have, for whatever reason, honestly never seen the embrace of Christ or the church as a personal religious obligation.

Pope John Paul II invokes this Catholic understanding in hopeful and moving ways in his book, *Crossing the Threshold of Hope.* He notes the common elements of belief between Christianity and what we often call "pagan" religions.

"The Catholic Church rejects nothing that is true and holy in these religions," he says, because we are "guided by the faith that God the Creator wants to save all humankind in Jesus Christ."

We don't know how God does all this. But we do know, the pope continues, that "Christ came into the world for all these peoples. He redeemed them all and has his own ways of reaching each of them" in the present age of salvation history (pages 80-83).

It's a striking way of acknowledging that God has told us much about some details of his saving love for us; but he still "has his own ways" of doing things. If that is true anywhere, we would expect it to be true in his plan for the salvation of the world through Jesus Christ. Pope John Paul expresses our belief that this is indeed the case.

Roman Catholics, other Catholics

Is there a difference between a Catholic and a Roman Catholic? What is the meaning of "Roman"?

The word "catholic" means "universal." It was first applied to Christians by St. Ignatius of Antioch around the year 100. Roman Catholics sometimes tend to consider themselves "the" Catholic church of the world. While we are the largest in numbers, other Catholic churches are united with the bishop of Rome, but distinct churches in themselves. There are the Melkite, for example, Armenian, Maronite and Ukrainian Catholic churches, and many more. These churches, including the church of Rome, have their roots in varying styles of liturgy and expressions of faith that developed in different centers of Christianity during its early centuries.

Such churches are not branches of the Roman Catholic Church. They are of equal dignity and rank with the Roman church and with each other. (See, for example, the Vatican II Decree on Eastern Churches, No. 3) In this context, the designation Roman Catholic distinguishes our part of the universal church from other Catholic churches.

World Council of Churches

I was told recently that the Catholic Church is about ready to join the World Council of Churches. This puzzles me greatly. How could our church become a member of a Protestant organization like this? Is this where ecumenism is leading us?

The World Council of Churches, founded in 1949, is a partnership "of churches which accept our Lord Jesus Christ as God and Savior." Its purpose is to promote Christian unity, and to aid cooperation among the churches in doctrinal research, relief and welfare programs, missionary activities and other common projects.

From the beginning, even though it numbered some Orthodox and Anglican groups among its members, the WCC was primarily Protestant-oriented, dealing mainly with problems that concerned Protestant churches. During the 1960s, however, Pope Paul VI and

WCC officials began a close working relationship, especially in areas involving social justice and peace, a relationship that continues under Pope John Paul II.

Consultants and observers from both groups work together, and apparently agree there is no theoretical reason the Roman Catholic Church should not join. The problem with Catholic membership is practical. Membership in the Catholic Church totals more than the entire membership of the churches presently part of the WCC. In fact, more than half of all the Christians in the world are Catholics.

A serious question is therefore: How can a church of this size and scope share membership with the WCC without, in effect, dominating the whole organization? This is why Pope Paul said in 1969, during his visit to WCC headquarters in Geneva, that the time is not ready for a decision on the matter.

WCC leaders generally agree. Dr. Eugene Carson Blake, then secretary general of the organization, said at the time, "How does a church of approximately the size of the total fellowship of the World Council best cooperate with or have relationships with the World Council, which consists of 240 churches in 80 or 90 countries?"

By now, the WCC consists of nearly 300 churches, with 450 million members, in 100 countries.

Eventually it will be the Catholic Church's decision to ask to join. Until an answer to these practical questions is found, however, we'll have to be satisfied with continued informal, but close, collaboration.

Sharing non-Catholic communion

When Catholics attend a non-Catholic wedding in a Protestant church as part of the wedding party or family, may they receive communion distributed at these services?

I heard this is permitted as long as they do not believe they are receiving the body and blood of Christ. What is the Catholic Church's teaching on this?

The policy you heard about is not Catholic teaching, and distorts both Catholic understanding of the Eucharist and norms for interfaith communion. The most up-to-date and complete explanation of Catholic concerns and policies on this subject is in the 1993 Ecumenical Directory. The following points are most relevant to the issues you raise.

The sacraments, especially the Eucharist, are intended to be signs of the unity in faith, worship and community life which exist among those who receive them. Eucharistic communion is therefore linked to full, visible communion in the church itself.

At the same time, the Catholic Church believes that baptism brings people of other churches and ecclesial communities into a real, if imperfect, communion with the Catholic Church.

These two principles are the foundation of Catholic policies concerning access to eucharistic Communion. In light of these principles and other Catholic doctrines concerning the sacraments and their validity, for example, the requirement that the eucharistic celebration be presided over by a validly ordained priest, the fact that there is not a common faith in the eucharistic presence of Christ would be a primary reason for not receiving communion in the other Christian worship.

If we accept the Christian tradition that eucharistic Communion is a symbol of unity in faith, Catholics may ask for the sacrament only from a minister in whose church these sacraments are valid, or from one who is validly ordained according to Catholic teaching on ordination.

Catholic Communion by Protestants

How about the other way around? May non-Catholics receive Communion at a Catholic wedding?

To minister Catholic Communion to Protestants, four conditions must be present. First, the non-Catholic must be unable, in the circumstance, to go to a minister of his or her own church or religious community for the sacrament.

In addition, the individual must ask for Communion on his or her initiative, have a faith in the Eucharist in accord with Catholic belief, and be properly disposed spiritually for reception of the sacrament.

Bishops' conferences or individual diocesan bishops may establish supplementary norms "for judging situations of grave and pressing need and for verifying the conditions" required. Catholic ministers must judge individual cases and administer the sacraments in accord with these further norms, if they exist.

Otherwise, says the Directory, ministers of the sacraments are to judge according to the norms of the Directory, as I indicated them above.

Up to now, the United States Conference of Catholic Bishops has not established additional norms. Some diocesan bishops have established norms for their dioceses, or have reserved to themselves judgment as to the presence of the necessary conditions. Others have not.

I know of instances in which bishops have, for example, allowed non-Catholic parents to receive Communion at the marriage of their Catholic son or daughter, non-Catholic spouses to receive at the funeral of the Catholic husbands or wives, non-Catholic graduates to receive with their classmates at a baccalaureate Mass, and so on.

When particular norms are not established by the Bishops' Conference or the local bishop, the priest himself should judge individual cases according to norms of the Directory (130) I pointed out above. The 1993 Directory expands on, and in some cases slightly modifies, previous ecumenical guidelines, including those in canon law. (Directory, 129-132)

Eucharist and "one faith"

I cannot understand how holy Communion can be given to Protestants even in cases when the church says this is permitted. Isn't Communion supposed to be a sign of unity? If we are not united, isn't it wrong to act as if we were?

This question particularly involves one of the conditions required before Protestants may receive Communion in the Catholic Church, that is that they "have a faith in the sacrament in conformity with that of the church."

There are many levels and degrees of Christian unity. I'm sure, for example, that you disagree on some important, if not essential, religious convictions with people you are at the Communion table with each week. Yet you would probably say that you agree on the "basics."

What are these basic Christian beliefs? Undoubtedly, the most fundamental are a belief in God the Creator and in his redeeming love for mankind; in Jesus, the incarnate Son of God, as our Savior and Lord; that by his death, resurrection, and glorification with the heavenly Father, Jesus has united us with himself and with each other in a way that transcends all hope and power without him; that we are reborn into eternal life with him through baptism; that we celebrate and keep alive this redemptive act of Jesus by offering and eating the Eucharist as he commanded at the Last Supper; that in this Eucharist it is truly himself — his body and blood — that is our offering and our food, and that we are destined through faith, hope, and mutual love to be together with Christ, our brother, in eternal life.

All Protestants hold most of these truths as sacredly as we do, and many Protestants believe *all* of them as explicitly and as sincerely as we do. Surely it is quite an array of awesome doctrines to be united about.

There are other considerable beliefs which divide us, mainly in the area of church structure, such as the nature of the ministerial order, the role of the spiritual head of the church in the person of the Roman Pontiff, sacraments, and so on. While acknowledging these differences, the Vatican Council and recent popes have insisted that it is equally important to acknowledge in word and action, wherever possible, the much greater elements which unite us as all "brothers and sisters in Christ."

We must keep in mind that the Eucharist relates in a special way to the Mystery of the Church and is the sacramental sign *par excellence* of visible unity. Even here the church says we must acknowledge our common faith, especially if that faith includes similar beliefs concerning the Eucharist, and if the other prescribed conditions for inter-Communion are present.

Can I receive Communion?

My son, who was in college, was killed playing basketball. I am Baptist, but I attend Mass regularly in the parish church near us. All of my young children are Catholics, as was my son who died. My Catholic husband again goes to Mass with me every Sunday and I'm grateful for that.

To take Communion at Mass, do you have to be Catholic? I would really like to receive.

I am deeply sorry for the hurt you are suffering because of the death of your son. Through your participation at Mass, you have obviously come to recognize to some degree why Communion holds such an important place in the hearts of Catholics. It is the main way in which we, in our worship, unite ourselves to the death and resurrection of Christ, which we offer again to the heavenly Father in every celebration of the Eucharist.

Because of your family's situation and the Catholic practices you already observe, I am prompted to ask that you consider becoming a full member of the Catholic faith

As I explained above, it is true that except for special situations, only people of the Catholic faith should receive Communion at Mass. I suggest you go to one of the priests you know and discuss your situation with him, if you have not done so already. You would like to participate and share in the Mass as intimately as possible; he will help you do that.

Communion at funeral

A dear friend and I attended the funeral of another friend in the Catholic Church. My friend is Lutheran and devoted to her church.

At Communion time, this lady went up to receive and the priest gave her holy Communion. How could she receive in the Catholic Church if she is not Catholic? I didn't question her about it for fear of hurting her feelings.

Unless special conditions were present she should not have received Communion. In fact, many Lutherans are equally strong in their restrictions about their members' reception of Communion in other churches, or about people of other faiths receiving Communion in the Lutheran Church.

Your friend did what she did in a spirit of friendship, reverence and Christian faith. Since the situation is not likely to be repeated and since there seems little chance of misunderstanding by others, I believe you acted prudently in not attempting to correct her.

The priest, of course, had no way of knowing she is not Catholic. Priests usually must assume that anyone who approaches for holy Communion is a practicing Catholic.

How many sacraments?

A few Catholics are in a discussion group with some Protestant couples. A question arose recently about the sacraments. Where do we get seven? If Christ instituted them, why do Protestants recognize only two?

There was no actual enumeration of seven sacraments until more than 1,000 years after Jesus' resurrection. During those centuries, however, the Christian church recognized that among all its religious ceremonies, some rites established a unique contact with Christ, and were intimately connected with peak experiences in the lives of Christians — birth, life, growth, worship, forgiveness, sickness and death.

As early as the year 200, the theologian, Tertullian, wrote about the special goodness of those marriages which the church blesses and seals and which the heavenly Father ratifies.

Around 1150, another noted theologian, Peter Lombard, researched all this Christian experience and came up with a list of seven sacraments. The list was accepted by St. Thomas and other theologians. No serious disagreement was raised until the Protestant Reformation nearly 400 years later. Interestingly, while the Western (Latin) and Eastern churches fought violently over many matters of faith, this is one thing they agreed on.

The reasons most Protestant churches acknowledge only two sacraments (baptism and the Eucharist) are complicated. Mainly it is because these are, even in Catholic doctrine, the focal sacraments of the Christian life and because they are more obviously founded on explicit texts in the Gospels. It's worth noting that certain Protestant communities increasingly provide rites for other "sacraments." Some Lutherans and Presbyterians, for example, celebrate a rite for confession, and Anglicans for the anointing of the sick.

The list of seven sacraments was defined as Catholic faith by the Councils of Florence in 1439, and Trent in 1547.

Catholic Anglican agreements

Is there any difference remaining between Episcopalian and Catholic teachings? An Episcopal friend tells me her priest says that most differences, especially about holy Communion, have been resolved in recent discussions. Is she right?

Some remarkable agreements have been reached in Anglican-Roman Catholic discussions during the past several years. A few years ago, for example, the U. S. Anglican-Roman Catholic dialogue, made up of bishops, other clergy and theologians of both churches, published several "affirmations." They affirm together that:

1. In the Eucharist, the church makes present the sacrifice of Calvary and is empowered by the Holy Spirit to make Christ present and to receive all the benefits of this sacrifice.
2. In the Eucharist, Christ makes himself present sacramentally when the bread and wine are changed into his body and blood.
3. After the Eucharistic celebration the body and blood of Christ may be reserved for Communion of the sick and may be reserved for adoration, as an extension of the worship of Jesus Christ at the celebration of the Eucharist.
4. Only a validly ordained priest can be the minister who brings into being the sacrament of the Eucharist and offers sacramentally the redemptive sacrifice of Christ which God offers us.

Participants in the dialogue concluded that "the Eucharist as sacrifice is not an issue that divides our two churches." A short time later the president of the Pontifical Council for Promoting Christian Unity told the Anglican-Roman Catholic International Commission that agreement between the two churches had been greatly strengthened. While much remains to be done and prayed for, there is no question that this and similar agreements are major events as we move with hope toward the unity for which Jesus prayed at the Last Supper.

The Presbyterian Book of Common Worship

You wrote once about a new book by a Protestant denomination that had something like Mass prayers in it. A Protestant couple tells us they know nothing about it, and have a hard time believing it. Frankly, so do we. Is there such a book? If there is, can they buy one?

I'm sure you are speaking of the Presbyterian *Book of Common Worship* published in 1993 by the Cumberland Presbyterian Church and the Presbyterian Church (U.S.A.). I imagine they would be more than reluctant to say it contains Mass prayers.

What is noteworthy, however, is that the new worship book assumes Sunday worship will normally include a celebration of word and sacrament, loosely what Catholics would call a Liturgy of the Word and a Liturgy of the Eucharist.

This understanding of worship is not entirely new for the Presbyterian Church. An earlier worship book took major steps in this direction about 25 years ago. It's a safe guess, however, that the contents of the 1993 volume would astonish most Protestants, and certainly most Catholics, whose image of Protestant worship does not fit what this ceremonial calls for. It incorporates an order of worship that has been common in the Roman Catholic and Anglican bodies, and for a long time in certain other churches, particularly Lutheran.

Perhaps most interesting, at least for Catholics, is the inclusion of 24 eucharistic prayers, plus ceremonies for care and anointing of the sick, for forgiveness and reconciliation of individual penitents and for traditional Christian observances such as Ash Wednesday and the Easter triduum.

The book also contains psalms and prayers from the Liturgy of the Hours, the Revised Common Lectionary (very similar to our schedule of scriptural readings) and much more.

Whatever our doctrinal differences may be with other Christian denominations, we can only be happy and hopeful over this venture of the Presbyterian Church, and what it can mean for the development of liturgical worship. In offering congratulations to those who developed and published the book, the U. S. Bishops' Committee on the Liturgy noted, "This new service book is sure to have great influence on many other Protestant churches in the country."

The *Book of Common Worship* is available for $25 from Presbyterian Publishing House, 100 Witherspoon St., Louisville, KY 40202-1396.

Catholic and Muslim unity

Recently, I heard the Nation of Islam leader speak. I became impressed with what he said, and even more with his closing prayer, quoting Jesus, and saying nothing belittling to Christians or Jews. I know nothing about this religion, but can see why many African-Americans have joined. What would prevent Catholics and Muslims from uniting? Catholics and Protestants have not made all that much progress. After listening to this man, maybe unity with the Muslims is more attainable.

Some sort of peaceful relationship between the Catholic Church and Islam would indeed be an awesome achievement. Catholics, about 1.058 billion, constitute the largest single religious denomination in the world. Muslims run a close second, about 1.033 billion. They are the only religious groups with over 1 billion members world wide.

It's no wonder that everyone from the pope on down, on the Catholic side at least, looks with hope on any sign of dialogue between the two faiths. I'm afraid, however, that any stable, effective religious collaboration or union between the Catholic Church and Islam is more difficult than might sometimes appear.

Many points of similarity do exist. With Judaism and Christianity, Islam is one of the three great monotheistic religions in the world, all in one way or another looking to Abraham as the founder of their faith.

The Muslim creed is simple: There is no God but Allah, and Mohammed is his prophet. Each day devout Muslims recite often the prayer *Allahu Akbar*, God is the most great.

All three of these faiths look to Jerusalem as a spiritual focus of their religion. The second most sacred mosque of Islam is the Dome of the Rock, built on the site of Solomon's temple in Jerusalem, where, it is traditionally believed, Abraham intended to sacrifice Isaac, where

Jesus walked and taught, and where (according to Muslim tradition) Mohammed ascended into heaven in 632 A. D.

Frequent prayer, generous and personal care of the poor, fasting, and belief in one God are pillars of Islamic faith. Officially at least, economic justice, equal dignity for women far beyond what was acceptable in the surrounding male-dominated cultures, and racial equality are among the demands Mohammed made on believers. The insistence on racial equality, incidentally, is one reason mainstream Islam even today rejects the Black Muslim movement for its discrimination and segregation.

The obstacles to effective dialogue are many. For one, Muslims reject belief in the Trinity, and thus many other core Christian doctrines, the divinity of Jesus Christ among them. Nevertheless, God's plan for salvation includes all who acknowledge the Creator, says the *Catechism of the Catholic Church*, "in the first place among whom are the Muslims." . . . "Together with us they adore the one merciful God, mankind's judge on the last day." (No. 841, quoting the Vatican Constitution on the Church, 16)

Unity between our two faiths doesn't appear imminent. But God accomplishes remarkable things when he is ready to move.

Recent Catholic-Lutheran agreement

When I was growing up, several good friends were Lutherans. Some of us are still close. We didn't go into the Lutheran church, and they would never come to ours, though none of us quite understood why.

So you can understand why the recent (1999) agreement between Catholics and Lutherans is surprising. Are there no "official" differences between us any more?

The convergence between these two faiths is truly historic. The new document, released Oct. 31, 1999, deals primarily with justification, one of the most crucial doctrinal elements in the division between Lutherans, and many other Protestants, and Catholics for the last 500 years.

What is justification, and how does it happen? What is it that "justifies" us, forgives our sins and brings us holiness by the gift of new life in Jesus Christ?

Luther and his followers claimed this gift was purely from God's generosity. No action of ours could merit it; we receive it and accept it only by faith (*sole fide*) in the compassionate mercy of God. Catholic theology, on the other hand, while insisting that justification is an unmerited favor from God, tended to put more emphasis on the importance of human actions.

The Council of Trent (1545-1563) taught, for example, that individuals dispose themselves for justification by penitence, hope, faith, keeping God's commands and intending to begin a "new life" (Session 6, chapter 6 and canon 9). True, the church had insisted for centuries that even those initial steps toward God are possible only by his grace. Nevertheless, there appeared to be division between the two positions.

There's an unhappy human inclination that when we disagree with others, especially in a climate of hostility, we bolster our side by putting the most negative possible interpretation on their words. This was much the situation in whatever "dialogue" took place during most of the past 500 years. In recent decades, thankfully, another principle has taken control. If you genuinely seek the truth, it says, and not just the upper hand, before you disagree with someone be sure you can repeat back to him, to his satisfaction, what he has said. Often, our antagonist will respond: No, that's not exactly what I mean; let me make it more clear.

Such discourse follows the pattern urged by Pope John Paul II in his 1995 encyclical *Ut Unum Sint* (That They May Be One). "Theological dialogue," he directed, "must take account of the ways of thinking and historical experiences of the other party." Pursuing their theological exchanges with this in mind, Catholics and Lutherans involved in the dialogue gradually discovered that their ideas on this subject are not that far apart; they are only arrived at from different directions. By grace alone, by faith in Christ's saving work and not because of any merit on our part, states the agreement, "we are accepted by God and receive the Holy Spirit, who renews our hearts while equipping and calling us to good works." God's grace is total gift; we live out that gift by our good works.

The prominent American Jesuit theologian, Cardinal Avery Dulles, speaking on this new consensus, notes that the decrees of Trent remain Catholic teaching "but should not be used as the standard for measuring Lutheran doctrines expressed in relation to a different historical perspective." Trent, he says, was scholastic and heavily influenced by Greek metaphysics, whereas Lutheran thought-form was more personal and existential. It is now recognized, he adds, that "even Trent" was "not the last and ultimate word" in stating theological positions.

Major hurdles remain between the churches, not least of which is "selling" the agreement to many Catholic and Lutheran theologians who are not comfortable with it. That the consensus is an ecumenical breakthrough of monumental proportions, however, cannot be denied. As little as 30 years ago, it would have been thought impossible. Where the Holy Spirit will take us next remains to be seen.

Are Protestants heretics?

Why don't we hear the word heretic anymore? With so many crazy teachings today, I think it's a sign of how far we've come in not knowing what we believe. Our catechism called Protestants heretics. Aren't they considered this any more?

Also, why all the Protestant hymns at Mass? I once asked a priest years ago why we couldn't sing "A Mighty Fortress is Our God" and he said it was because it was written by a heretic.

First, let's clear up that word "heretic." With all respect to your memory, I don't believe any catechism ever called all Protestants heretics. A heretic, by traditional definition of the church, is one who knowingly and obstinately denies some doctrine that he knows is revealed by God, and which is proposed as an article of Catholic faith by the church. If you consider that definition carefully, it does not apply to sincere Protestants. In fact, there might be serious question whether, at least today, it applies to anybody.

You ask why the word isn't used much anymore. Beyond the reason just given, I believe the church (which means all of us) realizes these days that this kind of labeling and name-calling accomplishes little toward the cause of truth or charity. In the earliest years of the Protestant revolt from the Catholic faith, there may have been some justification for this either-or drawing of lines. The situation then was different from now in a multitude of ways.

Protestants and Catholics still differ on significant beliefs, generally dealing with the Eucharist and the structure of the church as an institution. These differences may not be ignored or shrugged off. However, both groups of Christians finally seem more ready to acknowledge that substantial points of doctrinal agreement are more numerous, and just as significant, as points of disagreement. The feeling seems to be, among the leaders and members of the communities involved, that when our larger "enemies" are the common enemies of all Christians, it is of small value to attempt to pinpoint heretics.

As for your other question, what makes a hymn Protestant anyway? If the words are doctrinally and spiritually suitable, and if its music is of appropriate quality, a song may be used in Catholic worship no matter who wrote it or who used it first.

Happy interfaith marriages?

I recently broke an engagement because of religious differences. My parents were of different faiths and we children were raised in both churches. I remember the confusion of it all. As an adult, I chose to go to the Catholic church. Shortly before we were to be married, my fiance began pressuring me to drop my religion and indicated he would return to the Baptist Church. I refused.

After the break, his brother told me they were taught that all Catholics went to hell. He also said his brother wasn't very stable, and was frightened by loving someone who may never be "saved." Can Protestants, especially Baptists, ever have a successful marriage with a Catholic? Would differences make a miserable marriage?

As you probably do also, I have dozens of friends and co-workers who are in healthy interfaith marriages. To my knowledge, however, not one of them would deny that differences in religion place tensions and strains in a marriage that are normally not present when both partners are of the same faith. It is not unusual for these strains to be more than the husband and wife can handle.

Much depends on the nature and extent of the difference of faith and the degree of conviction with which each party adheres to that faith. It is not possible to draw general conclusions beyond stressing the absolute necessity for the prospective husband and wife to discuss thoroughly and honestly all faith differences that will affect their marriage and their role as parents, and to do this before committing to a marriage.

Younger or inexperienced people tend to underestimate the influence of their spiritual backgrounds on their deepest, often unrecognized, desires for themselves, their spouses and their families. If parents have passed on to them any depth of religious culture, then their understanding of God and how he relates to us and we to him, the ways we encounter Jesus and commit ourselves to him and to his people, the place of the church and its caring love for us in our lives, and even whether any of these elements of faith are important or not — all these will determine what a prospective spouse expects to give and to receive during the marriage. To ignore these realities and these expectations can be disastrous.

These differences may occur just as seriously between Protestants of different faiths as between a Catholic and a Protestant. One must admit, particularly today, that even two baptized Catholics may be so at variance in their religious understanding and practice that their union might need to be approached, for all practical purposes, as an interfaith marriage.

To answer your question, people of differing faiths can have a successful marriage, but only on the condition that their convictions are strong, that the demands of their consciences are clearly known to each other, and that they have each assured themselves that they will be able to pursue a good fruitful married life without either of them betraying their hopes or their beliefs.

Today more than ever such prayerful reflection and honesty is essential to a successful marriage.

If you meet someone else and marriage appears even a remote possibility, don't wait until you're engaged to begin this kind of discussion.

Mass at interfaith marriage

I am Catholic. My fiance has no denomination but attends Mass and loves the Catholic Church. The priest tells us that, since my fiance is not Catholic, we cannot have a Mass. We are both disappointed. However, several people, including a nun, told me it isn't that way anymore. What is the rule?

Nuptial Masses are sometimes allowed at the wedding of a Catholic and non-Catholic. However, Mass is not automatically possible at every interfaith marriage. Two major conditions are required. (Directory 129-131,159)

First, the non-Catholic should be a baptized Christian. Normally, only a Christian would understand and believe in the religious significance of the Lord's Supper, and therefore appreciate in some proper way its re-enactment in our eucharistic celebration.

Second, both partners must desire and freely request that their marriage be celebrated within the Mass. The intent here, of course, is to be sure that the sensibilities of the non-Catholic and his family are honored, and that both partners see the ceremony as a commitment to God and each other in the sacrament of marriage. (See Rite of Marriage, introduction, no. 8)

Both requirements also aim at eliminating the Mass as simply a social adornment making the marriage ceremony more ostentatious. Decisions on this matter should be reached in consultation with the priest performing the wedding, who ultimately is responsible for assuring that requirements are fulfilled.

Anglican and Roman priests

We have many friends who are members of the Anglican Church. While we go to each others' churches sometimes, we realize we should not receive communion in these other churches since there is a problem about the recognition of the Anglican priests.

Has there been, or will there be, any change in Catholic teaching about Anglican priests?

The story of the Roman Catholic Church's concern about the Anglican orders, which is the center of your question, is long and complicated.

The primary official document of the Roman Catholic Church on the subject is the decree, *Apostolicae Curae*, of Sept. 18, 1896, in which Pope Leo XIII declared that the defects in the ordination of Anglican bishops and priests are so critical that Anglican orders must be judged invalid.

The Holy Father gave two reasons for this judgment. The first was a presumed disagreement about the nature of the Eucharist, especially the relationship of the sacrifice of the Mass to the sacrifice of Christ on Calvary.

The second was an apparent difference of belief about the origin of the order of bishops and priests. Pope Leo concluded that there was a serious divergence between the Anglican belief and the Roman Catholic position — which is that the commission of bishops and priests derives from the same commission which Jesus gave to his apostles.

Since Vatican Council II, Roman Catholic and Anglican scholars have devoted years to a restudy of these differences, and have found they are perhaps not nearly as great as they seemed at the time of Pope Leo. The Anglican-Roman Catholic International Commission, appointed by Pope Paul VI and the Archbishop of Canterbury, concluded several years ago that the judgment of Pope Leo XIII should be put "in a new context" for the church today.

It is impossible here to explain these agreements in more detail, but they are expressed in two documents which you can obtain, each treating one of the major differences that I mentioned above. They are titled, The Agreed Statement on Ministry and Ordination, and The Agreed Statement on Eucharistic Doctrine. (USCCB Publications, 3211 Fourth St., NE, Washington, D. C., 20017)

Officially the matter is still being weighed. There is no change at this time in the position of the Roman Catholic Church regarding Anglican orders.

Protestant use of Catholic church

Our Catholic newspaper informs us that a bishop allowed the use of his cathedral church for the consecration of an Episcopalian bishop. This astonished me. I realize it is a good gesture on the part of the Catholic bishop to create good will and understanding, and that in time we may all be one. But, for now, today? Does a bishop have a right to permit this?

Any Christian raised in the Catholic versus Protestant atmosphere that lasted nearly 400 years (and which in great degree ended only around the time of Vatican Council II) needs serious study and reflection to understand what the Catholic Church and others are doing today.

For now it is sufficient to admit that, on all sides, this opposition was fed by much uncharitableness and untruth about each other. Whatever may have been in the past, all Christians, thank God, are taking a new look at the prayer and wish of Jesus that his followers be one, and that they be identified by their love for one another.

The Catholic bishop in this case acted in accord with regulations of our church, which are made in the spirit of love and reconciliation.

The Ecumenical Directory of 1967 stated: "If the separated brethren have no place in which to carry out religious rites properly and with dignity, the local ordinary may allow them the use of a Catholic building, cemetery or church." (n. 61. The 1993 Directory n. 137 says the same.)

Later explanations of this regulation point out that initiatives in sharing facilities can be undertaken only with the authority of the bishop of the diocese. It is impossible for any such regulations to be specific to cover all cases. The bishop must make his decision in response to a local need or an emergency.

The Catholic Church is attempting everything possible to follow the guidance of the Holy Spirit in bringing about eventual Christian unity. The 1967 Directory is among the documents at the base of the 1993 Directory.

"Fraternal charity in the relations of daily life is not enough to foster the restoration of unity among all Christians," it states. "It is right and proper that there should also be allowed a certain sharing of spiritual activity and resources — that is, Christians should be able to share that spiritual heritage they have in common in a manner and to a degree permissible and appropriate in their present divided states.

"Some, even very many, of those elements and endowments which together build up and give life to the church herself can exist outside the visible boundaries of the Catholic church. These elements, which come from Christ and lead to him, rightly belong to the one church of Christ; they can contribute appropriately to our petition for the grace of unity; they can manifest and strengthen the bonds which still bind Catholics to their separated brethren."

The event you ask about is by no means a first. Sharing churches with other faiths has occurred often. Among other examples, in the 1960s, an American archbishop permitted the ordination of an Anglican bishop in the Roman Catholic cathedral because the Anglican cathedral was too small. The archbishop attended the ceremony.

Can Catholics join the Rotary Club?

I have found your answers on the Catholic Church and the Masons enlightening. What can you tell us about the Odd Fellows? Are they a Masonic group? My husband has been invited, and we want to do the right thing.

We also heard that the church once prohibited membership in the Rotary Club. Is this correct?

The Independent Order of Odd Fellows was one of several organizations — the Knights of Pythias was another — established in the 19th century, modeled more or less on Freemasonry, but aimed at the working classes. Dues were less, and membership and activities were less restricted and regimented.

Membership in the Odd Fellows has never been, even in the past, as forbidden as membership in Freemasonry.

Rotary was founded in Chicago in 1905 to promote a spirit of friendliness, service and honesty among businessmen. Rotary organizations have always tried to be faithful to that spirit. Thousands of cities in the United States and foreign countries are proud to have a Rotary club as part of their community life.

In 1929, for reasons never officially given, the Vatican's Sacred Consistorial Congregation declared that priests and bishops should not be members of Rotary. At the time, the apostolic delegate in the United States explained that the ruling did not apply to the United States. Twenty-one years later, however, on Dec. 20, 1950, the Congregation of the Holy Office reiterated and expanded the ban. Not only were priests forbidden to join, Catholic laymen were warned against affiliating with any Rotary International group.

Again, no reasons were given. When the 1950 decree was issued, many American priests and bishops held active and influential positions in Rotary. Some were founding members of Rotary clubs.

Unofficial explanations were offered in the Vatican newspaper — Rotary was Masonic, "naturalistic" and anti-Catholic — all of which were vigorously protested by Catholic and other Rotarians. Most likely, Rome's actions against Rotary resulted largely from a book by an Irish priest, Father E. Cahill, S. J., identifying Rotary International (along with the Boy Scouts, Girl Scouts and the Salvation Army) as a form of "White Masonry," secretly controlled by and promoting Freemasonry.

While no official reversal has been forthcoming, the church today clearly has no desire to forbid or discourage membership in Rotary. In 1965, in an address to Rotarians, Pope Paul VI alluded to "possible problems" in the past, but praised the wisdom and ideals which characterize Rotary International. Once again, priests, bishops, and Catholic laymen share in those activities.

It may be helpful to note that the church's *Code of Canon Law* mentions no forbidden organizations explicitly. It simply prohibits membership in an "organization which plots against the church" (canon 1374). (Regulations about membership in Masonic organizations are discussed in chapter 8.)

Protestant monks and sisters?

Are there any Protestant groups of sisters or monks today? I have heard there are, and that they are flourishing better than Catholic sisters. Is this true?

At the time of the Reformation, monasteries and convents were outlawed in most Protestant regions, especially in England. A few, however, lasted up to the present, though their membership is small.

During the 19th century, a major revival of the religious life developed in England, with many Anglican-Episcopalian orders of men and women being formed in Europe and the United States

Since World War II, a remarkable increase of interest and reappraisal of the importance of religious community life for both men and women has occurred in Europe and, on a much smaller scale, in this country. Dozens of orders and brotherhoods have been founded by the Lutheran and Reformed churches, among others. Nearly all place heavy emphasis on spiritual renewal and the contemplative life. Many have contributed to the ecumenical and liturgical renewals of the past 50 years.

Catholic officials, including the pope and monastic scholars, acknowledge often that Catholic spirituality today owes much to some of these Protestant orders, especially in understanding the role of religious communities.

Since most Protestant communities are newer and smaller, they frequently avoid much of the turmoil from which larger, well-known Catholic orders are suffering. All communities, however, both Catholic and Protestant, feel the pinch of the times, admit they have much to learn from each other, and agree that arguments about which is "getting along better" are presumptuous and futile.

Joining non-Catholic ceremonies

What is the Catholic position about participation as Catholics in ceremonies of other faiths?

Prayer services involving Catholics and Protestants are fortunately frequent today. These services focus on common interests such as peace, Christian unity, social problems, and similar concerns. In this type of ceremony, Catholics are not only permitted, but encouraged, to share, whether in a Catholic or Protestant church or other location.

Catholics may also attend official liturgical ceremonies of another faith on occasion, for any good reason — friendship or relationship with a member of that congregation, duties of public office, or even out of a desire to be better informed. "Official" ceremonies are those carried out according to the proper books and rites by the ministers — such as the usual Sunday worship, the rite of the Lord's Supper, and so on.

Participation in (receiving) the sacraments of another church, such as baptism or the Eucharist, is generally not permitted. Theologians of most churches agree with the Catholic position on this matter since Vatican II: "Celebration of the sacraments is an action of the celebrating community, carried out within that community, signifying the oneness of faith, worship and life of the community." (Directory 102-128)

Catholic witness at Protestant baptisms

Non-Catholics are permitted to be Christian witnesses for a Catholic baptism. How about the other way around? May a Catholic be godparent for a child being baptized into the Lutheran Church?

It is possible for Catholics to do what you suggest at a Protestant baptism. Catholic understanding is that, normally, godparents at baptism should be members of the church or ecclesial community in which the baptism is being celebrated. One reason is that sponsors are present not only as relatives or friends of the family. They also represent that particular community of faith, that "family of believers." As such, they commit themselves to support the child as it matures in faith and becomes a full member of the community in which the baptism is taking place.

However, it is also Catholic belief that a valid baptism, in any Christian faith, makes one part of the larger community of believers in Christ. For this reason, and because there may be other ties of friendship and family, a Catholic can be a Christian witness at a Protestant baptism if, of course, the other church allows this participation. These guidelines are found in the Directory (96-98).

"Catholic" in Apostles' Creed

During a funeral in a Protestant church, the congregation prayed the Apostles' Creed just as we say it, including "I believe in the holy catholic church." They're not Catholics, so why do they recite this prayer?

The word "catholic" (Greek *catholikos*) means universal or general. By about the year 100, the Christian community was already sometimes referred to as the catholic church, meaning it was for all people, not just for certain classes or certain places.

The Apostles' Creed did not, as was once believed, derive from the apostles themselves. It went through a few minor changes even after its first use, in about the form we have it, around the year 200. So it's not surprising that it contains the phrase "catholic church."

When Protestants use this creed, they mean the words in their stricter original meaning, not in reference to the Roman Catholic Church.

Hanukkah and Christmas

Around Christmas time, there is much in the papers and on television about the Feast of Hanukkah. Are these two feasts connected?

The eight-day festival of Hanukkah, often called the Festival of Lights, commemorates the rededication of the temple in Jerusalem about 165 B.C. This rededication, described in the Book of Maccabees, followed a period of religious repression and is therefore particularly a celebration of religious freedom.

Hanukkah, unlike most other major Jewish feasts, is a family affair, celebrated for the most part in homes rather than in temples or synagogues. An additional candle is lit on each of the eight days, symbolizing the growth of holiness that should occur during the feast, and gifts are exchanged — in some homes on each of the eight days, which I suppose, gives the Jewish children some kind of edge over Christians.

The theme and use of light are also prominent in the customs and liturgy of Advent and Christmas. Apart from this symbolism, however, and the fact that both occur about the same time of the year, there is no connection between the two celebrations.

Ecumenism and women's ordination

Some years ago the Anglican Church Board approved the ordination of women to the priesthood. This surprised me. I have been interested for a long time in the ecumenical movement, and this should set it back a hundred years. Why did they decide to allow this now? Do you think it ends hope for the reunion of the Anglican and Roman Catholic Churches?

No, I don't think it ends the hope of reunion between the two churches. Some assumptions behind your question are, however, perhaps more important than the questions themselves.

First, while the reunion of Christians should be a fervent prayer and goal of all followers of Christ, our first responsibility in whatever church we are, is to be faithful to the traditions and inspirations of the Holy Spirit as we find them in our own particular community. Christian unity, in whatever form it gradually comes about, will be the work of the Spirit, not of our human ingenuity at compromise.

Those most deeply involved and experienced in ecumenical labors have long since learned this truth. Fidelity to what we believe, along with an open charity and humility toward what other Christians have to say to us and with us — these are the tools the Spirit uses to bring us together.

Thus, if our Anglican brothers and sisters, or even a significant group of them, honestly feel this is the way for them to go, all things considered, then decide they must — regardless of possible ecumenical repercussions.

As for ending hopes for reunion of our two churches, this would presume that we know what a "united" Christianity will look like. But do we?

According to papal statements in recent years, it appears the Roman Catholic Church will not allow the ordination of women. From past experience we know that, while tradition is a significant theological argument, it is not always a final argument. Might not the Roman Catholic Church, for instance, preserve its present policy, and still be able to live with a united Christendom in which one branch allows women priests — much as it has for centuries lived with other branches which allow married priests — while it continues to require that its own priests be celibate males?

Unthinkable? I'm not so sure. The Holy Spirit has already brought us far along the way to healing the shameful division in the family of Christ, a long way that 40 years ago would have been called ridiculous and impossible.

So we keep moving, and give the Spirit the benefit of the doubt. There might be something big going on that will astound us even more.

Orthodox and intercommunion

Does the Catholic Church deem it acceptable for Roman Catholics to receive Communion at an Orthodox Mass? Can one fulfill the Sunday obligation by attending an Orthodox Mass?

For those not familiar with the terminology, the word Orthodox generally refers to those Eastern Christian Churches not in full communion with the Latin, or Roman, Catholic Church. The Vatican II Decree on Ecumenism points out a special relationship with these churches, with whom we still have a close agreement in faith.

"Through the celebration of the Eucharist of the Lord in each of these churches, the church of God is built up and grows in stature," it says. "Although separated from us, these churches still possess the true sacraments, above all — by apostolic succession — the priesthood and the Eucharist" (15).

This communion in matters of belief and tradition affects sharing our respective liturgies. Whenever necessity requires, or when it serves some spiritual advantage, Roman Catholics who cannot approach a

Catholic minister for some reason, may receive the sacraments of penance, Eucharist and anointing of the sick from a priest of an Eastern Orthodox Church. (Directory, 122)

Likewise, Catholic ministers may administer the same sacraments to members of the Eastern churches who ask to receive them and who are properly disposed (Directory 123, 125).

Because the policies of some Orthodox churches are more restrictive than those of the Latin Church, a Catholic who wishes to receive Communion with Orthodox Christians must respect the wishes and discipline of that particular church and refrain from receiving if that church restricts the sacrament to its members. In the same way, Catholic ministers who offer Communion to Orthodox Christians should be aware of restrictions on the other side and avoid any suggestion of proselytizing (Directory, 124).

The limiting conditions for participation indicated above do not apply to Eastern churches which are in communion with the Latin Church. The Sunday Mass obligation, for example, may be satisfied by assistance at Mass celebrated "in any Catholic rite" (canons 923 and 1248). This would apply to the Latin Church and those Eastern churches in communion with Rome. Except possibly for the circumstances I explained, the obligation for Sunday Mass would not be fulfilled at liturgies in other Eastern churches.

Mass for non-Catholic spouse

My husband died a few weeks ago. Our family wanted a Mass offered for him. The priest in my own parish refused, but the priest in the neighboring parish readily agreed. I was confused. What are the rules about offering a Mass for a deceased non-Catholic? He was a baptized Christian.

A Mass offered for a non-Catholic Christian is permitted. In June, 1976, the Vatican Congregation for the Doctrine of the Faith liberalized the law in this matter following requests in various countries for Catholic priests to celebrate Mass for deceased persons who were baptized in other denominations. This happens particularly, it noted, when the person who has died showed special respect and honor for the Catholic religion, or held public office in the service of the whole community.

Such Masses, private or public (announced in the parish bulletin, for example), not only are permitted, they can be unreservedly encouraged, said the decree, for reasons of patriotism, friendship and gratitude, if the family or friends request it, and if in the judgment of the bishop there is no danger of scandal.

Assuming these two requirements were met, the decision of the priest to offer Masses for your husband was proper. (Directory, 120)

Mormon baptism of the dead

Friends who are Mormons say they baptize people even after they are dead. Early Christians did that, they claim, and they continue the practice.

Where does such a belief come from? Our friends tell us this is one reason the Mormon church has massive genealogical records, to identify ancestors who may still need baptism. Our discussions about our faiths are always frustrating.

In his first letter to the Corinthians, St. Paul described at length how the resurrection of Jesus is essential to our faith. If Christ has not been raised, he said, our whole religion is absurd. "So too in Christ shall all be brought to life." (15:22) At one point, he uses a puzzling argument. If we are not raised from the dead, "what will people accomplish by having themselves baptized for the dead? If the dead are not raised at all, then why are they having themselves baptized for them?" (15:29)

This perplexing verse has provoked endless speculation. One of today's experts on the letters to the Corinthians argues that the passage is not authentic, claiming that baptizing the living for the dead is so foreign to Paul's theology he would never have alluded to such a practice even as an argument. The predominant interpretation, however, seems to be that some early Christians did have themselves baptized for deceased non-Christians, which is not to say that Paul promoted or approved the practice.

The Mormon policy of baptizing the living for the dead grows out of a theology of faith and salvation that is wholly alien to other Christians. (Mormons often seem to wish to identify themselves in some way as Christians.)

The Church of Jesus Christ of Latter-day Saints was founded or "restored" in 1830 by Joseph Smith, who, according to his own testimony, discovered near Palmyra, N.Y., a set of golden plates on which was inscribed the Book of Mormon, sometimes erroneously called the Mormon bible.

Briefly, according to Mormon teaching, there is not one God; there are several gods who, through countless generations, produce innumerable "children." These gods, or Fathers, through a sort of sexual relationship with female counterparts, bring into existence other beings, including Jesus and other earthly inhabitants, who take bodies here after (for some of them at least) a pre-existence in heaven. Those who reach the most exalted states of "salvation" become in their own right gods or Fathers to others, in and through the continuation of the family unit in eternity. (Mormon Doctrine and Covenants 131-132)

For adherents, "there is no salvation of this type outside the Church of Jesus Christ of Latter-Day Saints" (Mormon Doctrine p. 670). This explains the well-known Mormon promotion of the family, and why devout Mormons want their deceased ancestors to be baptized, even by proxy. Ancestors entering the Mormon Church this way, it is believed, will have the opportunity to reach the "celestial" level of eternity.

On June 5, 2001, the Congregation for the Doctrine of the Faith ruled that Mormon baptisms cannot be considered valid. Among other reasons, explained the Vatican newspaper, the baptism formula is not a true invocation of the Trinity because, according to Mormon teaching, Father, Son and Holy Spirit are three gods who formed a divinity when they decided to unite; and god the Father has a wife with whom he shares responsibility for creation.

As you have found, useful and fruitful discussion on these matters is uncommonly difficult. Words like God, savior, heaven, faith, mean something vastly different to Mormons than they do to us. Understanding them, or bringing them to understand other Christians, is nearly impossible without long and honest dialogue on what is meant by every word used. Not many on either side can overcome that hurdle.

Rosicrucians

What is the Ancient Mystical Order Rosae Crucis (the Rosicrucians)? What is the church's position on this organization?

The Ancient Mystical Order Rosae Crucis (AMORC) is a modern form of gnosticism (from the Greek word *gnosis*, knowledge), which has cropped up through the ages in many forms and in many places. We read even in the New Testament of the problems the early church had with Gnostic groups.

The type of gnosticism varied, but always the promise was to open up the secrets of the universe through a profound mystical experience.

The initiates, those "in the know," possessed a grasp of man and the world that remained unintelligible to the rest of the human race.

The Order of the Brotherhood of the Rose Cross supposedly appeared about 500 years ago, though many of the earliest documents are now known to be hoaxes written much later. As it now exists, the AMORC was organized about 100 years ago. Units ("colleges") are organized in the United States and Europe. Rosicrucian General Statutes identify it as part of Freemasonry.

What doctrines there are in AMORC are a strange mixture of Christian and non-Christian ideas. Many elements are incompatible with Christian faith. There is, for example, a strong pantheistic strain in such movements holding that all creation, the human race included, is somehow an extension or "part" of "God." Such doctrines do not appear in so many words, but they are implied throughout the philosophy.

The church has not taken an official position on the Rosicrucians, just as it has not on numerous other quasi-religious groups. It would seem impossible, however, to accept and believe at one and the same time the truths of the Catholic faith and the teachings of the Ancient Mystical Order.

CHAPTER 11

PRAYER
AND DEVOTIONS

Do Prayers affect God?

Could you explain how our prayers affect God's activity in the world? We ask for recovery from illness, help in safe traveling, and to be protected from rainstorms. Are these things in which God meddles — or do we really think we will change his mind? Aren't we asking for a miracle when we pray, if it doesn't happen to be "God's will?"

It isn't so much a matter of changing God's mind as of recognizing that his providence and care for us include his awareness of our prayers, our desires and our longings. We are dealing here with at least two great mysteries. One is the mystery of God's knowledge of all things, along with his unconditional love and care, his faithful, unfailing tenderness in our regard.

The other is the mystery of man's free will, which means there is some way men and women work together with God in shaping their individual lives and destinies. Ours is a genuine personal freedom, not just a game of "let's pretend," a freedom which involves above all a personal relationship with God. It includes sharing with him our joys and sorrows, our hopes and disappointments, our wonders and our regrets — all of which is nothing else but prayer.

This is, of course, why Jesus urges us so often to pray fervently and why he prayed so frequently himself. What the heavenly Father plans and what he does depends very much on what we show is important to us in our prayers.

How prayers are answered?

Concerning your response to the question about prayer, doesn't God know what's best for us, and won't he do that if he really loves us regard-

less of what we ask for — or for that matter, whether we pray at all?

Obviously, God loves all people. Scripture tells us that he views all of his creation as good, and this goes most of all for human beings who are made most like him in their ability to know and to love, to relate to one another as persons. Because of that love, he always wants what is best for us.

Many elements essential to our relationship to God enter our lives with prayer, not least of which is the desire for the things God wishes to give us, desires which must be in our hearts if we are to be able to receive his gifts.

Did it ever occur to you that what is best may be different if we are praying desperately for something than if we are not? We are individuals, all different, even in our deepest relationship with God and the world. Our humility before God, our trust in him, our conviction in faith and love that something will be good for us, for our children whom we love, or for the people for whom we care very much — all this goes in to determine what is really best for us in God's eyes here and now.

This surely does not mean that we ought always to receive exactly what we want, as we want it, if we pray hard enough. But prayer, and that means above all a habitual prayerful attitude before God, affects us deeply so that we are not the same persons we would be if we did not pray. Therefore, what is best for us will be different, too, in God's eyes as well as our own.

Devotion or superstition?

You wrote about the church's regulation that Catholics should not receive Communion more than twice a day. You commented that the church knows from experience that some Catholics tend to multiply good things, even Communion, in ways that are not spiritually healthy.

What other activities are you thinking of? At what point are they not spiritually healthy?

Numerous examples come to mind. I'm sure you are familiar with at least some of them.

Perhaps the most obvious is chain letters concerning prayers to be said, or Masses to be attended. Readers send me samples of these constantly. Recipients are urged to say a certain number of prayers to St. Jude or St. Anthony, our Blessed Mother or another saint, and pass the letter on to a given number of friends. If they "break the chain" by failing to recite the prayers or send the message on, bad things will happen. Someone threw the letter away, so the story goes, and dropped dead four days later. Or conversely, an individual carried out the instructions and inherited $100,000.

Those who carry on this kind of correspondence usually consider themselves devout Catholics and often defend their actions with the excuse that anything is good if it gets people to pray more. Obviously the church favors prayers. We have rosaries and novenas and other traditional, repetitive methods of expressing our persevering confidence in God's love. Jesus himself not only approves, but encourages us to pester God aggressively with our prayers. (See, for example, Luke, chapter 11 and 18)

However, the chain appeals described here have more to do with magic and manipulation of God than with genuine religious devotion and trust.

Other sacramentals, (actions, statues, medals, sacred pictures that may enhance our spiritual lives) are also a frequently abused part of Catholic spirituality. Like prayer, used properly they can be a joyful, almost playful, exercise of faith and appreciation of the good things God has given us.

Many Catholics, for example, and sometimes other Christians I know of, if they get desperate enough place a statue of St. Joseph in their home or on their property as a sign of their prayer that they sell their home. From our Catholic view of things at least, this makes good devotional sense. As one Catholic high school student put it when someone claimed these practices are superstitious: "That's not superstition, that's what makes being a Catholic fun."

It is not unheard of, however, for some enthusiasts, Catholic or not, to promote, even sell, "lucky statues" of St. Joseph, complete with instructions. I think all would agree this goes beyond legitimate, prayerful devotion.

Lourdes, France, is one of the major Catholic shrines in the world. The spring of water where the mother of Jesus appeared to St. Bernadette has been the site of many spiritual and physical cures. Today, however, "Lourdes water" has become a major industry, and the groups involved are not always non-Catholic. One newspaper advertises crosses with "lucky water of Lourdes" in each cross. Among the benefits promised are "miracles of good luck at numbers, racetracks and lotteries." Some groups offer "free" Lourdes water and its benefits, or other religious articles, to all who contribute a minimum "offering."

One reader sent me an offer she received for a medal of Our Lady of Medjugorje. Several recipients "became lucky and succeeded in everything," says the ad. A few days wearing it "may" bring you "everything you really need: health, love, fortune," on condition, of course, that you never take it off. All this is yours if you send $19.95 and consider joining a pilgrimage to Yugoslavia.

At what point does this sort of "religion" cease being spiritually healthy?

St. Thomas Aquinas says it is when anyone carries religion too far, and gives more importance to externals of religious observance than to what is going on in the heart. (S.T. II-II, q. 93, a.2)

In other words, it happens when we no longer see our relationship with God as an interpersonal one of trust, love and caring, and begin to treat God as some "thing," a guaranteed source of magic if only he is invoked and "worked" with proper invocations or rituals.

All this is one more indication that we Catholics today need to read carefully and discriminately whatever affects our faith, no matter how spiritual and devout the source seems to be.

Prayer for deceased son?

A year ago my son was killed instantly in a motorcycle accident. Although he was raised a Catholic, he had neglected his religion, at least outwardly, for eight years.

Beyond the terrible blow of his death, I am more concerned with his spiritual welfare. Can my prayers, offering Masses, and so forth, bring him God's pardon? I shall continue to pray regardless, but I hope your answer will be able to strengthen my belief in the hereafter.

I am sorry for your hurt. The sudden death of a son or daughter is always a terrible tragedy; yours is even more painful because of the spiritual concerns.

It may be helpful to remember two things. First, as a parent you are at least somewhat aware of the many complicated factors that might today lie behind a young person's neglect of his religious faith and practices. I do not say, of course, that such neglect is a good thing. By no means, however, does it necessarily or even usually reflect rejection of God. Each person's relationship to God is unique and personal. And it always exists under at least some influence of the faithful love God has for each of us.

Second, we must remember that in hearing and answering our prayers, God is not bound by the limits of time, past or future. The prayers we offer, in addition to whatever intercessory power they have in the present moment, can be "answered" by God long before they are actually said.

This may sound complicated, but it is an insight of faith that we Christians have always acted upon.

The official prayers of the church at Masses for the dead for example, repeatedly imply (by praying for "forgiveness" and so on) an extension of that prayer back to that person's time on earth and his or her preparations for death.

In other words, we pray for a happy and holy death long after the person has died, something which logically and faithfully follows from what we believe about God. Thus, at least one of the things you are praying for at this time is that God might grant the grace of essential faith, hope and love in your son's life and as the time came for him to die.

This to me is one of the most consoling aspects of our faith. It is, among other things, what we mean when we say we believe in the supreme Lordship of God, and in the communion of saints.

Stations of the Cross

I am doing some Lenten study on the Stations of the Cross. Why were they not carried over to the Protestant churches if they originated before the reformation? Is there a connection between the stations and the path to Calvary followed by modern visitors to Jerusalem?

The devotion we know as the Stations (or Way) of the Cross was one of many forms of devotion developed during the very late Middle Ages, generally the 1200s or 1300s. Politically, culturally and religiously those were tumultuous and painful times for the vast majority of ordinary people. Practicing and passing on faith was enormously difficult.

Into this picture came, among others, St. Francis of Assisi and St. Dominic and their followers, who helped popularize such expressions of faith and prayer as the Christmas creche (St. Francis) and the rosary (Dominicans). The Stations were one of these devotions, serving both as prayer and a sort of catechism about the sufferings of the Lord. Various Franciscan communities, who already held responsibility for the holy places in Jerusalem for Latin Rite Catholics, helped popularize the devotion.

The Stations once included seven falls under the cross. Another form was a total of 43 separate stations. But the 14 stations as we know them became fairly stabilized by Pope Clement XII in 1731.

For some years now, most publications of the Stations of the Cross have included a 15th station, or meditation, calling to mind Christ's victory over death in the resurrection.

The city of Jerusalem was leveled by the Roman armies about 40 years after the death of Jesus, making the precise locations of the falls of Jesus on the way to Calvary nearly impossible to determine. The markings of the 14 stations along the Via Dolorosa (Sorrowful Way) in old Jerusalem are comparatively recent. The accuracy and even historical validity of some of them are open to considerable question. Nevertheless, the Stations of the Cross remain one of the richest ways in our tradition to reflect on our Lord's suffering and death.

The reasons Protestantism did not continue many devotional traditions such as the Stations are complicated. Several Reformed churches mistrusted the use of pictures or other images in worship and prayer. This may be part of the answer. Another could be that the Stations have always included incidents which come out of Christian tradition but are not found in the Gospels.

Our fourth station, for example, commemorates Jesus meeting his mother. Luke notes that Jesus stopped along the way to speak to "many women who mourned and lamented him," but he doesn't say Mary was among them. John places her at the foot of the cross, but not on the road. With the Protestant emphasis on Scripture as the rule of faith, it is perhaps understandable that some of these popular devotions would not be picked up in their spirituality.

The story of Veronica wiping the face of Jesus is also not in the Gospels.

What is the Magnificat?

I am a young Catholic mother and have had no Catholic education except some Sunday school. I have seen references several times to the "Magnificat." Can you explain what that means?

In the first chapter of St. Luke's Gospel, we find the story of the visit of Mary, the mother of Jesus, to her cousin, Elizabeth. In response to Elizabeth's greeting, the Gospel places on the lips of Mary a beautiful prayer or hymn which is found frequently in our Catholic liturgy and other devotions.

In Latin, the hymn begins *Magnificat anima mea Dominum* (my soul proclaims the greatness of the Lord). It is often referred to as the Magnificat.

You speak of yourself as a young mother. You may be too young to remember that not many years ago, Catholic people were much more familiar with Latin terminology. Phrases like *Pater Noster* (Our Father), *Kyrie eleison* (Greek for "Lord have mercy") and many others were everyday terms for Catholics. Sometimes Catholic writers and liturgists forget there is a new generation of Catholics like yourself for whom these words and titles are completely unfamiliar.

Novena devotions

When I was younger, about 30 years ago, my parish had novena devotions one night a week. Other churches had similar devotions on other nights. Do any churches hold novenas like that anymore? Why were they discontinued? I used to look forward to these ceremonies.

I'm not sure anyone knows the whole answer to that one. Perhaps it's something like asking why, for no apparent reason and with no change in the teaching of the church about when to receive the sacrament of penance, people stopped going to confession with anything like the former frequency. No one has the answer to that either.

My opinion is that a major explanation for the decline in extra-liturgical devotions such as these lies in the greatly increased emphasis on the eucharistic liturgy since Vatican II. Before the liturgical changes of the past decades, the Mass was viewed far more than it is today as the priests' personal action, and Masses were generally limited to early morning, particularly on weekdays.

Today, most peoples' devotional lives are more Eucharist-centered. Many who in former days might have attended novena devotions now participate in evening Masses. The eucharistic sacrifice often constitutes an integral part of important afternoon and evening religious gatherings, which was impossible before Vatican Council II.

Add to this the emphasis on Scripture as the primary inspiration of Catholic spirituality, and several significant social developments (such as changes in parish structure and reluctance of people to go out at night) and you probably have most of the reasons why the kinds of devotions you speak of have declined in American Catholic life.

Nine First Fridays

I am still one who likes to make the nine First Fridays, but I don't know anything about where and when these promises were made. What did Christ promise about this devotion?

The practice of the nine First Fridays resulted from revelations apparently made by Jesus to St. Margaret Mary Alocoque about 300 years ago. St. Margaret Mary was a French Visitation nun who had a strong devotion to the heart of Jesus as a symbol of God's love for us. At his urging, after these revelations, devotion to the Sacred Heart of Jesus was established in the church, including the Feast of the Sacred Heart which we celebrate in June.

According to St. Margaret Mary, Jesus made 12 "promises" to those who honor his Sacred Heart. The last of these was this: "I promise you, in the exceeding mercy of My Heart, that Its all-powerful love will grant to all those who go to Communion on nine First Fridays of the month the final grace of repentance; they shall not die in Its disfavor nor without receiving the Sacraments, My Divine Heart becoming their assumed refuge at that last moment."

The practice is, in other words, a sort of novena — a nine-time prayer which Christians have used for centuries as one of the ways of emphasizing the importance of perseverance and trust in our prayer to God.

One must remember that, at the time of these revelations, holy Communion was rarely received by many Catholics, especially in France, where the severe Jansenist heresy was strongest. Neglect was such that once a year was often considered enough, even for the "most worthy." The weekly, even daily, Communion common among practicing Catholics today was all but unheard of.

As a private revelation, these promises are not an obligatory part of Catholic belief or practice. However, devotion to the Heart of Jesus, as the sign of our Lord's love, is now an important and special part of Catholic tradition. In approving and promoting it, the church indicates that it contains nothing contrary to our faith, and that it may be devoutly believed and practiced.

Holy water

Why does the church use holy water, and what are the effects of its use for those of us who believe it combats evil? I saw a pamphlet which says the "devil hates holy water" and that we can sprinkle holy water for a blessing to our loved ones who live far away from us. What do you think of these beliefs?

The pamphlet from which you quote contains some questionable comments about the use of holy water, making it sound almost like a spiritual rabbit's foot.

In all uses of sacramentals, including holy water, we must keep straight exactly what a sacramental is in the church's tradition. A blessed medal, picture, or holy water, is a material item over which the church has prayed a blessing, asking God to accept the prayers of the church for those who reverently use it.

For a sacramental such as holy water, therefore, the devotion, faith and charity of the person using it is augmented and supported by the prayers of the church. There is no magic-like power in the water itself.

Use of holy water in the proper manner has great spiritual benefit. It can be a striking reminder of our baptism and of the commitment to Jesus we made in receiving that sacrament. It can symbolize and strengthen our faith in the forgiving love of God, and therefore assist us in a spirit of conversion that brings with it the forgiveness of sins.

Again, all this prayer and good intention is enriched immeasurably by the blessing of the church, which carries with it the assurance of the prayers of all our fellow Catholics and Christians. Properly used with these intentions, there is nothing superstitious about holy water or any other sacramental. Some over-zealous devotees of certain sacramentals occasionally come close to stepping over the line.

Religious candles

Where did our use of candles at Mass come from, and are they still required? There seems to be no consistency about the number of them, or even whether there should be any at all.

Christian use of candles was taken over from the Romans who used them on a variety of civic and religious occasions. The practice is, however, part of a much larger human tradition.

The natural symbolism of light has been recognized by nearly every religion since time immemorial. Even pagans lit lamps over tombs, expressing belief in some sort of continued existence for the deceased. Light, particularly a living flame, signified life, hope, joy, divinity, courage — in other words, nearly everything human beings have considered good and beautiful.

Some of this symbolism may be sensed from the fact that the lighted ceremonial candle for evening prayer developed into our paschal candle. These lights were also used in funeral ceremonies, before the tombs of deceased Christians, and in front of the image of martyrs and other saints. They symbolized then what they still do for us: light (Christ), life, hope, resurrection and faith.

Candles have been used at Mass in some way since the seventh century, and are still required, though regulations concerning them are considerably simpler than in the past.

Care of palms

Please explain the proper use of the palm we received on Palm Sunday. How long should it be kept, in what way, and how should it be disposed of?

Palms distributed on the Sunday before Easter remind us of our Lord's death and resurrection, and of our share in his passage from death to life. Any reverent way of keeping these palms in our homes with this kind of prayerful and devout intention is fine. Some people place them behind a crucifix, others place them with a picture that is particularly meaningful, still others merely hang them on the wall or keep them on a desk or table.

As anything that is blessed, palms lose their blessing when they lose their identity. The proper way to dispose of a palm, therefore, is either by burning or breaking it up. The remains may then be thrown away.

Advent customs

What is now the proper arrangement for an Advent wreath? Formerly we used three purple candles (or white candles tied with a purple bow) and one pink. In recent years I have seen other forms of the Advent wreath, sometimes with all white candles and blue bows. What is proper now?

There is no official form of the Advent wreath. It can be for our homes a beautiful and meaningful symbol of the spirit of Advent, but its arrangement is only a matter of custom.

The observation you make about Advent, however, is significant in light of the developing flavor of the church's observance of this important time of year.

In times past, Advent was seen as somewhat of a mini-Lent, a time of penance and self-denial, but with a tinge of joy in the background — perhaps symbolized most by the rose vestments the priest wore at Mass on the third Sunday of Advent, and by the rose candle lit on the Advent wreath that day.

As the church's liturgy developed over the past century or so, particularly in the last several decades, the predominant spirit of Advent is one of joyful waiting and hope. This theme clearly appears in the

Scripture readings for weekday and Sunday masses as well as in the other liturgical texts for this season.

He descended into hell?

In the Apostles' Creed we say, "He descended into hell." Would you explain why we say this? Jesus was the only perfect person on earth. He never sinned. Why would he have to go to hell?

The word "hell" as it is used in the Apostles' Creed does not mean the "hell of the damned," which it usually means in current English. Our word "hell" comes from an old Teutonic word *hela*, which means a hidden, or covered, place. In earlier English literature, it was used to describe any kind of pit, dungeon or dark hole.

The use of the word in our English translation of the Creed is unfortunate, but has been traditional for so long it will hardly be changed now. The word is a translation from a Latin (also Greek and Hebrew) word which means the "lower regions" — a generic name for the place where people would go after death without regard to a condition of reward or punishment.

Rosary

Is it necessary to say all five decades of the Rosary at the same time? I sometimes say only a decade each day. Is that all right?

There is no required way to say the Rosary. In fact, different countries, different Catholic cultures, sometimes vary in the sequence and number of prayers — though all are based on 150 Hail Marys and reflections on the chief events in the life of Christ.

Regular praying of the Rosary, all of it or any part of it, was and still is a powerful prayer and a marvelous way to express one's love for our Lord and his mother.

The usual form of the Rosary in most English speaking and many other countries is as follows:

The events are divided into the five Joyful Mysteries: the Annunciation, the Visitation, the Birth of Our Lord, the Presentation of Jesus in the Temple, and the Finding of Jesus in the Temple.

The five Sorrowful Mysteries: the Agony of Jesus in the Garden, the Scourging at the Pillar, the Crowning of Jesus with Thorns, the Carrying of the Cross, and the Crucifixion.

The five Glorious Mysteries: The Resurrection of Jesus from the Dead, the Ascension, the Coming of the Holy Spirit upon the Apostles

(Pentecost), the Assumption of Mary into Heaven, and the Crowning (Glorification) of Mary in Heaven.

The praying of each "mystery" consists of one Our Father, ten Hail Marys, and one Glory be to the Father. The Rosary usually begins with the Apostles' Creed, three Hail Marys and one Glory be to the Father.

Hail, Holy Queen

Is it true that the prayer "Hail, Holy Queen" has been deleted from the Rosary? If so, why?

The "Hail, Holy Queen" was not deleted from the Rosary; it was never in any official way part of the Rosary. As I said, the prayer we call the Rosary has taken many forms. The core seems always to have been 150 Hail Marys (15 decades) in imitation of the 150 psalms; people who could not read might say the Hail Marys instead. Another similar prayer of 150 Our Fathers was popular for a time in some parts of the church.

In various times and places, additional prayers before, during and after the Hail Marys became common. The "Hail, Holy Queen" is one of them.

This particular ending has been widely used in our country in the past decades, but is not universal. Not long ago, I was at the Vatican on an occasion when Pope John Paul II led the Rosary. He did not use this prayer at the conclusion.

Another Sign of the Cross?

Some of us attended a discussion workshop at one of our schools. When times came to pray, the leader said, "In the name of the Creator, Redeemer and Sanctifier."

When we asked, we were told this is a different way of making the Sign of the Cross. Since then I've heard it again. Is this really another Sign of the Cross? One priest said he thought we should not use it, but he didn't say why.

The prayer you quote, invoking God under those titles, can be a good one. Obviously there is nothing wrong with it as it stands. A problem arises, however, when it is presented as an equivalent or substitute for our traditional Sign of the Cross.

Most Catholics and other Christians know that the mystery of the Holy Trinity, three persons in one God, is the fundamental doctrine of our faith. The fact that there is "within" God an eternal community of existence, a mutual exchange of life and love that is what we call three Persons, is something we would know nothing about unless Jesus himself had told us. Theologians refer to this inner divine life as God's action *ad intra*, on the inside.

This inner life of God — Father, Son and Holy Spirit, to use the Gospel's words, is the core of all Christian beliefs. Without it all other crucial elements of our spirituality and faith — the Incarnation, Eucharist, sacraments, the church as we know it — would be unthinkable.

Since the beginning, Christians have approached this mystery with the utmost reverence and care. It was in the name of the persons of the Trinity that Christians were, and still are, baptized into the faith of Jesus Christ. It is in their name, as in the Sign of the Cross, that all Christian prayer and important action take place.

In light of the centrality and importance of this great mystery, it is significant that the "new" Sign of the Cross is not an explicit invocation of the Trinity at all. True, our creeds sometimes attribute creation to the Father, redemption to the Son and sanctification to the Holy Spirit. (See the Nicene Creed, for example, which nevertheless first stresses the inner Trinitarian life of the Father, Son and Holy Spirit.) But these attributes or titles all involve actions that theology calls *ad extra*, outside of God. As such, they are actions of all three Persons, not only of one. In other words, they are not Trinitarian actions, but "God" actions.

In fact, one need not even believe in three divine persons to use this revised prayer. Jehovah Witnesses, for example, reject belief in the Trinity, but staunchly believe God is their creator, savior and sanctifier.

These differences may not appear significant to many of us, but to equate Creator, Redeemer and Sanctifier with Father, Son and Holy Spirit is theologically and spiritually questionable, and contrary to Christian and Catholic tradition. It ignores the relational interior activity of God which is central to our faith in the Trinity.

The Serenity Prayer

I belong to three Alcoholics Anonymous groups. One of our favorite AA prayers is the Serenity Prayer. Several of us tried to find out where it came from, but no luck. Someone told us it was written by St. Francis.

The Serenity Prayer is one of those that could probably be traced back centuries in some form or other. As we have it today, it seems to have been authored by Reinhold Niebuhr, an American Protestant theologian who died in 1971.

In 1934, about the time AA was founded, he wrote it as: "God, give us the serenity to accept what cannot be changed; give us the courage to change what should be changed; give us the wisdom to distinguish one from the other."

Parents' blessing during a wedding

Our son is getting married, and I am wondering how to give a parents' blessing to the couple. My sister and I were married at the same time, and our father had us kneel and pray, and blessed us. It meant a lot, and I would like to do this for our son. Can you suggest anything to help us do something like this?

First of all, no officially approved ceremony is necessary for the blessing you mention. Either by yourselves or in conjunction with the parents of your son's fiance, you could prepare and minister such a blessing using Scripture passages, prayers (traditional or some you make up) and other appropriate words and actions. As parents and as fellow Christians, this would be a wonderful and proper way for you to express your love, prayers and hopes for the bride and groom.

Your question gives me an opportunity to call attention to an excellent book published under the auspices of the bishops of the United States, *Catholic Household Blessings and Prayers*. This excellent volume contains varieties of blessings, celebrations of special times and seasons, and prayers, all designed for use within family surroundings.

In a section titled "Blessings Related to Marriage" you will find what you're looking for, the blessing of an engaged couple, to be celebrated by both families if possible, perhaps at a meal together.

The Forward and Introduction briefly discuss family prayer, and how to use the book to the best spiritual advantage. Since we're on the subject, a few lines from this book are worth quoting:

"Begin to pray beside your children even when they are very young. Pray in your own words, by all means, but pray especially the words of the church. Pray because you yourself need to pray. Then, as your children grow, invite them into this prayer.

"Bless them each night. Pray at table with them each evening. Let them hear you singing the songs of faith and reading the Holy Scriptures. Let them know that fast and almsgiving, care for the poor and the sick, and daily intercession for justice and for peace are what you hold most dear."

The publication is a response of the American bishops to a 1984 *Book of Blessings* published by the Vatican Congregation for Divine

Worship, which suggested that local churches adapt and expand the rites for local use.

The idea of lay men and women giving "official" blessings of the church perhaps still seems strange to some Catholics. While priests or deacons, if they are present, normally preside at blessings, the church does not exclude others from doing so.

Lay men and women, says the Vatican edition, "in virtue of the universal priesthood, a dignity they possess because of their baptism and confirmation, may celebrate certain blessings... by use of the rites and formularies designated for a lay minister. Such lay persons exercise this ministry in virtue of their office (for example, parents on behalf of their children) or by reason of some special liturgical ministry or in fulfillment of a particular charge in the church" (*Book of Blessings*, General Introduction 18).

Catholic Household Blessings and Prayers is an asset for families, and for individuals and couples without children as well. It is published by the U.S. Catholic Bishops' Conference and should be available through any book store.

Cursillo

What is a Cursillo? How does it differ from a retreat?

Since it is designed to help examine and improve one's life as a Christian, a Cursillo has some similarities to a retreat, but also many important differences.

Started in Spain (its full name is *Cursillo de Christianidad*, literally, a short course in Christianity), it is a program to discover, or rediscover, one's beliefs and responsibilities to God and other people as a Christian. An individual makes only one Cursillo in his life, though he or she may be part of a team presenting the program many times.

There are also follow-up meetings (reunions) and regular large gatherings (ultreyas) of those who have made a Cursillo to preserve and develop the spirit of community and mutual support the program is intended to promote.

Another difference is that the 15 talks contained in the three-day program are standard as to subject, but are prepared and written personally usually by five priests and 10 laymen or women who give them.

As anything else, of course, details and quality of the Cursillo programs differ from place to place, depending on leadership personnel, general interest, and other factors.

Charismatic Movement

How does the Charismatic Movement coincide with the teaching of the Catholic Church and the teaching of Jesus Christ? Many priests and bishops go along with it, while many do not approve of it because it's too emotional. Jesus said we must become like little children, and little children surely do not become emotional.

I'll pass over your last sentence. You must be acquainted with children different from the ones I know.

The Charismatic Movement takes its name from the Greek word *charisma*, which means a free gift, a favor. In the church, it has meant a special talent or power given to certain people by God for the service of the rest of the Christian community, the church.

Some charisms are for service in the church (governing, for example), others for teaching or preaching, and others for more spectacular purposes such as healing, speaking in tongues, and prediction of the future.

These gifts of the Holy Spirit were especially necessary in the early days of the church when Christian people had not yet experienced many of the signs of Christ's presence that intervening history has offered. But such charisms are still useful even today as a source of faith and hope to those who experience them and use them well.

They are also important to the institution of the church, with which they will nearly always be in tension, as a reminder that the Holy Spirit "blows where he will" and that his actions are not limited to popes, bishops and others.

Already in the New Testament, St. Paul warned against two main dangers in the charismatic activities in the church. An individual may easily fool himself about the genuineness of his special gifts, especially the more spectacular ones. Also, every gift is suspect if it does not serve the whole community by aiding the spirit of co-operation, love and mutual support. If the Charismatic Movement or any other movement becomes divisive or elitist, that's the best proof that there is something wrong with it.

One reason that bishops, priests and others may differ on their view of charismatics is that they can differ on their vision of the church. Charismatic groups themselves differ in their spirit and in their understanding of where they fit into the rest of the Christian community.

Read First Corinthians, chapters 12-14, for St. Paul's comments on charisms. As St. Augustine said once in a homily, God gives different charisms such as healing, tongues and others, to different people. As different parts of our body have different functions, people in the church have varying gifts. Whether or not one has the gift of healing, or any other charism, has nothing to do with personal holiness. All various gifts of the Spirit, working together, make us the living Body of Christ.

Focolare Movement

Our Catholic newspaper quotes a woman in our diocese who spoke of her discovery of the Focolare Movement, and how it gave her strength to live what she believed. I've never heard of this group. Is it a retreat program?

Focolare is one of several movements or types of spirituality which have done much in this century for lay men and women to deepen and enrich their Christian lives.

The name comes from the Italian word for fire and is said to suggest the meaning "carriers of fire." Officially the Worldwide Focolare Movement (Work of Mary), it began in Italy during World War II when a few young girls sought a way to bring about the unity on earth for which Jesus prayed.

Through the years, this theme of unity has become the cornerstone of its ideals, with the conviction that the only solid base of unity, the one reality that will last, is God himself. The movement has flourished particularly since Vatican Council II when its ideals were seen to be stressed often in the council fathers' commitment of the church to the cause of political, social and religious harmony and unity among the people of the world.

Focolare has a number of movements or groups within itself. Some single members, called Focolarini, live in separate communities (Focolare Centers). While they work in businesses or other professions as other lay people, they follow the evangelical counsels of poverty, obedience and chastity.

Another group are volunteers who attempt by their lives to transform all of human activity according to the Gospel and the spirit of the movement.

The first official approval of the movement by the church came from Pope John XXIII in 1962. In 1978, Pope Paul VI also encouraged the movement, saying, "Be faithful to your inspiration which is so modern and so fruitful."

Here in the United States, Focolare operates a publishing house and sponsors a monthly magazine, *Living City*, promoting the activities and spirituality of the movement.

Headquarters are in Rome, but it has national offices in several countries. One of six in North America may be reached at Box 496, New York, N.Y., 10021.

Rapture in prayer

Some Protestant friends of mine tell about a "rapture" that takes place in their church. I've heard this mentioned a few times by other people also. What is this rapture?

Rapture is another word for a condition that Christian mysticism more generally refers to as ecstasy. In certain stages of prayer, it is not uncommon that the individual becomes so absorbed in God and things of heaven that he goes into a form of trance and is literally out of touch with the senses of hearing, sight and touch.

The word ecstasy comes from a combination of Greek words that literally means "standing outside of" one's self.

While real mystical ecstasy may accompany higher forms of contemplation, some degree of this experience is not uncommon in Christian prayer life. When it does accompany or result from genuine prayer, it is always the work of the Holy Spirit leading the soul to a greater union with God.

The experience of people who have written about this, however, proves that it is not always a pleasant one. In fact, the word rapture more commonly identifies the forms of ecstasy that are more violent or painful.

The church respects this kind of manifestation of the work of the Holy Spirit in our movement toward God. It is also aware that the externals of genuine ecstasy can often result from psychological causes, not necessarily from any religious experience.

Another rapture

I believe you misinterpreted the meaning of rapture. To most "born again" Christians, rapture means only one thing, and that is the "great snatch" when Christ comes to take us who live, and his church, out of this world "to meet the Lord in the air."

The subject of the rapture is discussed at length today because they feel the signs of the Great Tribulation Period (Seventieth Week of Daniel) are close at hand. I am sure this is the rapture to which your writer referred.

Rapture in our Christian tradition does also embrace the meaning you indicate: The final coming of Christ to take the world to himself and lift all humanity with him to the heavenly Father. The Catholic Church considers the final coming of Christ the climax and completion of all human history.

To be honest, however, it learned centuries ago not to take too seriously the dire predictions that the heavens are about ready to drop, and that the end of the world is just around the corner. It has lived through hundreds of such predictions that have come and gone.

Whether the end of the world comes one year, or a hundred thousand years, from now doesn't really make that much difference. The more critical concern is whether we individually are prepared for the "end," for the close of our personal pilgrimage on this earth. Our life as Christians must always be guided by faith in the supreme Lordship of Jesus which will come to its perfection when he comes again. How soon that coming will be isn't at all important.

Understanding indulgences

Gaining indulgences was a big thing when I was young. We heard about them during the Jubilee Year (2000), so I assume they're still valid. Is there some reason the church doesn't discuss them much any more?

Indulgences are traditionally described as partial or total remission of temporal punishment due to our sins because of prayers or good works performed by a Christian.

The church is, as you observe, cautious in speaking of indulgences today because that area of our faith has been badly misunderstood in the past, with tragic consequences. Indulgences are a "delicate theme," says Pope John Paul II, "about which there have been historic misunderstandings which negatively left their mark on communion among Christians." Abuses in the granting of indulgences were among the issues that led to the Protestant Reformation.

Traditional Catholic teaching on this subject is based on two Christian truths. First, every sin not only disobeys God's law, it violates the harmony of creation established by the Creator and is, at least to some degree, a rejection of his love. Complete conversion, therefore, includes a reintegration of that divine order, a process involving some cleansing (purgation) either in this life or at death.

Pope Paul VI in The Doctrine of Indulgences (1967) called for reform of the whole indulgence structure. Pope John Paul, picking up on that theme before the recent Jubilee Year, pointed out that an indulgence is not a quick ticket to heaven, but is a help for real conversion of heart. "Those who think they can receive this gift simply by fulfilling a few exterior requirements are wrong," said the pope. Receiving an indulgence "is not automatic, but depends on our turning away from sin and conversion to God."

In his 1967 restructuring, Paul VI reduced the number of indulgenced prayers and good works. "The main concern has been to attach greater importance to a Christian way of life and lead souls to cultivate a spirit of prayer and penance, and to practice the theological virtues (faith, hope and love) rather than merely repeat certain formulas and acts." (Manual of Indulgences, 1967)

He listed three categories of daily life as deserving of indulgence. 1) Invoking God's mercy and protection while fulfilling one's responsibilities and enduring difficulties. 2) Offering oneself and one's possessions, in a spirit of faith, to people in need. 3) Voluntarily foregoing some pleasure in a spirit of repentance and sacrifice.

A revised manual of indulgences published in September, 1999, in anticipation of the jubilee, continued the spirit of the earlier manual, and added a fourth indulgence category: Giving public witness to one's faith by frequent reception of the sacraments and by proclaiming one's faith to nonbelievers by word and example.

Partial indulgences are granted using only those words, with no confusing mention of days or years as was common previously. Contrary to what many Catholics thought, an indulgence of one year, for example, did not mean "one year off of purgatory." It meant, rather, whatever alleviation of purgative suffering might be achieved by one year of fasting or other penance.

The church today takes great pains to keep the understanding of indulgences in harmony with the Gospel and teachings of Vatican Council II. (Quotations from Pope John Paul II are from his audience address Sept. 29, 1999)

Personal spiritual growth

What advice would you give to a person who sincerely desires to grow spiritually? Would making a private retreat be a good start?

Our spiritual life and our growth in it is a many-faceted reality. It includes knowledge and trust in God, our increasing realization of the presence of God in the events of our daily lives, especially in ourselves and in those around us, and a spirit of hope and faith in the power of what is offered to us in the Gospel as essential elements of our Christian commitment.

Growth comes through prayer, reflection and action, and depends greatly on the circumstances of our personal life — about which, incidentally, you mention nothing.

The best step at the moment would not necessarily be a retreat, but some thoughtful reflection and consultation with someone in whom you have confidence, possibly a priest or religious, or lay person, you can talk to about your ideals and concerns. They will assist you in evaluating where you are, the expectations you have of yourself, and what expectations others around you may have. Much depends on whether or not you are married, have children, and their ages. Your own age and experience of life are important factors.

Please think it over in these terms and ask a priest or someone for an appointment, talk with him and allow him to offer some thoughts and options for you to pursue.

Presider for Benediction

Our discussion group was talking about lay people now leading many activities, including prayers, in our parish. What about Benediction? Some said a eucharistic minister can officiate at Benediction; others said not. Who is right?

According to the Ritual for Exposition of the Blessed Sacrament, the ordinary minister of this ceremony is a priest or deacon. Before the end of adoration, the priest or deacon blesses the people with the Blessed Sacrament and places it back into the tabernacle.

If there is no deacon or priest, or if they are for some good reason unable to officiate, the following persons may expose and repose the Holy Eucharist for public adoration: 1) An acolyte, that is one who has been installed in this role by the church, not simply an altar server. 2) A "special minister of Communion." 3) A member of a religious community or of a lay association of men and women devoted to eucharistic adoration, if this individual has been appointed by the local bishop.

These people may open the tabernacle and place the ciborium on the altar, or place the Host in the monstrance. At the end of adoration time, they replace the Blessed Sacrament into the tabernacle. They should not, however, give the blessing with the sacrament (Holy Communion and Worship of the Eucharist Outside Mass, n. 91)

Pagan feasts worked for church

You explained why we celebrate the birth of our Lord on Dec. 25. It took the place, you said, of the pagan Roman feast honoring the birth of the Unconquered Sun at the beginning of winter. It seems to me a strange thing that such a feast as Christmas should substitute for honoring a pagan god. Why would the church do that?

It might appear strange to us, but it would not be to the Christians of the time. When the birth of Christ began to be celebrated with a specific feast about 300 years after our Lord's death and resurrection, it was not the major celebration it is now. The church in those days often had a much different attitude toward things pagan than we might assume.

In the year 601, for example, Pope Gregory the Great, in his instructions to St. Augustine and other missionaries to England, told them that under no circumstances should temples to idols be destroyed. They should be sprinkled with holy water, and altars should be set up in them. Seeing their temples are not destroyed, he said, the people may be more ready to return to them "to know and adore the true God." Since they have a custom of sacrificing oxen to demons, he added, "let some other solemnity like the dedication of the church or a martyr's feast be sustituted on the same day."

They can decorate the churches as they did before, he instructed, even kill and use the animals as food, not in sacrifice, but as a way of giving thanks to the Giver of all gifts. (Letter of Gregory to Abbot Mellitus and Augustine)

Rather than considering it a danger or scandal, they saw in this sort of "ecumenism" a help to spreading the Gospel and in making their faith attractive to the people they were hoping to convert. More feasts and other Catholic traditions than most of us realize are traceable to this strategy of our Christian forebears.

Belief in guardian angels

What can you tell us about guardian angels? When I was a youngster in school (1930s), we were taught that these angels were "to light and guard, to rule and guide" mortals through life on this earth. I have attempted to find more information in your columns and other places, but there isn't much solid information. What is the official position of the Catholic Church on guardian angels? Dogma? Just theological opinion?

The belief in guardian angels is indeed one of the loveliest and most humanly consoling elements of our Christian tradition. The conviction of followers of Jesus that each human person is given an angel to guard him or her and be a spiritual companion through life is but one extension of our conviction that God has a personal, daily, intimate concern for our good and our happiness.

Perhaps one reason you are disappointed in the amount of material available about guardian angels is that there just isn't that much to say, apart from pointing out the evidence for this belief through the centuries. It is an explicit Catholic doctrine, based largely on evidence from the Bible, that angels, bodiless creatures who possess an intelligence and free will beyond that of the human, really exist. That some of these angels are "guardians" of individual persons or groups is not defined Catholic dogma, but has been a continuous, almost instinctive part of the Christian way of thinking practically from the beginning.

Jesus himself, discussing little children, speaks of "their angels" who look upon the face of the Father in heaven. (Mt. 18:10) Early Christians in Jerusalem, seeing Peter at their door, couldn't believe he had escaped from prison; Luke tells us they thought they were seeing "his angel." (Acts 12:15)

Later on, at least from the second century, one theologian or father of the church after another relates this same Christian view. The great Scripture commentator and spiritual writer, Origen (born about 185), in his commentary on the book of Numbers, writes: "For each of us in the church of God, no matter how small, there is a good angel of the Lord who stands daily before the face of God to rule and move and govern, to correct our actions and intercede for us in our sufferings."

Origen's limiting of guardian angels to those in the church is not shared by the greater part of Christian tradition. The more universal belief is represented by St. Jerome (died 420): "What a great dignity of souls, that each person has, from birth, an angel assigned as guardian!"

The word "angel" comes from the Greek word *angelos*, messenger. This identifies them with how they relate to human beings, since they so often bring God's power and message to earth. Guardian angels are, in our Christian insights, God's messengers *par excellence*, his envoys beside us throughout life.

While the doctrine of guardian angels is not an "article of faith," and acceptance of that belief is not an essential of Christian and Catholic life, in my view those who dismiss it are missing a rich and joyful treasure of our Christian heritage. The prayer you quote from, which is several hundred years old, I also learned in the 1930s; I still pray it regularly. A feast in honor of the guardian angels is celebrated on October 2.

Disposing of blessed articles

My husband purchased an old altar from a parish church some time ago. Now he wants to turn it into a bar and the idea upsets me. Isn't that a sacrilege? We're not even supposed to throw away a crucifix or holy pictures. An altar is much more sacred.

An altar should never be put to common use like this. The importance of recognizing the special nature of blessed or consecrated things increases with the closeness they have to the Mass and the Eucharist. Your husband would, I'm sure, agree it would be wrong to start using chalices as beer mugs!

So what to do? When anything is taken apart, melted, or otherwise radically changed, it is no longer considered blessed. Thus, while it would be wrong to use an altar as a bar, it would not be wrong to use the materials from an altar for something else, including a bar — as long as common sense is used and any scandal or misunderstanding is avoided. After all, it is the altar that is blessed, not the wood and nails.

The same applies to other blessed items. Unless one owns a warehouse, there's a limit to how many blessed candles, crucifixes, statues, rosaries and holy pictures one can accumulate over the years. When they no longer have a use, it is proper to break or tear them so they lose their identity as a candle or picture, and discard them. Their purpose is to increase our faith and assist our spirit of prayer and devotion. When they have served that purpose and become worn out or are to be replaced, there is no irreverence in disposing of them appropriately.

CHAPTER 12

SAINTS

❧

Praying to the Saints

I am not a Roman Catholic. I've never received a sufficient explanation why Catholics pray to the saints and give them so much tribute. I believe that Jesus Christ is the one mediator between God and man.

The relationship with the saints cannot be understood without recalling a truth found often in the New Testament. All who believe in Jesus, who acknowledge him as Savior and live according to his teachings, form a special, very close family, whether they are living or dead, and "with" God, as St. Paul puts it. As Paul also said often, all Christians are in some way saints in that they share in the sanctity and love of the Father, along with and in Jesus, with whom they are united by ties of loyalty and love.

The people we usually call "saints," however, are individuals their fellow Christians acknowledge as having lived the Christian life in an especially holy way. When we pray to them, we do it to be glad with them and ask them to add to our prayers their own intercessions to Jesus, and through him to the heavenly Father, for whom they have proven their love.

One Protestant lady with whom I was speaking about this recently put it perfectly: "Then it's really just asking these holy people to talk to God with us, and for us, for the things we need! That's beautiful, because it's just what we do with people who are close and dear to us here on earth."

Perhaps much of the problem is in the phrase "pray to." In present English usage, it often implies the kind of adoration and relationship that belongs uniquely to God. It is particularly important, therefore, to understand precisely what is meant by "praying to" the saints.

Book of saints?

In the church's celebration of feasts of saints, is there a rotation of feasts as there is for the Sunday Scripture readings? Is there a book of saints similar to one I have which is almost 50 years old? Does it relate to our present calendar?

In the most recent revision of the church calendar (which takes place every few hundred years to eliminate confusion which develops with the addition of new saints), several dates were changed. There is no rotation from year to year. Each saint's feast is celebrated each year, unless that feast is superceded by a Sunday or other more solemn feast.

A few books describing the lives of the saints according to the present church calendar are now available. The classic in this field, however, remains Butler's *Lives of the Saints.* The four-volume set, recently updated, covering the entire year is relatively expensive, but well worth saving up for. It presents information not only on the major saint of each day (the one whose name appears on Catholic calendars) but on other lesser known but equally inspiring holy men and women whose feast falls on the same date. The set may be ordered through almost any Catholic book store, which will have other biographies of saints to choose from.

Why Catholics have statues

What light can you throw on why Catholics have statues in their churches and most Protestant churches do not?

Images of Jesus and the saints have been used for decoration and devotional purposes since the beginning of Christianity. Today only the most uninformed person gives credence to the accusation that Catholics worship these statues or pictures.

Several hundred years ago, the Council of Trent explained the practice perfectly: "The images of Christ, the Virgin Mother of God, and of the other saints are kept and honored in churches not because it is believed that there is any divinity or power in these images, or that anything may be asked of them, or any faith be put in them. The honor shown to them is really being given to the persons whom they represent. Through these images which we kiss, and before which we bow with bared heads, we worship Christ, and not the saints whose likenesses they display."

Even many Catholics do not realize that the church is very careful about what images are allowed for public veneration. All pictures or sculptures must be approved by the bishop or other proper authority.

The reasons most Protestant denominations do not allow images in their churches are varied. One is that early in the Protestant Reformation there was much misunderstanding about the meaning of honoring images of Jesus and the saints. "No statues" became a symbol of protest against the church of Rome.

Perhaps a more significant reason is that many early Protestant leaders, especially Calvinist and other Puritan traditions, considered any display, color, or emotion, such as might be encouraged by statues and pictures, out of place in religious worship.

All Saints is for all saints

I am a lifelong Catholic who thought the feast of All Saints was to honor canonized saints. Recently we were told in a catechumen class that the feast was to honor all the people in heaven, even our parents who have died. It's a beautiful thought, but what is the church's understanding of this feast?

From the earliest centuries the intention of this Christian feast was to honor all who are in heaven with God. It started as a way of honoring many martyrs whose existence was perhaps unknown to the church, whose names were known only to God. By the fifth century, the celebration (on the first Sunday after Pentecost at that time) included non-martyrs as well, and became known as the Sunday of the Nativity of All Saints, nativity meaning the day of death, of birth into eternal life.

As the prayers and preface of the feast of All Saints make obvious, this continues to be the significance of our All Saints celebration. The canonization process as we know it is not very old. For hundreds of years, saints became "official" by general acclaim of their holiness among Christian people of their region, or perhaps of the whole church.

The feast reaches even to us still alive on earth. St. Paul, in his letters, refers to the Christians to whom he is writing as "saints." The word comes from the Latin *sancti*, holy ones.

For him, as for the church in its liturgy today, those who believe the good news of Christ, who are united in baptism and faith to him and who work for the coming of his kingdom, are already in some way God's holy ones. (See, for example, Sunday Preface I and Eucharistic Prayer IV) To that degree at least, the feast of All Saints on Nov. 1

extends to all who are still on life's journey, but who are attempting to live faithfully in the life and grace of Christ.

Any poor Catholic saints?

Can a poor Roman Catholic have a chance to become a canonized saint? Such people do not belong to church societies, do not do much volunteer work, do not attend fairs and luncheons because they cannot afford it, and often don't come in contact with the pastor. All a poor Catholic can do is attend Mass on Sundays and holy days, practice the teachings of the church, raise his children to know their faith, and do small kind deeds the best way he can. Is the Catholic Church fair in picking out canonized saints? God shows no such partiality.

Probably the most striking and happy note about your letter is that you seriously consider yourself at least a potential saint. You mention the "only" things a poor person can do. Those aren't as insignificant as you seem to imply. Follow through on them and you can't miss.

You have a couple of misconceptions, however, about canonized saints. One is that there are no poor people among them. The list of poor saints is so huge, one wouldn't know where to begin.

It is true that most canonized saints, particularly in the last several hundred years, have been members of religious orders, or people of some prominence in the church. That is partly because the process of canonization is so long and so complex that a number of people must be interested in the project, and able to carry it through many years for a successful canonization procedure. It is not all that rare, though, for relatively unknown men or women, lay person or religious, to be officially declared a saint.

In canonizing saints the church does not say these are the only holy people, or even the most holy people, in the world. It is likely that among the saintliest persons are millions unknown to all but a few family members and friends, but whose closeness to God will shine brilliantly throughout eternity.

When the church canonizes anyone, she says only that the individual led a Christian life of sufficient and evident heroism that we can be sure that person is in heaven, and that we on earth might in many ways use that saint's life as a model for our own.

Maybe you will never have a church built in your honor. But, to paraphrase an old saying, some of my best friends are uncanonized saints.

Communion of saints at prayer

My Presbyterian daughter professes to be a devout Christian. She questioned me when I said I pray to St. Jude. "Why do that when you can go directly to God? After all, he is all knowing and all powerful," she said. How would you answer such a query?

Has your daughter ever asked you to pray for her? Or has she asked anyone else to join her in prayer for something she really wanted? If she has, you could make the same objection to her. Why not go directly to God?

The long Christian tradition of praying to the saints is another facet of our request for prayers from each other. As God's family, we can approach him together to strengthen our own faith and increase our desire for the good things that God can give to us.

The "communion of saints" which we profess in the Apostles' Creed means that the union of faith and love which the family of Christ enjoys goes beyond the limits of death. Since those in heaven are with God, it is only natural and profoundly Christian that we ask their help and prayers for anything important to us, just as we ask the help and prayers of the people who are still with us on earth.

Mary, the mother of God?

I am a Protestant reader of your column. Most things about the Catholic faith, even your dogmas, I can agree with. But calling Mary the mother of God turns me off. How can anyone be God's mother?

Your misgivings are understandable. On the face of it, such a title for Mary sounds ridiculous, if not blasphemous.

When Catholics speak of Mary as the mother of God, they do not mean that she was God's parent from eternity, but that she was the mother of Jesus when he came to earth. Since Jesus was God from the first moment of his coming in the womb of Mary, she is correctly called God's — that is Jesus' — mother.

Perhaps it will help if you understand how that phrase was first officially applied to her. In the early centuries after Christ, a Christian sect called Nestorians taught that when Jesus was born he was just a man. As he grew up, they said, God "saddled" him somehow (this was the actual word used in those days; God "saddled" him like a man saddles his horse), and "used" him to perform the work of salvation.

The main body of early Christians had come to realize and believe that Jesus was both God and man from the very beginning of his life.

They recognized that Nestorian doctrine was dangerous to the theology of salvation. If Jesus was not really God, or was not really and fully human, something essential was lacking in the saving work of reuniting God and the human race, which we believe was accomplished by Jesus.

The matter came to a head in 431 at the council of Ephesus, the third ecumenical council. After long and heated discussion, the council decided that the shortest way to pinpoint the basic belief that Jesus is truly God is to say simply: Mary is the mother of God — not from eternity, of course, but as he comes into this world in his human nature, in the womb of Mary. No one can accept that brief statement without believing that Jesus is both divine and human. He had a *mother* as we did, and therefore he is one of us. And yet the child of that mother was *God*, not because of a later doctrine, but as he came from her womb.

The Greek title *Theotokos* (God-bearer) was already commonly applied to Mary in Christian worship and devotion long before the Council of Ephesus.

So as you can see, the title "Mother of God" came into Christian doctrine as a vital part of belief about Jesus himself, not primarily as a way to honor Mary. It does, of course, reflect much honor on her to have had such an intimate share in God's plan of salvation.

Mary in our faith

How can the church urge that we pray to Mary, as the pope does when he recommends prayer to her for an increase in vocations to the priesthood and religious life? Isn't it true that Catholics pray to Mary? I don't believe the Bible says she is divine.

We do not believe Mary is divine. She is a human being who needed the saving graces of her Son just as we do. While the church has always reserved a special dignity and honor for our Blessed Mother, we pray to her in much the same way as we pray to the other saints, or for that matter, as we "pray" to other Christians when we ask them to pray for us.

Since the earliest decades, Christian people have honored the Virgin Mary as the greatest of saints because of her pre-eminent fidelity to God and her Son, attested to often in the New Testament, and because of her intimate relationship with Jesus, who took his human flesh from her.

For us there is an even more personal reason. Since he received from her his life as the incarnate Son of God, and since Jesus shares his life with those who believe in him, she is also *our* mother. The church has, in fact, always recognized those words to John from the cross, "Behold your mother," as addressed to the whole Body of Christ on earth, whom she loves, cares for and prays for as her own child. This is the reason for one of the loveliest titles we have for Mary, calling her our Blessed Mother.

Pope John Paul II echoed this tradition in his 1987 encyclical, Mother of the Redeemer, which incidentally is the most biblically and ecumenically oriented document on Mary in the history of the church. It should be required reading for anyone interested in her place in our faith.

The church, says the Holy Father, "sees Mary maternally present and sharing the many complicated problems which today beset the lives of individuals, families and nations; she (the church) sees her (Mary) helping the Christian people in the constant struggles between good and evil, to ensure that it 'does not fall,' or if it has fallen 'to rise again.'"

Unfortunately some devotees, in their over-enthusiasm or sometimes lack of knowledge of Christian beliefs, lose this Catholic balance. They occasionally express ideas at odds with Catholic belief. Some go so far as to suggest that if Jesus is "threatening" us or is reluctant to help, we need only go to Mary and she will obtain what he will not.

Suffice it to say here that Jesus is Mary's savior as he is ours (see Luke 1: 47), and that as God he is the source and infinite exemplar of whatever saving love she or any of the rest of us may have. To even imply that she outshines him in mercy or compassion and that if we're really in trouble she will do for us what he will not, only dishonors the Mother of Christ.

As long as we keep this perspective, the honor that we give to Mary can be nothing but a source of joy and pleasure to her Son. Beginning with the Gospels themselves, she has never been in any competition with him, nor has he with her.

Immaculate Conception in the Bible?

I realize we have Scripture and tradition as a basis for our beliefs. But when someone not of our faith asks for proof of the Immaculate Conception of the Blessed Virgin Mary from the Bible, what should be our answer?

There is no proof, in the ordinary sense of the word, of the Immaculate

Conception in the Bible. But this is not strange; every Christian believes a number of things which, even if he does not realize it, cannot be proven from the Bible.

Some texts from Scripture, however, strongly suggest or imply a belief by the earliest Christians in the Immaculate Conception of Mary, that she was sinless by the saving grace of Jesus from the time of her conception in the womb of her mother. Passages in the first part of St. Luke's Gospel concerning her and her relation to Jesus indicate a conviction by the first Christians that she was an exceptionally holy person who shared in a particularly intimate and total way in the victory of our Lord over sin, perhaps even to being totally free from any stain of moral imperfection or offense. But these texts are not what one could call proofs.

The more detailed theological implications of Mary's holiness and of her sharing in the work of Jesus as Savior, while hinted at in Scripture, were only gradually clarified and understood by the church through the centuries.

Wrong Gospel for December 8?

The Gospel for the feast of the Immaculate Conception, Dec. 8, is the story of the Annunciation, when Jesus was conceived by the Holy Spirit. The Immaculate Conception, at least as I understand it, celebrates the conception of Mary in the womb of her mother, St. Anne. Why doesn't the church correct that?

You ask a good question. In fact, the Gospel of that day (Luke 1:26-38) with the dialogue between Mary and the angel Gabriel at the time of the conception of Jesus, may be one reason many are confused about the Immaculate Conception.

First, there is, of course, no part of the Gospels that goes back to the time of Mary's own conception and birth. This is understandable; the New Testament, particularly the Gospels, is not about her, but about her son Jesus. She comes into the picture only in relation to him.

We would expect, then, that the Gospel of that feast would be a passage that reflects that relationship, and would also tell how early Christians, out of whose lives the Gospels arose, saw her and the special gifts God gave her. We must always return to the truth that, while we honor Mary as the greatest of the saints and as the recipient of the holiest gifts of God's grace, these gifts and her consequent holiness were given by the Father to honor his Son, who would become man through her.

It is the clear teaching of the church that all of Mary's glory, including her sinless conception in the womb of her mother, came through the foreseen merits of Christ, to make her a "worthy dwelling place for Christ, not on account of her own bodily endowments, but because of that grace which was hers from the beginning." (Pope Pius IX in his declaration of the dogma of the Immaculate Conception in 1854.)

Understanding this, it is clear why the church would choose this passage of Luke for Dec. 8. Every word and phrase overflows with biblical themes proclaiming the greatness of our Lord and Mary's sharing, as participant and recipient, in his redemption of the world.

Gabriel's words to Mary, "The power of the most high will overshadow you," are a clear echo of the overshadowing cloud or light, the "glory of the Lord," which stood over the Ark of the Covenant in the Exodus, and later in the temple of Jerusalem. For the Jews, this hovering sign marked the presence of God himself. (See, for example, Exodus 40:35.)

Luke's readers saw his words in light of this tradition, a new overshadowing revealing a new "Ark of the Covenant" in which, or rather in whom, the Lord God himself was present.

It would be difficult to find a more appropriate Gospel passage to celebrate the sinless entering into this world of the one who was to become this new Ark of the New Covenant.

Where was Mary born?

On a trip to Greece we were taken to an island where the Blessed Mother was said to have been born. If this is true, how did she come to Bethlehem and Nazareth?

To the best of our knowledge, Mary was born in Jerusalem. While there may be some doubt about that, I know of no tradition that places her birth in the area you indicate.

Perhaps you're thinking of the ancient city of Ephesus which, according to some traditions, was the home of John the Evangelist in his later years. Since Jesus shortly before his death on the cross gave Mary into John's care, this tradition could also place Mary's final days in Ephesus. It is more commonly believed, however, that she spent her last years in or around Jerusalem and died there.

Is there a tomb of the Virgin Mary?

Our Catholic paper printed an ad by the Israel Ministry of Tourism,

*which said that in Jerusalem you may visit Mary's tomb. I believe in the
assumption and feel that Mary had no need of a tomb. Did she die? Did
she have a tomb? Was she buried?*

There is on the southwest side of old Jerusalem, on the hill called
Mount Zion, a church named the Dormition ("falling asleep") of the
Virgin. Christians frequently referred to death as sleep, awaiting the
resurrection.

That church's background goes back 1,500 years, particularly to a
series of fifth-century writings historians collectively refer to as the
Transitus Mariae, the passage of Mary. Christians wanted to know
more about the death of the mother of Jesus, and these works, which
are inventive and largely fictitious, responded to that desire.

They describe Mary's last hours in detail, how her death was fore-
told, how the apostles miraculously gathered around her, how Christ
took her soul to heaven while the apostles buried her body in the valley
of Jehosaphat, how the Holy Spirit intervened when Jesus tried to burn
her body, how after some time her body was assumed into paradise,
and so on.

During the fifth, sixth and seventh centuries, a feast of the
Dormition on Aug. 15 was established in parts of the Christian world
honoring all her prerogatives as our Lord's mother, including her glorification in body and soul. More than 1,000 years ago, the title of that
celebration was changed to the feast of the Assumption.

The crypt in the church of the Dormition in Jerusalem contains a
sculpture of Mary lying peacefully in death. But no one today hints
that this is the location of Mary's tomb, or even that there is a tomb.

Did Mary actually die? The question has been debated for centuries. The church has not declared authoritatively one way or the other.
When Pope Pius XII defined the dogma of the Assumption in 1959, he
reviewed the history of belief in the Blessed Virgin's assumption, but in
the solemn definition itself he avoided the point about her death. He
said simply that Mary, "having completed the course of her earthly
life" (in Latin, *expleto terrestris vitae cursu*), was taken body and soul
into heavenly glory. That's where the matter rests.

Our Lady of Guadalupe

*Our liturgy planning group was discussing the feast of Our Lady of
Guadalupe on Dec. 12. We think of this as a Mexican feast and celebration. Why is it celebrated and so popular in the United States?*

There are at least two good reasons. First, millions of U. S. citizens of Mexican descent and other Spanish-speaking Americans are understandably and properly proud of their religious and other customs and feasts. They have helped make the devotion of Our Lady of Guadalupe popular in our country.

Second, and probably more important, the feast is as much ours (the United States and Canada) as it is anyone else's. When the Blessed Virgin appeared to the Indian Juan Diego on the hill of Tepeyac near Mexico City, the year was 1521, nearly 100 years before the pilgrims landed at Plymouth Rock.

At that time, the present boundaries of nations in the New World did not exist. Thus the event at Guadalupe and numerous miracles of faith that this shrine has occasioned during the past 400 years remain spiritually significant not only for Mexico, but for all the Americas.

Did Our Lady of Guadalupe appear pregnant?

For many years Our Lady of Guadalupe has had a special place in my prayers. Someone remarked that when she appeared to Juan Diego in Mexico, she was pregnant. Is that true?

It may be. A publication on Our Lady of Guadalupe (by Jeanette Rodriguez, University of Texas Press) discusses at length the many Christian and Indian signs and symbols on the well-known image of Our Lady of Guadalupe. Some of them would indicate a pregnant woman. Around her waist is what appears to be a maternity band, or *cinta*. In Spanish, *estar en cinta* means to be pregnant.

Below the band is a small flower which, to the Nahuatl Indians, signified the sun god. Its presence on her womb indicated to them that she was pregnant. Some doubters maintain these items were added to the picture later. Many believe they were present from the beginning. Up to now, at least, no one has found a way to be certain.

Decline in honor of Mary?

Is the Rosary a thing of the past? This past October, no one had a rosary in his hand at church. Are people losing their devotion to Our Blessed Mother when they don't say the Rosary?

I agree with you that people say the Rosary less now than they did 40 years ago. However, I'm not sure that indicates any less love of Mary, or of our Lord.

The Rosary developed over about 400 years (the 12th to the 16th century) when Catholics were almost completely cut off from meaningful participation in the liturgy. Indeed, the period was one of the low points in seeing the Mass as a community celebration.

Because of this, and because most persons couldn't read anyway, various devotions arose as a substitute for taking a more direct part in the liturgy, especially the Eucharist. The 150 Our Fathers (later 150 Hail Marys) were sometimes called the "poor man's breviary," they matched the 150 psalms said by clerics or others who could read.

Interestingly, saying the Rosary together was one of the first ways, in modern times, that Catholics began to do anything together aloud at Mass, and to see the Mass as something more than just another private prayer, which is the way some spiritual books described it before the present liturgical renewal.

As the Mass and other sacramental ceremonies become more significant in our lives, it is understandable that certain devotions which partially substituted for them would decline in use.

I really don't believe there is a great loss of honor and love for Mary. She will inevitably hold a high place in any religion that believes her son is God. The Rosary has been, and still can be, a tremendous help to Christian growth. But I wouldn't identify Our Lady's position in the church with how many Rosaries are said every day. (See more on the Rosary in chapter 11)

Believing in private revelations

The flood of news some Catholics receive about appearances of the Blessed Virgin and Jesus and saints is unbelievable and confusing. You have said that none of these visions put obligations on us about what to believe or what to do. But some people are so insistent. Either do this, or don't do that, or you will make Mary unhappy, or you will go to hell. Is there any way to tell if any of these are really, as they say, "messages from heaven?"

Before anything else, it is worth emphasizing one point you make. No private revelations, even the authenticated ones, impose any new beliefs or obligations on Catholic Christians. They may remind us of the importance of prayer and penance and good works, which we know already from the Gospels and from traditional practices of the church. That is good, of course.

Two major observations or cautions may help you and your

friends. First, those who desire special revelations or messages from God beyond what we already possess, don't have very nice things said about them by the great Christian spiritual writers in our Catholic tradition. Such searches and expectations of personal announcements from God are usually considered signs of a weakness of faith.

St. John of the Cross, for example, second to none in the history of Christianity for his mystical experiences of God and for his reputation as a spiritual director, knew God can speak to us any way he wishes. Yet, he claimed, God has spoken in total completeness in his Word; in his Son, he has given and said to us everything he would wish.

"Anyone who would seek some new vision or revelation from him would commit an offense," according to this great authority on spiritual life. "No soul who does not deal with them (inner messages) as the work of an enemy can possibly escape delusion in a greater or lesser degree." (*Ascent of Mount Carmel*, chapters 22 and 29) Maybe that's putting it a little strongly, but such phenomena obviously didn't impress St. John much at all.

Second, one sure sign that a personal revelation is suspect, if not outright fraud, is that the recipient attempts to bind other people to obligations because of it.

In my opinion, one of the most readable and common-sense books available on this subject is *A Still Voice: A Practical Guide on Reported Revelations*, by Father Benedict Groeschel. A clear sign suggesting that a revelation is false or actually fraudulent is, according to him, "the recipient's insistence that the decisions of others must be made on the basis of what is allegedly revealed to the visionary." (pg. 114)

Those who, by every evidence, actually did receive genuine personal revelations from God, St. Teresa of Avila for example, made no such demands. These impositions on others are, however, a common tactic of those, past and present, who claim visions and revelations which eventually prove to have no supernatural foundation.

I sympathize with your frustration and wonder at the, at best, naivete of so many people. It's important these days to keep your balance.

Private revelations — Fatima

Our local newspaper and some recent books include information about Fatima, the appearance of the Blessed Mother, and the miracles that were supposed to have happened there. The church I attend tells people that the first Saturday devotion (receiving Communion on the first Sat-

urday of each month, which Mary was supposed to have requested at Fatima for world peace) is only a private devotion.

What is the church's teaching about Fatima? Whatever became of the letter that was to be opened in 1960?

The church always respects the role of prophets. It realizes, however, that individuals can easily fool themselves into thinking that God is giving them private messages in support of their own prejudices. From the evidence of my own mail, I can testify that there is hardly a weird idea possible in the field of religion that someone doesn't believe God has told him or her to preach.

Some private revelations (Lourdes is perhaps the most famous) the church has officially approved. Some, such as the alleged appearances of Our Lady at Necedah, Wis., in the 1950s, it has officially rejected. About many of them — including alleged apparitions and other manifestations at San Damiano; Canton, Ohio; Woolongong, Australia; Madero, Mexico; Medjugorje; Limpias, Spain; Rwanda, and numerous others — the church either says nothing or makes no decision one way or the other.

When the church approves such messages, all it says is that there is nothing in them contrary to Catholic faith or morals, and that following the suggestions in these messages can be helpful in our efforts toward holiness. If it enhances one's spiritual life and one's love of God and neighbor, that is good. It is essential to remember, however, that the church never imposes a special belief or practice contained in these revelations as obligations for all Catholics. The Mass and sacraments, the teachings of the Gospel, and universally accepted traditional practices of our faith are basic for everyone. Apart from them, no one is obliged to accept or follow anything in private revelation, though a proper respect for the fact that God can speak to us this way is proper for us, as it is for the whole church.

Now about Fatima. Church officials, including popes, have indicated acceptance of the fact that the mother of Jesus appeared to the three shepherd children at Fatima, Portugal, during 1917, urging prayer and penance by all Christians for world peace. Many people in the decades since then have been inspired to these spiritual good works by the message of Fatima.

Again, however, no Catholic is obliged to observe special practices, devotions or prayers suggested at Fatima, except insofar as they are already contained in our responsibilities as Catholic Christians. In that sense, Fatima, and everything connected with it is private revelation.

The letter you speak of, containing the "third secret" of Fatima, written by one of the young sheperds, Sister Lucia, was kept in the Vatican after 1957. Its contents were published in June, 2000.

In an accompanying commentary, Cardinal Josef Ratzinger, prefect of the Congregation for the Doctrine of the Faith, called it a symbolic prophecy of the present struggles with evil political systems and of the ultimate triumph of good. Like any private revelation, said the cardinal, the Fatima message offers a help for living our faith, but it creates no new obligations for Catholics. The message of Fatima invites us, he said, to trust in Christ's promise that the final victory is his. The full text of the message is on the Vatican website.

Fatima: adoration of Mary?

I belong to an interdenominational prayer group. I'm amazed at the misconceptions Protestants still have about Catholics, especially about our veneration of the saints.

It would be easy to explain usually, but then there are articles such as the one in a Catholic paper recently about Our Lady of Fatima that confuse Catholics as well. The article said that during one of the apparitions to the children, Mary asked for adoration of herself.

Any Christian knows that the only being we should adore is God. What is the Catholic doctrine on this?

Whoever wrote or translated the article you saw was guilty of some sloppy use of words. Christian theology has a specific Latin word (*latria*) to designate the kind of honor or worship due to God alone. Another word (*dulia*) designates the honor given to saints. There are degrees of honor, of course, depending on the dignity of a particular saint.

As the greatest of the saints, Mary reaches the highest honor (*hyper dulia*) in the church apart from Jesus himself and the Father and the Holy Spirit. But the church never forgets that she is only human, and that as she said in the Magnificat, (Luke 1,47), God is her Savior as well as ours.

Unfortunately, our English language doesn't have words with such clear-cut theological meanings. Dictionaries give some definitions of worship and adoration which might apply to saints, or even special people on this earth, as well as to God.

Generally, however, we try to reserve these words for God, and use others like honor, veneration or devotion when referring to the saints.

Not all writers, even Catholic writers, carefully respect this distinction. When they happen not to do so, we should recognize it as a slip of the pen, or maybe over-enthusiasm, not an attempt to introduce a new doctrine about the mother of God.

Appearances of Mary at Necedah

Your explanation about private revelations and our attitude toward them was helpful. We get confused by so many conflicting reports on different shrines and apparitions. Can you tell us about the reported appearances of the Blessed Virgin at Necedah, Wis.? Does the church still refuse to approve the visions there?

The story of Necedah and the series of rejections by church authorities of Mrs. Mary Van Hoof's claim that the Blessed Virgin Mary appeared to her in 1950 is unfortunate and sad.

Within five years after the alleged appearances of Mary, officials of the LaCrosse, Wis., diocese investigated the situation and concluded that the visions and revelations were without supernatural basis and were false. In 1969, the bishop of that diocese reached the same conclusion after another investigation. In 1975, he was forced to place leaders of the shrine under personal interdict, meaning they could not receive the sacraments.

In the spring of 1979, the Necedah group made its final break with the church by inviting someone who claimed to be the "Archbishop and Metropolitan of North America, American National Catholic Church, Roman Catholic Ultrajectine" to bless and consecrate the shrine. The alleged archbishop then left a "priest" at the shrine to care for the pilgrims who might come.

Since then the self-proclaimed bishop, who was apparently a Catholic layman, has severed his connection with the shrine, as has another man who claimed to be a priest and bishop, and some others who were associated with the alleged apparitions. Mrs. Van Hoof died in 1984.

Visions at Garabandal

What is the church's position on the apparitions of the Blessed Virgin at Garabandal? I know the church treats these things in a low-key way, but a film I saw on this subject moved me deeply and I'd like to learn more about it.

Garabandal is another of those shrines at which, after extensive investigation by competent religious and scientific authorities, claims of some supernatural activity proved groundless.

For several months, beginning in 1961, children in the town of Garabandal in the Diocese of Santander in Northern Spain, were said to have seen visions of the Virgin Mary. During these appearances Mary is reported to have repeated much of the message of Fatima — the need for prayers and conversion of life if the human race is not to suffer greatly from disasters imminent in the world.

In March, 1967, Bishop Vicente Montis of Santander, reported the following after his own investigation: "There have been no apparitions of the Blessed Virgin, of Michael the Archangel, or of any other celestial person; there have been no messages. All of the reported happenings in that area have a natural explanation."

I must repeat what I have said before. When local church authorities find no evidence of a supernatural character in these appearances, they mean precisely that and nothing more. Unless explicitly stated otherwise (as it has been in some instances), the church does not mean to forbid Catholics from observing the spiritual advice involved, which most often is simply restressing the need for prayer and penance, which is and always has been an integral part of a good Christian life.

Bayside

Someone sent me material advertising appearances of the Blessed Virgin in Bayside, N. Y. I know this is possible, but some information sounds strange to me. Has the church approved this shrine?

Beginning in 1970, a lady in Bayside, Veronica Leuken, claimed a series of visions of Our Lady and Jesus. These supposedly occurred during prayer vigils held about twice a month to which people from surrounding states and cities were invited. Following the visions, during which the voices of Jesus and Mary sometimes were taped, long quotes were published, running hundreds of words, of what Jesus and Mary supposedly said.

The rambling "revelations" covered everything from abortion to the imminent catastrophic punishment of the world by God. They were against just about everything from Communion in the hand and lay ministers of the Eucharist, to rock music and ecumenism, and even against joining a particular farm cooperative in New Hampshire. Much was made of numerous so-called miraculous pictures. Included in the alleged revelations were poems allegedly dictated personally by Mary, or sometimes by St. Theresa of the Child Jesus. The vigils and supposed apparitions took place at Flushing Meadows, site of the New York World's Fair just next to Shea Stadium, former home of the New York Giants.

On Sept. 27, 1975, according to Mrs. Leuken, Mary revealed that three high Vatican officials (Cardinal Jean Villot, Archbishop Agostino Casaroli and Archbishop Giovanni Benelli) in league with Satan, had drugged the real Pope Paul VI and kept him a prisoner in the Vatican. The one who appeared in public, according to Mrs. Leuken, was an impostor changed by plastic surgery to look like Pope Paul, but who was actually an agent of the devil. The theory was "proven" to Mrs. Leuken's satisfaction by a series of pictures of the "real" and "fake" pope.

In 1973, officials of the Diocese of Brooklyn, where Bayside is located, concluded that no credibility could be given to the events there. The chancellor of the diocese at that time reported: "The conclusion we reached independently was that the Bayside apparition was the result of a lot of imagination after reading a lot about Lourdes and Fatima."

This remains the official position of the Brooklyn Diocese. Mrs.Leuken is now deceased, but devotees from all over the country still visit the shrine.

Devotions to Mary

I am enclosing a booklet on devotion to the Flame of Love of the Immaculate Heart of Mary. After asking permission, I passed it to two prayer groups. Our spiritual director told us it was all right, but said we had to be careful. I have refrained from passing any more leaflets. Do you know of this devotion? Is it all right to share with others?

Some privately advanced devotions to Mary and other saints fall victim to two dangers; the booklet you sent is a classic illustration of both. They tread close to outright superstition, and they confuse our relationship with the saints, again including Our Lady, with Jesus himself.

Certain special forms of prayer have become accepted by long tradition in the church. Even these, however, must be understood correctly or they can sound like some sort of magic.

Novenas are a good illustration. Nine days of prayer, as a sign of faith and expression of persevering trust in God's love, can be an excellent way of laying our petitions, praise and thanksgiving before Our

Lord. However, we do not attribute anything miraculous or automatic to the number nine.

The particular devotion about which you inquire is one of those which gets so wrapped up in pious specifics, it becomes hard to distinguish from plain superstition.

We are told, for instance, that "families who keep the holy hour of reconciliation on Thursdays and Fridays will receive a special grace through which I (Mary) will free a member of their family from purgatory within eight days, if only one of them keeps one day of fasting on bread and water."

Those who fast on bread and water on Mondays will, we are told, free the soul of a priest from purgatory. Those who say three Hail Mary's "mindful of my Immaculate Heart's flame of love, will free one soul from purgatory, and those who say one Hail Mary during November will free 10 souls from the place of suffering." (Another thing common to most of these unusual devotions is their eccentric fascination with purgatory.)

There's nothing in Catholic tradition or teaching to give basis or credence to this brand of spirituality.

Even more serious, and clearly in contradiction to Catholic teaching, is the tendency to compare the mercy and love of Mary with that of Jesus, with Jesus coming out on the short end. Some may remember the queer legend repeated by some promoters of the Rosary that describes Mary using the rosary to lift through the back window of heaven those whom Jesus had rejected at the front door. On this the instigators of the Flame of Love devotion mince no words.

The cult derives from messages Our Lady allegedly addressed to six Hungarian children some years ago. The revelation includes the following: "My children, my holy son's hand is prepared to strike down. It is difficult to hold him back. Help me! If you ask my Flame of Love for help, together we can save the world." Such nonsense would be ludicrous if it were not that some Catholics really take it seriously. The errors, even heresies, in this kind of thinking are so numerous and complex one hardly knows where to begin to refute them.

The Flame of Love pamphlet claims to be printed with permission of a diocese in Hungary. Given the disturbed circumstances of the church in that nation during that time, one cannot know by whom, or under what circumstances, such permission may have been given.

I find it hard to believe that legitimate Catholic authorities anywhere would sanction such a garbling of Catholic teaching and spirituality.

American saints

Can you tell us how many canonized saints there are from the United States?

Five U. S. citizens have now been canonized: Mother Frances Xavier Cabrini, who died in 1917, was the first, in 1946; John Nepomucene Neumann (died in 1860), bishop of Philadelphia, in 1977; Elizabeth Seton (died 1821), in 1975; Rose Philippine Duchesne (died 1852), in 1988, and Katharine Drexel (died 1955) in 2000.

Is St. Patrick still a saint?

An argument arose in our group whether or not St. Patrick is still considered a saint. Some say he is no longer considered as such by the Catholic Church, but the rest of us say that is impossible.

Some years ago, following extensive scientific research in the catacombs and other ancient locations, Catholic Church officials acknowledged serious doubts about the existence of certain early "saints," at least with the names traditionally given them. The mistakes came mainly from misinterpreting inscriptions on tombs and misreading old documents.

St. Patrick was not one of these. He is among another group of saints whose feast days were dropped from the universal church calendar for automatic observance by Latin Rite Catholics everywhere. Many saints' feasts were eliminated this way, or otherwise de-emphasized, in order to give greater focus to saints more familiar in each part of the world, and that more liturgical attention might be given the seasonal celebrations of the mysteries of Our Lord — Christmas, Lent, Holy Week, Easter and others.

Though not in the general church calendar, however, these feasts can still be celebrated in countries and localities which desire to do so, as St. Patrick's Day is in most parts of the United States on March 17.

St. Gerard

My husband and I desperately want a child. Someone gave us a prayer to St. Gerard to say for this intention. Who was he, and why is he a patron for people like us?

St. Gerard Majella was an Italian lay brother and mystic who died at the age of 29 in 1755. After a childhood filled with an unusual share of mental and physical hardships, and after being rejected by the Capuchin monks because of ill health, he was finally accepted in the Redemptorist novitiate as "a useless lay brother."

So many miracles were attributed to him that even in his lifetime he became known as the wonder-worker. Then and after his death, a number of these miracles involved situations which caused him to become the special patron of couples who seemed to be unable to have children. He is also known as the patron of women preparing for the birth of a child. His feast is Oct. 16.

Veneration of relics

Could you give some information about the church's position on relics of the saints? I am puzzled why we do not encourage the veneration of relics. I believe they are special gifts from God. Is there a special prayer one can say, for example, when venerating a relic of our Lord?

The veneration of relics is one of those areas of Christian belief and practice which possess a solid theological and spiritual foundation, but which experience proves also have an almost built-in temptation for misunderstanding and abuse.

As most Catholics know, veneration of the bodies of the saints, especially martyrs, goes back to the very early church. Sometimes the blood of the martyrs was collected on a cloth to be kept as a reminder to the Christian community of that individual's fidelity and courage in professing the faith. Later the Eucharist was celebrated and churches were built over their tombs.

Already by the 800s and 900s, problems began to surface. Possession of bodies of certain saints became a source of prestige for churches and monasteries. When St. Thomas Aquinas died in the Cistercian monastery of Fossa Nuova, it is reported that the monks there decapitated his body to be sure of keeping his remains. The tug of war between the Cistercians and Dominicans for St. Thomas' body continued for decades after his death. Buying and selling, even stealing bodies or parts of bodies of saints, became common. Transfer of relics became a major international business. To this day church law explicitly forbids "alienation" or permanent transfer of major relics from one place to another without the pope's permission (canon 1190).

It's not surprising that this strange sort of dealing with the bodies of saints should be reflected in popular piety of the Middle Ages and beyond. Veneration of relics gave rise to all kinds of feasts, shrines and pilgrimages. Possession of relics even became one of the marks of affluence and power. In 1392, at a royal feast, France's King Charles VI distributed to guests ribs of his holy ancestor, St. Louis. Some opposition to these practices was always heard, but even popes eventually became nearly powerless to do anything to discourage them. Mishandling, and the sale, of relics became one of the abuses attacked by leaders of the Protestant Reformation.

In 1563, the Council of Trent offered three positive reasons for venerating the bodies of the saints. They were living members of the Body of Christ, they were temples of the Holy Spirit, and are destined to be raised and glorified by him. (Session XXV) These motives remain valid. But experience understandably makes the church careful, lest this less central aspect of Catholic devotion again assume an importance and meaning way out of proportion.

The concern is evident in several ways. Some carefully controlled options for veneration of relics which were offered in former church law are not even mentioned in the present *Code of Canon Law*. This may be due as much to the decline of the importance of relics in popular Catholic devotion, as to any other reason.

The church's current norms and grants for indulgences do not include any prayers or actions relating to relics of the saints. Veneration of relics can be a means of praising the goodness of God, and of honoring our brothers and sisters who are saints. It is critical, and obviously not always easy, to preserve that focus.

Luther a saint?

I heard recently that the Catholic Church is thinking of canonizing Martin Luther! How is it possible for the church to make a saint out of someone who lived like he did, and who caused such a terrible break from the Catholic Church?

I hardly know where to start this one. It may ease your mind to know that, rumors to the contrary, no one, Catholic or Protestant, is pushing to get Martin Luther canonized, to my knowledge.

Among facts widely acknowledged by historians today are that much of what has been written about Luther's personal life is unfounded, and that many of his "heretical" teachings (about faith and the Eucharist, for example) are compatible with Catholic doctrine when they are understood as he understood them, not as some of his early opponents interpreted them.

Pope Paul VI and Pope John Paul II have said we all have much to repent in the tragic separation between Catholics and Protestants. They refer in part to the fact that the church was in many ways in a sorry condition at the time. A sweeping reform was long overdue, but even heroic efforts of courageous Catholic reformers like St. Bernardine and St. Catherine of Siena achieved only limited and local results. Something like Luther and his movement was probably inevitable to make the renewal happen.

This is, of course, not to defend everything Luther did and taught. It does, however, put his life, and what he "caused" in a more charitable light. Lutherans themselves do not, I believe, admire him as a saint, or as the perfect ideal of a Christian, but as a man who reacted with courage and intelligence to a personal and Christian crisis.

Communion of saints and praying for the dead

I would like to know more about helping loved ones by praying for them after they have passed on. Many other religions believe that when someone dies, it is too late. Where in the Bible would I find something to back our beliefs about praying for the dead?

From the beginning of the Christian era, Christian people have believed in the "communion of saints," a union with those who have died before us, as well as those who are presently in the Body of Christ on earth. They understood this to mean that prayers offered to God for those who have died, as well as for those still alive, are proper and effective in God's providential care for his people. This was true from the earliest decades of the church. But you won't find much, if anything, about it in the Bible.

Some have seen hints of the validity of this beautiful Christian tradition in a few Scripture passages, such as the reference in the book of Maccabees, that it is a "holy and wholesome thought to pray for the dead." (As one of the deutero-canonical books, Maccabees is not traditionally in the Protestant Bible.)

However, Christian belief in the communion of saints, and other beliefs following from that, are not primarily based on anything in the Scriptures. They come out of the instincts inspired by the Holy Spirit as the church gradually reflected on what Jesus said and did, and how those realities should affect the way his people live and pray.

It is helpful to remind ourselves that not until the Protestant Reformation did some people begin to require that a truth appear in the Bible before it could be valid Christian belief and practice. Today most Protestants agree that this is not the way to approach or understand Christian faith. Even Christians who claim to believe only what is in the Bible actually believe many things that are not there.

Perhaps most obvious of all, where in the Bible does it even say there should be a Bible in the first place? Nowhere in the New Testament do we have a record of Jesus writing anything (except on the ground in the event of the woman caught in adultery) or asking his disciples to write anything. It was simply assumed to make sense, in light of the obvious intentions of Jesus, that some things be put into writing and recognized as normative by the church to lay out the parameters for Christian belief and practice.

As discussed more at length in the first chapter, anything contrary to those parameters would be at least suspect, but not every Christian truth was expected to be in those writings. This is the way the church understood the Scriptures as Christian "inspired writings," and this is the way the church understands them today.

The same goes for our belief in the communion of saints and prayer for the dead. If there is anything the resurrection of Jesus told the earliest members of our faith, it was that the walls between heaven and earth are not impregnable. In some mysterious plan of Divine Providence, there is communication between the life of eternity and the shadows of that life which we share in this world.

All the rest of what Jesus said and did, his relationships with the early Christians and their understanding of their intimacy with him as the risen Lord, would make no sense if there were not such a thing as the communion of saints as the church has understood it, and a recognition of that union in our community of prayer with those who have gone before us.

CHAPTER 13

DEATH AND BURIAL

∽

A fear of eternity

Sometimes it seems that I am the only one who worries and is depressed by eternity and life hereafter. It frightens this man of 73 that we will go on and on after death. My choice would be a reunion with our departed family and call it a day. My weary bones say I have been around long enough. Almost every month one of my former schoolmates takes his leave. I'm ready to join them except for the specter of eternity.

Believe me, you are not alone. Something of your experience is shared by everyone, especially as she or he advances in years. Your question is simply your way of expressing one of the major elements in the age-old experience of the human family, the fear of death. It is not so much death itself, but the wonder of what is on the other side that can give one the shivers. Even Jesus could not explain that fear away and he did not try. However, one of his favorite expressions was, "Don't be afraid." And there is nothing about which he was more emphatic in that statement than about the fear of death.

I believe his entire attitude can be summarized like this: "I can't begin to explain to you what is on the other side of death. I can only tell you, as I have tried to prove, that the heavenly Father loves you and that where you are going will be your home as it will be mine. Just try to do as I have told you, and then trust me."

That may sound extremely simple, but it really is what we well might call the last will and testament of Jesus. I urge you to read the Gospel of St. John, chapters 13-17, where Jesus attempts, among other things, to prepare the disciples and us not only for his death but also for our own. Everything revolves around his promise that he is going before us to prepare a place for us, that where he is we also will be, and that his joy will be ours to the full.

As I have said before, Jesus does not tell us much about life after death, probably because he knows we could not understand if he tried.

Only a few saints claimed to anticipate the experience of death with total joy. For the rest of us, what God asks is a calm, grateful acceptance of his will, and trust that the Father will surely answer the moving prayer of Jesus that all his family, all his friends, will be in his company in the glory of eternity. (John 17:24) That may not be all we would like to know about eternity, but it far surpasses what the human race once dreamed it would ever know.

Funeral Mass passe?

Many Catholics in our area have only a funeral service at a funeral home, with a priest present. Is there a reason? Is there a trend against bringing the deceased person to the church for a funeral Mass?

There is no significant trend in that direction to my knowledge. The celebration of the Eucharist in church, with the body of the dead person present, remains the ideal and normal Catholic ceremony before burial. It is a significant act of prayer for the one who has died, and of faith and hope by those who are left behind.

The official rite of burial does provide for a funeral service outside of Mass. I have officiated at such ceremonies on days when a funeral Mass is not allowed, or when the desires of the family or other special circumstances make that funeral rite more appropriate. This may be the explanation for those occasions you have encountered.

Incense at funeral Masses?

Please explain the use of incense, especially at funeral Masses. Why does the priest incense the casket?

The use of incense in religious ceremonies as a symbol of prayer and worship of God began in ancient times. Pagan rites often included incense, and it is referred to in Scripture in connection with Jewish Old Testament worship. (See, for example, Exodus 30:34-38)

At first Christians refused to use incense because of its connection with pagan Roman worship, but incense later became common, especially at Mass. It is both a symbol of prayer to God and of honor to holy things, which is why the altar, the people, the body of the deceased at funeral Masses, the Easter candle and other sacred objects are often incensed during our liturgies.

How long to pray for deceased

I have a question about our prayers and Masses for the dead. How long should these continue? My mother died over 50 years ago, my father, 35.

We know few specifics of life after death, what things happen or when they happen. As far as we are able to calculate, there is nothing like "time" in our sense of the word — hours, days, years — in eternity. We supposedly will be out of a dimension where such measures of time make sense.

Thus, any answer to your question cannot be based on the duration of events after we die. The church in its prayers and liturgies basically just walks around that question and continues to pray always for those who have died. The Eucharistic Prayers at every Mass are a good example. At least two good reasons exist for this tradition. First, our prayers for the dead, as all our prayers, go to a God who is eternal, who has no beginning and no end. For God there is no past or future. All, from the beginning of time to the end of the world, is one eternally present moment for him. When we pray, therefore, considering that universal reach of God's presence and being, our prayers are not limited by time. They extend back to the beginning of an individual's life, through to the end, and into eternity. This is not speculation: It follows from what we know about God. Prayers we offer years after a person's death can be "applied" by God to when that person was still alive.

Second, prayers for loved ones who have died are also prayers of thanks, praising God for his goodness to that individual and for all the good done for others through and in that person's life on earth. For both of these reasons, and there are more, your continued prayerful remembrance of your parents and others makes excellent spiritual and religious sense.

Funeral services for non-Catholic

Can the funeral of a non-Catholic ever be held in a Catholic church?

Under certain circumstances it is possible for funeral services to be conducted for a non-Catholic in a Catholic church. Priests often officiate at funerals of those not of our faith, especially when the person is a relative or is otherwise close to a member of the Catholic parish, and when the family requests it. Usually these ceremonies are conducted in the funeral home, but there is nothing in church law that would forbid holding such a service in church. Naturally, the ceremony would rarely, if ever, include the offering of the Eucharist, but it could include other appropriate Scripture readings and prayers.

The decision on each case would be subject to the discretion of the pastor or perhaps the local bishop. (See also chapter on ecumenism.)

Funeral Mass for "former Catholic"

A friend of mine, a former Catholic, died recently. I say "former Catholic" because for years she did not go to Mass. She requested that she not be brought into church after her death. In spite of this, there was a funeral Mass for her. Is this usual practice? Would a person like this always have a funeral Mass?

When a person dies after years of neglect in the practice of his or her faith, every benefit of doubt is given in determining the type of funeral rite that is provided. Often the children of such individuals are aware of situations in the family that color the attitude of the dead person quite differently than the person appeared to outsiders, possibly even to the parish priest.

On the other hand, the church does not feel it has a right to impose religious ceremonies on people who explicitly and with full consciousness reject them. It does not presume to judge how that person stands before God, but the church believes it must respect the clear intent and will of the individual expressed when that person was alive.

It is impossible to evaluate the circumstances of the individual and family you mention. In fact, I would guess that many elements of that person's religious and family life are unknown even to you as a close friend. I assume, as I suggest you do also, that the parish priest on the scene acted with as great a concern as possible for the woman who died, and for her family and friends.

Meriting Catholic burial

My former husband, whom I married in the church at a nuptial Mass, died recently. We were divorced 30 years ago and three years later he married a Catholic woman in a Baptist church. He never practiced his faith as far as I know. Recently he became ill, and died in a coma without regaining consciousness. How could he be given the last sacraments and be buried from the Catholic Church?

There may be much about his last years and days that you do not know. Offhand, I can think of several circumstances that might explain his burial from the church. Perhaps some of these would be unknown outside of those closest to him in his final hours.

Catholic burial never implies approval of an individual's actions; even less does it imply any judgment of him one way or the other. The church accepts the person as one of its children, as a brother or sister of Christ, and prays for and professes its faith in the loving mercy of God.

You were deeply hurt by the divorce and the wounds obviously are still not healed. But I hope you don't begrudge him either the church's prayers or your own.

Husband remarried

I am indignant about the answer you gave to a woman who was divorced 30 years ago, whose husband remarried in the Baptist Church, died in a coma, and was buried in the Catholic Church.

My husband of 21 years insisted on a divorce last year. I finally agreed. He remarried immediately in a Protestant church. I continue as a devout Catholic.

Do you mean to tell me that if he continues as he is until death, circumstances could allow him to receive the last rites? Why should I continue to follow my vows if this is the case? That does not make any sense.

You have been badly and painfully hurt by your former husband. But above everything else, don't let bitterness rule your life. You will hurt yourself more than you will hurt him.

The person who asked the question had no intimate knowledge of the final days of her deceased former husband. As I indicated, unless individuals were with that person almost continually through the final hours, and unless they were privy to all the thoughts and words of the dying person, they might be unaware of circumstances which could open the way for Catholic burial.

The individual may have given signs of sorrow to one person or another, or might even have received the last sacraments, including the sacrament of penance, sometime before death. Repentance for wrongs that have been committed is possible all the way up to the time of death. Basic charity demands that we desire this even for our worst enemies. In granting Christian burial whenever it can give an individual the benefit of any doubt, the church implies no judgment of that individual's soul.

As for why you should continue acting in one way when your former husband acts in another, the answer is very simple: You believe you are doing what is right. When you die, you will be asked by God to give an accounting not of someone else's life and actions, but of your own. As I said at first, don't let your anger cloud that fact or diminish the fullness of the life that remains for you to live.

Burial of a non-Catholic

I am a Catholic and my husband is not. May he be buried in a Catholic cemetery? If not, would it be against the laws of the church for me to be buried in a non-Catholic cemetery?

Christians always have shown concern that their funeral rites for their dead brothers and sisters reflect their beliefs about the sacredness of the human body and the resurrection. This moved them to arrange special places to bury their dead, a custom we continue to the present.

However, the church's policies are not so strict as to preclude either of the options you suggest. People who are not Catholics may normally be buried in a Catholic cemetery.

Also, Catholics (again a common example may be a spouse, or a convert whose family plot is in another cemetery) may be buried in a non-Catholic cemetery. In the latter case, the grave is blessed at the time of the burial, as it would be in a Catholic cemetery. (CCL 1240)

Each diocese has regulations which may differ slightly from some others. It's best to ask your parish priest about details.

Is Mass for non-Catholics also?

My Protestant employer recently passed away. Today one of my Catholic co-workers and I were discussing the appropriateness of having a Mass offered for him and sending a Mass card to the family. Is it all right to do this? Do the merits of a Mass for the dead apply to those who are not Catholic?

I hesitated before including this question, frankly because of some embarrassment about it appearing in this book. I mean no disrespect to you, nor do I ridicule your concern and your honest question. That question, after all, results from a mentality which was not of your making, but which we recognize resulted from an attitude influenced by the Catholic Church's efforts to preserve its identity and theological positions after the Protestant Reformation.

Having said that, I also must say that your question reveals so many misconceptions about the church and about our faith that I hardly know where to start.

First, Masses may be offered for the intention of those who are not Catholic. As I explained in the chapter on ecumenism, it may even be announced publicly if two conditions are fulfilled:

1. The request should be made by the family, or at least explicitly approved by them. This is to assure that the non-Catholic's family will not be offended by something they do not believe in, and perhaps might reject.
2. There should be no scandal resulting either for Catholics or for those of other faiths because of the announced intention of the Mass. (Decree of the Congregation of the Doctrine of the Faith, 1976. See also 1993 Ecumenical Directory, 120)

The church thus recognizes in one of many ways that it has no corner on God's love or on Christ's redeeming grace. Nor does it determine the directions in which the grace and love of the crucified and risen Christ, celebrated and represented in the Eucharist, will go.

Jesus Christ died for the whole human race, as St. Paul and the rest of the New Testament attest time and again. If the Mass is the re-offering of that once-and-for-all sacrifice to the heavenly Father, then every Mass is for all humankind too. No one, nothing of creation, is excluded.

Our belief is reflected frequently in the documents of Vatican Council II. "As often as the sacrifice of the cross in which 'Christ, our Passover, has been sacrificed' is celebrated on an altar, the work of our redemption is carried on. . . All men are called to this union with Christ who is the light of the world, from whom we go forth, through whom we live, and toward whom our journey leads us." (Dogmatic Constitution on the Church, par. 2 and 3)

The Catholic Church tries not to violate another human being's conscience, or that of the family, even after he or she has died. Its own belief, however, is clear: The love of Jesus shown on the cross and remembered and renewed in the Eucharist, is as big and embracing as the world.

Church's position on cremation?

I am a senior citizen and wish to know about cremation. How can it be permitted now if the church once did not allow it? What happens to the ashes? I've been thinking about being cremated, but some of my family is against it. Would there be a funeral Mass after cremation?

Cremation was formerly forbidden by the church because it was promoted years ago, especially in Europe, by groups who used cremation as an argument against belief in the resurrection. How could God possibly collect all those ashes and smoke together to make us rise again?

It's been a long time since that argument was raised seriously by anyone. So cremation is no longer forbidden, provided the individual involved and his family intend no disrespect or contempt for the body or for our faith. In fact, the funeral rite of the church explicitly provides for cremation ceremonies. (See Introduction to the Rite of Funerals and CCL 1176)

Two documents, The Order of Christian Funerals, and Reflections on the Body, Cremation and Catholic Funeral Rites, published by the bishops of the United States in 1997, outline the church's practice for funeral liturgies and burial. The following points are primarily from the latter document.

Church teaching still prefers traditional burial of the body of the deceased. Economic, geographic, ecological or family factors, however, sometimes make cremation the only practical choice. At the present time, more than one-fifth of American Catholics choose cremation.

Even when cremation is chosen, the church urges that, if at all possible, the body of the deceased person be present for all funeral liturgies (vigil service, Mass, and prayers of commendation at the end of the funeral liturgy), with cremation following. When circumstances require cremation beforehand, it is appropriate that the cremated remains be present for all the funeral rites, and then be buried in a cemetery or mausoleum. In other words, cremated remains should be treated with the same respect given to the deceased body.

The church has no rules, incidentally, concerning a casket. Religious customs on this matter differ from country to country. Nor, to my knowledge, does any state in our country require a casket if the body will be cremated. A few states do expect a body to be shipped to the crematory in a casket or other suitable container. Funeral directors will supply information about what is required locally.

Fifteen centuries ago, St. Augustine noted that our Christian funeral rites are more for the living than for the dead. The point made by the holy bishop was that we need the reminders that come to us in the presence of the body of a friend, in the Eucharist we offer, and in the placing of the body in the grave. All Catholic funeral liturgy, from wake to burial, spells out those reminders in the context of Jesus' own death and resurrection.

One final reminder: When family is involved, one should discuss the matter thoroughly with them and make sure they are psychologically and spiritually comfortable with cremation arrangements. Should we ever lose contact with those spiritual realities that confront us in death and in the liturgies of burial, we would lose something precious in our Christian lives.

History of cremation

I still get arguments from fellow Catholics, including a couple of priests, that cremation is not allowed by the church. Could you be more specific about when the church allows cremation, and how it happened to put such emphasis on ordinary burial in the first place?

It seems that Christians adopted the practice of inhumation (traditional burial) from the ancient Romans, who adopted the custom in order to have more elaborate and demonstrative funerals.

Whenever feasible, this form of burial became common for nearly all Christians, even in those parts of the world where different funeral customs prevailed.

Burial of the dead was so common in Western society that no laws prohibiting cremation were proposed until the late Middle Ages. The most stringent regulations appeared only about 100 years ago. The first general legislation banning the burning of bodies as a funeral rite came from the Vatican's Holy Office in May, 1886, noting an anti-religious and Masonic motivation behind the movement. The *Code of Canon Law* of 1918 continued the ban because cremation was still considered a flagrant rejection of the Christian belief in immortality and the resurrection. That code forbade Christian burial to anyone who ordered that his body be cremated. (Exceptions were always made for times of urgent public crisis, epidemics, war, etc.)

In 1926, the church repeated the warning, noting that because of the virulent anti-religious motivation of most cremation proponents, its promoters were "enemies of Christianity."

With the decline of the anti-Christian symbolism of cremation, regulations are far less strict. The Holy Office in 1963 recognized there may be personal reasons for desiring cremation — financial, emotional, hygienic, and others. It presumes that people who request cremation are doing so in good faith, not out of some irreligious motive. The practices explained in the previous question are based on that assumption.

Organ and body donations

Is it permissible for a practicing Catholic to will his or her body to science? I would like my body used for the betterment of humanity after I am finished with it. I am also concerned about the effect on my grieving relatives.

It is lawful and can be a generous act of charity to donate one's body, or a needed organ or tissue (cornea, skin, heart valves, etc.) at the time of death. The use of organs and bodies for transplants, education and research remains significant, even though medical schools themselves rely heavily today on models which simulate most major physical structure and functions.

If the decision is made for such a donation, record is kept by the individual or the family, and the body is removed for that purpose immediately after death.

In my opinion, you are wise to consider not only your own feelings, but those of your relatives as well. The funeral and burial rite can help them deal with the grief resulting from death, and also help them accept the reality of death — their own as well as yours. I agree that you should discuss your thoughts with them and learn their feelings before you make a decision.

A Uniform Donor Card providing for the gift of part of one's body to a living person who needs it, or all of one's body for education-research, may be obtained from Living Bank, Box 6725, Houston, Texas, 77265. Many regional donation centers also exist, and most states have donor forms on the back of, or attached to, driver's licenses. Ask your funeral director, and be sure to tell your family of your desires.

Organ and tissue donations approved

What is the current Catholic Church view on organ donations after the death of an individual? If it is permissible, what is required before such a transplant?

The Catholic Church supports the principle and practice of giving an organ of one's body to another. Circumstances must be examined, however, to determine whether or not taking an organ from one person and giving it to another is morally proper.

This may become complicated, since it deals with questions involving certainty of death if the giving of the organ depends on the donor's death; physical effects on the donor if the donor is living; degree of hope for a successful transplant; informed consent, and so on.

The *Catechism of the Catholic Church* notes both positive and negative aspects of such decisions. Organ transplants conform with the moral law and can be meritorious as long as the physical and psychological dangers to the donor are proportionate to the benefit for the recipient.

Amid today's public disputes about such issues as assisted suicide, the catechism needed to point out that it is morally unacceptable to directly cause a disabling mutilation or death of a human being, even if that might help, or delay the death of, another person (no. 2296). It is impossible to discuss all these circumstances in an adequate way here.

Over a lifetime of active love and sacrifice, we in one way or another help each other all the time. If something that has been ours in life can still do good for someone else, before or after death, why not? Many people have given you part of their lives already. Without these you would not be alive today. If medical science allows us to extend that gift even to the bodies which God has given for our stewardship, it is something to be grateful for, to use thoughtfully but generously.

Pope John Paul II repeated this position not long ago, speaking of the shortage of available donors for patients awaiting transplants. It is a matter of Christian generosity, he said, and "no solution will be forthcoming without a renewed sense of human solidarity" based on Christ's example, which can "inspire men and women to make great sacrifices in the service of others" (April 30, 1990).

Can Catholics avoid wakes?

My husband and I oppose wakes for the dead. When we die, we'd like our caskets closed, with no wake, and a service at the funeral home by a priest.

Sometime after the funeral, our loved ones would go to Mass and offer it for the one who has died. Would such a funeral arrangement be permitted by the church?

I realize you are simply exploring the idea. Remember, however, that the funeral ceremony is not primarily for the dead, but for those who are left behind. Prayers for the deceased individual and for all the dead are included in the funeral rite. But more significant is the aid the funeral liturgy gives to those who are still alive, to confront the priorities of which death reminds us, and allow our grief to be worked out in a Christian context,

This may not be important to you. It may be extremely important to your children, grandchildren, and friends who will be reminded of some important truths by their encounter with the death of someone they love. The ritual you wish to avoid may not mean much to you. It may, however, be the most valuable final gift you leave your family.

Funeral liturgy after miscarriage

Three years ago, my first pregnancy ended tragically in a miscarriage at home. My husband and I were devastated and were left trying to decide how to humanely dispose of the body. Our parish priest told us that the Catholic Church makes no provision for miscarried babies. Why is there no service of any kind to memorialize our children who die before birth? Some form of liturgy would aid the grieving process parents face. What do hospitals do with a fetus after miscarriage?

The special hurt that results from the death of one's child before it is born deserves to be recognized and soothed by the community's prayer and liturgy. Perhaps your priest was not aware that Catholic funeral guidelines adapt in several ways to experiences like yours, which unfortunately are not uncommon.

Full funeral rites may be celebrated for children whose parents intended them to be baptized, but who died before baptism. Since there is no requirement that the body be present, a funeral or memorial Mass is appropriate after a miscarriage. Other ceremonies, with prayers and Scripture readings chosen to meet the particular needs of the family and friends, are possible and appropriate. These provisions are explained in the church's Order of Christian Funerals, in the section on funeral rites for children.

According to directions followed in Catholic (and many other) hospitals, if they can be identified, deceased fetuses are normally given proper burial as is "consonant with the dignity of the human body."

Catholic burial after suicide

*Last year our 22-year-old son committed suicide. He seemed happy, was
an altar server, helped around church, and had a good job and a lady
friend. Needless to say, we miss him dearly. I go to Mass daily and offer
my Communion for him. When he died, many priests assured us that our
Lord would welcome him home. He must have been very troubled over
something, but some people say the sin of suicide is never forgiven. That
would be more than I could bear.*

*How is suicide treated in the Catholic faith? Is Catholic burial always
permitted? Will he be allowed to go home to our Father? I pray every day
that he has found the peace he couldn't find on this earth.*

I am pleased you had priests who supported you in such a good way. I
hope you take faith and confidence in what they told you.

The *Catechism of the Catholic Church* reflects the same theology
when it says we each have responsibility for our lives, but we should
not despair of the salvation of persons who take their own lives. By
ways known to him alone, God has ways of providing for them spiritually, and the church always holds them (as it does all the departed) in
its prayers. (2283)

Much of the Catholic Church's beliefs on the subject are reflected
in its funeral policies. Canon law lists those who are to be deprived of
Catholic rites. Among these are "manifest sinners for whom ecclesiastical funeral rites cannot be granted without public scandal." (canon
1184) Insofar as they are covered at all, people who commit suicide
would be part of that group. Are such people really open "sinners"
whose Christian burial would give scandal? Particularly today, bishops
and other pastors generally believe just the opposite. The scandal
would be if a Christian burial were refused. They correctly act with
awareness of our limitations in knowing what really happened spiritually, and with particular care for those left behind.

Taking one's own life is a serious matter. But how much was the
individual capable of reflection on what he or she was doing? How
much true consent of the will was there?

I have had the sad experience of dealing with suicide many times
in my 47 years as a priest. Circumstances surrounding these deaths
gave strong hints to everyone who knew them that the deceased were
hampered mentally or emotionally, often to a severe degree, at the time
of death. Sometimes those hints are overt, with erratic behavior pointing to some crippling psychological dysfunction. Sometimes they are
less obvious, when such a self-destructive action contradicts every

experience with that person. There is no evidence of any plan or reflection beforehand. To all appearances, something inside just snapped, and we likely will never know what that might have been.

In offering Christian burial rites, we make no judgment on the individual's relationship with God. Again, as it does for all of us, the church begs God's mercy for the deceased and for those who have been hurt by the death. It seems to me the encouragement your priests gave you was based on solid Catholic belief about God, and what we understand today about such suicides as your son's.

Suicide in Christian history

I have been told that suicide is not sinful. I always believed it was a sin against the fifth commandment, thou shalt not kill. Someone said that suicide was once approved by Catholics. Is this true?

Before responding to your question directly, something needs to be said that many Catholics, indeed other Christians as well, sometimes find hard to believe. The moral code taught by the Catholic Church and other Christians did not fall full-blown into our laps.

Jesus gave us the two foundational principles of morality: Love God above all things and your neighbor as yourself. Throughout its 2,000 years, the church has meditated and reflected on those principles as it tried to discern how they apply to the myriad cultural, personal, social and religious conditions in which Christians find themselves. The area of morality about which you speak is a good example. During the great Roman persecutions, killing oneself in the face of imminent torture and death was looked on with praise.

Bishop Eusebius of Caesarea (died in the year 340) provides our best window into the first Christian centuries in his *History of the Church from Christ to Constantine.* Christians praised those martyrs who endured horrendous tortures before they died. He tells of others, however, who "unable to face such a trial, and before they were caught and came into the hands of their would-be destroyers, threw themselves down from the roofs of tall houses, regarding death as a prize snatched from the scheming hands of God's enemies."

Women were praised for throwing themselves to their death rather than submit to abuse. One woman, about to be apprehended and subjected to dishonor and torture, stabbed herself to death. "By deed that spoke more loudly than words," says Eusebius, "she proclaimed to all men then living or yet to come that the only unconquerable and indestructible possession was Christian's virtue" (Book XII, XV).

Suicide was not the only area of morality about which our Christian forebears held ideals less refined than our own. Eusebius describes how, when the persecutions ended and the "enemies of true religion" were captured, these enemies were themselves subjected to "elaborate tortures" and executed. None of us today would sanction these barbarous attitudes toward other human beings, though they are all too common among Christians even in our own generation. We need to be aware that we do not necessarily enjoy options in the way we treat ourselves and others simply because Christians of another time acted in a particular way.

To be specific, the church's teaching, based on God's lordship over our lives, is that any attempt to take one's own life is objectively seriously sinful. The individual's subjective responsibility depends on many factors. We have learned much as a community of faith about applying Gospel values to human life. If history has anything to teach us, it is that even now we have not learned it all.

Aftermath of suicide

Did you ever feel like a nothing? Like a blank piece of paper? I've been alive for 22 years and I feel like I've never made an impression on the world.

My brother killed himself, and now I cannot. After he died my family was crushed; they'll never be the same. I can't do that to them again. Does God test everyone this way? Is it my imagination, or are other people in this world relatively happy? How can I get help?

Your letter is proof again of how much we need each other on this earth. It also proves how impossible it is for us to judge another person's life, or even in many ways our own.

For better or worse, we are deeply involved with each other. You need to talk to someone who loves you and is concerned about you, to air your feelings of guilt and frustration. I'm not sure who that might be for you, but please do not rule out your own family too quickly.

Too often after a tragedy such as your family has suffered, parents and children tend to hide their feelings from each other out of loving concern not to add their own problems to the emotional hurts already suffered by other members of the family. Tenderness and thoughtfulness are called for here. But sometimes one member's willingness to expose his or her fears and hurts can help others do the same, to the mutual support and encouragement of everyone.

Beyond that you might talk with a friend or with a priest in whom you have confidence, your own parish priest or someone else.

Above all, know that there is real hope for you. The feelings of desolation and depression you express are common, even normal, in a time of grief and loss such as you and your family experienced.

Burial at sea

I am interested in ocean burial. Does the Catholic Church have any objections to this idea?

Christian funeral customs always reflect Christian faith in Christ, our conviction about the dignity of our human person and belief in life after death. For these reasons, the church discourages practices that might, in a frivolous way, begin to reflect dishonor on the dead or seem to minimize beliefs which are precious to us.

It is within this context that your question must be approached. If a good and valid reason suggests it, there is no rule against burial at sea. It is done thousands of times in emergency situations, particularly in time of war. This type of burial, therefore, would not always be wrong.

I suggest you consider your reasons carefully and discuss the matter with your parish priest, who would be responsible for carrying out your wishes within the framework of our Catholic liturgy for the dead.

Won't take care of health

I irk my relatives and friends because I won't seek medical help for any illness. They claim it's stubbornness. My argument is, I'll go next week if my time is up whether I go to a doctor or not. Am I right or wrong?

Sorry, but you don't give anywhere near enough information for an answer to be very helpful. How serious is your illness? How much help will medical assistance be? How old are you? And what responsibilities to others have you in your present situation?

A father at age 45 with six growing children obviously has a more serious obligation to seek medical assistance for a serious illness than does an old man of 80 whose children are all adults.

However right or wrong your conclusion may be, I can't say much for your argument. By the same logic, you could drive your car recklessly, or stop eating, arguing that when your time is up, you'll die anyway. We are obliged to take reasonable care of our health and protect it as well as we can, whether the dangers to it come from inside or outside.

Living wills and power of attorney

Newspapers in our state print many stories about living wills and other documents people can sign to prepare for a serious illness. The more I think about it, the more concerned I am. Do you think it is wise for a person to have such a "will?"

Living wills are one form of advance directives, various methods of determining which types of medical technology and treatment should not be used if a person suffers a critical, perhaps terminal, illness, but is unable to make necessary health care decisions himself or herself.

A living will is a personal document indicating to the physician, family, or health care institution which life-sustaining or life-prolonging treatments should be withdrawn in a terminal illness.

The other most widely discussed advance directive is the "durable power of attorney for health care." This names another person as your substitute to make critical health care decisions if you are unable to make such decisions yourself.

Many states have legal procedures to provide a health care surrogate. In at least one state, if an individual has no living will or durable power of attorney, the hospital or other health care provider must find the highest person on a list (guardian, spouse, adult child of the patient, etc.) to serve as substitute decision maker.

There is no universal agreement on the value, appropriateness or necessity of these advance directives. For one thing, the motivation is not always pure and good. Some organizations who are laboring vigorously for permissive euthanasia laws and for physician-assisted suicide, consider living wills, for example, a first step toward their more sinister goals.

The largest concern, in my judgment, is the inevitable confusion and fuzziness about what exactly is being signed away. The person who makes a living will is rejecting some unspecified future treatment in some unspecified future circumstance.

In addition to other obvious difficulties, a legally executed living will might force a good physician, or at least lead him to feel forced, to act against his better medical and human judgment, even one made in consultation with the family of the patient.

Under any such arrangement, the patient and others designated are morally obliged to base their decisions on several fundamental truths. First, all human life is a gift from God that must be treated with respect and reverence in every circumstance. Second, death is for us not an absolute evil to be frantically delayed as long as possible at all costs. We believe that death is the beginning of eternal life, not the end of existence. And third, each of us has the right and obligation to be in charge of the health care we receive, whether we make the decisions ourselves or arrange for others to make them in our stead. All these factors need to be prayerfully and carefully pondered in each life-and-death decision.

The complexity of all this is multiplied by the fact that most states now have legal guidelines to determine who has what rights and obligations in critical health decisions. These legal guidelines differ from state to state.

State Catholic conferences in many parts of the country have prepared, or are preparing, explanations of these questions in light of moral concerns and individual state laws.

To discover what is or is not possible where you live, and what the consequences of your own advance directives may be, you need to contact an attorney, or perhaps a priest who would be conversant with such matters, or the chancery of your diocese.

Why no flag on casket?

When a casket is brought into church for a funeral Mass, it is covered with a white shroud. In the case of veterans, the American flag is removed and the white shroud is placed over the casket. Many veterans and veterans' organizations want an exception to this for veterans whose caskets are covered by the American flag. They wish the flag to remain on the casket during the funeral Mass.

Where should our veterans go to have this exception made official so deceased veterans will have the American flag covering their caskets during the funeral rites?

The American (or other national) flag may be placed over the casket until the body enters the church, and at the time of burial, when it is folded and presented to the surviving family.

There is no provision, however, in Catholic ritual for replacing the white pall with the flag during the liturgy in church. When the pall is used along with the sprinkling of water, it is a symbol of the water and white cloth at baptism. It expresses the baptismal faith of the Christian who is being buried, and the faith of the others present for the liturgy.

As a Christian and as a human being, the deceased individual owed many loyalties — to God, to his or her spouse and children, to others who rightfully depended upon him or her for love and care, to work and profession — and, of course, to a patriotic commitment to honor and preserve the country's ideals of justice and freedom. One of the primary intentions of our Catholic funeral liturgy is to acknowledge and thank God for this particular Christian's faithful adherence to all these commitments and loyalties.

It is a virtuous and sometimes heroic act to serve one's nation in whatever capacity, including militarily. We honor and express our gratitude for that patriotism by appropriate rites at the time of burial. It is not appropriate, however, to single out that one aspect of Christian generosity as primary focus of the funeral Mass and other burial liturgies. In the funeral liturgy, the church attempts to honor and remind us of all the ways we must respond to our Lord's command to love God and neighbor.

What happens to our soul?

Some friends and I were discussing what happens to your soul when you die. I thought the soul goes immediately to heaven. Another thought one's soul remains sleeping until Jesus comes again, then we go to heaven, but it will feel like you have been asleep for only a second. Who is right?

Most of what you ask cannot be answered with anything more than speculation. A few considerations, however, might throw some light on your discussion. Both our spiritual and material parts, traditionally referred to as body and soul, are essential for our human nature, whether here or in the next life. In other words, it seems there can be no such thing as a human soul floating around without a body. If a soul does not have some relation to a body, it is not a human soul. Whatever it is, if such a separate existence were even possible, it would not be a human being.

Without getting too philosophically technical, all this follows from the church's traditional explanation of our human nature in terms of the Greek metaphysics passed down to us by Aristotle and Thomas Aquinas, in which elements called matter (body) and form (soul) are the inseparable, interwoven counterparts of all material beings. This all fits and presupposes what we profess in the Apostles' Creed: I believe in the resurrection of the body.

Your friend's comment about being "asleep for only a second" is interesting. Putting all the above together, many have suggested that when we die, our next conscious moment will be the resurrection, our rising to the new life that Paul attempts to describe in the second letter to the Corinthians (chapter 15).

It seems to make sense, insofar as any explanation we might make of the next life can make sense, given our limited experience in this one.

Views on eternity deny doctrine?

Your response about what happens to our souls when we die raises some serious questions. You acknowledge that most questions about eternity can be answered in detail only with some amount of speculation. But you quote people who theorize that the next conscious moment after death could be the resurrection. Don't these opinions deny such Catholic doctrines as prayers for the dead, the communion of saints, the judgment, purgatory, or the fact that some people, great saints maybe, go to heaven immediately? Are all the dead in some giant dormitory until the end of the world?

Your concerns seem to be based on an assumption that somehow there must be time — days, weeks, years — after death, similar to the time divisions we experience in this life. As you said, I noted that any answer we can give as to what and how things happen in eternity involve some speculation. But speculation is not simply pulling ideas out of the blue sky. It's using what we know to try to explain things we don't, and cannot, understand now.

For example, we know that time-related items — words like immediately, until, before, after — cannot be simply transferred to the framework of life after death, to eternity. Eternity, or infinity, by definition cannot be divided into parts; there can be no half, or one 365th, of eternity.

Thus, can there be any unqualified "past" or "future" in eternity? It's a different way of thinking than we are used to. But Pope John Paul II, who discussed these matters at length not long ago, noted that when we use words, even biblical words, to describe eternal realities, it is essential to realize we are speaking symbolically and figuratively. Therefore, said the pope, the words need to be interpreted symbolically.

For example, even though we speak of "going to" heaven, or "being in" heaven, or about the "fires of hell," he explained, heaven and hell and purgatory are not abstractions or physical places, at least in our experience of place. They are relationships, or lack of relationships, with the Holy Trinity.

When Jesus or the creed speak of his sitting at the right hand of the Father, we instinctively know those words are to be understood metaphorically, symbolically. Thus, scriptural language describing eternal realities cannot be interpreted literally. They are God's attempts, through the sacred authors, to somehow put into human language realities which are ultimately humanly inexpressible.

None of these limitations contradict or minimize Catholic doctrines. They simply say in another way something we already know, that God's world, his framework of time and space, is not ours. To require that we interpret these time-related words literally, to insist, for example, that we will literally wait around for centuries after death anticipating the resurrection or whatever else may come, would be to circumscribe God, to enclose and limit his actions inside our earthly time frame.

It deserves repeating that when our Holy Father says purgatory "is not a place" but a "condition," a "process of purification," he is saying nothing new in Catholic teaching. It does not deny that after sinning in this life, a remission of temporal punishment, a purification from our imperfections, may take place upon death, and that this suffering can be lessened, as the pope says, "through prayer and works of love."

To cite Pope John Paul once more, descriptions of heaven and other eternal realities will always remain inadequate. It is good to remember this. Trying to participate in those realities by imitating Christ and sharing in his Paschal mystery is more important than describing them. (The citations from Pope John Paul are mainly from his addresses during papal audiences on July 21 and 28, and August 4, 1999.)

Deceased babies are not angels

My baby died while I was in labor three months ago. My husband and I believe she is a saint in heaven, but we have this ongoing disagreement with my mother and her friends, who claim she is an angel.

Two friends claim to have seen my baby; one says she's flying around the feet of the Blessed Mother, is now 2 years old and has gold wings. This sounds absurd to me and drives me crazy. How could two human beings conceive a child who turns into an angel?

In an effort to be helpful, well-intentioned people frequently say strange things to survivors after death, especially the death of a child. Things like "God wanted her more than you did." Or, "she is now an angel with God."

Some remarks may be consoling; some are not. But many have no basis in Christian theology or Catholic belief. The one you mention is among them.

Your observations on the subject are right on the mark. The soul of a deceased human being, young or old, is not a free-floating spirit that takes on an angelic nature. Even after death it remains a human soul, with all that involves. (See previous questions.)

According to Aristotle, what we call the human soul is the "form" of the body. That means it is what makes our bodies human bodies, rather than tulips or monkeys. In other words, wherever and however it exists, our soul, the spiritual "part" of us, is and remains human. Whether in this world or the next, it is never complete, never completely human, without some relationship to a body.

This fact is proved by, if nothing else, the resurrection of Jesus to a new life. According to the Gospels, he possessed a distinctly different kind of body, but a human body nevertheless, which he was quick to point out could eat, speak, be seen and touched.

Most Catholics and other Christians realize all this, I believe. But, as you say, it is possible to become confused if we forget that some kind words at the time of death are just that, expressions of sympathy and consolation, not statements of theology.

Passive euthanasia

A newspaper referred to what was called "passive euthanasia." The article seemed to say that this kind of euthanasia is morally permissible. If it's mercy killing, it's still wrong isn't it?

Passive euthanasia is a phrase used occasionally in medical and moral literature to describe a situation in which a person is allowed to die rather than be provided with treatment or medication that would keep him alive. It is opposed to active euthanasia (or mercy killing in the traditional sense) in which death is brought about by positive, deliberate action of a physician or other person.

Using the word euthanasia in this double sense can be confusing. There is a huge difference morally between the two. For example, to administer a fatal drug to a suffering person (active euthanasia) may be called "merciful release" or any number of other pleasant sounding names. But it is intentional killing of another human being. It has almost always been recognized as seriously wrong by the human race in general, by moral theologians, and — until recently at least — by the medical profession almost without exception.

On the other hand, it is not always morally necessary to use every conceivable means to keep a sick person alive a while longer. Treatment which would be extraordinary under the circumstances because of immense cost, extreme pain, little hope for success, or other reasons, need not always be used.

A very old person might know, for example, that his life could be prolonged for several months by a very expensive and exhausting operation. He would not be obliged to submit to that operation, nor would his doctor be obliged to perform it against the patient's desire.

Such decisions can be complicated and difficult. What might be extraordinary and not required for an aged grandmother, could be different for a younger father who still has a wife and family depending on him for support.

Passive euthanasia, then, is not necessarily mercy killing. Whether it is right or wrong depends on the circumstances.

CHAPTER 14

ETCETERA

∾

Doubting the existence of God

I am 14 years old and have recently been having doubts as to the existence of God and Jesus and all the other characters of the Bible. I used to be devoted, said my prayers every night and every morning and participated fully at all the Masses. I know that faith is believing in something you cannot see, but I am finding it very hard.

It started one day at Mass when I got to thinking: What if we're all worshiping something that doesn't exist? I started feeling silly, like I was taking part in something that had no meaning.

Here are some questions I hope you can answer for me. If there is a God, why is there so much bad in the world? Is everything in the Bible true? How do we know ours is the right religion?

Why doesn't Jesus appear on earth every once in a while just to visit? What exactly is the Holy Spirit? What was Jesus' job on earth? Wouldn't everything still be the same if he would not have come? Couldn't God allow reincarnation?

Most of the queries you have (the ones I listed here are only about a third of them) reflect questions that have intrigued men and women as long as the human race has existed. It's impossible to respond to all of them, but anyone who has not seriously asked these questions has not yet begun to live a deliberate adult life. The fact that you are asking them should in itself be thrilling for you.

You are at an age when you begin to wonder about many significant things in life, most of them involved with the emotional, physical and social changes you are experiencing. You are probably either a freshman or sophomore in high school, which means a lot of adjustment there also. So don't be disturbed at finding yourself confronting large concerns about God and the meaning of life openly and squarely.

It is a sign of your developing maturity that you are doing so.

In this as in other facets of your life, have confidence and trust in the people who love you, especially your family, close friends who may be a little older, your parish priest, and others. You are smart enough to know that the big questions of life do not have easy one-paragraph (or even one-book) answers. A bit of study, prayer and the kind of wisdom that comes from thoughtful living help us toward finding those answers and, maybe even more importantly, help us to accept the relationships with God and those around us which make it possible to integrate those answers into our lives.

You may also be consoled by knowing that millions of good faith-filled Catholic men and women have lived through the same process of doubting and wondering that you now experience. In other words, you must have enough insight to recognize the kind of answers you are looking for are beyond you right now, but you are beginning to find them much more than are a lot of other people. It is valuable to keep your inquisitiveness without losing sight of your own real faith, and the faith of others whose lives reflect for you one solid truth: God and his love really do exist.

As one who still enjoys finding fuller and better answers, I believe you are on the right track. At this point for you, that's more important than knowing all the answers.

Unconditional love

I've noticed priests and other teachers use the term unconditional love. Is that found anywhere in Scripture? If so, where? What is meant by the term, and why do we seem to hear about it so often in relation to God?

Unconditional love means a love that is not subject to any conditions or "ifs." Many relationships we identify as love are conditional ones: I will love you if you do this, or as long as you behave this way or that.

The most genuine and total love is unconditioned. We are told often, especially in the New Testament, that our love for God must be total and unconditional, and that our love for one another must imitate his love for us.

Even in the Old Testament, God insists on the totality of that love. Particularly after Hosea, and later in the book of Deuteronomy, the mutual love which God sees as the relationship he desires between himself and his people becomes more and more evident.

The most astounding proofs of the enormity and generosity of God's love are in the New Testament, particularly in Jesus' words about how God's love for us can be measured only by the love which he has for the Father and the Father for him from all eternity.

"As the Father has loved me, so I have loved you," he told his disciples. He later prayed "that they may be one as we are one" so the world would know "that you loved them as you loved me."

That is genuine unconditional love, the measure Jesus gives for our love of one another.

God is Truth: What does that mean?

A question has baffled me for years. The Old Testament says God is the source of all Truth. His word and law are Truth. He is Truth. It's probably a stupid question, but what is Truth?

That's not a stupid question at all. Usually when we use the word "truth," we mean it as related to something we know or speak. If I tell someone the sun rises in the east (from our earth perspective, at least), we say that is true, it fits the facts; or put more formally, it conforms to reality, it matches what is really out there.

When we speak of Truth with a capital "T", however, we mean something more. When Scripture refers to Truth in the way you describe, it is not speaking of something that only mirrors reality, but of reality itself, total reality, total being. In other words, the being we call God.

Throughout the Bible, God describes himself with two especially identifying qualities, loving tenderness and absolute faithfulness. In Hebrew, the words are *hesed* and *emet*. They occur in the Old Testament, particularly in the psalms, and parallel words abound in the New Testament in the words and actions of Jesus.

While attributes of God cannot be isolated from one another, it is the second of these qualities, God's unfailing fidelity, that we connect most to his Truth. We are able to trust him without conditions, have total confidence in his tender love for us, because if he were not faithful to his promises, he would quite literally stop being God.

The letter to Timothy puts it graphically. We ourselves may be unfaithful, but God can only be faithful. For him to act against what he has said and done would be a cosmic lie, a violation of ultimate reality and Truth, by which God would seem to deny, disown, his own self (2 Tm. 2:13). How that all works out, that God is a faithful judge and also a faithful redeemer, we do not know. But the fact is inescapable in the Scriptures.

We can barely grasp all of this even in a small way. The full understanding of a Truth which encompasses all that exists or could exist is beyond our experience or comprehension. Which is why God made it at least a little easier for us, wrapping it all up in human language in the human nature of his Son.

Your question is appropriate to reflect on anytime we celebrate the Incarnation. The Truth you ask about is not simply knowing about reality, about God. This Truth is precisely the being who is the solid ground of all our hope and faith. The one who reveals himself in the Incarnation sends to our earth not just information, but the promise of sharing a life beyond our imagining and someone who can give us a hint of what it will be like.

At the Last Supper, with charming naivete, Philip says to Jesus, "Lord show us the Father, and that will be enough for us." The Lord answered: "You still do not know me? Whoever has seen me has seen the Father." In other words, when you see me, Jesus says, you see all there is to see.

When Jesus says "I am the Truth" (Jn. 14:6), he is not claiming simply to know everything. He is proclaiming that all of what is real, all that has being, dwells among us in him, the Word made flesh.

What do we mean by Trinity?

In the Blessed Trinity, did God the Son exist in heaven as separate from God the Father before coming to earth? If so, what was his function in heaven? Did God the Holy Spirit exist in heaven separate before being sent to earth? What was his function?

All three Persons must have existed from the beginning. I just don't understand their purpose in heaven. I also don't understand why God the Father waited all those generations before sending the Son. Didn't he know from the beginning of time that people would never be able to keep the old covenant?

In the Trinity we are dealing with the central mystery of Christianity, something utterly beyond our comprehension. Human experience or language can only remotely (the theological term is "by analogy") touch that Supreme Reality.

We believe in one God. Many who are not Christians share that belief. It is one that human beings can arrive at from common sense and intelligence. In fact, throughout history, people have reasoned their way from what they saw and experienced in the world around them to the conclusion that there had to be an intelligent, personal Being who brought it all into existence.

It was only Jesus, however, who let us in on the rest of the story. "Within" this one God there exists, from all eternity, a community or interchange of life and love involving the three persons we (following Jesus' own words) call Father, Son and Holy Spirit. This aspect of God's most intimate inner life is what we name the mystery of the Trinity. Without our Lord's telling us, we could never have known about it.

What their "function" might be within that divine life we can barely speculate. The Nicene Creed, based on Scripture and other Christian tradition, tells us that in some mysterious way the Son is "begotten" by the Father. The Word comes into being by God's infinite knowledge of himself. The Spirit "proceeds from the Father and the Son," from the love between them, a Love so complete and perfect that it literally is another person in the one God — the Spirit (sigh, breath) of love between the Son and the Father. And all this from eternity, without beginning, without end. Three Persons, each of them God, identified by Jesus as somehow distinguishable from each other and yet not three Gods, but one. Some of the early Greek Fathers of the church chose an amazing Greek word for this inner, eternal life of Persons of the Trinity, *perichoresis*, literally, "they danced together."

Jesus did not let us in on all this just to satisfy our curiosity. As Christians, our spirituality, our prayer life, our holiness begins with the astounding truth that through and in Christ we share intimately in that inner life of God. "As the Father loves me so I love you," said Jesus. He prayed "that they may be one as you, Father, are in me and I in you. . . I in them and you in me that they may be perfectly one." (See chapters 15 and 17 in the Gospel of John.)

Thus, easier to understand than their eternal "function" with each other may be the function of the divine Persons in our behalf: The Word made flesh revealing the unfathomable life of the Father, with the Spirit, as Paul says, the binding force uniting us to each other and to them in eternal love.

As for the rest of your question, perhaps all we can say here is that God usually seems to adapt his revelation to our human condition. He generally gives us only what we can handle at one time, even if it did take eons, including nearly 2,000 years of "old covenant" to prepare us for the main event. After all, we believe that because of the eternal "present moment" with which God sees all past, present and future, the saving grace of Jesus Christ was already at work in the hearts of the very first human beings. So, at least from this viewpoint, what was the hurry?

Where does evil come from?

The creation hymn of Genesis where God creates the world informs us that God surveyed the cosmos and saw "it was very good" (Gn. 1:31). How is it that all creation proceeded (proceeds) from the Creator, and yet is evaluated as both good and evil? It seems that everything that comes from God should be good. Wouldn't all created things be basically good?

Your question takes us to the heart of one of the foundational theological statements in this creation story.

These Genesis stories were formed within a strongly monotheistic Hebrew people, who lived among cultures with vastly different beliefs and theologies. One of these differences centered on the problem of evil. Every people in history who wrestled at all with spiritual concerns has asked the question: How do we explain the presence of evil, hurt, alienation in the world?

Every sane human being claims to want only peace, harmony, love and goodness. Yet, put two of us in the same room for long, or two nations on the same earth, and you soon have misunderstanding, viciousness, hatred and killing. How does one explain that?

The most common explanation, outside of "one God" religions like Christianity, Judaism and Islam, has been some form of dualism. There are out there somewhere, so this belief goes, two powers or gods, one good and one bad, (sometimes several of each) always struggling with each other for dominance or control. The good god is the source of happy situations, so we placate him, pray to him and sacrifice to him. The bad god causes all evil, so we placate him too, in order to minimize his bad intentions toward us.

All this may sound bizarre, but it's true, and in fact is still present in our world. Many of our own responses to God as Christians carry echoes of this kind of thinking about God our Father, precisely one of the attitudes toward God which Jesus came to correct with his "good news."

From our knowledge of contemporary religious outlooks at the time the book of Genesis was formed, we know that one great purpose of these stories was to place Hebrew belief in one God over against the beliefs of their neighbors. When God created the world, he didn't fight or hassle with any other god as the pagans believed. He simply said: "Let it be," and it was. Furthermore, when this world came from his creative will it was "good" to its core, all good, and finally as you say, "very good."

Then where, according to this Hebrew story, did moral evil, human evil, come from? It came not from God, but from us! The one God loved us enough to want us able to respond to that love, and so gave us a free will. We are able to say yes to God, or no. And all our hurt, all moral evil, comes from the fact that we, all of us, out of selfishness and pride deep within, occasionally and to some degree, do say no in our hearts and with our lives.

This is the Genesis lesson about good and evil. The world, the cosmos and every corner of it, comes from the hand of a God who can make nothing bad. In other words, we cannot look outside for someone to blame for our troubles, although we persist in doing that.

Adam, which means in Hebrew "the man," and his wife turned their backs on the Friend with whom they walked and talked in the cool of the evening. They refused to accept the realities of creation, and thought they could be "like gods" (3:5). As God told Cain after the death of Abel, sin is a demon lurking at your door and you must master it (4:7).

Imprimaturs

Most books written by Catholics and dealing with religious subjects used to have an "imprimatur." Now I see many which do not. Has there been a change? If so, what does an imprimatur mean today? Which books have them?

A clear change has occurred recently in the church's understanding of an *imprimatur*. For a long time an imprimatur (Latin for "it may be printed") was given, usually by a local bishop, to declare the book or pamphlet was free of doctrinal or moral errors. Normally accompanying it was a *nihil obstat* (Latin: "nothing stands in the way"), a statement by someone versed in theology, meaning basically the same thing. Neither the imprimatur nor the nihil obstat implied agreement with the content or opinions, merely that nothing in the writing contradicted Catholic doctrine.

In recent years the Vatican has changed the understanding of an imprimatur. In 1983 and 1984, for example, in connection with the removal of the imprimatur from a book of introduction to the Catholic faith, the Sacred Congregation for the Doctrine of the Faith (CDF) made clear that an imprimatur was only required for books not only theologically correct, but having a methodology rendering them suitable as catechetical texts. The imprimatur, in that particular case, should be removed, the CDF wrote to the archbishop of Newark, N. J., "since even a (theologically) corrected version would not be suitable as a catechetical text." (March 29, 1983)

Early in 1985 the CDF repeated its concern for methodology in catechetical texts in granting imprimaturs. This is one reason many recent books dealing with Catholic spirituality, morals and doctrine do not carry an imprimatur. An example of this change is the book you are now reading. Since it is not a text formally organized for systematic catechetical instruction, church officials in several parts of the country recommended that a *nihil obstat* and imprimatur were not necessary or appropriate. Previous editions, substantially the same as this, did have both. Uncertainty remains today over the exact nature of an imprimatur and which books may or must have one.

Writings found by archeologists

Several years ago I read that Jewish archeologists discovered evidence of writings related to Jesus dating from the first century. These were to be released later, but I've heard nothing on the subject since. What might these be?

During the past few decades, archeologists have discovered numerous writings apparently dating from around the time of our Lord. To my knowledge, however, none of them deal in any explicit way with Jesus and his life, unless they are documents already familiar to historians.

Throughout Christian history, considerable attention and respect was naturally afforded anything that would enlighten us about Jesus. Full texts of many documents have been handed down in other writings, even though the original has never been found. Some modern discoveries seem to give us parts of some of these documents, but contain nothing specifically about Jesus that we did not already know.

Texts of the Dead Sea Scrolls, discovered after World War II in the southern part of the Holy Land, speak of a Teacher of Righteousness. Certain scholars conjectured at first that this teacher might be Jesus, or at least a man closely connected with him. Experts now agree that this is not so. The Teacher of Righteousness, whoever he was, died some decades before our Lord, and apparently had no more connection with him than any of the other holy men living in first century B.C. Palestine.

Church's stand on astrology

Could you clarify the stand of the Catholic Church on belief in and use of astrology? Many of us have become confused lately about our church's position.

On the subject of astrology, it is helpful to keep a few facts in mind. From ancient times until only about 200 years ago, the study of the influence of stars and planets on human activity was treated as a genuine, legitimate science. Many great names in physics and astronomy, like Copernicus and Galileo, believed in it, taught it, and practiced it by casting horoscopes.

Most political and religious leaders, including popes, governed much of their activity by horoscopes. Pope Julius II set the day of his coronation according to the advice of the astrologers.

All this was possible because of their limited knowledge of the heavens. As the science of astronomy developed in modern times — particularly after the invention of the telescope — the discovery of thousands of new planets, stars and other objects in space caused the collapse of astrology as a science. The entire supposed "system" fell apart.

The church officially opposes astrology because of two dangers. If the stars governed all mankind's actions, free will would be meaningless. Also, some claimed that the power of Satan and other evil spirits was behind this astrological influence, and that astrology was therefore the devil's way of infiltrating human life.

These concerns remain at the base of whatever reservations the church has about astrology and of its warning that it can involve sinful superstition.

In spite of the array of inconsistencies and contradictions contained in astrology, more than a few people are getting rich because it still fascinates millions. Maybe they're only curious. Or maybe they're just anxious to discover somewhere "out there" the cause of their problems.

Should we give to "panhandlers"?

The New Testament says we should give to anyone who asks. There are a lot of panhandlers in the city where I live. But I would rather give to charities that help the poor and homeless and to the missions. I'm under the impression that some who ask for money spend it on liquor. I want to give where it will do the most good. Am I obliged to give to everyone that asks?

We need to consider some basic Christian truths when confronting these situations. We give to those in need because, as you say, we are obliged to by our Lord. The poor and the hungry are Christ, he told us, and what we do for them, we do to and for him.

Furthermore, any graces God gives us are to be used, not saved up for a more ideal situation that better fits our views. The opportunity to assist someone in need is such a grace. When grace-filled invitations present themselves, it's not wise to tell God this is not exactly what we had in mind. We need to do the best we can and not wait for something better. If there is a next time, and there may not be, the graces and gifts to do what God wishes us to do will be there when that time comes. And it may be another "panhandler."

If we're always determined to be "safe" in what we give, probably not many chances will come our way. It's usually hard, often impossible, to know for sure where our help "will do the most good." Even charitable and missionary organizations cannot guarantee everything will be perfect, that only "deserving" people (whatever that means) will benefit from our gifts. Jesus does not ask us to sit in judgment of the lives of those who come to us for help. Maybe some of the desperate and destitute people we see need a bit of wine more than they need other things.

In any case, while we should use some common sense, appropriate use of what we give is not ours to judge; it is a concern between the recipient and God. Our task is to respond generously to the graced opportunity when it stands in front of us.

On a personal note, I have often and honestly attributed much of whatever good has happened in the parishes I have served to the fact that we tried never to turn anyone away who asked for help, but to give what was possible, even if sometimes only a kind word. Such an attitude is possible and, I truly believe, greatly rewarding for all of us. I'm glad you are exploring the best way to do this. God wonderfully blesses such efforts.

A Catholic position on humanism?

A friend of mine in college says that humanism is the answer to all human relations. Someone else said it is pure existentialism, unChristian and unCatholic. Our study club had quite a violent argument about the meaning of existentialism, and for that matter, humanism. Is there a Catholic position on humanism? What does it mean?

Both existentialism and humanism have a rainbow of meanings; some are compatible with Christian beliefs and some are not. Fundamentally, however, existentialism may be described as a form of humanism, so let's limit ourselves to that second word and its meaning.

Humanism is basically the belief or philosophy that the greatest good of man is the perfection of himself as a human being. All good, all morality, according to this idea, is simply what will make a man or woman more perfectly human, more able to be whole in their knowing and loving and feeling.

Put that way, there is nothing unChristian about humanism; it is solid Catholic doctrine. Pope Paul VI said in his encyclical, The Development of Peoples, in all the church's labors for truth and justice "what must be aimed at is complete humanism. . . the integral development of the whole man and of all men." St. Irenaeus was, I believe, the first to say, "The glory of God is man fully alive."

This is echoed in the Vatican Council II decree, The Church in the Modern World, in which hope is seen for mankind because "we are witnesses of the birth of a new humanism, one in which man is defined first of all by his responsibility toward his brothers and toward history." (no. 55)

This kind of humanism, therefore, is not only permissible, it is essential if the human family is to develop on this earth in a healthy manner.

On the other hand, some brands of humanism, in the past as well as today, view the works and goals of the human family without regard to any relationship to a Creator, to a Savior, to a life beyond this world. This view of men and women is opposed to Christian beliefs, and often has been explicitly condemned by Catholic and other Christian authorities.

Shalom

We recently received a plaque for our home with the word Shalom. We've seen it often, even in church, but what does it mean?

Shalom is the Hebrew word for peace. At least this is the way it is usually translated, but there really is no English word that carries its rich meaning. The word means completeness or wholeness, a situation in which everything is there that should be there, and in proper order and balance. It could refer to an individual or a group.

Shalom is considered one of God's greatest gifts, and the word was (and still is) used commonly among Jews as a greeting or expression of good wishes. It would have been the word Jesus used at the Last Supper: Shalom (peace) I give to you, my shalom I leave with you. Or when he greeted his apostles on the evening of the resurrection: Shalom — peace be with you.

"Pagan" feast?

Why do so many Catholic theologians make us believe that great Christian feasts are really just pagan feasts that the church took over? Now I read (in an article on Lent) that Easter is connected with pagan celebrations and that the name of the feast is from a pagan god.

The reasons for celebrating our major feasts when we do are many and varied. In general, however, it is true that they often have at least an indirect connection with pre-Christian feasts celebrated about the same time of the year — feasts centering around the harvest, the re-birth of the sun at the winter solstice (now Dec. 21, but Dec. 25 in the old Julian calendar), the renewal of nature in spring, and so on.

Our Easter is directly related to the Jewish feast of Passover which our Lord and his disciples celebrated shortly before his death. In turn, Passover, which is a joyful festival of freedom and hope, was probably celebrated in the spring not only because it was naturally appropriate, but particularly as the Jewish version of similar spring feasts celebrated by the pagans around them, and in which they were forbidden to participate.

The name Easter may have come to the Christian liturgy by way of an old Teutonic word for dawn, *eostarum*. However, from the time of St. Bede, the sixth century church historian, the more popular explanation is that the word comes from the name of the Anglo-Saxon goddess of spring, Eastre.

Who can distribute ashes?

We moved to another and smaller parish several months ago. On Ash Wednesday we were surprised that lay people distributed ashes. Shouldn't only priests do this? The lay people were some who usually help give Communion.

Most Catholics would be as surprised as you, since few parishes have used lay ministers for bestowal of ashes up to now. In a response to the American Bishops' Committee on the Liturgy, dated Jan. 30, 1975, the secretary of the Congregation for Sacraments and Divine Worship indicated that "Extraordinary (eucharistic) ministers cannot bless the ashes but may assist the celebrant in their imposition, and even, if there is no priest and the ashes are already blessed, impose them himself."

Deacons also may assist in giving ashes, even though they are not mentioned explicitly in this response. The response would provide also for other lay persons to help distribute ashes if there is pastoral need.

Many pastors are reluctant to ask their lay eucharistic ministers to assist with the ashes, partly I suppose out of concern for the sensibilities of their parishioners who, as you, would find it startling.

But it is allowed. Possibly the explanation in your case is that you are in a smaller parish; if there are fewer priests than in your previous parish (perhaps only one), it may be necessary for your pastor to utilize the assistance of lay ministers more often. This need will doubtless increase with the decreasing number of priests in coming years.

Date of Easter

The dates for Lent and Easter change all the time. Who determines when these feasts will be celebrated each year?

Though there is some divergence in parts of the Christian world, our celebration of Easter is on the first Sunday after the first full moon following the vernal equinox. The vernal equinox, which we ordinarily refer to as the first day of spring, is on or about March 21.

The dates for Lent, Ascension and Pentecost are determined by counting backward or forward from the date of Easter.

Lent and the Sacred Triduum

Could you please tell us when Lent officially ends now? Is it after the Holy Saturday Vigil Mass?

Lent now ends on Holy Thursday. Those of us who are older will recall that for a long time Lent ended at noon on Holy Saturday. This happened because the great liturgies of Holy Thursday and Holy Saturday were twisted out of shape and were celebrated in the morning of those days.

Before this, the long tradition of the church was that the Sacred Triduum (literally the sacred "three days") formed a separate holy time between Lent and the beginning of the Easter season.

Now, the Mass celebrating the institution of the Eucharist again takes place on Holy Thursday night, and the Easter Vigil is back where it traditionally belongs, during the night between Holy Saturday and Easter Sunday.

The General Norms for the Liturgical Year and Calendar, promulgated by Pope Paul VI in 1969, state: "Lent lasts from Ash Wednesday to the Mass of the Lord's Supper exclusive" (no. 28).

In other words, Lent ends before the Mass on Holy Thursday evening. The Triduum itself begins with the evening Mass on Holy Thursday and reaches its high point in the Easter Vigil, which begins the Easter season.

The Easter Vigil

Our parish puts heavy emphasis on Holy Saturday, so much so that it seems to overshadow Easter Sunday. Is Holy Saturday a more important day in the church than Easter? If so, why?

To understand my response, it is essential to realize that any Catholic born before the 1950s grew up during a period when the church's Holy Week liturgy had deteriorated almost beyond recognition. We are now beginning to get back to what it was, and always should have been.

Easter was the earliest feast celebrated in the church, since it celebrated our Lord's victory over death. The main, often the only, celebration of this feast was during Holy Saturday night, the night of the resurrection, what we now know as the Easter Vigil Liturgy. That night, with the lighting of the Easter candle and other lamps, the reading of the scriptural stories of God's revelation of his love, the baptism of new Christians and celebration of the Eucharist, was the perfect way to enter the joy of Easter.

As time went on, for a variety of reasons, this and many other magnificent liturgical treasures of our church became all but forgotten. For the Easter Vigil, the low point came during the past few hundred years, including the first half of this century. Prompted partly by the fact that Masses could not be offered after noon, the glorious celebration of the Easter Vigil was compressed into an hour or two early on Holy Saturday morning, with the priest reciting all the Scripture readings and blessings by himself in Latin, and then a simple Mass, much like any other weekday Mass of the year.

With no exaggeration, it was a caricature of what once was and now is gradually becoming again the high point of our Christian liturgy, the supreme act of worship of the year. In that situation, with the

Easter Vigil gone, the Sunday morning Masses were, of course, the only Easter Masses.

Starting years before Vatican Council II, the church realized the time had come to restore the Holy Week liturgies, with the Easter Vigil as the top priority. Now this central celebration of our Lord's resurrection is again taking its place as the focal liturgy of the year; all others either lead up to it or are built upon it.

I hope you can see, then, that the Easter Vigil Service is not a "Holy Saturday Mass." It is the Easter Mass and celebration *par excellence.*

Priests are sometimes amused or saddened by people who ask, "Does the Easter Vigil Mass count for Easter Sunday?" The answer is that the Easter Vigil celebration is the first and main Eucharist of the entire Easter season. All others, including those on Easter Sunday morning, only continue the celebration that begins on that holy night.

I hope you take the opportunity to share in that liturgy next Easter. If your parish does it at all well, you'll begin to realize what the church has been missing for too many centuries.

INRI — IHS

What do the letters INRI stand for on the top of the crucifix? Sometimes the letters are IHS. I've been told that means "I have suffered." Is this true?

The Gospel of John (19:19) tells us that Pilate placed an inscription on the cross of Jesus which read, "Jesus of Nazareth the king of the Jews." The other Gospels have a similar passage.

The letters you indicate are an abbreviation for those words, which in Latin are *Iesus Nazarenus Rex Iudaeorum.*

The symbol IHS is the first three letters, *iota, eta* and *sigma,* of the name of Jesus in Greek. This symbol was used long before the English language developed, so it could not have been an abbreviation for English words.

Skull and crossbones crucifix

At the bottom of my crucifix is a skull and crossbones. Why are these on a crucifix?

The Gospels of Matthew, Mark and John give the name of the place of crucifixion as Golgotha, an Aramaic word which all three translate as the Place of the Skull. Luke, in his narration of the passion and death of the Lord, identifies the place by the Greek word for skull, *kranion*. Latin translations of Scripture continued the tradition by naming the place *Calvaria*, Latin for skull, which eventually gave us our English "Calvary."

Various reasons for the name have been proposed through the years. Perhaps one of the most likely comes through the great scripture scholar Origen (died 254), who recounts a legend that our Lord's death took place on the spot were Adam was buried. No evidence exists for such a theory, but the story seems to have inspired the skull and crossbones in many Christian depictions of the crucifixion.

Understanding heaven, hell, purgatory

Belief in the resurrection of the body is central to Christian faith. I know it refers to a "spiritual body," but could you explain this belief in light of what Pope John Paul II has said. According to him, heaven and hell are states of being, not physical places, generally downplaying the terrors of hell. The Catechism of the Catholic Church, *however, which the pope introduces as "a sure norm for teaching the faith," takes the traditional approach that says heaven is a "place" (no. 326) and that the teaching of the church affirms the existence of hell (no. 1035). How can these two viewpoints be reconciled?*

We find here another of those occasions when our Holy Father challenges us to take a fresh and thoughtful look at what we say we believe. When we hear key words of our faith, we often pay more attention to familiar and popular images than to the doctrines themselves. "Heaven," "purgatory," and "hell" are all strongly evocative words for Christians. A little reflection should warn us to be cautious, however, about the pictures and ideas these words inspire.

What Pope John Paul II has done is make explicit what has been implicit all the time. Does anyone really believe, for example, that heaven and hell are places in our ordinary sense of that term? Are they somewhere out in material creation on an unknown planet? In a galaxy on the other side of a distant black hole?

The same must be said for purgatory. It is not a "place," he explained, but a "condition" of purification for the saved whereby Christ "frees them from their imperfections." As the catechism says, purgatory is a process of purgation, of cleansing.

The Gospel stories of his appearances and actions after the resurrection make clear that the risen Jesus (as we will in our risen bodies) exists in a frame of space and time outside our normal experience. He did not physically dash in and out of human perception with the speed of light. He simply was not there, visible and touchable, then he was there.

Interestingly, the catechism references you give imply that we need to walk carefully here. When it says heaven is a "place," it puts the word in quotation marks, indicating that, in this context, it does not have its usual meaning. Similarly, in the words of the catechism, the condition of self-exclusion from communion with God is what we call "hell."

As for the graphic biblical descriptions of heaven and hell, John Paul II repeats the best long-standing Scripture scholarship when he says the symbolic and metaphorical language we find in the New Testament attempts to put into human words the reality of eternal "joyful communion with God," or "the complete frustration and emptiness of a life without God."

Far from downplaying the terrors of damnation, he contends that "the situation in which one finds himself after freely and definitively withdrawing from God, the source of life and joy," can only be approached figuratively with images like "inextinguishable fire" and "the burning oven."

Are any human beings (Judas? Hitler? Stalin?) actually in this condition of eternal separation? As he has in the past, the pope reminds us that this "remains a possibility, but is not something we can know."

We would do well, it seems to me, to dwell more on the conclusion Pope John Paul draws from seeing heaven and hell not as places of merriment forever or eternal fire, but having or not having "a living personal relationship with the Trinity." We should pay more attention, he suggests, to significant spiritual moments in this life: The pain brought about by sin, the satisfaction we experience in doing good. The happiness and distress of this life are clues to the next.

The suffering caused by sin, he states, is often said to "make life hell," whereas when we enjoy properly "the good things that the Lord showers upon us every day of our earthly lives, we have begun to experience the joy and peace which will be completely ours in the next life." The pope hopes we will all profitably reflect on that truth. These remarks were given by our Holy Father at his Wednesday general audiences on July 21 and 28, and Aug. 3, 1999.

Purgatory and prayers for the dead

You quoted the pope and the Catechism of the Catholic Church *that purgatory is a process (purification) therefore not necessarily a place or location. As evidence that purgatory is a definite place, note our Blessed Mother's words at Fatima in apparitions approved by the church: Lucia (one of those who saw the visions) asked Mary about a friend who had died. Our Blessed Mother said, "She is in purgatory (a place), and she will be there until the end of the world (a duration)."*

You have raised the question: Could that purification take place in the process of death itself, or in an instant after death as our sinfulness confronts the infinite holiness of God? If that were true, all our Masses and prayers would be only for those who are dying at that particular instant. What you and the pope said about purgatory cannot be true.

My purpose when dealing with matters of faith is to explain as clearly, concisely and accurately as possible the traditions and official teachings of the Catholic faith. For this reason, I rarely, if ever, advert to private visions and revelations, simply because they never add to or subtract from what we already know from church teachings or the sacred Scriptures.

This does not mean such revelations cannot be spiritually helpful for some people. It says only that, even for those apparitions and messages which are "approved" by the church (Lourdes and Fatima, for example), it is not necessary for Catholics to believe anything new that was said, or even that the apparitions actually happened. This is not lack of belief that such events can happen. I personally am convinced the two I mentioned, and some others, are authentic appearances of our blessed Mother. We simply need to keep all this in perspective.

The essential fact is that we have all we need for salvation in the Scriptures, the sacraments, and the official teachings of the church through the centuries. As Pope John Paul II noted during his 1983 visit to Fatima, when the church accepts or approves a message such as Fatima, "it is above all because the message contains a truth and a call whose basic content is the truth and the call of the Gospel itself." In other words, the church accepts Mary's call to prayer and penance precisely because that call already sounds in the Gospels. As for specifics, about the nature of purgatory for example, these revelations shed no doctrinally essential light.

Franciscan Father Benedict Groeschel points out in his excellent book, *A Still Small Voice: A Practical Guide on Reported Revelations*, that even the most well-known seers, to whom some persons give almost reverential credence, sometimes contradict each other in "facts" they recount from their visions. Reports, based on their visions, on the time of the death of the Blessed Virgin Mary, for example, vary from 21 years after the death of Christ (Mother Mary of Agreda) to a year and a half (St. Elizabeth of Schoenau) and elsewhere in between. St. Catherine of Laboure, who originated the "miraculous medal" following one of her visions, when confronted with the error of certain of her predictions, admitted she got some facts of the revelation wrong. "This admission of simply 'getting it wrong' on the part of this simple visionary is something we should never forget," maintains Father Groeschel.

About your prayer dilemma, it is no problem. Since all time, past and future, is one present moment to God, all our prayers, whenever they are said, go to a God who is not limited by "when" they happen to be offered. Can you actually imagine God saying, "It's too bad your prayers are late; if you had said them yesterday, or last year, I could have done something about it?" Our prayers and Masses for the living or the dead "go back" over their entire lives, their final illnesses and their entrance into eternity.

Who doesn't get to heaven?

My dad is agnostic and my mother is Southern Baptist. I became a Catholic a few years ago. Recently, we took my mother with us to Mass, then went with her to the Baptist service. After detailing the beauty of the golden streets of heaven, the pastor said, "Some things you won't see in heaven. You won't see Adolph Hitler... You won't see Jeffrey Dahmer." We took offense to that. Who is anyone to tell us who is in heaven and who is not? What is the Catholic Church's position about who goes to heaven and who doesn't?

I'm not sure how that pastor's remarks square with Baptist teaching, but they do not reflect the belief of the Catholic Church, nor, I think, of most other Christian denominations. The church teaches, and always has, that human beings have it in their power deliberately and completely to turn away from God. They can reject his invitation to friendship and life by a radical selfishness which definitively separates them from other people and from God. Thus, hell is theoretically possible for any of us, if we end our lives totally rejecting goodness, rejecting God.

The question is whether any human being has ended life on earth in this condition. We do not know, nor can any human insights or knowledge tell us. Some people are, from our perspective, possibly good candidates, among them maybe Hitler or Stalin or Dahmer or Judas. But the secrets of their hearts are hidden from us, nor do we have a clue about what the grace of Christ might have accomplished in their final moments and hours.

Pope John Paul II movingly speaks of this mystery in his book, *Crossing the Threshold of Hope*. "Can God, who loves man so much," he asks, "permit the man who rejects him to be condemned to eternal torment? The silence of the church is, therefore, the only appropriate position for Christian faith. Even when Jesus says of Judas, the traitor, 'It would be better for that man if he had never been born' (Mt. 26:24) his words do not allude for certain to eternal damnation." (p. 186)

Again, we simply do not know.

Will dogs be in heaven?

Our family dog, which was loved by us all, died recently. Now the children are asking whether dogs and other animals go to heaven. I want them to have peace of mind, and also know God loves them.

It's amazing how children often go to the heart of a theological question. Of course, when we get down to it, we don't really know. I wouldn't be at all surprised to see dogs, and trees and flowers, in heaven.

Heaven is where we will all be perfectly happy. If we really think we need a dog to be perfectly happy, I'm sure God will see that we have one. I don't believe anyone could argue with that.

Questions about what eternal life with the Lord will be like are treated brilliantly and with wide scholarship in the book, *Land of the Living*, by Father James O'Connor (1992, Catholic Book Publishing Company). In his Forward, the late Cardinal John O'Connor speaks of the harmony Christ will bring to that transformed but enduring universe. Explicitly referring to dumb animals, he writes, "If, indeed all things were made 'through him,' and if he is the same yesterday, today and forever, then should it be out of the question that all things will somehow endure?"

While the church has no explicit teaching on your question, that in a nutshell reflects the way most Christians have answered it through the centuries.

What will heaven be like?

In your answer to a mother whose children wondered whether they would have their dog in heaven, you said you wouldn't be surprised to see dogs and trees and flowers in heaven. I thought heaven was just being with God. Will we need more than God to make us happy? I think your answer is misleading.

I think you're leaving out an important truth of faith, that we will share in the resurrection of the body. We know little about what our bodies will be like in their exalted condition after the resurrection. We do know, however, that they will be our bodies — like Christ's, with eyes, ears, mouth, touch, and other senses that are part of our human nature.

If the resurrection means anything, these senses and organs will not be atrophied and useless. Our eyes will see, our ears will hear, our tongue will taste. As Jesus apparently tried to prove to the disciples after he rose from the dead, to deny these things would be to deny the resurrection.

Yet, apart from the human nature of Jesus, God is pure spirit. What then would there be in heaven to hear, feel, taste and touch? True, the essence of heaven is our presence with God. Is it possible, however, that God might even then reveal himself to us in ways similar to, if immeasurably beyond, the ways he reveals himself to us here on earth? After all, even in heaven our minds and wills will still be created minds and wills; we will never know and love God as he knows and loves himself, with one eternally perfect act of comprehension and union.

How then will God reveal himself to us? One thing we do know. Having taken our human nature, he has a tremendous respect for it. It is our best Christian guess that he will use it, all of it, even in heaven.

If this sounds strange, perhaps one reason is that we do not respect and reverence our human nature as much as God does. More than one saint (and theologian) has suggested that one of the great surprises of heaven may be in how many respects it resembles our life on earth, with trees, flowers, smiles — and maybe even dogs.

What happens at the final judgment?

On the last day, at the final judgment, will all our sins be made public to everyone? I am 85 years old and always believed that, but my children tell me they do not. Is this still part of Catholic doctrine?

That is at best a limited and incomplete way to describe Catholic teaching about what will take place at "the end of the world," whatever and whenever that may be. The central truth about the "last judgment" is that Christ will come in his glory, and, as the *Catechism of the Catho-*

lic Church puts it, "in the presence of Christ, who is truth itself, the truth of man's relationship with God will be laid bare."

In other words, we will, as fully as created human nature can do so, see things as God sees them. We will understand, as the catechism says, the fullest consequences of the good things we have done or failed to do in our earthly life.

This awareness can motivate us to conversion, to commit ourselves "to the justice of the kingdom of God," to do our best to live now the kind of life we will hope to have lived when that time comes. But that judgment is not something to panic about or fear. It is not likely that, under this kind of scrutiny, any of us humans will be concerned about what other people think. We will all be too humbled by the majesty and beauty and love of God, too awed by the unimaginable debt we each owe to his mercy and goodness.

This is the real drift of the church's understanding of the "final" event when God "will pronounce the final word on all history. We shall know the ultimate meaning of the whole work of creation and of the entire economy of salvation, and understand the marvelous ways by which his providence led everything toward its final end. The last judgment will reveal that God's justice triumphs over all the injustices committed by his creatures and that God's love is stronger than death." (Catechism 1038-41)

To put it briefly, great truths will be revealed at that time. Our limitations and failures will be a long way from the focus of attention.

Membership in the Knights of Columbus

I would like to know if a man can be a member of the Knights of Columbus if he is divorced. Does it matter any more if a Knight is divorced, even living with someone else?

The Knights of Columbus fraternity desires that its members be Catholic men who are living their religion faithfully in every way. It is not always easy, however, to assure this is happening, especially when the matter is one of personal private conscience.

Your basic question is: Who may be a member of the Knights of Columbus? The regulations of that organization state: "Only practicing Catholics in union with the Holy Spirit shall be eligible to and entitled to continue membership in the order." Another rule asserts that any member who fails to remain a practicing Catholic in union with the Holy Spirit shall automatically forfeit membership in the Knights.

There was a time when those who were known not to have fulfilled their Easter obligation, or who were divorced and remarried, were promptly expelled from the K of C, generally with the consent of the local pastor or chaplain.

After receiving your letter, I asked a spokesman for the Supreme Council of the Knights of Columbus to describe their policy today. He noted that the Catholic attitude has changed considerably in the past two decades, at least in that the church no longer excommunicates those who obtain a divorce and remarry. In fact, the church encourages them to continue the practice of their faith as best they can.

"This more compassionate and hopeful view also has been adopted by most of the Knights of Columbus councils," he said. "There is more concern about bringing the individual back to church and to the sacraments so he indeed will be a practicing Catholic, rather than in rejecting him from our society. One possible exception to the policy would be a case of serious scandal."

National K of C officials have concluded that it is difficult, if not impossible, to establish a hard and fast rule which would govern every case and still be fair to everyone. Consequently, they leave implementation of any penalties to the local grand knight and the chaplain.

Volunteer to help other countries

Does the Catholic Church have a group of missionaries or volunteers working in poor countries? I feel like God is asking me to put aside my worldly ways and help out. How can I get more information?

In my view, the best places to start are with two agencies with enviable records of service to other countries. They are the Catholic Relief Services and the Catholic Medical Mission Board.

You're probably familiar with CRS through the collection taken up around the nation each year for its work. In addition to emergency disaster assistance, it attempts to initiate long-term developments in deprived regions of the world.

CRS maintains offices or local representation in about 70 countries, so it needs a small army of volunteers (and paid workers) of all kinds — skilled and unskilled, professional and nonprofessional. You may obtain more information from the headquarters at 209 W. Fayette St., Baltimore, MD, 21201.

The Medical Mission Board provides medical supplies and offers medical and paramedical personnel for hospitals, clinics and dispensaries in many countries. Not all workers need training specifically in medical care. Write to the director of the Catholic Medical Mission Board at 10 W. 17th Street, New York, N. Y. 10011.

Two publications with helpful information are also available.

One is *Response*, a volunteer directory published by the Catholic Network of Volunteer Service. It lists the purpose, requirements, financial and living arrangements, training expectations and other information for dozens of volunteer programs in the United States and foreign countries, with lengths of service varying from several weeks to several years. The majority have Catholic affiliation; a few are under Protestant or non-denominational auspices. Write to CNVS, 41211 Harewood Road N. E., Washington, D. C., 20017; 800-543-5046.

Another is *Connections*, a publication of the St. Vincent Pallotti Center for Apostolic Development (Box 893, Cardinal Station; Washington, D. C., 20064; phone 202-529-3330). *Connections* carries basically the same information as *Response*. Many listings overlap, but each publication includes programs not in the other. Openings are available to teenagers, senior citizens and everyone in between.

As the presence of these directories indicates, lay volunteers, short and long-term, have become a significant factor in the life of the church today. Every indication is that their importance will continue to grow.

The Pallotti Center and the Catholic Network (and I'm sure there are others as well) deserve our thanks for making this information so readily available to American Catholics and others.

Shroud of Turin

What is the Catholic Church's present teaching about the Shroud of Turin? Is it now accepted as the cloth in which Jesus was wrapped after the crucifixion?

The so-called Shroud of Turin, which bears the image of a human person and is alleged by some to have been wrapped around the body of our Lord, apparently appeared in Europe sometime during the Crusades.

The Archdiocese of Turin has possessed the shroud for centuries. In 1988, officials there authorized a carbon-dating of the cloth by three scientific laboratories, working independently. The tests indicated a 95 percent certainty that the cloth was made between the years 1250 and 1390. These findings have been disputed by other experts, but the Catholic Church has no official position on the origin or age of the shroud.

Index of forbidden books

I am a convert of several years to the Catholic faith. A few days ago a friend mentioned the Index of Prohibited Books. Is there such a list of forbidden books? What does that mean?

Almost from the beginning, the Catholic church has recognized that what people read greatly influences their faith, for good or bad. This is one reason Christian people were always so careful that translations and copies of the sacred Scriptures were as accurate as humanly possible.

Among the most colorful documents we possess from early Christian centuries are letters that flowed between early theologians and saints arguing over the most appropriate translation of a word in the Bible. This concern was then directed toward other writings. The Index of Prohibited Books was later a list of books relating to religion, Christian religion particularly, that members of the church were not to read without sufficient preparation and background.

The Index continued, in one fashion or another, up to our time. Gradually, particularly in the last century, this prohibition against printing, selling or reading certain books was mitigated and now is repealed altogether. The 1983 *Code of Canon Law* contains no provisions for the prohibition of books.

Approval by proper church authorities is still required for certain types of publications, either before or after they are printed. These include mainly editions of the Bible, liturgical and devotional books, and books intended to be used as texts for religious instruction (see CCL 824-828). These provisions are considerably less restrictive than the previous church law. The church today retains the same concerns for the integrity of our faith as in the past. The shift is toward a different understanding of the way church law should reflect that concern.

Ku Klux Klan

A friend of mine from a southern state claims that Catholics are members of the Ku Klux Klan. I thought this was an anti-Catholic group and that Catholics were forbidden to belong.

The KKK was part of the wave of anti-Catholic bigotry which lasted through several decades of the last century in our country. It was one of four or five major "native American" organizations which sprang up after the economic panic of 1819, and reacted to the large immigration of mainly Catholic Europeans.

There have been two major Ku Klux Klan (the name derives from the Greek word *kyklos*, circle) organizations. The first, formed after the Civil War, was an extremist white supremacy organization which at one time involved most whites in the south. Through terror, lynching, torture and other cruelties, the Klan "protected" white people, and opposed all reconstruction efforts of federal and local governments. This Klan finally disbanded about 1877.

The second organization began during and after World War I, inspired by economic, political and social breakdown, and the growing nationalism of that period. It was plainly an anti-black, anti-Catholic, anti-Jew, anti-foreign movement which by the mid 1920s boasted nearly five million members and, in some areas, exercised great political power.

No one has attempted to explain how Christian beliefs and practices can coexist with the policies and activities of the Klan.

Devil worship

Is it possible for someone to be possessed by the devil? Is there a rite of exorcism performed by the priest in such a case? What about the so-called Black Masses? Are they creations of a fiction writer?

The Black Mass is no fiction. For centuries up to and including the present, a central liturgical ceremony of many Satanists, or devil worshipers, has been a parody of the sacrifice of the Mass. Often an attempt is made for these sacrilegious services to obtain and desecrate a consecrated host from a true Mass.

The question about possession is harder to answer. Belief in angels and demons ("fallen angels") is consistent in Christianity since the time of Christ, and existed before that in the Old Testament. The exact nature of these beings, however, is unknown. There is little in church doctrine about them, though it is common teaching that they are intelligent personal beings.

Partly because of the need for more theological study about good and bad angels, many questions remain unanswered about diabolic possession, the physical control of a human being's body by a devil or demon. One thing is certainly true: With the advance of knowledge about psychological and nervous disorders, many strange happenings once attributed to the devil are known to have other possible, natural explanations. In addition, our present awareness of the possibility of mental telepathy (transfer of thought from one mind to another) and telekinesis (mental transfer of physical energy) makes the detection of true possession very difficult.

The rite of exorcism is a series of prayers, blessings and commands used by a priest or bishop to expel evil spirits in a case of possession. This official ceremony is rarely used today, and may be performed only with the permission of the bishop. An effective exorcism is considered by some theologians as perhaps the only sure proof of true diabolic possession.

Diabolical obsession

A review of the book, The Exorcist, *mentioned diabolical obsession. Is it the same thing as possession?*

No. Possession means control or near control of a person's body from the inside, as it were, by an evil spirit.

Obsession is the term traditionally used for a phenomenon experienced by some persons in which individuals are violently molested physically in circumstances that seem to point to evil spirits as the cause. It is more an external than an internal influence.

Gregorian calendar

A religious tract someone gave me contains many insulting things about the Catholic Church, especially about the pope. Most are ridiculous. It says, however, that several hundred years ago, one pope (Gregory XIII) foisted a new calendar on the world out of spite against the Protestants, and to make a feeble attempt to save the declining prestige of the papacy. What about this?

If your reading of this tract is accurate, the resurrection of this old controversy is almost eerie, somewhat like charging that Columbus' claim that the earth is round was only religious propaganda.

In the first century before Christ, Julius Caesar revised the calendar to correct serious errors in the old system. Several centuries later, it became obvious that this Julian calendar also had serious defects. The solar year had been computed at 11 minutes and 14 seconds too long. This doesn't sound like much, but it means a full day every 128 years. By the time of Pope Gregory XIII (who became pope in 1572), the "legal" calendar lagged 10 or 11 days behind true sun time and caused considerable confusion politically, religiously, and of course, scientifically.

A series of efforts to reform the calendar stretching back 200-300 years had failed. So Gregory determined the time had come to act. After consultation with universities and scientists throughout the western world, our present calendar (with leap years, etc.) was developed — including the complete elimination of 10 days in October, 1582. Oct. 5 became Oct. 15.

Most European nations accepted the new calendar at once, but some Protestant governments refused, particularly in Germany and England. They labeled the new arrangement the work of Satan, claiming the pope was preparing a blood bath of Protestants, and even that the end of the world was imminent because of Gregory's fooling around with Mother Nature.

Only vigorous defense of the new calendar by renowned scientists like Tycho Brahe and Johann Kepler gradually brought these opponents to acknowledge that change was necessary and had nothing to do with religious sectarianism.

Today, no civilized person denies that the Gregorian calendar reform constitutes a praiseworthy and significant accomplishment in modern history.

Who was "Bloody Mary?"

Who is the Catholic queen that the "Bloody Mary" is supposed to be named after? At least this was what I was told a few nights ago by some drinking buddies.

You're thinking of Queen Mary of England, who ruled from 1553 to 1558. Twenty years before she took the throne, her father, King Henry VIII, formally rejected the Catholic faith and took most of the country with him.

When she became queen, Mary tried to reverse the process and as part of her severe program, several hundred "heretics" were burned at the stake, most of them peasants. Burning heretics was a popular idea in those days with both Catholic and Protestant governments. History has often referred to this queen as "Bloody Mary," though her primary mistake in the eyes of most countrymen was that she burned the wrong people.

The name was given to the modern drink perhaps because of its color.

Healing on television

What is the Catholic Church's view on miracle services performed on television by many ministers? I know that whenever there is an alleged miracle, the Catholic Church expects much proof before said miracle is claimed authentic. Is this necessary if there is simple faith that God can heal and will heal? Why cannot we accept these healings without all the proof?

The Catholic Church believes that miracles of healing are not only possible, but are much more frequent than many of us suspect. The rite for the sacrament of the anointing of the sick, for example, clearly states the church's prayer and expectations for healings of various kinds as a result of the petitions made by the people of God.

The church is concerned, however, because true miracles (healing or otherwise) are not haphazard, frivolous intrusions by God into nature. As Jesus made clear, miracles are above all signs — signs of our heavenly Father's presence, and signs of his lordship and supreme power over evil. This is why he once told the people, "If you do not believe me, believe the works that I do." His miracles showed that Jesus was the messenger and Son of God he claimed to be.

Experience teaches us that many events can appear to be miracles when they are not. "Mysterious" cures often have non-miraculous physical or psychological explanations. Religious con-men have sometimes staged outright fake "miracles" to establish their religious credentials.

The church therefore intends no disrespect to God or man when it exercises, and suggests, caution in accepting at face value every apparent miracle that comes along. It has too much belief in God's power to allow supposed exercises of that power to be used as entertaining curiosities or religious gimmicks.

Human life in outer space?

Astronomers tell us that in our part of the universe there are millions of stars which, like our sun, have planetary systems which could support life. Assuming that some of them have life forms capable of rational thought, what would be their relationship to salvation as we know it? Did the death and resurrection of Jesus save them, too? I can't imagine Jesus having to die a thousand times, once on each planet.

I can't either. On the other hand, if I didn't know otherwise from faith,

I couldn't imagine God coming to this planet, taking a human form, and dying even once.

About the only claim we can make for sure in such matters is that nothing in Catholic and Christian faith denies the possibility of rational "human-like" creatures in other parts of the cosmos.

God's creative imagination and power is certainly not exhausted by the human realities we experience on this earth. There might be countless other life forms having the faculties necessary to know and love and relate to the Creator in a conscious way. What "salvation" might mean for these creatures we have no clue.

Considering the exuberant generosity with which God seems to shower life of all kinds so lavishly on the world around us, one might be excused for strongly suspecting that this divine extravagance isn't limited to our time and place. Beyond that, any theory about whether or how that might happen is pure speculation.

Some people claim it is typical human arrogance even to question the existence of other conscious life. We cannot be, they say, the only fish in such a big pond. It seems to me that is not a strongly imposing argument. It pretends to know much more about what God expects and receives from his creation, including ourselves, than we will probably ever know this side of eternity. Again, conjectures are fun, but it's good to remember that's all they are.

How did we get B.C. and A.D.?

Would you explain how B.C. (time before Christ) and A.D. (time after Christ) is measured? There seems to be confusion about dates in the Bible and in other events we read about in ancient history.

Keeping track of times and dates in history is more complicated than most people realize. In Old Testament times, most dates were based on a particular ruler or king ("in the 11th year of the reign of King Darius"), or major events such as the Babylonian exile in the sixth century B.C. The religious calendar used by Jews today, supposedly based on the time from the creation of the world, began to be used only about 1,000 years ago. The "date" of creation was computed by adding up all references to years and ages in the Hebrew Bible, especially the book of Genesis.

Early Christians employed a variety of methods to record history. Some used local Greek calendars, some the most common Roman method of dating events from the founding of the city of Rome about 735 B.C. (using initials AUC, probably *anno urbis conditae*). Other

Christians counted years from the supposed date of the birth of Abraham, still others from the schedule of taxation under Emperor Diocletian in the third century.

Our method of dating events from before or after the birth of Christ came as a by-product of attempts to settle the bitter controversy between the Eastern and Western churches over the date of Easter. A Roman monk, Dionysius the Little, began this way of dating in the sixth century. Many historical sources available to us today were unknown in his time, resulting in his setting year one of the Christian era six or eight years later than it should have been.

Thus the birth of Christ took place, according to our calendar, about 7 B.C. It took centuries for the new way of numbering years to be accepted even in the Christian world. The fact that it took hold at all is greatly due to the eighth century historian St. Bede, who utilized this method of dating in his *Ecclesiastical History of the English People* and other historical writings..

Believing in dreams

An article about dreams, in a Catholic magazine, said we should think about our dreams, "befriend" them, and that we would learn much this way. I thought that it was superstition to pay attention to dreams.

To think about our dreams, even to learn something from them, is not sinful. We have ample proof even in the Bible that God uses dreams to help people understand his will for them.

Psychological sciences still cannot tell us very much about where dreams come from, or what makes them happen. It is now widely agreed, however, that reflection on one's dreams, trying to enter into their imagery and moods, and to understand them, can contribute much to a person's self-knowledge, perception of emotions, and what is going on in his or her life. One author, who has written much on the subject of psychology and religion, coined the term "befriend a dream" — which is probably where your article picked it up.

Some persons responsible for formation in religious orders and communities have found that "listening" to dreams, even sharing them simply and nonjudgmentally with another, may be helpful to both persons.

Of course, dreams could be used wrongly, for example if one pretended to tell fortunes from them, or if one allowed himself to become obsessed with a fantasy world. But it would be just as wrong not to accept dreams as a natural, if puzzling, part of life, or to assume that there is automatically something magical, even diabolical, about them.

Can we bless God?

During the Stations of the Cross and other prayers, we say, "We adore Thee, O Christ, and we bless Thee." I can't understand what talent or ability I have to bless Christ. Isn't it wrong to say we bless Christ, or God?

In a way it is wrong. The Latin word *benedicere* usually means to bless in the commonly understood sense, to communicate life or some other good to another. It also, however, may mean to thank someone, or to acknowledge another's power and goodness. The phrase "Blessed be God," for example, which we find often in the psalms and in the New Testament, is a prayer of praise and recognition of the goodness of God, and of the benefits he has bestowed on us. The phrase carries the same meaning in our prayers.

Reincarnation

Please explain the teachings of the church on reincarnation. A friend has questioned me about it, and I'm not comfortable with my answers. I understand some Christian groups believe in a kind of reincarnation and say there's no problem.

The word "reincarnation" means "coming again in the flesh." As you suggest, writings promoted by some groups currently on the Christian scene do sound something like reincarnation. But its not at all clear, to me at least, what they mean.

According to the teachings of several religions or philosophies, particularly in ancient cultures of Asia, all living beings exist in a cycle of deaths and rebirths. This happens to everything, including divine beings, humans, animals and plants. When one life is finished, they return to another form, higher or lower, depending on how they lived their previous existence. This applies in a particular way to human beings. By the law of what Hindus call "karma," one's earthly life does not cease at death. Individuals return in another form, usually unaware of their previous existence, though their new life is radically affected by their failings in the past. This process is believed to lead in some mystical way to the absorption of all being into "absolute reality," which finally will be the only reality there is. All else will be fantasy, an illusion.

These few sentences cannot do justice to an ancient, many-faceted and intricate worldview of a large part of our human family as it searches for answers to life's great questions. Where did we come from? Why are we here? Where are we going? What else is out there? Whence comes evil? How does what we do here affect what comes after? These are the cosmic mysteries people have probed for tens of thousands of years.

If we reflect on even the few words of explanation I give here, the beliefs of these cultures include insights about our human condition that may have value for all of us. This should not surprise us. As Pope John Paul II repeats in his book *Crossing the Threshold of Hope*, speaking specifically of some Asian religions, the Holy Spirit works effectively in cultures and religions even outside the visible structure of the church; the church rejects nothing that is true and holy in these religions. The Spirit uses for good purposes these *semina Verbi* (seeds of the Word), which constitute a kind of root of salvation present in all religions. (pages 80-81)

Just as clearly, however, the doctrine of reincarnation runs contrary to Catholic doctrines such as the immortality of the soul, the final resurrection of each of us, the finality of death, and our personal, conscious responsibility, in cooperation with God's grace, for our definitive destiny after death. For these and other reasons, embrace of reincarnation in any traditional sense of that word is incompatible with Catholic and Christian faith.

Why does God allow worry?

If God loves us, why does he allow people to suffer mental torment and worry? Why are hospitals filled with people who are sick, or who are physical wrecks because of unbearable inhibitions, guilt, lack of self-confidence, loneliness and frustration? This God must be sadistic rather than loving.

In his providence, God has enabled humanity to grow much through the centuries in its capacity to deal with the evils that plague it, including the ones you mention. Advances in sciences of all sorts make possible our management, if not cure, of physical and emotional illnesses that once were mysteries, and perhaps bearers of certain early death. Our first responsibility, then, is to avail ourselves of the care and cure that can help us cope with and heal our hurts.

Your question goes much deeper than that. The most perceptive people in history have wrestled with what is called the "problem of evil" — why is there suffering and evil in the world, and where does it come from? No one has arrived at a totally satisfying answer.

Among the theological issues addressed in the creation story of Genesis is that of the origin of evil. About the only answer it could give is that suffering and pain do not come from God, from whose hand all things are good. Evil arises rather from inside us, from our disobedience and disorientation from the purpose of creation.

Jesus could not remove suffering and death from our human condition, even for himself. For the first time, and for all time, he brought to a pained humanity the promise of meaning, healing and hope in its hurt. But he did not create a new Garden of Eden.

The suffering you abhor would lead us to a sadistic God only if the pain were inflicted by him. It is not. Indeed, God could stop it only by removing our opportunity for free choices, which would mean taking away our potential for love. God allows us to hurt ourselves and does all he can to reduce the hurt and ease the pain (which is what Jesus is all about) because he knows that in the end, the love that grows amidst that pain will make it all worthwhile. Of that, our Lord himself is the supreme proof and assurance.

Display flags in church?

Many churches have an American flag in the sanctuary all the time. I see it less and less, especially in new churches. A priest said he did not think it was permitted, but was not sure. Are there any rules on this?

As older Catholics will remember, display of the American flag in churches became widespread around the time of World War II, when we were encouraged to exhibit the flag in public buildings. Even then, the custom held only in the United States. Catholics in other nations consider display of their national flag in church, at least in the sanctuary, inappropriate and foreign to the spirit of the Eucharist which knows no national or other political boundary. In most churches of Italy, for example, one rarely, if ever, sees an Italian flag.

As for official regulations, first of all, the General Instruction of the Roman Missal, which gives primary guidelines for everything relating to the Mass, does not list flags or other national symbols as among accoutrements to be in the sanctuary area for the Eucharist.

In 1982, the U. S. Bishops' Committee on the Liturgy responded this way to a question similar to yours: "When Catholics assemble for worship, they bring with them their cultural, ethnic and national identities. These traits should not be devalued or denied unless, of course, there is something in them which is truly inimical to the gospel of Christ. Still, the liturgy of the church which is expressed in the various cultures of the people must always reflect a church which is truly Catholic." (See BCL Newsletter, Dec. 1982)

To display the flag or other symbol of our nation and its ideals at the time of major celebrations or holidays is appropriate. As for permanent display, however, though some churches have done it and still do it, there is no authorization and never has been. Whether and how to display the national flag in church is left to the judgment of the local bishop.

Crucifix, with corpus

In non-Catholic churches the crosses do not display the body of Christ. My friends who attend there give me the reason that they believe Jesus is living. We believe he is living, too. When did the Catholic church begin using the crucifix?

The practice of portraying the body of the crucified Lord on the cross began relatively recently — if one can call about 700 years ago recently.

During the first 600 years or so after Jesus' death and resurrection, portraying the body of Christ on crosses was rare. The conviction that the death of Christ was part of the whole paschal, or Easter, event was so deep in the church that heaviest emphasis was placed on the resurrection.

In the fifth and sixth centuries, crosses were adorned with precious jewels for the same reason. In fact, when the body of Christ began to appear more frequently on crosses, it was often the risen living Lord that was shown, rather than the dying or dead Christ that became common later.

Around the 1200s, the passion of Christ became more central in Christian theology and spirituality. Crucifixes graphically displaying the suffering Christ became popular and remained so until our own time.

With today's renewed emphasis on the resurrection and its central place in the history of salvation, something like jeweled crosses and crucifixes with the body of the risen Christ are seen more and more, even in Catholic churches.

Requests from charities

Almost every day we receive requests from at least one Catholic charitable organization. From what we read, we suspect that most of what we give is used up by the fund-raising organizations. We are happy to help, but want the bulk of our donations to go to the charitable purpose we intend.

Your concerns are legitimate in light of numerous questionable groups presenting themselves today as charitable organizations. Even when the organization involved is a highly reputable Catholic community or association, you still like to know what is being done with your money.

When you have these questions, write to the organization itself for more information on how donated money is disbursed. There is nothing wrong, in itself, in enlisting the assistance of fund-raising companies. Their techniques and experience can be helpful, and there is no reason to condemn missionary societies for using other companies to assist them in raising the funds they need. It is your money, however, and you have every right to ask how much of this money is being used for the purpose you believe you are offering it.

Carrying our crosses

Jesus says we are to take up our cross and follow him. Where does this cross come from? Is it God's will for you? Is it man's doing? Or just circumstances?

The crosses which burden each of our lives come usually from three directions. The first and most common are those which result from normal daily living. These may be physical realities, such as illnesses and material disasters of various kinds. Or they may be the burdens of emotional, intellectual and spiritual frailties which cause pain to ourselves and others.

The second source of crosses is hurt done to us, deliberately or indeliberately, by the sinfulness of others, especially by those closest to us.

The third type of cross, which I believe are for most people the heaviest, are those which result from our own sinfulness and infidelities; in other words, from our own (vague perhaps, but nonetheless real) consciousness of having contributed to the lack of harmony and peace in our own and others' hearts and lives.

It is the prevalence and weight of these last crosses which make it necessary for God to insist as often and strongly as he does on the limitless power of his forgiving and healing love. When people deny or doubt that they can ever be forgiven of some particularly hurtful sin or fault, I am convinced that most of the time they really are wondering whether even God can make things right again. It is, I believe, one of the great acts of faith and one of the great steps toward holiness, to trust that he can and will bring about this healing and wholeness.

To answer your questions, any and all of these may be crosses Jesus asks us to take up daily and follow him. They may not be the ones we would choose, or the ones we think "fit" us. But they happen to be ours. And in some way we find they do fit us uniquely, as do the graces we receive to carry them.

The Catholic Abraham Lincoln

I am sending an article from a "Catholic" publication. It claims that Abraham Lincoln was brought up a Catholic, but fell away from the faith because of the influence of some "secret society." They quote bishops who seem to have a little knowledge of the facts, and a pioneer priest, Father St. Cyr. My wife, a distant relative of President Lincoln, does not agree. Is there evidence to support this claim?

Yes, an Abraham Lincoln was Catholic, but the Catholic Lincoln did not become president of the United States. Sources which claim our 16th president was Catholic are confusing him with his cousin, with the same name, who is buried in an obscure pioneer cemetery in central Illinois.

There were at least three Abraham Lincolns. The first, grandfather of the president and of the Catholic Abraham, lived in Virginia. In 1782, he sold his farm, moved the family to Kentucky, and in 1788 was killed by an Indian. This grandfather Abraham had three sons, among them Thomas, father of the president, and Mordecai, who became a convert to Catholicism when he married Mary Mudd, daughter of a prominent Catholic family. Their marriage is on record at Bardstown, KY.

In 1830, Mordecai moved his family — Mordecai Jr., the Catholic Abraham, James, Elizabeth, Mary and Martha — to Hancock County in western Illinois where they and other Catholic settlers founded St. Simon the Apostle Chapel. Mordecai Sr. died shortly after the great snow of 1830-31. Meanwhile, Mordecai's brother, Thomas, married Nancy Hanks, who gave birth to the future president Feb. 12, 1809, in Hodgenville, Kentucky. Nancy died later, and the family moved to Illinois.

There is no record that President Lincoln himself ever joined any church, though he was familiar with and fond of the Bible. (His wife, Mary Todd, attended Presbyterian services in Springfield, Illinois, and in Washington.)

During the 1830s, the pioneer priest Father Irenaeus St. Cyr offered Mass among the scattered Catholic settlements along the Mississippi Valley from St. Louis north to Chicago. Historians have reason to believe his memory became rather hazy in his old age. He spoke of President Lincoln's immediate family, but it seems certain that his recollections were rather of the Catholic Lincolns in Hancock County, where he labored as a well-known early missionary.

I have visited the cemetery where the Catholic Abraham is buried, at the site of St. Simon Chapel, which has long since disappeared. For many years now, the burial plot has been a cow pasture. The tomb of his famous cousin is a short distance away in Springfield.

Chain letters

What should I do with a letter I received? It assures good luck if I say a prayer which was included, make 20 copies and send it to others within 96 hours. It promises good luck if I do what it demands, and bad luck if I don't. The letter says some man lost his wife six days after receiving the letter because he failed to send copies to other people. However, before her death he received $7,750,000.

My religious instinct tells me to throw these things in the garbage, but can you explain why a Catholic would send such a letter?

I can't imagine why anyone, Catholic or not, would send this letter. This particular chain letter, one of dozens forwarded to me during past years, is typical in that it assumes enough people are sufficiently gullible and ignorant to make the game worthwhile.

Most chain letters, even though they are nearly always one hundred percent superstitious, at least make a pass at something that sounds religious. The letter you sent with your question does not even attempt that, apart from the fact that it is "signed" by St. Jude!

If people are naive and uneducated enough to give credence to this type of mail, they probably will not be influenced by anything you or I or anyone else says. Throw such letters away. Only the U. S. Postal Service gains from them.

Halloween and All Saints

One of our children's teachers told her class that Halloween was a religious feast in times past. But there was no explanation. I asked our pastor. He told us it had something to do with the feast of All Saints the next day. Tricks and treats, and dressing up like ghosts seem strange if there is something religious about it.

Halloween does have a connection with All Saints Day. The old English word "hallow" means to make holy or consecrated. As an adjective it means something that is holy or blessed, as in the Our Father, when we say "hallowed be thy name."

Thus, the feast we know as All Saints (Nov. 1) was for centuries called Hallow-Mass, or All Hallow-Mass, the Mass celebrating all the blessed, all the saints.

Halloween is a shortened form of Hallows-Even, the evening before Hallows day. It has been called that for at least 200 years.

How did Halloween become the night disembodied spirits roam the earth? Like many other popular celebrations, for this one, too, we can probably thank the Irish. In the ancient Celtic calendar, Nov. 1 began the new year. As with nearly every culture we know of, including our own, the first day of the new year and the evening before were times of revelry— dancing, singing, games and not uncommonly generally making a fool of oneself. So it was with the Celts. They picked up such partying, even then apparently as part of a religious tradition, including a Hallow Even fire which they inherited from the ancient Druids. As one 19th century writer put it, "Halloween is the carnival time of disembodied spirits."

While Christians have honored the martyrs and other saints from the earliest centuries, no one is sure precisely how the feast of All Saints developed in the Western world.

In more recent years, Halloween has again become connected with the next day's feast, remembering and honoring the "disembodied spirits" we know as the saints, the followers of Christ who have preceded us into eternity.

Among many Catholic people even to this day, especially in countries of Hispanic tradition, the evening before All Saints is a full night of remembrance and prayer at the graves of their dead. In a beautiful and thoroughly Catholic way, in touch with their ancient respect for ancestors who have gone to God, they praise the "hallowed" ones who, as the Eucharistic Prayer puts it, have gone before us with the sign of faith and rest in the sleep of peace.

Parousia, second coming of Christ

What is the church's teaching on when the second coming of Christ will take place? Watching Christian evangelical television, I notice emphasis is placed on the theory that events taking place today bring us close to the end times described in the books of Daniel and Revelation.

They also describe the "rapture of the church," the tribulation period, the defeat of the Antichrist in Armageddon, the second coming of Christ, etc. Is there a Catholic book that addresses itself to this subject?

Yes, there is a good book. It's called the Bible. In it Jesus says very clearly, "You know neither the day nor the hour." According to long Christian tradition, even the rest of the Bible doesn't take us much closer to the answer.

Most of the book of Revelation and a good part of the book of Daniel are made up of a type of literature well known during the century or so before and after Christ, called apocalyptic. Apocalyptic writings contain a wide variety of symbols and visions, many of them quite bizarre, supposedly with veiled occult or divine messages. Often an angel or other messenger is introduced to explain the message, though often the explanations sometimes are hardly more clear than the vision itself. We find all this both in Daniel and Revelation.

It is no exaggeration that groups of Christians have had a field day with all those visions for the past 18 or 19 centuries. In every century, even every generation, one finds movements which make frightening predictions of the end of the world. These come from people who, deliberately or not, play on the emotional shakiness of people who are afraid of the times, perhaps superficial in their knowledge of their Christian faith, people easily convinced that the world has never been so evil, which somehow is supposed to bring about God's vengeance by his burning the earth to a crisp.

The list of these "predictions" in history is almost endless. One example is particularly interesting. Revelation 20:4 speaks of a period of 1,000 years between the first coming of Christ and his return. If some Christians today are still trying to maneuver that figure to refer to the present time, one can imagine the situation when the actual year 1000 was approaching a thousand years ago.

Other predictions may have been wrong, said many "prophets" of the day, but now the real year 1000 is at hand. The world, indeed Christianity itself, is in such a mess, they preached, that the final battle in the valley of Mageddo (Armageddon) between the good and the bad (Rev. 16:16) is imminent.

Obviously they were wrong, as have been a host of others in the centuries that followed.

To answer your question, the church has no teaching about the specific time of the second coming of Christ and the events that might accompany it. It is, in fact, a curiosity-type concern which even Jesus did not seem especially anxious to address, perhaps because it can more easily distract than help us in our daily Christian living in the world.

As I have mentioned before, the end of the world, for which Jesus asked us to prepare carefully and well, is not the day the world burns up, but the day each one of us leaves it.

Lord's Prayer reworded?

A column in a Catholic paper suggested that we change the wording of the Our Father. Isn't the way Christ said it (Matthew 6:9-13) good enough?

I'm afraid you are under several misconceptions concerning the Our Father. First of all, no one knows for sure what exact words our Lord used when he gave us what Christians commonly call the Lord's Prayer. Jesus did not speak English. What we have are translations from the Aramaic that Jesus used, or even translations of translations.

Since any good translation from one language to another involves an interpretation not merely of words but of ideas, the exact wording of something like the Our Father will differ greatly according to who is doing the translating. The various English editions of the Scriptures do differ greatly from each other.

As it is, the form of the Lord's Prayer Catholics are accustomed to is different from the one you refer to in the Gospel of Matthew — and even more different from the form given in the Gospel of Luke (Luke 11:2-4).

Leaders of all Christian churches acknowledge the desirability of a common text, but it's easier said than done. Since all Christians know the Lord's Prayer if they know any prayer, emotional and devotional ties to the words they are accustomed to are very strong.

What is the "kingdom of God"?

My question is about "thy kingdom come" in the Our Father. Those words seem to say the kingdom of God is in the future, at the end of the world, which is what I always thought. However, a priest speaking at our church during Lent said the kingdom is here and now. He quoted Jesus saying the kingdom is among you. Now I'm not even sure I know what the kingdom of God is.

The Gospels, Matthew particularly, speak of the kingdom as a truth which frames and forms our relationship with God here and in eternity.

One difficulty is that the kingdom of God, or kingdom of heaven, is quite a fluid term in the New Testament. Jesus never actually defines it. Rather, he alludes to it with a variety of images and stories that give us something of a multicolored description of what he means.

The kingdom of which Christ speaks is, first of all, not a place, nor is it a static condition, something finally finished here, or perhaps even in the future. God's reign, his loving rule and power over all creation, is active and dynamic, an ongoing reality continually operative in everything he is creating.

Neither is it something new. God has always been Lord of the universe and of the human family, in a specific way of the Hebrew people, who, nevertheless rebelled against him. From the beginning of his public life, Jesus declares that the rule of God continues now; we must reform our lives to recognize his reign and to reestablish the harmony of creation destroyed by sin.

In fact, the core of the good news ("gospel") is that this God whose reign we honor is a gracious, loving, merciful and joyful Father who is revealed in the life and words of his Son — as in the great parables such as those in Luke 15.

Ultimately it is this conviction, that the infinite Mystery surrounding us is a benevolent one, that allows Jesus to urge us to trust, not to be afraid. Whatever happens, we are sure of the Father's presence and power active in the world. As the preface of the feast of the Kingship of Christ puts it, the kingdom he proclaims is one of justice, love and peace. All these are active, on going realities that, at least here, are never totally perfect, always moving toward fuller realization.

The New Testament indicates often that this reigning presence of God is not something we merit or "build." It is his work, a pure gift to his people when they try to live as a community of charity and faithfulness. When we look at it this way, as part of the mystery of God's creating love, perhaps we can understand at least a little how the reign of God will always be here, and always be coming, as long as the Creator continues his work.

The more we are aware of the power of this divine rule among us now and of its continuance in eternity, the greater is our confidence that, in Paul's words, nothing can separate us from the love of God that comes to us in Christ Jesus our Lord.

"For thine is the kingdom..."?

I am a eucharistic minister in a nursing home. In our prayer service I always use the Our Father. One non-Catholic resident who often joins in our prayers asked why we do not add "For thine is the kingdom, the power and the glory forever and ever."

The sentence you ask about — ending the Our Father — began to be used in Christian liturgy very early in the Christian era, probably because similar formulae had been common in Jewish worship for centuries.

Eventually some perhaps overzealous copiers of the Scriptures (this was long before the printing press) began adding these words after the Lord's Prayer in Matthew (6:9-13) as a gloss — a marginal "interpretation" or pious note, inserted sometimes possibly just to break the monotony of a tedious job.

In later centuries many glosses, including this one, found their way into the Bible text itself. This was the situation when the King James Authorized English translation was published in 1611. Since this version of Scripture was in general use by Protestants for more than 300 years, and since it included this one-sentence addition to the Lord's Prayer, the addition became part of what is often called the "Protestant Our Father."

As scholarship developed, however, it became clear to all that this addition was not really part of Scripture, but was inserted afterward. Therefore, Protestant Bibles after the King James version, including the most recent, have eliminated the sentence from the Scripture text, mentioning it at most in a footnote as an unauthentic addition to the biblical text.

Bible translations under Catholic auspices never included the sentence. Thus, since it is not actually scriptural, it has not been part of the "Catholic" Our Father.

We do, of course, continue the ancient liturgical tradition even today by saying this prayer of praise together at Mass shortly after the Our Father. Oriental rite Catholics and other Catholic cultures around the world still use it regularly.

Does God tempt us?

How do we explain the words in the Lord's Prayer, "Lead us not into temptation?" Surely God does not try to lead us into sin.

You are right, of course. The Letter of James in the New Testament says clearly, "God is not subject to temptation to evil, and he himself tempts no one" (1:13).

That section of the Lord's Prayer seems to be a mistake in translation which has persisted in English Bibles, both Protestant and Catholic, for hundreds of years. It's not possible to explore here why the change occurred, but more correct translations began to appear only in the 1960s.

The (Protestant) *New English Bible* reads "the test" instead of "temptation." The (Catholic) *New American Bible* now has the words "do not subject us to the final test" in both Matthew (6:13) and Luke (11:4). These and other recent translations of the Lord's Prayer in the Gospels are somewhat closer to the real meaning.

The *Catechism of the Catholic Church* gives an enlightening explanation of this text in its commentary on the Our Father. It acknowledges first of all that no one English word, like "temptation" or "test," can convey the rich meaning of the Greek word. In this sixth petition of the Lord's Prayer, we ask God to keep us from the way that leads to sin, to help us unmask the lie in every temptation whose object appears to be good, but in reality leads to death.

In other words, Christ unites us here with his battle against evil and his agony, and urges us to the vigilance that keeps our hearts in communion with his (catechism 2846-2849).

Does God determine time of death?

Do Catholics and other Christians maintain that God determines, or merely knows, when an individual will die? At funeral Masses, the priest has said the person's death at this time was God's will. It seems then that God does determine the time of death.

On abortion, however, the church seems to say the opposite. The idea that these children can, in fact, be saved suggests God does not decide when life will end. If he did, then would not the aborted baby have died anyway?

God's will could work in different ways. He could decide everything on the spur of the moment, choosing whatever seems likely to make someone happy. That might make all creation rather haphazard and unpredictable, but I suppose it is possible. In the real world that exists, however, God's will is most manifest in the way he created this universe, how he makes it "work." Every movement of every galaxy and every subatomic particle, and everything in between, takes place within the framework of God's creative order and harmony.

The inventor of the gasoline engine created nothing new. He merely discovered (uncovered) something that was there all the time, but we didn't know it. If you combine carbon atoms with atoms of other elements, put the result under pressure and ignite it, the mixture will explode and expand to move an engine's piston.

All creation is like that. Cancer cells and the AIDS virus are disastrous for us, but when they destroy parts of our bodies, they are only acting according to their nature. Like gasoline molecules, they are doing what their created makeup says they should do. Cancer research, in fact, is based on the expectation that specific molecules and cells will act in a certain way. Scientists look to find the secret of exactly what that way is, and then introduce other substances whose makeup is such that they attack and hopefully destroy the cancer.

We're not used to thinking about the earth this way. But God's will, for humans and for everything else, is established by his creating the universe as he did. It may sound unfeeling to put it this way, but when a moving train hits a human being, God does not step in at that moment to decide it's time to die. Whatever tragedy happens is just reality. It's what naturally happens when two such bodies collide.

As I said, God could, if he wished, involve himself directly in every event that takes place in creation and manipulate cancer cells, for instance, so they don't destroy one's ovaries or liver. He doesn't do that, however, at least routinely. It would destroy all predictability in nature, all possibility of knowledge and intelligent use of the things around us on earth.

Here especially, it seems to me, we need a lot of humility. We acknowledge that while great personal tragedies and calamities cause us terrible pain, we come to accept, and believe, that God's ways of placing equilibrium and harmony in our world is for our greatest good and happiness, while we are here and after we leave.

What I have said points to the real evil that lies beneath all killing. Whether unborn infants, the old and sick, or the convicted criminal, to deliberately, unnaturally and violently end a human life is a dreadful violation of God's providential will for each of us. That will is not capricious or fickle. It permeates, and is disclosed by, the creation he has given us to live in.

Are miracles possible?

Doesn't your explanation of God's will imply we should simply sit back and take what comes? Shouldn't we sometimes even pray for miracles?

Miracles, wondrous events that mysteriously but unmistakably preclude all natural explanation, are always possible. And we can pray for them. It is, after all, still God's world, and his continual recreation. Lourdes and some other shrines offer countless instances of remarkable events that contradict all medical and scientific expectation of what "ought" to happen. Withered arms and legs become healthy and whole overnight. Carcinomic neoplasms that should inevitably be fatal disappear instantaneously.

These are without question God's doing. To seek such blessings in prayer is a sign of Christian faith and hope.

It remains, however, that miracles or instant interventions into the workings of the world, are not God's usual ways. As the Genesis creation story tells us, God looked at what he had made and declared it good, very good. He was wonderfully satisfied. As far as we can tell, it is the same Wisdom that gave existence to this infinitely complex universe that allows it to live and breathe and act according to the "laws" he placed there in the first place.

Voluntary evil human actions, when human beings do inhuman, wicked harm to each other, are another question. As with the rest of creation, when we act against what human nature was created to be, bad things happen not because God decrees a punishment, but simply because sin, evil, is destructive. How God's knowledge and will mesh with human free will in all this is a mystery I don't think anyone has, or perhaps even can, satisfactorily unravel.

Body, blood of Christ?

We believe that during the Eucharistic Prayer of the Mass, the bread and wine each become the body and blood of Christ. Why then do eucharistic ministers say "Body of Christ" when ministering the host, and "Blood of Christ" when ministering the cup? Why not just "Body and Blood of Christ"? The present practice can lead people to believe that the bread is the body only, and the wine the blood only.

I believe most Catholics are sufficiently grounded in their eucharistic faith not to be confused by the words of the Communion ministers. The way they readily accept the host and the cup, separately or together, as the body and blood of the Lord is proof enough of that. You do raise a significant point, however, concerning our Lord's intention and graciousness in giving the Eucharist as the food and drink which forms us into the Body of Christ on earth.

For at least the first 12 centuries of Christianity, people regularly received Communion under both kinds, bread and wine. It was assumed that this is the fullest response to our Lord's command to eat his flesh and drink his blood. (John 6:53) For reasons too complex to discuss here, by the 13th and 14th centuries Communion with bread alone became increasingly common. The sacrament was received less and less often, until even men and women religious considered once a year more than sufficient.

This later prompted some leaders of the Reformation to contend that Communion under the form of bread alone was invalid, since Jesus said we must eat his body and drink his blood. In reaction, Catholic authorities discouraged, even forbade, Communion with both forms, to emphasize that Christ is wholly present under each species, bread and wine.

The custom continued until Vatican Council II, when the bishops of the world restored the practice of Communion under two species, and recommended instruction explaining, among other things, how Communion with both bread and wine better reflects Catholic eucharistic theology and spirituality. The "one bread and one cup" we share make us into, and declare that we are, the Body of Christ.

St. Augustine, in an Easter homily about the year 410, spoke movingly of this function of the Eucharist in Christian life. "This bread," he said, "is the body of Christ, to which the apostle (Paul) refers when he addresses the Church: 'You are the body of Christ, and his members.' That which you receive, you yourselves are by the grace of the redemption, as you acknowledge when you respond Amen." In other words, according to Augustine, the Amen we say at Communion proclaims first of all that we are the Body of Christ, as we receive and are formed into Christ by his Eucharistic Body.

The American Bishops' Committee on the Liturgy (BCL) gives this as the reason ministers of the Eucharist do not say, "This is the body of Christ" or "This is the blood of Christ," but simply "The body of Christ" and "The blood of Christ."

It seems perhaps a trivial difference, but it expresses a remarkable reality of faith. What we receive in Communion, we ourselves already are, the Body of Christ, a truth we acknowledge when we respond with our Amen. (*The Body of Christ*, BCL, 1977, pages 22-23)

While, therefore, the eucharistic bread and wine are each the entire living Christ, together they recall more explicitly and symbolically the words of Jesus: This is my body given for you, and my blood shed for you. The words of the eucharistic ministers before Communion reflect that truth.

Belief in Santa Claus

My question isn't very deep, but with Christmas coming, I am concerned about the attitude of some friends who don't want their children to "believe in Santa Claus." From almost infancy, they tell their children there isn't really a Santa, that it was all made up to sell more things at Christmas time. I think they're missing something, but I'm not sure how to tell them. What do you think?

I too think they're missing something, very big. It's always risky to analyze fantasies, but maybe it's worth trying for a moment. Fantasies, perhaps especially for children, are critical ways of entering a world, a real world that is closed to us in ordinary human language and happenings. They are doors to wonder and awe, a way of touching Something otherwise out of our reach. Santa Claus, I believe, is like that.

No one has expressed this truth more movingly and accurately, in my opinion, than the noted British Catholic author G. K. Chesterton, in an essay years ago in the London *Tablet*. On Christmas morning, he remembered, his stockings were filled with things he had not worked for, or made, or even "been good" for. The only explanation people had was that a being called Santa Claus was somehow kindly disposed toward him.

"We believed," he wrote, that a certain benevolent person "did give us those toys for nothing. And... I believe it still. I have merely extended the idea.

"Then I only wondered who put the toys in the stocking; now I wonder who put the stocking by the bed, and the bed in the room, and the room in the house, and the house on the planet, and the great planet in the void.

"Once I only thanked Santa Claus for a few dolls and crackers; now I thank him for stars and street faces and wine and the great sea. Once I thought it delightful and astonishing to find a present so big that it only went halfway into the stocking.

"Now I am delighted and astonished every morning to find a present so big that it takes two stockings to hold it, and then leaves a great deal outside; it is the large and preposterous present of myself, as to the origin of which I can offer no suggestion except that Santa Claus gave it to me in a fit of peculiarly fantastic goodwill."

Are not parents of faith blessed countless times over to have for their children (and for themselves) such a fantastic and playful bridge to infinite, unconditionally loving Goodness, the Goodness which dreamed up the Christmas event in the first place?

Call Santa Claus a myth or what you will, but in his name parents and, for that matter, all of us who give gifts at this special time of the year, are putting each other in deeper touch with the "peculiarly fantastic goodwill" which is the ultimate Source of it all. Plus, it's fun!

I hope your friends reconsider.

Suicide bombers

How does God deal with suicide bombers who believe they will go to "paradise" and be with Allah? How can they go to hell if they don't even believe in it? For that matter, how can anyone go to hell who doesn't believe in it? Sometimes I think hell is only for bad Catholics.

Many have written to me since the Sept. 11, 2001, terrorist attacks, asking basically the same question. I am not qualified to explain Islamic beliefs on the subject, but Catholic teaching has some interesting and valuable things to say about it.

Contrary to the assumptions of many, including even to this day a fair number of Catholics, the Catholic Church holds that all persons who sincerely attempt to follow the dictates of their conscience, what they believe to be right and good, are saved. This concept is by now well entrenched in church teaching.

The *Catechism of the Catholic Church,* in a section I have quoted earlier, says it clearly. "Those who, through no fault of their own, do not know the gospel of Christ or his church, but who nevertheless seek God with a sincere heart and, moved by grace, try in their actions to do his will as they know it through the dictates of their conscience — these too may achieve eternal salvation." (n. 847, quoting the Vatican Council II Constitution on the Church)

Pope John Paul II elaborated on this in his message for the World Day of Peace, Jan. 1, 1999. Speaking about religious freedom, he concluded, "People are obliged to follow their conscience in all circumstances and cannot be forced to act against it."

All this assumes, of course, a diligent and honest attempt to inform one's conscience with all the grace and wisdom possible, and then to live one's life in accord with what is seen as "religious duty," however the individual sees that duty. Some will claim that no human being could honestly envision as morally good the inhuman and appalling acts of cruelty we experienced on that day — acts which, incidentally, are perpetrated in countless other nations of our world to this hour, by people other than Muslims.

More than a few Americans, among them religious leaders, have publicly proclaimed that all the dead terrorists are burning in hell, and those still alive will do so. Arrogance like this is unworthy of any thoughtful human being, let alone any Christian. Judgments about the condition and fate of other people's souls are wholly beyond our reach. The pretense of having sufficient knowledge and wisdom to make such judgments invades territory that belongs to God alone.

God created all of us, including the terrorists, out of love. And Jesus, as St. Paul declares, died for each of us. It is, therefore, the worst sort of blasphemy to dare to tell God which of his children he will reject, or to tell Jesus which of those for whom he died must be condemned.

To be sure, whether an individual explicitly believes in hell or not, someone of any or no religion is capable of rejecting God and his law by a deliberate, radical, eternal choice of evil over good. But that is not the whole story. We must also confront our complete ignorance of how God's grace and truth may have transformed a person, not only during his or her life, but also in the last moments. We believe God performs incredible miracles of mercy.

Who knows which ones took place here? We don't know, of course, and will never know in this life. But it is with these instincts of faith and hope, aware that we all desperately need his mercy, that the church has us pray, just after the consecration at Mass, that God will bring our deceased "brothers and sisters, and all the departed," all the people in the world who have died, into the light of his presence.

INDEX

A WORD ABOUT CROSSROAD

Crossroad offers the finest in attractive, thoughtful, and hopeful books on spirituality, religion, and theology. We invite you to look at the following pages for other books of interest to Catholics and others interested in the Catholic faith.

For more information about these and other books, visit us online at:

www.cpcbooks.com

or call 1-800-707-0670 to request our catalog.

Of Related Interest

Pope John Paul II
Edited by Carl J. Moell, S.J.
HOLY FATHER, SACRED HEART
The Complete Collection of John Paul II's Writings
on the Perennial Catholic Devotion

Pope John Paul II has given the devotion to the Sacred Heart a special place in his spiritual life and public ministry for decades. In *Holy Father, Sacred Heart,* Carl J. Moell, drawing from his experience working with the Society of Jesus in Rome, gathers together every teaching the Holy Father has proclaimed regarding this most intimate of Catholic devotions. From the Pope's speeches before audiences of millions, to his personal prayers and writings, *Holy Father, Sacred Heart* is the perfect treasury for everyone devoted to the Sacred Heart of Jesus Christ.

0-8245-2147-1, $24.95 paperback

William J. O'Malley, S.J.
WHY BE CATHOLIC?

"A dazzlingly original and extraordinarily powerful summary of the meaning of the Catholic heritage, remarkably free of catechetical gobbledegook and theological gibberish."   — Andrew Greeley

0-8245-1362-2, $18.95 paperback

crossroad

Of Related Interest

Joseph M. Champlin
MYSTERY AND MEANING OF THE MASS
Revised and Updated Edition!

Why does the priest kiss the altar? Why does he pour water in the cup? Why do we strike our breasts before communion? In essence, how can we best understand the Mass and the intricacies of its many components? This acclaimed primer explains it all — from the particulars of the ritual and symbols, to the history and theology behind them.

0-8245-2296-6, $9.95 paperback

Chris Aridas
YOUR CATHOLIC WEDDING
A Complete Planbook

Revised and Updated Edition

A handy guide for couples, family members, and priest in the preparation for a Catholic wedding. It includes the entire liturgical rite with options, practical details of church arrangements, an insightful commentary, and valuable checklists.

0-8245-1675-3, $12.95 paperback

crossroad

Of Related Interest

Elizabeth Ficocelli
SHOWER OF HEAVENLY ROSES
Stories of the Intercession of St. Therese of Lisieux

Therese of Lisieux — Therese of the Little Flower — is universally recognized as one of the most influential saints of recent times. Since her death at an early age, countless miracles, healings, and life changes have been attributed to her inspiration and grace. In this book, Elizabeth Ficocelli, who herself experienced such a miracle, gathers together stories of Therese's grace, the "roses" she promised to send from heaven to the faithful. The book includes black and white art relating to Therese and photographs relating to the miracles.

0-8245-2256-7, $14.95 paperback

Robert Ellsberg
ALL SAINTS
*Daily Reflections on Saints, Prophets,
and Witnesses for Our Time*

Winner of the 1998 Christopher Award

From Therese of Lisieux to Mother Teresa, from Moses to Gandhi, this inspiring treasury combines traditional saints with other spiritual giants whose lives speak to the meaning of holiness for our time.

"A wonderfully broad, knowing, and narratively compelling look at human goodness as it has been tested by life. This book will give us the very best kind of moral and spiritual education." — Robert Coles

0-8245-1679-6, $24.95 paperback

crossroad

Of Related Interest

Ann Ball
THE OTHER FACES OF MARY
Stories, Devotions, and Pictures of the Holy Virgin around the World

Everyone knows about the famous apparitions of Mary in Medjugorje, Lourdes, and Fatima. But many regions of the world have their own appearances of Mary, from the German Virgin who Unties Knots, the Queen and Protectress of Nigeria, and the wheat-bearing Mary (Japan). In this remarkable book, Ann Ball, one of the most distinctive voices in popular Catholic writing today, shows us the other faces of Mary: some sublime, some unusual, and all a tribute to the enduring power of the Mother of God around the world. Each piece includes a devotion, a story, and comment from a local source. Includes photos.

ISBN: 0-8245-2255-9, $14.95 paperback

Robert Royal
CATHOLIC MARTYRS
OF THE TWENTIETH CENTURY
A Comprehensive World History

Robert Royal presents the first comprehensive history of the twentieth-century martyrs. This volume traces specific situations all over the world, recounts how martyrdoms occurred, studies the political systems, and offers a rich collection of individual biographies.

0-8245-1846-2, $39.95 hardcover

crossroad